Fundamentals of American Government

Fundamentals of American Government

NATIONAL, STATE, AND LOCAL

CULLEN B. GOSNELL, *Emory University*

LANE W. LANCASTER, *University of Nebraska*

ROBERT S. RANKIN, *Duke University*

GREENWOOD PRESS, PUBLISHERS
WESTPORT, CONNECTICUT

Preface

The original version of this book dealt solely with the national government of the United States and attempted to meet the needs of those institutions which allot a single semester to that part of the general subject of American government. Since the book's appearance there has been a wide demand for an edition which deals also with government on the state and local levels. Six chapters have been added to meet this demand. They do not examine state and local government in detail, but it is the hope of the authors that the enlarged version will serve as a satisfactory introduction to the subject.

The readers of any book are entitled to know the authors' point of view and their reasons for the emphases they give. It is our position, since government in the United States is conducted through machinery which is not only extremely complex but continually changing both in the number and designation of its parts and in the relationships between them, that to describe it in detail would have two principal disadvantages. In the first place, such an encyclopedic treatise would lay upon the student the heavy burden of discriminating between the important and the unimportant in a vast array of facts—a task for which few young students are equipped. In the second place, even if it were possible to master the details of such a description, the resulting picture would be accurate for only a moment. It seems to us unreasonable to ask the students to memorize facts which will soon cease *to be* facts. A certain amount of memorization cannot be avoided—but it should be held to a minimum.

On the other hand, it would be unrealistic to assume that the subject could be mastered by understanding a few general "principles." In every government there *are* principles, of course, but to approach the study of politics only from this point of view would seem to have at least two defects. One is that principles have no life of their own apart from the specific machinery in which they are embodied. It is hard, for example, to understand the principle of the separation of powers without knowing a good deal about the actual working of the three branches of government. If the principle is to be more than a dry formula this sort of knowledge is necessary. The other weakness of a purely theoretical approach is that principles themselves undergo subtle changes as new

v

devices and adjustments are worked out to meet new problems. For example, the principle of federalism still has considerable vitality despite the pressures of opposing centralizing forces. But the operation of these forces compels us from time to time to rephrase the federalist principle.

In short, it has been the purpose of the authors to avoid, on the one hand, too great an emphasis on the details of governmental machinery and, on the other, an exclusive preoccupation with principles. They have sought to give a realistic description of the conduct of government in the United States without losing sight of the way in which its operation is influenced by a widespread belief in certain theories. The task of relating theory and practice accurately is a hard one, and how well the authors have succeeded must be left to the judgment of others.

The authors wish to record here their indebtedness to Mrs. Miriam Roher Resnick for her careful editing of parts of the manuscript; to Dr. W. Brooke Graves, of the Library of Congress; to Mr. David Estes of Emory University Library for bibliographical and other assistance; to Professor Robert J. Morgan of the University of Nebraska; to Mr. George Barnes of the Emory Law School; and to Mr. James L. Hamrick, Dr. William Seyler, and Dr. A. B. Winter who, while research assistants at Duke University, rendered valuable services.

All the authors took part in the planning of the book and the various contributions have been carefully correlated. Mr. Gosnell wrote Chapters 7, 8, 9, 12, 13, 14, 19, 24, 25, and 26; Mr. Lancaster wrote Chapters 1 through 5, 22, 23, 29, 30, and 31; and Mr. Rankin, Chapters 6, 10, 11, 15 through 18, 20, 21, 27, and 28.

CULLEN B. GOSNELL
LANE W. LANCASTER
ROBERT S. RANKIN

Contents

CHAPTER 1 *Natural Rights*

We are about to study the machinery and the working of the American government, and we begin quite reasonably with an examination of our Constitution. Within broad limits, it is the Constitution that determines what and how public policies shall be decided on, how they shall be carried out, and how, in doing these things, citizens shall have their wishes consulted and their rights respected.

The Nature of a Constitution

Every nation has a constitution. It used to be common to draw a distinction between written and unwritten constitutions, that of the United States being described as written and that of Great Britain as unwritten. There is a sense in which this distinction is a valid one for, in the United States, there is a document which we call the Constitution; whereas in Great Britain there is no such written statement of governmental principles, the working of the government being determined to a very considerable degree by custom. However, if custom is important in Great Britain, it is also significant in the United States; and, if there is in Great Britain no single document called the constitution, there are many written laws, inscribed over the centuries which, taken together, amount to something like a scheme of government. In other words, a reading of our Constitution would not give a very adequate idea of how power is exercised here; and a knowledge of political customs in Great Britain has to be supplemented by acquaintance with many documents. Each country has both a written and an unwritten constitution. In short, a nation's constitution is the sum total of all those provisions, whether written or unwritten, in accordance with which governing power is organized and the relations of the government to the citizens are determined. Thus, a constitution, as we in the Western world understand it, is both a grant of powers and a series of limitations on those powers—limitations intended to protect the citizens from irresponsible officeholders.

1

An examination of any constitution will show that it embodies certain fundamental principles. These principles may not be realized in practice— as we think is the case in such nations as Soviet Russia or the former Nazi Germany; but a statement of them *does* tell us something about the aspirations of a people, and without knowing them we can scarcely understand how a government operates.

Leading Principles of the American Constitution

There will be found in the American Constitution a number of principles which may be regarded as fundamental and distinctive. Some of these have to do primarily with the manner in which authority is organized, others with restrictions upon the power to govern, in the interests of the governed. Actually, these two kinds of principles cannot be separated except for discussion; since it is clear that a special way of organizing the machinery of government has some other purpose than to make it easy for students to draw diagrams and charts. Among these other purposes may be named (1) provision for the orderly and predictable exercise of governmental power; and (2) seeing to it that those with power do not oppress the citizen. It is evident that these objectives are closely related. For instance, as will be pointed out in the proper place, the division of the powers of the national government into legislative, executive, and judicial, with the accompanying checks and balances, was intended not only to establish an understandable organization, but even more, to make it hard for office-holders to obtain excessive power with which to oppress the people.

The leading principles in accordance with which the national government is organized are (1) the doctrine of the natural rights of the individual as against government; (2) the doctrine of the separation of powers and checks and balances; (3) the practice, developed by usage, under which the courts, and especially the Supreme Court of the United States, determine finally whether acts of the legislative and executive branches are in harmony with the Constitution, and hence enforceable; (4) the principle of popular sovereignty or the final legal supremacy of the people; (5) the "rule of law," that is, the principle that the government itself shall be subject to law; and (6) the principle that governing authority shall be divided between the national and the state governments. The last is not simply a way of bringing about a division of labor. It is now commonly defended as a way of preventing the concentration of power in the hands of a government geographically remote from the bulk of the population.

There is not, of course, universal agreement either as to the validity of these principles or as to whether government in practice is conducted in accordance with them. Many people do not believe in them at all, or at least are very critical of some or all of them. Some accept a few of them and reject the others. Many more, at various times, pretend to believe that those in office try to ignore or evade them. These principles have all, however, become such integral parts of our tradition that there is general agreement that they represent desirable bases for free government. And there is an equally general willingness to believe that most officials accept them in good faith, even though they may on occasion find irksome the restrictions implied in them.

The Doctrine of Natural Rights

The doctrine of natural rights asserts that there are certain rights belonging to man simply because he is a human being. These rights are against government and not against other men. They are commonly asserted to be based upon "nature" or to have been instituted by God. They are held to have belonged to men in the so-called "state of nature" in which men were said to have lived before there was any government. When governments were set up, men presumably continued to possess these rights and did not give them up to the regulating power of government. Indeed, the believers in the doctrine assert that government exists to *secure* these rights. Probably as good a general statement of the doctrine as can be found is that in the Declaration of Independence: "We hold these truths to be self-evident, that all men are created equal, that they are endowed by their Creator with certain unalienable Rights, that among these are Life, Liberty, and the pursuit of Happiness. That to secure these rights, Governments are instituted among Men. . . ." It is evident from this that the rights of men were believed to have been conferred by God, and that government, far from having power to abridge or abolish them, was created for the express purpose of making each man more secure in his possession of them.

During the eighteenth and the early part of the nineteenth centuries, those members of the educated classes who could be called liberal were for the most part believers in the reality of natural rights. Those who were religious traced these rights to God; those who were skeptics found their guarantees in the natural order of the universe. Even conservatives often believed in natural rights, although they were likely to give such rights a different content, believing, for example, that monarchy or a class system was natural, and that what we call democracy was against nature. It was in this climate of opinion that the American Constitution was drafted. By the early part of the nineteenth century, in the United States at least, there came to be rather general agreement that men had a natural right to worship according to their own beliefs; to express their opinions orally or in writing so long, at any rate, as they did not assail the character of others; to enter into contracts with respect to legitimate objects; to combine with others for legal purposes; and to be guaranteed the usual procedural safeguards in the courts. It was also generally believed that government rested on the consent of the governed, that the people were the ultimate sovereigns in the community, and that they had the right to change the form of government when it deliberately violated their rights.

Although, as will be suggested later, belief in the objective reality of natural rights is not as universal as it once was, there are many who not only defend the traditional rights as vital to freedom and progress, but would add still others. Thus we hear demands for the right to work, to security in old age, to a living wage, to strike, and pleas for other rights even more vague. Some of these newer rights have indeed found expression in a few of our state constitutions, and many national and state statutes would seem to be based upon an acceptance of the reality and desirability of these newer rights.

The Modern Content of Natural Rights [1]

Religious Freedom. In many ways the most fundamental right secured by the national Constitution is that of religious freedom. The First Amendment to the Constitution provides that "Congress shall make no law respecting an establishment of religion, or prohibiting the free exercise thereof." The intent of this provision is clear enough, even though its application has not been without difficulties. Congress is forbidden to give public support to any sect, either by supplying it with funds or by making it in any sense the official faith of the country. That is, it would be unconstitutional for Congress to support, out of taxes, a particular church; impose an oath of office which would be repugnant to members of any faith; or in other ways give preference before the law to members of any religious body. To do these things would, of course, place some denominations under more or less serious disabilities. The American state thus tolerates all religious beliefs and practices, at least so long as the latter do not involve a disturbance of public order.

In the twentieth century we find it difficult to imagine Congress doing any of the intolerant things mentioned in the preceding paragraph, and so we are prone to believe that the First Amendment is providing against something not likely to happen. It must be remembered, however, that, over perhaps most of the world, religious toleration is either nonexistent or at any rate a very new thing. A religious "establishment" actually existed in England in 1789—and still does; and certain denominations had a preferred status in some of the thirteen original colonies. And in any case, it is clear that nothing like liberal democracy can exist unless a very large measure of religious toleration is established. This is true because one's

---

[1] The list of specific rights discussed here is not intended to be complete, but only illustrative. A comprehensive treatment will be found in Chap. 9.

religious beliefs are at the center of his view of life. Even if a person makes no attempt to force his beliefs on others, he will at least hold them tenaciously, resist any efforts to suppress his expression of them, and do what he can peaceably to make them prevail.

For these reasons, when those in office are legally required to subscribe to a specific religious dogma, all dissenters are excluded from any hope of obtaining power and are, in a sense, lawbreakers. For centuries it seemed natural that the state should support by taxation, and by its army, a particular religion—usually that of its ruler. All who dissented from the official faith were considered not only bad men but probably traitors also. The truth of this is witnessed to by centuries of religious quarrels within the various European countries, and by a series of bloody religious wars between nations. Lacking an internal agreement about the most fundamental concern of human life, it was obviously impossible for men to settle *any* domestic question by peaceful negotiation. If men feel strongly that they have the only true method of salvation, they cannot regard their religious beliefs as proper subjects for political compromise or even political discussion.

By the late seventeenth century, influential European scholars and statesmen had rather generally come to the conclusion that religious belief could not be compelled and that the only feasible public policy was one of toleration. In most of the Western world it had become evident that no church was able to impose its will on nonmembers and hence that it would be best to stop trying to do so. This view was held even by many people who were devoutly religious. For example, the French lawyer Jean Bodin (1530–1596), to whom we owe the classic statement of the modern theory of political sovereignty, came out for the supremacy of his King, largely because he sought a rallying point for patriotic Frenchmen which would put an end to internal disputes over religion. In spite of this, Bodin remained a faithful son of the Church. On the other hand, much of the willingness to tolerate differing beliefs sprang in large measure from a decline in religious faith—at least among the classes influential in government. Among such persons toleration was the offspring of indifference.

Whatever may be the historical reasons for the policy of toleration expressed in the American Constitution, there are still many to whom religion is an important and serious matter. For these it is by no means easy to distinguish between the things that are Caesar's and those that are God's. Religious faith, if deeply held, and the demands of the state may conflict at many points. A sincere belief in any religious dogma demands control over the *whole* of life and is almost certain sooner or later to cause the believer to deny the rightfulness of state authority over at least the most crucial matters. No member of the Society of Friends (Quakers), for example, can regard as legitimate the demand of the state that he engage in combatant military service. The commandment "Thou shalt not kill" is more persuasive with him than the call of his country.

Under our law, however, religious freedom is not absolute. Polygamy has been outlawed, with the approval of the Supreme Court, even though it was once sanctioned by the teachings of a religious sect. Some form of military service may be compelled, even against the scruples of believers in pacifism; and although such persons may not at present be required to perform combatant service in the Armed Forces, it may be assumed that this concession will be withdrawn when and if the national safety shall require truly universal service. Sects and persons whose beliefs cause them to oppose vaccination may be compelled to submit to it in the interest of the public health. The sterilization of the unfit, under safeguards acceptable to the courts, is permitted against the contention that it is a violation of natural law or natural rights. The difficulty of reconciling the demands of religious faith and the requirements of public policy is nowhere better shown than in the flag-salute cases involving the Jehovah's Witnesses. In 1940 the Supreme Court upheld a state law requiring students daily to salute the flag and pledge their allegiance to the nation, in spite of the argument that to do these things was a kind of idolatry, a putting of the flag and the nation above God Himself. Three years later the Court reversed itself, holding that the salute violated religious convictions and that its omission did not threaten the national interest to any significant degree.[2] When the highest court in the land finds itself in such difficulties, it is evident that the distinction between religious liberty and the legitimate demands of political authority is not an easy one to make.

On the general question of the right to religious freedom, one is safe in saying, first, that the courts will generally refuse to enforce laws which have the effect of giving any advantage to one sect over another; and second, that no act can be excused on the ground that religious faith requires its performance, if it seems to the courts to violate the general laws of the nation. Beyond this, it appears clear that, to date, the community consensus in favor of toleration is so firmly established that the bias of the courts is in favor of freedom and generally against attempts to interfere with it—unless an overwhelming public interest makes such interference desirable or imperative.

Freedom of Speech and the Press. Immediately following the guarantee of religious freedom, the First Amendment denies to Congress the power to make any law "abridging the freedom of speech, or of the press." This covers any expression of views, whether oral or written, and includes the graphic arts such as painting, sculpture, and the movies. So far as the

---

[2] These two cases are: *Minersville School District v. Gobitis,* 310 U.S. 586 (1940) and *West Virginia Board of Education v. Barnette,* 319 U.S. 624 (1943).

national government is concerned, it rules out anything like a prior censorship of expression. It is not, however, absolute in its protection. The common law gives a right of civil action to anyone who claims that the words or writings of another have injured him in his reputation or his property rights. Under certain circumstances to be discussed later, Congress may punish seditious utterances.

Freedom of speech and writing is a corollary of the proposition that free government is government by discussion. It assumes that if citizens are fully informed about public matters, they will reach decisions which, if not always sound, will at least be accepted. This assumption is based on the fact that full opportunity has been given to all persons to present their views and, if possible, to win to their side those holding different opinions. The alternative to this sort of unrestricted discussion would be the imposition, by those with force enough to accomplish it, of their own views, right or wrong, sound or foolish. To be sure, the freedom described above allows the circulation of a bewildering variety of opinions, not all of them calculated to contribute to reasonable decisions; but this is the price which must be paid for freedom. The only real safeguard against what seems often to be the irresponsibility or even viciousness of writers, radio commentators, and politicians is the cultivation of a more critical attitude on the part of the public to whom their words are addressed.

Power tends to corrupt; and officials can be required to exercise government authority with restraint and responsibility only if others are completely free to criticize them without fear of reprisals. For this reason, freedom of expression, in all its forms, is the most powerful weapon in the hands of a political opposition and is some guarantee at least of temperate government. It is not difficult to understand why the first victims of such tyrants as the European dictators were the newspapers, magazines, theatres, and movies.

The right of free speech and press is important, however, in nonpolitical matters. Most of us have come to feel, almost naturally, that a man is something less than a complete human being if he is not permitted to write a book, produce a play, or paint a picture which expresses faithfully his own ideas; even though what is produced may cause pain or disgust to others who do not sympathize with his opinions or who have not shared his experiences. It is felt, moreover, that a people's culture acquires richness and variety in direct proportion to the freedom allowed to writers and other artists, and that much would be lost if this freedom were restricted by official censorship or punishment. This freedom may allow the production of much which the judgment of history will pronounce to be rubbish; but, until we have exact standards in such matters, liberty must be as broad as possible lest, through the zeal of some official censor, works of genius fall under an official ban.

It is obvious, of course, that no society can permit the exercise of the right of free expression under circumstances where such use threatens public order or safety; but drawing the line in specific cases is often hard. Someone has to decide when it is dangerous to say or print certain things, and once this is admitted, the door may be opened to official abuse. The authority which makes this decision in the first instance may be a chief of police, a mayor, or a governor; but ultimately it is the Supreme Court of the United States whose rulings are binding on all state and Federal authorities.

The rule now adopted by the Supreme Court as a guide is that freedom shall prevail—except in circumstances where the speech or writing in question constitutes a "clear and present danger" to orderly government or the public safety. But just what *is* a "clear and present danger"? It has long been held that freedom of speech does not excuse an appeal to citizens to obstruct the drafting of troops when the nation is actually at war, since no chances can safely be taken when the very existence of the nation is at stake. But, since democracy is based upon the desirability of allowing for peaceful change by persuasion, what are we to do with persons holding and expressing opinions contrary to those held by the majority which supports the government in power and its policies? Suppose a man or a party proposes the abolition of the usual rights of property, or the setting up of a dictatorship. Is he to be allowed to express these opinions and make converts? After all, these views are probably no more entitled to be called "wrong" or "unpatriotic" or "wicked" than were some of the things said about the institution of kingship at the time of the American Revolution —by men who, of course, under English law, were rebels and traitors.

It is by no means easy to answer this question. Freedom of speech, if it is to amount to anything, must be freedom to say what is unpopular; it can not consistently be limited to saying those things which are generally accepted. For example, the Communist Party is a legal organization in most of the states of the American Union, and, although its views are shared by only a tiny number of Americans, these views, *so long as they are only views,* would seem to be entitled to be expressed under the guarantees of the First Amendment. On the other hand, certain things may be said under circumstances in which clearly illegal actions are pretty sure to follow. In such cases the courts, while reflecting the traditional popular bias in favor of freedom, cannot be blind to the probable consequences of these expressions.

The now famous case of the eleven American Communist leaders, convicted in 1950 of conspiracy to advocate the violent overthrow of the United States government, illustrates the present view of the Supreme Court. These leaders were found guilty, in the trial court, of such conspiracy and of teaching the necessity and desirability of revolution. It is to be noted that no *actions* were charged, only agitation. Now it is clear from what we have reason to believe is true of the Soviet Union, that if the Communist Party should secure power here it would quickly destroy all civil rights in the United States. Nevertheless the eleven defendants availed themselves of the guarantee of free speech in the First Amendment to demand their release.

This defense the Supreme Court refused to accept. In upholding the conviction of the accused, it said [3] that their formation

. . . of such a highly organized conspiracy, with rigidly disciplined members subject to call when the leaders . . . felt that the time had come for action, coupled with the inflammable nature of world conditions, similar uprisings in other countries, and the touch-and-go nature of our relations with countries with whom [the convicted persons] were in the very least ideologically attuned, convinces us that their convictions were justified on this score.

Two things may be inferred from this opinion. The first is that ordinary members of the Communist Party, apparently, would not have been punished for expressing their belief in the principles of the Party. It was the probability of prompt and decisive action by a determined and ruthless leadership that weighed heavily with the Court—which could not but be aware of what such leadership had done elsewhere in the world. The second inference is that peaceful study and teaching of Communist ideas would not have been held a crime. In short, the Court was trying to preserve some freedom to hold and express unpopular views, while preventing the kind of advocacy which presumably had a chance of passing rapidly into violent action against legitimate political authority. The line between conspiracy and action is difficult to draw, but the most liberal must admit that there are some chances which no government can afford to take. No one knows, of course, whether the danger of violence was as real as the Court seemed to think. But it must be assumed that, with the record before them, the Court acted in a reasonable fashion.

Procedural Rights. The rights discussed above are called "substantive" rights. In addition to these, the Constitution provides for certain devices intended to protect the citizen against arbitrary and unreasonable acts of public officials. These are found in the Bill of Rights and in Sections 9 and 10 of the first article, and are known as "procedural" rights or guarantees. Some of these procedures must be followed in the national courts, some are applied specifically to actions in the state courts. Even in those cases where the provisions of the Constitution do not apply to the states, most of the same safeguards are effective in the states, either by their requirement in the state constitutions or by interpretations of the United States Supreme Court which are binding upon the states.

[3] *United States v. Dennis,* 341 U.S. 494 (1951).

Neither the state legislatures nor Congress may pass bills of attainder or ex post facto laws. A bill of attainder is an act of a legislative body inflicting punishment without trial before a court. The only punishments which a legislative body can impose directly are the censure and the expulsion of its own members and the impeachment of executive and judicial officers. Even in case of contempt of its procedure, the accused must be tried in the regular courts; and in the case of impeachment, conviction may carry no punishment beyond removal from office and disqualification for holding office in the future. Bills of attainder were occasionally used by the British Parliament until well into the eighteenth century, to punish persons who could not be reached in any other way—for the most part, unpopular public servants who probably could not have been convicted in the regular manner. The penalty was death, confiscation of property, and the "corruption of blood." Bills of pains and penalties, involving punishments less than death, were in the same general category. That the prohibition against bills of these sorts has not lost its point even in the twentieth century is indicated by the fact that an attempt by Congress to punish three federal officials, specifically named in a statute, by denying them salaries, was declared unconstitutional by the Supreme Court in 1946 on the ground that such an act amounted to a bill of attainder.[4] An ex post facto law makes punishable as a crime an act which was not illegal at the time it was committed; or increases the penalty of an act; or so alters the rules of evidence as to make conviction easier. If such laws were not forbidden, it is easy to see that the way would be open to serious oppression.[5]

A considerable number of provisions intended to protect citizens against hasty or arbitrary acts on the part of officeholders are found in the Constitution. While it is not strictly accurate to speak of these provisions as establishing natural rights, it is difficult to see how the substantive rights could be vindicated if the procedures required by them were not available. In all federal crimes the accused is entitled to be indicted by a grand jury and to trial by a petit jury if he demands the latter. Trial by a jury is considered a protection to the accused, since the jury may be regarded as a body representing the community and likely to be a counterweight against a too strict interpretation of the law by the judge.

The Constitution further provides that "the privilege of the writ of habeas corpus shall not be suspended, unless when in case of rebellion or invasion the public safety may require it." The writ is an order of a court, directed to a police officer or other official having a person in cus-

[4] *United States v. Lovett*, 328 U.S. 303 (1946). It would have been entirely legal to abolish the positions held by these three men.

[5] This prohibition does not apply to laws dealing with civil matters. A tax law, for example, may be retroactive.

tody, requiring him to present the prisoner in court so that the reasons for his arrest may be inquired into. The court is required to issue the writ when proper cause is shown. If examination shows that the prisoner is being held contrary to law, his immediate release will be ordered. If there is reason to believe that a jury would convict on the basis of the evidence presented by the police officials, the prisoner will be held for trial with or without reasonable bail. It is easy to see that, so long as the courts are open and the writ is available, it is a powerful obstacle to the imprisonment of people who may be guilty of no offense except unpopularity with officials or the public.

The Reality of Natural Rights

It was made clear at the outset of this discussion that the rights we have been describing are alleged to have existed before there was any government and that they were therefore not granted by government. Quite to the contrary, it is maintained that government exists in order, among other things, to make their enjoyment more secure. Believers in the reality of natural rights hold, in other words, that they are rooted in the very nature of things and are for that reason beyond the reach of government.

In so far as these rights are said to belong to man in a presocial state of nature, it is perhaps sufficient to say that such a state is purely imaginary. Such evidence as we have seems to show that men have never existed outside society or without government, however rudimentary the latter may have been in the most ancient times. Actually one cannot speak of rights as belonging to isolated human beings. They are the result of men's living together. So long as Robinson Crusoe was alone on his island, he was, apart from the culture which he carried with him as a citizen of England, simply an animal having the same right as any other animal— that is the right to get whatever he could in the general scramble. In other words, he had power rather than rights, and took what he wanted if he had the strength to do it. The use of "rights" in such a context would be a mere abuse of language.

It is only in society that rights appear; and it is society, speaking most frequently through government, that determines the limits of rights. Furthermore, society usually imposes duties corresponding to the rights which it allows. If I have a right to property, I am, by implication, forbidden to invade the property of others, or so to use my own property as to injure the property of others. On no other terms than these may I claim rights. Parents have certain rights with respect to their children but, in the present state of the conscience of the Western world at least, these rights do not include that of keeping them in ignorance, neglecting their health, or setting them to work at an early age.

Now the Constitution of the United States, in some cases, sets forth these rights in absolute language. Thus, "Congress shall make no law respecting an establishment of religion." In practice, however, none of these rights is absolute. The courts ordinarily will uphold them, and the bias of our people favors their preservation in full vigor. It may as well be admitted, on the other hand, that whether or not they will be available depends upon circumstances. In some cases, for example that of the Communist leaders discussed above, the courts have to choose between the liberty of individuals and what appears to be an overriding public interest. Where that interest seems clearly threatened by the conduct of such individuals, the rights of the latter will be abridged or denied. What this means, then, is that social utility actually determines the limits of individual freedom. Of course, some specific person or persons will have to render the decision, and for that reason there is some danger that freedom will be unduly restricted. No human device escapes the possibility of being abused. All one can say is that the procedures established in the United States, for the trial of persons accused of abusing the rights guaranteed them, are calculated to minimize this danger. For those individuals to whom these procedures seem inadequate, the way is always open by peaceful persuasion to alter them. Hence it is difficult to defend any appeal to physical violence in a country whose Constitution may be changed by orderly and peaceful means.

Belief in the objective reality of natural rights is simply an illustration of our tendency to assert that certain liberties *ought* to exist whether they actually do or not. Taken together, these imagined liberties describe the kind of society in which the men who believe in them would like to live. This kind of society is alleged to be both natural and reasonable. And indeed, though in actual practice governments are compelled to apply the test of public welfare, with all the good will their officials can muster, this does not mean that there are no natural rights in some understandable sense. In fact, there is little point in talking about demonstration or proof in such matters. Those who believe that there are such rights, objectively, are simply saying that they *ought* to exist now, and *would* exist if the governments of the world were patterned after their own finest dreams and deepest convictions. They are asserting that there is a Law behind the law of men, before the bar of which even the sovereign state may be called to justify its acts.[6] Against such assertions, all merely logical arguments spend themselves in vain. Men who believe in the reality of natural rights *do* exist, and it is well that they do. The willingness of men now and in the past to suffer and even die for such beliefs is the strongest guarantee that individual liberty will always have defenders. The existence of such

[6] Plato asserted something like this when he had Socrates say: "You must contrive for your future rulers another and a better life than that of a ruler." *Republic*, Book VII, p. 521.

men and women is also some assurance that what may be called the conscience of mankind will steadily compel the state to act in conformity with the highest ideals of political life.

REFERENCES

As indicated in the text, modern writers on rights do not rest their case on a belief in the objective reality of rights; the following are suggested as good modern discussions of the substance of rights.

Carl Becker, *Freedom and Responsibility in the American Way of Life* (1945).
Zechariah Chafee, *Free Speech in the United States* (1941).
Osmund K. Fraenkel, *Our Civil Liberties* (1944).
W. Gellhorn, *Security, Loyalty, and Science* (1950).
Arthur N. Holcombe, *Human Rights in the Modern World* (1948).
John Stuart Mill, *On Liberty* (1859).
The President's Committee on Civil Rights, *To Secure These Rights* (1947).
D. G. Ritchie, *Natural Rights* (1897).

CHAPTER 2 *Popular Sovereignty*

The Development of Political Democracy

No solution of political issues is more frequently offered in the United States than that the issues in question be referred to the "people." This recipe is suggested, and for the most part accepted, with a finality which leaves no doubt that in the public's belief and feeling the doctrine of popular sovereignty is firmly rooted. And rightly so. The United States is a political democracy, a society in which the people rule.

It is true, of course, that the framers of the Constitution had no intention of establishing any political system which would be recognizable today as democratic. Yet those who stress the conservatism of the founders would do well to note that the Constitution, by its own terms, is the creation of the people—"We, the people of the United States . . . do ordain and establish this Constitution."[1] The men of 1787 had many reservations about the political competence of the mass of the population, but they did not press them and, the above language having been used, it has not been found possible in practice to avoid its plain implications. These words have been cited, from generation to generation, to justify every extension of political power to the mass of the population.

To understand the revolutionary nature of this language, a glance at history is required. Even when the Constitution was being drafted, although aristocratic influence was still strong in the colonies, political power was nevertheless more widely distributed here than in any nation in the world. Over the entire European continent the masses of the population were hardly better than beasts of burden. They were illiterate, badly fed, miserably housed, and, what was worse, for the most part beyond hoping for escape from the lot to which "Divine Providence" had consigned them. Even in relatively enlightened England where, a century before, a

[1] It is only fair to point out that the first draft of the Preamble named the thirteen states, and this language was changed to "We, the people of the United States" because no one knew which of the states would actually ratify the Constitution.

14

revolution of sorts had occurred, the vast mass of the people were completely excluded from political power. Politics was an intricate game, played by lords and "gentlemen" with little regard for the vague wishes or the welfare of the masses. In a population of eight millions, scarcely a quarter of a million were qualified to vote for members of Parliament; and that body itself was controlled by a few hundred titled landholders or wealthy merchants. Except as a reservoir of possible violence, the "people" did not count.[2]

For centuries this system was regarded as completely natural. Ruling was the business of kings, fighting was that of nobles, and hard work was that of simple folk. Kings reigned "by the grace of God," however graceless or ungracious their actual conduct might be. The throne was buttressed by the concentric circles of the aristocracy, and the entire structure was supported by the ill-requited labors of millions of peasants and craftsmen. Louis followed Henry, and Karl gave way to Frederick, on the thrones of Europe—with all of the inevitability of the procession of the seasons. Thus it had always been; thus it must be for the indefinite future.

It is true that there was in Europe a vague tradition that the people were the source of power, but this had grown shadowy as the centuries passed. In theory the late Roman Emperors exercised powers committed to them by the people; but their successors in the national states of Western Europe paid scant attention to theory. Even though lip service might now and then be paid to the idea that kings were responsible for the welfare of their subjects, there was nowhere any belief that the people had anything to say about the conduct of their rulers, much less the choosing of them. To assert, even as late as 1787, that government was an affair of the "people" was as shocking to traditionalists as were the doctrines of communism a century and a half later. When a believer in such moderate democracy as Thomas Jefferson was elected President in 1800, American conservatives solemnly predicted that his accession to power would enthrone the "swinish multitude" and put an end to public order and decency. In this setting, then, to proclaim that the fundamental law of the United States was made by the people was an enormous advance.

What Is Sovereignty?

There is perhaps no term in political science and law about which more has been written than "sovereignty." Much of this exposition is extremely hard going indeed, filled as it is with finespun distinctions and hairsplitting definitions. For our purposes it is perhaps enough to say that in every

[2] For pictures of English society and politics in the eighteenth century see W. E. H. Lecky, *History of England in the Eighteenth Century;* Louis Kronenberger, *Kings and Desperate Men;* and L. B. Namier, *The Structure of Politics in the Reign of George the Third.*

political order there is an authority which has no *legal* superior and which is therefore the final source of all law. This authority is called the sovereign.

The term itself is usually associated with the French writer Jean Bodin, who defined it as "perpetual power of commanding in a state." Bodin lived at a time when his native country was being torn by religious warfare and when feudal magnates were attempting by force to retain exclusive power within their territorial holdings. To Bodin this meant hopeless anarchy and perpetual confusion, to be avoided at all costs. For this reason he sought some point about which all parties and interests might rally, and he found it in the King—to whom he attributed supreme legal power.[3]

Whatever difficulties may be involved in discussing the idea of sovereignty, the fact remains that in every state there is somewhere an authority which has the last word. In Great Britain the highest legal authority is Parliament. Many years ago it was said that Parliament could do anything but make a man a woman. This is only a whimsical way of saying that any act of Parliament, no matter how ridiculous or unjust it may strike one, cannot be *legally* reversed by any other earthly power. No court can declare it void, and it cannot be repealed except by Parliament itself. If citizens do not like it, two possible courses of action are open to them. They may bide their time and choose a new Parliament which will repeal the obnoxious law; or they may stage a revolution. Parliament, however, being supreme, may declare its own term perpetual and fill vacancies without recourse to a general election. This is not likely to happen, of course; but the point is that it would be perfectly legal and quite beyond the reach of any other governmental authority, all other authorities being by definition mere creatures of the sovereign. And revolution is, of course, an assertion of political and not of merely legal power. This is not to say that the rights of Englishmen are without safeguards or that what is legally possible is at all likely to happen. It is true that the British Constitution does not permit the courts to restrain Parliament nor does it contain other mechanical checks on the power of that body; but public opinion, custom, and tradition have proved quite as effective safeguards of popular rights against governmental tyranny as have such institutions as the separation of powers and judicial review in the case of the United States.

Sovereignty in the United States

In the United States, largely because of our federal system, the legal sovereign is more difficult to find; but it *can* be found if one tries hard enough. We live under a Constitution which is, by its own terms, the "supreme [that is, sovereign] law of the land." This supreme law did not,

[3] Students of political theory find inconsistencies in Bodin's discussion of sovereignty, but for our purposes the statement above may be allowed to stand.

of course, make itself; therefore, if we can find its maker, we have found the sovereign. More to the point today, if we can find the authority which can change the existing Constitution, that authority is sovereign. Since the Constitution was ordained and established by the people, then the people are sovereign. Just how they act in their sovereign capacity is a matter which may be left for later discussion.

The average man naturally does not take time out from his business and amusements to indulge in any such analysis. If he is asked who has supreme power, he is likely to answer, "Congress," "the state legislatures," or "the Supreme Court." For all practical purposes this answer does well enough. If he should rationalize his answer, he would say something like this: The Constitution tells Congress and the state legislatures what they may and may not do. Under this authority a law has been passed, and the Supreme Court of the United States has said that it is not contrary to the commands of the Constitution; therefore I must obey it.

What is missing in this answer is the recognition of the fact that the sovereign people may, if it seems best to them, enlarge or restrict the powers of every agency of the government of a state or of the United States. The people, to be sure, must act in a way specified in the Constitution. But if two-thirds of the House of Representatives and the Senate of the United States, and a majority in three-fourths of the state legislatures or state conventions, agree to an amendment, *any change whatsoever* may be made in the powers of the government or in the rights of the citizen. Behind the will of legislatures, executives, and judges is the permanent will of the ultimate sovereign. Against acts of *government* the citizen may successfully assert rights; against the *sovereign* he has no rights. The maker of the "supreme law of the land" is obviously beyond the reach of law, all rights depending absolutely upon its will.

One illustration may suffice to make this clear. Congress is forbidden by the First Amendment to the Constitution to make any law abridging the freedom of the press. Let us suppose the people to be convinced that censorship of the press is necessary or desirable. An amendment providing for such censorship, if adopted by the prescribed procedure, would then become a part of the supreme law of the land, and all officials would be obliged to enforce any law passed to carry it out. The amendment itself would deprive all persons of any right to protest in the courts, since it is clear that no one has any legal right against the sovereign creator of the supreme law, upon which *all* legal rights depend. The people, of course, may revolt if they think they can do so successfully, but a revolution is, by its very nature, an illegal proceeding and therefore not to the point here.

In the light of this discussion it is clear what the citizen means when he confesses his obligation to obey a law. What he is saying may be put in this way: The legislatures and the courts alike acknowledge their loyalty to the supreme law. They will not willfully disobey or misinterpret it. They have done their best to meet a situation or correct an abuse—by following a procedure intended to allow the public to express its views. Having acted in this way, they are more likely than not to have passed a reasonable law which I ought to obey. This law is sovereign—not in the sense that it may not be reversed by the people, but in the sense that, every precaution having been taken, it seems to agree with the will which the sovereign itself would express if a direct appeal to the sovereign were made.

Who Are the People?

It is much easier to say, in discussing supreme power, that it rests with the people than it is to say who the people are in a political or governmental sense. Many of our sharpest political controversies have involved this question. The Civil War, indeed, turned on the question as to whether the people were the people of the individual states or the people of the whole United States. It is unnecessary here to examine these controversies. It is enough to say that once power is attributed to the people, the pressure will be continuous to make the term include all people, or at least all law-abiding and competent adults. The basic drive in every democracy is toward equality; and those persons at any given time who find themselves excluded from political power will insist upon their inclusion, precisely because so long as they are excluded, they have good reason to believe that their interests will be neglected and they will be at a disadvantage in comparison with those who possess the vote.

That this pressure for political equality is a reality is best illustrated by the progressive extensions of the suffrage here and elsewhere. Political leaders at the time of the adoption of the Constitution generally meant by "the people" the white, adult, male property owners. The ownership of property meant having a "stake" in the country and was also commonly held to indicate enough intelligence to use the vote wisely. Thus John Jay remarked that those who own the country should rule it; while Jefferson's plan for making landownership easy was, in reality, based on the same theory of political competence. No one, of course, thought of extending the vote to "persons of color." And yet, with the passing of the years, all these excluded groups—the propertyless, women, and Negroes—themselves legally incapable of setting in motion the machinery of constitutional amendment, managed to get themselves included among the holders of political power. Today, so far as the letter of law and constitutions is concerned, substantially all adults may qualify for the vote. Complete formal political democracy has been achieved.

The Exercise of Sovereignty

The doctrine of popular sovereignty means at least that, in some intelligible sense, government is conducted in accordance with the will of the people. When we examine such questions as to *what* people are active in ruling and *how* they exercise their legal powers, troublesome difficulties arise. A little observation shows that by no means all of the people take part in such formal procedures as elections, although voting is the most obvious way to use political power. Even the excitement of a presidential election brings to the polls only a little more than a majority of those qualified to vote; while party primaries normally arouse considerably less interest. The record of voting on measures referred to the people, in those states having the initiative and referendum, is often even more disappointing. Victorious primary aspirants and measures, more often than not, are the choice of a *majority of a minority* of the total electorate. Even the distinctive act of popular sovereignty—the amendment of the Constitution —may conceivably be the act of a minority.

It would be wrong to conclude from such a recital, however, that popular sovereignty is only an attractive fiction. Voting is only one way by which the people intervene in governing; and the political parties which compete for their allegiance are only one device for discovering and marshaling their views. It is well known that in established democracies like Great Britain and the United States, no revolutionary changes follow even the most sweeping party victory. At best the new rulers will differ from the old principally in emphasis with respect to policies on the main lines of which they both agree. Almost no laws are actually repealed, in spite of the way in which the party orators have denounced certain of them as unjust, unconstitutional, unworkable, and what-not in the heat of the campaign. Enforcement by the victorious party may be somewhat less vigorous, and some minor amendments may be adopted but, on the whole, things will go on much as before.

What this means is that the whole process of primary elections, conventions, and campaigning is directed to finding a majority which can be united behind a party policy. Obviously this policy cannot be an extreme one. What actual rulers are seeking, when they try to build majority support for their views, is the solution of a concrete problem. The suggested solution must be one which, while calculated to please the majority, will not outrage the minority. Most responsible politicians and statesmen have, after all, very modest objectives. They are not expecting to find perfect solutions for issues on which people feel strongly; for they know that in an imperfect world such solutions are not to be found, and that, if they were found, they would not be accepted by anything like a majority.

In a political democracy at least, public men have to begin with two assumptions. The first of these is that there is a consensus of opinion concerning the *kinds* of matters which may be the subject of legislation. For example, the Constitution of the United States denies to Congress—and, by interpretation, to the states—the authority to set up a religious establishment or to interfere with the expression of religious views. This is not merely a formal matter of constitutional law; it represents a well-settled popular conviction concerning the proper sphere of government. Because of these facts religious belief is not a proper subject for legislation, and any politician proposing to act in this area would find himself violating a consensus. The Constitution and public opinion are also hostile to any sudden or frontal attacks on the system of private property. It might be possible, as a matter of theory, to introduce something like communism into the United States by slow and successive changes in the law of property, but any attempt to do so at once would meet with complete defeat.

The second assumption of democratic politics concerns the desirability of doing things in a fair and orderly fashion. There must be well-nigh universal belief, for example, that voting is preferable to fighting. Even the minority on any given issue shares in this consensus, if for no other reason than that it hopes one day to be the majority. Indeed it must be insisted that there can be nothing like democracy unless complete freedom of expression is granted to the minority. This is true not only because such freedom is necessary in the process of solving problems, but also because grievances cannot even be discovered unless all persons and groups are permitted freely to express their views.

The bearing of this upon the doctrine of popular sovereignty should be clear. Politicians and statesmen may not always know precisely *who* the people are or *what* they want but, in their constant search for a supporting majority, they acknowledge that the people are the masters of government. The politicians may guess wrong, of course, and it is not hard to cite instances when the popular will was flouted; but, over the years, government and law in the established democratic countries are seen to be related to the wishes of the people. In the process of discovering what these wishes are, an election is perhaps only a formal and dramatic registration of opinions—arrived at by debate and discussion which go on constantly *between* elections. This discussion goes on not only among individual party members, but also within hundreds of organizations and associations likely to be involved in emerging public problems. The massive force called public opinion is formed by such discussion. The parties attempt to marshal this opinion, and an election is one way of measuring its force and direction—perhaps the only strictly authoritative one, but not the only one.

These perhaps somewhat abstract statements may be illustrated by the history of almost any important public policy. Eleven years elapsed between the passage of the so-called Wagner Act (National Labor Relations Act) and the Taft-Hartley Act (Labor-Management Relations Act), which was in effect an amendment of the Wagner Act. During all of these years the alleged unfairness of the Wagner Act was before the public—or at least before those large groups in the population which had a stake in the orderly relations between workers and employers. Such organizations as the American Federation of Labor, the Congress of Industrial Organizations, the National Association of Manufacturers, and the Chamber of Commerce of the United States, were active in presenting their views to the general public and to congressional committees. Farm organizations and many other groups were also active in this long debate. The arguments and appeals of these various groups, it is important to note, were so phrased as to fit into what was felt to be the established consensus with respect to the proper relationship between labor and management.

Both sides in this long discussion appealed to the general belief in fair play and to the necessity of preserving something like free enterprise both for employers and workers. In Congress itself, each chamber passed its own version of a new labor law, that of the House being more restrictive toward labor than the one adopted by the Senate. The Taft-Hartley Act itself was formulated by a conference committee in which the contrasting views of the two chambers were compromised. This act was vetoed by the President, only to be repassed by the constitutional two-thirds vote in each house. This vote was a bipartisan one, it being found impossible for the majority party alone to carry the measure. A few years' experience with the act revealed the need of further changes, and to these the two parties, each with its own emphasis, may be confidently expected to turn in future Congresses.

This brief review of the adoption of a single measure is important as showing two things. In the first place, the process involved in adopting any important national statute is a long and complicated one in which elections and formal voting are, on the whole, minor parts. In the second place, the defenders of quite different views are careful to respect the limits set by public opinion to permissible action. Behind the formal apparatus of debate, committee hearings, conference action, and Presidential veto, and the informal activity of lobbyists, stands the determination of the people that moderation shall prevail; and this determination is ordinarily decisive with those who register decisions formally in statutes.

Of course, the enactment of a statute is not technically an example of the exercise of sovereignty, which occurs only in the formal amendment of a constitution. The example above, however, illustrates, it is believed, the central fact of popular sovereignty—namely, the role of the public in compelling policies to be adopted only after every opportunity has been afforded to discover the sort of solution which the mass of the people would approve. There was no popular vote on the Taft-Hartley Act. It could not even be alleged that the previous congressional elections had turned, in any direct way, on the issue. The fact remains that those active in advancing and opposing the act were constantly aware that public opinion insisted on a solution that would not do violence to accepted standards. The politicians, who are our experts in this sort of thing, are constantly aware of its steady pressure. The people at least tell them what they dare not do.

Popular Sovereignty and Majority Rule

It was remarked above that, for practical purposes, the people rule by a process which aims at finding a majority in favor of a solution to a specific problem. It has often been pointed out that a majority may be as tyrannical as an absolute monarch or an irresponsible oligarchy. But democracy for the most part involves not so much government by a majority as by *a series of majorities*. There is, in other words, no fixed and unchanging majority and therefore no strong probability, except in times of great crisis, of systematic oppression of minorities. Any suggested solution of a concrete problem is bound to be opposed at once by those individuals and groups likely to be injured by its adoption. All of these are selfish and many of them are powerful, but no one of them can have its way without forming alliances with others who exact changes in the original proposal as the price of their cooperation. Farmers, business and professional men, laborers, religious groups, and so on, find themselves at various times on different sides or in close partnership as issues change. This is what we mean by saying that "politics makes strange bedfellows." Furthermore, there is no firm unity about any of these great interests. Labor is divided, as is well known, between the American Federation of Labor, the Congress of Industrial Organizations, the Railway Brotherhoods, and many independent groups. Business is likewise not a single interest, but is in fact shot through with antipathies. And farmers find their spokesmen in at least three major and many special propaganda and lobbying organizations.

Under such conditions we have majorities forming, reforming, and dissolving, and an almost infinite variety of compromises being entered into as one or another suggested policy produces its effect on group life. Politics is indeed a struggle for power; but total victory is impossible for any fixed majority, and will be for so long as men and associations of men are permitted freedom in expressing their views. There is about this constant struggle inevitably an air of shoddiness offensive to the idealistic, since compromise by its very nature involves some departure from absolute principles. Politics is, in the words of an English statesman, "the passionate pursuit of the second-best." On the other hand, solutions based upon principles seem possible only in an absolute state. Out of the unlovely contests, which to the hyperesthetic disfigure our public life, is derived liberty. We may well be alarmed if our politics produces a stable and consistent majority and a hopeless minority. If history makes anything clear, it is this—that the division of a nation into two or more irreconcilable groups, each unwilling to accept half a loaf, is the prelude to violence ending in absolutism.

Democracy and Leadership

The disorderliness in the formation and execution of policy, which seems to be inevitable in a free political society, has on many occasions led to demands that we get rid of politicians and put "experts" in charge. The earliest classic example of this appeal occurs in Plato's *Republic*, where it is suggested that the woes of the state will be ended only when philosophers are kings or kings have the spirit of philosophy. By "philosopher," Plato meant a political *scientist* in the strictest sense of the word. Such a scientist, Plato believed, would have precisely the same sort of knowledge about affairs of state as do mathematicians or physicians or chemists about their sciences. If such knowledge were actually attainable, there would be, of course, no more reason to question the decisions of rulers than there would be to argue whether two and two make four. There would be rules about governing as unquestionable as those about surveying or chemical analysis.

Since Plato's time, few generations have passed without the demand being made that "those who know" should do the ruling. The benevolent despotisms of eighteenth-century Europe were attempts, by rulers possessed of unlimited power, to apply the principles of "reason" to affairs of state. More recently, the Nazi and Fascist regimes were said to be founded on the superior wisdom and public spirit of so-called elites— small groups capable of rising above the superstitions and the petty prejudices of the masses, and of understanding the "real" interests of society. In our own day, a good deal of the more vocal criticism of the "crooked politicians" is accompanied by the suggestion that the latter be turned out and their places filled by people who know what is best for the country.

A number of things may be said about this general point of view. In the first place, it may be suspected that the demand for government by "experts" more often than not arises from an unwillingness to bear the responsibilities for thought and action which free government entails. There is, no doubt, a real possibility that men shrink from liberty as thus understood. If enough do so, we can be assured that they will cease to govern themselves. In the second place, the record made by the "experts" and those who "know the answers" is not impressive. The trumpeted claim that Mussolini made the trains run on time has, with the passing of the years, come to be a measure of the *pettiness* rather than the greatness of Italian fascism; a defeated, prostrate, and impoverished Italy is its more natural fruit. To give an additional example, the rigid bureaucracy created by Frederick the Great has been said, with justice, to have been responsible for Prussian feebleness before the armies of Napoleon within twenty years of the death of the "enlightened" despot. Most fundamental of all, however, is the obvious fact that politics and government are *not* sciences. Planning a bridge is relatively easy; but it takes wisdom of a higher order to calculate the strains and stresses present in even simple domestic and international issues. If there were rules in such matters, comparable in their simplicity to those of the engineer, there would obviously be no such thing as politics.

It may well be, of course, that truly scientific rules for governing will eventually be discovered by psychologists and other social scientists, but this is surely in the distant future. Until such rules are available and, what is more to the point, generally accepted, there is nothing for it but to continue the search for the "second best" solution of problems as they appear. And in free governments at least, the leaders in this search will continue to be the despised politicians, the only political elite in democratic society. It is the function of the politician, in cooperation with the people, to ask the right questions about public problems and suggest the acceptable answers. If he fails at this, his failure is ordinarily the reflection of confusion or irresponsibility on the part of the voters. All that the politician or any other elite has any moral right to do is to propose solutions; and this right belongs to the humblest member of society. There is still, even in a fantastically complicated world, much in Jefferson's remark that, on most public questions, the ploughman is as likely to be right as the professor.

The Democratic Faith

Every form of government rests in the last analysis upon faith. There is no way by which one form can be proved better than another. The English, who live under the formal rule of a monarch, have a feeling about kings and queens which, being after all largely irrational, cannot be argued about. What one gets used to, will seldom be made to seem better or worse by scientific analysis. Democracy is no exception to this rule. It rests upon certain unprovable assumptions about the nature of man and of human values—assumptions which men accept almost wholly because they are emotionally or spiritually satisfying, and never because their correctness can be demonstrated. What are these assumptions in the case of popular government?

The central article in the democratic faith is the belief in the equality of men. This is not to say that men are equal in wisdom or strength or skill, since it is obvious to the most doctrinaire democrat that this is not true. But the believer in democracy does hold that each individual ought to have equal opportunity to realize his own personality, so long at least as he does no injury to the prospects of others. The convinced democrat will not admit the legitimacy of any aristocracy of birth, race, wealth, or creed standing in the way of each man's use of his talents. The Western world, of course, is never without groups and individuals claiming special privileges, including a superior right to rule; but it is clear that democracy means, above all, hostility and resistance to such claims. In practice, equality means, and perhaps can only mean, equality before the law. Even this, as we know, is not by any means always realized. Persons of wealth and social prestige have an advantage in courts and legislatures over their more needy and humble fellow citizens; but, by and large, we still believe that "justice is the constant will to give each man his due," and we feel openly or secretly ashamed when our system fails to measure up to this standard.

The sincere democrat believes further that individual men and women, while likely to be carried away by appeals to their prejudices or emotions, are, after all, rational creatures capable of understanding and solving the practical problems of individual and social life. This does not mean that the people know the right answers to complicated administrative problems or even that they can pass upon the details of questions of policy. What it *does* mean is that they are as likely to reach reasonable conclusions, when they have the facts, as are "experts" or "leaders." Even so conservative a man as Edmund Burke could say what has not yet ceased to be true:

I am not one of those who think that the people are never in the wrong. They have been so, frequently and outrageously, both in other countries and in this. But I do say that in all disputes between them and their rulers, the presumption is at least upon a par in favor of the people. . . . The people have no interest in disorder. When they do wrong, it is their error, and not their crime. But with the governing part of the state, it is far otherwise. They certainly may act ill by design, as well as by mistake.

This wise remark may well be pondered by all who hanker after a Duce, a Führer, or the "man who knows what ought to be done."

A final article in the democratic faith asserts that basically man is good and therefore capable of altruism and of conduct in accordance with a system of moral law. This optimistic belief is not inconsistent with the recognition of the fact that men are selfish and seek first their own advantage. What it means is that, to have any political society *at all,* the majority of men are obligated and are willing to think at least part of the time in terms of the *general good*. This involves no impossible self-sacrifice. All government involves some restraint; and it is clear that most people more or less willingly submit themselves to such restraint, if for no other reason than that by so doing their own interests are advanced. Thus, the payment of taxes is painful, and if men were completely unsocial they would resist taxation. Yet most men have enough sense of the value of the public services which taxes supply, to pay them with a minimum of grumbling. Of course, this willingness may be explained by saying that taxes buy safety and comfort for the individual; but there is surely more to it than that. It is not merely fanciful to say that most men have some sense of the value of order and education and commodious living. A society as completely self-centered as "the state of nature" pictured by the philosopher Hobbes, would be a society of animals, and animals obviously have no civic spirit.

Requirements of Successful Democracy

Democracy is the creed of a small minority of the world's population. It has had its principal successes in western and northern Europe and in North America, and has won few converts elsewhere. This fact leads one to the conclusion that there are special circumstances, not met with universally, without which it cannot succeed. Some of these circumstances should be examined.

First of all, if the people are to rule, they must be informed about public questions. This means not only that formal education must be available, but that informal channels of information, such as the radio, the press, and public discussion, must be kept open and free. It is the function of schools to preserve and transmit a nation's tradition and to give pupils such an intellectual training as will enable them to deal critically with political issues and to form sound judgments about would-be leaders. In short, the intelligent voter must possess considerable information about government and have a mind capable of discriminating between alternative solutions offered for public problems. An ignorant and uninstructed population cannot operate democratic institutions and is certain to be ruled in a dictatorial fashion.

In the second place, a considerable measure of economic security is necessary if democracy is to work. A population occupied solely in a search for a mere existence will have neither the energy nor the leisure to understand public issues. It is perhaps not too much to say, indeed, that free government is a sort of luxury which only relatively rich peoples can enjoy. Where the masses live on the edge of starvation or discomfort, there will be little interest in the discussion of questions of government. On the contrary, their very insecurity is likely to drive them to accept the rule of dictators who promise to lighten their burdens. If the masses in Latin America and Asia submit meekly to the rule of one or a few, it is not because of any special perverseness; men whose attention is centered on the next meal do not find the ballot significant.

Finally, democracy works best in those countries where there is so complete an agreement on fundamentals that public controversies turn on questions of secondary importance. The existence of such a consensus has been noted above, but its importance will bear reemphasis. The significance of this sort of general agreement may be illustrated by a hypothetical example. If people did not in the main believe in the desirability of the private ownership of property, it is clear that robbery, theft, burglary, and embezzlement would be so widespread as to make order impossible. Likewise, if large numbers of people are without faith in the good will of the majority and in the reasonableness of its policies, the only way out is armed conflict. The minority in the Southern States felt, after the election of 1860, that their interests would be ignored by a majority whose motives they questioned. Although greatly inferior to the North both in population and war potential, the South fought rather than submit. Violence being, of course, the negation of peaceful persuasion and discussion, is incompatible with a democratic regime.

It follows from this that the sorts of matters on which peaceful compromise is difficult or impossible must somehow be excluded from the arena of political controversy. These matters are, of course, precisely the ones that touch men most closely—religion, the management of property, and the form of government. Once such matters are no longer admitted to be legitimate subjects for debate, the issues left are of second-rate importance. But this does not mean that the latter affairs are of no importance at all and therefore that political struggles in a democracy are only sham battles. Such issues as taxation, foreign policy, public improvements, education, and social security *do* affect deeply the prosperity of individuals and classes. The energy with which these are debated at this very hour is sufficient evidence of their significance. Those who insist that every public issue be one of "fundamental" importance need to be reminded that such issues cannot be settled democratically.

The Outlook for Democracy

Some measure of democracy has existed in different parts of the world at various times in the past. In a few places it still exhibits vigor and adaptability. Nevertheless, its brief existence in the past, and its present position as the creed of a minority, prevent our taking its successful future for granted. As a matter of historical fact, modern political democracy achieved its principal triumphs at a moment of time not likely to be duplicated in the foreseeable future. This triumph was, for a brief moment in history, so unquestioned that its permanence could reasonably be assumed.

During the latter half of the nineteenth century, every circumstance conspired to make men believe that, in the course of another hundred years, the system of government which was so closely connected with the prosperity of Western Europe and the United States would be carried by our merchants, our scientists, and our missionaries to the far corners of the earth by the arts of peaceful persuasion and economic penetration. The plough, the cash register, and the Bible were to do the work hitherto confided to the sword.

We know now that no such conquests lie ahead of democracy. It now stands over against bodies of dogma which speak with an authority of which democracy is by its nature incapable—a specious authority, perhaps, but one which is nevertheless compelling with many of the despised and rejected of the earth. A creed such as democracy is at a tremendous disadvantage with communism and fascism. This is true because, at bottom, democracy is skeptical and experimental and, in its methods, untidy and at loose ends. It does not promise certainty about anything, but only holds out freedom in the human search. It demands work and attention and some public spirit of its citizens.

The new political and economic faiths attract followers by their very claims to certainty. Their leaders promise plenty and glory and ask only for the surrender of rights in return for freedom from responsibility. To people who have never *had* rights as we understand them, this surrender is not an impossible one. Even within the democratic nations there are frustrated and unhappy people to whom the appeal of the new faiths has compelling charm. To such people the claims made for democracy by the successful and the comfortable do not seem valid. The unhappy and the embittered may well be the spearhead of an attack on traditional loyalties already weakened by other factors. At the very least, they would constitute the followers of those who prefer their own dominance to the preservation of the democratic way.

In all the democracies there are developments which do not augur well for the future of democracy. One of these is the threat to a genuine consensus, inherent in the complexities of the modern economic and social system. The division of labor in modern industrialism may have destroyed that community of interest upon which democratic citizenship is based. When men think of themselves first as bankers, miners, farmers, steelworkers, or manufacturers and only secondly as citizens, it will be more and more difficult to appeal to them in terms of a higher unity than that which binds them together in occupational and professional groups. If this should turn out to be the pattern of the future, it will be impossible to compromise group interests by democratic means. There will be nothing for it but for someone to "take charge" and impose order at any cost.

A second threat to the perpetuity of democratic government arises from the growing complexity of the governmental process. The ordinary citizen, immersed, as he necessarily is, in earning a living and amusing himself, does not have the time to secure any serviceable understanding of the vast and intricate machinery which governs him and supplies him with necessary or desirable public services. One measure of his disillusionment and sense of helplessness is afforded by his declining interest in the electoral process. The most vigorous propaganda efforts of the political parties bring to the polls barely half of the qualified voters in general elections, while primaries attract far fewer participants. Accompanying this declining interest is a growing cynicism. It is widely believed that elections settle nothing except that one group of "professionals" shall enjoy the sweets of office rather than another, that jobs and not principles are at stake, and that, therefore, there is little point in bestirring oneself.

This may all be very wrongheaded from the point of view of the enthusiastic believers in democracy, but it cannot be condemned out of hand as merely perverse. In any case, we can be certain that if the people do not use what opportunities they have to control public decisions, these decisions will be made by persons whose motives may be suspect. Those who control a government such as that of the United States possess vastly greater power than belonged to the absolute rulers of the past. Each new function of government adds to this power. If officeholders are subject to no such checks as are involved in the voters' power to turn them out, the temptation to use this power to their own advantage may well be too great to be resisted. Democracy may thus be lost by default.

Finally, democracy is threatened by our growing nationalism in the face of threats from alien creeds and powerful foreign enemies. The greatest problem a free people faces is that of preserving, at one and the same time, their national integrity and their traditional individual freedoms. Democracy has always meant the freest possible experimentation with ideas, and also a generous hospitality even to those ideas which seem not only strange but actually dangerous. In times of stress there is always a strong temptation to suppress unpopular views—in the name of principles asserted to be of permanent validity. At such times the strongest appeal, of course, is to the sentiment of patriotism. At its worst this sentiment may be made to correspond to a unanimity which a free society can rarely if ever attain. If, in order to combat ideas thought wrong, the individual is completely swallowed up by the state, as was the case under the recent European dictatorships, free government will have come to an end. Just where to draw the line between allowable freedom to criticize, and direct assaults on the national safety, is admittedly a difficult question. The historic temper of American democracy, however, requires that some chances be taken even with respect to vital matters, in order that the liberty of the individual may be preserved. If this liberty cannot somehow be retained even in the midst of dangers, its reconquest may be difficult or even impossible when these dangers have passed.

All this is, of course, quite frankly speculation. We do not know the actual strength of antidemocratic influences. In our "time of troubles" they may seem stronger than they really are. Against their threat must be balanced the possibilities of survival inherent in our long attachment to the democratic way. Moreover, our pragmatic cast of mind may well be hostile to the mystical appeals of the new political and economic dogmas so attractive to other peoples. Faith in popular rule is, after all, a matter of belief, not a "scientific" principle. Perhaps, no more than other beliefs, will it be lightly abandoned.

REFERENCES

Stuart Chase, *Democracy under Pressure* (1945).
E. Pendleton Herring, *The Politics of Democracy* (1940).
A. D. Lindsay, *The Modern Democratic State* (1947).
John Stuart Mill, *Considerations on Representative Government* (1861).
J. Roland Pennock, *Liberal Democracy* (1950).
Graham Wallas, *Human Nature in Politics* (1908).
Frederick M. Watkins, *The Political Tradition of the West* (1948).

CHAPTER 3 *The Separation of Powers*

The Problem of Free Government

Those who set about to create a government for a free society are confronted by two problems. In the first place, they must give the rulers enough power to do an efficient job. Secondly, they must so limit the exercise of this essential power that it will not be used to oppress the individual for whom the government exists. These objectives are, of course, hard to reconcile simply because political power is morally neutral and may be used either for "good" or "bad" purposes. There may be general agreement among the people as to what is "good" or "bad," but this definition may not be the one arrived at by officials.

Political power might be used consistently with the general well-being and in conformity with popular wishes if every official understood accurately the desires of the public. No official can have this perfect understanding. There are many reasons for this. The official may simply be ill-informed concerning public opinion as was, for example, Sir Samuel Hoare in 1935, when he saw his notorious "Hoare-Laval deal" repudiated by an indignant Parliament in which his party had a safe majority. Or, an official may be ambitious for more power than public opinion is willing to allow him. Or, he may, because of an otherwise praiseworthy zeal to do a good job, propose things which the public is not ready to approve, as was apparently the case when President Franklin Roosevelt suggested remodeling the Supreme Court.

As active and experienced politicians, the makers of our Constitution were aware of these difficulties. They were also for the most part men of learning who knew in detail the record of usurpation exhibited by governments in the past. More to the point, they had crossed swords in the immediate past with arrogant and arbitrary English colonial governors. Besides all this, they knew that they were exceeding the strict letter of their instructions in drafting a *new* Constitution. They knew especially that the powerful national government which they were suggesting would be

31

subject to severe criticism when it came before the state conventions for acceptance or rejection. It is also true that they themselves believed in individual liberty and were therefore suspicious of strong government. In brief, as statesmen their problem was to create a government strong enough to survive, and as politicians they had to create one that would be acceptable to those who were to live under it.

The problem which faced the men of 1787 has never been better stated than by the author of No. 51 of *The Federalist:* [1]

In framing a government which is to be administered by men over men, the great difficulty lies in this: you must first enable the government to control the governed; and in the next place oblige it to govern itself. A dependence on the people is, no doubt, the primary control on the government; but experience has taught mankind the necessity of auxiliary precautions.

The second sentence here is significant. The writer admits that the people are the final controllers of the government, but he feels that this is not enough, and that "auxiliary precautions" are needed. The chief of these "auxiliary precautions" is the apparatus of the separation of powers and the system of checks and balances.

The writer in *The Federalist* felt that popular control would have to be supplemented by some mechanical contrivance for two reasons. In the first place, in common with most educated men of the day, he did not fully trust the people. In 1787 democracy was a new idea and the adoption of even a little of it was looked upon as a leap in the dark. In the second place, it did not seem feasible to secure popular control by providing for the direct election of national officials. Some other method of control must be found.

The Meaning of the Separation of Powers

In order to prevent the concentration of governing power in the hands of one or a few officials, the Constitution provides for a separation of powers. What does this mean? It means, in general, that the powers assigned by the Constitution to the legislative, executive, and judicial branches of the national government shall be exercised solely by the branch to which they are committed, no other department sharing in this exercise.

If this is thought of as a way of dividing up the work of government, there is nothing very new or significant about it. In the ancient world, Aristotle made some such division, and a hundred years before the Constitutional Convention of 1787 the philosopher John Locke described government in somewhat similar terms. What is distinctive about the separation of powers, as conceived by the men of 1787, is that it is *a doctrine of liberty*. To defend the device as serving the cause of liberty, the founders

[1] There is doubt as to whether Hamilton or Madison wrote this paper.

of the American Republic frequently quoted as an authority the French philosopher, Montesquieu (1689–1755), who had written in *The Spirit of the Laws:*

When the legislative and executive powers are united in the same person or body, there can be no liberty, because apprehension may arise lest the same monarch or senate should enact tyrannical laws to execute them in a tyrannical manner. Were the power of judging joined with the legislative, the life and liberty of the subject would be exposed to arbitrary control, for the judge would then be the legislator. Were it joined to the executive power, the judge might behave with all the violence of an oppressor.

The authority of a philosopher was hardly needed, however, to support a position on these matters which had been arrived at as a result of concrete experience. Colonial history had been filled with clashes between the various branches of the state governments, and the "fathers" had been personally concerned in some of these clashes. In fact, most of the state constitutions drawn up during the Revolution provided for the separation of powers. Perhaps the clearest of these statements is that found in the Massachusetts constitution of 1780:

The legislative department shall never exercise the executive and judicial powers or either of them; the executive shall never exercise the legislative and judicial powers or either of them; the judicial shall never exercise the legislative and executive powers or either of them to the end this be a government of laws and not of men.

In addition to all of these considerations it must be said that public men generally wished to avoid a concentrated government, because they feared it would be a meddlesome government. It must be remembered that in 1787 the Western world was only beginning to emerge from a long epoch of overgovernment, examples of which were ready to hand in the navigation acts which had so plagued the colonists throughout the eighteenth century. The rising manufacturing and trading classes in the new country did not relish a government strong enough to halt the growing tendency to greater commercial freedom. This sort of consideration may have been in the mind of Madison when he argued that the powers granted to the new national government were few and clearly defined. In any case, a device such as the separation of powers would at least make government a cumbersome business and perhaps minimize the dangers which men feared.

The Mechanics of the Separation of Powers

There is in the Constitution itself no direct statement of the doctrine of separation of powers. It is inferred rather from the sentences with which the first three articles of that instrument begin:

All legislative powers herein granted shall be vested in a Congress . . . The executive power shall be vested in a President of the United States of America . . . The judicial power of the United States shall be vested in one Supreme Court, and in such inferior courts as the Congress may from time to time ordain and establish.

On the basis of this arrangement the doctrine has from the first been clearly established as a principle of governmental organization and has been enforced by the courts exactly as any other legal rule. One of the many statements of it is found in the judgment of the United States Supreme court in *Kilbourn v. Thompson:* [2]

It is believed to be one of the chief merits of the American system of written constitutional law that all the powers intrusted to government, whether state or national, are divided into the three grand departments, the executive, the legislative, and the judicial; that the functions appropriate to each of these branches of government shall be vested in a separate body of public servants; and that the perfection of the system requires that the lines which separate and divide these departments shall be broadly and clearly defined. It is also essential to the successful working of this system that the persons intrusted with power in any one of these branches shall not be permitted to encroach upon the powers confided to the others, but that each shall by the law of its creation be limited to its own department and no other.

When one considers closely the mechanics of the separation of powers, it is seen to exhibit great ingenuity. First of all, the President, each branch of Congress, and the judges are chosen in different ways, so that the authority of each may be traced to a different source. Next, the President is elected by an indirect process which is supposed to make him independent at once of the people, the Congress, and the state legislatures. It was argued at the time and is still asserted that this method of choice placed the President above the level of ordinary partisan and sectional controversy and made it possible for him to mediate among various clashing interests, thus protecting the general public interest. As to Congress, the House of Representatives was to be chosen by such citizens as the states might permit to vote for their own lower houses, and was thought of as representing the people at large. The Senate, with a view to making it more "aristocratic," and therefore a check on the "democracy" of the lower chamber, was to be chosen by the state legislatures which were assumed to be more conservative.[3]

[2] 103 U.S. 168, 190–191 (1880). There is a more modern discussion in *Hampton v. United States,* 276 U.S. 394 (1928).

[3] The Senate is now, of course, chosen by a direct vote of the people in the several states and can scarcely be said to be either more conservative or more aristocratic than the House of Representatives.

The national courts were to be filled by Presidential appointment, checked by Senate confirmation. Judges were to serve for good behavior and their salaries were to be beyond the immediate reach of the Congress. Additional safeguards against the accumulation of power are to be found in the fact that each branch of the government is chosen for a different term—the House for two years, the Senate for six years with one-third of the body renewable every two years, and the President for four years.

It is clear that any designing leader or group of leaders, desiring to master all the branches of government by using the regular elective processes, would have to win two Senatorial elections and two House elections while controlling the Presidency. At the end of the four years required to accomplish this, the schemers would be faced with a new Presidential election. Even if success crowned these efforts in choosing the political branches of the government, the plotters would in all likelihood find in office judges hostile to their program.

It goes without saying, perhaps, that if political or social conditions were desperate enough to invite such a bid for dictatorship, little heed would be paid to the letter of the Constitution. Nevertheless, the separation of powers has even in ordinary times been a serious obstacle to plots of this sort. It has also been, except in times of crisis, effective in preventing governmental "meddling," since it is often very difficult to get all three branches of the government to act in concert.

The Checks and Balances. The most convinced believers in the doctrine of the separation of powers acknowledged that an absolute separation of the three departments of government would make government itself impossible. It was therefore necessary to introduce modifications of the pure doctrine by setting up what are called the "checks and balances." The justifications for this departure from the pure principle are most interesting. No claim is made in *The Federalist,* for example, that officials are to be guided in their acts by any special care for the public interest. They may, in fact, be completely patriotic and unselfish, but the founding fathers did not count on their being so, expecting rather that in general they would be selfish and jealous of their respective powers. The matter is thus put in No. 51 of *The Federalist:*

But the great security against a gradual concentration of the several powers in the same department consists in giving to those who administer each department the necessary constitutional means and personal motives to resist encroachments of the others . . . Ambition must be made to counteract ambition. The interest of the man must be connected with the constitutional rights of the place. It may be a reflection on human nature, that such devices should be necessary to control the abuses of government. But what is government itself but the greatest of all reflections on human nature. If men were angels, no government would be necessary.

Thus the President may express his view of the public good by vetoing a measure passed by Congress. Incidentally, in using his veto, he is partaking in the legislative process, a fact which itself shows that his functions are not wholly executive. The Congress, if it can muster a two-thirds vote, may then enforce its views by overriding his veto. Or, the Senate may refuse to confirm nominations made to it by the President, or to approve treaties negotiated by the President, and thus influence the conduct of the executive branch of the government. In all of these actions, each branch of the government may be looked upon in the first instance simply as defending its own constitutional prerogatives. The hope is that, in doing so for quite selfish reasons of corporate or personal pride, the liberty of the individual citizen will be protected. As *The Federalist* puts it, "the private interest of every individual shall be a sentinel over the public rights."

A Contrast. Perhaps as good a way as any to illustrate the significance of the separation of powers in action is to contrast it with the quite different system of British government. In Britain there are, of course, legislative, judicial, and executive officers, but they enjoy no such independence as is correctly attributed to similar officers in the United States. It is true that both American and British writers at the end of the eighteenth century spoke of the British Constitution as being "balanced," but even then this had largely ceased to be true. Men on both sides of the Atlantic were too close to government to see that the legislative branch in Britain had already made itself supreme and that the fusion of powers was already wellnigh complete.

In Great Britain today the day-to-day conduct of government is in the hands of the Cabinet. This body, numbering from 20 to 25 members, is to all intents and purposes a committee of Parliament, not formally chosen by that body, but acceptable to it and holding office and power only so long as it can keep the confidence of the lower chamber, the House of Commons, the House of Lords having lost most of its influence on public affairs. The Prime Minister is the head of the Cabinet by virtue of his leadership of the majority of the House of Commons. The formal executive, the Queen, must in practice name as ministers those persons whom the Prime Minister suggests.

Ministers, however, although they hold executive posts, are not merely executive officers. They have, under modern conditions, a practical monopoly in proposing public laws, as well as substantially complete control of the budget. The Ministry may be dismissed by an adverse vote in the House of Commons but, since ministers control the machinery of that chamber, this is not likely to happen and, as a matter of fact, ministries in recent years have lost office only as a result of a general election. The royal veto has not been used since 1707. This, as is the case with all the other legal powers of the Queen, may be exercised only on the advice of ministers, and such advice is not likely to be offered with respect to measures already suggested by ministers and pushed through Parliament by them.

As for the courts, they are powerless to check the Cabinet. Parliament is the legal sovereign in Great Britain, with power not only to enact ordinary statutes but to amend the Constitution itself. Whatever Parliament, under the leadership of the Cabinet, enacts, is constitutional, and the judges may not inquire into the content of laws, no matter how unwise or unfair they may consider them. The most that a British court can do in interpreting an act of Parliament is to hold that an official in acting under its authority has exceeded the powers granted by it. This is quite a different thing from holding the act unconstitutional. A Cabinet in harmony with a majority of the House of Commons can thus do what it likes with the Constitution.

The British system, then, is one in which all legislative and executive powers are united in the Cabinet, which exercises them as it sees fit, subject only to the approval of the House of Commons. This approval is almost never withheld since the majority party controls the procedure of the House. Only if the Cabinet should grossly misinterpret the wishes and the temper of the House is the latter likely to turn upon its chosen leaders and compel their resignation. In practice, then, the only safeguard of the citizen against arbitrary acts of the Cabinet is to choose a Parliament which will repudiate such acts by refusing to support ministers responsible for them. This means, of course, that the defense of liberty which we seek in part through the separation of powers and the system of checks and balances is secured in Great Britain through the pressure of public opinion.

There are special reasons why reliance on the force of public opinion has been an adequate protection for individual liberty in Great Britain. The area of the kingdom is not much greater than that of a middle-sized American state. Ethnically the homogeneity of the population is much greater than in the United States, what with our many racial and national minorities. The economy is almost wholly industrial and the sectional differences that plague American politics are of little significance. All of these factors make it possible to attain and preserve a political consensus within the limits of which all parties operate. In view of the far greater complexity of political life in the United States, it may be reasonably argued that something like our cumbersome and mechanical system of safeguards, embodied in the separation of powers, is necessary to work out a consensus.

How the System Works in Practice. As was remarked above, the scheme of the separation of powers is modified by the system of checks and balances by which the exercise of power by one department may be blocked by a "rival" department having the constitutional right to refuse to assent and thus to compel reconsideration. The net effect of this system has been to encourage, in fact to make necessary, a very considerable degree of what amounts to common consultation among the several branches with respect to suggested public policies. Superficially, this consultation may seem to be only organized quarreling, but actually it amounts to a real, though awkward, discussion. This may be illustrated by a few examples.

Let us assume that a powerful "pressure group" succeeds, by the familiar tactics of propaganda, in securing the enactment by the House of Representatives of a measure which, although of primary interest and value to a minority, may be made to appear of value to the nation as a whole. Other minority interests will, of course, be dissatisfied with such a decision. Consider, for example, the quite different views of desirable public policy held by railroads, airlines, and the trucking industry. The interests defeated in the House will take their cause to the Senate where, of course, they will put *their* case in terms of the *national* good. Since the Senate is somewhat differently constituted and its members are chosen for different terms, there is always the hope of defeating the offensive measure there. If the Senate does defeat the measure, there may be ground for assuming that the House had in fact miscalculated the balance of forces engaged in the controversy.

If the Senate, however, refuses to "check" the House and also passes the bill, it then goes to the President. It is commonly assumed that the President, as the one national officer chosen by the whole people, will take a less partial view of the matter than either house of Congress. This may or may not be true, but, in any case, he may be expected to know what are the forces aligned on both sides of the issue. If he rejects the measure, that is the end of it unless it is reintroduced in another Congress, or unless its friends can secure a two-thirds vote of each house to pass it over his veto—something normally hard to do.

The result of this cumbersome process is that no public policy on the issue involved is possible, at least for the moment. A great deal of time and energy has been expended, much money has been spent in urging the measure's passage or defeat and in conducting hearings before committees, tempers are frayed, and considerable confusion may have been created in the mind of the public. The contrast with the apparent smoothness of the British system, where the ministry may ordinarily expect the support of its followers, is striking. But it may well be that no public consensus on the issues actually existed. In a country as vast in area and as complex in its pattern of sectional and economic interests as the United States, the formation of a clear public mandate requires more time than in a homogeneous society. To the impatient persons who are sure that they know what should be done, the working of the separation of powers and of the system of checks and balances seems little less than a nuisance; to the cautious and to those who do not feel so much confidence in their own wisdom, it may seem that Congress, as the Grand Inquest of the Nation, exists to defeat as well as to accept proposed laws. And it may be added that in times of crisis and danger the separation of powers has not prevented quick and decisive action. When the people know what they want, the device does not defeat their wishes.

A further illustration, in reverse as it were, may be given. Our President is elected on a party platform and on the basis of personal statements as to desirable public policies. Once in office he seeks to have his views embodied in statutes and, as the only national official chosen by all the people, he may appear justified in expecting the other branches of the government to cooperate with him. In any case, he may feel that his own party in the Congress should support him. For a variety of reasons, however, that body may reject the Executive's proposals or amend them in an unacceptable fashion. As the representatives of the varied and complex interests of the country, members of Congress may honestly feel that public opinion is not yet ready to go all the way with the President. There is also in every body like Congress a corporate sense of pride which causes it to reject any proposal likely to redound to the credit or increase the prestige of another branch of the government. This may operate even if both President and Congress are of the same political faith, and many a widely popular President has learned that the "honeymoon" with Congress is a brief one. For these reasons, especially if the proposed policy is of doubtful wisdom or has been little discussed, it is always possible to claim on behalf of the legislative branch that the "private interest of every individual is a sentinel over the public rights."

The Separation of Powers and Administrative Agencies

The separation of powers is, however, a more steadily influential force than is indicated by these somewhat dramatic examples. The grant of legislative power to Congress seems on the surface to prevent its exercise by either of the other branches. That this is not its effect is evident when one observes the extent to which actual government is conducted through rules and "directives" issued by the administrative agencies of the national government. These rules have the force of law and yet do not proceed from the legislative branch at all, or at least not directly. The reasons for this resort to what has been called administrative legislation are not far to seek.

In working out the provisions of a statute, Congress cannot possibly know all of the concrete situations, of almost infinite variety, to which it will have to be applied. Congress has before it some abuse to be remedied, or some conflict between powerful groups in society which must be adjusted in the interest of justice, smooth administration, or public order. As among various ways of correcting an abuse or compromising a conflict, it cannot be known in advance how one or the other may succeed. Congress could not know these things even if it had time to examine all aspects of the problem, and it never has time to do much more than consider its general outlines.

For these reasons Congress has more and more had to content itself with providing in general terms for the solution of the problem before it, turning over the details to administrative officials to be dealt with by appropriate rules and regulations. Are such rules and regulations legislation? If they are held to be so, then it is the executive branch that is making law; and Congress is likely to look with suspicion and distrust upon administrative directives which may more or less seriously modify the general policy contained in the statute. Members of Congress, and many others fearful of "bureaucracy," take the view that the rules of procedure of legislative bodies provide safeguards against arbitrary action which are largely lacking when rules binding upon citizens are made and issued by the administration. There may be much or little substance to such a view, but there can be little doubt as to its persuasiveness with many parts of the public.

The many hundreds of men in the national civil service who make these rules and regulations are permanent employees, in practice guaranteed security in their posts and, in any case, not responsible to the interests affected by their orders with anything like the immediacy felt by members of Congress. These latter every few years must face the voters, and daily they are bombarded by demands that the law be applied with less vigor to interests within their constituencies. Moreover, the experts who man the executive departments are almost by definition antidemocratic in their attitude. The mere fact that they *are* experts sets them apart from the common run of people. Their experience does not involve the endless compromising which is the essence of practical politics. They are likely to believe that two and two make four, whereas in politics the sum often turns out to be three or five! Among such men there may arise an impatience with bumbling government *by* the people as contrasted with some neat plan of government *for* the people.

It is easy to caricature the civil service, as Dickens did in writing about the Circumlocution Office, and as lesser men have done since his day. Suspicion of the methods and motives of civil servants arises primarily from the extreme complexity of many of the matters with which they habitually deal. It is not easy to make these matters clear to laymen, so that in time they come to be regarded as mysterious and somehow sinister. The civil servant then becomes a dealer in a modern kind of black magic and is condemned as a "bureaucrat." Many bureaucrats seem actually to be rather timid people far from tyrannical in their attitude. Even the friends of the permanent service, however, sense the danger that it may escape popular control and are busy seeking to prevent such a development.

Congressional Control of Administration. The devices available to Congress for seeing that its intent is not perverted or defeated by the administrative power to make rules and issue directives are not particularly effective. The committee hearings on the passage of an act and upon appropriation bills afford members a chance to question civil servants, but this seems of doubtful value. Congressional committees are not usually assisted by the kinds of advisers and investigators competent to meet on equal terms the experts who speak for the executive agencies. Only the few members of Congress who have devoted themselves to long study of an agency are capable of asking intelligent questions. Actually, when Congress wishes really to inform itself as to the needs and the work of a department, its committees resort to "borrowing" experts from the department itself.

There is always available to Congress, of course, the prerogative of withholding funds from a department which has incurred its displeasure. In practice this weapon can hardly be used with either efficiency or justice in view of the inability of the lay members of Congress to make an intelligent judgment concerning the reasonableness of an agency's request for funds. As a way of disciplining the bureaucracy, it is blundering, awkward, and unjust. Finally, Congress may conduct full-scale investigations of executive agencies through special committees of either house. Many investigating committees in recent years have "made the headlines," and their work in a general way is familiar to millions. It is not necessary to say that most of these investigations bear only indirectly on the real problem involved here, which is that of supplying some day-to-day oversight of the administration.

The Courts and the Separation of Powers

The problem of controlling the civil service in the interests of democracy and responsibility is one which involves not only an oversight of the rulemaking power. Many of the great agencies used in the enforcement of the law or in the conduct of the business operations of the national government have also long exercised what amounts to judicial power. Before we discuss attempts to solve the problem of controlling the administration, it is necessary to give attention to the way in which the executive and the judicial powers have also been mingled in the ordinary operations of the government.

The part played by the courts in the operation of the scheme of separation of powers and the system of checks and balances is ordinarily not dramatic, for clashes between the judicial and the other branches are not frequent. The action of the courts, especially the Supreme Court, in passing upon the constitutionality of acts of Congress is, however, an important part of the process of discussion and consultation which accompanies the shaping of many important national policies.

In a few cases administration has been completely halted by a decision holding void a statute passed by Congress and approved by the President. Thus, that part of the early New Deal program which embodied the National Industrial Recovery Act was struck down by the Supreme Court within two years of its passage, partly on the ground that Congress had by that law delegated to the President its power to make what amounted to laws, thus flagrantly violating the principle of the separation of powers.[4] It was action by the Supreme Court in this and other cases which led to the attempt by President Franklin Roosevelt in 1937 to change the membership of the Court. Although this assault on the Court was unsuccessful, it is widely believed to have been influential in causing the Court to take a more friendly attitude toward other New Deal legislation. Within a few years several changes occurred in the membership of the Court, giving it a decidedly liberal outlook.[5]

Declaring congressional acts void, while dramatic and productive of much praise or denunciation at the time, is, over the years, an unusual happening. Of more interest to us here is the way in which the courts have found rivals in the administrative agencies. This rivalry springs from the possession by those agencies of something like a judicial power of their own. National bureaus and commissions do not and, in practice, cannot stop with the issuance of rules and directives. As enforcing agencies they must often determine facts and pass judgment upon matters of guilt and innocence. In doing these things they act much as the regular courts do and thus exercise executive, legislative, and judicial powers. On the surface no clearer case could be made for the charge that the principle of the separation of powers is being flouted.

The thing to be remembered in a discussion of this point is that the kinds of cases handled day by day in the bureaus and regulatory commissions of the national government involve important property and individual rights. If these rights could be determined by Congress directly, those claiming them might have the satisfaction of feeling that their cases had been presented to a representative body zealous to protect them. For reasons referred to above such a determination is impossible. Congress has been compelled by the pressure of business to turn over to the civil service not only the authority to issue what amount to minor laws, but also the authority to pass upon the rights and obligations created by such laws. It is true that these minor laws must be consistent with the statute under the authority of which they are issued, but whether or not they are so

[4] *Schechter v. United States*, 295 U.S. 495 (1935).

[5] Thus, in 1935 and 1936, the Court held unconstitutional eleven acts of Congress which were parts of the New Deal, whereas since 1937 only two such decisions, and these in minor matters, have been rendered.

consistent is itself a very difficult question. A few illustrations may be helpful.

The Federal Trade Commission is empowered by act of Congress to prevent unfair competitive practices in interstate commerce, and to do this in proper cases by issuing orders to "cease and desist" from practices deemed unfair. For example, how far may a cigarette advertiser go in making claims for the harmlessness of his product? In such cases the Commission has to make a finding of fact, sit in judgment on the accused, and finally perhaps ban its product from the channels of interstate trade until it has mended its ways. The immigration authorities in the Department of Justice have power to deport aliens under circumstances set forth in the statutes. The State Department has considerable discretion in granting or denying passports for travel abroad. The Securities and Exchange Commission may deprive brokers of their licenses and exclude certain securities from trading on the exchanges. The determinations of these agencies may have every appearance to the outsider of being fair and in line with the public interest, but to the person or corporation affected they may spell the difference between prosperity and bankruptcy, freedom or arbitrary restraint.

Perhaps the principal question of constitutional law which has been before Congress for the past twenty years has been the legitimacy of the exercise of both legislative and judicial powers by administrative agencies. The issue has involved not only the natural suspicion of Congress that its constitutional powers are being exercised by persons only indirectly responsible to it; it raises the even more important question as to whether persons whose affairs are judged by administrative tribunals are being arbitrarily deprived of vital rights without the safeguards existing in the procedure of the regular courts. Tribunals composed of permanent officials have tended to develop their own rules of procedure and these rules are believed by many—and especially by lawyers bred in the tradition of the common law—to be less careful of private rights than the older judicial rules.

In addition to these factors is the practice once common of permitting an administrative body, in the exercise of what is called its quasi-judicial functions, to pass upon the application of rules which it has issued under its quasi-legislative powers. If the same body both makes and enforces a rule, there is at least ground for believing that it is acting as judge in its own cause, thus violating one of the oldest precepts of the common law. In any event, there is at least the possibility that administrative officials, especially if they are possessed of missionary zeal, may abuse such powers, so that, on strictly public grounds, the suspicions of both Congress and the judges may seem to be justified.

The Control of Administrative Discretion

The solution of this problem is extremely difficult. Congress by its own admission cannot legislate on details, and yet wishes to retain adequate and intelligent control of the substance of law. The courts are not equipped to deal with the mass of complicated and technical detail involved in administering laws respecting industrial and business operations. Some flexibility in enforcing such policies is admittedly desirable; and, on the other hand, protection of the individual's rights is essential.

The latest comprehensive attempt to deal with these problems is the Administrative Procedure Act of 1946. This act followed several years of discussion, in and out of Congress, of the alleged evils of administrative lawmaking and adjudication, especially in such important regulatory bodies as the Interstate Commerce Commission, the Federal Trade Commission, and the National Labor Relations Board. Extensive reports on administrative procedure had been made by committees named by the Attorney General and by the American Bar Association, and an earlier act of Congress greatly restricting the quasi-judicial powers of executive agencies had failed of passage only because of the veto of President Franklin Roosevelt.

In general, the Administrative Procedure Act does three things. First, in the case of "administrative lawmaking" it provides a settled procedure for the formulation and publication of rules issued by administrative bodies. There must be a prior consultation between the agency and the persons or interests to be affected by the proposed rule; there must be a public notice of a hearing before the rule may be published, so that all likely to be affected may appear and have their "say"; the rule itself must be published in the *Federal Register;* [6] and there must be a waiting period between the publication and the enforcement of the rule.

In the second place, the act provides for a separation between what may be called the prosecuting and the adjudicating functions of administrative agencies. This is to meet the objection that the same persons were both making and enforcing rules. In effect, this requirement of the act sets up within the agency the principle of the separation of powers, as the finding of the facts and the framing of accusations are handled by one person and the adjudication of the case by others.

Finally, the act considerably enlarges the scope of judicial review of administrative decisions. It is difficult for a layman to discuss the precise effects of the act in this area and we can deal only in generalities. Prior to its passage, however, the decisions of administrative officers and tribunals

[6] The *Federal Register* was established in 1936 for the publication of all Presidential and other Executive and administrative orders. It is issued daily and it is significant to note that it exceeds several times in bulk the annual output of statute law.

were final in a great variety of cases, the assumption apparently being that within the agency's own procedure existed adequate safeguards for the protection of individual rights. As a matter of fact, the Attorney General's Committee on Administrative Procedure, referred to above, reported that in practically all cases the agencies were most scrupulous in giving the affected parties full and sympathetic consideration. In any case, the act itself specifies the kinds of cases which may be appealed to the regular courts. In general, it seems still to be true that the finding of an administrative body as to *fact* is final, unless the record shows the finding to be arbitrary or the procedure used clearly unfair. It is, however, apparently somewhat easier for those with a grievance to get a case to the courts by alleging lack of due process in the agency's procedure or some other denial of accustomed rights guaranteed by the Constitution.[7]

In addition to these strictly legal safeguards against administrative irresponsibility, some informal devices have been developed. Public agencies, no matter how efficient their staffs may be, frequently feel the need of more adequate knowledge of the highly technical matters which they are set to regulate. The most likely place to find this information is in industry itself. Hence it comes about that for many years the government departments have habitually consulted the affected interests prior to the issuance of rules or regulations. The most usual avenue of approach is through the trade associations into which all important industrial enterprises are now organized. There are strong reasons for this kind of cooperation. The government needs the practical advice which it can get from such sources. It is also likely to find its work made much easier if it can secure the prior acceptance of its proposed regulation by the affected businesses.

There is also considerable use made of advisory committees, drawn from the interests affected and attached to the appropriate agency. An example of this is the Advisory Council on Social Security, which is made up of representatives of employers, labor unions, and the general public, and is attached to the Social Security Administration. Although such committees have only advisory powers, they are valuable in quickly making available expert knowledge of the business concerned. At the same time they afford direct representation of such interests in the work of administration.

The use of these devices of consultation is a way of regularizing "lobbying" by special interests. It is important to these interests to be able to present their views to the administration. Consequently wide use is made

[7] It is interesting to note that in 1946 the British Parliament also passed an act for adopting and publishing subordinate legislation. The act makes it possible for Parliament to debate more readily obviously undesirable rules and to question the responsible minister about them. On the subject of this act see J. A. Corry, *Elements of Democratic Government,* Chap. 16, "The Administrative Process," new ed., 1951.

of consultative and advisory committees in Great Britain as well as in the United States. The arrangement has obvious dangers. Regulated interests, of course, want power, at least enough power to get the sort of regulation they desire. They will therefore be tempted to influence in their favor the personnel and procedure of the regulating authority, and it will take able administrators to prevent this sort of development. It may be said, then, that these advisory committees are valuable adjuncts to more formal mechanisms of control, but that they are not answers to the problem discussed here.[8]

The strong feelings aroused during the long controversy preceding the passage of the Administrative Procedure Act, and still being heatedly expressed, are themselves eloquent commentary on the modern status of the doctrine of separation of powers. On the one side are ranged the legal traditionalists and the defenders generally of old-fashioned political theories. Some critics of the act have been unkind enough to say bluntly that its provisions for judicial review were drawn with the idea of making more business for lawyers! On the other side are to be found the believers in the kind of government activity which can be carried out only by an active executive. In short the old doctrine has become a modern political issue of the first importance.

Modern Government and the Separation of Powers

The truth of the matter seems to be that we are trying to retain an eighteenth-century device intended to hamper government, in an age when people seem to demand *much* government. An economy as complex as that of most modern states cannot be regulated effectively by a government constructed on the theory of separation of powers. The doctrine assumes that there is little urgency about policy or little complexity in administration. This view is wholly unrealistic in these modern, complicated times. Ours is an era of speed, urgency, high pressure. Many governmental functions must be performed quickly. They cannot await the leisurely consultation which the scheme of separation of powers enforces upon public men.

In 1789 neither legislation nor administration bore any resemblance to the same functions as we know them in the twentieth century. Legislation in the administration of George Washington was by any standard a simple matter. A glance at the early statute books makes that clear. Administration in the same era was largely a matter of law enforcement in a society in which there were few factories, no industrial corporations, and little

---

[8] Two excellent treatments of this point are E. Pendleton Herring, *Public Administration and the Public Interest,* 1936, and Avery Leiserson, *Administrative Regulation,* 1942.

wealth except in land. Government rendered few services and these were of a simple character.

Today, at an equal pace with the development of industry and technology, the concentration of economic and financial power, and the rise of sectional and class conflicts, government has undertaken nothing less than the regulation and direction of the national economic life. The enforcement of law by the imposition of penalties is less important than a day-by-day oversight of complex industrial and economic processes deeply affecting individual and group welfare. This supervision can hardly be provided for by statute law; it requires an active executive power freed of some of the traditional legal and formal restraints of a government divided sharply into three branches. Nor is this all: government today directly provides services and manages great economic enterprises—the national parks, the Tennessee Valley Authority, the post office. In doing such things it requires the same sort of freedom that is possessed by private corporate enterprises of comparable size and complexity.

To the overly romantic it may seem regrettable that science and technology have created a society such as we have, though few even of these individuals seem to wish to return to the tallow candle, the stage coach, and the rudimentary medicine of the eighteenth century. In any case no such return is possible, and we must make our peace as best we can with the governmental complexities which these changes have produced, just as we have to get on with similar complexities in private business.

An extensive civil service, hierarchically organized and vested with wide discretion, is required by every large enterprise, private or public, under today's complex modern conditions. In 1789 a few hundred clerks, performing routine functions minutely prescribed by acts of Congress, constituted the entire public service. There was no Securities and Exchange Commission because there were no securities and no exchanges; there was no Tennessee Valley Authority; there were no monopolies, no demands for "social security," no railways, telegraphs, telephones, radio, or television networks to regulate—not to mention the dozens of other functions of almost infinite complexity taken on by government since then in response to demands felt by Congress to be just or at least entitled to be met.

If we want to get rid of the "boards, bureaus, and commissions" which we have heard denounced so vociferously by certain politicians and journalists, there is no way to do it but to repeal most of the social and economic legislation of the past three-quarters of a century. This is not likely to be done. Unless it is, civil servants will have to be given what amount to legislative and judicial powers, and we shall have to do our best to see that these powers are exercised in a responsible fashion. The separation of powers is no longer a feasible instrument to accomplish this end. In fact the edges of the doctrine are now badly blurred. Judges do and must legislate in the act of interpreting the law. The law itself must be made in part by administrators in the act of executing it. Rights must be determined by the same officials as an incident to the law's enforcement. The traditional classification of governmental "powers" no longer fits the facts. Enough of the original vigor of the doctrine of separation remains to put the bureaucracy on guard and to preserve a substantial judicial independence, but not enough to prevent the dominant opinion of the nation from having its way with respect to services about which men and women feel deeply.

REFERENCES

Paul H. Appleby, *Policy and Administration* (1948).
Edward S. Corwin, *The Constitution and What It Means Today,* 8th ed. (1946).
The Federalist, Nos. 47–51.
Carl J. Friedrich, *Constitutional Government and Democracy,* rev. ed. (1950).
E. Pendleton Herring, *Public Administration and the Public Interest* (1936).
Charles S. Hyneman, *Bureaucracy in a Democracy* (1950).
James M. Landis, *The Administrative Process* (1938).
Howard L. McBain, *The Living Constitution* (1927).
J. Roland Pennock, *Administration and the Rule of Law* (1941).
Carl B. Swisher, *American Constitutional Development* (1943).

CHAPTER 4 *Judicial Review and the Rule of Law*

The Meaning of Judicial Review

A distinctive American contribution to the art of government is the doctrine and practice of judicial review. By judicial review we mean the authority belonging to the courts to declare acts of the legislative branch of no effect when, in the opinion of the judges, such acts are inconsistent with the requirements of the Constitution. It includes also, of course, the authority to nullify executive acts purporting to be authorized by such legislation. Although the final judgment in cases of this sort is made by the Supreme Court of the United States, judicial review is a prerogative of all courts from the highest to the lowest, being attached, by custom and tradition, to the judicial branch of the government. Even a justice of the peace may exercise this authority in proper cases although his decision, of course, would certainly be appealed.

When a court declares a legislative act unconstitutional, what it does technically is to refuse to enforce it on the ground that its inconsistency with the Constitution deprives it of the character of law and therefore of any binding force. The courts, of course, have little physical force at their disposal to carry out their decrees and, as a matter of theory, an executive officer might ignore their judgments. This has actually happened in a few cases, as, for example, in a famous case in connection with which President Andrew Jackson wrathfully remarked that "John Marshall has made his decision, now let him enforce it." In the vast majority of cases, however, the prestige of the doctrine is so great that a pronouncement of the courts is accepted as final even when the act declared unconstitutional is a popular one.[1]

[1] The Supreme Court's view of the nature of its action in holding an act void was well expressed in a case decided in 1936. This decision declared unconstitutional the act of Congress levying processing taxes on certain farm products as a means of raising revenue with which to pay benefits to farmers. "When an act of Congress is appropriately challenged in the courts as not conforming to the constitutional mandate, the judicial branch of the Government has only one duty—to lay the article of the

49

Origins of Judicial Review

The national Constitution itself makes no clear grant of authority to the courts to review legislative acts. If there is any constitutional basis for the authority it must be grounded on an interpretation of two statements in that document, neither of them definite enough to be good evidence of the specific intent of the framers. The second section of Article III, referring to the judicial power of the United States, contains these words: "The judicial power shall extend to all cases, in law and equity, arising under this Constitution. . . ." It might possibly be inferred from this that the Constitution itself was to be the standard by comparison with which legislative acts were to be judged, but students of the subject do not believe that the words inevitably lead to such an interpretation.[2] In Article VI, the Constitution provides:

This Constitution, and the laws of the United States which shall be made in pursuance thereof; and all treaties made, or which shall be made, under the authority of the United States, shall be the supreme law of the land; and the judges in every State shall be bound thereby, anything in the constitution or laws of any State to the contrary notwithstanding.

It might be argued from this that the fathers intended the courts to have the authority to declare void the acts of state legislatures, but such an interpretation by no means follows inevitably, and, in any case, power over acts of Congress is not conferred. At the very most, the language of the Constitution is too ambiguous to support an argument that judicial review is specifically provided in that instrument.

An inquiry into the possible expectations of the framers of the Constitution is somewhat more rewarding. Many years ago, the historian Charles A. Beard, after a careful study, came to the conclusion that a majority of the members of the Convention of 1787 favored judicial review or, at any rate, expected it to be one of the functions of the courts.[3] It may be further noted that many of the members were aware of the fact that state courts had already in a few cases exercised what looked at least very much like judicial review of state acts. All of this evidence, however, lacks compelling force—at least in terms of the present scope of judicial review.

What came to be the official view of the Supreme Court of the United States was stated by Hamilton in No. 78 of *The Federalist.*

Constitution invoked beside the statute which is challenged and to decide whether the latter squares with the former. All the court does or can do is to announce its considered judgment on the question." *United States v. Butler,* 297 U.S. 62–63 (1936).

[2] Much later, however, Chief Justice Marshall said that "a case in law or equity . . . may truly be said to arise under the Constitution or law of the United States whenever its correct solution depends on the construction of either." *Cohens v. Virginia,* 6 Wheat. 264 (1821).

[3] Charles A. Beard, *The Supreme Court and the Constitution* (1912).

The interpretation of the laws is the proper and peculiar province of the courts. A constitution is, in fact, and must be regarded by the judges, as a fundamental law. It therefore belongs to them to ascertain its meaning, as well as the meaning of any particular act proceeding from the legislative body. If there should happen to be an irreconcilable variance between the two, that which has the superior obligation and validity ought, of course, to be preferred; or, in other words, the Constitution ought to be preferred to the statute, the intention of the people to the intention of their agents.

The view here set forth by Hamilton was accepted by Chief Justice John Marshall in the first case in which an act of Congress was held invalid, in words that are almost a paraphrase of Hamilton's language: [4]

It is a proposition too plain to be contested, that the Constitution controls any legislative act repugnant to it. . . . It is emphatically the province and duty of the judicial department to say what the law is. Those who apply the rule to particular cases must of necessity expound and interpret that rule. If two laws conflict with each other, the courts must decide on the operation of each.

If, then, the courts are to regard the Constitution, and the Constitution is superior to any ordinary act of the legislature, the Constitution, and not such ordinary act, must govern the case to which they both apply.

Hamilton and Marshall both assert that the Constitution has the character of fundamental law superior to statutes, and that conflicts between the two orders of law may be settled by the courts in the discharge of their ordinary duties, precisely as if two contradictory statutes were involved. No claim is made that judges are in some mysterious way superior to legislators, but only that the Constitution is a rule for their guidance of transcendent, binding authority. Their act in declaring a statute void is one not of will but of judgment, and their decision is arrived at with all of the preciseness and inevitability attached to a logical syllogism.

Whatever future experience may have done to these doctrines, they were certainly novelties of constitutional law in the late eighteenth century. It is true that the great oracle of the common law, Sir Edward Coke, had in 1610 expressed similar views. In the famous case of Dr. Bonham, the Lord Chief Justice had said that "it appears in our books that in many cases the common law will control Acts of Parliament and sometimes adjudge them to be utterly void; for when an Act of Parliament is against common right or reason, or repugnant or impossible to perform, the common law will control it and adjudge such act to be void." It is also true that this argument had been relied on by James Otis in his attempt to outlaw writs of assistance during the pre-Revolutionary quarrel with England. The opinion of Coke, however, was what the lawyers call "dictum"—something said in passing and not necessary to the decision of the case in hand—and was

[4] *Marbury v. Madison*, 1 Cranch 137 (1803).

largely disregarded in England both when announced and during the ensuing century. As to Otis's plea, it came at a time when the colonists had lost their argument on strict legal grounds and were beginning to justify rebellion by appeals to political theory. In any case, it is beyond doubt that the Glorious Revolution of 1688 established the absolute legal supremacy of Parliament. In England at least Coke's argument soon lost any influence it may have had as legal dogma.

As a matter of fact, by the date of our Constitution legislative bodies on both sides of the Atlantic had engrossed the bulk of the powers of government. No one in England seriously questioned the sovereignty of positive law as enacted by Parliament. The great Blackstone in the main clearly asserted that no ordinary court could question the validity of an act of Parliament.[5] The French political philosopher Rousseau (1712–1778) in his *Social Contract* had parliamentary supremacy in mind when he remarked that the English were free only at the moment of a general election and then used their freedom to enslave themselves by choosing an omnipotent Parliament. Among the American states in the period immediately preceding the Constitutional Convention of 1787 the legislatures were substantially sovereign bodies, completely dwarfing the two other branches of government. If continuity with English precedents had been preserved, judicial review as we know it now would not have developed. This continuity was broken by peculiarly American circumstances.

The Establishment of Judicial Review

The first development preparing the way for the acceptance of the doctrine was the changing conception of the nature of a written constitution. The colonies, forced by the exigencies of separation from the mother country to construct new governments, looked upon their first constitutions as assertions of popular power rather than as arrangements of any special sanctity. It was not long, however, until the Constitution came to be thought of as a superior grade of law proceeding from the sovereign people. It was a logical step from this conception to the conclusion that laws enacted by the people's agents, the legislatures, were of subordinate rank and to be held of no effect when inconsistent with the supreme law.

In the second place, the activities of many of the state legislatures during and immediately after the outbreak of the Revolution were such as to cause the conservative elements in the population to seek some means to control them. The passage of acts staying the foreclosure of mortgages and providing for paper money unsupported by a metallic basis was a direct threat

[5] It was as the first Vinerian professor of law at Oxford that Blackstone delivered the lectures later published (1765–1769) as his *Commentaries on the Laws of England.* This work continued for well over a century to be the leading general legal treatise in both Britain and the United States. As late as the present writer's youth, men studying law were referred to as "reading Blackstone," and often literally did so.

to the interests of the creditor class which, as is well known, was prominent in the convention that framed the Constitution. One device to halt such legislation was the executive veto which was introduced into both national and state constitutions. It cannot be demonstrated that conservatives directly demanded judicial review as a means of thwarting "radical" policies, but experience within those states controlled by the debtor class at least prepared the minds of men for acceptance of the doctrine when it was officially announced by John Marshall.

It is also true that in the 1780s a number of decisions were rendered by state supreme courts in which something very like the full-blown doctrine was applied. In 1786, for example, the supreme court of Rhode Island declared void a paper-money law of the state, and in the following spring the highest court of North Carolina outlawed an act of the assembly on the specific ground that it violated both the state constitution and the Articles of Confederation. One of the lawyers in the latter case was a delegate to the Constitutional Convention and, since reports of both cases were printed in the Philadelphia newspapers in 1787, members generally may be assumed to have known about them. Counsel against the legislative acts in both cases developed their arguments along the same line as that taken by Hamilton in No. 78 of *The Federalist*.

Judicial review became a part of our constitutional law—in fact, its very cornerstone—with the announcement of the judgment of the Supreme Court of the United States in the case of *Marbury v. Madison* in 1803. William Marbury had been appointed justice of the peace in the District of Columbia by President John Adams at the very end of his administration. His commission had been signed by the President but had not been delivered to him when Jefferson took office March 4, 1801. Marbury brought an action directly in the Supreme Court to compel Madison, the new Secretary of State, to hand over his commission. In bringing his suit he relied upon a section of the Judiciary Act of 1789 conferring original jurisdiction in mandamus cases on the Supreme Court.[6] The Court ruled that his appointment was completed, that he was entitled to his commission, and that mandamus was the proper writ in such cases. It refused to issue the writ, however, on the ground that the act under which Marbury brought his suit was unconstitutional in attempting to give the Supreme Court *original* jurisdiction in mandamus cases whereas the Constitution itself provided that it should have in such cases only an *appellate* jurisdiction.

The decision of Marshall in this case was not based upon a review of precedents, for none was cited in its support. The opinion was in fact an exercise in logical reasoning which, it must be admitted, is persuasive. Once one grants that the statute in question is inconsistent with the con-

---

[6] The writ of mandamus which Marbury sought is an order issued by a court to compel a person, usually a public official, to perform a nondiscretionary duty.

stitutional provision applicable, said the Chief Justice, the Court has no choice but to uphold the Constitution and strike down the statute. The presumption here is that the Constitution is an expression of the will of the sovereign people while the statute is the act of their agents, the Congress. In such cases, there can be no doubt but that the will of the sovereign is to be preferred and enforced. Furthermore, continued the Chief Justice, this is a government of limited powers and it would be fruitless to set limits upon the Congress if that body could ignore them.

Although the judgment in this celebrated case established the practice of judicial review in our constitutional law, it is interesting to note that this part of the decision was at the time subjected to little or no criticism. Chief Justice Marshall, a Federalist sympathizer who had been appointed by John Adams, was deeply distrusted by Jefferson and his followers, but he was attacked, not for holding that the Supreme Court could set aside an act of Congress, but rather because he was willing to issue the process of the Court against such a high executive officer as the Secretary of State and because of his alleged sympathy with "aristocratic" views. Actually, although the argument of unconstitutionality was presented to the Supreme Court on several occasions in the next half century, no congressional act was again declared void until 1857 when, in the Dred Scott case, a badly divided Court denied to Congress the power to exclude slavery from the territories. Between the close of the Civil War and 1900, 24 acts or parts of acts were declared unconstitutional. Between 1900 and 1934 about 40 such decisions were rendered. Within the four years immediately after inauguration of the so-called New Deal, eleven acts of Congress were struck down by the Court.

Since the practice of judicial review accepts literally and completely the proposition that the national Constitution is the supreme law of the land, it follows that state as well as congressional legislation may be tested by its conformity with the Constitution as that instrument is understood by the Supreme Court. Seven years after *Marbury v. Madison,* the Court held unanimously that an act of a state legislature attempting to recover lands granted by the state was in violation of that portion of the national Constitution prohibiting the states from passing laws impairing the obligation of a contract.[7] The effect of these two decisions which became precedents for many judgments in the future was to constitute the Supreme Court the final arbiter of the constitutional law of both the states and the United States. In other words, what Congress, the state legislatures,

---

[7] *Fletcher v. Peck,* 6 Cranch 87 (1810). There was in this case ample evidence that the lands in question had been granted by a corrupt legislature. The Supreme Court held nevertheless that the grant was valid, saying that "the grant when issued conveyed an estate in fee simple . . . clothed with all the solemnities which law can bestow. This estate was transferable; and those who purchased parts of it were not stained by that guilt which infected the original transaction."

county boards, and local councils may or may not do is a question finally answered by the nine Justices of the Supreme Court of the United States. The law and the Constitution are what the judges say they are.

The Employment of Judicial Review

Since 1789 Congress has passed about 30,000 public acts. Of these the Supreme Court has declared about eighty unconstitutional. Looked at in this way the Court's authority has been used very sparingly. In this connection, however, two things should be emphasized. The first is that many of the acts struck down were of first-rate importance, involving weighty economic interests and the political and economic hopes and fortunes of large numbers of persons. One need cite only such decisions as those in the Dred Scott case, the income tax law of 1894, and the New Deal legislation of the 1930s to grasp the larger political significance of judicial review. Furthermore, with the passage of time and the closer integration of the economic and social structure of the nation, the judgments of the Court will grow more and more vital. In the second place, the mere possession of this authority by the courts is more or less constantly in the minds of lawmakers and for this reason affects the form and content of proposals before Congress and the state legislatures.

It follows from this that every judgment of the courts, and especially of the Supreme Court, on matters affecting large interests, is certain to involve the judiciary in politics. In the strictly partisan sense of the term, the Supreme Court has been above politics; in the wider sense, any body with such authority cannot avoid making decisions which have political implications. It is in a very real sense a superlegislature and as such is necessarily involved in controversy whenever the issues with which it deals are ones about which men feel passionately. Presidents have of course been aware of this in exercising their power of appointment and have normally sought out men likely to share the views of the administration in office. When President Franklin Roosevelt sought to add six members to the Court in 1937, it was surely no secret that, if the power he sought were granted by the Congress, the new members to be named would join with the more "liberal" members of the existing Court in upholding the legislation to which the administration had committed itself. Before President Theodore Roosevelt named Oliver Wendell Holmes to the Court in 1902 he made careful inquiries of Senator Henry Cabot Lodge as to whether Judge Holmes agreed with him "on the great issues of the day."

Congress itself has not scrupled to interfere on occasion with both the personnel and the jurisdiction of the Supreme Court. During its history the size of the Court has been changed no fewer than seven times and there is reason to believe that on every occasion the change was prompted by the desire to secure decisions of a certain sort. It must be remembered also that both the structure and the jurisdiction of the federal court system are subject to the authority of Congress. Presumably there must always be a Supreme Court, since the Constitution itself provides for it, but Congress is free to contract or expand its appellate jurisdiction as well as that of the lower federal courts as seems wise to it. On at least one occasion, in fact, Congress so altered the appellate jurisdiction of the Supreme Court as to prevent its reviewing an act which was already before a lower court for adjudication.[8]

Most of these specific incidents are only illustrations of the general issue involved in the existence and exercise of judicial review. Controversies about this authority can scarcely be avoided in a nation presumably devoted to the principle of majority rule. There *is* something undemocratic about permitting nine men, serving for life and chosen by appointment, to nullify policies which proceed from bodies representing the mass of the voters and presumably expressing their will. Concerning this dilemma all one can say is that the people have in general acquiesced in the check imposed by the courts. There has actually been little or no demand for abolishing judicial review, its continuance being assumed even by various schemes for altering the personnel and jurisdiction of the courts.

The Rationale of Judicial Review

In general, two views have been held with respect to the process by which the courts reach a judgment as to the constitutionality of a legislative act. One follows closely and literally the argument of Hamilton and Marshall to the effect that the process of testing a statute is an exercise in legal logic, the conclusion of which follows inevitably from certain premises. In this view the courts act quite impersonally, much as a mathematician would in solving an equation. This is obviously an oversimplification of the process of judicial review. Neither the facts before the courts nor the words of Constitution and statutes are fixed and bloodless abstractions. Controversies do not get to the higher courts unless men honestly differ about the meanings of terms and feel deeply about the definitions of those terms which the courts are urged to accept. The process of interpreting the Constitution is not an operation in legal mathematics; at the very least it is an act of statesmanship, that is, of political judgment. The important question is whether the courts are better agencies for making such judgments than the other branches of the government.

At the other extreme are those persons who maintain that judges' decisions are determined by their station in society, their party or personal or class prejudices, even by the state of their digestion. This is to assert that judicial review amounts merely to an asserting of will, a will no more

[8] *Ex parte McCardle*, 7 Wall. 506 (1869).

entitled to respect than that of the legislature. This is also, of course, an oversimplification. It may as well be admitted that judges, like other men, are the products of their environments, and of the family, educational, economic, and professional influences to which they are exposed. In an imperfect world there are only approximations to complete disinterestedness, never its perfect attainment. In the United States judges have been chosen less perhaps because of legal learning and purely professional eminence than because they were what for want of a better term we call men of affairs.

It is also true, of course, that the words which judges deal with in construing the law are capable of an almost infinite number of interpretations. If this were not so, indeed, few controversies would ever reach the appellate courts. Consider, for example, the possibilities inherent in such words as "liberty," "commerce," and "due process of law," about which most constitutional cases in recent years have turned. Able and disinterested men, in Congress and the state legislatures, on the bench and at the bar, can and do honestly differ as to their meaning.

In every government operating under a written constitution *some* authority must pass finally upon the effective meaning of these and many other terms. A very strong argument can be made for putting the power to do this in the hands of the judges. The circumstances of their appointment, at least in the case of the national government, are calculated to protect them from the more crass forms of political and partisan pressure and to lift them above the passions of the hour. Federal judges serve during good behavior, have their salaries guaranteed against diminution by Congress, and may be removed only by the cumbersome process of impeachment. Much weight must also be attributed to the fact that judges are members of an ancient profession and as such conscious of the force of the tradition of their craft. Not all lawyers, it is true, are loyal to their obligations as officers of the court, but it may be assumed that the majority of those who reach the bench are aware of the significance of their position. It is not being wholly fanciful to regard them as the defenders of the Constitution and the conscience of the nation.

This does not mean, however, that judges are either the embodiment of pure reason or forever indifferent to the forces which play upon the "political" branches of the government. They know what is going on in the world as well as, or perhaps better than, the active politicians in the legislature, and they are not without ability to sense the force and direction of social movements which find expression in statute law. In the last analysis the judicial veto is a suspensory one. A former distinguished Justice of the Supreme Court wrote many years ago these eloquent words about the place and function of judges in our system: [9]

[9] Benjamin N. Cardozo, *The Nature of the Judicial Process*, p. 168, 1921.

The great tides and currents which engulf the rest of men do not turn aside in their course and pass the judges by . . . The law, conceived of as a real existence, dwelling apart and alone, speaks through the voices of priests and ministers the words which they have no choice except to utter.

In any discussion about the desirability of judicial review the practical question to ask is whether the final word is to be spoken by the direct representatives of the people in legislative or executive offices, or by the judges who are less immediately responsive to what appear to be popular desires. Preference for one system or the other doubtless depends largely upon one's temperament and upon the urgency one feels about the adoption or defeat of proposed policies.

The Rule of Law

One of the leading principles emphasized in all legal and political systems derived from England is that which goes by the name "rule of law." In a general way the rule of law simply means that the law and not men should rule, that known rules of procedure and not the personal will or whim of officials should control in all exercises of governmental power. The germ of this idea is to be found in the *Politics* of Aristotle. After examining the claims to power of the one, the few, and the many, the Greek philosopher reached the conclusion that law and not men should rule. This was preferable, he thought, because he believed that there was something of the beast in the rule even of the best of men. By contrast, he said, law is "reason unaffected by desire" and hence a safer sovereign than even the wisest man or group of men. While the idea embodied herein is no longer stated in the language used by Aristotle, the modern rule of law in English-speaking countries is really only an elaboration of it.

During the late Middle Ages and the early modern period, when kings were looked upon with awe, the tradition persisted that even the monarch was not absolute. He was held to be subject to law, the latter term meaning essentially the custom of the folk, which was felt to be binding upon the high as well as upon the low. So pervasive had this idea become that the French lawyer, Bodin, while assigning to his king supreme law-making power, nevertheless asserted that the king could not act contrary to what he called the constitutional laws of the realm (*leges imperii*)—in other words, established custom and procedure. Long before Bodin's day the English jurist, Bracton, had declared that the king was subject to the law. This view was well established in the thinking of English lawyers and publicists before the end of the sixteenth century. When King James I angrily asserted that the independence of his judges meant that he was *under* the law, which, he declared, was "treason to affirm," his Chief Justice Coke replied: "Thus wrote Bracton: 'The King ought not to be under any man, but he is under God and the law.'" The Stuart monarchs were not temperamentally constructed so as to accept this view readily, but by 1688 it was established beyond doubt in the jurisprudence of Britain, one ruler having lost his head and another his throne by stubbornly opposing it.

In American and English law the proposition has again and again been successfully asserted that no official may act without authority of law, no matter how desirable in any individual case his proposed action may be. It is *law* that is to rule, not the *will* of any man, no matter how wise or well-disposed he may be. This aspect of the general rule has in modern times been given classic expression by the late Professor Albert V. Dicey: [10]

. . . no man is punishable or can be lawfully made to suffer in body or goods except for a distinct breach of law established in the ordinary legal manner before the ordinary Courts of the land. In this sense the rule of law is contrasted with every system of government based on the exercise by persons in authority of wide, arbitrary, or discretionary powers of restraint.

In the United States the rule is inextricably associated with the doctrine of the separation of powers, the principal purpose of which has been to prevent the exercise of personal power as distinct from power in accordance with law. It is the object of this constitutional contrivance to prevent the exercise of arbitrary power by requiring the adoption of rules only after a process of debate, deliberation, and conference intended to maximize reason and minimize mere will. The close connection between the rule of law and the separation of powers has been emphasized hundreds of times by the American courts. One of the most eloquent explanations of the purpose of the latter doctrine is that given a quarter of a century ago by Justice Brandeis: [11]

The doctrine of the separation of powers was adopted by the convention of 1787, not to promote efficiency but to preclude the exercise of arbitrary power. The purpose was, not to avoid friction, but by means of the inevitable friction incident to the distribution of the governmental powers among three departments, to save the people from autocracy.

The most recent reaffirmation of the rule of law in this sense occurred under dramatic circumstances. In the spring of 1952, President Truman, acting under his alleged authority as President and Commander in Chief, seized the steel industry of the country and directed the Secretary of Commerce to operate it. The ground for this action was the necessity of insuring a supply of steel for civilian and defense uses. The President relied on no act of Congress for authority but simply upon powers purported to belong to him as President and Commander in Chief. The Supreme Court denied that the President, *simply as President and Commander in Chief,*

[10] Albert V. Dicey, *Introduction to the Study of the Law of the Constitution,* 8th ed., pp. 183–184, 1915.
[11] *Myers v. United States,* 272 U.S. 52 (1926).

had any constitutional authority to do what he had attempted, and ordered the return of the steel industry to its private owners. It is true that the Court's decision was based very largely upon its understanding of the doctrine of separation of powers, yet the rule of law was clearly in the mind of Justice Jackson when he wrote: [12]

The essence of our free Government is 'leave to live by no man's leave, underneath the law'—to be governed by those impersonal forces which we call law. Our Government is fashioned to fulfill this concept so far as humanly possible. The Executive, except for recommendation and veto, has no legislative power. The executive action we have here originated in the individual will of the President and represents an exercise of authority without law. No one, perhaps not even the President, knows the limits of the power he may seek to exert in this instance and the parties affected cannot learn the limit of their rights. We do not know today what powers over labor or property would be claimed to flow from Government possession, if we should legalize it, what rights to compensation would be claimed or recognized, or on what contingency it would end. With all its defects, delays, and inconveniences, men have discovered no technique for long preserving free government except that the Executive be under the law and that the law be made by parliamentary deliberations.

Such institutions may be destined to pass away. But it is the duty of the Court to be last, not first, to give them up.

It is obvious that the purpose of the rule of law is to prevent precisely the sort of conduct observable in dictatorial governments. The rule itself has nothing to do with the severity or even with the apparent arbitrariness of statute law. For example, the criminal laws of Great Britain were notoriously savage in the eighteenth century when the rule was well established. The point is, however, that no one was in doubt as to the provisions of the law and that there was, on the whole, nothing arbitrary about its administration. On the continent at the same time there were no legal guarantees of individual rights, and the property, personal liberty, and even the life of the citizen could be taken away at the unfettered will of the Crown. When the Bastille fell in July, 1789, it contained fewer than a dozen prisoners, yet its capture by the Paris revolutionists was rightly heralded as a stroke for liberty since it stood as the symbol of a lawless system under which French subjects could be deprived of their liberty at the pleasure of the King or of anyone powerful enough to gain the ear of majesty. In spite of the misery and squalor of large numbers of Englishmen at this period, their essential rights were recognized and safeguarded, and they could be punished only for infractions of known laws after a trial by jury. It is no wonder that such eminent Frenchmen as Voltaire and Montesquieu were loud in their praises of English liberty.

The rule of law as enforced by American courts is also effective against

[12] *Youngstown Sheet and Tube Co. v. Sawyer,* 343 U.S. 579 (1952).

arbitrary acts of legislatures, although it is clear that in its usual application it has been directed against the pretensions of executive and administrative officials. In our history it is the latter who have been feared and suspected. Legislatures may act despotically, but it has always been assumed that the opposition of wills in a representative body will lead eventually to a compromise acceptable to all sides. In our system, however, the courts have not hesitated to declare void legislative acts which struck them as arbitrary or unreasonable. The "due process of law" required by both the Fifth and the Fourteenth Amendments to the national Constitution means not only that a certain valid procedure must be followed in enforcing a statute, but also that the statute itself shall be so free of ambiguities and so clear in its requirements that all persons affected may know in advance their rights and obligations. Whether or not such clarity exists is a question for the courts, which do not hesitate to strike down statutes which lack it.

We have discussed the rule of law in this chapter because it is a peculiarity of our system that the rights of the citizen are not drawn directly from constitutional guarantee but are enforced by the courts in the exercise of their ordinary jurisdiction. The importance of this point is clear when we recall that, although many modern constitutions contain elaborate bills of rights, no adequate machinery exists for enforcing them. From the American point of view, at least, the "rights" enumerated in the Russian Constitution of 1936 are without substance, since no independent judiciary exists to enforce them as against the government. The following language of Dicey applies to the United States as well as to England: [13]

We may say that the constitution is pervaded by the rule of law on the ground that the general principles of the constitution (as for example the right to personal liberty, or the right of public meeting) are with us the result of judicial decisions determining the rights of private persons in particular cases brought before the courts; whereas under many foreign constitutions the security (such as it is) given to the rights of individuals results, or appears to result, from the general principles of the constitution.

The rule of law in the United States thus grows out of concrete controversies between citizens and officials and is determined by a judiciary as independent of both as human contrivance can make it and as human frailty will permit. In such cases the officials have no rights arising from their official position; they may not plead the orders of their superiors in extenuation of acts which would be illegal if performed by other persons; and, with the sole exception of the President himself, they may be brought before the court precisely as if they were private persons. The judgments of the courts in cases involving the rights of citizens give substance and authoritative meaning to formal statements of rights which, in countries of

[13] Dicey, *op. cit.*, p. 191.

a different tradition, are open to invasion by the temporary holders of political power.

The Present Status of the Rule of Law. The rule of law, in common with every other mortal device, must adjust itself to changes in the world outside the courtroom in which it is spelled out in actual controversies. It was worked out as one of the incidents in the long struggle of our British forefathers with willful kings long since laid in the dust. But kings are not the only would-be tyrants; they are only highly placed ones. The urge to dominate afflicts all or nearly all who hold power and official position. The motive in one case may be self-aggrandizement, in another desire for financial gain, in another the well-intentioned wish to impose one's view of what is good for others. All of these breed impatience with the slow and bumbling processes of the law and tempt men to take short cuts. These considerations are specially pertinent in modern governments with numerous responsibilities to carry and complicated functions to perform. The discharge of such functions cannot abide the slow processes by which statutes are made. Officials require discretion and, once discretion is granted, it may be abused. Will may be substituted for judgment and rights may be compelled to yield to force or to alleged superior knowledge.

Something was said about these possibilities in the discussion of the doctrine of the separation of powers. There it was pointed out that executive and administrative officers must, because of the urgency of the matters with which they deal, have a freedom of action which the strict application of the rule of law seems to deny them. To some extent these officers must make, interpret, and enforce the law if they are to perform promptly and efficiently the duties committed to them. To some extent the role of the ordinary courts as guardians of rights must be modified. The legislature, overwhelmed by a multitude of duties, must to a degree delegate its authority and content itself with what may be only a shadowy oversight of the bureaucracy.

It is easy to conclude from these developments that the pillars of the temple of free government are crumbling. This, however, would be more than a little hysterical. The evils charged against the bureaucracy are easily magnified by partisans and traditionalists. To the extent that they are real they are often chargeable not so much to the bureaucrats as to the legislature's failure so to organize itself as to perform effectively its own historic function of supervision. Nor is it too much to say that safeguards for individuals exist in large measure within the procedures of the administration itself. In any case, although we may expect an increase in the power of the administration, the belief that government should be under the law is too deeply lodged in our tradition and modes of thought to be easily surrendered. "The King ought not to be under any man, but he is under God and the law."

REFERENCES

Charles A. Beard, *The Supreme Court and the Constitution* (1912).
Benjamin N. Cardozo, *The Nature of the Judicial Process* (1921).
Robert K. Carr, *The Supreme Court and Judicial Review* (1942).
Albert Venn Dicey, *Introduction to the Study of the Law of the Constitution,* 8th ed. (1915).
C. A. M. Ewing, *The Judges of the Supreme Court, 1789–1937* (1938).
Hamilton, Jay, and Madison, *The Federalist,* No. 78.
O. W. Holmes, Jr., *Collected Legal Papers* (1922).
R. H. Jackson, *The Struggle for Judicial Supremacy* (1941).
J. Roland Pennock, *Administration and the Rule of Law* (1941).
Carl B. Swisher, *The Growth of Constitutional Power in the United States* (1946).

CHAPTER 5 *Federalism*

The Meaning of Federalism

One of the fundamental features of our constitutional system is that government shall be organized on the federal principle. Since the United States is one of the oldest and certainly one of the most successful of federal states, it is important to know the nature of this sort of political organization.[1] "Federalism" is a term used to describe *one* of the ways in which the power to govern may be partitioned between a central or national government and the governments of the areas (states, provinces, departments, and so on) into which the national territory is divided.

Every country as a matter of fact is divided into more or less numerous units, each of which has certain functions to perform, the importance and number of these functions varying from nation to nation. In some countries the powers exercised by these units are granted by the national government which has the legal authority to decrease or increase these powers or even to abolish them without the consent of the member units. Where this is the situation, it is customary to speak of the state as unitary, because there is in fact only *one* government—that of the nation as contrasted with a federal state in which numerous governments are found. A good example of such a state is Great Britain. In that kingdom the legal supremacy of the national Parliament is complete, and whatever powers may be exercised by shires, cities, and boroughs are conferred by Parliament, which may at any time, on its own motion, enlarge or abolish these powers. It goes without saying that Parliament does not attempt to destroy these units and govern

[1] Throughout this chapter the author has used the word "national" to refer to the central government, although in popular usage the word "federal" is employed. Strictly speaking, there is no such thing as federal government or unitary government or confederate government—there are federal, unitary, and confederate states. Again, strictly speaking, the members of the American Union are not states as the word "state" is used in political science, since they do not possess what the formal treatises call sovereignty.

64

directly; but the important point is that it may do so if it wishes as no legal power exists anywhere to prevent it.

At the other extreme, there have been political organizations called alliances in which there were very rudimentary central organs with some restricted powers respecting foreign affairs and mutual defense—organs created by action of the individual members and completely subject to their will. Examples may be found in military and diplomatic alliances and in such associations as the League of Nations and the United Nations. These are not true states, of course, since each member of the alliance retains complete control over its own domestic concerns and is attached to the alliance only so long as it wishes to remain a member.

Proceeding up the scale, we come to the type of state organization called a confederation. This is usually created by units that have a good deal in common in the way of language, culture, and commerce and therefore have at least some desire for unity. Still, in such an organization the "national" organs are only slightly developed and the balance of power and authority remains with the member units. A good example is the United States during the period when the Articles of Confederation were in effect (1781–1789). The war of the Revolution was waged by what amounted to an alliance among the thirteen former British colonies. This alliance was converted into something a bit stronger under the pressure of the war, which persuaded the now independent states to enter into what was called a "firm league of friendship" and to create reluctantly a central government of sorts.

For our purposes the important thing about the government under the Articles of Confederation was the weakness of the central government and the very large body of powers retained by the individual states. No power existed in the government of the Confederation to act directly upon individual citizens or to compel the states to comply with resolutions adopted by the Confederation Congress. There was no effective executive head of the Confederation and no system of Confederation courts. In short, the real power to govern lay with the individual states. This was a little better than an alliance but not much. It was the well-known weaknesses of the Confederation that led to the Constitutional Convention of 1787 and finally to the new government which went into operation in 1789. This new state was a *federation*.

Now, a federal state is one whose government has a distribution of powers placing it somewhere between a unitary state and a confederate state. Keeping in mind that all definitions are probably too neat to cover the facts, we may define federalism as follows: A federal state is one in which the powers of government are divided between the central and the local authorities in a manner which may not be changed by either government acting alone, and in which each government, when exercising its constitutional powers, is independent of the other. In the United States the division of powers between the national government and the state governments is made by a written constitution, and this division may not be *formally* changed except by amending the Constitution itself—a process in which both the national Congress and the states *as such* are involved.

Under our federal system, for example, the power to enact divorce laws is not one of those granted to Congress or prohibited to the state; therefore, it belongs to the state legislatures and, no matter how desirable uniformity in the matter may seem to be, Congress may not enact valid laws on the subject. To transfer the power to Congress would require a formal amendment to the Constitution. To put the matter the other way about, Congress has the express power to enact bankruptcy laws and has acted under that power; now, no matter how dissatisfied the states might be with the national law, they could not transfer this power to their own legislatures except by setting in motion the machinery of constitutional amendment, although, if the national laws were all repealed, the states would be free to act.

It would be erroneous, however, to assume that it is always necessary to amend the Constitution before the national government can enact laws or engage in activities formerly regarded as belonging exclusively to the states. Under the broad powers granted to it by the Constitution, Congress has been able to enact legislation on such subjects as social security, labor, agriculture, and the regulation of securities and exchanges, thus vitally affecting the distribution of powers and functions between the states and the national government.

Origins of American Federalism

As a matter of theory, it would have been simpler for the makers of the Constitution to have created a national government alone, with the individual states regarded simply as convenient districts within which to administer national law. This would have been a neater and tidier way to solve the problem of government. The reasons why this was not done were very practical ones. The delegates to the convention in Philadelphia in 1787 represented states which were already going concerns. Each had a complete government and each exercised powers which might be fairly called "sovereign" such as the coining of money, the levying of taxes, even the conclusion of treaties. The delegates themselves were active politicians in their own states, well informed about local problems, and loyal to the existing system. To put it more bluntly, each was an integral part of what we should today call the political machine of his state.

There was, it is true, a very considerable desire on the part of many of the delegates for some strong, common agencies of government that would make possible certain recognized national objectives. But this was in conflict with the fear of other delegates that a strong central government would weaken the state governments. Because of this divergence the delegates who believed in a stronger central government had to tread warily. They were actually not commissioned by their states to create a *new* government and they were wise enough to know that any scheme which they might devise could come into effect only by the consent of men already influential in state politics. Alexander Hamilton put the matter very realistically in the first number of *The Federalist:*

Among the most formidable of the obstacles which the new Constitution will have to encounter may readily be distinguished the obvious interest of a certain class of men in every state to resist all changes which may hazard a diminution of the power, emolument, and consequence of the offices they hold under the state establishments.

What Hamilton is saying is that state officials could not but be suspicious of a national government powerful enough to make their own status less important. They quite naturally feared the possible coming of a "king that knows not Joseph"!

In a sense it is correct to say that most of the papers in *The Federalist* were written to allay the suspicions of local politicians and to minimize the dangers to the states from the stronger central government provided by the new Constitution. Three of the papers (Nos. 44, 45, and 46) were devoted wholly to the guarantees made to the states by the Constitution or to the reasonableness of the restrictions upon the powers left to them. The framers, however, were more than mere politicians seeking victory for their cause. They sincerely believed that the mortal danger of civil war or foreign conquest awaited the new nation if a more adequate government were not quickly supplied. Moreover, almost none wanted a completely centralized state, even the most nationalistic of them having a considerable degree of devotion to their own states. It was on the state level, in fact, where men for many years believed that the most distinguished public careers would be realized.

In short, the principal problem faced in 1787 may be stated thus: How to secure a government strong enough to protect certain clearly national interests and likely to survive in a dangerous international situation, and capable at the same time of winning the support of men who could not but look upon any new departure as likely to defeat their established expectations in public life.

Federalism in the Constitution

It is evidence of the strength of local feeling that there was no serious discussion in the Convention of 1787 of proposals which might have lowered the dignity of the individual states. It is true that Hamilton regarded the state governments with scorn and proposed subjecting them to rather complete central control; but, while many applauded his eloquence and admired his youthful brilliance, none followed his suggestions.

The Constitution itself assumes the existence and perpetuity of the states. In fact, without them the new government would have been unworkable. United States Senators were to be chosen by the state legislatures; qualifications for voting, even for the national House of Representatives, were left to be determined by the individual state legislatures; amendments to the Constitution were to be adopted by the states, either through their legislatures or through special state conventions; the states were to decide how Presidential electors were to be chosen; and, in case no Presidential candidate received a majority of the electoral vote, the state delegations in the House of Representatives, *voting as units*, were to make the choice. In these and other ways, the states were woven firmly into the constitutional fabric.

The chief protection to the states, however, was thought to be found in the fact that the powers of the national government were limited strictly to those delegated to it in Article I, Section 8. These powers of the new national government were to be incapable of increase except by the amending process. It was further assumed that, these powers being delegated to the Congress in express words, all others were to remain with the states. Since this latter argument was not convincing to the believers in state rights, assurance was made doubly sure by the Tenth Amendment, adopted in 1791, which states that "The powers not delegated to the United States by the Constitution, nor prohibited by it to the States, are reserved to the States respectively, or to the people." This was presumed to render impossible any "usurpation" of additional powers by the national government.

In a general way it may be said that the words of the Constitution give to the national government power over those matters of common interest to the whole population, while leaving to the states the care of those matters touching most closely the daily life of the people. The powers delegated to the national government were regarded by the defenders of the new scheme of government as fewer in number and of less genuine importance than the latter. Thus, James Madison argued:

The powers delegated by the proposed Constitution to the federal government are few and defined. Those which are to remain in the State governments are numerous and indefinite. The former will be exercised principally on external objects, as war, peace, negotiation, and foreign commerce, with which last the power of taxation will, for the most part, be connected. The powers reserved to the several states will extend to all the objects which, in the ordinary course of affairs, concern the lives, liberties, and properties of the people, and the internal order, improvement, and prosperity of the State.

There is no reason to doubt the complete sincerity of this and similar arguments. No one in 1787 could have foreseen the circumstances which in a century would give a new meaning to the "few and defined" powers of the national government, and make their exercise a real or apparent threat to the balance between nation and state which the original Constitution attempted to set up.

To the framers of the Constitution it was clear that certain powers were by their very nature national. For example, the powers to conduct war and to provide a defense establishment were generally admitted to require centralized management. The same was conceded to be true of the conduct of foreign affairs. Both of these functions had belonged to Congress under the Articles of Confederation, although the Confederation government was without adequate power to discharge them efficiently. In transferring them to the new and distinctly more powerful national government, the Constitution simply provided for the better execution of powers generally recognized as belonging to the Union rather than to the individual states.

A number of powers delegated to the national government were closely related to the conduct of business operations. Even in 1787 commerce and shipping had begun to grow beyond the purely local market and to become national in their scope. Many of the members of the convention which drafted the new Constitution were themselves engaged in foreign and interstate commerce and knew from experience the difficulties involved in trying to comply with thirteen different sets of laws in carrying on their ordinary operations. For, under the Confederation government, Congress had no effective power to prevent the several states from levying taxes on each other's products at the state lines or from imposing vexatious restrictions on imports from other states. While such policies were, it is true, prohibited by the Articles, Congress really had no effective power to prevent their adoption. There was not even a national judicial system, so that disputes arising in the course of trade had to be submitted to the courts of the various states, where justice to an "outsider" could not be assured.

Because of this situation the new national Congress was given authority to regulate foreign and domestic commerce, to coin money and regulate its value, to make uniform bankruptcy laws, to fix the standard of weights and measures, and to grant patents and copyrights—all matters in which uniformity on a national scale was regarded as necessary to the smooth functioning of the economy. In addition, provision was made for a *national* judiciary with jurisdiction over disputes involving citizens of different states. At the same time the states were forbidden to levy import or export duties except under the control of Congress, to coin money, to issue bills of credit, to make anything but gold or silver legal tender in the payment of debts, or to pass laws impairing the obligation of contracts.

The grant to the new national government of an independent taxing power was perhaps the one that aroused the greatest suspicion among those who defended the old order, even though it is easy enough now to see that a government without this power is no government at all. Under the Articles of Confederation the Congress could simply *ask* the states for funds, the method by which money was to be raised being no concern of the national government. Since Congress had no power to compel the states to heed its request, it is not surprising that the response of the states was both sporadic and inadequate. The new tax power was to operate on *individuals* and the national taxes were to be collected by *national* officers. The supporters of the new Constitution defended this grant of power by arguing that it would normally be used principally in connection with the regulation of commerce or, at all events, as incidental to other specifically delegated national powers. It was said, in other words, that taxes would normally be indirect, laid on imports or as excises on articles of consumption, and that direct taxes, as we know them today on April 15th of each year, would be exceptional, if, indeed, they would ever be resorted to. Although this argument was advanced with complete sincerity, history, as we know, has proved it to be poor prophecy.

Federalism and Individual Liberty

It must not be concluded from this description of the division of powers between the national and state governments that federalism provides simply for a division of labor. It has always been defended as a device for protecting the individual, and is thus a part of our theory of individual liberty. It is argued that, by leaving in the hands of state officials the management of those affairs touching the citizen most intimately, the people will be better able to enforce responsible government than would be the case if such matters were controlled by distant officers, not chosen by the people and not easily held responsible by them. In this way the danger of arbitrary rule by unsympathetic officials was to be prevented by breaking the lines of power at a point close to the local voters.

Federalism and Governmental Efficiency

As to efficiency, it was believed that officers near to the people would know their wants and needs better than those at the national capital. In a nation of continental extent there are significant differences among the various local communities and only a decentralized government can take proper account of these differences. The reasonableness of this argument is even today recognized by the national government in its arrangements for administering certain programs supported in part by national funds. Old-age assistance, as well as aid to the blind, to dependent children, and to the permanently and totally disabled are all in the first instance in the hands of county or other local authorities. The same thing is true of the secondary road program of the national government, under which the roads to be included in the system are chosen in conferences between local or state officials and representatives of the national Bureau of Public Roads. If national grants are ever made for the support of the public schools, the case for decentralized administration can be urged persuasively on the ground that local advice will be indispensable as a way of taking into account local needs and wishes.

All of these arguments were presented at the time of the adoption of the Constitution. As time went on others were developed. For example, it is today widely believed that the states are useful, even vital, areas within which important political and economic experiments, such as the unicameral legislature, workmen's compensation legislation, or public ownership of economic enterprises, may be carried out—experiments which might well be dangerous if they could be attempted only on a national scale. Again, it is alleged that the states serve as valuable training grounds for politicians and administrators, the most competent of whom in time find their way into the national arena. There are in the state legislatures, for example, about 7,500 members. In addition there are several hundred judicial, executive, and major administrative officers at the state level. Most of these men are ambitious for higher preferment. The successful emerge as members of Congress, Federal judges, or national administrators. The process may be likened to that by which a Joe DiMaggio or a Babe Ruth finds his way to the major leagues from the sandlot teams in a thousand American cities and villages.

The preoccupation of the politicians with what Hamilton called the "power, emoluments, and consequence" of local and state office need not lead us to cynicism about public affairs. We should do well to admit that it is only through playing the political "game" on the local level that men and women prove themselves capable of tackling problems of a higher order. Whatever we may think of our Senators and Representatives at Washington in our more disillusioned moments, they are the best that our public life produces. Whatever skill they have is made possible by a political system which provides 48 stages upon which many players may strut their hour, to be heard no more, or to move on to our political Broadway on Capitol Hill.

The Federal System and National Interests

A very large measure of decentralization was made necessary by the facts of geography and technology in 1787. In an age when it required thirty hours to go from New York to Boston by the fastest conveyance, most problems *were* local and it could be argued that the powers of the states should be left largely as they were. Moreover, if the founding fathers had believed in centralization, and most of them did not, a stronger national government would not have been accepted by the state conventions which were called to ratify the new Constitution.

Since all forms of government are devised primarily to fit an existing set of conditions, they are certain to change as conditions change. If a constitution has no formal provision for change, informal devices will be found to bring government sooner or later into conformity with the needs and desires of society.

Federalism in the United States has been no exception to this general rule. We know that the national government is doing more things, spending more money, and coming much closer to the people than was contemplated by the framers of the Constitution. That government now engages in such activities as public health, agriculture, poor relief, highway construction, labor relations, and many others, although a reading of the words of the Constitution would lead one to infer that these functions belong exclusively to the state governments. And yet, the Constitution has been formally amended only once with respect to the federal principle. The Eighteenth Amendment, adopted in 1919, forbade the manufacture of and trade in intoxicating beverages, and Congress was given concurrent power with the states to make the prohibition effective. Fourteen years later this amendment was rescinded by the Twenty-first, and the former balance of state and national powers was largely restored.

Other ways besides the amending process have been found, however, to bring the powers of the national government into harmony with acutely-felt needs of the people. Thus, although there is not a word in the written Constitution authorizing the national government to act with respect to any of the matters referred to in the preceding paragraph, Congress, by the use of its broad powers to tax and to regulate foreign and interstate commerce, has been able to enter these areas when it has believed the national interest required it. What is more, with minor exceptions the exercise of Congressional power in these new fields has been sustained by the Supreme Court against the contention that the rights of the states have been invaded.

National Regulation of Interstate Commerce. One of the principal difficulties encountered by business men under the Articles of Confederation was the mass of conflicting regulations of business enforced by the individual states. It was uneasiness and vexation about this situation, in fact, which brought about the Annapolis Convention of 1786, a meeting which led directly to the Constitutional Convention of the following year.

The Constitution which was submitted for ratification to the state conventions included a clause conferring upon Congress the power "to regulate commerce with foreign nations and among the several States. . . ." In defending this, Hamilton wrote in No. 11 of *The Federalist* that "a unity of commercial, as well as political, interests, can only result from a unity of government." What Hamilton meant was that political power should be commensurate in its range with the matter which it is permitted to regulate. In this case, the power of Congress to regulate commerce must grow at equal pace with the growth of that commerce, and not be confined to the forms of interstate and foreign business as they existed in 1787. In interpreting the Constitution, the Supreme Court has consistently accepted this argument.

In a long line of decisions defining the "commerce power" the Court has steadily expanded Congressional control over trade. Most business transactions are now subject to national regulation, while such significant aspects of the labor contract as collective bargaining, hours, wages, working conditions, and the conduct of strikes in large sectors of American industry have been largely withdrawn from the jurisdiction of the states. In short, it is no longer simply commerce that is being nationally regulated but the whole complex mass of transactions covered by the word "business." Perhaps we should say that commerce, no matter what it may have meant in 1789, has come to mean everything connected with manufacturing, buying, and selling, even if it involves intercourse between the states only remotely.

Let us illustrate. Manufacturing would seem to be something different from trading and so, if regulated at all, to be subject to state rules. Indeed the Supreme Court so held in a controversy before it in 1895 and its judgment in that case was affirmed twenty years later. In 1937, however, in a series of decisions passing upon the constitutionality of the National Labor Relations Act, it reversed its former stand. The Court held that a strike in a steel plant in Pennsylvania, because it affected the flow of raw materials into the state where the plant was located and of the finished product into the channels of interstate commerce, could be taken under the jurisdiction of the National Labor Relations Board. In other words, a strike is an obstacle to interstate commerce which Congress may take steps to remove in the exercise of its power to "regulate commerce among the several States." Later decisions defined the word commerce still more liberally. For example, it was held that elevator operators in a building occupied in part by a firm engaged in interstate trade, were subject to national supervision with respect to some portions of the contract of labor with their employers. What these decisions mean is that the national power is at last as extensive as the business system itself. The individual states may and do still enforce laws with respect to business, but, as a growing proportion of transactions involves interstate operations in some degree, what share is left to state control is of declining importance in the total economy.[2]

[2] If possible the student should read the decisions in the following cases: *United States v. E. C. Knight Co.,* 156 U.S. 1 (1895); *Hammer v. Dagenhart,* 247 U.S. 251 (1918); *National Labor Relations Board v. Jones & Laughlin Steel Corp.,* 301 U.S.

Before leaving the general question involved here, two things may be said. In the first place, the national government has increased its activity in many fields simply because problems were involved with which the states could not effectively cope since they transcended state boundaries. An example of this is agricultural policy. Undoubtedly some aspects of farming may reasonably be left to the care of the states; but it is difficult to deny that farm credit, farm marketing, and the control of agricultural prices enter so deeply into national economic policy that they require uniform treatment. It may be argued, of course, that these matters ought not to be subject to public regulation at all; but to abandon such controls seems unlikely so long at least as other sectors of the economy demand and receive government support. For good or ill, the modern world is not at present moving in the direction of such abandonment. In the second place, the fact seems to be that many of the states have failed in spite of their legal powers to cope efficiently with problems within their own boundaries. In some cases this failure may be attributed to sheer administrative incompetence; in others to a lack of local funds. For example, even if we grant the desirability of public housing, most of our states have neither the money to finance an effective housing program nor the administrative staff capable of supervising it.

The National Government and the General Welfare. Standing first among the powers delegated by the Constitution to the national Congress is the power to "lay and collect taxes, duties, imposts, and excises to pay the debts and provide for the common defense and general welfare of the United States. . . ." Carelessly read, this clause seems to confer upon Congress a vast, almost unlimited power to make laws for the general welfare. This, however, is clearly an error, for if Congress possessed any such indefinable power, the enumeration of specific powers that follows this clause would be superfluous, and the states would be mere administrative units. What the clause does mean is that Congress may tax the inhabitants and spend the proceeds for whatever it may regard as the general welfare, so long at least as this does not involve any direct invasion of powers reserved to the individual states. Congress may not, for example, legislate concerning the training of musicians, but it may aid the states in promoting musical education, if the Supreme Court can be persuaded to regard such a policy as contributing to the general welfare.[3]

Yet the use which Congress has made of this power has been as centralizing in many ways as its use of the commerce power. With respect to

1 (1937); *Kirchbaum v. Walling,* 316 U.S. 517 (1942). The Fair Labor Standards Act of 1938 (52 Stat. L. 1060) exempts certain classes of workers from its operations. These classes indicate in a general way the kinds of business still more or less under state supervision.

[3] Congress may, of course, exercise all the powers of a state legislature in the District of Columbia, and with respect to the Territories of the United States.

the latter it is always possible to argue that the regulation of such matters as industrial strikes or the rights of elevator operators is justified by their more or less close relationship to the conduct of interstate commerce, and that therefore state laws are inadequate. In spending money for the general welfare, however, it makes little difference whether the object of the expenditure is among the specific matters over which Congress has power, or is one normally under state control.

National Grants for the General Welfare. Examples of the use of the power to tax for the general welfare are numerous and well known, and nearly all of them involve functions which would seem clearly to be among those reserved to the states. The national social-security program provides for the annual payment from the national Treasury to the states of hundreds of millions of dollars for assistance to the aged poor, dependent children, the blind, and the permanently and totally disabled. Before the passage of the Social Security Act in 1935, poor relief was regarded as a local function, as it had been for centuries.

The new idea is that the unfortunate are often the victims of the defective working of a *national* economic system and that therefore the nation as a whole has an obligation to help them; or that, in any case, their need is the concern of all citizens no matter where they may live. Congress, as spokesman for all of us, provides for such persons by granting to the states financial aid up to a certain proportion of the total amount of expenditures for their relief by the states, on condition that the states and their local units administer the program in accordance with rules laid down by the national Social Security Administration. Welfare officials are still locally chosen, but the program itself is *national*, not local.

The story is the same with respect to highways. Beginning in 1916 Congress has annually appropriated millions of dollars to be spent by the states in the construction and maintenance of roads. At present these grants total nearly half a billion dollars a year. In the early highway-aid acts, the expenditures were made to improve "post roads," Congress having the express power in the Constitution to "establish post offices and post roads." It was not long, however, until this ceased to be even a pretense, and money is now spent to the extent of more than $150 million a year on minor roads which may or may not be used in carrying the mails. The states must "match the federal dollar" from their own funds and all money spent, both state and national, must be spent in accordance with rules promulgated by the Commissioner of Public Roads in Washington.

These and a dozen other programs conducted by the states with the financial assistance of the national government are perfectly natural developments in an age when society is so complex and so closely knit that few functions are purely local in their bearing. Such programs may be justified by the fact that the wealth and taxpaying ability of the states vary enormously, much more so than their respective needs for certain governmental services. The nation as a whole can not be indifferent to the poverty of a state if that poverty means poor roads, poor schools, poor health facilities, and widespread destitution—all of which adversely affect national well-being. What we are doing is to permit Congress to tax the richer sections of the country and to use the proceeds to aid those less fortunate. The willingness of the more prosperous areas to make this sort of contribution is evidence of a growing consciousness of national unity. The demand heard in some quarters that the whole system of grants-in-aid be abandoned is wholly unrealistic.[4]

There is little doubt that the system of national grants-in-aid is not only here to stay, but also that it is likely to be expanded. The next function to be aided probably will be public elementary and secondary education. Beginning with the depression of the 1930s, there has been a growing belief in many influential quarters, especially among the organized educators, that only by national aid can minimum educational opportunities be provided in poor states. Nearly every recent Congress has had before it bills providing for large grants to improve education by this device. Such bills have failed of passage partly because of the desire to keep down expenditures in a period of international crisis and partly because controversies have arisen over religious and racial issues. When the latter are somehow successfully compromised, and the national military needs are less urgent, substantial aid to local schools will become a reality.

Implied Powers and Federalism

The shift of powers from the state to the national government has been accomplished primarily because the Supreme Court, as the umpire of the federal system, has interpreted liberally the "commerce" and the "general-welfare" clauses in the written Constitution. The possibility of such a liberal interpretation is concealed in the very last of the clauses delegating powers to Congress. After enumerating no fewer than 17 functions entrusted to Congress, an eighteenth clause is added in Article I, Section 8, conferring the power "To make all laws which shall be necessary and proper for carrying into execution the foregoing powers, and all other powers vested by this Constitution in the government of the United States, or in any department or officer thereof."

A division of powers made in writing necessarily requires that some authority interpret the words used. If a power is not granted to Congress in specific language, it may still be one which it is "necessary and proper"

[4] In 1950 the total of national grants to the states was $1,960,000,000. The system of grants has gone even further in other nations, being highly developed in Great Britain and in the British dominions. In the United States itself, *state* aids to local units in 1950 amounted to slightly more than $4 billion.

for Congress to have in order to "carry into execution" one of its express powers. But *some* authority must exist to say whether the proposed power *is* necessary and proper. Ordinarily, the first interpretation is made by Congress itself in passing the law, since it must be assumed that Congress will not deliberately violate the Constitution. But the final authority cannot lie with Congress, since to leave it there would make that body judge of its own powers and thus deprive the states of all assurance that their reserved powers would be preserved.

Under our system as it has developed the ultimate interpretation is made by the Supreme Court. If the Court is convinced, for example, that a corner in cotton on the commodity markets, or a strike in a steel mill, is an obstacle to the free flow of commerce among the states, then it holds that Congress may act to remove such an obstacle by passing a law "necessary and proper" to make good its express power to regulate commerce among the states. Likewise, if it seems to Congress that parcels should be carried in the mails and the Supreme Court agrees, then the act establishing the parcel post becomes a necessary and proper law for carrying into execution the power to establish post offices and post roads. If the Court is convinced that aid to the states is a necessary and proper way to advance the general welfare, the grant-in-aid system receives its final legal ratification.[5]

Whatever one may think of the expansion of national power, it cannot be doubted that such expansion would have been much more difficult without the "necessary and proper" clause. Nor has the Supreme Court put a strained interpretation on the language of the written Constitution. There is nothing perverse in holding that Congress has authority to do what it can to prevent a crippling strike in a nationwide industry such as steel. A stoppage in such an industry would soon affect the flow of trade almost if not quite as seriously as a railroad strike. As a matter of fact, scarcely any industry of consequence is without national significance, and it is not unreasonable to hold, as the Court has consistently done, that the regulative power should be coextensive with the problem requiring attention.

Decentralizing Factors

Whether national regulation will be efficient is, of course, another question, and there are some who think there is danger of overloading the national administration to the point where it cannot function effectively. There can be little doubt, however, that leaving regulation to the individual

---

[5] The grant-in-aid system was by implication upheld by the Supreme Court in *Massachusetts v. Mellon* and *Frothingham v. Mellon*, 262 U.S. 447 (1923). To the contention that national grants could be used to "invade" state powers, the court replied that such a result could be avoided by the states simply by their refusing to accept the grants. At present, however, all of the aided programs are being administered in practically all of the states.

states would amount to no regulation at all. It is perhaps not going too far to suggest that much of the opposition to national controls and much of the demand that powers be restored to the states proceed from interests who want no regulation of any sort. In this connection it is worth pointing out again that the demand for national regulation came originally from business men who had had enough of conflicting and punitive legislation by the states. By the same token there are important interests today that do not wish to return to this sort of anarchy. Commerce is not what it was in 1787 and the Supreme Court at any rate recognizes that fact.

It may be true that, as the functions of the national government increase in number and complexity, it will find itself overloaded and incapable of doing a good job. The remedy for this does not lie, however, in a return of functions to the states. It is to be sought rather in other directions. First of all, it seems feasible to decentralize national administration to the point where the authority to make decisions will be closer to the interests affected. National authorities are aware of this possibility. Even now many national departments operate through numerous regional offices readily accessible to such interests and competent to make final decisions in many classes of problems.

More important than administrative decentralization is the steady growth of cooperation between the two levels of government. Experience has shown that national participation in functions hitherto regarded as state or local does not necessarily mean the end of state influence. Existing arrangements in many fields show that we have a *cooperative* federalism rather than a suspicious competition between the nation and the states. For example, cooperation is widespread in those functions where national aid is available to the states. Welfare, highway, and agricultural experts from both governments work together amicably in administering the various programs. The same sort of relationship exists with respect to functions where there are no financial grants involved. Thousands of local law-enforcement officers have been trained by the police academy maintained by the Federal Bureau of Investigation and there is a considerable degree of cooperative administration between state and Federal officers in the various food and drug and wildlife services. In these and other fields there is a steady exchange of information and services and a cooperation in planning and execution, few questions of precedence being raised on either side.

Obligations of the National Government to the States. Federalism has historically involved a delicate balancing of state and national powers. In the case of the United States the provisions for maintaining this balance are more numerous than the ones we have already discussed. A mere statement concerning the division of powers is not sufficient to guarantee a federal system. The national government must perform certain functions calculated to protect the states as independent entities. On the other hand, the states must be prohibited from doing certain things which would threaten the integrity of the national powers. Let us glance first at the obligations toward the states assumed by the national government under the Constitution. These are found in Article IV, Sections 3 and 4 of that document.

First of all, guarantee of the territorial integrity of the states is supplied by the provision that "no new State shall be formed or erected within the jurisdiction of any other State; nor any State be formed by the junction of two or more States, or parts of States, without the consent of the legislatures of the States concerned as well as of the Congress." Little comment on this provision is needed, for if the national government were free to alter state boundaries, the way would be open to a vexatious and perhaps fatal interference with state powers. An additional safeguard of state integrity is found in Article V which provides that the process of amendment may not be used in such a way as to deprive a state of its equal representation in the Senate.

The national government is also required to protect a member state of the Union against invasion and to assist it in suppressing violence within its borders. The first of these obligations is not likely to create difficulties, since an invasion of a state would be also an invasion of the United States and would undoubtedly be met by the national military power. In the case of the suppression of domestic violence, the request for national assistance is made to the President by either the state legislature or the governor. Whether or not the national army is to be sent into the state rests in the discretion of the President who may refuse to act if he believes the state capable of meeting the situation with its own forces. National military forces may be sent into a state by order of the President without any request by the state authorities or even over their protests if national property is threatened or national functions, such as commerce or the transmission of the mails, are interfered with.

The national government is also required to guarantee to each state a republican form of government. The question as to whether such a government actually exists within a state has been seldom raised, although it conceivably might be in the future. A republican form of government seems to be any government in which political power rests ultimately with the people, irrespective of merely formal changes in the organization of the state government. Thus a state may use the initiative and referendum with respect to its laws or constitution, or adopt the unicameral legislative system, or permit its cities to adopt the city-manager plan, without ceasing to be republican in form. The decision in this matter is made by Congress. If that body receives and seats the senators and representatives of a state, then, so the Supreme Court has held, its government is assumed to be republican.[6]

Constitutional Restrictions on State Powers

There are certain things which the states must not be permitted to do in a federal system if that system is to endure. It must be remembered that the 10th Amendment, which was intended to protect the reserved powers of the states against invasion by the national government, specifically refers to the fact that some powers are prohibited to the states in the body of the Constitution. Most of these are powers which if exercised by the states could only end in disruption of the Union.

The states are forbidden in absolute language to enter into "any treaty, alliance, or confederation" or to make any "agreement or compact" among themselves without the consent of Congress. The general intent of these provisions is to prevent arrangements of a political nature with foreign states, or political alliances among the states themselves.

It is obvious that no state of a federal character would long endure if its member states were free to make treaties with foreign powers. Within the confines of the Union itself, however, many questions arise which, while not national in character, affect more than a single state. With respect to such matters there can be no objection to compacts or agreements among the states most concerned. About 120 such compacts and agreements now exist. The best known of these are the one finally concluded in 1928, between the seven states through which the Colorado River flows, for the assignment of water rights, and the compact between New Jersey and New York in 1921 creating the Port of New York Authority for the construction and management of port facilities. Other compacts exist in all parts of the Union for the allocation of water rights, control of stream pollution and waste in oil production, the better use of fisheries, and the improvement of dairy-production standards.

Interstate compacts are difficult to negotiate and administer and some students do not feel encouraged as to the future possibilities of the device; but there will undoubtedly be further experimentation with it. The consent of Congress to such agreements may be given in advance or upon their completion, and in at least two cases blanket approval has been given in advance with respect to marine fisheries and water-pollution compacts. It is possible that the use of compacts may slow the drift toward centralization by providing a regional solution for certain problems which might otherwise be turned over to the national government. On the other hand, those impatient with state action regard regional compacts merely as way-

---

[6] The leading court decisions are *Luther v. Borden*, 7 How. 1 (1849) and *Pacific States Tel. & Tel. Co. v. Oregon*, 223 U.S. 118 (1912).

stations on the road to what they consider a more desirable national control. In any event, in the light of our experience to date, it is reasonable to believe that many more compacts will be completed in the future.[7]

The individual states are prohibited either by the express words of the Constitution or by judicial interpretation from so using their tax power as to interfere with the operations of the national government or to affect adversely any function subject to national regulation. State export and import taxes, once more or less common, may not be laid without the consent of Congress. To discourage the use of such taxes it is further provided that their proceeds beyond the costs of administration shall be paid into the national Treasury.

Aside from this limitation in specific words, restrictions on state-taxing power arise out of interpretations of the inherent nature of a federal system. Both national and state governments possess the power to tax, and if either were permitted to use it without regard to the functions of the other, the federal system would come to an end. Unrestrained national power could destroy the state governments; unlimited state power could paralyze the government of the Union.

The question as to what objects may constitutionally be taxed by either government is, like all questions of taxation, a complicated one, and to all general statements there are exceptions. We must confine ourselves here to generalities, however, if we are not to be bogged down in legal details. First of all, the property of the national government is exempt from state taxation. Congress may permit such taxation if it wishes, but it has not done so with respect to any property used directly in the performance of national governmental functions. The real property and the stock of national banks were many years ago made taxable by state and local governments, but such banks are after all private ventures and not public agencies. The *general* rule is that the states are without power to tax the property of national agencies.[8]

The states are also forbidden, as a result of well-settled judicial interpretation, to use their tax power in such a way as to interfere with "national instrumentalities." This principle was first laid down by Chief Justice John Marshall in 1819 in the famous case of *McCulloch v. Maryland.* This case arose over the attempt of the state of Maryland to tax the notes of the Bank of the United States, a part of the stock of which was subscribed by the national Treasury. The power to collect such a state tax was denied on the ground that to permit it would allow the states to de-

---

[7] See the biennial issues of *The Book of the States* (Council of State Governments, Chicago) for lists of interstate compacts in force, and Frederick L. Zimmermann, *The Interstate Compact since 1925,* Council of State Governments, Chicago, 1951.

[8] For a good many years now the Tennessee Valley Authority has, under congressional direction, paid sums of money in lieu of taxes to the states in which it has acquired land and other real property.

stroy national agencies simply by laying upon them prohibitive taxes. For more than a century this reasoning was applied so literally as to deny to the states any power to tax the salaries of employees of the national government or the principal or income of federal securities, on the ground that the former were instrumentalities of the national government, and that securities were necessary to the national borrowing power with which the states could not validly interfere.

For many years this theory worked in favor of the states also. About fifty years after *McCulloch v. Maryland,* it was held by the Supreme Court in *Tax Collector v. Day,* on precisely the same theory as that announced by Marshall, that a national income tax could not be laid upon the salary of a state official. The result of this reasoning was that until 1939 neither the states nor the Unites States could tax the salaries of each other's employees or the income from their respective securities. This quite understandably struck many people as unfair, and an act of Congress finally asserted the right of the United States to tax the salaries of state and local officials. This act was upheld by the Supreme Court, and since that date both governments have been free to tax the salaries of public employees, although Congress has not as yet levied a similar tax on the value of or income from state or local securities.[9]

The States and Interstate Trade. Since the power to regulate interstate commerce is one committed to Congress by the Constitution, it follows that the state governments may not interfere with its exercise or act so as to change regulations adopted by the national government. The general principle here is not difficult to state, although in applying it intricate problems arise. Trade beginning and ending within a state is not subject to Congressional regulation. If, however, at any stage such trade crosses a state line, or involves persons or property destined for points outside the state, or in any other manner takes on an interstate character, the entire transaction is regarded by the courts as interstate and hence subject in all its incidents to national control. It is only necessary to recall the cases involving interstate commerce referred to above to conclude that purely intrastate trade is today of declining importance. The states may not burden interstate commerce by taxation; and all state regulations intended to protect the life and property of state citizens, such as safety and sanitary laws, are valid only so long as the courts regard them as reasonable and

---

[9] The leading cases are *Graves v. The People of the State of New York* and *State Tax Commission of Utah v. Van Cott,* 306 U.S. 466, 511 (1939). What these decisions really held was that the taxation of salaries was not a burden on either government, but was an obligation which public employees must share along with all other receivers of income. It is perhaps unnecessary to add that if either government taxed the employees of the other at discriminatory rates, it would be invalid, not only as a burden upon the government's functions but also, presumably, as a denial of due process of law or of the equal protection of the laws.

Congress has not acted on the same matters. Many state laws of this type, enacted ostensibly as health and welfare regulations or as tax measures, have had the effect of erecting trade barriers between the states. A few years ago such legislation threatened to become widespread, but fortunately state officials have come to recognize its harmful effects and the trend has been stopped. This subject is discussed in a subsequent chapter in more detail.

Money and Contracts. In order to make uniform the standard of value, the states are forbidden to coin money or to emit bills of credit. Bills of credit were instruments formerly issued by the states and backed by their credit, promising to pay the amounts indicated, and intended to circulate as currency. Unless the power over money and its value is centralized in one authority, all transactions are bound to be precarious. The individual states may still charter banks which exist alongside national banks, but state banks are no longer permitted to issue their own currency.[10]

Almost equally important in guaranteeing the stability of property rights and business transactions is the provision found in Article I, Section 10 of the Constitution prohibiting the states from passing laws impairing the obligation of a contract. Ordinary agreements for the payment of money, the rate of interest, and the sale of property are protected by this provision. The case is somewhat different when corporate charters and permits and licenses are involved. A charter was long ago held to be a contract which the state could not change. It is now the rule however, that even contracts of this sort may be altered by the state in the interests of the public health, safety, or welfare. Thus a state law or constitutional amendment may destroy the liquor business even though those engaged in it conduct their business under state charters, on the ground that the public welfare overrides any private rights arising from the charter. Likewise a license to practice a profession is now regarded as a species of property which the state may regulate in the public interest so that, for example, a lawyer who abuses the privilege conferred by his license may be disbarred upon proof of his unfitness. From the point of view of federalism, the general effect of the provision is that business men and others may operate throughout the Union with assurance that legal agreements will everywhere be respected and enforced.[11]

[10] By a decision of the Supreme Court in 1869 state bank notes were made subject to a prohibitive national tax, which, of course, made their issue unprofitable.

[11] During the depression of the 1930s the Supreme Court sustained a Minnesota law allowing an extension of two years in the time during which debtors might redeem property about to be taken under foreclosure proceedings. This law obviously tampered with the provision of mortgage contracts, but the court took the view that the extension was reasonable under emergency conditions, especially since the amounts due creditors in principal and interest were not reduced. *Home Building and Loan Association v. Blaisdell*, 290 U.S. 398 (1934).

The Fourteenth Amendment and Federalism. Finally, restrictions of very great importance are placed upon the state governments by that portion of the Fourteenth Amendment which provides that no state shall "deprive any person of life, liberty, or property, without due process of law; nor deny to any person within its jurisdiction the equal protection of the laws." The present meaning of these words is fully discussed elsewhere in this book. Here it is enough to say that the effect has been to prohibit the invasion of personal rights by the states in the exercise of any of their powers of government. From the point of view of federalism, the vital significance of these provisions is that the Supreme Court has so interpreted them as to create rules of nationwide application protecting the fundamental liberties of the citizen as those liberties are understood in successive epochs. In this sense these provisions are centralizing. But it is important to point out that the national authorities have been more zealous in guarding the rights of the citizens than have the states. If the Fourteenth Amendment has centralized power, the results in this area of human affairs have justified centralization. On the whole the national courts have been better interpreters of the national conscience than have the state and local authorities.

It might be concluded from what has been said that there has been a steady and irresistible march of political power to Washington and that it is therefore unrealistic to speak as if federalism had any real substance. To conclude, however, that the states are "through" would be premature. In the first place, government in general has grown in the extent, variety, and costliness of its functions, and the state and local units have shared in this growth. Thus, in 1915 the expenditures of the 48 states amounted to only half a billion dollars; in 1950 they reached more than eleven billion. This is one measure of the growth of public regulation of economic life. In the second place, the growth of national power and influence has had the paradoxical effect of reviving local units. The programs now jointly financed by the national and state governments involve in their actual administration a very considerable measure of decentralization, and this has had the effect of touching into life many local units long considered moribund. Moreover, federal standards of administration have had a tonic effect on local personnel and methods. In budgeting, accounting, purchasing, and the choice of employees, many a local unit for the first time has approached a level of efficiency which students a generation ago thought unlikely to be realized. These reciprocal influences of the national and state governments point up the obvious fact that there is no way to freeze inter-governmental relations in a federal system. Although "centralizers" and believers in "home rule" in the heat of partisan struggle may talk as if they had found a sure-fire recipe for stabilizing these relations, it is clear that no such prescription exists. By its very nature federalism means that the distribution of functions among the various levels of government is subject to constant alteration as conditions and needs ceaselessly change.

In 1863 the distinguished English historian Freeman published a book entitled *A History of Federal Government from the Foundation of the Achaean League to the Disruption of the United States.* Although the victories at Gettysburg and Vicksburg in the same year made sure that there would be no disruption of the American Union, Freeman *could* call history to support his prophecy, for federalism has nearly always failed to maintain the necessary balance between the center and the periphery. It is a testimony to the political inventiveness of our people and our politicians that the temptation to centralize, standardize, and concentrate has been resisted.

REFERENCES

George C. S. Benson, *The New Centralization* (1941).
Jane P. Clark, *The Rise of a New Federalism* (1938).
E. S. Corwin, *The Commerce Power versus States' Rights* (1936).
James W. Fesler, *Area and Administration* (1949).
Hamilton, Jay, and Madison, *The Federalist.*
K. C. Wheare, *Federal Government,* 2d ed. (1951).

CHAPTER 6 *Interstate Relations*

In any federal state the maintenance of friendly and cooperative relations between the different units that make up the federal system is vital. This is particularly so when those vary in area and in population to the degree that exists among the states of the American Union. Except in the case of the Civil War, all disputes between states have been settled amicably and today there exists among them a spirit of friendship and cooperation. Citizens develop pride in the accomplishments, the government, or the scenic beauty of a particular state, yet the differences between states tend to disappear. A motor trip across the continent will show that no state has a corner on all good things, and if the traveler were not informed by highway signs that he was crossing from one state to another he would not be aware of that fact. The traveler is also impressed by the lack of frontier guards, by the absence of passports and, save for highway regulations and for certain quarantine laws, by complete freedom of transit between states.

Included in the Constitution of the United States are certain broad regulations governing the states in their relations with one another. In addition, there are statutes, customs, and extralegal forms of interstate relations that have developed through the years. It has been stated that in the federal system there is no small, no large, no weak, no powerful state but that they are all equal. Like many broad statements, this one has an element of truth and also much that is false in it. The states, irrespective of size and population, are equal before the law. Constitutional provisions that apply to any state apply to all states. All states have the same obligations and none is privileged. They are members of "an indestructible Union composed of indestructible States" [1] although, by amendment to the Federal Constitution, the powers and responsibilities of the states in the Union may be altered.

[1] A statement used by Chief Justice Salmon P. Chase in writing the opinion of the Supreme Court in *Texas v. White*, 7 Wall. 700, 725 (1869).

It is in Article IV of the Constitution that the rules governing inter-state relations may be found. In order to promote better relations between states, it is stipulated that the citizens of one state shall have the same privileges and immunities as citizens in the other states, that full faith and credit must be given to the public acts, records, and judicial proceedings of other states, and that fugitives from justice from one state shall be returned by the asylum state.

Privileges and Immunities

A state must accord citizens of other states the same rights and privileges as those it gives to its own citizens. It is difficult to define exactly what these privileges are but one court has said that included are the right to travel or reside in another state, to have access to the courts, to acquire and dispose of property, and to be taxed as citizens of that state.[2] These are but some of the privileges and immunities; there are many more. Not included in this number is the right to participate in elections; residence must first be acquired. Hunting and fishing licenses are usually sold to out-of-state residents at higher rates than those accorded citizens of the state. Although the right has been modified to some degree, a state may reserve certain natural resources of the state for the use of its own citizens.[3] In general, however, citizens of one state, while in another state, receive the same basic privileges that are given to the citizens of that state.

Full Faith and Credit

The constitutional fathers, fully aware of the troubles that states had with one another under the Articles of Confederation and realizing that states and citizens of a state would have many business matters that would extend into the jurisdiction of other states, included within the Constitution guarantees of fair treatment. Certainly a state does not act entirely to itself but must live with other states in a friendly and cooperative manner. In so doing both the state and the citizens receive benefits. The first section of Article IV, therefore, requires that "Full faith and credit shall be given in each State to the public acts, records, and judicial proceedings of every other State." Congress is then given the power to set down by general law the rules governing the manner in which these public acts and proceedings shall be authenticated so as to take effect in all other states.

Pursuant to this grant of power, Congress, beginning in 1790, has enacted several laws requiring the seal of the state to be affixed, the cer-

---

[2] *Corfield v. Coryell,* Fed. Case No. 3230 (1825).

[3] A different conclusion was reached in *Toomer v. Witsell,* 334 U.S. 385 (1948), where the state of South Carolina was not allowed to regulate shrimp fishing off the coast to the advantage of South Carolina citizens.

tification by the proper judge or agency secured, and observance of other regulatory provisions.[4] These regulatory acts are concerned with court decisions, records, and all public documents that pertain to civil matters and do not extend to those of a criminal nature. Without these requirements, citizens might easily escape their legal responsibilities simply by crossing a state line. Speaking generally, the states have benefited greatly by having this statement in the Constitution although at times many have rebelled in giving full faith and credit to something that would not be permitted under their own laws. Questions of the proper jurisdiction of courts also frequently interfere with the smooth working of genuine full faith and credit.

It is most difficult to give an accurate definition of the meaning of full faith and credit. The minutes of the Constitutional Convention show only one interpretation of the statement.[5]

Mr. Wilson & Docr. Johnson supposed the meaning to be that Judgments in a State should be the grounds of actions in other States & that acts of the Legislatures should be included, for the sake of Acts of insolvency. . . .

One of the most frequent uses of the full-faith-and-credit clause concerns property damages resulting from automobile accidents. Should you be hit by an out-of-state driver and should the local court award you damages, the fact that the driver is from another state in which all his property is located does not free him from meeting his obligations imposed by the court. It is the duty of the courts in the sister state to aid you in collecting the judgment awarded to you.

Illustrative of the Supreme Court's interpretation of full faith and credit is a suit brought in a Wisconsin court to secure damages arising from an automobile accident that occurred in Illinois. Mr. Hughes, a citizen of Wisconsin, was killed in the accident. The administrator of his estate brought suit in the courts of Wisconsin to recover damages. The complaint was based on an Illinois statute under which it was possible to recover damages in any court for a wrongful death occurring in that state. Wisconsin law, however, provided that no action could be brought in a Wisconsin court for a wrongful death occurring outside the state. Therefore, the Wisconsin courts dismissed the case. The Supreme Court of the United States reversed the Wisconsin findings, holding that the Illinois statute was a public act within the meaning of the full-faith-and-credit clause of the Constitution; therefore, action could be brought in Wisconsin. Said the Court: [6]

[4] Stat. L. 122 (1790), 2 Stat. L. 298–299 (1804), 28 U.S.C.A., Secs. 1738–1739.
[5] Max Farrand, *The Records of the Federal Constitution,* Vol. 2, p. 447, Yale University Press, New Haven, Conn., 1937.
[6] *Hughes v. Fetter,* 341 U.S. 609 (1951).

Acts of other states must give way . . . to the strong unifying principle embodied in the Full Faith and Credit Clause leaning toward maximum enforcement in each state of the obligations or rights created or recognized by the statutes of sister states.

In the field of commercial law, it has been the practice of the Supreme Court to require other states to defer to the law of the state of incorporation or to the law of the place of contract. With respect to workman's compensation the Supreme Court has been reluctant to impose a rigid requirement of full faith and credit lest it prevent a workman from taking advantage of whatever state provisions give him the greater protection.

Full Faith and Credit and the Validity of Interstate Divorce. Where marriage and divorce laws are concerned, the Supreme Court's position has been most uncertain.

Rules regulating the granting of divorces vary from state to state. New York grants divorces only on the ground of adultery, while other states have as many as 14 different acceptable grounds for divorce.[7] In states where divorce rules are rigid, many residents leave to secure a divorce elsewhere. Such out-of-state divorces are possible if at least one party to the divorce establishes residence in the more liberal state. The granting of divorces in recent years has become a business. In order to attract this lucrative traffic, some states have lowered residence requirements and have made it easy to secure a divorce. In Florida, residence may be established in a three months' period; Arkansas requires two months' residence before commencing action while Nevada residence may be established after a six-week sojourn. A person can file suit immediately after the establishment of residence, receive his or her decree the same day that the divorce is granted, and remarry immediately. Other states are loath to recognize divorces granted in this fashion to persons who, according to Justice Frankfurter, desire to thwart the will of the state and evade state law, "to change their spouses rather than to change their homes."[8]

When one party to a marriage leaves a state, establishes domicile in another state, and applies for a divorce, he or she secures an *ex parte* divorce. During the nineteenth century, some states refused to recognize such divorces unless the other party to the divorce appeared or was served personally within the jurisdiction of the granting court. In other words, each state determined for itself the extent to which it would honor the faith-and-credit requirements of the Constitution in divorce decrees.[9]

[7] New York, Civil Practice Act, Art. 68, Sec. 1147; Kentucky, Revised Statutes, 1948, Chap. 403, Sec. 403.020 (2117).
[8] *Sherrer v. Sherrer*, 334 U.S. 343, 361 (1948).
[9] Under present-day rules it is possible for a person to have a legal spouse in one state, a second legal spouse in another and possibly a third within another jurisdiction. It has been said facetiously that a citizen may be lawfully married in one state, a bigamist in another and a "trigomist" in a third.

Early in this century the Supreme Court held that when each of the two parties to a divorce obtained a decree, each in a different state, the decree secured from the court having jurisdiction of the marriage domicile would be the divorce to be recognized.[10] Later in *Haddock v. Haddock*, Chief Justice White, speaking for the Court, held that the state of the marriage domicile does not have to recognize a divorce granted in another state unless it chooses to do so. In refusing to compel New York, the state of the marriage domicile, to recognize a divorce secured in Connecticut by one party to the marriage the Court concluded, "We hold that the decree of the court of Connecticut . . . was not entitled to obligatory enforcement in the State of New York by virtue of the full faith and credit clause." [11]

Nearly forty years later, the Court appeared to reverse itself when it decided that North Carolina was compelled by the full-faith-and-credit clause to recognize a Nevada divorce.[12] The Court was unwilling to continue exceptions to the full-faith-and-credit requirement and also was appalled by the disastrous effects upon the lives of innocent persons as a result of the Haddock decision. True, the "strict" states would have their divorce rules undermined to a certain degree by the "liberal" states but, according to Justice Douglas, this was a part of the price of the federal system.

But North Carolina refused to surrender. Now it contended that the Nevada court did not have jurisdiction since the parties to the divorce action had not acquired bona fide domicile in that state. This time the Court held that North Carolina was compelled to give full faith and credit to the Nevada decree only if the Nevada court had jurisdiction of the divorce proceedings, and that in order to secure jurisdiction, bona fide domicile had to be established in Nevada. This, the Court found, had not been done.[13]

In another case a married woman living in Massachusetts took up residence in Florida in order to institute a divorce action. When the case came to trial in Florida her husband appeared to contest the divorce. On appeal to the United States Supreme Court the divorce granted by the Florida court was upheld on the ground that the husband had had his day in court and the matter was *res adjudicata*.[14]

The conclusions that may be reached from this brief history of interstate divorce before the Supreme Court are two:

[10] *Atherton v. Atherton*, 181 U.S. 155 (1901).
[11] *Haddock v. Haddock*, 201 U.S. 562, 606 (1906).
[12] *Williams v. North Carolina*, 317 U.S. 287 (1942). The question of jurisdiction was not raised in this case.
[13] *Williams v. North Carolina*, 325 U.S. 226 (1945).
[14] *Sherrer v. Sherrer*, 334 U.S. 343 (1948).

1. A divorce obtained without establishing bona fide domicile is not legally binding.

2. When the absent spouse participates in the divorce proceedings and has his day in court, the divorce decree must be recognized in all states.

Full faith and credit remains a constitutional requirement that is difficult to enforce. A possible solution is an amendment to the United States Constitution giving Congress the power to make uniform rules for divorce. Until public opinion is aroused to demand such a law, there is little possibility of securing uniform divorce laws or of avoiding disputes over the validity of interstate divorces.

Interstate Rendition

Persons charged with crimes have, from the time this country was settled, fled great distances not only to make their arrest difficult but also to escape from the jurisdiction of the colony or state where the crime was committed. The process by which a fugitive is returned for trial is termed interstate rendition. Frequently the term "extradition" is used to describe both the international and interstate process. However, the two are distinguishable by the fact that international extradition depends upon treaty, contract, or stipulation, while interstate rendition rests upon the supreme law of the land and the acts that have been passed pursuant to it.

The first written agreement in America providing for interstate rendition was in the Articles of the New England Confederation, signed in 1643. This was used as the basis for Article 4 of the Articles of Confederation which also provided for the return of fugitives who were guilty of treason, felony, or other high misdemeanor. Under the Articles, the demand for the return of a fugitive was to be made by the state executive rather than by judicial authorities.

There was little debate in the Constitutional Convention over interstate rendition. The statement used in the Articles of Confederation was incorporated in Article IV, Section 2, of the Constitution with the substitution of the term "other crime" for "high misdemeanor." The final draft of this article states: "A person charged in any State with treason, felony, or other crime, who shall flee from justice, and be found in another State, shall on demand of the executive authority of the State from which he fled, be delivered up, to be removed to the State having jurisdiction of the crime." This clause does not confer a right, and there is no express grant to Congress of legislative power to execute this provision. Therefore, it, in itself, was not sufficient to control rendition. As a result, Congress, in 1793, passed supplementary legislation which has continued to be the law of the land to the present day.[15] This act requires the executive authority of the de-

[15] Rev. Stat., Sec. 5278, 5279; 18 U.S.C.A., Secs. 3182, 3194.

manding state to ask for the return of the fugitive and then states that it shall be the duty of the executive authority of the asylum state to arrest the fugitive and secure his return. Until the Fugitive Felon Act of 1935,[16] the states themselves had the sole responsibility of carrying out the process of interstate rendition.

This is the procedure for securing the return of a fugitive: Suppose a man has committed a crime in Indiana and has fled to Kentucky. The sheriff of the county in which the crime was committed asks the governor of Indiana to make a formal request of the governor of Kentucky for the return of the fugitive. The governor of Kentucky may or may not grant this request. If he does, the fugitive is arrested. He then has the opportunity of asking for a writ of habeas corpus from a local court on the ground that he was not in the state when the crime was committed or that he is the wrong party. If the writ is not granted, he is held until officers from Indiana come to Kentucky and return the fugitive for trial in the court with proper jurisdiction.

In spite of attempts to close all loopholes in the procedure many people still escape punishment by crossing state lines. In the first place, the governor of the asylum state may refuse to honor the request for rendition. The Constitution says the fugitive shall "be delivered up . . . ." and the Supreme Court of the United States has interpreted this phrase as meaning he should be returned but that it is not mandatory.[17] Many instances have occurred when governors have refused to honor requests. When Luke Lea was hiding in the mountains of Tennessee in order to avoid prison sentence in North Carolina he is reported to have received a telegram from "Ma" Ferguson, then governor of Texas, offering him asylum and protection in her state. The same Texas governor refused a request made by Governor Al Smith of New York simply because Governor Smith previously had refused to return a fugitive from Texas found in New York State.[18]

A second means of avoiding return is for the fugitive to secure a writ of habeas corpus on the ground that he is not a fugitive from justice or that he is the wrong party.

Within recent years, judges of courts have been loath to return fugitives from justice unless convinced that the fugitive will receive a fair trial in the demanding state. In *Commonwealth v. Superintendent*, the state court held that when a judge is satisfied that feeling in the demanding state indicates that the fugitive will not get a fair trial, the judge can discharge him from custody.[19] Undoubtedly a writ should be granted in a case like this;

[16] 48 Stat. L., 782, 18 U.S.C.A., Sec. 1073.

[17] *Kentucky v. Dennison*, 24 How. 66 (1860).

[18] This occurred during the famous controversy between Governors Smith and Ferguson in the Canada kidnapping case in 1925.

[19] *Commonwealth v. Superintendent*, 152 Pa. Super. 167, 31 A.2d 576 (1943).

nevertheless, it sets up judges of one state as examiners of the judicial structure of other states. It is not hard to see that this might lead to many difficulties.

In order to close the gaps that existed for so many years in the process of interstate rendition, attempts were begun in 1887 to secure the enactment of uniform state extradition acts. A suggested uniform act was drawn up in 1926 and has been revised several times since then. However, this act has been approved by only 35 states and while it minimizes the problem it does not go far enough.[20]

A second attempt to improve rendition procedure involves a Federal statute. In 1935 Congress passed the Fugitive Felon Act which made it a Federal offense for a person to cross a state line after committing a crime.[21] The constitutionality of the Federal act has been upheld many times in lower Federal courts. The Fugitive Felon Act is an exercise of Congress's power to regulate interstate commerce. Certainly, if Congress under the Mann Act could regulate the transportation of women for immoral purposes across the state line as a part of interstate commerce, it could also regulate fugitives from justice who cross state lines.[22]

Unfortunately state executives have not made extensive use of the Fugitive Felon Act in securing the return of fugitives. Jealous of their powers as state officers, they have preferred, in most instances, to continue to use the old system without asking for help from the Federal government.

Interstate Boundary Disputes

Disputes over boundary lines continually arise among the several states.[23] It is an unusual session of the Supreme Court that does not have at least one boundary dispute. The casual observer might think that the settlement of hundreds of boundary disputes would mean fewer to be settled in the future. Yet boundary disputes continue to arise. There remain many vague and indefinite boundaries which, if the disputed area becomes valuable, will result in interstate disputes and possible judicial settlement. The Red River controversy between Texas and Oklahoma, for example, was brought about as the direct result of the discovery of oil in the Red River Basin.[24]

[20] New signatories have been acquired yearly. See *Your Government,* Bulletin of the Bureau of Government Research, University of Kansas, Feb. 15, 1952.

[21] 48 Stat. L. 782, 18 U.S.C.A., .Sec. 1073.

[22] *United States v. McClure,* 15 F. Supp. 931 (1936).

[23] Chief Justice Taft remarked, in an opinion, "By far the greater number of suits between States have been brought for the purpose of settling boundaries. . . ." *North Dakota v. Minnesota,* 263 U.S. 583 (1924).

[24] The dispute over the boundary line between Oklahoma and Texas was a bitter one and engendered much animosity. From 1919 until 1930 the Supreme Court issued 12 decrees and opinions on this one controversy. See George C. Lay, "The Red River Valley Controversy between the United States, Texas and Oklahoma,"

Disputes over the location of boundary lines are resolved in the following ways. First, interstate compacts are used. Under this method, the states, with the consent of Congress, agree by compact to set up boards and commissions to determine boundary lines. This procedure was followed during colonial days. Nine boundary compacts were entered into between colonies and four were made during the days of the Articles of Confederation.[25] However, many disputes that arise over the compacts are referred to the Supreme Court for final settlement.

Second, interstate boundary disputes are settled in court. They reach the Supreme Court under both its appellate and its original jurisdiction and afford an outstanding example of the Court's role as an arbiter between states. In settling these disputes, the courts frequently use commissioners and agents who make surveys and perform technical services that become the basis of the final decision. The cost of a survey of this type is met by equal payments from the states themselves.

The use of natural barriers as boundaries is understandable but such boundaries are the source of many disputes. Water boundaries have been particularly unsatisfactory. Only four states, Montana, Wyoming, Utah, and Colorado, do not have water boundaries and the first three have never had a boundary dispute before the Supreme Court. The Mississippi River acts as a boundary line for 10 states and the Missouri and the Ohio Rivers for five states each. River beds change through the forces of erosion, accretion, and avulsion. When changes occur through erosion and accretion, the boundary also changes. When a boundary river suddenly abandons its old channel, and forms a new one through the process of avulsion, the boundary line remains unchanged. Thus, a good map of the Mississippi River basin will show that Tennessee, Arkansas and other states have small plots of territory on the opposite side of the river for, although the channel of the river was altered by avulsion, the original boundary line remains unchanged.[26]

The settlement of such interstate disputes by the Supreme Court affords a splendid example of how units of a federal system live within the law. It also illustrates the value of the constitutional means at the disposal of the states for the settlement of many of their troubles, namely, the interstate compact and the Supreme Court's function as an arbiter.

American Law Review, Vol. 63, pp. 180–199, 1929. See also W. C. Carpenter, "The Red River Boundary Dispute," *American Journal of International Law*, Vol. 19, pp. 517–529, 1925.

[25] For the early history of the use of Interstate compacts see Felix Frankfurter and James M. Landis, "The Compact Clause of the Constitution, A Study of Interstate Adjustments," *Yale Law Journal*, Vol. 34, p. 685, 1925.

[26] *Arkansas v. Tennessee*, 246 U.S. 158 (1918); *Cissna v. Tennessee*, 246 U.S. 289 (1917).

Interstate Trade Barriers

An interstate trade barrier has been defined as: ". . . any State statute or regulation which, on its face, or in practical effect, (tends) to operate to the disadvantage of persons, products, or services coming from sister States, to the advantage of local residents, products and business. . . ." [27]

An increase in interstate trade barriers was one of the principal problems leading to the Constitutional Convention at Philadelphia in May, 1787. The economic paralysis inherent in trade barriers caused the framers of the Constitution to place the regulation of commerce across state lines in the hands of the Federal government.

In spite of sporadic attempts by some states to establish trade barriers for the benefit of home industries, fortunately such legislation was not widespread until the depression years following 1929. Then, because of slack business, widespread unemployment, and declining tax revenues, business interests and state officials pushed legislation and other regulations to protect them against competition with out-of-state products. They soon learned that this was a game which other states also could play.

Four types of powers reserved to the states under the Constitution were used for these restrictive measures: (1) the power of taxation; (2) the state's police power in the protection of health and sanitation, including quarantine and inspection; (3) licensing and general regulatory powers in the interest of public safety and morals; (4) the sovereign proprietary powers with regard to the conservation of natural resources and the ownership of public works and property.

The taxing power was employed in a number of ways. Taxes were imposed to exclude competitive commodities in favor of home products. Other taxes did not overtly discriminate against out-of-state products, yet operated as barriers because of their multiplicity, diversity, and cumulative burden on interstate commerce.

Quarantine and inspection laws operated in many fields, but had their greatest effect in the dairy, nursery, livestock, liquor, and general-foods industries, where they were effectively used as trade barriers. A California measure which would have placed a form of quarantine upon persons desiring to enter the state was declared unconstitutional by the Supreme Court. In order to discourage the entrance into the state of persons who might become public charges, the California legislature enacted a measure setting up penalties for individuals who might bring indigent persons into the state. Edwards, a resident of California, was found guilty of bringing in an indigent person from Texas.[28] When his conviction was appealed to

[27] *Interstate Trade Barriers,* U.S. Department of Commerce, Marketing Laws Survey, p. 2, 1942.

[28] *Edwards v. California,* 314 U.S. 160 (1941).

the Supreme Court, the state law was declared unconstitutional as an interference with interstate commerce. The states may regulate the health and welfare of their citizens, but the transportation of persons is commerce and migrations of people are a national and not a state concern. A pauper, the Court said, does not constitute a moral pestilence and while it is true that a state may solve its own problems, this type of regulation goes too far. It must give way to the power of the Federal government to regulate interstate commerce.

Licensing and general regulatory laws were particularly effective trade barriers with respect to liquor, insurance, margarine, and general foods, and they were employed extensively to burden itinerant merchants and out-of-state motor vehicles.

Proprietary powers were employed as trade barriers primarily when the states, as purchasers, gave preference to their own residents and state-produced products.

In 1940 it was found that 1,489 state statutes operating in some 10 different fields might be employed as trade barriers. Motor vehicles were affected by 301 such statutes; dairy products by 209; oleomargarine by 245; livestock and general foods by 138; nursery stock by 145; liquor by 125; commercial fishing by 35; insurance by 69; there were also 109 use taxes, and 113 general preference statutes.[29]

The constitutionality of these statutes depended upon the particular law involved, but in the absence of congressional action the courts employed certain general criteria. In the exercise of their general police powers in the field of taxation and regulation, states are forbidden to impose burdens on interstate commerce which are direct and substantial. Until Congress occupies the field, states may regulate interstate commerce in an indirect and insubstantial manner. When the discrimination against interstate commerce is obvious on the face of the statute it is unconstitutional. The courts will look into the facts of each case to determine the extent to which the statutory provision in question operates to burden interstate commerce. The court will go behind the face of the statute to its practical effect. No state, in its dealings with another state, may place itself in a position of economic isolation.

Since 1939 the states have shown a tendency to resist proposals that would increase trade restrictions among them. Restrictive measures have been removed in some instances although many still remain. The courts have been prone to adopt two solutions to trade-barrier problems. They have either invalidated certain types of state trade-barrier laws as contravening the provisions of the commerce clause, or else they have tossed the problem back into the lap of Congress. In either event, the Federal power over interstate commerce is there to be exercised.

[29] *Trade Barriers among the States,* p. 5.

Two courses are open as a means of handling any trade-barrier problem. The one is Federal action. The other is for the states, either jointly or individually, to realize the transitory value of trade barriers and to maintain the far greater advantages that result from the removal of all restrictions upon interstate travel and commerce.

Interstate Compacts

In their relations with one another the states have devised, through practical experience, several agencies through which interstate activities may be conducted and cooperation secured. Most important are interstate compacts, for which the Constitution itself makes provision. It assumes the use of such agreements by providing that "No State shall, without the consent of Congress . . . enter into any agreement or compact with another State, or with a foreign power. . . ." [30] For many years the states made little use of this provision except with relation to boundary problems. [31] But in recent years many problems have arisen in our complex society that transcend state lines and yet are not national in scope. The interstate compact has been advocated and to a limited extent has been used as a practical and a constitutional method of solving these varied problems.

Many relationships among the states do not, of course, involve anything so formal as compacts. Matters which are purely local in character, and which do not threaten to disturb the constitutional division of powers, are in many cases adjusted by agreements entered into between the appropriate state officials.

Whenever the need for formal action is apparent it has been customary for the states to make compacts with each other. [32] The terms "agreement" and "compact" are not defined in the Constitution but have been described as contracts between states that may be enforced in the courts. There are two restrictions on the making of interstate compacts. First, no political compacts are permitted. The danger of political compacts between states is clearly shown by the Civil War. The second restriction is that the consent of Congress is required to make interstate compacts valid. But approval may be given by implication. In the famous case of *Virginia v. Tennessee,* the Supreme Court held the compact valid although approval was not given directly. It was implied when certain legislation passed by

[30] Article I, Sec. 10, par. 3.

[31] For the first 110 years under the Constitution approximately 17 compacts were authorized or consented to by Congress. From 1900 to 1951, 104 were authorized or consented to by Congress, 55 of them during the last 15 years. *The Book of the States, 1950–51,* p. 22, Council of State Governments, Chicago, 1951.

[32] There are two excellent accounts of the use of interstate compacts: Felix Frankfurter and James Landis, "The Compact Clause of the Constitution," *Yale Law Journal,* Vol. 34, pp. 685–758, 1925; and Frederick L. Zimmermann and Mitchell Wendell, *The Interstate Compact since 1925,* Council of State Governments, Chicago, 1951.

Congress was based on the acceptance of the terms of the compact.[33] The trend has gone even further: certain types of compacts are considered to have the approval of Congress simply because that body has not expressed disapproval. Also Congress may give its consent in advance.[34]

One of the most important of recent compacts is the Southern Regional Educational Compact. Approved by 14 Southern states, the stated purpose of this compact was to secure the establishment of regional professional and graduate schools that would serve all the states participating under the provisions of the compact. The consent of the House of Representatives was secured without difficulty by the adoption of a joint resolution. The Senate, however, never acted favorably upon the resolution. In that body opposition arose over the inclusion of the subject of education, a matter of state concern, in the provisions of the compact. Other Senators were afraid that the real purpose of the compact was to continue segregation in the schools and that Senate consent might be considered to be approval of segregation.

In spite of the failure of the Senate to take action, the Southern states have assumed that the consent of Congress is unnecessary because of the subject matter and have proceeded to act under the terms of the compact.

In the early days the chief subject of compacts was boundary lines. Today compacts deal with stream pollution, the allocation of water, education, and other subjects. In addition to giving its consent, the Federal government may participate as one of the parties to the compact.

A recent interstate compact is a splendid example of interstate action and of the means available for the enforcement of the provisions of the compact. With the consent of Congress, West Virginia and seven other states entered into a compact to control pollution of the Ohio River basin. They created a commission consisting of representatives from each of the eight states and the United States and agreed to delegate certain powers to it and to appropriate funds for administrative expenses. The state auditor of West Virginia refused to issue the necessary warrant; and when the issue was brought before the West Virginia State Supreme Court, it held that this legislation was an unconstitutional delegation of legislative power and violated certain provisions of the state constitution. The United States Supreme Court, in overruling this decision, held that a compact is in effect a legal contract and "just as this Court has power to settle disputes between States where there is no compact, it must have final power to pass upon the meaning and validity of compacts." The Court refused to permit one state to nullify the terms of the agreement by stating it "cannot be nullified unilaterally, or given final meaning by any organ of one of the

[33] *Virginia v. Tennessee,* 148 U.S. 503 (1893).
[34] See Edward S. Corwin and Jack W. Peltason, *Understanding the Constitution,* p. 39, William Sloane Associates, New York, 1949.

contracting states." The Court was fully aware of the importance of compacts and said a compact is more than a subtle device for dealing with interests confined within a region; it also safeguards the national interest.[35]

It is possible that compacts may find a significant place within our Federal system. There is danger that too many levels of government may be established but the compact clause of the Constitution "permits infinite governmental flexibility in the combination of area administration, and local initiative." [36] It is being used more and more and with an ever-broadening subject matter.

Governors' Conference

In addition to the instruments provided in the Constitution for the conduct of interstate relations, there have developed down through the years other instruments which were neither contemplated nor provided for in the Constitution. Extralegal in character, many have served the states and the nation effectively and to a good purpose.

Theodore Roosevelt, while President of the United States, called a meeting in 1908 of the governors of the several states to consider the subject of conservation. The conference was held in Washington for three days and was so successful that it was decided that in the future an annual meeting of the chief executives of the 48 states would afford an opportunity for them to discuss common problems that concern interstate relations, Federal-state relations where cooperation is needed, and any other matter related to the improvement of state government. With the exception of a very few years, annual meetings have been held since then and an organization has been perfected. Financial support is obtained from annual dues paid by the individual states. The program of the annual meeting is devoted both to serious work and to entertainment. No vote is taken on any matter that pertains to politics and the atmosphere is informal. This description of a meeting of the governors appeared in *Life* magazine: [37]

> For four days at White Sulphur Springs, W. Va., last week there was a rare and heartening gathering of politicians—the 42nd annual Governors' Conference. What was rare and heartening about it was that, instead of partisanship, politicking and partying, the Conference was characterized by a genuine spirit of cooperation. Among the governors who came . . . it was hard to tell Democrat from Republican.

[35] *Dyer v. Sims,* 341 U.S. 22, 28 (1951).

[36] Frederick L. Zimmermann and Mitchell Wendell, *The Interstate Compact since 1925,* p. 126, Council of State Governments, Chicago, 1951. The use of interstate commissions and a possible increase in the number of interstate compacts, particularly with respect to public power and river-control projects, was forecast when President Eisenhower assumed office. State and regional representatives will make up these groups, along with Federal members whose job would be to advise, *Newsweek,* Nov. 17, 1952, p. 23.

[37] *Life,* Vol. 29, No. 1, p. 13, July 3, 1950.

Like sober businessmen the governors sat at conference tables and swapped ideas on mutual problems. They talked over state government reorganization, water resources and truck regulation— "You get behind one of those things on the highway," said Browning of Tennessee, "and the only way you can pass is on a parallel road in the next county."

Americans are great joiners and maintain an intense belief in associations with annual meetings and programs. In addition to the governors, the secretaries of state, the chief justices, and the attorneys general, the state budget officers, purchasing officials, and others have their own organizations and meet at stated times.

Regional groups also have been organized. Possibly, the governors who meet in regional associations to consider specific problems accomplish more than is generally accomplished at national conferences. However, all these organizations illustrate the importance of cooperation among the states which comprise the Federal system.

National Conference of Commissioners on Uniform State Laws

Since the middle of the nineteenth century, the possibility of securing uniformity in state law through adoption of an identical act by all the states has intrigued many persons. Much confusion has resulted from differences and conflicts in the laws of the various states on a given subject. David Dudley Field first saw the possibility of eliminating such confusion when the penal code that he drafted in 1857 for the State of New York was adopted by other states. Progress in securing uniformity was slow until the American Bar Association became interested and called the first Conference on Uniform State Laws in 1892. Nine states were represented then but today the attendance at annual conferences includes representatives from all states, the District of Columbia, and the territories. The national conference meets three days before the annual meeting of the American Bar Association. Thus excellent attendance has been secured. The 63rd annual meeting of the conference was held in 1954.[38] Commissioners are usually appointed by governors who act under legislative authorization. In most instances those selected are lawyers of standing and experience who serve without pay.

The number of commissioners from a state varies from one to six. The primary purpose of the conference is to promote uniformity in state laws on subjects where uniformity is deemed desirable and practicable. Other purposes of the conference are to draft model acts and to promote the uni-

---

[38] For a detailed account of the work of the National Conference, see *The Handbook of the National Conference of Commissioners on Uniform State Laws and Proceedings of the Annual Conference.* This handbook is published annually. See also *The Book of the States,* which is published biennially by the Council of State Governments, Chicago.

formity of judicial decisions. The Conference of Commissioners on Uniform State Laws has been asked to sponsor uniform measures upon many subjects and for various reasons. Today the conference will not of itself sponsor a uniform act unless there is a strong demand for such a measure.

The subject matter of uniform acts is wisely limited to those matters where lack of uniformity is injurious to the states and to the citizens of the states. The commissioners, as a rule, try to avoid novel subjects and controversial questions of a political nature. The acts that the conference has prepared deal with law rather than administrative procedure and are made as brief as possible.

The work of the conference is done largely by committees. At its regular meeting the conference divides itself into three general committees. One is concerned with legislative drafting, another with uniformity of laws and judicial decisions, and the third concerns itself with interstate compacts. Special and sectional committees are appointed to prepare acts on particular subjects. Usually several years elapse before any agreement can be reached on a proposed measure. It must be approved not only by the committee but also by the entire conference by a majority vote and with at least 40 delegations approving the act. It is then presented to the states for adoption.

Altogether, the National Conference of Commissioners on Uniform State Laws has recommended approximately 100 uniform acts. Many of these have become obsolete and at present only about 25 are recommended. Progress toward uniformity in separate state action is slow and even when uniform statutes are adopted by states, entire uniformity may be defeated by decisions of state and territorial courts and by the interpretation of administrative officials in applying the law in special instances. However, the Negotiable Instruments Act has been adopted by 53 jurisdictions, the Warehouse Receipts Act by 51. One state has approved 46 of the proposed uniform laws and 12 states have adopted 30 or more. The conference at times has had as many as 45 committees working on proposed uniform and model laws. While the conference recognizes the possibility of the use of interstate compacts, most of its work has been done in promoting uniform and model acts.

The Conference on Uniform State Laws is performing a valuable service in the field of interstate relations and has done much to eradicate the confusion that results from statutory conflicts.

The Council of State Governments

In the early 1920s, a member of the Colorado state senate became disturbed over the fact that members of that body, in debating a matter of state policy, knew nothing about what other states were doing to solve the same problem. He therefore wrote to all the members of the different state legislatures urging the formation of a national association, and called an organizational meeting to be held in 1926. The American Legislators Association, as this organization was called, held annual meetings but failed to secure much support until 1933 when it was decided to make state administrative officers eligible for membership. A year later the association changed its name to the Council of State Governments. It continues to function under that name today, with a definite organization, a secretariat, and a national conference which is held once every two years.

The purposes of the council are (1) to provide a clearing house for information and research for the states, (2) to serve as a medium for improving state legislative and administrative practices, (3) to maintain an instrumentality for encouraging full cooperation among the states in the solution of interstate problems, and (4) to serve as a means of improving Federal-state and state-local relations.

The Council of State Governments is composed of state commissions which have been established by the governments of each state. A typical commission is one made up of 10 legislators and five state administrators. Biennially a General Assembly of the States is held with delegations attending from the state commissions. The council has a board of managers that determines policy, an executive committee, an executive secretary, and a permanent secretariat located in Chicago. Two publications are sponsored by this organization, *State Government,* a monthly, and the *Book of the States,* which is published biennially.

The financial support of the Council of State Governments comes from the states themselves. Although Congress has been asked for financial support, none has been received and today the council does its work as an agency "for the states, supported by the states."

In addition to its general functions the council has been engaged in special research projects for individual states and also offers assistance in the preparation of interstate compacts. The council has acted as an agent in establishing nationwide programs requiring state and national cooperation, and it maintains an information service.

Initially the Council of State Governments was an association by which members of state legislatures could look beyond state lines and find out how other states were solving common problems. Today, among its major functions is the promotion of better interstate relations. Its work received impetus from those who believed that it might serve as a substitute for centralization of power in the hands of the national government.

REFERENCES

William Anderson, *Federalism and Intergovernmental Relations* (1946).
Erwin W. Bard, *The Port of New York Authority* (1941).

Council of State Governments, *Federal-State Relations*, published as S. Doc. 81,
  81st Cong., 1st sess., 1949.
————, *Trade Barriers among the States*, Proceedings of the National Conference
  on Interstate Trade Barriers, Chicago, 1939.
M. E. Dimock, and G. C. S. Benson, *Can Interstate Compacts Succeed?* (1937).
W. B. Graves, *Uniform State Action* (1934).
Thomas S. Green, Jr., *Liquor Trade Barriers* (1940).
R. H. Jackson, *Full Faith and Credit: The Lawyer's Clause of the Constitution*
  (1945).
J. B. Moore, *A Treatise on Extradition and Interstate Rendition*, 2 vols. (1891).
National Resources Planning Board, *Interstate Water Compacts, 1785 to 1941*
  (1942).
J. A. Scott, *Law of Interstate Rendition* (1917).
Tax Institute, *Tax Barriers to Trade* (1941).
Vincent Thursby, *Interstate Cooperation* (1953).
Frederick L. Zimmermann and Mitchell Wendell, *The Interstate Compact since
  1925* (1951).

CHAPTER 7 *The Establishment of the Constitution*

William Gladstone once said that the Constitution of the United States "is the most wonderful work ever struck off by the brain and purpose of man." Apparently he intended this statement as a high compliment, but it was an orator's oversimplification. Gladstone implied that the Constitution was the instant product of the framers who convened in Philadelphia in 1787, springing full-blown from minds united in a glorious unanimity of purpose. The facts, alas, teach otherwise.

The American Constitution was no different from any other political achievement of the past or the present. In the first place, it was far from "original." Its framers inherited their ideas from political experience centuries older than themselves. In the second place, it was conceived in anything but unanimity. Its immediate progenitors, in convention assembled, represented only a fraction of the people of the colonies. They fought bitterly among themselves over its principles and its details. And when the time came for the adoption of the Constitution by the people, limited though the suffrage was, still there was a hard, close fight to achieve the necessary ratifications. The only differences between the American Constitution and, say, one of the more controversial Federal laws of the 1950s are that the Constitution has been proved by the years to be an enduring and serviceable instrument and that it has served as the foundation for the development of a mighty nation.

Historical Origins

English. It is to Gladstone's own country that we are greatly indebted for the rich institutional heritage which was translated into the Constitution of the United States. While the American governmental system is quite different from the English, certain fundamentals were drawn from Britain. It was there that constitutional government developed. After the Glorious Revolution of 1688, John Locke set forth in his *Second Treatise*

104

on Civil Government the classic defense of what had happened, thus providing us with a catalogue of the constitutional genes common both to England and to our country.

Representative government is America's prime inheritance from England, whose Parliament is often referred to as the "Mother of Parliaments." Representative government as it is known in England today had its beginnings in the thirteenth century, although it is not entirely fanciful to trace it to the much earlier Saxon popular assemblies. In 1254 probably the first elected representatives were chosen, when knights from the shires were selected to meet with the barons and prelates to consider the request of Henry III for men and money to carry on a war against France. In 1265, Simon de Montfort's Parliament, summoned to meet at Westminster, contained for the first time representatives of the boroughs and towns.[1] The Model Parliament of 1295 is significant in that it was the first one in which there was representation of all classes.

At the beginning the English Parliament was not a positive law-making body. It functioned only as a sort of consultative agency requested from time to time to consent to certain proposals. Eventually it was able to pass on policies by its control over the purse, and thus became a legislative body in every sense. When the colonists came over from England representative government was foremost among the political institutions they brought with them.

America is indebted to England also for the idea of limited government and civil rights. It was in such great documents as Magna Charta, the Petition of Right, and the Bill of Rights, to mention only a few, that what became known as the rights of Englishmen were recognized. Magna Charta was referred to by Pollock and Maitland "as the nearest approach to an irrepealable 'fundamental statute' that England ever had." In Magna Charta, King John, whose reign had been replete with wrongs and abuses, agreed to limitations on his power, conceding certain fundamental rights to his subjects. Among other things, the king agreed that the English Church should be free; no taxes should be imposed on the kingdom "unless by common council of our kingdom" except for certain specified purposes; requisitions for "corn or other provisions" by constables or bailiffs could not be made without offering compensation immediately, unless the seller agreed to a postponement of payment; and to "no one will we sell, to no one will we refuse or delay, right or justice." The Petition of Right of 1628 bound the king not to levy taxes without the consent of Parliament, not to billet troops in private homes, not to declare and enforce martial law in time of peace, and not to throw his subjects into prison on a blanket charge.

[1] See Edward M. Sait, *Political Institutions: A Preface,* pp. 496–497, Appleton-Century-Crofts, Inc., New York, 1938.

The Bill of Rights of 1689 came after the abuses of the reign of James II and his overthrow during the Glorious Revolution. This document proclaimed that henceforth no laws could be suspended except by Parliament, no taxes could be collected without the approval of Parliament, appropriations for the army could be made only for one year at a time so that there could be no standing army without Parliament's consent, and no excessive bail could be required. It also assured free elections for members of Parliament, as well as freedom of debate and the right to bear arms. After the Glorious Revolution, too, executive powers came to be exercised by a committee of Parliament which became known as the Cabinet. Thus there developed a government by the consent of the governed. While Parliament became legal sovereign, back of the legal sovereign was the political sovereign or the people. Although Parliament could change the Constitution at will, nevertheless it was in effect restrained by the principles found in Magna Charta, the Petition of Right, and the Bill of Rights.

Not only did America fall heir to representative government as developed in England and to the rights of Englishmen as laid down in the great documents just described, but the system of English common law as interpreted by the courts was also transplanted to this country. By this judge-made law individual rights were further expanded and limitations were placed on government.

In a very real sense our Republic was built on English foundations. The fact that England retained its monarchical system does not detract one iota from the debt we owe to England. It took centuries for the Englishman to build his system of government. It evolved slowly, "broadening down from precedent to precedent," to borrow the words of Tennyson. The colonists had this rich fundamental heritage upon which to erect the edifice of the American system.

Colonial and State Origins. More immediately, the American system grew out of American colonial and state experience. As Simeon Baldwin said, the germ of the American Constitution was to be found in the colonial charter. The charters of Connecticut and Rhode Island, which were in effect in 1776, became state constitutions with little or no change. Representative government was firmly entrenched in the colonies. In 1776 and the years following, all of the former 13 colonies established constitutions with three departments of government—executive, legislative, and judicial. The legislatures were generally bicameral in form, although Georgia and Pennsylvania provided for unicameral legislatures. Some of the state constitutions, notably that of Massachusetts adopted in 1780, provided for the separation of powers; whether this principle was expressed or not, it was implied in all of the others. The executive was granted only limited powers and all state constitutions contained bills of rights.

Declaration of Independence. On July 4, 1776, the representatives of the 13 original colonies adopted and proclaimed to the world the Declaration of Independence, which ranks with the Constitution adopted 11 years later as one of the cornerstones of our government. Though it was drafted by Thomas Jefferson, most of the ideas were those of John Locke. Charles A. Beard implied in his *Republic* that the Declaration, along with the Preamble to the Constitution, made it unnecessary to have a Bill of Rights in the Constitution, though it was later added in the first 10 amendments. Here is one of the most significant statements from the Declaration:

We hold these truths to be self-evident, that all men are created equal, that they are endowed by their Creator with certain unalienable Rights, that among these are Life, Liberty, and the pursuit of Happiness. That to secure these rights, Governments are instituted among Men, deriving their just powers from the consent of the governed, That whenever any Form of Government becomes destructive of these ends, it is the Right of the People to alter or to abolish it, and to institute new Government, laying its foundation on such principles and organizing its powers in such form, as to them shall seem most likely to effect their Safety and Happiness.

In this brief excerpt are embodied the basic principles of constitutional free government. Here we find such ideas as popular sovereignty, natural rights, and the right of revolution. Professor McLaughlin said: [2]

The document is of very great moment in American history because of the philosophy of government set forth in the opening paragraphs . . . It was the philosophy—the political thinking—of compact and natural rights, the philosophy which justified rebellion or revolution against tyranny, which announced the principle of the popular origin of government and proclaimed the doctrine that governments were possessed of *derived* authority—a doctrine, then and now, of pivotal importance in American constitutionalism. The passages in which these principles were proclaimed were clear and powerful; they expressed the beliefs and the theories held by the American people. Jefferson merely made use of commonly accepted ideas concerning the origin and nature of government.

Articles of Confederation. The immediate forerunner of the American Constitution was the document, Articles of Confederation. Agreed to by Congress on November 15, 1777, the Articles were ratified and put into force March 1, 1781. They called for a loose confederation of the 13 states, which was known as the United States of America. According to Article II: "Each State retains its sovereignty, freedom and independence, and every power, jurisdiction and right, which is not by this confederation expressly delegated to the United States, in Congress assembled." Of course this

[2] Andrew C. McLaughlin, *A Constitutional History of the United States,* pp. 101–102, Appleton-Century-Crofts, Inc., New York, 1935.

was contradictory, as no state could give up powers and at the same time retain its sovereignty. The purposes of the Union as outlined in Article III were for the common defense, "the security of their liberties, and their mutual and general welfare." Article V called for a Congress composed of not less than two or more than seven delegates from each state to be selected as the state legislature "shall direct," and each delegation was to have one vote.

Article VI provided for certain limitations upon the states, to the effect that they could not have diplomatic representation abroad, conclude treaties or alliances with foreign nations or with each other, lay any imposts or duties "which may interfere with any stipulations in treaties" entered into by Congress with foreign nations; or keep an army or navy without the consent of Congress; or engage in war without the assent of Congress. Under Article VIII, all national expenditures were to be defrayed by requisitions levied upon the states. There was only one department of government—the legislative. Executive and judicial departments were lacking.

The new government was in operation only a very short time before insurmountable difficulties arose. A condition of near anarchy prevailed in interstate relations and in relations with foreign countries. States erected tariff walls against each other and violated treaties wholesale.

The Articles had so many weaknesses that the compact was doomed to failure as an instrument of practical government. There was no coercive force to deal with the states and compel them to obey the laws. The powers of Congress were insufficient. Congress could not levy taxes or regulate commerce, make laws governing coinage, determine the budget, or fix the size of the armed forces without the assent of nine states. And the Articles could not be amended without unanimous consent, which was impossible to secure.

Yet the Articles of Confederation marked a step forward in American constitutional development. Perhaps, as the historian Van Tyne has indicated, the Articles were valuable in marking the transition from provincialism to nationalism.[3] The former colonists were fearful of a strong national government at the outset and would not have tolerated anything more than a weak confederation.

The Philadelphia Convention

The failure of the Articles of Confederation led such outstanding men as George Washington, John Jay, and James Madison to insist as early as 1783 and 1784 that a stronger government should be established. In a letter to John Jay on August 1, 1786, Washington said:

[3] Claude H. Van Tyne, *The American Revolution*, Harper & Brothers, New York, 1905.

Your sentiments, that our affairs are drawing rapidly to a crisis, accord with my own. What the event will be, is also beyond the reach of my foresight. We have errors to correct. We have probably had too good an opinion of human nature in forming our Confederation. Experience has taught us, that men will not adopt and carry into execution measures the best calculated for their own good, without the intervention of a coercive power. I do not conceive we can exist long as a nation without having lodged somewhere a power, which will pervade the whole Union in as energetic a manner as the authority of the State Governments extends over the several States.

But all the leaders were not in accord with Washington and Jay. Jefferson, for one, maintained that the loose confederation was the best system in existence. He wished to keep government close to the people and was fearful that the liberties of the people would be endangered by concentration of power at the top. Fortunately, the thinking of Washington, Jay, and Madison predominated.

Spurred on by the demands of these leaders, the states did act. On January 21, 1786, an important resolution by James Madison was passed by the General Assembly of Virginia. It called for the selection of certain men as commissioners to represent Virginia in a meeting of commissioners, selected from other states, at a time and place to be named, for the purpose of considering measures to effect the uniform regulation of trade and commerce. The direct result was the Annapolis Convention of 1786. Since only five states were represented, the commissioners decided to take no action on the objectives set forth, but they urged that a general convention of the states be convened at Philadelphia in May of 1787 to consider these and other grave matters. Seven state legislatures—those of Virginia, New Jersey, Pennsylvania, North Carolina, New Hampshire, Delaware, and Georgia—took steps to be represented at Philadelphia. Congress, impressed, formally called for a convention on February 21, 1787. The call stated that the "sole and express purpose" of the convention was that "of revising the Articles of Confederation." Then five other states took legislative action. Only Rhode Island held out and did not send representatives.

The Constitutional Convention assembled at Philadelphia on May 14, 1787, but since a majority of the delegates had not arrived the meeting was adjourned until a quorum was finally present on May 25. On that day, according to Madison's notes,[4] Gouverneur Morris's motion that a president be elected by ballot was agreed to and Morris immediately nominated Washington, who was chosen unanimously. This was a fortunate choice, for Washington was held in such high regard by all the delegates that he was able to hold the Convention together through some stormy debates that almost wrecked it.

[4] Considered more reliable than the official Journal.

While 74 delegates were chosen to represent the states, 19 did not serve. Only 55 attended the sessions of the Convention, and 39 signed the document. Ages of the members ranged from twenty-seven to eighty-one.

The Makers of the Constitution. The Convention was not representative of the people. While it included able men as well as some of mediocre ability, practically all the delegates came either from professional ranks or from the propertied classes, with lawyers predominating. Although the tidewater areas were well represented, no wage earners or representatives of the frontier were to be found among the delegates. For the most part, the membership of the Convention was made up of the well-to-do, not to say the wealthy. Among those who played conspicuous roles in the Convention were James Wilson and Robert Morris of Pennsylvania, and James Madison and George Washington of Virginia. While Alexander Hamilton was probably the most brilliant, he was such an extreme nationalist that he had little following. Still, more than any other person, he deserves the credit for ratification of the Constitution. Edmund Randolph and George Mason of Virginia took leading roles at the beginning, but both refused to sign the final document. Men like Luther Martin of Maryland and John Lansing and Robert Yates of New York resorted to obstructive tactics and hindered the work of the Convention much more than they aided it. Conspicuous by their absence were the radicals Samuel Adams, Thomas Jefferson, and Patrick Henry.

Sketches of the delegates made during the session by Major William Pierce of Georgia are quite revealing. His pen pictures of two great leaders and of two lesser lights are especially interesting and enlightening. Of James Madison, he said: [5]

Mr. Maddison is a character who has long been in public life; and what is very remarkable every person seems to acknowledge his greatness. He blends together the profound politician, with the scholar. In the management of every great question he evidently took the lead in the Convention, and tho' he cannot be called an orator, he is a most agreeable, eloquent, and convincing speaker. From a spirit of industry and application which he possesses in a most eminent degree, he always comes forward the best informed Man of any point in debate. The affairs of the United States, he perhaps, has the most correct knowledge of, of any Man in the Union. He has been twice a Member of Congress, and was always thought one of the ablest Members that ever sat in that Council. Mr. Maddison is about 37 years of age, a Gentleman of great modesty,—with a remarkable sweet temper. He is easy and unreserved among his acquaintance, and has a most agreeable style of conversation.

[5] This and other sketches are from Charles C. Tansill (ed.), *Documents Illustrative of the Formation of the Union of the American States,* H. Doc. 398, 69th Cong., 1st sess. 1927, pp. 96–108.

And of the President of the Convention, Pierce wrote:

Gen'l Washington is well known as the Commander in Chief of the late American Army. Having conducted these States to independence and peace, he now appears to assist in framing a Government to make the People happy. Like Gustavus Vasa, he may be said to be the deliverer of his Country;—like Peter the great he appears as the politician and the Statesman; and like Cincinnatus he returned to his farm perfectly contented with being only a plain citizen, after enjoying the highest honor of the Confederacy,—and now only seeks for the approbation of his countrymen by being virtuous and useful. The General was conducted to the chair as President of the Convention by the unanimous voice of its members. He is in the 52nd year of his age.

On two less illustrious delegates, William Houston of Georgia and Roger Sherman of Connecticut, he commented thus:

Mr. Houstoun is an attorney at law, and has been a Member of Congress for the State of Georgia. He is a gentleman of family, and was educated in England. As to his legal or political knowledge, he has very little to boast of. Nature seems to have done more for his corporeal than mental powers. His person is striking, but his mind very little improved with useful or elegant knowledge. He has none of the talents requisite for the orator, but in public debate is confused and irregular. Mr. Houstoun is about 30 years of age of an amiable and sweet temper, and of good and honorable principles.

Mr. Sherman exhibits the oddest shaped character I ever remember to have met with. He is awkward, unmeaning, and unaccountably strange in his manner. But in his train of thinking there is something regular, deep, and comprehensive; yet the oddity of his address, the vulgarisms that accompany his public speaking, and that strange new England cant, which runs through his public as well as his private speaking make everything that is connected with him grotesque and laughable;—and yet he deserves infinite praise,—no man has a better heart or a clearer head. If he cannot embellish he can furnish thoughts that are wise and useful. He is an able politician, and extremely artful in accomplishing any particular object;—it is remarked that he seldom fails . . . In the early part of his life he was a shoe-maker;—but despising the lowness of his condition, he turned almanack maker, and so progressed upwards to a judge. He has been several years a Member of Congress, and discharged the duties of his Office with honor and credit to himself, and advantage to the State he represented. He is about 60.

Charles A. Beard advanced the thesis in his *An Economic Interpretation of the Constitution of the United States* that the framers were persons of property who stood to profit by the formation of a strong national government and hence had an economic stake in the new Constitution. While the charge is not without truth, it is overemphasized. The fact is that a number of wealthy men like Randolph and Mason refused to sign the document, and the latter fought ratification in the Virginia Convention.

Madison expressed his confidence in all the framers by saying they were "pure in their motives." Even a more impartial critic, Lord Bryce, said: [6]

There were no reactionary conspirators to be feared, for every one prized liberty and equality. There were no questions between classes, no animosities against rank and wealth, for rank and wealth did not exist.

The task of the framers proved to be a difficult one. There were many sharp clashes in the Convention, and had it not been for the presence of cool heads, the Convention would have failed in its task. The most serious disagreement was between representatives of the small states, who urged equal representation of the states in the legislative department, and those speaking for the large states, who stood for representation according to population. Still another clash was over whether slaves should be counted in apportioning members of the lower house on the basis of population and in levying of direct taxes. The compromises which resulted will be treated in some detail later in this chapter.

It must be made clear that it was not the intention of the framers to create a democratic government; quite the contrary. The vast majority of the delegates were afraid of popular rule and expressed their concern about the dangers of mobocracy. The delegates wanted a stable government and security for property. It seemed to most of them that these objectives could best be assured by a stronger national government.

Plans for a Constitution. A number of plans were brought forward for consideration. Of these, the Virginia or Randolph plan (largely the work of Madison) and the New Jersey or Paterson plan received serious consideration. It was, in fact, from these plans that the Constitution was drawn.

The Virginia or Randolph plan favored the large states. This plan embodied the following elements:

1. LEGISLATIVE. A bicameral legislative body in which representation was to be based on population or contributions. The legislative branch to exercise all the powers vested in Congress by the Confederation and also to legislate in all fields in which the state legislatures were incompetent. This body to be empowered to veto all state laws which in its judgment contravened the Articles of Union.

2. EXECUTIVE. A national executive, elected by Congress, to enforce the national laws and to exercise all executive powers vested in Congress by the Confederation.

3. COUNCIL OF REVISION. A council of revision composed of the executive and a convenient number of the national judiciary empowered to review all acts of the national legislature before they should become effective,

[6] James Bryce, *The American Commonwealth.* Vol. 1, 2d ed., p. 22, The Macmillan Company, New York, 1889.

and "every act of a particular legislature before a negative thereon should be final." If the council should veto any of these acts, such action would amount to rejection unless overridden by a certain vote of the members of each branch.

4. JUDICIARY. A judiciary composed "of one or more supreme tribunals, and of inferior tribunals," the judges of which were to be elected by the national legislature and to serve during good behavior.

5. ADDITIONAL POWERS OF NATIONAL GOVERNMENT. The correction and enlargement of the Articles of Confederation so as to include the purposes for which instituted, that is, "common defence, security of liberty, and general welfare."

The Paterson or New Jersey plan differed in several ways from the Randolph plan. Its salient features were:

1. Revise and enlarge the Articles of Confederation so as "to render the Federal Constitution adequate to meet the exigencies of Government and the preservation of the Union."

2. In addition to the power vested in the United States by the Articles, add the power to pass acts for raising revenue, the power to regulate commerce with foreign nations, and the power to regulate interstate commerce.

3. A plural executive elected by the United States in Congress with important appointment, military, and law-enforcement powers.

4. A supreme court with judges appointed by the Executive and holding office during good behavior.

The Compromises. The matter which produced the greatest controversy was the question of the basis of representation. As we have seen, the Virginia plan called for two houses, membership in both of which was to be based either on population or contributions, while the New Jersey plan assumed that the one-house system, as under the Articles, would continue, with equal representation for all states. Debate on this matter was acrimonious and the Convention came near to going on the rocks as a result. Finally, Johnson of Connecticut came forward with a compromise which was accepted. This plan called for a national legislature composed of two houses—a house of representatives and a senate. Membership in the house was to be apportioned among the states according to population, while in the senate the states were to have equal suffrage. This was later known as the Great Compromise.

There were other compromises of less importance, such as that for counting the slaves in the apportionment of representatives. Delegates from the slave states insisted that all slaves should be counted, but representatives of the free states demurred. Moreover, the slave-state delegates insisted that slaves should not be counted for taxation, while their Northern cousins insisted equally that they should be. The dispute ended in a compromise whereby each slave was to be counted as three-fifths of a person in the apportionment of representatives and direct taxes.

Other compromises had to be worked out, and some of them were very difficult, especially the one affecting the executive—the term, number, and method of selection. Finally, a single executive selected by an electoral college for a four-year term was decided upon. Another compromise of some importance dealt with the slave trade. Certain interests demanded that no limitation be placed on the trade. A compromise was effected whereby the slave trade could not be outlawed prior to 1808.

The Convention finished its work on September 17, after having been in session approximately four months. The new document was transmitted to Congress with a letter attached from George Washington. Resolutions were passed by the Convention suggesting that Congress submit the new Constitution to state conventions for ratification.

In presenting a new Constitution, the Convention went beyond its instructions. It had been generally understood that the Convention was charged with the task of amending the Articles only and not with making a new document. Nevertheless, Madison makes out a good case for authorization to make a new Constitution. In *The Federalist,* No. 40, he points out that the act of the Annapolis Convention and the recommendatory act of Congress of February, 1787, gave a mandate to the Convention to

. . . establish in these states, *a firm national government;* second, that this government was to be such as would be *adequate to the exigencies of government,* and *the preservation of the union;* third, that these purposes were to be effected by *alterations and provisions in the Articles of Confederation,* as it is expressed in the act of Congress; or by *such further provisions as should appear necessary,* as it stands in the recommendatory act from Annapolis; fourth, that the alterations and provisions were to be reported to Congress, and to the states, in order to be agreed to by the former and confirmed by the latter.

Such great leaders as Washington and Hamilton were convinced that a new Constitution was essential to the welfare of the new nation. John Jay pointed out in *The Federalist,* Nos. 2 to 5 inclusive, the inadequacies of the Articles as to foreign relations. Whether Madison was right or wrong, the fact remains that outstanding leaders realized that mere revision of the Articles would be insufficient.

Adoption of the Constitution

The Philadelphia Convention provided in Article VII of the Constitution that the new document should go into effect as soon as it was ratified by nine state conventions. On September 28, 1787, Congress passed a resolution calling for transmission of the Constitution together with a report from the Convention to the legislatures of the several states so that they might submit it to the conventions of delegates selected by the people.

Bitter struggles for ratification took place in some of the states, notably Virginia and New York. Delegates were selected on the basis of whether they were for or against ratification. In New York, 46 delegates were returned who opposed ratification and only 19 in favor. Here Governor Clinton and his lieutenants, Lansing and Yates, with the strong support of the agrarian element, bitterly assailed ratification. New York was a key state because of its geographical location. It had to be won over in order to make the union a success.

It was because of the critical importance of the impending struggle for ratification that *The Federalist* papers—a great classic in political science —were written. Governor Clinton had assailed the new Constitution in late September, 1787, under the name of "Cato," and Hamilton replied under the pseudonym of "Publius." After this, John Jay and Madison joined Hamilton in defense of the Constitution. Altogether, 85 papers were written by these three men—all appearing in the New York papers under the name of "Publius." Most of these papers were written by Hamilton and Madison.

Undoubtedly, *The Federalist* papers tipped the balance in New York in favor of ratification and they played a conspicuous part in ratification elsewhere, especially in Virginia and Pennsylvania. After charges by opponents in the state conventions that the Constitution provided for consolidated government and endangered the liberties of the individual by the failure to include in it a bill of rights, ratification finally was accomplished, although in New York the final vote was a close 30 to 27. A change of only two votes would have spelled defeat. It was the masterful leadership of Hamilton that accounted for the triumph.

In the Virginia convention a battle raged with unceasing fury. Madison and Marshall were locked in combat against Patrick Henry and George Mason. Henry used all the weapons in his arsenal. His fire was centered on the failure of the convention to include a bill of rights. In demagogic fashion, Henry argued that a large federal army might swoop down upon the people and destroy their liberties.[7] He urged that ratification be withheld until a bill of rights was added. In both the Virginia and New York conventions there were demands for another convention to meet the criticism. But Madison was not to be outdone and his side eventually won out. However, he was impressed with the demands for a bill of rights and it was he who later introduced in Congress the resolution calling for the first ten amendments.

Less intense but still rather sharp was the struggle in the Pennsylvania

[7] In a letter to Madison dated December 20, 1787, Jefferson had also expressed dissatisfaction that a Bill of Rights was omitted. See S. K. Padover (ed.), *The Complete Jefferson*, pp. 120–123, Duell, Sloan & Pearce, Inc., New York, 1943.

convention. James Wilson led the fight for ratification and success crowned his efforts.

Bancroft's statement that "from the ocean to the American outposts nearest the Mississippi one desire prevailed for a closer connection" hardly squares with the facts. There was a sharp division among the people as to ratification, and two opposing camps resulted. There were the Federalists who favored the Constitution and the Antifederalists who opposed. Geographically, the back country people were against ratification; those of the seaboard were for it. The dispossessed or debtor classes who wanted easy money were Antifederalists, while the well-to-do were Federalists. The former wanted more paper money and freedom from regulation, while the latter wanted a strong national government and sound money. Among the Federalists were merchants, bankers, manufacturers, shipowners, speculators, holders of government securities, planters, and all privileged classes who were interested in security. The Antifederalists included small landowners and propertyless people in the towns, that is, the "have-nots." But some prosperous men, including Jefferson and Patrick Henry, who feared that the Federal government would be just as scornful of the people's rights and liberties as the British Parliament had been, opposed ratification.

It is impossible to ascertain just what proportion of the people favored ratification of the new Constitution. Because of stringent property qualifications, it is doubtful if more than one-fourth of the adult males participated in the election of delegates to ratifying conventions in the states. More specifically, it is estimated that of the 4 million population, 160,000 voted for delegates, and of this number 100,000 cast their votes for delegates known to support ratification. Eventually, the necessary nine ratifications were obtained, and other states followed. North Carolina and Rhode Island did not ratify until after the Constitution had gone into effect.

REFERENCES

Max Beloff (ed.), *The Federalist* or *The New Constitution* (1948).
W. W. Croskey, *Politics and the Constitution in the History of the United States,* 2 vols. (1953).
Elliott's Debates.
Max Farrand (ed.), *The Framing of the Constitution of the United States* (1913).
———, *Records of the Federal Convention of 1787* (1911).
Journal of the Federal Convention (kept by James Madison) (1898).
John Locke, *The Second Treatise of Civil Government and a Letter Concerning Toleration* (1946).
Walter Hastings Lyon, *The Constitution and the Men Who Made It* (1936).
Andrew C. McLaughlin, *A Constitutional History of the United States* (1935).
Charles Louis de Secondat Montesquieu, *The Spirit of Laws* (1899).

CHAPTER 8 *The Development of the Constitution*

In a broad sense, the Constitution of the United States is more than the written document composed of seven articles and twenty-two amendments; it also includes decisions of the Supreme Court interpreting its meaning, certain basic laws passed by Congress, usages and customs, executive ordinances, and treaties. Considered in that manner, the difference between our Constitution and England's is not so great.[1] Judge Cooley defined a constitution as "the body of rules and maxims in accordance with which the powers of sovereignty are habitually exercised." And Woodrow Wilson described the Constitution as a "vigorous taproot" from which has evolved "a vast constitutional system—a system branching and expanding in statutes and judicial decisions as well as in unwritten precedent."[2]

The Constituent Power

In addition to the methods of amendment and revision of the Constitution described below, it should be noted at the outset that the people of the United States have the right to alter their form of government through the exercise of their "constituent power." The idea of a constituent power was stated by Locke, and reasserted by such founding fathers as James Wilson and George Mason. As Professor Carl Friedrich has so well said: [3]

No matter how elaborate the provisions for an amending power may be, they must never, from a political viewpoint, be assumed to have superseded the constituent power, for the constituent power is the power that made the constitution. It remains forever in the people, who cannot be bound by their ancestors to any existing governmental pattern.

[1] In his *Usages of the American Constitution* (Oxford University Press, London, 1925), Herbert W. Horwill contends that there is no distinction between written and unwritten constitutions.
[2] Woodrow Wilson, *Congressional Government*, p. 9, Houghton Mifflin Company, Boston, 1887.
[3] *The New Belief in the Common Man*, pp. 129–130, Little, Brown, & Company, Boston, 1942.

117

The right of the people to alter, change, or abolish their government whenever they so desire rests essentially upon the right of revolution. Locke insisted that if the rulers became tyrannical and failed to respect the natural rights of the people, the latter could take back the power of government which they had only temporarily lodged in their rulers. And so it is with the American people. If the government should overstep its bounds and sweep away the liberties of the people as guaranteed in the Bill of Rights, then the people could resume their original powers. Abraham Lincoln referred to this constituent power in his first inaugural address, when he said:

This country, with its institutions, belongs to the people who inhabit it. Whenever they shall grow weary of the existing Government, they can exercise their *constitutional* right of amending it, or their *revolutionary* right to dismember or overthrow it.[4]

If revolution did occur and succeed, the people would be free to set up any form of government they desired, including a monarchy or dictatorship. Fortunately, this has never been done and most Americans hope it will never be necessary. As long as the officers of government act according to law and respect the people's liberties, this residual power will not be exercised. But it is well for those who govern to know it exists.

The Amending Power

The most obvious, and the most formal method of changing the meaning of the Constitution is through the process of amendment laid down in Article V. Under the Constitution, amendments may be proposed by a two-thirds vote of both houses of Congress; or, upon application of two-thirds of the state legislatures, a convention may be called by Congress for the purpose of proposing amendments. In order to become a part of the Constitution, an amendment must be ratified by the legislatures of three-fourths of the states or by constitutional conventions of the same number of states. Congress decides upon the method of ratification. To date, only one amendment—the Twenty-first—has been submitted to state conventions.

In *Hawke v. Smith*[5] the Supreme Court held that an amendment did not have to be submitted to a referendum of the people of a state, but might be ratified either by state legislatures or by conventions. In another case the Court held that Congress could fix the time limit for the states to ratify an amendment.[6] Furthermore, in *Coleman et al. v. Miller et al.*,[7] it was held that once a state has ratified an amendment, it may not sub-

[4] Italics supplied.
[5] 253 U.S. 221 (1920).
[6] *Dillon v. Gloss*, 256 U.S. 368 (1921).
[7] 71 P. 2d. 518 (Kans. 1937).

sequently rescind its action. However, a state may reject an amendment and later reverse itself.

Because only 22 amendments have been added to the Constitution since 1789, there are those who believe that the amending process is too cumbersome. John Marshall once voiced this opinion and proceeded to expand the Constitution by judicial interpretation. Professor Carl Friedrich agrees with Marshall and suggests that the freer method of amendment in use in Switzerland and in some of the states would probably be better. But if an easier method were adopted, there might be danger of legislating in the Constitution, a practice which many of the states have followed.[8]

The First Ten Amendments. The first 10 amendments, which are, in effect, a Federal Bill of Rights, were proposed in 1789 and adopted in 1791. They were offered by James Madison to meet the objections voiced in state conventions by Patrick Henry and others. These amendments limit the Federal government only. However, the "due process" clause of the Fourteenth Amendment, which does apply to the states, has been interpreted broadly by the Supreme Court, and its effect has been to enforce upon the states some of the same obligations as those exacted from the Federal government in the Bill of Rights. Amendments I through X and XIV are discussed in detail in Chap. 9.

The Eleventh and Twelfth Amendments. The Eleventh Amendment, proposed in 1794 and adopted the next year, came as the result of an important decision of the Supreme Court in *Chisholm v. Georgia.*[9] In this case, the Court held that a citizen of one state could sue another state in the Federal courts. The amendment outlawed future suits of this sort and also provided that no citizen or subject of a foreign country could sue any one of the states. When the Principality of Monaco attempted to bring suit against one of the Southern states for redemption of securities held by it, the Supreme Court held that such a suit could not be entertained without the consent of the state, even though the suit was not expressly barred by the Eleventh Amendment.[10]

The Twelfth Amendment, proposed in 1803 and adopted shortly thereafter, came about as a result of confusion in the presidential election of 1800. Originally the Constitution provided that each elector should cast his vote for two persons without designating which was his choice for President and which for Vice-President. In the election of 1800, the candidates of the Republican party, Jefferson and Burr, received 65 votes

[8] The easily amended constitutions of many states have become filled with minor details, some of transitory importance. Once those provisions find their way into a constitution, they are difficult to remove and the constitution becomes clogged with trivia which more properly belong in legislation.

[9] 2 Dall. 419 (1793).

[10] *Principality of Monaco v. Mississippi,* 292 U.S. 313 (1934).

each, although the former had been nominated by his party for the Presidency and the latter for the Vice-Presidency. In the ensuing election in the House of Representatives, Burr came close to election over Jefferson. In order to obviate such a situation, the Twelfth Amendment specifies that an elector must vote for one person for the Presidency and another for the Vice-Presidency. This amendment also provides that when the election is thrown into the House, the choice is between the three highest candidates for the Presidency instead of the five highest, as originally specified. Furthermore, the Twelfth Amendment provides that to be eligible for the Vice-Presidency, a person must be qualified for the Presidency.

The War Amendments.[11] The Thirteenth, Fourteenth, and Fifteenth Amendments are known as the War Amendments. They resulted from the War Between the States and had to do largely with the rights of the Negro. The Thirteenth Amendment freed the slaves and authorized Congress to take steps for the punishment of anyone holding another in involuntary servitude except for punishment of crime. The Fourteenth Amendment made the Negro a citizen and extended certain civil rights to him, while the Fifteenth Amendment was designed to give him the right to vote. Recently the Supreme Court held that the white primary is unconstitutional under the Fourteenth and Fifteenth Amendments.[12]

The Sixteenth Amendment. The Sixteenth Amendment, proposed in 1909 and ratified four years later, authorized Congress to levy an income tax. The need for the amendment grew out of the case of *Pollock v. Farmers' Loan and Trust Company,*[13] in which the Supreme Court had declared unconstitutional the income tax law of 1894. In a 5-to-4 decision the Court had held that a tax on income from land was a direct tax, and hence must be apportioned among the states according to population. The effect of the Sixteenth Amendment was to render apportionment unnecessary and therefore to validate congressional taxes on income from whatever source derived.

The Seventeenth Amendment. This amendment, providing for popular election of United States Senators, was proposed in 1912 and was adopted within 359 days. Originally Senators were elected by the state legislatures. Before this amendment was adopted, however, many states had already enacted laws which gave the voters the choice of United States Senators. In 29 states the party nominees for the office were chosen in a direct primary, and while the results were not legally binding on the state legislatures, generally they were followed. Two states adopted preferential elections which were binding on the state legislature.

---

[11] The Thirteenth Amendment was proposed in 1865, the Fourteenth in 1866, and the Fifteenth in 1869. All were ratified within two years after they were proposed.
[12] For further discussion see Chap. 9.
[13] 157 U.S. 429 (1895).

The Eighteenth Amendment. The amendment prohibiting the manufacture and sale of intoxicating liquors was proposed in 1917, during the First World War, and adopted the following year. It proved to be the most controversial amendment ever adopted, and in 1933 was repealed by the adoption of the Twenty-first Amendment.

The Nineteenth Amendment. This amendment ushered in woman suffrage throughout the nation. Proposed by Congress in 1919, it was ratified in 1920.

The Twentieth Amendment. Generally known as the "lame duck" amendment, this measure was initiated in Congress by Senator George Norris and passed in 1932. It was adopted less than a year after proposal. It provides that members elected to either House shall take office on January 3 following the general election. Formerly, members who were defeated (known as "lame ducks") continued to serve throughout the session of Congress which opened in December following the election and continued until March 4 of the next year, while newly elected members did not start their service until the next session of Congress, usually thirteen months after their election.

The Twenty-first Amendment. As stated above, this amendment repealed the Eighteenth Amendment. Proposed in 1933, it was ratified the same year.

The Twenty-second Amendment. The Twenty-second Amendment prohibits any President from serving more than two terms. Also, a person who has served more than two years of another President's term may be elected for only one additional term. An exception was made of President Truman, during whose term the amendment was proposed. Thus the highly controversial third term has been outlawed. Only Franklin D. Roosevelt was ever elected for more than two terms. Urged by many of the leaders in his party, Roosevelt stood for a third term in 1940 and was elected over Wendell Willkie, who made the third term his chief issue. Roosevelt was elected to a fourth term in 1944 when the country was in the midst of World War II. Until Roosevelt's time, no one had successfully defied the tradition against a third term. General Grant was put forward in 1880 for the Republican nomination, but failed to get it. In 1912 Theodore Roosevelt made a bid for a third term, but he fell short of election, although he received both a larger popular vote and a larger electoral vote than the nominee of the Republican party.[14]

Development by Judicial Interpretation

The meaning of the Constitution is to be found not by reading the text alone, but by reading the decisions of the Supreme Court as to what the

---

[14] After his election in 1904, Roosevelt stated that he would consider this term to which he had just been elected a second term and that he would not run again.

Constitution means with regard to specific issues which have arisen from time to time. Former Chief Justice Charles Evans Hughes once said, "The Constitution is what the Supreme Court says it is." This is necessarily so, because such terms as "interstate commerce" require definition and application to specific issues. Judicial interpretation has been the most important method of determining the meaning of the Constitution.

Under the leadership of Chief Justice Marshall the Supreme Court adopted a policy of broad interpretation of the powers of the Federal government. During Marshall's long tenure from 1801 to 1835 the Court handed down a number of significant decisions bearing on national powers. In *Marbury v. Madison*,[15] the Court enunciated for the first time the doctrine of judicial review. While the Constitution did not specifically authorize the courts to rule that an act of Congress was unconstitutional, the Court found that this power was there by implication. The power of reviewing and annulling acts of Congress was long used sparingly by the Court. Only two acts were declared void before 1865.

Another momentous decision of this period was that of *McCulloch v. Maryland*,[16] in which a tax levied by Maryland on notes of the Bank of the United States was challenged. Maryland insisted that Congress had no power to establish the bank in the first place. No mention of a bank was contained in the Constitution. To this contention, the Court replied that the power of the Congress to establish a bank was implied in the "necessary and proper" clause of Article I, Section 8, paragraph 18 of the Constitution. It was in this clause, in conjunction with certain express powers like the power to borrow money on the credit of the United States, that the power lay. "Let the end be legitimate," said the Court, "let it be within the scope of the Constitution, and all means which are appropriate, which are plainly adapted to that end, which are not prohibited, but consist with the letter and spirit of the Constitution, are constitutional." This broad interpretation is called the doctrine of implied powers.

National power was still further expanded in the Court's interpretation of the commerce power. In *Gibbons v. Ogden*,[17] the Court, with Marshall again speaking, handed down a sweeping decision on the power of Congress to regulate commerce among the states. A New York state law gave Ogden the exclusive right to operate steamboats in the waters of the state, while Gibbons was operating steamboats in the coastal trade under an act of Congress of 1793. Ogden had applied for a writ of injunction against the violation of his exclusive right by Gibbons, and the New York court granted the writ. After stating that the power to regulate commerce with foreign nations was exclusively vested in Congress, the Supreme

[15] 1 Cranch 137 (1803).
[16] 4 Wheat. 316 (1819).
[17] 9 Wheat. 1 (1824).

Court went on to hold that Congress had the same power with respect to interstate commerce:

The subject to which the power is next applied is to commerce "among the several states." The word "among" means intermingled with. A thing which is among others is intermingled with them. Commerce among the states cannot stop at the external boundary line of each state, but may be introduced into the interior . . . We are now arrived at the inquiry, what is this power? It is the power to regulate; that is, to prescribe the rule by which commerce is to be governed. This power, like all others vested in Congress, is complete in itself, may be exercised to its utmost extent, and acknowledges no limitations other than are prescribed in the Constitution. These are expressed in plain terms, and do not affect the questions which arise in this case, or which have been discussed at the bar. If, as has always been understood, the sovereignty of Congress, though limited to specified objects, is plenary as to those objects, the power over commerce with foreign nations, and among the several states, is vested in Congress as absolutely as it would be in a single government, having in its constitution the same restrictions on the exercise of the powers as are found in the Constitution of the United States.

Thus the commerce power of Congress is exclusive with respect to matters requiring uniformity. In line with this decision, the Supreme Court was later to hold in the Shreveport Case [18] that Congress could even regulate *intrastate* commerce where it bore a substantial relation to interstate commerce. A temporary halt was called on the broad interpretation of the commerce power in *Hammer v. Dagenhart,*[19] when the Court held that commerce did not include manufacture. The wider view was again accepted in *United States v. Darby Lumber Company,*[20] reversing the Dagenhart decision. The Darby Lumber Company, a Georgia lumber concern, had refused to abide by the Fair Labor Standards Act providing for payment of certain minimum wages. The Court now held that manufacturing was so closely related to commerce that Congress could regulate at least certain aspects of it. The Court said:

The motive and purpose of the present regulation is plainly to make effective the congressional conception of public policy that interstate commerce should not be made the instrument of competition in the distribution of goods produced under sub-standard labor conditions, which competition is injurious to the commerce and to the states from and to which the commerce flows.

It is to the constitutional power to tax and to regulate commerce that the Federal government owes most of the powers which it has exercised (and which the Court has upheld) under the New Deal and the Fair

[18] *Houston, East and West Texas Railway Company v. United States,* 234 U.S. 341, 342 (1914).
[19] 247 U.S. 251 (1918).
[20] 312 U.S. 100 (1941).

Deal. But precedent had already been clearly set—witness the earlier notable cases of *Champion v. Ames*,[21] *Hoke v. United States*,[22] and *McCray v. United States*,[23] in which the power of Congress to ban lottery tickets, "white slavery," and oleomargarine from interstate commerce had been sustained.

Development by Statute

The Constitution of the United States is a short document containing only the basic provisions concerning the powers and framework of the Federal government. It is well that this is so, for the fundamental law should not include legislation. The founding fathers were wise to leave to Congress the task of filling in the details, thereby making the Constitution more elastic and adaptable to the changing problems of society.

Thus, Article III, Section 1, of the Constitution merely says that "The judicial power of the United States shall be vested in one Supreme Court, and in such inferior courts as the Congress may from time to time ordain and establish." Notice that this section does not state how many judges shall constitute the Supreme Court, how much their salaries shall be, who shall preside over the Court, and so on. Nor is the number of inferior courts specified—their constitution, number of judges, salaries, and organization. All these details are left to Congress. Neither does the Constitution provide for the specific jurisdiction of the various courts, nor (in the original Constitution) confer exclusive jurisdiction on the Federal courts. The jurisdiction of the Federal judiciary is broadly sketched in Article III, but Congress decides just what jurisdiction each court shall have, except that the Constitution does provide that the Supreme Court shall have original jurisdiction in all cases affecting ambassadors, other public ministers, and consuls, and those in which a "State shall be party." Article III, Section 2, provides that the Supreme Court shall have appellate jurisdiction in all other cases "with such exceptions, and under such regulations, as the Congress shall make." Does this mean that Congress could take away all of the appellate jurisdiction of the Court? Some authorities, including Professor Robert E. Cushman, think it does.

A good example of expansion of the Constitution by statute is the Judiciary Act passed by Congress in 1789. This act provided for the organization of the Supreme Court and inferior courts. It fixed the number of judges of the Supreme Court and the judges' salaries, otherwise provided for the Court's organization, and set forth its jurisdiction.[24] The methods

---

[21] 188 U.S. 321 (1903).
[22] 227 U.S. 308 (1913).
[23] 195 U.S. 327 (1904).
[24] In providing for original jurisdiction as to writs of mandamus, the Congress exceeded its powers, or so the Supreme Court held in *Marbury v. Madison*, 1 Cranch 137 (1803).

of appealing cases from the lower courts were prescribed. Inferior courts were established by the same act and their organization was also laid down in detail. This act has been amended from time to time. Several times Congress has passed laws changing the number of members of the Supreme Court. However, in 1937, when President Roosevelt proposed the addition of six new members after the Court had declared several New Deal measures unconstitutional by a divided vote, such a step was regarded as revolutionary. It was rejected by Congress after a debate that rocked the country.

Even though the Federal courts have sprung largely from legislation, rather than from the Constitution, they have become such indispensable parts of our system that they are actually constitutional in character. Thus, when Congress legislates with regard to them, it is, in effect, amending or at least expanding the original Constitution.

Another significant statute which expanded the Constitution in no small way was the Election Disputes Act of 1887. In 1876, 21 electoral votes were disputed by the followers of Tilden and Hayes. On the first count, Tilden had 184, or one short of a majority, while Hayes had only 164. The matter was finally submitted to an electoral commission composed of 15 members, which awarded the disputed votes to Hayes. This settlement left a bitter taste in the mouths of Tilden and his followers, for they felt that Tilden had been cheated out of the election. It was to forestall the possibility of another such fiasco that the Election Disputes Act of 1887 was passed. It provides for the certification by state authorities of the electoral votes of each state. Considering the importance of its subject matter this statute must be looked upon as constitutional in character.

Customs and Usages

In several instances usages or conventions have supplanted portions of the Constitution. Charles A. Beard has commented, "The customs of our Constitution form as large an element as they do in the English Constitution." [25]

Election of the President. For example, it was clearly the intention of the framers of the Constitution that the college of electors should be free to choose a President, for it was their belief that an indirect system of election would be best. They thought that the presidential electors would be better *qualified* than the voters to choose a man for this high office. Said one of the framers, "It would be as unnatural to refer the choice of a proper person for President to the people as to refer a trial of colors to a blind man." Even Madison entertained a certain amount of distrust of the people. Accordingly, it was provided that the state legislatures should

[25] *American Government and Politics,* p. 60, The Macmillan Company, New York, 1921.

decide how the presidential electors were to be chosen and that they should meet in their respective state capitals and cast their ballots for two persons. The electors were to exercise an independent choice.

But the founding fathers did not foresee how the American political system would develop. As political parties evolved, candidates were nominated and the presidential electors were instructed how to vote. Gradually popular selection of the electors supplanted election by state legislatures, and it became an inflexible custom that electors must vote for the choice of the people of their respective states. In 1820 one elector exercised an independent choice and voted for a person other than the one for whom he was instructed to vote. And again in 1948 a Tennessee elector voted for Strom Thurmond although the people of the state had voted for Truman. These electors had a perfect legal right to cast their votes contrary to the wishes of the people.[26] However, the electors do usually follow party instructions in spite of the fact that the framers intended that they should be independent. The role of the elector was well described by Woodrow Wilson as follows: [27]

But now he is merely a registering machine—a sort of bell-punch to the hand of his party convention. It gives the pressure and he rings. It is, therefore, patent to everyone that that portion of the Constitution which prescribes his functions is as though it were not.

The Vice-President. Although the wording of the Constitution appears to indicate that it was the intention of the framers that on the death or resignation of the President, the Vice-President would become acting President, usage has established that he shall take the title of office and become President. Article II, Section 1, states:

In case of the removal of the President from office, or of his death, resignation, or inability to discharge the powers and duties of the said office, the same shall devolve on the Vice President, and the Congress may by law provide for the case of removal, death, resignation, or inability, both of the President and Vice President, declaring what officer shall then act as President, and such officer shall act accordingly, until the disability be removed, or a President shall be elected.

Nothing is said about the Vice-President becoming President in case of a vacancy in the office of President. The statement in the Constitution simply is that the powers and duties of the office "shall devolve on the Vice President." The apparent intention was that the Vice-President should become only an acting President. Usage has decreed it otherwise, however, and the Vice-President has taken the title of President when

---

[26] In 1952 certain Southern legislatures, including those of Georgia and South Carolina, attempted to turn back the hands of the clock by providing that their electors should have a free choice in the electoral college.

[27] Wilson, *op. cit.*, p. 250.

vacancies have occurred. The practice was started by John Tyler when he succeeded Harrison after the death of the latter. On April 6, 1841, Tyler took the oath of office as President of the United States and three days later issued a proclamation stating that he had been called to the office of President.[28] Many of the members of Congress, including John Quincy Adams, believed that Tyler should have been designated only as acting President. In their eyes, Tyler usurped the office of President. But whether this was correct or not, the fact remains that Tyler became President and thus started a usage that has continued through the years.

The Cabinet. Although the Cabinet originated in the early days, there was no provision for it in the Constitution. Apparently it was the intention of the framers that the Senate should act as an advisory body to the President, but Washington had some unfortunate experiences in trying to consult with the Senate and finally gave up in disgust. From that day, consultation with the Senate as a body was discarded. Even though the President consults with individual members of the Senate, particularly with the leading Senators of his party, the Cabinet early displaced the Senate as a formal advisory body. Originating in 1791, it was first called a "Cabinet" in 1793. The first legal sanction of the term was in a Supreme Court decision in 1803. In 1829 the word "Cabinet" appeared in a presidential message to Congress. William Howard Taft said: "The Cabinet is a mere creation of the President's will. It is an extra-statutory and extra-constitutional body. It exists only by custom. If the President desired to dispense with it, he could do so." [29]

The President may invite whomever he wishes to the meetings of the Cabinet—usually held twice a week. Franklin Roosevelt invited not only the heads of the 10 executive departments to attend his Cabinet meetings but several other chief officials as well.

The American Cabinet, however, is very different from that of Great Britain, which runs the government and exercises very important legislative and executive powers. The American Cabinet neither has any powers as a Cabinet, nor is it the principal source of advice for the President. The most important policies are rarely decided in the Cabinet, and often are not even discussed there.[30]

Appointments and Removals. While Article II, Section 2, of the Constitution provides that the appointing power of the President shall be exercised "by and with the advice and consent of the Senate," actually the President does not consult with the Senate as a body before submitting nominations, though he often consults with individual Senators. The

[28] Horwill, *op. cit.*, pp. 70–71.
[29] William Howard Taft, *Our Chief Magistrate and His Powers*, p. 30, Columbia University Press, New York, 1916.
[30] For further discussion of the Cabinet, see Chap. 14.

phrase "advice and consent" historically meant only an act of approval or disapproval. Hamilton stated in *The Federalist* that since the power to nominate or to choose was vested in the President, members of the Senate would not attempt to dictate nominations. Nevertheless, the custom has grown up for the Senators of the party in office to select the persons to be appointed to Federal offices in their own states, such as judges, district attorneys, marshals, collectors of internal revenue, and others. This custom has been enforced by the practice of the Senate, known as senatorial courtesy, under which it will reject a nominee of the President if he is objected to by a Senator of the state in which he is to serve. This unwritten rule is customarily invoked only by members of the same political party as the President. Senators of the opposite party seldom invoke it, for they do not select the Federal officeholders in their states.

Senatorial courtesy was at work as early as 1789, when the Senate rejected the President's nomination of Benjamin Fishbourne to be port commissioner of Savannah, simply because the two Georgia Senators had another candidate. A more modern example occurred in 1950 when the two Georgia Senators objected to the nomination of Neill Andrews for a judgeship in their state, not because he was in any way unqualified, but because they had recommended another person. The Senate obliged them and rejected Andrews, and subsequently President Truman nominated their candidate, who was approved. In 1951 a similar case arose when Senator Douglas objected to two nominees to Federal judgeships in Illinois because his own recommendations had not been accepted by the President. The Senate turned down the President's choices.

Thus, by usage, "The right to reject, which the Constitution vests in the Senate, has become the right to select." [31]

Concerning removal of Federal officers, the Constitution is silent, except for the provision on impeachment. The issue arose in the first session of Congress. After a notable debate which lasted for four days in the House, it was decided that the President has an inherent power to remove officers whom he appoints. This decision was frequently challenged in the Senate on the ground that the right to participate in appointments implied a similar power over removals. During Johnson's administration an act was passed prohibiting the President from making removals without the concurrence of the Senate. Later this legislation was repealed in part. It was not until 1926, in the famous case of *Myers v. United States* [32] that the Supreme Court ruled on the issue, holding that the President had an inherent removal power which could not be curtailed by Congress. This

[31] This is the remark of Senator Hatch before the Senate in 1943 when he opposed the McKellar bill requiring senatorial confirmation for thousands of administrative employees. See *Congressional Record,* 78th Cong., 1st sess., June 13, 1943, p. 5822.

[32] 272 U S. 52 (1926).

decision was later modified in *Rathbun v. United States*,[33] when the Court held that Congress could prohibit the removal of members of independent regulatory commissions except for reasons stated in law.

Other Usages. There are many other usages, but only a few can be mentioned here.

1. While the Constitution does not specify that the Speaker of the House of Representatives shall be chosen from the membership of the House, custom has invariably so decreed.

2. According to the Constitution, all revenue bills must originate in the lower house and the framers intended that the House of Representatives should exercise a dominant voice in such legislation. Actually, the Senate has exercised an equal power over revenue legislation and at times has so greatly revised the House revenue bills that only the title remained unchanged.

3. While the Constitution specifies that a member of the House of Representatives must reside in the state which he represents, it does not provide that he must be a resident of the district. And yet custom has required that Representatives must reside in the district which they represent.

Expansion by Treaty. The best example of the development of the Constitution by treaty is the Migratory Bird Treaty of 1916, concluded between the United States and Great Britain. Because migratory birds were in danger of extermination unless common measures were taken, the treaty provided that both nations should take steps to control the hunting seasons for such birds as doves and waterfowl. Each government was to recommend the necessary laws to its legislature. In compliance with the treaty, Congress passed the Migratory Bird Act in 1918. Then in the case of *Missouri v. Holland*,[34] the state of Missouri sought an injunction to prevent Holland, a Federal game warden, from enforcing the act and the regulations made under it by the Secretary of Agriculture. Among other contentions, Missouri insisted that the statute was an unconstitutional interference with the rights reserved to the states by the Tenth Amendment. Certainly this would have been a valid contention before the treaty was made, since the control of wildlife resided in the states.

But the Supreme Court decided against Missouri. The Court said, in part:

Here a national interest of very nearly the first magnitude is involved. It can be protected only by national action in concert with that of another power. The subject matter is only transitorily within the state and has no permanent habitat therein. But for the treaty and the statute there soon might be no birds for any powers to deal with. We see nothing in the Constitution that compels the gov-

33 295 U.S. 602 (1935).
34 252 U.S. 416 (1920).

ernment to sit by while a food supply is cut off and the protectors of our forests and our crops are destroyed. It is not sufficient to rely upon the states.[35]

Executive Ordinance. Not so important as the other methods, perhaps, but still worth mentioning is the development of the Constitution by executive ordinances. Some important statutes leave broad discretionary power to the President. The Reorganization Act of 1939 is a sample. This act vested in the President wide power to reorganize the administrative agencies of the Federal government. For example, the Coast Guard was transferred from the Navy Department back to the Treasury Department under the power given to the President by this law.

These various examples of constitutional expansion lend substance to the Wilsonian description of the Constitution as merely a "vigorous taproot." The Constitution is, indeed, far more than the seven articles and their twenty-two amendments. But even if due account is taken of the statutes, judicial decisions, usages and customs, treaties and executive ordinances which comprise today's Constitution, no one can say with certainty that the identical Constitution will be in effect in the next decade or even next year. The United States Constitution is a living document, and like any vital organism it is subject to constant change. No one can know for certain today the direction in which the courts or Congress or the people will bend the Constitution tomorrow.

REFERENCES

Edward S. Corwin, *The Constitution and What It Means Today* (1948).
Walton Hamilton and Douglass Adair, *The Power to Govern: The Constitution —Then and Now* (1937).
Herbert W. Horwill, *The Usages of the American Constitution* (1925).
Lester B. Orfield, *The Amending of the Federal Constitution* (1942).
Carl B. Swisher, *American Constitutional Development* (1943).
Benjamin F. Wright, *The Growth of American Constitutional Law* (1942).

[35] In 1954 a highly controversial amendment to the Constitution proposed by Senator Bricker of Ohio was being considered. Under this proposal, executive agreements limiting powers of the states could not be entered into without the consent of Congress.

CHAPTER 9 *Citizenship and Individual Rights*

Who *are* citizens—in the United States? To whom does the term apply? The answer is simple. It matters not what color of skin a person has, or who his parents are: if he was born within the United States *he is a citizen* provided his parents were subject to the jurisdiction of the United States when he was born.

In recent years this sweeping principle has governed the determination of citizenship in our country. But it was not always so. The original Constitution did not define clearly the qualifications for citizenship. Consequently until the issue was resolved by the Fourteenth Amendment, which was adopted after the War between the States, there were two schools of thought.

One held that only those who qualified as citizens under the laws of the states in which they resided were citizens of the nation. This position was upheld by the Supreme Court in the famous Dred Scott decision. The opposite view was that citizenship in the United States did not depend on state laws. The Fourteenth Amendment settled the matter. It defined United States citizenship, and expressly provided that the citizens of the nation are also citizens of the states in which they reside. Thus the amendment forbade the states to deny citizenship to Negroes.

Citizenship by Birth

The Supreme Court made the matter clear in 1898 in the celebrated case of Wong Kim Ark, an American-born Chinese who had been denied re-entry into the United States, after a short visit to China, on the ground that he was not a citizen of this country. The Court emphatically re-affirmed the man's right to citizenship. Wrote Justice Gray: [1]

The Fourteenth Amendment of the Constitution . . . contemplates two sources of citizenship, and two only: birth and naturalization. Citizenship by

[1] *United States v. Wong Kim Ark*, 169 U.S. 649 (1898).

131

naturalization can only be acquired by naturalization under the authority and in the forms of law. But citizenship by birth is established by the mere fact of birth under the circumstances defined in the Constitution. Every person born in the United States, and subject to the jurisdiction thereof, becomes at once a citizen of the United States, and needs no naturalization.

The only exceptions to the rule are persons whose parents were not subject to the jurisdiction of the United States. For example, a child born of British parents in the British diplomatic service in this country would not be a citizen of the United States.

Not only persons born in this country but also children born to American parents abroad are American citizens. This follows the ancient rule of law which held that nationality was based on descent or parentage. And yet, while a child born of American parents residing abroad is normally regarded as an American citizen, this is subject to certain exceptions and conditions. Under a law of 1934, a child born abroad of American citizens does not acquire citizenship in this country unless one of his parents has resided in the United States prior to his birth. If either of the parents is an alien, the child, if born subsequent to May 1934, must reside continuously in the United States for five years previous to his eighteenth birthday, and at the age of twenty-one he must take an oath of allegiance to the United States.

Citizenship by Naturalization

This country's peculiar role as a melting pot springs from the fact that in addition to being born here there is a second way of attaining United States citizenship. A person born elsewhere but desiring to live here and become a part of our society may be naturalized according to certain procedures laid down in the Constitution and laws of the country.

There are two kinds of naturalization—collective and individual. An entire population may become citizens of the United States, either by a treaty of cession or by an act of Congress. For example, when Alaska was purchased from Russia in 1867, it was specified by the treaty of cession that the people of that territory should become citizens. By act of Congress in 1925 the American Indians were made citizens, and in 1927 the people of the Virgin Islands had citizenship conferred on them in the same manner.

Individual naturalization is open to all aliens who can prove certain qualifications which Congress deems necessary to good American citizenship. The basic procedure is simple. After five years of continuous residence in this country and six months in one state, any alien eighteen years of age or over may file a petition for citizenship, attaching a certificate proving that he entered the United States lawfully. After investigation and a preliminary hearing, a final hearing before the Federal District Court or a state court of record takes place. This happens not less than ninety days after the original application was filed. Then, if the applicant and his two citizen witnesses satisfy the court that he meets certain qualifications, the oath of citizenship is administered, a certificate of citizenship is issued, and the new citizen takes his place along with natural-born citizens of the United States.

Surrounding those "certain qualifications," however, have been lively controversy and many Supreme Court attempts to define and redefine what is the sine qua non for attaining naturalization. At the present time, a petitioner for citizenship must be of good moral character. He must be able to read, write, and speak English. He must understand the history, principles, and form of American government, and must swear to uphold those principles. He must not have deserted the Armed Forces or have evaded a wartime draft. He must not have applied for exemption from military service because he was an alien. He must neither be an anarchist, nor any sort of totalitarian such as a Communist, nor ever have been associated with revolutionary or totalitarian organizations or aided in propagating their views. He must renounce any title of nobility and must not be a citizen of a country with whom this country is at war. He must also state his attitude toward bearing arms.

About the question of a prospective citizen's willingness to bear arms in defense of the United States much controversy raged for many years. The naturalization laws enacted by Congress have required that before an alien could be admitted to citizenship he had to declare on oath in open court that he would "support and defend the Constitution and laws of the United States against all enemies, foreign and domestic, and bear true allegiance to the same." The Supreme Court more than once held that unwillingness to go to war (even in the case of a forty-nine-year-old woman) was a bar to citizenship. This hotly contested dictum was reversed at last in 1943, when one Girouard, a Canadian and a Seventh Day Adventist, applied for naturalization in the District Court of Massachusetts. While he was willing to take the oath of allegiance, he refused to agree to bear arms, on the ground that it was contrary to his religion. Reversing its previous position, the Supreme Court ruled that the required oath did not include the bearing of arms in defense of the country, and that pacifists could be naturalized. In this opinion the Court laid down a new, modern version of the essentials of good citizenship: [2]

The nuclear physicists who developed the atomic bomb, the worker at his lathe, the seaman on cargo vessels, construction battalions, nurses, engineers, litter bearers, doctors, chaplains—these, too, made essential contributions. And many of them made the supreme sacrifice.

[2] *United States v. Girouard,* 328 U.S. 61 (1946).

Congress put its own version of this dictum into law in the McCarran Acts of 1949 and 1952. The law says that conscientious objectors on religious grounds may be naturalized but pacifists who base their objections on political, sociological, or philosophical grounds are barred.

Another restriction on applicants for citizenship used to stem from the racial origin of the immigrant. Until 1952, groups who were barred at one time or another included Negroes, Japanese, Chinese, Filipinos, Koreans, and North American and Asiatic Indians. Now the racial restrictions have been dropped almost entirely and any person, no matter what his color, may be naturalized, provided he meets the other legal requirements.

There was a time when an American woman lost her citizenship if she married an alien, but such is not the case today. American women who marry aliens may now retain their citizenship, while foreign women marrying American citizens may acquire citizenship in one year instead of in five.

There are, then, three ways of becoming a citizen of the United States. First, all persons, regardless of color or race, who are born in the United States and subject to its jurisdiction are citizens. Second, all persons born abroad of American parentage are, subject to certain conditions, citizens of this country. Finally, a foreign-born man or woman who meets the legal requirements may be admitted to citizenship by the process of naturalization. Citizenship of the United States and that of the individual states have become practically identical; any citizen of the nation becomes a citizen of a state immediately upon taking up residence in that state.

Loss of Citizenship

Neither a native-born citizen nor a naturalized one is necessarily a citizen for life. He may lose his right to call himself an American if he is naturalized by another country or takes an oath of allegiance to a foreign government or if he formally renounces American citizenship before the proper authorities. He forfeits citizenship also if he enters the armed forces of a foreign country, holds civil office under a foreign government, or votes in a political election in a foreign country. A child loses American citizenship if his parent is naturalized by a foreign state.

A naturalized citizen may lose American citizenship in still other ways. Citizenship is cancelled if it is shown that he obtained his naturalization papers fraudulently or illegally, or if he moves permanently from the United States within five years after naturalization. The McCarran Act of 1952 also specified that citizenship will be revoked if a naturalized citizen joins a revolutionary or totalitarian organization within five years after he obtains citizenship or if, when accused of subversive activity, he is convicted of contempt for refusing to testify before a congressional committee within 10 years after receiving citizenship.

Duties of Citizenship

Not only does the citizen have rights, but he has corresponding duties and obligations. A citizen must observe the laws and, in the case of a man, perform military service when called upon by his government, although this does not mean that conscientious objectors must bear arms. The highest form of citizenship, however, involves much more than the performance of these basic duties. The effective citizen also participates actively in community and civic affairs, becomes informed on public issues and makes his contribution to an intelligent public opinion, stands up for the rights of citizens and the well being of his community, and in many instances exercises leadership by serving as an officer of public or civic bodies or by standing for public office. It would be a mistake to regard activities of this kind as merely the performance of a public duty; they also provide the opportunity to qualified citizens to render service which is richly rewarding in human satisfactions. Democratic government cannot succeed without the active, informed, and intelligent participation of its citizens.

The Vote

The right to vote is the cornerstone of democratic government. In the United States, the decision as to who may vote is left by the Federal Constitution almost entirely to state determination. Article I provides that the qualifications for voting for members of the House of Representatives shall be the same as those prescribed by the several states for the election of the most numerous branch of the state legislature. This rule also governs the election of United States Senators. The Constitution contains no provision concerning who may vote for Presidential electors, but provides that they shall be *appointed* in such manner as the state legislatures shall determine. In the early history of the country it was the usual practice for Presidential electors to be chosen by the state legislatures. The framers of the Constitution did not foresee that custom would reduce the electoral college to a mere formality and change the election of the President and Vice-President from an indirect to a direct system.

Today the same qualifications for voting apply to all officers alike, Federal and state, and these qualifications are determined by the states. The Fifteenth Amendment, however, forbids the states to deny or to abridge the right to vote on account of race, color, or previous condition of servitude, and the Nineteenth Amendment prohibits discrimination on the basis of sex.

Qualifications for Voting. In the early history of the Republic the suffrage was greatly restricted. Most states required property qualifications for voting, and a few imposed religious tests as well. Universal manhood suffrage was ushered in during the Jacksonian era—at first in the frontier states. Later it spread to the Atlantic seaboard. At the end of the War Between the States, Negroes were given the franchise, but subsequently they were deprived of this right in most Southern states in spite of the specific constitutional prohibition of discrimination on the basis of race.

The principal means used by Southern states to disfranchise the Negro was to impose a literacy test for voting. Such a test is entirely legal and is found in 18 states including many outside of the South. There, however, it has sometimes been administered by local registrars in an arbitrary and discriminatory manner. Literate Negroes have often been rejected when they applied for registration at the same time that illiterate whites were permitted to register without taking a test at all or because their grandfathers had been voters. In several Southern states, such as Alabama, Georgia, and Mississippi, a political-knowledge test is used, although it is only one of several alternative requirements. Any voter who is of good character and who understands the duties of citizenship under a republican form of government may qualify to vote under the provision. This is another wide opening for discrimination against Negroes, especially where registrars have ample discretionary power as in the South. Another device used to disfranchise the Negro in the South, recently held unconstitutional, has been the Democratic party's "white primary." Since the Democratic primary in most Southern states determines the final results, and the general election is largely a formality, persons who were debarred from voting in the Democratic primary were virtually disfranchised.

Requiring prepayment of a poll tax—in several states as much as six months before the election—is another device to discourage Negroes from voting, but it has had the same effect on many white voters as well. At one time practically all the Southern states and a few Northern states required voters to pay a poll tax in order to qualify to vote. In recent years Florida, Georgia, Louisiana, North Carolina, South Carolina, and Tennessee have abolished the poll tax, but it continues in effect in Alabama, Arkansas, Mississippi, Texas, and Virginia. Wherever the poll tax has been repealed, registration and voting have increased—by as much as 50 per cent in some states. There has been a strong movement for the enactment of a national law outlawing the poll tax as a qualification for voting for national officers. Such bills have passed the House of Representatives only to be defeated in the Senate through the use or threat of a filibuster by the Senators from the South. Authorities differ as to whether such legislation would be constitutional.

Prior to the adoption of the Nineteenth Amendment in 1920, only a few states permitted women to vote. Although woman suffrage has not purified politics, as predicted by its ardent advocates, yet the effect of women on public life has been wholesome. Numbers of women have been elected to office and many have made notable contributions to public life. The League of Women Voters has done much to interest and educate women on public issues. There are many women who take their politics more seriously than their spouses do.

Practically everywhere voters are required to register in order to vote. The purpose of the requirement is to provide a list of qualified electors prior to the election, and thus to permit investigations if fraud is suspected. Formerly, voters were usually required to register every year, or every two or four years, depending on the state law. Now most states have permanent registration laws whereby the voter remains on the registration list so long as he continues to reside at his registered address and votes at least once every two years. In many states the voter is required to sign the registration record, and this signature is compared with his signature when he applies at the polls to vote, thus preventing others from voting under his name. Various means are taken to purge the lists of the names of persons who have died or moved away, but in many states the registration officers are lax in their duties and much dead wood is carried on the registration lists.

In both Georgia and Kentucky the voting age is now eighteen; in all other states it is twenty-one. While it is difficult to draw conclusions as to the result of lowering the age qualification, it has been suggested in a number of states, and a constitutional amendment providing for voting at eighteen has been proposed by President Eisenhower to Congress. All states now limit the franchise to citizens, although formerly aliens who had declared their intention to become citizens were allowed to vote in some states. Residence in the state for a specified period varying from six months in some states to as much as two years in others, is universally required.

Nonvoting. Today the greatest problem concerning suffrage is not who is qualified but, rather, the failure of many qualified voters to vote. Nonvoting is increasing. In so-called minor elections it has become a serious problem. In Presidential elections, which generally bring out a much higher vote than state and local elections, only 50 to 60 per cent of the eligible voters have cast their ballots in recent elections; in other elections it is not uncommon for the vote to drop as low as 25 per cent of those who are qualified. The vote in primary elections, often more crucial than the final elections, is usually only about half that cast in the general election. And in the South, where the final election is usually taken for granted, the number of voters who cast their ballots is generally very small.

There are many causes of nonvoting. They include apathy, disgust with politics, absolute control by one party in some areas, too many elections and too long ballots, poor registration systems, too-lengthy residence requirements, and arbitrary disqualifications for voting. Abroad, voting is often compulsory, but there is little support for such a requirement here. Perhaps the basic remedy for nonvoting is to educate our children more thoroughly in the duties of citizenship. A large vote is almost useless unless the voters are informed on the issues and candidates and are thus able to vote intelligently for the kind of leadership they believe the country, the state, and the community need.

Civil Rights

When the American colonists declared themselves free and independent of England in 1776, their greatest fear was of tyrannical government. Not only were they concerned about the tyranny of kings, but of Parliament as well. These fears are reflected in the Declaration of Independence, in which the doctrine of the equality of men and of their natural rights was proclaimed. Accordingly, all the state constitutions included a bill of rights patterned after such great documents as the British Magna Charta of 1215 and the Bill of Rights of 1689. The bill of rights in Virginia's constitution of 1776 stated that "all men are by nature, equally free and independent, and have certain inherent rights," of which they cannot by compact divest their posterity, and "that all power is vested in, and consequently derived from the people." It also guaranteed freedom of religion, freedom of the press, trial by jury, and protection against excessive bail, general warrants, and so on.

The original Constitution of the United States did not include a bill of rights, although it did provide for the writ of habeas corpus, and prohibited ex post facto laws and bills of attainder. The failure to include a bill of rights almost brought about its defeat in some states, notably Virginia. Patrick Henry, one of the most vigorous opponents of ratification in the Virginia convention, pointed out the dangers of setting up a central government without proper guarantees of the rights of the people. The Federal government, he declared, could swoop down upon the defenseless people with a great army and strike terror into their hearts. It was only with the assurance that a bill of rights would be added to the Constitution that Virginia finally ratified it. Soon after the new Constitution went into effect Congress submitted ten amendments which were quickly ratified by the states and came to be known as the Bill of Rights.

In order to secure individual rights against arbitrary action by the executive and legislative departments, the people must look to the courts. And the courts have, on the whole, guarded well these liberties and rights. State as well as Federal courts are expected to uphold the individual rights guaranteed by the Federal Constitution. The Supreme Court of the United

States is the final arbiter. In the past twenty-five years it has handed down decisions which preserved the so-called "preferred rights"—freedom of speech and thought, freedom of assembly, freedom of the press, and freedom of religion.

Guarantees against the Federal Government. Article I, Section 9, of the Constitution provides: "The privilege of the writ of habeas corpus shall not be suspended, unless when in cases of rebellion or invasion the public safety may require it." As explained in Chap. 1, this means that a person may not be held in prison without sufficient cause. When a writ of habeas corpus is issued, the authorities must bring the prisoner before the judge issuing the writ and show sufficient grounds for keeping him in prison, otherwise the judge will order his release.

It is in the Bill of Rights, or, strictly speaking, the first eight amendments to the Constitution, that the bulk of civil rights are stated, *i.e.*, guarantees against Federal interference. These rights may be divided into substantive and procedural.

Substantive Rights. Substantive rights are "the rights to the enjoyment of fundamental privileges and immunities equally with others."[3] They are guaranteed in the first three amendments. The First Amendment provides for what are sometimes called the four freedoms—freedom of religion, freedom of speech, freedom of the press, and freedom of assembly. The first three rights have been treated at length in Chap. 1.

In a democracy the right of assembly is of great importance, for a free play of ideas is essential. Nevertheless, good order is also essential, and for this reason freedom of assembly must be regulated to safeguard the security of persons and property.

In *Crandall v. Nevada*[4] the Supreme Court held that the right to petition Congress was also a privilege and immunity of United States citizenship. The right to petition is used to air grievances and to secure their redress, as well as to promote constructive legislation. Its importance not only to citizens but to the operation of the legislative body is obvious.

Procedural Rights. The right of a person to have his case tried by a court of law according to the procedure provided by the Constitution and the law is a procedural right. Several of the first ten amendments guarantee such rights for accused persons. The Fourth Amendment prohibits unreasonable searches and seizures. Law-enforcement officers cannot enter a person's premises and search them without sufficient cause and without a proper warrant secured for that specific purpose. This assures the individual that no general or blank warrants will be issued, a practice which was common in colonial days. However, an officer may

[3] See Edward C. Smith and Arnold J. Zurcher, *A Dictionary of American Politics*, p. 295, Barnes & Noble, Inc., New York, 1944.
[4] 6 Wall. 35, 44 (1868).

search without a warrant a vehicle which he has reason to believe is carrying outlawed commodities;[5] furthermore, implements of crime, as well as government property, may be seized without a warrant at the time a subject is arrested.[6]

The Fifth Amendment states that no person may be tried in a Federal court "for a capital or otherwise infamous crime, unless on a presentment or indictment of a grand jury," except in the armed forces.[7] Further, no person shall "be subject for the same offense to be twice put in jeopardy of life or limb." Thus, a person tried for a capital or "infamous crime" [8] and acquitted may not be tried again for the same offense. But there is no double jeopardy when there is a mistrial or where the jury is illegally constituted, or where conviction is set aside by a higher court on appeal. Moreover, the same act may be an offense both against state and Federal law. In *United States v. Lanza* [9] it was decided that conviction in a state court for an offense is no bar to trial and conviction by a Federal court for the same act if it is also a Federal offense, and vice versa, for the same offense may be against both jurisdictions. It is highly unlikely, however, that a person who is tried and convicted by either jurisdiction will be tried by the other.

The Fifth Amendment also guarantees that no person "shall be compelled in any criminal case to be a witness against himself." This provision against self-incrimination originated in England in the late sixteenth century because of the arbitrary methods instituted by the ecclesiastical courts. In accordance with decisions of the Supreme Court, no accused person may be compelled to testify in his own case, nor may a witness be compelled to answer questions which might be used in future prosecutions, nor as a rule, may the accused or a witness be required to produce books and papers which might incriminate him.[10] However, a witness must make it clear in testifying that he claims immunity.

The Fifth Amendment provides that no person shall "be deprived of life, liberty, or property, without due process of law." The same words are found in the Fourteenth Amendment, which applies to the states. The "due-process" clause is one of the most important provisions in the Federal Constitution, on the interpretation of which a large proportion of

---

[5] *Carroll v. United States,* 267 U.S. 132 (1925).

[6] *Adams v. New York,* 192 U.S. 585 (1904), and *Harris v. United States,* 331 U.S. 145 (1947).

[7] In some of the states, persons may be indicted by the district attorney as a result of facts he gathers as to guilt of the accused person.

[8] "Infamous" means a crime for which a person if found guilty is subjected to punishment by imprisonment, loss of civil or political liberty, or hard labor. (See Edward S. Corwin, *The Constitution and What It Means Today,* p. 163, 10th ed., 1948.)

[9] 260 U.S. 377 (1922).

[10] See *Boyd v. United States,* 116 U.S. 616 (1886) and *Counselman v. Hitchcock,* 142 U.S. 547 (1892).

constitutional decisions have been based. For many years this provision was regarded as merely guaranteeing to the individual his day in court and the protection of the customary judicial procedures. Then, shortly before 1900, the Supreme Court began to hold that laws regulating business or fixing the rates of public utilities in a manner which it regarded as unreasonable or confiscatory were a denial of due process of law. On this ground the Court held unconstitutional a number of state regulatory laws. Since 1937, however, the Court has reversed itself and has returned to its earlier, more limited interpretation of the due-process clause.

By the Sixth Amendment, one of the most important from a procedural standpoint, the accused in criminal cases is granted the right to "a speedy and public trial, by an impartial jury of the State and district" where the alleged crime took place. Furthermore, it is provided that he shall be informed "of the nature and cause of the accusation," that he shall "be confronted with the witnesses against him," and that he shall have "compulsory process for obtaining witnesses in his favor, and . . . have the assistance of counsel for his defense."

Jury trial in Federal law means a trial by a jury of 12 persons and the verdict must be unanimous as to guilt.[11] While the judge may comment on the law involved, as well as on the facts, he must make it clear in each case that the determination of facts is up to the jury. Although the jury is supposed to be drawn from all walks of life in the community, "blue ribbon" juries are permissible under certain circumstances.[12] Jury trial may also be waived by the accused. "Speedy trial" does not necessarily mean that the accused must be tried within a certain specified time, but within a reasonable period. Nor does a "public trial" mean that all of the public is permitted to be present, but rather that representatives of the public, including friends of the accused, may attend.[13]

The assurance that the accused shall be tried in the state and district where the crime occurred is to make certain that the trial is to take place in the vicinity where the accused is known, presumably where he has friends. But this rule is not always followed, especially where persons are accused of conspiracy to break the laws of the United States, or of perpetrating fraud against the Federal government. The defendant is assured the privilege of legal counsel so that he will be certain to be aware of all his rights. The Seventh Amendment provides for jury trial in civil cases where the damages claimed amount to over $20. The Eighth Amendment guarantees the accused against the exaction of "excessive bail" and against "excessive fines" and "cruel and unusual punishment." What is excessive

---

[11] See *Bauman v. Ross*, 167 U.S. 548 (1897); *Bailey v. Anderson*, 326 U.S. 203 (1945); and *Thiel v. Sou. Pac. Co.*, 326 U.S. 217 (1946).
[12] *Fay v. New York*, 332 U.S. 261 (1947).
[13] Corwin, *op. cit.*, p. 177.

bail is left to the discretion of the courts. "Cruel and unusual punishment" would be a penalty too heavy for the particular offense involved.

Federal Guarantees of Civil Rights against State Action. In order to protect citizens of the United States, especially Negroes, against arbitrary and unreasonable action by the states which might deprive them of their civil rights, the Fourteenth Amendment was added to the Constitution in 1868. It provides in Section 1: "No State shall make or enforce any law which shall abridge the privileges or immunities of citizens of the United States; nor shall any State deprive any person of life, liberty, or property, without due process of law; nor deny to any person within its jurisdiction the equal protection of the laws."

While the first eight amendments to the Constitution fully safeguard citizens of the United States against Federal encroachment on their civil rights, there is no equal constitutional bulwark against the encroachments of the states. There are those who have insisted that the Fourteenth Amendment covers the same civil rights as are listed in the first eight amendments, but the Supreme Court of the United States has taken a different view.[14] In his dissenting opinion in the Slaughterhouse Cases,[15] Justice Field contended that the framers of the Fourteenth Amendment had wrought a constitutional revolution by providing that all the civil rights of citizens of the United States should be guaranteed against the states in the same manner as they were guaranteed against the Federal government; but although Justice Field was joined by three of his colleagues he was in the minority. It is true that in a piecemeal manner many of the civil rights protected by the first eight amendments are now protected also against the states' inroads under the Fourteenth Amendment. But while all the *substantive* rights are thus guaranteed against arbitrary state action, the *procedural* rights are not.

Although the Supreme Court failed to go along with the broad view expressed by Justice Field, the Court later used the due-process clause as a springboard for the so-called constitutional revolution. Beginning in 1925 with *Gitlow v. New York*,[16] when the Court held that freedom of speech and freedom of the press were protected by the due-process clause of the Fourteenth Amendment against unreasonable state action, it went on to hold in various cases that all the four freedoms of the First Amendment limit state action. Although in *Gitlow v. New York* the antisyndical-ism law of New York was upheld, still the Court asserted that freedom of speech and freedom of the press are protected by the Fourteenth Amendment. Thus the Court ushered in a new era in constitutional interpretation, in which the civil liberties of individuals were to reach new heights.

[14] See *Maxwell v. Dow*, 176 U.S. 581 (1900).
[15] 16 Wall. 36 (1873).
[16] 268 U.S. 262 (1925).

A few years after the Gitlow case, the Supreme Court held unconstitutional in *Near v. Minnesota* [17] a Minnesota law which provided for the suppression, as a public nuisance, of any "malicious, scandalous and defamatory newspaper, magazine, or other periodical." With Chief Justice Hughes speaking for the majority, the Court said:

> This statute, for the suppression as a public nuisance of a newspaper or periodical, is unusual, if not unique, and raises questions of grave importance transcending the local interests involved in the particular action. It is no longer open to doubt that the liberty of the press and the liberty of speech is within the liberty safeguarded by the due process clause of the Fourteenth Amendment from invasion by state action.

Later, in *Grosjean v. American Press Company* [18] the Court declared a Louisiana tax on newspaper advertising null and void on the ground that the purpose was to regulate the press. Here the Court said that "a free press stands as one of the great interpreters between the government and the people. To allow it to be fettered is to fetter ourselves." License taxes imposed by cities on the sale of leaflets by Jehovah's Witnesses met the same fate as the Louisiana tax, because they obstructed the dissemination of ideas. Professor Corwin raises the question of whether the freedom here upheld includes the right to propagate religious ideas.

The Court has also gone a long way in upholding the freedom of speech and of thought. Returning to the Holmes doctrine of clear and present danger, the Court in *Herndon v. Lowry* [19] held null and void a Georgia conspiracy law which made "utterances advocating the overthrow of organized government by force" a criminal offense. Angelo Herndon had been convicted in a Georgia court for distributing communist literature. The Supreme Court declared that this law deprived Herndon of his constitutional right of freedom of speech. And years later, in *Terminiello v. Chicago*, [20] the Court declared a Chicago ordinance unconstitutional on the ground that it invaded the right of free speech. In this case Terminiello had been indicted and convicted for violation of an ordinance which provided that anyone "who shall make, aid, countenance or assist in making any improper noise, riot, disturbance, breach of the peace or diversion tending to a breach of the peace" shall be deemed guilty of disorderly conduct. Terminiello had made a speech which led to a riot outside the hall where he was speaking. Justice Douglas, who gave the majority opinion, held that dispute was a proper function of free speech and that one should not be punished for exercising it "unless shown likely to produce

---

[17] 283 U.S. 697 (1931). The newspaper involved in this action had charged that the law-enforcement officers of the community were in league with criminals.
[18] 297 U.S. 233 (1936).
[19] 301 U.S. 242 (1937).
[20] 337 U.S. 1 (1949).

a clear and present danger of a serious substantive evil that rises far above public inconvenience, annoyance, or unrest."

But in this case the Court was sharply divided, Justice Jackson entering a vigorous dissent in which he was joined by others. The result was that the decision was modified in *Feiner v. New York*,[21] in which the Court upheld a conviction for a similar offense. Speaking for the majority, Chief Justice Vinson upheld the conviction on the ground that the guarantee of freedom of speech does not offer a cloak under which to incite a riot.

The Supreme Court has similarly applied to the states the limitations of the First Amendment as to the abridgment of freedom of religion. In *Minersville School District v. Gobitis*[22] the Court upheld a regulation of a school board requiring all school children to salute the flag, but three years later this decision was reversed in *West Virginia State Board of Education v. Barnette*.[23] Both of these cases were brought by members of Jehovah's Witnesses who insisted that the requirement to salute the flag was contrary to their religious principles and beliefs. In the latter case the Court said:

> The very purpose of the Bill of Rights was to withdraw certain subjects from the vicissitudes of political controversy, to place them beyond the reach of majorities and officials and to establish them as legal principles to be applied by the courts. One's right to life, liberty, and property, to free speech, a free press, freedom of worship and assembly, and other fundamental rights may not be submitted to vote; they depend on the outcome of no elections.

Local government ordinances restricting the distribution of religious tracts and the playing of religious records in public places also have been declared unconstitutional. The decisions in these cases seem clearly to show that the guarantee of the freedom and practice of religion of the First Amendment is equally applicable to the states under the Fourteenth Amendment.

The First Amendment requires separation of church and state. In the case of *Everson v. New Jersey*,[24] a tax payer challenged a New Jersey law which authorized local school boards to make rules and contracts for the transportation of school children. Acting on the authority of the law, a township education board had authorized reimbursement of parents for the transportation of their children to schools on buses operated by the public transportation system. This included reimbursement to parents who sent their children to parochial and private schools as well. Everson challenged the statute chiefly on the ground that it was a law respecting "the establishment of religion." He contended that it violated the principle of

[21] 340 U.S. 315 (1951).
[22] 310 U.S. 586 (1940).
[23] 319 U.S. 624 (1943).
[24] 330 U.S. 1 (1947).

separation of Church and State guaranteed by the Fourteenth Amendment with respect to the states. While the Court, with Justice Black speaking, upheld the New Jersey law by a 5-to-4 vote, it did make an enlightening statement as to the meaning of "establishment of religion" when it said: [25]

Neither a state nor the Federal government can set up a church. Neither can pass laws which aid one religion, aid all religions, or prefer one religion over another. Neither can it force nor influence a person to go to or remain away from church against his will or force him to profess a belief or disbelief in any religion. No person can be punished for entertaining or professing religious beliefs or disbeliefs, for church attendance or non-attendance. No tax in any amount, large or small, can be levied to support any religious activities or institutions, whatever they may be called or whatever form they may adopt to teach or practice religion. Neither a state nor the Federal government can, openly or secretly, participate in the affairs of any religious organizations or groups or vice versa. In the words of Jefferson, the clause against establishment of religion by law was intended to erect "a wall of separation between Church and State."

The Court later held that the action of a local Illinois school board in permitting religious instruction in the public schools did violate the principle of separation of Church and State. In the case of *Illinois ex rel. McCollum v. Board of Education* [26] the plaintiff brought suit against the Champaign Board of Education, attacking the provision for religious education in the public schools. The Champaign Board of Education permitted religious instruction in the schools by representatives of any and all sects during school hours, although this instruction was taken by pupils on a voluntary basis. The Supreme Court of the United States held that religious instruction could not be carried on in the public schools, even when extended alike to all sects, saying:

The operation of the state's compulsory education system thus assists and is integrated with the program of religious instruction carried on by separate religious sects. Pupils compelled by law to go to school for secular education are released in part from their legal duty upon the condition that they attend the religious classes. This is beyond all question a utilization of the tax-established and tax-supported public school system to aid religious groups to spread their faith. And it falls squarely under the ban of the First Amendment (made applicable to the States by the Fourteenth) as we interpreted it in *Everson v. Board of Education.*

The Court went on to hold that the board in giving religious groups an opportunity to propagate religious doctrines in the public schools had violated the principle of separation of Church and State. On the other

[25] *Everson v. Board of Education,* 330 U.S. 15–16 (1946).
[26] 333 U.S. 203 (1948).

hand, the Court dismissed a suit attacking a New Jersey statute which provided for the reading of five verses of the Old Testament without comment at the opening of public-school exercises.

The Supreme Court had held in the Slaughterhouse Cases that peaceable assembly was a fundamental right of national citizenship; and this right was extended in *De Jonge v. Oregon.*[27] De Jonge had been convicted for conducting a communist meeting contrary to the Criminal Syndicalism Act of Oregon. In this case the Court held that "consistently with the Federal Constitution, peaceable assembly for lawful discussion cannot be made a crime." Thus even the right of Communists to hold peaceable meetings was upheld.

It is clear that the Supreme Court has interpreted the Fourteenth Amendment so broadly that it covers practically all of the substantive rights of citizens of the United States. On the other hand, the interpretation does not include guarantees, to the citizen in state actions, of all the *procedural* rights which he enjoys in Federal matters. The Supreme Court has held that the states must provide citizens with a fair trial, a hearing before a court and adequate counsel, and may not extort a confession from an accused person by cruel means. But states are not required by the U.S. Constitution to provide a trial by jury or to use a grand jury for the indictment of persons for capital or infamous crimes, and the guarantees against self-incrimination and double jeopardy do not apply to the states.

Racial Discrimination. Not yet clear-cut is the Court's interpretation of the Fourteenth Amendment in so far as the civil rights surrounding racial discrimination are concerned. Under the provision of the Fourteenth Amendment that no state "shall deny to any person within its jurisdiction the equal protection of the laws," a number of suits have been brought attacking laws which discriminated against Negroes. A "Jim Crow" law of Louisiana which provided for segregation of Negroes and white people on passenger coaches of railroads was attacked, but it was upheld by the Supreme Court in *Plessy v. Ferguson*[28] on the ground that the law provided for equal but separate accommodations. However in *Missouri ex rel. Gaines v. Canada,*[29] the Supreme Court held that unless the state provided equal facilities for legal training in Negro universities, a qualified Negro student would have to be admitted to state institutions providing such training for white students. Such provisions must be made for equal training within the bounds of the state, the Court held. By later decision the Court has made it plain that segregation must be abolished on the graduate level unless equal facilities are provided in Negro schools.

Not until May, 1954, did the Supreme Court overrule *Plessy v. Ferguson*

[27] 299 U.S. 356 (1937).
[28] 163 U.S. 537 (1896).
[29] 305 U.S. 337 (1938).

as it affected the public schools. On May 17, 1954, in the segregation cases, the Supreme Court in one of the most momentous decisions of its history declared segregation in the public schools unconstitutional. In a unanimous opinion read by Chief Justice Warren the Court held that segregation contravened the equal-protection clause of the Fourteenth Amendment in four cases appealed from the states of Delaware, Kansas, South Carolina, and Virginia.

In another case, this time from the District of Columbia, the Court held that segregation in the public schools violated the due process clause of the Fifth Amendment. The Court, after hearings in 1955, decided to leave enforcement of its judgments to the Federal district courts. It is likely that considerable time will elapse before complete adjustment is effected in the states concerned, since political leaders loud in their opposition to integration are sure to command a significant following.

The Civil Rights Report. In 1946 President Truman appointed a Committee on Civil Rights, headed by Charles E. Wilson, to make a study of the problems concerning civil liberties and to make recommendations for legislation. A year later the committee published its report, *To Secure These Rights,* and on February 2, 1948, President Truman in a special message to Congress recommended the following 10-point program based on the report:

1. Establishment of a permanent commission on civil rights, a joint congressional committee on civil rights, and a civil rights division in the Department of Justice.

2. Strengthening existing civil rights statutes.

3. Providing for Federal protection against lynching.

4. Protecting more adequately the right to vote.

5. Establishing a Fair Employment Practices Commission to prevent unfair discrimination in employment.

6. Prohibiting discrimination in interstate transportation facilities.

7. Providing home rule and suffrage in Presidential elections for the residents of the District of Columbia.

8. Providing statehood for Hawaii and Alaska and a greater measure of self-government for our island possessions.

9. Equalizing the opportunities for residents of the United States to become naturalized citizens.

10. Settling the evacuation claims of Japanese-Americans.

Although President Truman laid this report before Congress early in 1948, and in spite of the fact that both major political parties adopted planks in 1948 urging action, no legislation has been passed. The President's program brought about a sharp division in the Democratic party, and the Southern Senators have successfully blocked all legislation by the use of the filibuster.

State Guarantees of Civil Rights. In addition to the Federal guarantees against the abridgment of civil rights by the states, the state constitutions and state laws usually contain similar provisions. Every state constitution contains a bill of rights. In general, state constitutions provide (1) that the four freedoms—speech, press, religion, and freedom of assembly—shall be protected; (2) that no person shall be deprived of life, liberty, or property without due process of law; (3) that the privilege of the writ of habeas corpus shall never be suspended; (4) that no ex post facto law, bill of attainder, or law impairing the obligation of contract shall be enacted; (5) that the people shall be secure in their persons, papers, homes, and effects against unreasonable seizures; (6) that a person accused of an infamous crime shall be indicted by a grand jury; [30] (7) that an accused person shall be tried by a jury, shall have the right of counsel, shall be confronted by witnesses, and shall be given a speedy public trial; (8) that no person shall be compelled to testify against himself; (9) that neither excessive bail, excessive fines, nor cruel and unusual punishment shall be exacted of any person; and (10) finally, that the right to bear arms is guaranteed.

To these usual guarantees the new constitutions of Missouri and New Jersey have added a number of others. The constitution of Missouri does away with all discrimination against women by assuring them of equal civil and political rights with men, provides for freedom of the radio as well as of speech and press, and guarantees the right of labor to collective bargaining. The New Jersey constitution also assures the working man of his right to collective bargaining and it further says that no person shall be limited in his privileges because of race, color, sex, religion, or national origin.

Although Congress has so far refused to pass a law guaranteeing fair-employment practices, a number of states have enacted legislation of this sort. Among them are Connecticut, Massachusetts, New Jersey, New Mexico, New York, Oregon, and Rhode Island.

The Outlook for Civil Rights. In an illuminating article, Professor Robert E. Cushman, a noted authority on civil rights, points out the gains that have been made in the half century from 1900 to 1950.[31] At the same time he lists the losses. Cited as gains are (1) the constitutional revolution wrought by the Supreme Court, beginning with *Gitlow v. New York,* in applying the part of the First Amendment relating to free press and free speech to the "liberty" clause of the Fourteenth Amendment, and

[30] Some states provide for indictment on information. An information is an accusation brought by the district attorney on his official oath, supported by evidence collected by himself or by police officers acting under his authority. A grand jury, on the other hand, is supposed to be a random cross-section of the population and in a sense to speak for the community.

[31] "American Civil Liberties in Mid-Century," *The Annals of the American Academy of Political and Social Science,* pp. 1–8, May, 1951.

continuing in a piecemeal manner until all the other limitations of the First Amendment are now brought under the Fourteenth Amendment; (2) the fact that "the courts have given us an impressive body of precedents, doctrines, and rules which clarify and protect freedom of speech and of press"; (3) clarification and protection of religious liberty by the Supreme Court; (4) the work of the civil-rights section in the Department of Justice in the enforcement of the peonage laws, the laws protecting the citizen in his right to vote for Federal officers, and the laws relating to police brutality and official participation in lynching; (5) impressive gains in securing the rights of the American Negro, as evidenced by such decisions as those in the white primary cases and such laws as those of New York and several other states banning discrimination in private employment, and (6) the interest of the United Nations in human rights.

On the debit side, however, Professor Cushman paints a gloomy picture. In spite of the gains in civil rights enjoyed by the Negro, he is still only a second-class citizen, says Professor Cushman. He mentions continued segregation and denial by hostile groups of the right to vote. Discriminatory treatment of other minority groups such as the Japanese, Mexican, and Indian populations is cited as another flaw in the civil-rights picture. Next, he points out threats to the freedom of the press as the result of the "extensive and highly discretionary censorship by the Postmaster General over published matter passing through the mails," a power which is permitted by Federal laws. The most serious threat, according to Professor Cushman, comes from "our nationwide and rapidly accelerating drive against communism and other forms of disloyalty and subversion." The campaign, he asserts, has four major methods or techniques. They are the legislative investigating committee such as the House Committee on Un-American Activities; [32] the more than 450 state and local measures dealing with subversive activities and communism; the loyalty and loyalty-oath programs of states as well as of nongovernmental organizations, and "the brutal and ignorant application of the doctrine of guilt by association as a test of loyalty." Growing out of this last threat is a fifth one, *i.e.*, the conception that it is "disloyal or subversive to criticize the government's program for dealing with subversion or the official agencies which are administering it."

Summing up, Professor Cushman finds the outlook for civil liberties is very dark indeed. He says:

The 1951 balance sheet of our civil liberties is rather disturbing. We seem to be moving into the red. The emotional climate in which we are forced to make decisions which affect our civil liberties is abnormal. American public opinion

---

[32] It is only fair to add, however, that some investigating committees have an excellent record in preserving a high standard of procedure. The work of the Chelf (later the Keating) committee in investigating irregularities in the Department of Justice especially deserves commendation.

has become diseased with regard to the whole problem presented by Communism and disloyalty. We seem to have lost our collective capacity for calm and wise reflection upon matters which call for the wisest of statesmanship.

I do not believe that civil liberty in this country can long survive without a continuing determination on the part of the American people to preserve it. A very heavy responsibility rests upon every individual and every organization capable of exerting any influence to help keep that determination alive.

Disturbed by the threats to freedom of thought and by racial discrimination in America, the 70 bishops of the Methodist Church made a significant pronouncement in a "State of the Church" address at San Francisco on April 23, 1952. This statement, read by Bishop Kern, was approved unanimously by the bishops. After calling attention to the evils resulting from our high-handed methods of combating communism, the Bishop went on to say:

The defense of this country against communism will not come through practicing the tactics of the police state. It will arise out of the wellsprings of liberty in the hearts of individual men who are untrammeled and uncontrolled, free to search for the truth as God gives them to see the truth and to utter it without fear or favor because they are Americans in the glorious tradition of free men.

Since this declaration was made in behalf of some 9 million Methodists throughout the country, it should have a far-reaching effect. Those who still remember the original meaning of civil liberty in the United States feel that many people have lost their perspective in the present crisis. Americans must realize that in spite of their current desire to wipe out communism they have an even more important responsibility not to depart from their great heritage of freedom. By disregarding fundamental rights and beliefs, we fall an easy prey to our enemies. The democratic way is not the way of repression and discrimination; it is the way of free thought and of equal treatment of all, regardless of race or creed.

REFERENCES

Carl L. Becker and Others, *Safeguarding Civil Liberty Today* (1945).
Robert K. Carr, *Federal Protection of Civil Rights: Quest for a Sword* (1947).
Zechariah Chaffee, Jr., *Free Speech in the United States* (1941).
Francis W. Coker, *Democracy, Liberty and Property* (1942).
Edward S. Corwin, *The Constitution and What It Means Today,* 10th ed. (1948).
Walter Gellhorn, *Security, Loyalty and Science* (1950).
————, *The States and Subversion* (1952).
Arthur Holcombe, *Human Rights in the Modern World* (1948).
Dudley O. McGovney, *The American Suffrage Medley* (1949).
United States President's Committee on Civil Rights, *To Secure These Rights* (1947).

CHAPTER 10 *Political Parties: Theory and Practice*

One writer on the subject of the political party in America refers to it as "something of a fraternal organization, something of a game, something of a circus." [1] Professors Merriam and Gosnell say that a political party is [2]

. . . in a sense a political church which does not require regular attendance or a very strict creed, but still provides a home and "looks after" the individual who pays the minimum of party *devoirs*, consisting in acquaintance with and occasional support of some one of its lords, even though a minor one. Or, changing the metaphor, the party is a sporting interest, like a baseball team in which the individual is interested from time to time.

More precise definitions are almost as numerous as writers upon the subject of American politics.

Political Parties Defined

In this classic definition of a political party Edmund Burke wrote that it is "a body of men united for promoting by their joint endeavors the national interest upon some particular principle in which they are all agreed." [3] This is a picture of an ideal party with unity which has rarely been attained in actual political life.

Twentieth-century writers on the subject of American political parties define them in a more realistic manner. Professor Holcombe described a party as: [4]

. . . a part of the whole body of people who have combined together in order to pursue more effectively their own particular interests. This they endeavor to do

[1] Henry Commager, "The American Political Party," *The American Scholar*, Vol. 19, p. 310, Summer, 1950.

[2] Charles E. Merriam and Harold Gosnell, *The American Party System*, 4th ed., p. 479, The Macmillan Company, New York, 1949.

[3] Edmund Burke, "Thoughts on the Cause of the Present Discontents," *Works*, Vol. I, p. 530, Little, Brown, Boston, 1865 ed.

[4] Arthur N. Holcombe, *The Political Parties of Today*, p. 9, Harper & Brothers, New York, 1924.

by the adoption of such expedients as seem most advantageous to themselves and most promising of success. They may or may not be all agreed on the choice of measures to gain their ends, but they must agree at least in preferring the superior effectiveness of concerted action, even at the cost of much compromising of differences among themselves, to an unrestrained but futile liberty of doing in politics exactly as they please.

More recent writings are in agreement with Professor Holcombe. Professor McKean says that "a party may be defined as an organized group of the electorate that seeks to direct some policies and to furnish the personnel of government." [5] According to Professor Bone, "When a group of persons band together to capture the control of government through elective process in order to further a set of interests they are appropriately called a political party." [6]

Each of these definitions must be supplemented by the definitions of political parties which are set down by state statutes, usually state election laws. The legislatures of the several states define parties quantitatively—not on the basis of party function or purpose, but on the basis of voting strength. If a body of citizens wishes to nominate a candidate to public office, and if it is large enough to justify public expenditure for ballots and counts, then it is invested with the status of party and is required to organize and conduct itself according to uniform rules.

Combining the various definitions, we may say that a political party in the United States is a legally recognized body of voters which seeks to control government policy by persuading the electorate to install its candidates as public officers.

Party History

Federalist-Republican Period. The historical development of American political parties may be divided, for the sake of convenience, into four principal periods.[7] At the outset of the initial period there were no recognized political parties. George Washington was twice elected to the Presidency by unanimous vote and, to a large extent, remained aloof from parties. Nevertheless, by the end of Washington's second term "the spirit of party" had manifested itself upon the political scene in the form of two distinct parties.

Under Hamilton's leadership the "Federalists" adopted a program which stood for a strong national government. On the other hand, a Jeffersonian

[5] D. D. McKean, *Party and Pressure Politics*, p. 15, Houghton Mifflin Company, Boston, 1949.

[6] Hugh A. Bone, *American Politics and the Party System*, p. 354, McGraw-Hill Book Company, Inc., New York, 1949.

[7] Wilfred E. Binkley, *American Political Parties: Their Natural History*, Alfred A. Knopf, Inc., New York, 1945, is a recent and excellent history of American parties. Edgar E. Robinson, *The Evolution of American Political Parties*, Harcourt, Brace and Company, New York, 1924, is an older but still useful work.

group of "Republicans" stood solidly for states' rights, strict construction of the Constitution, and a militia under state control. This Federalist-Republican divergence provided a real basis for the two political parties, one party being representative of wealth in commerce and industry, and the other of wealth in land. However, in 1800 the Republicans succeeded in capturing the Presidency for Thomas Jefferson, whereas Hamilton's death in 1804 left the Federalists without a recognized national leader. Additional props were taken from the Federalists when Jefferson invaded the realm of the Federalist program by purchasing Louisiana and when, in 1816, the Republicans passed a protective-tariff act and issued a charter to the Second Bank of the United States. By 1820 the Federalist party, without leadership and with no positive program, had passed from the American political scene.

Democratic-Whig Rivalry. After 24 years of continuous rule by the "Virginia Dynasty" and a brief "re-release" of the Massachusetts Adams family, Andrew Jackson captured control of the Republican party in 1828. By this time the Union had grown to 24 states; the balance of power had shifted from the Eastern seaboard to the West; throngs of the masses were enfranchised; and the official name of Jackson's party was changed to the Democratic party. The rise of Jacksonian democracy was typified by these changes. Jackson succeeded in welding into a party the small farmers of the West and South and the laboring masses of the East, and this combination continued to hold power until 1841. "Old Hickory," who had won laurels on the battlefield, directed his political fire against everything which he regarded as in opposition to the recently enfranchised masses. He gave the people a new deal but this made inevitable a new political alignment. Largely through the work of Henry Clay, the bankers and manufacturers of the East and the plantation and slaveowners of the South were brought together to form a new party called Whigs. The name of the party was new, but its foundations were reminiscent of the old Federalist party.

The Whigs succeeded also in securing the support of some antislavery and anti-Masonic sentiment.[8] And with the aid of two military heroes—"Tippecanoe" Harrison and Zachary Taylor, the "hero of Buena Vista"—the party won the Presidency in 1840 and in 1848. The Whigs constituted an unstable group, however, and were torn asunder in 1854 by the slavery question. "Of all our major political parties," writes Professor Binkley, "the Whigs were least successful in translating the pressures of their component interests into established national policies."[9]

Republican Supremacy. The slavery issue also played havoc with the Democratic party. In 1860 the party split into two factions: a Southern faction which called for protection of slavery in all the territories, and a

---

[8] McKean, *op. cit.*, pp. 395–396.
[9] Binkley, *op. cit.*, pp. 171–172.

Northern faction which stood for popular sovereignty, meaning that each state should on admission to the Union decide for itself the question of slavery. With sharp cleavage in the Democratic party along sectional lines, a new Republican party under the leadership of Abraham Lincoln emerged victorious in the Presidential campaign of 1860. The "Party of Abraham" drew its initial strength by balancing the interests of the small farmer in the West, antislavery enthusiasts, and labor and industry in the East. Postwar prosperity, laissez-faire economics and, for good measure, periodic waving of the "bloody shirt" enabled the Republican party to control the Presidency, except for the administrations of Cleveland and Wilson, until 1932. Frequently during this period, however, the Democrats controlled one or both houses of Congress.

New Dealism. Reaction against the great depression which began in 1929, coupled with the dynamic leadership of Franklin Delano Roosevelt, swept the long-ailing Democratic party to victory in the election of 1932. Roosevelt reverted to Jackson's magic formula of uniting the laboring masses in the East with Western and Southern agrarianism. During the first of his unprecedented four terms, he ushered in what he called a "New Deal" for the "forgotten man."

This was a spectacular revival of a political party which had been so long out of power. For a time it was a revival in almost a religious sense. The adherents of New Dealism believed in the tenets of their newly rejuvenated party with a messianic fervor. It was their conviction that they were saving the country from economic ruin and the threat of fascism. A whole new vocabulary of catch phrases, complete with several politically oriented songs, added color to the new picture, and a huge group of new civil servants, all passionate adherents of the new political order, gave it considerable substance.

The New Deal had to its credit, or discredit, depending upon one's political orientation, the bank holiday of 1933 and a host of new alphabetical agencies such as the NRA, the AAA, the CCC, the WPA, designed to revive the nation's flagging economy. It had the Social Security Act, the National Labor-Relations Act, the TVA, public-housing legislation, minimum-wage and child-labor laws, the defeated Supreme-Court-packing plan; the Presidential "fireside chat," and the whole experience of World War II.

On all these events and on political and governmental innovations too numerous to list here intense political heat was expended, not only by the proponents of the new order but also by its opponents. The anti-New Deal faction, which included the hard core of the Republican party plus some newly disaffected Democrats, became almost fanatical in its dislike for everything which smacked even faintly of New Dealism. Many a sneer decorated the faces of New Dealers discussing the vanquished "Tories."

Many an apoplectic flush emphasized the diatribes of enraged Republicans when confronted with some fresh Rooseveltian outrage.

By the time Harry Truman succeeded to the Presidency, upon the death of Roosevelt in 1945, the New Deal had become the Fair Deal. The depression was now only an unhappy memory, the need for fighting a war had to a large extent united the country, and the political fever of the early 1930s had dropped closer to the normal temperature of factional differences.

The Eisenhower Triumph. The election of 1952 resulted in a return to power of the Republican party. Actually it was more a triumph for Eisenhower than a victory for the Republican party and more a repudiation of Harry Truman than a defeat for Adlai Stevenson. Corruption in government, unsettled world conditions, the Korean War, high taxation, inept handling of civil rights, and general unrest and dissatisfaction were all blamed, whether deservedly or not, upon the Democratic party. The Republican party was able to attract sufficient votes from the opposition party to win handily. These needed votes came from the "bourbon Democrats" of the South, farmers, the wealthy and the well-to-do, ex-soldiers, and all who were dissatisfied. Indeed, the people were tired of Democratic rule and wanted a change. In addition, the personal magnetism and military reputation of General Eisenhower added greatly to his popularity. The victory restored life to the Republican party and did much to maintain proper balance in the two-party system. How successful the Republicans will be in keeping the reins of government in their hands depends on President Eisenhower's ability in solving exceedingly difficult foreign and domestic problems and his success in holding together in a single political machine the divergent, and at times antagonistic, groups of voters responsible for sweeping him and his party into power.

Third Parties. One of the fundamental characteristics of American politics is the two-party system. Third parties, nevertheless, have had a significant influence upon the determination of national policies and in more than a few instances have had an appreciable effect upon the outcome of elections. Probably the main contribution of third parties has been their introduction of many reform ideas which have subsequently been accepted by the two major parties. Abolitionism, woman suffrage, and prohibition are examples of such reforms.

A principal difference between the major and the minor parties has been that the former usually have represented cross sections of our varied society, while the latter have usually been parties of a single idea—abolitionism, prohibition, populism—and hence have represented only one element of society.[10] A second characteristic of third parties is that many of them

[10] Allan Nevins, "The Strength of Our Political System," *The New York Times Magazine,* July 18, 1948, pp. 5, 31.

have represented interests of only one section of the country. The States' Rights or "Dixiecrat" party in 1948 appealed only to Southern interests. Other third parties have been the result of fragments breaking away from one of the major parties—for example, the Progressive parties of 1912, 1924, and 1948.

The first third party was the Quiddist party of John Randolph of Virginia. The Quids broke with the Republican party in 1806 over such issues as corruption in the Yazoo land settlement, the Florida purchase, and non-importation measures against Great Britain. In 1808 the Quids selected James Monroe to run against Madison for the Presidency. Madison stole the Quids' trump card by making Monroe his Secretary of State. Another third party, the Anti-Mason party, was born out of protests against the Masons in particular and secret societies in general. The party received a respectable vote in the Presidential election of 1832, but thereafter most of its adherents were won over by the anti-Jacksonian Whig party. A Liberty party representing the antislavery ferment appeared in 1840. In 1848 the Free Soil party, with the motto "Free Soil, Free Speech, Free Labor, and Free Men," drew a sizable vote for former President Martin Van Buren and consequently ensured a Whig victory for Zachary Taylor. In 1856 Southern members of the Whig party who were unwilling to go over to the Democratic party formed the Know-Nothing or American party. Their candidate, ex-President Fillmore, received a good vote in most Southern states but captured only the electoral votes of the state of Maryland.[11]

The third parties of the period prior to the Civil War were idealistic. On the other hand, many of the third parties of the last quarter of the nineteenth century represented primarily some form of agrarian protest—for example, the Grangers, Greenbackers, and Populists. Of somewhat more recent origin are the Socialist and Communist parties. Socialist parties date from the establishment of the Socialist Labor party in 1877. The size of the Socialist party grew steadily until the elections of 1920 when its candidate, Eugene V. Debs, polled over 920,000 votes while imprisoned in the Federal penitentiary. In 1919 the Socialist party was split by the Communists, who desired affiliation with the revolutionary Third International. Subsequent strength in the Communist party has centered in New York City where it has on occasion wielded some influence in local elections.

In the 1952 Presidential election 12 persons were nominated for President by major and minor parties.[12]

[11] John D. Hicks, "The Third Party Tradition in American Politics," *Mississippi Valley Historical Review*, Vol. 20, pp. 3–28, June, 1933. For a more detailed account see William B. Hesseltine, *The Rise and Fall of Third Parties*, Public Affairs Press, Washington, 1948.

[12] In addition to the Republican and Democratic parties the following minor parties selected nominees: Progressive, Socialist, Socialist Workers, Church of God Bible, Socialist Labor, Greenback, Prohibition, Vegetarian, Washington Peace, and Poor Man's party. *The New York Times*, Nov. 2, 1952.

Many cities have no major party but only a number of minor parties. New York City politics, as an illustration, may be characterized by the existence of multiple parties. At one time or another Mayor Fiorello La Guardia ran on nine different party labels. In 1945 he was said to have boasted: "I could run on a laundry ticket and be elected." [13] One observer has ventured the opinion that the multiparty system in New York City is largely due to the size and complexity of the population, the existence of an active independent element, the particular nature of the election laws, and recent schisms within the ranks of organized labor.

The Two-party System in the United States

Numerous theories have been advanced to explain the two-party tradition which has dominated party history in the United States. A two-way split is not inherent in party government, and the answer to the question, Why is party affiliation in the United States dichotomized?, is an important one. Some writers attribute the two-party system to the two theories of the strict and loose construction of the Constitution, or the theories of strong central control versus democratic decentralization. Others attribute the system to the geographical sections in the United States; to the differences between the Hamiltonians and the Jeffersonians—people can admire one but never both; or to the cultural homogeneity brought about by the fact that there are no highly conscious racial, religious, or historical groupings in the United States as there are in the countries of Western Europe where the multiparty system has prevailed.

Many persons accept the theory that people instinctively or automatically divide into parties which correspond to the basic drives or instincts of mankind. This cleavage is often described as running roughly between the drives for maintenance of the *status quo* and the drives which seek change in the hope of improvement. Probably the most widely accepted explanation in a materialistic society like that of the United States is the economic theory as exemplified in the writings of Charles A. Beard. Professor Beard wrote that [14]

. . . although Jefferson . . . based his explanation of the source of party antagonism on a theory of human nature, it must not be supposed that he was unaware of the economic character of the masses aligned on his side. . . . He recognized that the divergence in views concerning human nature which caused the split into parties was not fortuitous, but ran along distinctly economic lines.

Added to the theoretical "explanations" of the two-party system are a number of mechanical factors which, if not the cause, have certainly con-

[13] Hugh A. Bone, "Political Parties in New York City," *American Political Science Review*, Vol. 40, p. 272, April, 1946.
[14] *Economic Origins of Jeffersonian Democracy*, p. 421, The Macmillan Company, New York, 1915.

tributed to the maintenance of two major parties. One of these is the election system. Our system of representation, based largely upon geographical districts with one person elected from each district, makes it extremely difficult for a minor party to elect a candidate. Moreover, election to the Presidency—the plum of all the electoral offices—is closely hemmed in by the Twelfth Amendment, which requires a clear majority in the electoral college (or in the House of Representatives with the Representatives voting by state if the electoral college deadlocks). If there were more than two parties of nearly equal strength, none of the candidates would be able to command a clear majority; thus there is always a tendency for minor factions to combine into major parties in order to gain the highest elective office.

The Composition of Political Parties in the United States

Since most political desires and grievances in the United States have traditionally been channeled through one of two parties, these parties have of necessity cut across nearly all class lines both socially and economically. Economically, persons of all shades of opinion—conservatives, liberals, progressives, and radicals—and of all occupational groups can be found in the ranks of both parties. "Wets and drys," nationalists and internationalists, states-rightists and advocates of greater Federal control, pro-laborites and anti-laborites, and the bipartisan farm bloc come from both parties. If set up in diagram form, party alignment would be exhibited vertically instead of horizontally. Although it is true that in a given year or a given era certain groups have tended to congregate under one party banner, groups do not consistently stay in one party.

There are many factors which have contributed to the cosmopolitan make-up of political parties in the United States. These factors include—among others—class, race, creed, sectionalism, hereditary allegiance, leadership, and party organization.

With regard to class, Americans have not embraced in large numbers parties based upon occupational or class grouping. The farmers, the workers, and the business and professional men believe that their protests can best be expressed by remaining with one of the two old-line parties.

In Europe religious political parties are more or less commonplace, but in America no party has arisen around the nucleus of a religious denomination. Members of all religious sects are found in both major parties, and any attempt on the part of a church to organize a party on a local or national scale would meet with general public disapproval. Religion, however, has been a factor in American politics from time to time. Anti-Semitism and anti-Catholicism have appeared sub rosa in important political campaigns and at other strategic points. Mormonism enters into Utah politics and the "Baptist bloc" has been influential in the upper South.

The Methodists were strong supporters of many Republican nominees during the twenties when prohibition was a bitter battle. Nevertheless, none of these religious groups nominally affiliated itself with either of the parties.

Racial and nationalistic groups have not tended to form separate parties either. Negroes, Germans, Italians, and other such groups are in the ranks of both political parties. Both party machines make strong drives in cities to capture these voters, but none of them can be counted upon consistently to deliver votes en bloc for one of the major parties. Only in the South is found an outstanding party alignment based upon racial extraction, a division which has enabled Southerners to exercise powerful influence in both of the major party organizations.

Another factor which obstructs the rise of minor parties is the widely prevalent conviction among independent voters that a vote for other than one of the major parties is "thrown away." Added to this are the handicaps of lack of experience and of assured financial backing, legal obstacles in state election laws which make it difficult for minor-party candidates to qualify for a place on the ballot, and the lack of patronage available to minor parties.[15]

Probably the two most vital factors in present-day party composition are sectionalism and hereditary allegiance. The fact stands out that most members of a party were born into it and are continuing to support it out of tradition and inertia. Although there is no mathematical proof of it, undoubtedly it is true that more voters come into American parties every year by the hereditary process than because of any other factor, or probably through any combination of other factors.

As for sectionalism, there are well-defined territorial areas almost exclusively controlled by one party or the other, so much so that for political purposes these areas may be regarded as combinations or groups of states without regard to state lines. People in different parts of the country recognize, without needing explanation, that different sections have different economic interests and different attitudes toward life, and that these tend to solidify under the banner of the party which offers the most consideration to their particular section. Professor Merriam has said that sectionalism is strongest politically when it is not merely sentimental but is allied with some specific issue which finds a local seat in a particular geographic location.[16]

The Solid South. The so-called "solid South" is the prime illustration of sectionalism in American political life. Since the Reconstruction period, the Republican party in the South has wielded little influence. The 11

[15] L. B. Wheildon, "Third Party Movements," *Editorial Research Reports,* Vol. 2, pp. 477–493, July 16, 1947; Murray S. Stedman and Susan Stedman, *Discontent at the Polls: A Study of Farmer and Labor Parties, 1827–1948,* Columbia University Press, New York, 1950.

[16] Merriam, *op. cit.,* pp. 108–109.

states of the former Confederacy are solidly Democratic in practically all local and state elections, and in national elections they are normally Democratic.

The reasons ascribed for this situation are various, but they all center around conditions peculiar to the Southern section of the country. First, there is the large Negro population whose economic and political control is feared by many Southern whites. Professor V. O. Key finds that it is primarily the whites of the "black belt" who give the South its dominant political tone.[17] The Republicans are the party of Negro liberation; ergo, the South favors the Democrats.

Southern economic rivalry with the North provides another powerful sectional drive. The South has been struggling for years to nourish its own industrial growth and thus to displace the mastery of the Northern industrialists. The rising Southern textile industry is the chief example of this economic battle. Since it is the Republican party which traditionally represents the interests of Northern big business, it follows that the Democratic party is the party of Southern allegiance.

There is a historical factor as well in the South's common memory of the War Between the States and in the still surprisingly strong emotions connected with it. This is another reason for its traditional repugnance toward anything smacking of Republicanism.

The one-party system in the South has had some notable effects upon national political life. Because the Republican party is so weak in that area, the general election in most parts of the South has been a mere formality; it is the Democratic primary which really decides the election. Thus, Southern congressmen are able to dominate congressional committees when the Democrats are in power, and thereby exert a commanding influence upon legislation. The chain of events is this: Committee chairmanships are determined by seniority. Southern legislators have to face their constituents only once during the election year—in the primary election, while legislators from other sections have to face real battles in both the primary and the general election. The Southerners, therefore, have a better chance for reelection and for building up seniority.

Is the one-party system on the way out in the South? The unprecedented number of votes cast in the South for the Republican candidate for the Presidency in 1952 has raised the hope of all good Republicans that the solid South is not so solid and that the rival party's hold can be broken.[18]

[17] *Southern Politics,* p. 5, Alfred A. Knopf, Inc., New York, 1949.

[18] The solid South has been cracked before. Harding carried Tennessee in 1920. In the election of 1928, Hoover was able to beat Al Smith in Florida, North Carolina, Tennessee, Texas, and Virginia. In all other Presidential elections the Democrats have scored impressive victories. As late as 1944, the Republican Presidential candidate received only 3,742 votes in Mississippi and 4,610 in South Carolina. Commenting on the Presidential election of 1924, the late Coleman Livingston Blease, Governor and

Eisenhower's victory in Florida, Tennessee, Texas, and Virginia, however, was based on division among the Democrats rather than on a tremendous growth of strength within the Republican party. The Democrats hope to fill the breach and heal wounds while the Republicans will exert every effort to make the division among the Democrats permanent and thereby strengthen the Republicans until the solid South is no more.

Party Organization

A distinguishing feature of American political parties is their hierarchical organization. This hierarchy has developed from the simplicity and informality of Samuel Adams's caucus and the committees of correspondence to the complex organizations of today, which in most states are regulated in great detail by statute. Through voluminous state election laws (those of New York run to over 764 pages) each state legislature controls the form of party organization within its own confines. Party structure varies considerably from one state to another according to whether the structure has been established by law or developed by usage, but the divergences from the typical organization are less important than the likenesses.

A cardinal political principle is that a definite party organization shall be maintained in every electoral area of the United States. From the point of view of party success, the most important unit in the party structure is not the top but the bottom one. Frank Kent calculated that the head of the lowest unit in the party structure—the precinct executive—could, as a rule, deliver enough votes to swing a normal precinct election through use of his relatives, friends, lodge brothers, and the election officials hired by city and county officials on his recommendation.[19]

As a result of the party's attempt to be represented wherever officers of government are elected and wherever votes are cast, party structure forms a rough pyramid with levels corresponding to the layers of government:

National committee

Senatorial campaign committee   Congressional campaign committee

State committee (also called state central, or state executive committee)

District committees of various sorts, such as congressional, judicial, state
    senatorial

County committee

Ward, city, town, township, borough, village, parish, and other com-
    mittees

---

later Senator from South Carolina, remarked: "I think Mr. Coolidge received 1100 votes in my State. I do not know where he got them. I was astonished to know that they were cast and shocked to know that they were counted." (Quoted in Paul Lewinson, *Race, Class, and Party,* p. 109, Oxford University Press, London, 1932.

[19] *The Great Game of Politics,* p. 22, Doubleday & Company, New York, 1923.

Precinct (also called election-district and division) committee or committeeman and committeewoman

Authority in the pyramid of committees does not flow from one level to
another. Beyond extending some financial support a national committee
does not control a state committee, nor does a state committee control a
county committee, and so on, down to the precinct level.

Precinct. The precinct is the smallest unit of party organization and,
from the point of view of party success, the most important. It is usually
composed of the voters who may conveniently vote at one place. This
number varies from as few as six or eight in certain mountain areas to
over a thousand in cities. The head of the precinct is known as the precinct
committeeman. Merriam and Gosnell describe the committeeman as "the
unit cell in the party structure . . . These committeemen constitute the
working force of the party." [20] Just above the precinct in party organization
is the ward or city organization, which coordinates all of the work done
by the precinct.

County Executive Committees. There are over 3,000 counties in the
United States and the major political parties have organizations in most
of them. Usually the precinct committeeman serves as a member of the
county executive committee. The county executive committees are headed
by county chairmen whom Professor McKean has described as "the colo-
nels of their respective political armies." [21]

District Committees. Between the county and state level in most states
there are various types of district committees which aid in the election of
members to the United States House of Representatives and in the election
of certain state officers and state senators. Each committee usually has a
chairman; the committee's function is limited in scope.

State Executive Committees. Party structure on the state level is headed
by the state party chairman and the state executive committee. The committees range in size from 11 to several hundred. The powers of the committees vary from state to state. In most states the executive committee
endeavors to maintain an efficient party organization throughout the state,
makes plans for holding the state convention, and serves as an administrative committee for the party during the time that the state convention is
not in session.

Senatorial and Congressional Campaign Committees. On the national
level each major party has a senatorial campaign committee and a congressional committee selected by the house concerned. The function of
these committees is to assist in the congressional elections with money and
speakers. Except in the financial sphere these committees have no organic
relationship with each party's national committee. The 1948 budgets for

[20] Merriam and Gosnell, *op. cit.*, p. 175.
[21] McKean *op. cit.*, p. 206.

the Republican senatorial committee and for the House committee were reported to have been $400 thousand and $600 thousand, respectively.

National Committee. The highest organization of each national party is the national committee, which is composed of one man and one woman from each state and territory. In 1952 the Republicans provided that hereafter states which go Republican shall be entitled to a third committee member. National committee members are nominated in any one of four ways. In 22 states or territories selection is by state convention; in 16 states the delegates to the national convention make the choice; in 9 states or territories the choice is made by the state executive committee; and in seven states or territories members are nominated by primary. All nominations by the states are confirmed either by the national convention or the national committee itself. The Democratic National Committee recently refused to accept a committeewoman from South Carolina because she openly supported the States' Rights candidate for President in 1948 and not the Democratic nominee.

The national committee makes arrangements for holding the national convention every four years, determines the date, and selects the city in which it will be held. Pending the report of the credentials committee, the national committee prepares a tentative roll of delegates. It designates the convention keynoter and other temporary officers. Finally, the national committee is authorized to fill vacancies on the national ticket which may occur either by the death or the resignation of one of the nominees. This important authority has been exercised on only one occasion. In 1860 the Democratic National Committee named Herschel V. Johnson of Georgia to run for Vice-President after Benjamin Fitzpatrick of Alabama had declined to be the running mate of Stephen Douglas.[22]

Government Control of Elections

State and local party organizations in the United States are largely autonomous bodies. "Decentralization of power," Professor Schattschneider writes, "is by all odds the most important single characteristic of the American major party." [23] Because of the decentralization of power within the party the relation of the party to the government has been primarily on the local level. Notwithstanding state and Federal regulation, local party officers tend to conduct party affairs much as they please. For example, the Green committee which investigated the elections of 1944 found in the state of Arkansas an "appalling indifference to and a flagrant disregard for the laws governing the conduct of elections." Among other "wholesale irregularities" the committee found examples of husbands voting by proxy

[22] McKean, *op. cit.*, p. 210.
[23] E. E. Schattschneider, *Party Government*, p. 129, Rinehart & Company, Inc., New York, 1942.

for their wives and the use of such illegal ballot boxes as a Prince Albert tobacco box and a cardboard candy box.[24]

State Control. State control of parties is exercised through state law and through judicial decisions. State statutory regulation began in the 1880s with laws respecting party membership and balloting. Now state statutes regulate enrollment, prescribe a minimum size for parties, regulate nominating procedure, provide for the various party committees and officers and how they shall be elected, and protect parties from impostors and from corrupt practices. Although legislatures do not have the authority to deny people the right to organize political parties, they enact in many states stringent "ballot laws" which have the effect of impeding new or third parties.[25]

In general the courts have no concern with the affairs of the political parties as long as the parties are fairly and honestly administered according to the law and do not threaten civil rights. The courts' policy of remaining aloof from "political questions," moreover, tends to minimize their entanglement with political parties. However, the courts are not infrequently called upon to determine who are the legally elected officers of a political party, and in several states recently the legislatures have provided for special tribunals in such cases.

Federal Control. Article I, Section 4, of the United States Constitution provides that the states may determine the time, place, and manner of holding elections for Senators and Representatives, but that "the Congress may at any time by law make or alter such regulations, except as to the places of choosing Senators." For many years, however, Congress ignored this source of authority and left control with the states. Most congressional regulation has had to do with the money spent in elections, a subject treated separately later in this chapter. In 1921 the Supreme Court held in the Newberry case [26] that Federal laws regulating the amount of money which could be spent in election campaigns by candidates for the Senate did not apply to expenditures in primary campaigns.

Apparently, congressional control of elections did not extend to primary elections. Twenty years later the Supreme Court abandoned this position and held that when a primary becomes an integral part of the election machinery or when actual choice of who is to hold office is made in the primary, the Constitution guarantees to citizens the right to participate.[27] Considerable litigation in the courts continued respecting Federal authority to control primaries. The source of these cases was the Southern ex-

[24] Senate Special Committee to Investigate Campaign Expenditures in 1944, S. Rept. 100, 79th Cong., 1st sess., 1945, pp. 36, 40, 42.
[25] Joseph R. Starr, "The Legal Status of American Political Parties," *American Political Science Review,* Vol. 34, pp. 439–455 and 685–699, June and August, 1940.
[26] *Newberry v. United States,* 256 U.S. 232 (1921).
[27] *United States v. Classic,* 313 U.S. 299 (1941).

clusion of the Negro from participation in the Democratic "white primary." In 1944 the Supreme Court cleared up the controversy with the decision in *Smith v. Allwright*.[28] In this case the Court ruled that "when primaries become a part of the machinery for choosing officials, state and national . . . the same tests . . . should be applied to the primary as are applied to the general election." The Court then said that if the state prescribes for primary procedure and discriminates against Negroes such action violates the Fifteenth Amendment.

The state of South Carolina was not to be balked by the Supreme Court. Its governor believed that if the state legislature should repeal all laws regulating primary elections the state might escape the effect of the decision. In other words, the Democratic party would become simply a private association, like the Elks or the Baptist Church, and be free to nominate candidates in any manner that it pleased. A Federal judge, however, enjoined the party from preventing Negro voting in the primary. In upholding the lower Federal court, Judge John J. Parker of the court of appeals said: "No election machinery can be upheld if its purpose or effect is to deny the Negro, on account of his race or color, any effective voice in the government of his country or the state or community wherein he lives." [29] In other words, "country clubs" were one thing but elections to public office were another, and the state could not divorce itself from them even if it desired to do so.

Party Finance and Corrupt Practices

Congress and the legislatures of practically all the states have passed laws designed to outlaw corrupt practices in elections. But the problem is still far from being solved. One might ask where party expenditures go. In the first place, notwithstanding the fact that every party makes use of considerable voluntary help, parties also employ such skilled persons as publicity men, writers for radio and television, stenographers, and now even comic book artists. A political party must pay well for services of this type. Second, the party must pay rent for offices and party headquarters, usually a hotel suite. Third, parties expend large sums for such propaganda purposes as advertising, banners, buttons, letters, posters, pamphlets, and radio and television time. One of the largest items today in presidential campaigns is for radio and television. Fourth, probably the greatest expenditure is for the hiring of workers on election day. There are over 140,000 election precincts in the United States. In a large city it has been estimated that a party spends about $125 per precinct for election-day workers. These workers help in various ways to get out the vote. While many of these costs are entirely legitimate, it is no doubt also true that a

[28] 321 U.S. 694 (1944).
[29] *Rice v. Elmore*, 165 F.2d 387 (1947).

good deal of money finds its way into the pockets of the politicians, big and small. Campaign funds are usually handled in cash in order to conceal both the origin and the destination of these funds. Such methods of finance put a premium upon various dubious practices.

Sources of Party Funds. Sources of party funds are diverse. First, the candidate often pays a large share of the funds expended on his behalf. Frank Kent describes the ideal candidate from the party point of view as a "fat cat," or one who can finance his own campaign and contribute to the party as well.

A second source of funds is the "shake down" or assessment of office holders. Both state and Federal laws make soliciting, assessing, or receiving political contributions from Federal or state employees by other officers or employees illegal. The Hatch Act of 1940 forbids any person, Federal employee or not, to receive or to solicit any contribution from any person receiving a benefit under a Federal relief project. The Federal laws on the subject are enforced, but state and local provisions in practice are often bypassed by the party's requiring the employee to contribute through a relative or by "inducing" the employee to make a "voluntary contribution." State employees are usually powerless to protest such assessments and doubtless feel an obligation to the party for their jobs.

A third source of funds is contributions from persons who have a "general interest" in the party. These contributions range from the small two-dollar gift up to the maximum contribution of $5,000 by the so-called party "angels." A fourth source is the "interest group" which has a direct *financial* interest in the outcome of elections. Although congressional and state laws in three-fourths of the states prohibit contributions from corporations, such laws have not prevented corporations from voting bonuses to officers who in turn make the contribution. Section 304 of the Taft-Hartley Act of 1947 specifically prohibited labor unions from making contributions. In a test case the Supreme Court held that Congress could not have had the intention of preventing labor unions from expressing their views in labor journals, but did not pass upon the constitutionality of this section.[30] As a result the Political Action Committee, an auxiliary of the CIO, is free to carry on political activities on behalf of the candidates whom it supports.

A fifth source of party funds may be described as miscellaneous. This includes funds raised at the Jackson, Jefferson, and Lincoln Day dinners where each person pays from $100 to $1,000 per plate. The city in which the party holds its national convention usually raises about $300,000 for the party.

Finally, certain types of assistance to parties may have the same result as a financial contribution. For example, advertising by the National Asso-

[30] *United States v. CIO*, 335 U.S. 106 (1948).

ciation of Manufacturers often has the effect of propaganda for the Republican party. The same is frequently true with respect to endorsement of candidates by the press.

Limitations on the Amount of Expenditure. In addition to attempts to regulate the sources of funds, both Congress and the states have passed legislation to restrict the total amount of money that parties and candidates may spend. The Federal Corrupt Practices Act of 1925 limits expenditures by candidates for the Senate to $10,000 and for the House of Representatives to $2,500. The law provides alternatively that candidates may spend 3 cents for each vote cast in the last general election, provided that such an amount does not exceed $25,000 for a Senatorial candidate and $5,000 for a House candidate. Most of the states have enacted similar laws. Legislation of this type is subject to two serious defects: first, the amounts authorized are in many instances absurdly small and, second, the limitations are held to apply only to expenditures by the candidate and the official party organization, thus permitting unlimited expenditures by others.[31]

The Hatch Act of 1940 provides that no "national political committee" shall receive contributions or make expenditures in excess of $3 million in any calendar year, and limits individual or collective gifts to $5,000 per year to any committee. The law is ineffective because it permits national, senatorial, and congressional campaign committees as well as state and local committees and "independent" groups, each to spend up to $3 million. Furthermore, the $5,000 limitation does not prohibit the members of large families from contributing $5,000 apiece, and thereby amassing a gigantic contribution. In 1944, for instance, the DuPont family contributed $128,000, the Pew family $108,000, and the Mellon family $68,000, to name just a few.[32]

Another problem which is hard to reach by law is created by individuals who make loans to parties or candidates. Laws limiting the amount which an individual may contribute do not, of course, apply to loans. If the party wins the election it has little difficulty in wiping out the deficit, for contributors are virtually assured of getting something for their money. But if the party loses it is another story.

National laws also require candidates and parties to give publicity to contributions before and after elections. Many states, however, simply require publicity in some form *after* the election, or merely require the filing of reports of receipts or expenditures. Professor Overacker finds that

[31] In addition hundreds of independent party organizations have been formed to raise money for candidates. For example, in 1944 there were such clubs as "Aviation Committee for Dewey," "Minute Women," "Southern Anti-New Deal Association," "Harry Truman's Campaign Fund," each of which presumably might spend up to $3 million.

[32] Louise Overacker, *Money in Elections,* p. 910, The Macmillan Company, New York, 1932.

often these publicity requirements are ignored.[33] Most observers believe that one of the better ways of reducing corrupt practices in elections would be to enact more stringent laws requiring publicity.

The 1952 Presidential campaign was bitter and prolonged and resulted in the spending of a record amount of money.[34] When legal limits were reached, new political groups were organized outside the party to spend additional sums. Although the evil effects of huge campaign expenditures are generally recognized, Congress has found no successful way of limiting them. One proposal is to shorten the campaign. The conventions could be held in late August and still afford enough time for a spirited and informative campaign. Certainly with the many new means of disseminating information, there is no real need for the long drawn out political campaign that was considered necessary when William Jennings Bryan was running for the Presidency.

Another suggested change is for the radio and television companies to be required to give time in equal amounts to the major political parties.

A third proposal is not only to shorten the campaign but to have the government bear the cost of this abbreviated contest in an impartial manner. It seems unlikely, however, that any of these suggested reforms will stand much chance of adoption until there is a wider appreciation of the undesirable effects of large campaign expenditures.

The Functions of Political Parties in the United States

In spite of the once widespread distrust of political parties, it would be difficult to imagine how representative government could function without them today. With all their defects and shortcomings, parties have come to occupy an indispensable place in both the theory and operation of popular government, and the fact that they are selfishly motivated by the desire to stay in or get into office does not make their work any less valuable.

Their more important functions are:

1. Selection and support of candidates for public office
2. Control of governmental machinery and formulation of principles and policies of government
3. Unification of the organs of government, and breakdown of the artificial barriers of the federal system and of the separation of powers
4. Compromise of clashing interests of section, class, race, and religion
5. Crystallization of public opinion
6. Intermediation between individuals and government
7. Political education
8. Criticism of the major party in power
9. Assistance to individuals, including charity
10. Rendition of special services in the election of the President

[33] *Ibid.*
[34] See Chap. 13 for a more detailed description of 1952 campaign spending.

After a brief look at each of these functions, the significance of American political parties in the democratic process will be apparent.

Designating and supporting candidates for elective office is so peculiarly a function of political parties that it has often been called the fundamental test of a party. Parties serve the desirable purpose of trying to present candidates for all the offices that are to be filled by election, or, in the language of practical politics, "to offer a full ticket." Furthermore, they fill appointive positions, although nominally and sometimes actually this is done by the official charged with the power of appointment.

Control of government and formulation of principles and policies of government may be considered respectively the means and the end of the party's activities. Some critics assert that parties never get beyond their immediate objective, or that once in possession of public office they forget their pledges concerning public policies. This aspect of party life brings into bold relief the two political types—the politician and the statesman. The politician is more interested in securing control of the offices for what benefits he may derive from them, while the statesman looks upon public power as a means of carrying out certain policies which he considers in the public interest. However, it is only realistic to recognize that the principal parties in a two-party system are created to govern the country and not to carry torches. The party in power is ordinarily less interested in changing the government than in operating it.

The framers of the Constitution believed that the system which they were setting up would prevent control of the government by factions. The system of separation of powers operates in theory to keep the various authorities in separate compartments, each endowed with certain powers and functions. Whether one views this arrangement with approval or disapproval, the conclusion must be inevitable that in the United States some degree of unity between the executive and legislative branches of government is not only desirable but necessary for a satisfactory operation of the government. When a working majority of the Senate and the House of Representatives is of the same party as the President, a concord is created which ordinarily leads to the adoption of the policies announced by the party leaders in the preceding campaign. Despite the political buncombe and vague generalizations which are present in all campaigns, each party does in a general way indicate the broad policies which it will follow if elected to office. *It should be well understood that deadlocks and disagreements are prevented, not by the governmental organizational framework or by legal provision, but only through the instrumentality of political parties.*

In the United States, the compromise of the clashing interests of the vast array of opposed groups seeking to direct public opinion to their own advantage is vital to the democratic process, and is one of the primary duties reserved to political parties. Conflicts between North and South, East and

West, city and country, labor and capital, Catholic and Protestant, wets and drys, are all brought together under parties which serve as the only representative medium through which disparate interests may be reflected and conflicting claims adjusted.

As catalysts of public opinion, political parties have become increasingly important. Present-day public questions often are so complicated and concern so many different interests and so many different levels of political action that the electorate or its representatives cannot pass upon them until they are simplified. After the stage of compromise and adjustment, parties serve in many instances to reduce conflicting opinions into yes-or-no alternatives, one accepting and the other rejecting the final proposal.

Parties also serve as intermediaries, as buffers, as adjusters between society and the individual. This function becomes more important as American society becomes more and more complicated and as government affects the life of the citizen in more and more ways. Professors Merriam and Gosnell have pointed out in their discussion of the role of the political party in American life that the party worker aids his constituent in his dealing with the government, whether the constituent be a poor peddler seeking a license or a rich speeder, and this aid is sometimes in the interest of justice, sometimes not. "There are many shades of activity, ranging from the imparting of information regarding governmental services and personnel to personal favors of an innocuous type, to dubious privileges, to illegitimate spoils, and graft of a systematic nature." [35]

Parties serve as political educators. In its advocacy of personalities and policies and in its efforts to persuade the voters to accept them, the modern political party carries on an elaborate educational program through the press, in public debates, on the platform, through radio, through television, and through personal contacts. The process is often crude and superficial; it is often an appeal to prejudice, instinct, hatreds, class rivalries, and jealousies, but it is also often stimulating and socially useful. [36]

Another function which the party performs—one which is vital to the democratic process—is criticism of the policies of the major party in power by the principal party out of power, and by such minor parties as exist and are interested. This criticism may be and often is biased and partisan, but it is valuable, nevertheless. Without criticism any official or party would be free to do anything with public funds and public policy.

The next function of the party is to provide aid to the needy and distressed, and thus cushion the impact of the economic system upon individuals. Every political machine does some direct charity work. Professor McKean points out that the depression which followed the stock-market crash of 1929 overwhelmed political organizations with appeals,

[35] Merriam and Gosnell, *op. cit.*, p. 478.
[36] *Ibid.*, p. 475.

so that the parties had to turn to legislation to provide public funds for relief.[37]

Under the provisions of the Constitution that the President shall be elected by a majority vote of the whole number of electors in the electoral college, or, in case no candidate receives a majority vote, by the members of the House of Representatives voting by states, it is difficult to see how a selection could ever be made without national party organizations through which individual candidates are presented to the voters. The requirement of a majority vote places a premium on nationwide publicity, organization, and support. Under normal American conditions, with two major political parties, there has not been a single instance of a failure to reach a decision in the electoral college since the present system was adopted in 1804.[38]

One of the functions of the modern political party is the control of power, for the party is the major social instrument for registering consent. Without political parties the emergence of democracy is difficult to conceive. Without an expanding use of political parties the survival of democracy is difficult to imagine. The party leaders in both major parties in the United States are fond of such phrases as "party principles," "party tradition," or "party heritage," yet compromise has been the major factor in holding the two-party system together.

REFERENCES

Herbert Agar, *The Price of Union* (1950).
Charles A. Beard, *The American Party Battle* (1928).
W. E. Binkley, *American Political Parties: Their Natural History* (1943).
Hugh A. Bone, *American Politics and the Party System* (1949).
George A. Graham, *Morality in American Politics* (1952).
Alexander Heard, *A Two-party South?* (1951).
A. N. Holcombe, *The Middle Classes in American Politics* (1940).
V. O. Key, Jr., *Politics, Parties, and Pressure Groups,* 3d ed. (1952).
————, *Southern Politics* (1949).
Samuel Lubell, *The Future of American Politics* (1952).
Charles E. Merriam and Harold F. Gosnell, *The American Party System,* 4th ed. (1949).
Peter H. Odegard and E. Allen Helms, *American Politics: A Study in Political Dynamics,* rev. ed. (1947).
E. E. Schattschneider, *Party Government* (1941).
Murray S. Stedman, Jr., and Susan W. Stedman, *Discontent at the Polls: A Study of Farmer and Labor Parties, 1827–1948* (1950).

[37] McKean, *op. cit.,* p. 27.

[38] In 1824 when the election was thrown into the House of Representatives there were not two parties in the field as now, and in 1876 the disputed election turned on the validity of certain election returns.

CHAPTER 11 *Pressure Groups*

History of Pressure Groups

Even before the adoption of the Constitution the significance of pressure groups and factions was recognized by the founding fathers. In a famous passage in *The Federalist,* James Madison pointed out the impact of such groups upon government and the reasons for their development. He argued that the proposed Union would be a means to "break and control the violence of faction" which he defined as "a number of citizens, whether amounting to a majority or minority of the whole, who are united and actuated by some common impulse of passion, or of interest, adverse to the rights of other citizens, or to the permanent and aggregate interests of the community." Madison's comments on the source and character of group differences reflected keen insight into "pressure politics" as it has developed in the United States: [1]

The latent causes of faction are . . . sown in the nature of man; and we see them everywhere brought into different degrees of activity, according to the different circumstances of civil society. A zeal for different opinions concerning religion, concerning government, and many other points, as well of speculation as of practice; an attachment to different leaders ambitiously contending for pre-eminence and power; or to persons of other descriptions whose fortunes have been interesting to the human passions, have, in turn, divided mankind into parties, inflamed them with mutual animosity, and rendered them much more disposed to vex and oppress each other than to cooperate for their common good. . . . But the most common and durable source of factions has been the various and unequal distribution of property. Those who hold and those who are without property have ever formed distinct interests in society. Those who are creditors, and those who are debtors, fall under a like discrimination. A landed interest, a manufacturing interest, a mercantile interest, a moneyed interest, with many lesser interests, grow up of necessity in civilized nations, and divide them

[1] *The Federalist* (with an introduction by E. G. Bourne), No. 10, pp. 62–70, M. Walter Dunne, Washington, 1901.

into different classes, actuated by different sentiments and views. . . . The regulation of these various and interfering interests forms the principal task of modern legislation, and involves the spirit of party and faction in the necessary and ordinary operations of the government.

That Madison's concern for these "factions" was not unfounded soon became apparent in the First Congress under the newly adopted Constitution. When the funding of the state debt was being debated, Senator William Maclay of Pennsylvania made the following notation in his diary under the date of March 9, 1790: [2]

In the Senate chamber this morning Butler said he heard a man say he would give Vining (of Delaware) one thousand guineas for his vote, but added, "I question whether he would do so in fact." So do I, too, for he might get it for a tenth part of the sum. I do not know that pecuniary influence has actually been used, but I am certain that every other kind of management has been practiced and every tool at work that could be thought of . . . officers of Government, clergy, citizens, (Order of) Cincinnati, and every person under the influence of the Treasury.

The term "lobby" seems to have crept into the American language in the late 1820s although it was originally used as "lobby-agent" and was applied to seekers after special privilege at the capitol in Albany, New York, where Thurlow Weed and others soon made the title well and unfavorably known.[3] The term was soon shortened to "lobbyist" and by 1832 its use was frequent in Washington. From the beginning it was a term of reproach and throughout the nineteenth century it was always so used. Walt Whitman declaimed against "bawling office-holders . . . kept editors . . . bribers, compromisers, lobbiers, spongers . . . the lousy combings and born freedom-sellers of the earth." [4]

From the time of the War Between the States to the present day the activities of organized political interests have been an essential part of American politics. In the latter half of the nineteenth century the operations of the railroads and other interests in both national and state legislatures and the political activities of such farm groups as the Grange became well known parts of American history.[5]

From these relatively small beginnings, pressure groups have reached staggering numbers. No one knows the exact number of such groups but estimates have been made by various authorities. For several years the

[2] *Journal of William Maclay,* Edgar S. Maclay (ed.), p. 209, D. Appleton & Company, New York, 1890.

[3] G. G. Van Deusen, *Thurlow Weed: Wizard of the Lobby,* pp. 212–230, especially Chap. 14, "The Lucifer of the Lobby," Little, Brown & Company, Boston, 1947.

[4] Karl Schriftgiesser, *The Lobbyists,* p. 6, Little, Brown & Company, Boston, 1951.

[5] E. Pendleton Herring, *Group Representation before Congress,* pp. 30–39, Johns Hopkins Press, Baltimore, 1929.

World Almanac has been building up a list called, "United States Associations and Societies," which currently has over 500 entries. A study published in 1941 listed approximately 500 organizations with permanent headquarters in Washington.[6] The U.S. Department of Commerce recently estimated that there were about 8,000 trade associations, about 30,000 associations related to agriculture, "well over 50,000" women's associations, and about 500 professional societies.[7]

With such a variety of groups to consider it is impossible to cover completely the activities and techniques used by all of them. Instead, attention will be given to a few of the outstanding organizations in each of the following classifications: (1) business, (2) farm, (3) labor, (4) veterans, (5) professional, (6) bureaucracy, and (7) religious.[8]

Business Groups

In their earlier manifestations, business groups in the United States were organized into trade associations which became increasingly important in the period following the War Between the States. By the 1890s the trade associations had become so widespread as to be a familiar feature of industrial organization in America.[9] It was the well-founded suspicion that such associations were attempting to "restrain competition" that ultimately led to the passage of the Sherman Antitrust Act. Paradoxically, the latter brought these trade associations into an even closer relationship with the Federal government.

The NAM. One of the most influential of present-day business groups, the National Association of Manufacturers, emerged from the disturbed conditions of the panic of 1893. It did not become a particularly significant group until it also became involved in labor questions in 1903. The NAM continued to expand during the second decade of the century, fluctuating somewhat with shifts in the business cycle and the aggressiveness of labor unions. During the post-World War I decade, however, the organization did not grow appreciably. With the upturn in labor-union membership and the organization after 1935 of the mass-production workers along industrial lines, and with the passage of national legislation favorable to labor, the

[6] Donald C. Blaisdell, *Economic Power and Political Pressures*, TNEC Monograph 26, 1941, pp. 197–201.

[7] C. J. Judkins, *Trade and Professional Associations of the United States*, U.S. Department of Commerce, Industrial Series, No. 3, 1942.

[8] This classification represents a consensus of the types covered in Dayton David McKean, *Party and Pressure Politics*, Houghton Mifflin Company, Boston, 1949; P. H. Odegard and E. A. Helms, *American Politics*, Harper & Brothers, New York, 1947; V. O. Key, Jr., *Politics, Parties and Pressure Groups*, Thomas Y. Crowell Company, New York, 1952; and Hugh A. Bone, *American Politics and the Party System*, McGraw-Hill Book Company, Inc., New York 1949.

[9] Clarence E. Bonnett, "The Evolution of Business Groupings," *The Annals of the Academy of Political and Social Science*, Vol. 179, pp. 1–8, May, 1935.

NAM began again to expand. It claimed a membership of 16,000 in 1948.[10]

A careful student of the NAM's activities recently concluded that its objectives have appeared to be fourfold: "(1) reduction of the bargaining position of organized labor, both with respect to direct employer-employee relations and to indirect governmental sources of union power; (2) minimization of the tax burden on industrial profits and managerial compensation; (3) elimination, modification, and prevention of public regulation of or government participation in industrial functions and processes; and (4) encouragement of direct and indirect public aid to industry if not in conflict with other objectives." [11]

The NAM relies heavily upon publications to influence public opinion. Members are kept informed on legislation and labor relations through the *NAM News,* published every week. Addresses by officers of NAM are printed in attractive format and mailed to members and civic associations. The research staff produces pamphlets, sometimes of considerable length, on a variety of subjects, always with a strong current of emphasis upon private enterprise and ownership and upon freedom in the choice of economic activity and endeavor. In addition, elaborate materials in social science are prepared for schools and colleges. . . . In the spring of 1946 the NAM spent upward of $400,000 in an effort to defeat the extension of price control. Full-page advertisements in newspapers blamed the lack of consumers' and producers' goods on price control and promised an abundance of products if price controls were lifted.[12]

After Congress passed the Federal Regulation of Lobbying Act in 1946, which required the registration of individuals and organizations attempting to influence congressional legislation, the NAM refused to register. In a suit filed in January, 1948, the NAM asked a special District of Columbia Federal court to declare certain sections of the act unconstitutional. Furthermore, the NAM contended that even if the act were constitutional, it could not apply to that group. The president of the NAM declared that his association was not bound by the act because it was a service organization with "relatively little interest in lobbying as it understood that term." [13] Statements of expenditures for legislative purposes have been filed under protest.

Chamber of Commerce of the United States. A second major national business-pressure group is the Chamber of Commerce of the United States, which was organized in 1912. Its formation was due to the "anti-big-business" attitude which Theodore Roosevelt had popularized, the threat implied by the growth and increased political activity of organized labor,

---

[10] "Renovation in N.A.M." *Fortune,* July, 1948 p. 72.

[11] Alfred S. Cleveland, "N.A.M.: Spokesman for Industry?," *Harvard Business Review,* Vol. 26, pp. 353–371, 1948.

[12] Bone, *op. cit.,* pp. 108–109.

[13] *New York Herald-Tribune,* Jan. 29, 1948. Constitutionality of the Lobbying Act will be discussed later in this chapter.

and the "instabilities of the market that produced state and local chambers of commerce." [14]

The Chamber's position is made clear by its official organ, *The Nation's Business.* Freedom of business from governmental regulation and control and the demand that government refrain from entering fields of activity in competition with private enterprise form the heart of the Chamber's program.

Committee for Constitutional Government. In addition to the NAM and the Chamber of Commerce, business interests in the United States have developed, in recent years, more subtle and in some respects more effective pressure groups. One of the most notorious of these has been the Committee for Constitutional Government which was established in 1937 by Frank Gannett, the publisher of a chain of newspapers. One of the CCG's first lobbying targets was President Roosevelt's "courtpacking" plan and when the latter was defeated the CCG assumed much of the credit for the conquest. The CCG accepts two types of contribution: the first is apparently designed to escape the provisions of the Lobby Act of 1946 which requires a listing of all contributions of $500 or more; that is, the Committee seeks contributions of $490 or less for its general fund. It also accepts contributions of more than $490 but these are taken only for the distribution of books and pamphlets. The contributor may distribute these books himself, or, as is more likely, leave it to the committee to do so. "In either case," the Buchanan Committee to investigate lobbying reported, "the committee treats the transaction as a book sale which it does not report as a contribution under the Lobbying Act." [15]

The Buchanan Committee found that between 1937 and 1944 the Committee for Constitutional Government had distributed more than 82 million booklets and other items of "literature" which were designed to influence legislation. The counsel for the House committee observed in June, 1950: [16]

Of particular significance is the fact that Edward A. Rumely and the Committee for Constitutional Government . . . in recent years have devised a scheme for raising enormous funds without filing reports pursuant to the provision of the Federal Regulation of Lobbying Act. This scheme has the color of legality, but in fact is a method of circumventing the law. It utilizes a system whereby contributions to the CCG are designated as payments for the purchase of books, which are transmitted to others at the direction of the purchaser, with

[14] Paul Studenski, "Chambers of Commerce," *Encyclopaedia of the Social Sciences,* Vol. 3, pp. 325–328, The Macmillan Company, New York, 1930.

[15] *Hearings before the House Select Committee on Lobbying Act,* 81st Cong., 2d sess., 1950, Part 5, pp. 143 ff.; *General Interim Report of the House Select Committee on Lobbying Act,* H. Rept. 3138, 81st Cong., 2d sess., 1950, p. 12. Hearings hereafter cited as *Buchanan Hearings;* and second document cited hereafter as *Buchanan Committee General Interim Report.*

[16] *The New York Times,* June 28, 1950, p. 24. In 1953, the Committee for Constitutional Government was vigorously supporting the proposed Bricker Amendment.

both the contributor of the money and the recipients of the books totally unaware of the subterfuge.

In spite of these techniques for evading the listing of expenditures under the Lobbying Act, the Committee for Constitutional Government did admit spending some $620,000 for lobbying purposes in 1949. This figure made the CCG second only to the American Medical Association which listed expenditures of $1,500,000 for the same period for the purpose of influencing legislation.[17]

In summary, it may be said that although complete unity does not prevail among the various business groups, broadly speaking their "legislative objectives" run along these lines: (1) the balancing of the Federal budget and the ending of deficit spending except in times of war; (2) the reduction of taxes and especially the elimination of excess-profits taxes; (3) the preservation of management's "right to manage" in its relations with its employees, including almost unanimous support for the Taft-Hartley Act of 1947; (4) the limiting of publicly-owned enterprises to a minimum so that these agencies will not offer competition to privately-owned businesses; (5) the adoption of a "realistic tariff" program which usually means a "protective" tariff of some kind; and (6) opposition to what is termed a "government-planned" economy.[18]

Farm Groups

In some respects farm organizations resemble the early trade associations which were formed by American businessmen. Such groups as the National Council of Farmer Co-operatives, the National Co-operative Milk Producers' Federation, and the National Beet Growers Association either function much like trade associations or are closely affiliated with such business groups.[19] Distinct farm organizations, however, are better illustrated by the National Grange Order of the Patrons of Husbandry and the American Farm Bureau Federation.

The Grange. The Grange was started in 1867 as an educational society for farmers on the pattern of the Masonic order. In its earlier days the Grange was noted for its belligerent radicalism and its anti-railroad attitude along with its demand for publicly-owned grain storage and milling facilities.[20] In recent years, however, the organization has tended to reflect the views of "traditional rural Republicanism."

American Farm Bureau Federation. The largest and most important of

---

[17] Schriftgiesser, *op. cit.,* p. 168.

[18] Bone, *op. cit.,* pp. 109–115.

[19] For an account of the political attitudes of these groups, see Wesley McCune, *The Farm Bloc,* Doubleday & Company, New York, 1943.

[20] Solon J. Buck, "Grange," *Encyclopaedia of Social Sciences;* Orville M. Kile, *The Farm Bureau Movement,* pp. 14–17, The Macmillan Company, New York, 1921; U.S. Department of Agriculture, *Farmers in a Changing World,* p. 948, 1940.

farm pressure groups is the American Farm Bureau Federation, which grew out of the "county-agent" system. In 1914 the Smith-Lever Act established a system of grants-in-aid to the state colleges of agriculture in support of a program of extension education in improved farming methods. With this encouragement the county-agent system spread rapidly, covering approximately one-third of the nation's counties by the beginning of 1915.[21]

Additional Federal funds and encouragement of the formation of farm bureaus in order to increase agricultural production stimulated the farm-bureau movement during World War I.

With the aid of officials of the U.S. Department of Agriculture, the American Farm Bureau Federation was launched in 1919–20. . . . In many States the county bureaus had a semiofficial status [and] in recent years there have been seven States that still require a county farm bureau as a local sponsoring body. . . . In many others however, the Farm Bureau has retained the advantages of a semiofficial status even after formal connections with the State and county governments were severed. As a consequence, in part, of these developments, the emphasis in the Farm Bureau program shifted from education to governmental activities, particularly the promotion of favorable legislation . . . This shift was dramatically symbolized by the formation and operation of the first "farm bloc" in the 67th Congress (1920–1922), in which the Farm Bureau was a major factor.[22]

Examples of "pressure tactics" by the Farm Bureau Federations (both national and state) are numerous. Although it does not openly endorse candidates after an election, the Iowa Farm Bureau Federation sets up committees of five members in each legislative district whose function it is to capitalize upon local support which Bureau members have given to the successful candidate. The qualifications of the members of these committees, according to Kile, are four in number: (1) they must be "willing to put Farm Bureau policies ahead of any personal interest"; (2) they must be from the same party as the successful candidate; (3) they must be men who "individually helped get the candidate elected"; (4) they must be politically potent in the district.[23]

In sum, the objectives sought by the various farm pressure groups include a demand for economic aids, social betterment, and improved living conditions.

Labor Groups

AFL. Although local trade unions in the United States date back as far as the 1790s and although a National Labor Union and the Knights of

---

[21] Orville M. Kile, *The Farm Bureau through Three Decades*, pp. 88–89, Waverly Press, Baltimore, 1948.

[22] D. B. Truman, *The Governmental Process*, pp. 91–92, Alfred A. Knopf, Inc., New York, 1951.

[23] Kile, *op. cit.*, pp. 381–382.

Labor had been formed in the 1860s, it was not until the formation of the American Federation of Labor in 1886 that labor found a comparatively effective national pressure agency. The trend toward political activity by the AFL was strengthened during World War I when the organization demanded safeguards for union activities in return for its vigorous support of the war. By 1920, AFL membership exceeded 4 million workers.

CIO. In the 1930s the passage of the National Industrial Recovery Act (1933) and the National Labor Relations Act (1935) served as a stimulant to union development. When the AFL seemed hesitant to take advantage of this stimulus, the Committee for Industrial Organization (later the Congress of Industrial Organizations) was formed. One of the most significant results of the formation of the CIO, in so far as pressure devices are concerned, was the establishment of the CIO Political Action Committee (PAC) in 1943 under the leadership of Sidney Hillman. To carry out its functions, the PAC created a vast organization with a national office in New York and 14 regional offices embracing all 48 states. Each union was asked to form its own political action committee, to which the national office supplied pamphlets, posters, radio scripts, slogans, songs, clipsheets, stickers, buttons, and organization manuals, together with the voting record of the local congressman seeking reelection. Altogether 85 million pieces of literature of all sorts were printed and distributed in 1944 alone, and there has been little letup in the volume of publications since then.[24]

Educational and Political League. In 1947 the AFL formed Labor's Educational and Political League and began a drive to raise one dollar from each of the Federation's millions of members. The avowed purpose of the League is to defeat "anti-labor" candidates and to elect nominees friendly to labor. William Green termed the step of "historical importance" and an unprecedented one for the AFL, for previously it had used only temporary partisan committees at election time. Spokesmen for both the AFL and the CIO, however, indicated that the creation of the League was not directed toward bringing about political unity within the ranks of organized labor.[25]

Public Affairs Institute. Just as business groups have recently resorted to subtle devices, such as the Committee for Constitutional Government, for pressure purposes, so certain labor organizations have established a Public Affairs Institute to perform a similar function. The Public Affairs Institute was founded in 1947 through a trust agreement signed by Dr. Dewey Anderson, executive director, and the late A. F. Whitney, president of the Brotherhood of Railroad Trainmen. The Brotherhood supplied the funds which were the central operating budget for the first three years

[24] Joseph Gaer, *The First Round: The Story of the CIO Political Action Committee,* Chap. 1, Duell, Sloan and Pearce, Inc., New York, 1944.
[25] *The New York Times,* Dec. 6, 7, 1947. Discussion of a union of the AFL and the CIO was considered in 1953, and again in 1954.

and which amounted to nearly $160,000; this money was parceled out between October, 1947, and March, 1950. Most of the Institute's other funds have come from labor unions, some of them being general contributions for operating expenses, but most of them being earmarked for specific research projects. Dr. Anderson, testifying before the Buchanan Committee, described the work of the Public Affairs Institute.[26]

The Public Affairs Institute operates strictly as a nonprofit research agency. It initiates its own research program. It does not sponsor specific legislation. It does not seek the passage or defeat of legislation by the Congress of the United States. As with . . . other similar nonprofit, active educational and research organizations, the Public Affairs Institute develops specific recommendations flowing from the research and study of a problem, recommendations which may require substantive legislation and changes in public administration to be effective and to make the conclusions of the research done of practical value. We do not shrink from this use of the research technique; on the contrary, it is our means of influencing the course of events and helping to shape public policy. This is what the application of social science is all about, and it is what distinguishes a research approach from a propagandistic approach to social-economic-political issues.

Research by the Institute has produced pamphlets on a variety of subjects including European recovery, the role of collective bargaining in a democracy, conservation of natural resources, the Hoover reports, distribution of the costs of health insurance, medical care for the individual, and the so-called "Bold New Program" or Point Four. Approximately 45,000 copies of these publications have been sold or distributed gratis to the press and radio, congressmen, teachers, and others.[27]

In summary it may be said that the political action of the American Federation of Labor has taken the form of pressure politics. Both the recently created CIO Political Action Committee and the AFL Political Education League have been in the pressure field rather than in that of promoting a separate "labor" political party. The political action of organized labor has undoubtedly been weakened by the political division within labor itself.

Veterans' Groups

American Legion. Oustanding among veterans' pressure groups is the American Legion, which was formed at the close of World War I by a small group of men who were seriously concerned about the "radicalism" of the postwar period.[28] Although the constitution of the Legion provides

[26] *Buchanan Hearings,* Part 7, pp. 3–5.
[27] *Ibid.,* pp. 65–69.
[28] Richard S. Jones, *A History of the American Legion,* pp. 22–39, The Bobbs-Merrill Company, Inc., Indianapolis, 1946.

that it "shall be absolutely nonpolitical," its role as a pressure group is well known.

At its first convention in Minneapolis in November, 1919, the Legion provided for a committee on legislation to represent the organization in Washington, "to establish a Washington bureau, rent offices and employ personnel . . . necessary for the furtherance of the legislative program of the American Legion." [29] The power of the Legion lobby was first felt in the winter of 1920 when Congress was considering the Sweet bill to increase the maximum disability payments to veterans from $30 per month to $80.

Although it might appear that such a well-organized and numerous group as the American Legion would be well-nigh invincible at the polls, the evidence seems to indicate otherwise. V. O. Key analyzed the effects, as indicated in election returns, of congressional hostility to the American Legion's bonus demands. He compared the fortunes of members of the House of Representatives who had voted to sustain Presidential vetoes of such measures, with those of congressmen who voted to override them just before the elections of 1922, 1924, 1928, 1930, 1934, and 1936. His findings indicate that the most important variable was whether or not a congressman carried the label of the party against which the political tide was then running. The Legion's general effect on the outcome was almost completely negligible.[30]

Despite this failure to elect congressmen, there is no doubt that the Legion and other veterans' groups have exerted effective pressure in such fields as pensions, bonuses, hospitalization, rehabilitation programs, postwar educational opportunities, preferences in the civil service, and similar benefits.

Amvets and AVC. From World War II, two major veterans' associations emerged: the American Veterans of World War II (Amvets) and the American Veterans' Committee (AVC). The Amvet program has centered around the preservation of civil liberties and the notion that "peace, lasting peace—should be the alpha and omega of every organization of veterans, irrespective of what war they happen to be alumni of." [31]

The AVC has broken sharply with the conventional procedures and principles of other veterans' organizations. "Under its slogan 'Citizens First, Veterans Second,' the AVC uses none of the semimilitary procedures characteristic of veterans' groups and refers to its local units as chapters instead of posts." It opposes a bonus and emphasizes that jobs, full-employment measures, and social security are more important in helping the

---

[29] *Ibid.,* p. 46.

[30] "The Veterans and the House of Representatives: A Study of Pressure Group and Electoral Mortality," *Journal of Politics,* Vol. 5, pp. 27–40, February, 1943.

[31] Letter of National Judge Advocate of Amvets to *The New York Times,* Aug. 13, 1946.

veteran's integration into the community than a program of rehabilitation and bonuses.[32]

Professional Groups

The "ancient and honorable" professions of medicine and law have both traditionally been subject to a considerable measure of regulation to ensure effective and scrupulous discharge of their public trust. In the United States the oldest continuing professional groups are the medical associations which emerged in the late eighteenth century and were primarily concerned with the quality of professional training and licensing.

The AMA. By 1912 the American Medical Association included in its membership approximately half the doctors in the United States, a proportion which has now risen to something over two-thirds, a remarkably complete coverage for any widespread group.[33]

After the policy of the AMA has been finally adopted, it is regarded as a one-party line, to be sold by many techniques besides repetition and rational persuasion.[34] The AMA's "party line" has been most concerned in recent years with opposing compulsory Federal health insurance. The association's propaganda has been based in part upon the assumptions, probably valid, that many Americans are opposed to widespread socialization of the economy, fear proposals that are regarded as "alien," disapprove of excessive government expenditures, dislike invasions of their privacy, and expect doctors to be motivated by the highest humanitarian ideals. The AMA's "educational" campaign against Federal health insurance cost the association over $1,500,000 in the year 1949 and made that organization the largest-spending pressure group from which the Buchanan Committee received information.[35]

The ABA. There were few important associations of lawyers in America until after the War Between the States. The American Bar Association was set in operation in 1878 by a group of men among whose first acts was the establishment of a committee on legal education and admission to the bar. The ABA has never numbered among its members more than one-fifth of the country's lawyers, although the coverage of many of the state and local groups is more nearly complete.[36]

One of the primary interests of the American Bar Association has been the promotion of professional standards. The association advocates higher

[32] Bone, *op. cit.,* pp. 191–192.

[33] Oliver Garceau, *The Political Life of the American Medical Association,* pp. 14, 130, Harvard University Press, Cambridge, Mass., 1941.

[34] Oliver Garceau, "Organized Medicine Enforces Its 'Party Line,'" *Public Opinion Quarterly,* Vol. 4, pp. 408–428, 1940.

[35] Schriftgiesser, *op. cit.,* p. 168.

[36] M. Louise Rutherford, *The Influence of the American Bar Association on Public Opinion and Legislation,* pp. 8–11, 12, 16–17, 19–34, The Foundation Press, Philadelphia, 1937.

standards for admission to the bar and recommends that official approval of law schools be withheld unless they meet certain requirements. Licensing, court procedures, personnel, administrative courts, and criminal legislation are some of the major areas in which state and local bar associations have become concerned with public policy. As in the case of the American Medical Association, so too in the American Bar Association a split has developed along conservative versus liberal lines. The liberals in the ABA formed the National Lawyers' Guild which, unlike the ABA, "has endorsed many legislative measures designed to extend the rights of workers and farmers." [37]

In spite of their occupational differences, such professional associations as the AMA, ABA, National Educational Association, American Dental Association, American Institute of Architects, and many others do appear to have certain common interests. Most of them, for example, are concerned not only with professional problems but also with the creation of favorable public opinion regarding their particular professions. That their interest in public affairs has frequently been worth while is indicated by the comments of two students of their political activities: [38]

In general, the pressure activities of professional organizations should not be viewed with alarm. In fact, the entrance of these associations into the governmental field, whether on their own initiative or by invitation of different governmental agencies, appears to be a very promising way of bringing the expert into the service of the government.

Bureaucracy Groups

When the Eighty-first Congress established its House Committee on Lobbying Activities the latter was authorized not only to investigate all lobbying by private groups but also "all activities of agencies of the Federal Government intended to influence, encourage, promote, or retard legislation." [39] This represented a specific recognition of the role that administrative agencies themselves play in helping to shape legislative measures and consequently public policy. Because American government has had such a strong tradition favoring the separation of powers, the role of administrative agencies and of the Chief Executive, the President, in influencing the legislature had long been overlooked.

After an administration bill is introduced into Congress, the administrative agencies concerned are usually called to testify before the congressional committee handling the bill. Although "Federal law forbids the use of an agency appropriation directly or indirectly to pay for any

[37] Bone, *op. cit.*, p. 173.
[38] H. F. Gosnell and M. J. Schmidt, "Professional Associations," *The Annals of the American Academy of Political and Social Science*, Vol. 179, p. 33, May, 1935.
[39] H. Res. 298, 81st Cong., 1st sess., reproduced in *Buchanan Hearings*, Part 1, p. 1.

service intended to 'influence a member of Congress to favor or oppose any legislation or appropriation,' " the administrator's testimony may be far more influential than the expenditure of funds, largely because the expert information which he is likely to have carries great weight with Congress.[40]

Administrative agencies may consciously or unconsciously become important lobbying groups merely by supplying information of various sorts. A careful student of government publicity has pointed out that its broad objectives are to distribute information among the clients of the agency; to catch and hold the attention of the larger public; to influence legislation; to reply to attacks upon the agency; to avoid unfavorable publicity; and to report, without particular aims, the routine news of government.[41] Virtually all administrative agencies have at some time sought to achieve one or more of these objectives and thus have used the same techniques as private pressure groups.

One of the agencies most frequently attacked for its lobbying activities was the Federal Security Agency. The attacks were leveled too at its former head, Oscar R. Ewing, who was an ardent advocate of public health insurance. Mr. Ewing and several other officials of the FSA made a six-week trip to England, the Continent, and the Middle East during the winter of 1949–1950 at a total cost to the government of about $10,000. The Buchanan Committee requested the General Accounting Office to investigate the Ewing trip, but the GAO, through the Acting Comptroller General, found no impropriety in the trip or the expenditures.[42]

After investigating the "lobbying activities of federal government agencies," the Buchanan Committee concluded: [43]

We believe that there are interests in this Nation other than those which can be mobilized along group lines, and we believe that it is the responsibility of Government—both morally and politically—to defend them. We believe, in sum, that Government must lead as well as follow; but at the same time we recognize that there are limits beyond which executive participation in legislative policymaking may impinge on the authority of Congress and thus endanger our constitutional system. We should be constantly watchful that these limits are not exceeded.

Religious Groups

General Grant is said to have remarked that "in the United States there are three great political parties: the Republican, the Democratic, and the Methodist Church." The writer who quoted the General agreed with the

[40] Bone, *op. cit.*, p. 208.
[41] James L. McCamy, *Government Publicity*, p. 21, University of Chicago Press, Chicago, 1939.
[42] *Buchanan Hearings*, Part 10, pp. 307–319.
[43] *Buchanan Committee: General Interim Report*, p. 62.

view that religion is a force in politics, but he felt that Grant incorrectly gave the Methodists a unique prominence because [44]

. . . it is inherent in Christianity to believe that the affairs of government can be ordered more perfectly and more in harmony with the will of God. It is a rare church convention . . . whose resolutions committee fails to secure the adoption of at least one declaration on national policy, one statement of opinion upon a question that is up for political settlement.

After the War Between the States the American Protective Association and the Ku Klux Klan were not only antiforeign but also strongly anti-Catholic.[45]

When Alfred E. Smith sought the Democratic nomination in 1924, his Catholic faith became a key item in the convention struggle. At least 14 religious organizations took an active part in the 1928 campaign, and they spent uncounted hundreds of thousands of dollars attacking Smith and supporting Hoover. One E. C. Jameson alone contributed $172,800 to various anti-Smith groups.[46] Smith's defeat in 1928 was due, at least in part, to the religious question. The memory of that defeat helped to weaken the candidacy of James A. Farley in 1940. Farley relates how Cardinal Mundelein thought it would be inexpedient for him to be a candidate for the Presidency in 1940. The Cardinal remarked that he hoped Farley would "do nothing to involve the Catholics of this country in another debacle such as we experienced in 1928." [47]

In the social-welfare field both Catholics and Protestants have supported cooperatives in the United States but they disagreed on the proposed child-labor amendment to the Constitution which the Protestants generally favored while the Catholics opposed it on the ground that it would tend to weaken the family. However, when Congress finally forbade child labor by statute in the 1930s and when the act was upheld by the Supreme Court, the Catholic organizations made no great protest.[48]

In foreign affairs, religious groups in the United States frequently become vitally concerned with certain policies. The maintenance of friendly relations with such Catholic countries as Argentina, Eire, and Spain is generally a matter of interest to Catholic groups within the United States. Protestant groups, on the other hand, frequently express concern over what they regard as Catholic suppression of Protestant groups in some

[44] Quoted from Stanley High, *The Church in Politics* (Harper & Brothers, New York, 1930), in McKean, *op. cit.*, p. 543.

[45] J. M. Mecklin, *The Ku Klux Klan,* pp. 157–205, Harcourt, Brace and Company, Inc., New York, 1924.

[46] Louise Overacker, *Money in Elections,* pp. 259–267, The Macmillan Company, New York, 1932.

[47] James A. Farley, *Jim Farley's Story,* p. 174, The Macmillan Company, New York, 1948.

[48] McKean, *op. cit.*, p. 553.

countries. The Council of Bishops of the Methodist Churches began a long resolution as follows: [49]

We are aware of the denials of religious liberty in many countries where Government, at the insistence of the Roman Catholic hierarchy, has passed legislation seriously limiting the freedom of other religious bodies.

We refer particularly to the Argentine, where law now requires the teaching of the Roman Catholic religion even in the schools of Protestant churches.

The situation in Italy and Spain denies to Protestants religious freedom which Protestants in the United States desire the Roman Catholics to enjoy.

Recognition of Vatican Controversy. One of the most virulent controversies of the past few years centered in this country's diplomatic representation at the Vatican. When the President's personal representative to the Vatican, Myron C. Taylor, withdrew from his post in 1950, it appeared that the conflict which had existed over whether or not the Vatican should be recognized had subsided. On October 20, 1951, however, President Truman renewed the controversy by nominating General Mark W. Clark, an Episcopalian, as the first United States Ambassador to the "state of Vatican City." The President declared that direct diplomatic relations would assist in combating the communist menace. Bishop Henry Knox Sherrill, President of the National Council of the Churches of Christ in the U.S.A., which represents 32 million Protestants, predicted that it would cause controversy and division among the American people. President Truman's own Baptist pastor, the Rev. Dr. Edward Hughes Pruden, said he had tried to dissuade Mr. Truman from this action. [50]

After the Senate had recessed without taking action on General Clark's nomination and after loud Protestant protests were made, the White House announced on January 13, 1952 that, at General Clark's own request, President Truman would not resubmit the nomination but would nominate somebody else later.

The Council of Bishops of the Methodist Churches, meeting in Atlantic City Jan. 14, said nomination of a substitute would "compound a blunder." The executive committee of the Friends General Conference (Quakers) has also gone on record as opposed to an Ambassador to the Holy See. But Francis Cardinal Spellman, Roman Catholic Archbishop of N.Y., said in Rome Jan. 16, that he "personally" considered it "appropriate for my country" to join 40 others represented at the Vatican. He called this recognition of the Holy See "as a state . . . not as a religion." [51]

The National Lutheran Council, in a resolution voted at its thirty-fourth meeting in Atlantic City, February 1, 1952, urged the President "not to im-

[49] *The New York Times*, May 8, 1947.
[50] *Facts on File Yearbook*, Vol. 11, p. 340, Facts on File, New York, 1951.
[51] *Facts on File Yearbook*, Vol. 12, p. 16, 1952.

pair national unity" by insisting upon establishing a United States Embassy at the Vatican.[52]

In March, 1952, when the State Department asked Congress to appropriate $70,000 to set up an Embassy at Vatican City, the House Appropriations Committee voted 19 to 17 against the proposal on the grounds that the Senate had not approved an Ambassador to the Vatican.[53] In early April the House of Representatives voted 159 to 82 to deny the requested funds unless the Senate approved an Ambassador. A few days later the Vatican, in a radio broadcast, gave the text of President Lincoln's letter authorizing appointment of the first United States Papal Representative in 1862.[54] The whole affair demonstrates the hauling and tugging between Catholic and Protestant groups and the attempts of these groups to exert pressure both on Congress and on the Chief Executive.

A recent study of church lobbying in Washington indicates that churches are interesting themselves in more and more legislative measures and that the number of church lobbyists is growing.[55] It is contended that Protestant groups set up no permanent lobbies for other than special causes before World War II largely because Protestant leaders believed that their constituencies would oppose such action. Today, however, "the demands of extremely varied groups are reconciled, repressed and compromised. To be without group representation is to be without a voice in an important phase of lawmaking. To have group representation is to lobby." [56] It is contended that only a few of the church lobbyists have registered under the Federal Regulation of Lobbying Act mainly because of the effect that this registration might have on the tax-free status of contributions to the denominations sponsoring the lobby.

Pressure Groups: A Problem and Proposed Solutions

In March, 1952, when the Senate was debating the future of the tidelands oil basin, Senator Holland received permission from the Senate to give floor privileges to a registered lobbyist for the National Association of Attorneys General in order to obtain advice and assistance. The episode created a considerable furor and the Democratic floor leader, Senator McFarland, later declared that the incident should not be repeated.[57] This affair dramatized both the importance and the complexity of the

[52] *Ibid.*, p. 67.
[53] *The New York Times,* Mar. 26, 29, 1952.
[54] *The New York Times,* Apr. 5, 8, 1952.
[55] Luke Ebersole, *Church Lobbying in the Nation's Capitol,* The Macmillan Company, New York, 1951.
[56] *Ibid.*, pp. viii–ix.
[57] *The New York Times,* Mar. 26, 27, 1952. The lobbyist was Walter R. Johnson, who is listed on p. 26 of the *Lobby Index, 1946–1949.* For a study of the "corrupting" influence of lobbying on Congress, see H. H. Wilson, *Congress: Corruption and Compromise,* Rinehart & Company, Inc., New York, 1951.

problem which organized interest groups present in American political life.

In the early years of the twentieth century numerous proposals were advanced for the direct representation of organized interest groups in the legislative body, the intellectual sponsors being a school of pluralists influenced by the English guild socialists.[58] The argument was that the territorial system of representation was a sham and that it should be abolished in favor of a system that allotted legislative seats to interest groups. Little has been heard of such suggestions in recent years but occasionally they crop up in the writings of a commentator who wants to do away with the supposed evils of "pressure" groups by having these groups elect the members of Congress.[59]

A second, and more widely accepted, method of dealing with organized interest groups has been the attempt to restrict their activities both at the state and national levels. Aside from passing general laws that make bribery of any public official a crime, most of these attempts deal with the relationships between interest groups and the legislatures. The Alabama constitution of 1874 made "corrupt solicitation" of legislators a crime, and in 1877 the Georgia constitution outlawed "lobbying." In 1890 Massachusetts passed the first statute regulating "legislative agents," and by 1950 38 states and Alaska had similar laws on their books. At the Federal level such statutes are of later date, aside from a rule adopted by the House of Representatives in 1876 for the Forty-fourth Congress, requiring "persons or corporations" to register counsel or agents representing them in connection with pending legislation.[60]

As early as 1907 bills were introduced in Congress to control lobbying and similar proposals have come up in most subsequent sessions. In 1935–1936 particular types of lobbyists were placed under congressional regulation, but it was not until 1946 that Congress enacted the first general statute regulating lobbying. It was the Federal Regulation of Lobbying Act which was a part of the Legislative Reorganization Act of that year.[61]

1946 Lobbying Act. The Federal Regulation of Lobbying Act of 1946 requires every person or group receiving or spending money for lobbying

[58] See, for example, Kung Chuan-Hsiao, *Political Pluralism*, Harcourt, Brace and Company, Inc., New York, 1927.

[59] Harvey Fergusson, *People and Power*, pp. 110–111, William Morrow & Company, Inc., New York, 1947.

[60] *Buchanan Hearings*, Part I, p. 52. An excellent survey of state legislation on lobbying is found in Belle Zeller's testimony before the Buchanan Committee, *ibid.*, pp. 58–97. See also the Council of State Governments, *Constitutional and Statutory Provisions of the States*, Vol. 9, "State Regulation of Lobbying," Chicago, 1951.

[61] Belle Zeller, "The Federal Regulation of Lobbying Act," *American Political Science Review*, Vol. 42, pp. 239–271, April, 1948. The analysis of the Lobbying Act is based on this article.

to keep detailed records. It regulates each lobbying organization by requiring it to file quarterly statements in Congress listing the names of persons who gave $500 or more to the organization, the total sum of all contributions, the names of persons to whom the money was distributed in amounts of $10 or more, the purpose of each expenditure, and the total of all expenditures. The act opens the filed statements to the public and it specifies that its provisions should apply to persons or groups who in any manner collect or receive money for the primary purpose of influencing congressional action or legislation. Political committees are exempt from the act but all other lobbyists are required to file quarterly statements with Congress giving expenditures and income and describing publications that they have issued. Penalties under the act include a fine of $5,000 and one year's imprisonment for failure to register; and a person convicted under the act may not engage in lobbying or appear before a congressional committee for three years after conviction, on penalty of $10,000 fine and five years' imprisonment.[62]

In a suit filed on January 28, 1948, the National Association of Manufacturers asked the court to declare certain sections of the Federal Regulation of Lobbying Act unconstitutional. The NAM argued that even if they were constitutional they did not apply to the association. A decision was handed down on March 17, 1952, by a special District of Columbia three-man Federal court. The court upheld the NAM's contention that Sections 303 to 307 and 310 were unconstitutional, on the grounds that the definition of a lobbyist was too indefinite. The court said that a criminal statute must define the crime with sufficient precision so that a person may determine whether his action is prohibited; otherwise the statute is repugnant to the due-process clause.[63]

A second objectionable feature of the Lobbying Act, in the opinion of the special Federal court, was Section 310, which provided that a person convicted under the act could not engage in lobbying or appear before a congressional committee for three years after conviction, on penalty of $10,000 fine and five years' imprisonment:[64]

Freedom of speech and the right of the people peaceably to assemble and to petition the Government for redress of grievances are guaranteed by the First Amendment to the Constitution. Congress is prohibited from making any law abridging these rights. The penalty provision of the Act, however, manifestly deprives a person convicted of violating the statute, of his constitutional right of

[62] 60 Stat. L. 839; 2 U.S.C.A. 261–270. The act is reproduced in *Buchanan Hearings*, Part I, pp. 8–10.

[63] *National Association of Manufacturers of the United States v. McGrath*, 103 F. Supp. 510 (1952). Key excerpts from the Court's opinion are found in *The New York Times*, Mar. 19, 1952.

[64] *NAM v. McGrath*, 103 F. Supp. 510, 514 (1952).

freedom of speech and his constitutional right to petition the legislative branch of the Government. This clause is obviously unconstitutional. A person convicted of a crime may not for that reason be stripped of his constitutional privileges.

The practical effect of the decision is to give a choice to the lobbyists. In anticipation that the Justice Department will appeal the decision and that the Supreme Court will uphold the decision, the lobbyist may stop reporting. Otherwise, he may play safe in case of a reversal. The sections requiring lobbyists to register are left intact, but the sections providing penalties for noncompliance have been declared unconstitutional by the special court. Technically, the law is still in effect, but no prosecutions can be brought in the District of Columbia since the court's ruling will prevail there. As Professor Schriftgiesser pointed out in a letter to *The New York Times*, April 13, 1952:

> The Court has ruled that Congress has the right to ask whence come its petitioners, and why, and for whom, but that it cannot enforce its demand for this knowledge. Part of the Act is clear, part is vague; but since the unconstitutional penalty section applies to the enforcement of both, it would seem that the *Lobby Act of 1946* is null and void.

If functional representation affords little relief from pressure groups and if constitutional difficulties of the kind cited in the NAM case prevail, how are unorganized elements in a democratic society to be saved from the organized? Two careful students of the problem have recently indicated that, in their judgment, the matter is not hopeless.

Professor Truman finds great hope in the view that in the long run the "potential groups" such as consumers and ordinary citizens will represent an effective brake upon the highly organized groups and help to enforce the "rules of the game," which, although vague at times, appear to be fundamental to a democratic society.[65]

Another student of the problem of pressure groups finds some hope in the "nationalizing" influence of the Presidency as a counterbalance to special interest groups.[66]

It would appear that the hope of a democratic society rests in its ability to arouse those broad public interests in order that the special, organized interests may be allocated their proper role in the community.

REFERENCES

Stephen Kemp Bailey, *Congress Makes a Law* (1950).
Hugh A. Bone, *American Politics and the Party System* (1949).

[65] Truman, *op. cit.*, pp. 534–535.
[66] E. E. Schattschneider, "Congress in Conflict," *Yale Review*, Vol. 41, pp. 181–193, Winter, 1952.

Stuart Chase, *Democracy under Pressure: Special Interests vs. the Public Welfare* (1945).

Luke Ebersole, *Church Lobbying in the Nation's Capital* (1951).

Joseph Gaer, *The First Round: The Story of the CIO Political Action Committee* (1944).

Oliver Garceau, *The Political Life of the American Medical Association* (1941).

E. P. Herring, *Group Representation before Congress* (1929).

Richard S. Jones, *A History of the American Legion* (1946).

V. O. Key, Jr., *Politics, Parties and Pressure Groups* (1952).

Orville M. Kile, *The Farm Bureau Movement* (1921).

————, *The Farm Bureau through Three Decades* (1948).

Earl Latham, *The Group Basis of Politics* (1952).

Wesley McCune, *The Farm Bloc* (1943).

Dayton David McKean, *Party and Pressure Politics* (1949).

Fred W. Riggs, *Pressures on Congress: A Study of the Repeal of Chinese Exclusion* (1950).

M. Louise Rutherford, *The Influence of the American Bar Association on Public Opinion and Legislation* (1937).

E. E. Schattschneider, *Politics, Pressures and the Tariff* (1935).

Karl Schriftgiesser, *The Lobbyists* (1951).

David B. Truman, *The Governmental Process* (1951).

Belle Zeller, *Pressure Politics in New York* (1937).

CHAPTER 12   *Congress: Structure, Composition and Organization*

Theory and History of Representation

Common Law. Men have not always been governed by laws deliberately made by a legislative body. During most of human history people have lived in accordance with unrecorded custom—accepted modes of action known to all and rarely committed to writing. When kings "made" law what they really did was to discover custom and give it authoritative form in writing. They had the help of assemblies composed for the most part of persons felt to be particularly conversant with the ancient customs of the realm. The notion that such assemblies should announce *new* rules would not have been understandable. Thus, in England until near the end of the fourteenth century we find kings promising, upon their accession, to keep the "ancient customs of the kingdom," or "of good King Edward," and so forth. After Parliament became a fixed part of the machinery of government it did not so much "make" law as codify existing custom. Even today in the Near East, in Africa, and in the Orient, hundreds of millions of people live not under laws consciously enacted but under the "yoke of custom." These customs are known by chiefs, kings, elders, and wise men, and they are obeyed without question by the multitude.

In the English-speaking world, lawmaking as we know it now, as distinct from "finding" and declaring custom, was the exception until almost the beginning of the 1800s. The English Parliament did not really concern itself systematically with legislation until it was reformed by the act of 1832. Law was developed by decisions of the courts and by occasional restatements of the common law in formal acts of Parliament.

Today the law of custom is still very much alive in English-speaking countries. It is known as the common law and it consists of those customary modes of conduct in human relations which have received the approval of the courts. Some of it has been codified by legislative bodies; the rest may be found in the volumes where the decisions of judges are printed.

In modern times, however, we also have statute law, the deliberate work of legislative bodies or of executive and administrative agencies which have been given subordinate lawmaking powers. In this category come acts of Congress and the state legislatures, municipal and other local ordinances, and orders, decrees, and proclamations issued by administrators under the authority of statute or ordinance. Formally, at least, statute law is made by assemblies of men and women who consciously seek solutions for problems brought before them. In this sense it is "made," not developed like the common law.

History of Lawmaking Bodies. The modern legislative body is not really very different from its prototype, the medieval English Parliament. That assembly was looked upon as a body representing the permanent interests of the nation. The Lords Spiritual and Temporal spoke for the larger landed interests of the realm; the House of Commons (*i.e.,* House of Communities, *not* the house of the "common people") represented the smaller rural proprietors in the counties and the rising business and trading classes in the towns. Since each of these interests was a corporate one, it was not felt necessary that numbers *as such* be represented. The county members spoke for all the middling landholders, the burgesses for businessmen everywhere, and the lords for their class wherever located. So far as there was any theory about the matter at all, it was that the king, before legislating, desired the counsel of his "people," their "representatives" being assumed to know the custom of the country.

Modern representative bodies differ from medieval ones principally in representing numbers of individuals rather than "estates" or categories of individuals. Thus, each member of the American House of Representatives has a constituency of roughly 350,000 persons, while a member of the British House of Commons sits for about 75,000. If the economic interest of a constituency is a unified one—that is, largely agriculture or industry—the member is, in a sense, a spokesman for an "estate" much as his counterpart was five hundred years ago. Such districts are, however, extremely rare, and the function of the member is correspondingly difficult, since he cannot expect to understand with anything like expertness more than a very few of the interests in his district. In a general way it may be said, then, that Congress is constructed on a system calculated to produce a cross section of public opinion rather than to represent the bewildering variety of special interests affected by law.

Nature of Congress's Functions

It follows from this that the function of our Congress may fairly be described as judicial. Few members are competent to speak with authority on the myriad proposals laid before them by the "interests" into which the general electorate is divided. It is true, of course, that bills are introduced by members and that sometimes the members have an almost expert knowledge of what these bills involve. The more usual situation, however, is that the members sit in judgment on proposals which they do not understand in any precise way but upon which they must reach decisions after hearing the evidence presented. Congress is made up of politicians and ideally, a politician is simply a man of good judgment. He is expected to "size up" the proposals before Congress, to evaluate the evidence presented pro and con, and to know how the suggested law is likely to affect the interests about which he is best informed. Congressional committees have been known to say in effect to groups arguing for and against a bill that, if they can agree on what the bill should contain, the committee will be likely to recommend substantially what they agree upon. Since what is satisfactory to the contending parties is apt to be something like the custom of the trade, even the modern legislature in such an instance is not so much making law as declaring what is already a kind of law for those most immediately concerned.

Much the same may be said about the legislative proposals suggested by executive departments. An administrator's experience is bound to reveal defects in existing statutes, and each session sees a flood of administratively proposed amendments to correct those defects. Essentially, it is the business of Congress to decide whether the suggested changes will actually do what is needed and how they will affect general policy. Many of these measures are scarcely law at all in the true sense. Rather, they are administrative "directives" such as are issued by those in charge of a large business. It is necessary in a democracy that the legislative body keep an eye on such measures, but it is asking too much to expect Congress to be very inventive about them.

All of this means that Congress, with certain exceptions, is not in any important sense an originating body. Most of its members are beyond the age when they have much faith in legislation. In spite of the popular charge that they are meddlesome busybodies, their tendency is to do little or nothing until prodded into action from the outside. As a result, most important legislative proposals begin in a problem, a grievance, or a hope felt by important organized groups, or they come from the administrative branch of the government. It is the proper business of members to bring to bear upon such proposals that wisdom about human affairs which mature life supplies in varying measure to those who make a career of politics. There is no escape from it—democracy means government by politicians. Our hope of improving government lies in improving our politicians or in selecting wiser men in the first place. We can best do this by cultivating wisdom ourselves.

The Structure of Congress

"All legislative powers herein granted," states Article I, Section 1, of the Constitution, "shall be vested in a Congress of the United States, which shall consist of a Senate and House of Representatives." Both the Virginia and the Hamilton plans for a constitution called for a two-house national legislature, while the Paterson plan envisaged a unicameral system. The Constitutional Convention decided upon a bicameral system during the first days of its deliberations.

There are several reasons why the bicameral system was adopted. In the first place, England had a two-house Parliament consisting of Lords and Commons, and this undoubtedly influenced the framers of the Constitution. In the second place, this system was used in the colonies and, more important, by all the states except two. In the third place, the leaders had the idea that there should be a second house where the members would be more experienced and more sophisticated in public affairs. And finally, the two-house system was hit upon as a compromise acceptable to both small and large states.

Bicameralism has steadily lost ground in other countries. In France, legislative power is concentrated largely in the hands of the lower house, while the upper house merely sifts and amends proposed legislation coming from the lower chamber. In England, where the House of Lords once enjoyed considerable prestige, that body has become increasingly insignificant. The act of 1911 stripped the upper house of all power to revise money bills and limited to two years the period during which it could delay the enactment of an ordinary law by the House of Commons. The Labor government in 1949 reduced the period still further, to one year.

Evolution of Congress

It was the evident intention of the framers of the Constitution that the Senate should constitute an executive council to the President, patterned after similar councils which had existed in most of the colonies. It was thus believed that its most important function should be to advise the President on matters such as appointments and treaties and that its legislative function should be secondary. During the early years of Congress most of the important pieces of legislation were introduced in the House, although the Judiciary Act of 1789 was an exception to this rule. The pattern designed by the framers, however, was upset in Washington's term. Although at the beginning of his administration he consulted the Senate frequently, his experience with the Senate as a consultative body was very unsatisfactory, and the time soon came when he ceased to consult it officially and turned to his department heads and to individual Senators for advice.

Today the Senate has become a senior partner in legislation. While the Constitution provides that all revenue measures shall originate in the House, the Senate freely amends such bills, and on occasion has even changed them entirely, retaining only the title of the bill passed by the House. Certainly it was not expected that the Senate would have an equal or even greater voice than the House in legislative matters.

Composition and Basis of Apportionment

The House. The House of Representatives was a rather small body at the beginning but today, with its 435 members, it is large and unwieldy. In 1789 there were 65 members, but Congress has increased its membership after most decennial censuses.[1] There was no reapportionment from 1850 through 1870 or following the census of 1920. After the census of 1910, the membership of the House was increased, for the last time, to 435. In 1929 Congress permanently fixed the membership at that number. At the same time Congress decreed apportionment of Representatives among the states after each census, so that those states which showed considerable gain might receive additional members, and those which showed only slight gain or none at all might either lose Representatives or retain the same number they had after the preceding reapportionment. For instance, California's population increased enormously in the decade from 1940 to 1950 and thus the state was given seven additional members in the House, while the most populous state in the country, New York, lost two.

Although Representatives are apportioned among the states according to population, every state must have at least one member. Under the 1929 act, the Census Bureau prepares a table after each census, showing the population state by state and the number of Representatives each state is entitled to in accordance with a formula of "equal proportion." Each state is first allotted one Representative, and the remaining 387 are divided into the total population to find the quota for each member. This information is sent to Congress by the President and the new apportionment goes into effect, unless Congress is dissatisfied and provides for a new plan.

Qualifications and Election of Members. Members of the House are elected for two-year terms. Candidates are nominated by political parties in direct primaries and the people choose among the nominees and independent candidates on the Tuesday after the first Monday in November of even years.[2]

Under the Constitution, persons who are qualified in the several states to vote for the more numerous branch of the state legislature are qualified

[1] While the Constitution does not expressly provide for reapportionment after each census, it is implied.

[2] In Maine the general election takes place in September.

to vote for members of the House. The qualifications thus are left to the states, but there are those who believe that Congress could, if it chose, determine qualifications. For instance, an anti-poll-tax bill was proposed in Congress and passed the House of Representatives. This measure would have forbidden states which have a poll tax to enforce it in elections for Federal officers.

The Constitution provides that a Representative must be at least twenty-five years of age, seven years a citizen of the United States, and an inhabitant of the state. By usage, he must be a resident of the district which he offers to serve.

The District System. In the early years states were not required to elect Representatives by districts and in some states they were elected from the state at large. An act of 1842 made it mandatory upon all states having more than one Representative to divide the state into districts of "contiguous territory." Acts of Congress in 1901 and 1911 added the proviso that districts be compact. But the requirement that districts be contiguous and compact had little effect. State legislatures continued to gerrymander districts for partisan advantage and in the reapportionment act of 1929 the requirement was omitted.

National law requires each state legislature to redistrict the state after every decennial census, and to establish districts with as nearly equal populations as possible. But the state legislatures have devised various means of redistricting to favor the predominant party. In some states the legislature has declined to redistrict the state over a period of years, with the result that some districts may have several times as many people as others. Thus the legislature of Illinois failed to redistrict the state for over 30 years because it would have increased the representation of the growing city of Chicago at the expense of downstate. If the legislature refuses to redistrict the state, nothing can be done about it; if the state is entitled to additional Representatives, they are elected at large.

Another method whereby redistricting is utilized for partisan advantage is by carving out the districts so that the party in power is able to carry a maximum number of districts with safe majorities. This practice, known as gerrymandering, derives its name from Elbridge Gerry, who was responsible for a redistricting of Massachusetts in 1812 which created one district that resembled a salamander, and was dubbed a "Gerrymander." An examination of the congressional districts today will reveal many with shapes as strange as Elbridge Gerry's salamander district. "Shoestring," "saddlebag," and "dumbbell" districts have been common. One district in California extends over 600 miles in length and is less than 40 miles wide at one point; another district in Los Angeles is said to resemble a poodle dog playing a piano. In some states the majority party has been able to redistrict the state so skillfully that the minority party is unable to elect any members to Congress, even though it may poll as high as 40 per cent of the vote.

Another device is to create a few districts which the opposition party carries by huge majorities, thus concentrating the strength of the opposition in these districts. Another form of misrepresentation found in many states is the use of "rotten boroughs," or districts with very small populations.

Some telling statistics attest the effects of these malpractices on the representative quality of the House of Representatives. While cities had 56.2 per cent of the population of the country in 1930, they had less than one-fourth of the Representatives in the lower house in 1936.[3] Fourteen of the 44 states with more than one Representative had districts among which the largest was over twice as large, population wise, as the smallest.[4]

Attempts to secure relief from unequal representation in Illinois have failed in the courts. Professor Kenneth Colegrove and others brought suit in 1946 in the Federal district court and, failing to secure relief there, appealed to the Supreme Court. In *Colegrove v. Green*[5] the Court held that this was a political question. Justice Frankfurter, speaking for a divided court (3 to 3), said:

Nothing is clearer than that this controversy concerns matters that bring courts into immediate and active relations with party contests. From the determination of such issues this Court has traditionally held aloof. It is hostile to a democratic system to involve the judiciary in the politics of the people.

The Court went on to say that the remedy lay with the Illinois Legislature, with Congress, or ultimately with the people. That certainly gave little consolation to the petitioners. But a vigorous dissenting opinion read by Justice Black, and concurred in by Justices Douglas and Murphy, held that the Court should intervene where a rotten-borough system led to glaring inequalities in the voting weight of citizens and to a denial of the equal protection of the laws.

The district system has many disadvantages. Not only does it lead to gerrymandering, rotten boroughs, and gross misrepresentation of voters but, even worse, it forces congressmen to emphasize local issues to the exclusion of state, national, and international matters, and to be provincial in their outlook. The success or failure of a member is often measured by what he does for his own district. If he gets a new post-office building, a dam, or other public works for his district, he is hailed as a big success. His votes on important national issues, however, such as aid to European

[3] James M. Burns, *Congress on Trial*, p. 52, Harper & Brothers, New York, 1949. Many of these cities, however, are located in districts where rural and not urban interests are dominant.

[4] *Ibid.*, p. 51.

[5] 328 U.S. 549 (1946).

nations or conservation of natural resources, attract little attention. Still another serious defect of the district system is that it greatly restricts the available talent. The inflexible custom of requiring residence in the district operates against the use of a state's best talent. Able and aspiring men are often unable to run for Congress until a vacancy occurs in their district, or they may be permanently excluded because they belong to a party which is hopelessly in the minority in their district.

The Constitution, it should be noted, does not require that members of Congress be residents of the district which they represent. It is only required that they be residents of the state from which they come. Local pride, however, has established the custom that the member of Congress must live in his district. Only in large cities have there been instances of the election of a nonresident. In contrast, in Great Britain it is customary for districts to elect nonresidents to Parliament. A similar rule in this country would unquestionably be desirable, but is quite unlikely to be adopted. Not only would such a plan make for wider use of available talent, but it might also make for a broader horizon for the Representative.

In all fairness some advantages of the custom of requiring Representatives to be residents of their districts must be mentioned. As will be seen later, much of the work of the Representative has to do with personal services for his constituents, and since a Representative of a district has a better opportunity to become acquainted with his constituents, he will be in a better position to render efficient service. Furthermore, by cutting the state up into districts, the diversified interests of the state may get better representation.

The Senate. The Senate is composed of 96 members, two from each state. In accordance with Article V of the Constitution of the United States, no state may, without its consent, be deprived of equal representation in the Senate. Until the passage of the Seventeenth Amendment, the two Senators from each state were elected by the state legislatures in the various states.

For many reasons Senators are freer to follow their independent judgments than Representatives and usually have a broader outlook on national problems. Since the term of a Senator is six years, he is more inclined to vote according to his own convictions on legislation, knowing that votes which are momentarily unpopular may be forgotten by the time of the next election. A Senator has a larger constituency than a Representative, since he represents his entire state rather than a local district, and this makes for a broader horizon. Describing the House of Representatives as "a working body under a singly unifying discipline," Woodrow Wilson said that the Senate on the other hand "is not so much an organization as a body of individuals." He added that "the Senate is as various as the country it represents. It represents the country, not the people; the country in its many diverse sections, not the population of the country." [6] Pointing out further that the House tends more and more to represent concentrated populations in the East and North and hence particular interests, Wilson says that the Senate, on the contrary, "is its indispensable offset, and speaks always in its make-up of the size, the variety, the heterogeneity, the range and breadth of the country, which no community or group of communities can adequately represent." [7]

The Senate represents the states and not just the people. This system of unequal representation was one of the great compromises agreed to in the Constitutional Convention and was necessary to the formation of the Union. Thus we have two Senators from Nevada representing 160,000 people, while only two represent the 15 million people of New York.

The founding fathers had several reasons for the establishment of the Senate. These reasons were set forth by Hamilton in *The Federalist*, No. 62. In the first place, he contended that

. . . a senate, as a second branch of the legislative assembly, distinct from, and dividing the power with, a first, must be in all cases a salutary check on the government. It doubles the security to the people by requiring the concurrence of two distinct bodies in schemes of usurpation or perfidy, where the ambition or corruption of one would otherwise be sufficient. . . . *Second.* The necessity of a senate is not less indicated by the propensity of all single and numerous assemblies, to yield to the impulse of sudden and violent passions, and to be seduced by factious leaders into intemperate and pernicious resolutions.

Hamilton's third reason was that such a body would supply the urgent need for able and experienced legislators. Finally, he contended that the Senate would provide stability in the government. While the turnover of Representatives would be considerable every two years, the Senate with longer terms of six years would experience few changes in personnel. Since only one-third of its members were to be elected every two years, it would be a continuously organized body.

In the past the Senate was often called a millionaires' club. Actually this is not true today even if it once was. While there are several millionaires in the Senate, it is composed for the most part of men of moderate means. In some respects the Senate is more conservative than the House, and because membership in it carries greater prestige, it attracts more able and experienced men.

Contested Elections

The Constitution provides, in Article I, Section 5, that "each House shall be the judge of the elections, returns, and qualifications of its own

---

[6] *Constitutional Government in the United States*, pp. 112–113, Columbia University Press, New York, 1911.
[7] *Ibid.*, p. 117.

members. . . ." As a rule, persons who meet the qualifications fixed by the Constitution are seated without question. Occasionally, however, newly elected members are rejected by the House and Senate. In 1900, Brigham Roberts was refused his seat in the House because he had practiced polygamy, and in 1928 both William S. Vare and Frank L. Smith were rejected by the Senate on the ground that they had spent too much money in getting elected. Theodore Bilbo was not seated after his election to the Senate in 1946 because of the charge that he had intimidated Negro voters in the primary of that year. He died before there was time actually to bring the matter to a vote. The Senate had simply refused to seat Bilbo until the charges had been thoroughly aired.

Although a member of Congress may be expelled by a two-thirds vote of the house to which he belongs, this drastic procedure has rarely been used. In 1951 Senator Benton of Connecticut urged the expulsion of Senator McCarthy, but no action was taken. Each house can punish its members for "disorderly behavior."

Occasionally, but very rarely, censure is resorted to as punishment of a recalcitrant member of Congress. Although the Senate used censure to show its disapproval of a member's conduct only twice before 1954, a select committee was named in that year for the purpose of recommending action on charges brought by Senator Ralph Flanders and others against Senator Joseph McCarthy of Wisconsin. As long as Senator McCarthy attacked outsiders he was not touched by the Senate, but action was taken when he began to abuse fellow Senators. The committee was composed of the following middle-of-the-road Senators of whom three were Republicans and three Democrats: Arthur Watkins of Utah, chairman, and Senators Carlson of Kansas, Stennis of Mississippi, Johnson of Colorado, Case of South Dakota, and Ervin of North Carolina. After several weeks of deliberation, during which the chairman and others refused to be bullied by Senator McCarthy, the committee made a lengthy report (65,000 words) in late September, 1954, recommending censure on two charges and severely taking Senator McCarthy to task on other charges although not to the point of censure. The two charges evoking censure were that McCarthy acted in contempt of the Senate in refusing to furnish information on his finances to the Gillette-Hennings Subcommittee on Privileges and Elections, and that he had abused General Ralph Zwicker during hearings held by McCarthy's subcommittee in February, 1954. When the Senate convened for consideration of the subcommittee's report in November, 1954, McCarthy was condemned by a vote of 67 to 22 on the first count, but the second count was dropped. However, McCarthy was condemned by the same vote on a new charge that he had abused the Watkins Subcommittee and other Senators who had opposed him.

Privileges and Immunities

Compensation and Allowances. Congress determines the salaries and allowances of its members. The present salary is $22,500 a year for both Senators and Representatives. The tax-free expense allowance in force until 1955 was abolished in that year and the entire $22,500 is subject to income tax. All members are also given a travel allowance of 20 cents per mile to and from Washington and their homes. In addition, members may receive pensions at the age of sixty-two if they serve as long as six years, provided they have contributed to a retirement fund. The annual contribution to the fund is $750. It is possible for a member to attain the maximum of $9,375 annually provided he has served 30 years or more. Free stationery is provided for the members and their mail goes postage free. A Representative is allowed $12,500 for the hire of clerical personnel, while a Senator receives $40,000 to $50,000 for this purpose and in addition is allowed an administrative assistant at $10,000 a year.

Immunity from Arrest and Prosecution. The Constitution provides that the Senators and Representatives "shall in all cases, except treason, felony, and breach of the peace, be privileged from arrest during their attendance at the session of their respective Houses, and in going to and returning from the same. . . ." However, under interpretation of the courts this immunity is virtually nonexistent, for it has been held in *Long v. Ansell* [8] that members are not exempt from civil and criminal process. The exceptions of "treason, felony and breach of the peace" have also been so construed as to include all criminal offenses.[9] Professor Corwin has stated that the immunity is no longer of any importance since imprisonment for debt has long since been done away with.

Nevertheless, a member of Congress does enjoy immunity from prosecution for acts committed while performing his legislative duties. Article I, Section 6, specifies that "for any speech or debate in either House, they shall not be questioned in any other place." This immunity covers not only speeches and debates, but written reports, voting, and any other act of a congressman in line with his legislative functions. For libelous remarks made on the floor a member cannot even be held accountable in the courts, even though such remarks were unnecessary from the standpoint of legislative duties.[10] But if such remarks are repeated outside by the member who made them, he is no longer clothed with immunity.

This immunity is abused now and then by members of both houses, and innocent people have been slandered by irresponsible men in Congress

[8] 293 U.S. 446 (1934).
[9] *Williamson v. United States,* 207 U.S. 446 (1908).
[10] *Cochran v. Couzens,* 42 F.2d 783 (1930).

without recourse for the victims. If this abuse continues, it is probable that sooner or later Congress will be forced to take corrective action.

Congressional Personnel

In both houses of Congress lawyers predominate, but there are also a number of farmers, business and professional men. So far, labor has not been well represented. Labor organizations have seldom undertaken in this country to elect their leaders to Congress. In Great Britain many labor officials are elected to Parliament, and in time this is likely to be true of Congress in the United States. Labor organizations watch carefully the voting records of members of Congress and mark them for defeat or return, according to their records. Below is a classification of the members of the Eighty-second Congress according to vocation:

Vocation	Senate	House
Lawyers	62	243
Businessmen	10	71
Press representatives	6	28
Educators	2	24
Labor leaders	0	9
Farmers	9	24
Physicians	0	7
Miscellaneous	7	29
Total	96	435

While members of both houses of Congress are sensitive to public opinion, members of the lower house are generally more so because they come up for election more often and they control less patronage. Because, through senatorial courtesy, a Senator has much to say about important appointments in his state, he establishes a powerful following during his term of office. Thus a Senator is difficult to purge once he has been elected and has entrenched himself, as President Roosevelt discovered in 1938.

There are all kinds of congressmen. There are men of great ability, moderate ability, and mediocre ability. Some are conscientious and hard-working, while others are lazy and indolent. Most members are devoted to the public interest, but a few are political opportunists, willing tools of special interests. A few may accept bribes, but the great majority have high ethical standards. Most members are hard workers and conscientious servants of the people. Many of their failures can be charged up to an outmoded system or to traditions and procedures unsuited to the great tasks facing Congress today.

A Congressman's Day

It has already been emphasized that the average member of Congress works hard. Of course, some work much harder than others. Here is the typical day of an able and conscientious man, Representative Henderson Lanham of the Seventh District of Georgia:

Log of My Activities during a Typical Day,
Tuesday, April 8, 1952

6:15–7:45—Arose, dressed in working clothes, and worked in my flower garden for an hour and a half. Gardening is a hobby, exercise, relaxation, and it keeps me in good physical and mental shape for office responsibilities.

7:45—Breakfast with my family; I discussed the threatened steel strike, a speech by Phillip Murray, and the evening's dinner engagement.

9:03—Arrived at my office and began checking the morning mail.

9:10—Veterans' Administration phoned concerning a pending claim of a veteran-constituent.

9:25—Post Office Department notified me a mail route in my District will be extended 5/10 of a mile.

9:26—Called Representative Tackett for information concerning a bill he had introduced and committee-hearing arrangements.

9:28—Army phoned concerning transfer of station for an enlisted man.

9:39—My secretary called the Radio Room, Old House Office Building, for an appointment for me to make a recording.

9:42—Called a constituent in Douglasville, one of the cities of my District, to notify him of the approved extension of mail route, and to discuss possible relocation of a post office building.

9:45—Foreign Affairs Committee, of which I am a member, called to remind me of a meeting at 10:00.

9:50—A constituent paid a personal visit to my office.

9:52—The Folding Room requested additional franks and envelopes to complete mailing order-forms for farmers' bulletins to rural constituents.

9:55—Left my office to attend meeting of the Agriculture Committee where I urged approval of H.R. 565, which would provide funds for wild-life conservation. From there, I went directly to my Foreign Affairs Committee.

9:56–10:30—My staff continued routine work, among things handled being: phone calls to and from the Army concerning transfer of an enlisted man; to the Army concerning an old application for hardship discharge; to the Navy concerning records review of an enlisted man carried as AWOL, a case in which a lawyer seeks a declaration of death to allow insurance payment to the serviceman's father; and to the VA concerning a scheduled appeal of a veteran's claim. My secretary found time to do some work on my personal scrapbook. Correspondence not requiring personally dictated replies was answered by my staff. Items of possible interest to me, appearing in daily and weekly newspapers in my District, were clipped and placed on my desk for later perusal.

10:44—I returned to my office from my committee meetings and began review of clippings and mail which came in the second delivery of the morning.

10:45—Three bells, the call of the House to meet at 11:00.

10:47—Placed a long distance call to the Chamber of Commerce, Rome, Georgia.

10:48–11:07—Dictation of correspondence of a policy nature or requiring a personal touch.

10:57—Called Bureau of Personnel, Department of the Navy, concerning an old case of an enlisted man.

11:08—Radio Room notified me I could record at 1:00.

11:09—Three bells, quorum call; I went to the House Floor.

11:10—Incoming call concerning change of enlisted man's service records.

11:24 and 11:26—Other incoming calls concerning service personnel.

11:35—Commissioner of Roads and Revenues, and State Senator, Cobb County, called me long distance; calls were transferred to me at the House Cloak-room.

12:55—Returned to my office, picked up prepared speech and mailing labels, and went to Radio Room; completed recording at 1:22 and returned to office.

1:25—Radio Room called that recordings were ready; one of my staff picked them up and mailed them promptly.

1:30—Decided not to take time for lunch, but ate an apple in my office.

1:35—Returned to the Floor and participated in questioning and debate concerning cuts in an appropriation bill for the armed forces.

1:55—Called the Veterans' Administration to express interest in insurance claim of a deceased veteran.

2:02—Called the Army concerning payment of accrued leave of discharged serviceman.

3:30—One bell, tellers call.

3:35—Army called my office to announce approved award of large claim for severance pay of disabled regular Army man.

3:40—A delegation of fifty-four from the Bremen High School, Bremen, Georgia, had me paged on the Floor, where I was throughout the afternoon. I escorted them to the House Gallery for a brief view of the House in action.

3:58—The high-school group visited my office and staff, departing at 4:15.

4:05—A member of my staff went to the office of the Captain of the Guard, Capitol, to retrieve a camera lost by one of the high-school students.

4:08—Excess order blanks for farmers' bulletins returned to my office by the Folding Room.

4:30—Returned to my office to sign daily outgoing correspondence.

4:42—Received telephone request for copies of Intermediate Reports published by the Expenditures Committee's Subcommittee on International Organizations, of which I am the Chairman.

4:48—Received call that lost camera had been returned to its owner.

5:00—Returned to the House Floor. During the afternoon, about 4:15, I had been photographed with a Cotton Queen.

5:46—The House adjourned till 10:00 the next day, and I returned to my office.

5:50—Departed for home, arriving there about 6:20.

6:30—Worked in my garden awhile as a break between the day's activities and the evening's engagements.

7:30—Left home to attend a dinner at the Shoreham Hotel given by the National Conference of Economic and Social Development, at which President

Truman was to have been guest speaker. Because of the steel strike emergency, the President was unable to attend. Secretary of State Acheson discussed assistance to underdeveloped countries. I discussed problems of their respective countries with representatives of Turkey, Brazil, etc.

10:30—Returned home. I listened to the late evening news broadcast and relaxed by listening to musical recordings before retiring about 11:30.

Obviously, a congressman needs to be a god, a nursemaid, an encyclopedia, a diplomat, an administrator, a legislator, a social worker, and a fount of kinetic energy, all rolled into one, and all at a salary of $12,500. If some of our Representatives are found lacking in one or another of these abilities, is it any wonder?

Organization of the House

Organization for Business. Unlike the Senate, the House of Representatives has to be organized anew after each election. Just before the opening of a new Congress on January 3 of odd-numbered years, the members of each party hold a caucus to agree upon a slate of officers whom they will support. When the House convenes on the appointed day, the Clerk of the preceding House presides until the Speaker is elected. Both of the major parties place candidates in nomination for the speakership, but the party having a majority of the membership always succeeds in electing its candidate. The Speaker takes the chair and swears in the members of the House for a new term. The election of minor officers then takes place. A majority spokesman offers a resolution providing that certain persons shall be designated as Clerk, Sergeant at Arms, Doorkeeper, Chaplain, and Postmaster, while a minority spokesman offers a substitute resolution including a slate of minority candidates for the same positions. The matter is put to a vote and the majority candidates are voted in. The House then notifies the Senate and the President that they are ready to do business.

The Speaker. The Speaker is still an important official, but he no longer wields the extensive powers which were vested in the office prior to the revolt of 1910–1911. Until then the Speaker was chairman of the powerful Rules Committee consisting of five members. He appointed all the committees. By virtue of these prerogatives he completely dominated the Rules Committee and exerted a great influence on all other committees. The other two majority members of the Rules Committee were known as the Speaker's assistants. Besides, the Speaker had absolute power of recognition. No one could speak without his approval. But in 1910–1911 a battle to clip the Speaker's wings was led by Representative George Norris. Insurgent Republicans and the Democratic minority joined in this fight and succeeded in taking away his power to appoint the members of committees, took him off the Rules Committee, and reduced his power of recognition. The Speaker is still the head of his party in the House, and at times he steps down from the chair to participate in debate. He continues to have considerable influence in arranging and supervising debate in the House.

The Committee System. Because of the size of the House, most of its work is done in committees. Under the Reorganization Act of 1946, the 48 standing committees of the Seventy-ninth Congress were consolidated into 19. The present standing committees of the House are Agriculture, Appropriations, Armed Services, Banking and Currency, Post Office and Civil Service, District of Columbia, Education and Labor, Government Operations, Foreign Affairs, House Administration, Interior and Insular Affairs, Interstate and Foreign Commerce, Judiciary, Merchant Marine and Fisheries, Public Works, Rules, Un-American Activities, Veterans' Affairs, and Ways and Means.

Whereas a Representative formerly served on as many as three committees, he now serves as a rule on only one, and thus can become better informed on the subjects assigned to that committee. Formally the members of the standing committees are elected by the House, but actually they are hand-picked by a committee on committees in each party. The Democratic members of the Ways and Means Committee, who are selected by the party caucus, constitute the committee on committees for the Democrats. The Republican committee on committees is composed of one member from each state having one or more Republican Representatives, and each member has as many votes as there are Republican Representatives from his state. The Republican Representatives from each state select the member of the committee from their state. The slate picked by each of the committees on committees is reported to the party caucus and invariably ratified. Each party is allotted members on all standing committees according to its proportion of the entire membership of the House. The House then formally approves the selections of the party caucuses.

A visitor may not be favorably impressed with the usual debate in the House because he does not realize that most bills have been thoroughly threshed out in committee. The public hearings conducted by the committees on legislative proposals are generally much more important than the subsequent debates on the floor of the House. On major bills, particularly those that are controversial, the committee hearings may extend over a period of several weeks or even months. In view of the importance of committee work, it is obvious why there is always a scramble for assignments to the major committees such as Ways and Means, Appropriations, Education and Labor, and Armed Forces.

In addition to the regular standing committees, special committees are appointed for a certain specific purpose such as to make an investigation.

Joint committees with members from both houses are utilized less frequently. The Joint Congressional Committee on Atomic Energy is a notable example.

Committee Chairmen. Under the seniority rule the chairmanship goes to the majority Representative who has had the longest continuous service on the committee. This rule lays emphasis on mere age rather than ability, and men who are ill-fitted for the job are occasionally chosen. This can be a serious matter. During World War II, for example, the chairmanship of the Senate Military Affairs Committee went to Senator Reynolds of North Carolina, who was the next in line, although he was not sympathetic with America's war aims. Regardless of which party is in office, the seniority system brings to the chairmanship of some of the powerful committees of each house persons who are not equipped to exercise the leadership needed, and at times persons who are opposed to the program of their party. Much of the criticism of Congress is due to the seniority system and faulty leadership. The chairmanships invariably go to members from "safe" districts; when the Democrats are in power, most of them are accorded to Representatives from the South, and when the Republicans capture control of the House, they go to solidly Republican sections. Regardless of which party is in control, there are large and important areas with few or no chairmanships.

Woodrow Wilson criticized Congress for its lack of unified leadership. Pointing out that the leaders of Congress are the committee chairmen, he decried the fact that "the chairmen of the Standing Committees do not constitute a cooperative body like a ministry. They do not consult and concur in the adoption of homogeneous and mutually helpful measures; there is no thought of acting in concert. Each Committee goes its own way at its own pace." [11] Perhaps the remedy for this situation would be the formation of a council of chairmen in each house which would hold meetings from time to time with the Speaker and majority leader. Some semblance of a unified program might be brought about in this manner.

The Senate's Organization

Since only one-third of the members of the Senate come up for election every two years, it has been continuously in existence since the formation of the government. It is presided over by the Vice-President, or in his absence by a President pro tem. The Vice-President, however, is not necessarily the leader of the majority party, and, in fact, ordinarily has little influence in the deliberations of the Senate. Although he is prominent in his party, he has no voice in debate and votes only in the case of a tie. Tradition requires that his rulings as chairman be impartial.

[11] *Congressional Government,* p. 61, Houghton Mifflin Company, Boston, 1887.

Committee System. There were 33 standing committees in the Senate until 1947, when they were reduced to these 15: Agriculture and Forestry, Appropriations, Armed Services, Banking and Currency, Post Office and Civil Service, District of Columbia, Government Operations, Finance, Foreign Relations, Interstate and Foreign Commerce, Judiciary, Labor and Public Welfare, Interior and Insular Affairs, Public Works, and Rules and Administration.

Each Senator serves on two standing committees. However, majority members of the District of Columbia Committee and of the Committee on Expenditures in the Executive Departments may serve on three committees.

The members of the various standing committees are chosen by a committee on committees from each of the two major parties. The Republican committee on committees is appointed by the chairman of the Republican conference. It is very small and varies in size from time to time. For instance, in the Seventy-sixth Congress it consisted of five members, while in the Eightieth Congress it was composed of eight Senators. This committee picks a slate of Republican nominees for the standing committees of the Senate, and sends it to the Republican conference for approval. The Senate Democratic steering committee constitutes the Democratic committee on committees. The members of the committee are appointed by the Democratic floor leader. The committee meets at the beginning of each new session and selects a slate of Democratic members for each standing committee.[12]

While the standing committees of the Senate are important, their role is somewhat smaller than that of committees of the House. Since the Senate is a much smaller body, its debates are much more meaningful than House debates. Many bills are amended on the floor of the Senate as a result of the debate. Nevertheless, Senate committees perform very important functions and make decisions of some consequence on legislation. Membership on such committees as Foreign Relations, Finance, Armed Forces, and others are much sought after by Senators.

Party Organization

In addition to the official organization of each House of Congress, there is also the unofficial party organization which in some respects plays an even more influential role. At the opening of each new session, the party members in each house meet in a closed caucus or conference to elect officers and to decide upon committee assignments, which are of utmost importance to the members of Congress. It is the invariable practice of

[12] Floyd M. Riddick, *The United States Congress: Organization and Procedure,* pp. 154–158, National Capitol Publishers, Washington, 1949.

each house to accept the committee assignments proposed by the respective party caucuses, and the nominees of the majority party for Speaker of the House and President pro tem of the Senate are always elected.

In each house there is a caucus (or conference, as it is called by the Republicans) of each party, consisting of all members of that party. A Senator or a Representative may often vote against the program of his party, but he remains nevertheless a member of his party's caucus despite his failure to support its policies. The action of Senator Wayne Morse of Oregon in withdrawing from the Republican caucus after he came out for the Democratic candidate for President in 1952 was highly unusual. The principal use made of the party caucus is at the opening of a new session, when it plays a key role in the selection of the officers of each house, and passes on committee assignments. It is also employed from time to time to decide upon party policies with regard to legislation. Formerly it was the rule for each party to hold caucuses before action was taken on any important measure, and members were obligated to carry out the decisions reached in caucus. This practice has fallen into disuse; party caucuses have been held less frequently in recent years, and rarely is any attempt made today to bind members as to how they will vote. The purpose of the caucus or conference today is to enable party members to confer about major legislative policies, to reconcile differences of opinion, and wherever possible to reach agreement which, though not binding, will generally be followed by party members. For many years the Democrats rarely used the party caucus on legislative policies, fearing that no agreement could be reached, while the Republicans made more use of it. This difference was probably due to the fact that the Republicans were less divided on domestic policies than were the Democrats, and hence better able to reach agreement.

Today each party utilizes a policy or steering committee in each chamber, these being in effect executive committees. They consider pending legislation and make recommendations for conference action, and to a considerable extent guide the party officers and individual members in legislative matters. The greatest use of the party-policy committee is to be found in the Senate, where each committee has an official status and its staff is paid out of public funds. The corresponding committees in the House have unofficial status and less use is made of them.

The official spokesman of the party in each chamber is its floor leader, who is elected by the party caucus. Each week while Congress is in session the President customarily consults with the "Big Four"—the Vice-President, the Speaker, and the majority leaders of each house. The majority leader of the Senate, if he can command the support of members of his party, determines to a large extent the order in which legislation will be taken up. He is expected to lead the debate for his party, and he speaks for the administration. When the Republicans came into power in 1953, the late Senator Taft of Ohio, leader of his party in the Senate, became the floor leader. Senator Barkley of Kentucky had earlier been the Democratic floor leader for a number of years before being elected Vice-President.

Formerly the Speaker was the leader of his party in the House and the most powerful officer of Congress. He carried out the decisions reached by the party caucus, and through him the party leadership exercised strong control. Today, the Speaker is still the party leader in the House and as such exerts great influence on the course of legislation, but his power has been considerably curtailed. With the decline of the role of the Speaker, there has been a corresponding decline of the strength of the party. Leadership is so divided that no one really can speak for the party and responsibility is greatly weakened.

The two most powerful members of the House, Republican Joseph W. Martin of Massachusetts and Democrat Sam Rayburn of Texas, have served alternatively as Speaker when their party was in power, and floor leader when it was in the minority. The minority leader is the official spokesman of his party, often leading or guiding the debate. Both majority and minority party leaders appoint assistants, who are known as party "whips." It is their function to round up members when important votes are being taken, to convey to the rank and file of the membership the decisions which have been reached by the party leaders, and also to inform the leaders concerning the attitudes of the members.

Although party alignment is very important in most legislative issues, and is rarely absent when major measures are under consideration, neither party today can control the votes of its members. The typical member of Congress is probably more influenced by what he regards as the interest of his own district, the position of powerful pressure groups, or his own judgment than by the position of his party. On farm issues representatives from agricultural districts of both parties can be counted on to support measures advocated by the leading farm organization, and similarly those from labor districts usually vote prolabor, regardless of whether they are Republicans or Democrats. Many writers have advocated that our party system should be reformed, and that the party leadership in Congress should formulate definite legislative policies for which the party would accept responsibility. It is difficult to see how this can be accomplished, however, without granting to the national party leaders in Congress greater control and discipline over the individual members of the party.

References on Congress are given at the end of Chap. 14.

CHAPTER 13 *Congress: Functions and Powers*

Our American Congress is not exclusively a lawmaking agency. Of course, its chief function is to lay down the broad policies under which the nation carries on its government. But it has other duties as well, some of them of vital significance not only to government but also to individual citizens and groups. A semilegislative function is Congress's role in the amendment of the Constitution. In addition, Congress has judicial, electoral, housekeeping, executive, and administrative functions, including approval of appointments, administrative oversight, and control of the executive branch. Finally, congressmen provide numerous services for their constituents.

Nonlawmaking Functions

Constituent. The first function of Congress, known as the constituent function, relates to the process by which the Constitution may be amended. Amendments may be proposed by both houses of Congress by a two-thirds vote provided a quorum is present, or Congress may call a convention for revision of the Constitution upon application of two-thirds of the state legislatures.

Judicial. Congress is empowered by the Constitution to exercise certain functions of a judicial nature, including impeachment of civil officers and passing upon the elections and qualifications of its own members. A civil officer who is derelict in his duties or guilty of serious crimes or misconduct is subject to impeachment.[1] In such a case, it is the duty of the House of Representatives to draw up an article or articles of impeachment against the erring official. These charges are heard by the Senate, with a committee of the House serving as prosecuting attorneys. Two-thirds of the Senators present must vote for conviction on one or more counts in order

---

[1] The word "impeach" simply means to accuse, so that, strictly speaking, only the charges preferred by the House of Representatives constitute impeachment. The process is comparable to indictment by a grand jury or to an "information" exhibited by a prosecuting attorney.

to remove an official; otherwise he is acquitted. Up to now, only one President—Andrew Johnson—has had impeachment proceedings brought against him. He escaped conviction by the narrow margin of one vote.

The framers of the Constitution regarded the impeachment power as an important one which would be freely used, but the facts have been otherwise. In the entire history of the country, proceedings have been brought against only 12 officers, and only four of these were convicted. Aside from President Johnson, 11 persons have been impeached. Nine cases involved Federal judges, one a member of the Senate, and one the Secretary of War. Experience indicates that this method is too cumbersome to constitute a real protection against the continuance in office of persons who should be removed. Executive officers are generally subject to removal by the President, without the formality of an impeachment proceeding, and military officers may be removed after a trial by court-martial.

The second congressional function of a judicial nature which is provided for in the Constitution is that each house shall be "the judge of the elections, returns, and qualifications of its own members. . . ." This matter is discussed in Chap. 10.

Electoral. Congress has the function, under the Twelfth Amendment, of canvassing the election returns for President and Vice-President. The President of the Senate, in the presence of the Senate and House of Representatives, opens the certificates of the electors and the votes are counted. If no candidate for President has a majority of the electoral votes, then the House of Representatives is directed to choose a President from the three candidates having the largest number of votes. In such a case the vote is taken by ballot, with one vote for each state delegation. A quorum is composed of a member or members from two-thirds of the states.

Rules. Each house adopts its own rules of procedure. It is of interest that the leading early treatise on the rules and procedures was Thomas Jefferson's *Manual of Parliamentary Practice,* which for many years served as the authoritative guide. Jefferson, it will be recalled, served as Vice-President during the term of John Adams. The Rules of the House of Representatives are adopted at the beginning of each new Congress and are usually the same as those of the preceding House,[2] while those of the Senate continue from session to session. Revision of the rules, however, may be undertaken at any time either house sees fit. Each house is empowered to compel the attendance of its absent members and also to punish its members for disorderly conduct.

Executive Functions. The Senate alone exercises certain executive func-

---

[2] The effective Rules of the House, however, consist not only of the so-called "Manual," but of a great mass of precedents drawn from the rulings of successive Speakers. These precedents now fill 11 large volumes and are being added to as novel situations arise in the ordinary work of the House.

tions. Appointments to the cabinet, judgeships, and other major appointments have to be confirmed by the Senate,[3] and all treaties except those of an executive nature must have its consent. When considering such matters, the Senate goes into executive session. Although formerly these sessions were closed to the public, appointments and generally treaties too are now considered in open session.

"*W.R., or Washington Representative.*" Another function performed by all members of Congress, especially members of the House, is that of serving as "W.R., or Washington Representative," as Senator Kefauver calls it. This means that the Representative acts as errand boy for his constituents. Constituents frequently call on members of Congress to take care of personal matters, such as government insurance, allotments, pensions, patents, hospitalization for veterans, securing rooms in a Washington hotel, or a thousand menial services. But no matter how trivial or how menial, the Congressman must respond at once. Some of these tasks now are performed by the secretarial staff or administrative assistant of a Senator, but Representatives are usually their own leg men.

Still, a congressman's function as "Washington Representative" has real importance. In this day of complicated bureaucratic government, citizens need such personal help by someone who "knows his way around." Of necessity, the Federal government has become so complex that the man in the street is generally utterly bewildered by it all. When he has a personal problem involving a government office, upon whom can he call besides the man or woman who represents him in Washington? No one knows how to pull the strings and get the needed service so well as a congressman.

However, the system has serious faults. Members of Congress have testified that as much as 80 per cent of their time is consumed in serving constituents, with only the leavings for their real job of lawmaking. Besides, a good deal of W.R. work is to exert political influence in order to get constituents special consideration or patronage appointments. Such activities smack unappealingly of ward politics.

In 1946 a Joint Committee on the Organization of Congress recommended, among other things,[4] that each Senator and Representative be authorized to hire an administrative assistant to help handle nonlegislative functions. Congress did establish such assistance for Senators but not for Representatives. So the burden of "W.R." has been lifted, at least in part, from senatorial shoulders but its full weight still remains on the members of the lower house.

Control of the Executive. In a democratic system such as ours it is a

---

[3] For a discussion of the Senate's power over Presidential appointments, see Chap. 14.

[4] The joint committee's report is discussed in detail in Chap. 12.

function of the legislative branch of the government to exercise a certain amount of control over the executive branch. This is to say that the executive branch is responsible to the legislature. But Congress is unable, even if it desired, to make a constant check of the work of the numerous administrative offices and agencies that constitute the executive branch of the government under the President. Members of Congress as individuals either have too much work to do or they lack the technical knowledge necessary to supervise closely these agencies and departments. Nor are committees of Congress equipped and staffed to do it. Congress must look elsewhere for aid in checking up on expenditures and for close and continuous supervision of administration. Accordingly, it has provided for a Comptroller General to keep track of expenditures and the courts have been given the power to review administrative rules and regulations.

One way in which Congress checks the executive branch is by control of the purse. It appropriates funds and levies taxes. The executive department is thus dependent upon Congress for funds with which to operate. While the President recommends an annual budget prepared by the Budget Director and his corps of assistants, Congress has the actual fiscal power. "He who controls the purse, controls the nation," so it is said. In the past, Congress often deliberately underappropriated funds for various agencies, in order to force them to come back for more money and thus to subject themselves again to legislative scrutiny before the year was out. The result was large deficiency appropriations. Recently, Congress has tightened up on deficiencies, and it is now a serious offense for an agency to overspend its funds without authorization.

The control of the purse is a basic power of Congress and all legislative bodies. But there is no effective over-all review of the budget by Congress at any time. Reviewing procedures are not well adapted to a budget of the present magnitude. Besides, the appropriations committees spend too much time on detailed items and too little time on the over-all picture. There are a dozen or more regular appropriation bills, as well as numerous special ones; expenditures are considered by numerous committees and subcommittees, each operating quite independently of the others; revenues are considered by another set of committees; and all committees of Congress act on bills which authorize the spending of money. The result is that responsibility in Congress for the fiscal affairs of the government is hopelessly divided. At the same time there is every inducement in the present system for individual members to go after appropriations of interest to their own districts. One of the common popular fallacies is that Congress is economy-minded; actually, it is quite the other way around, despite the usual fulminations about the need for cutting government spending.

Various reforms of the Federal budget system have been proposed. These include the use of a single or omnibus appropriation bill instead of a series of independent bills. Proponents of this change assert that it would lead to a consideration of the entire Federal budget at one time, instead of by piecemeal action. In 1950 all the regular appropriations were consolidated into a single bill, but the results did not live up to expectations, and the plan was abandoned the next year. The Presidential item veto has been urged for many years by students of public finance on the ground that it would enable the President to veto pork-barrel items of little merit, but the proposal has received meager support in Congress. Another proposal has been for Congress to set up its own budget agency to parallel the Bureau of the Budget. A bill of this kind has passed the Senate twice in recent years but failed in the House. Two budget bureaus in the place of one would hardly be an improvement, would in fact lead to worse confusion. The path of true reform lies in the direction of establishing more definite responsibility for federal financial policies, of curtailing pork-barrel expenditures, and bringing about more effective cooperation between the President and congressional leaders.

More recently the greatest offender in encroachment on the powers of the executive has been the Subcommittee of the Senate Committee on Government Operations, better known as the McCarthy committee. Since the Republicans came into power Senator Joseph McCarthy has become head of this subcommittee and has taken the play away from the House Un-American Activities Committee. He has become so aggressive that there is now a widespread demand that the activities of such committees be curbed.

Due to his concern about the usurpation of executive powers by the McCarthy subcommittee investigating government operations, President Dwight D. Eisenhower issued an order on May 17, 1954, to Secretary of Defense Wilson directing that he instruct his employees to refrain from quoting high-level conversations or communications in the Department in their testimony before the subcommittee. This statement was issued after an exhaustive study and report had been made to the President by Attorney General Brownell. In the course of his order, President Eisenhower said: [5]

It has long been recognized that to assist the Congress in achieving its legislative purposes every executive department or agency must, upon the request of a congressional committee, expeditiously furnish information relating to any matter within the jurisdiction of the committee, with certain historical exceptions —some of which are pointed out in the attached memorandum from the Attorney General. This administration has been and will continue to be diligent in following this principle. However, it is essential to the successful working of our system that the persons entrusted with power in any one of the three great branches of Government shall not encroach upon the authority confided to the others. The

[5] See *Congressional Record*, Vol. 100, No. 90, pp. 6263–6264.

ultimate responsibility for the conduct of the executive branch rests with the President.

Within this framework each branch should cooperate fully with each other for the common good. However, throughout our history the President has withheld information whenever he found that what was sought was confidential or its disclosure would be incompatible with the public interest or jeopardize the safety of the Nation.

The President went on to direct that employees in the Department of Defense not only refrain from testifying before the subcommittee as to high level conversations and conferences, but also not produce documents relating to these matters. This, he said, he was doing in the interest of "efficient and effective administration."

The President added: "I direct this action so as to maintain the proper separation of powers between the executive and legislative branches of the Government in accordance with my responsibilities and duties under the Constitution. This separation is vital to preclude the exercise of arbitrary power by any branch of the Government."

In his report, Attorney General Brownell pointed out that precedents had been established beginning with Washington and running down to the present day in which the President had refused to allow information to be divulged by any of the executive departments that was of a highly confidential nature and that might endanger the safety of the nation. Citation after citation was made by Brownell where the President had refused to divulge information of this sort.

The Eisenhower order upset the subcommittee investigating the difficulties between McCarthy and the Army. In fact it so upset the subcommittee that it suspended hearings for an entire week. During this time McCarthy demanded that the President revoke his order, but he was unsuccessful. Finally the hearings were resumed as the order stood.

Power to Investigate. A function which has become more and more important in recent years is Congress's power to investigate any matter which it considers pertinent to the welfare of the nation or the operation of the government.

"It is the proper duty of a legislative body," said Woodrow Wilson, "to look diligently into every affair of government and to talk much about what it sees. It is meant to be the eyes and the voice and to embody the wisdom and will of its constituents." [6]

Through its investigative power, Congress has reached not only into government agencies but into many organizations and many homes as well. It has commanded powerful publicity in the nation's newspapers and mag-

[6] Woodrow Wilson, *Congressional Government,* p. 303, Houghton Mifflin Company, Boston, 1887.

azines and on radio and television. Many political fortunes have been made or lost. The reputations of countless individuals have been hopelessly besmirched; some reputations have been enduringly brightened. Many a government program of national or international significance has been doomed or raised to importance through a congressional investigation.

A congressional investigation may be touched off, say, by widespread criticism of the work of some agency, such as the Reconstruction Finance Corporation. Congress usually assigns the job by resolution to a committee, most often a Senate committee. Most of these investigations are very useful, for the purpose usually is to seek information which Congress may use in legislation to correct the evils which have been laid bare. During World War II, the Truman committee rendered yeoman service in keeping a close check on war contracts and bringing to light unsavory practices. In 1950 and 1951 a committee investigating corrupt practices in the RFC likewise rendered a worthwhile service.

In investigations, witnesses may be called and required to testify under oath. A witness who refuses to testify or to produce records may be punished for contempt. This power of Congress was upheld in *McGrain v. Daugherty* [7] when the Court, with Justice Van Devanter speaking, said in part:

We are of the opinion that the power of inquiry—with process to enforce it— is an essential and appropriate auxiliary to the legislative function. It was so regarded and employed in American legislatures before the Constitution was framed and ratified. Both Houses of Congress took this view of it early in their history—the House of Representatives with the approving votes of Mr. Madison and other members whose service in the convention which framed the Constitution give special significance to their action—and both houses have employed the power accordingly up to the present time.

While the investigative function has, on the whole, been useful, still it has been abused. The best instance is the House Committee on Un-American Activities. Known as the "Dies committee" at the beginning (named for Martin Dies, its chairman), it has been made a standing committee of the House. In a period of over 10 years it has produced little or no legislation except a "rider" attached to an appropriation bill, the purpose of which was to eliminate three men from the payroll. In *United States v. Lovett* [8] the Supreme Court declared the rider to be an act of attainder and therefore unconstitutional.

Investigation is a proper function of Congress, yet all investigations should be conducted with a due regard for the rights of individuals. Certainly these committees should not be used for the purpose of forwarding

[7] 273 U.S. 135 (1927).
[8] 328 U.S. 303 (1946).

the political ambitions of any member or members at the expense of private citizens. When a committee allows reputations of citizens to be ruined by permitting unsupported rumors and charges to be aired, does not allow an accused person to be heard, and permits a chairman to make reports which the committee members have not seen, it is time to call a halt. Even though an accused may be heard, his answers may never catch up with the malicious charge. In contrast to the conduct of such committees as the Committee on Un-American Activities, it is somewhat reassuring to note that the Kefauver committee which investigated organized crime followed procedures which were more becoming the dignity of such a committee. Accused individuals were invariably allowed to be heard. Nevertheless, the televising of the proceedings has been criticized by bar associations and others not only as an encroachment on an individual's liberty but also for making a show out of what should be a serious, decorous investigation to ascertain facts.

It would appear that the Committee on Un-American Activities has clearly usurped the judicial power, for it has attempted to try suspected persons, not to investigate facts. Many people of good reputation have been seriously damaged by this committee. It is high time that Congress reconsider its function of investigation and that this device be restricted to legitimate purposes only. The proper place to try a person for crimes is in the courts, not in the Congress. Congress already has before it legislation which would lay down rules for the conduct of committee investigations, in order to eliminate some of the abuses.

Lawmaking

Overshadowing all other functions is Congress' responsibility for legislation. The procedures to be followed before a bill becomes a law are laid down in the Rules of the House of Representatives and of the Senate, discussed in detail in Chap. 12.

Congress shares its legislative power with the President, for the Constitution provides that "he shall from time to time give to the Congress information of the state of the Union, and recommend to their consideration such measures as he shall judge necessary and expedient." The President is also authorized to call special sessions of Congress and to adjourn both houses in case of disagreement between them "to such time as he shall think proper." Furthermore, the President may veto a bill passed by Congress and this may be overridden only by a two-thirds vote of both houses.

At times the Executive has exercised a powerful influence over legislation, notably in the administrations of strong presidents like Theodore Roosevelt, Woodrow Wilson, and Franklin D. Roosevelt. All three felt that Congress needed leadership and guidance and did their vigorous best to provide it. Wilson revived the practice of going before Congress in person

to deliver his message, thus materially helping to win support for his legislative program. Franklin D. Roosevelt also made personal appearances
before Congress and resorted to direct appeals to the people in "fireside
chats" over the radio. Not only did he suggest legislation, but he often had
drafts of proposed laws prepared by his staff and by the departments for
introduction by friendly congressmen. Certain important administrative
measures were called "must" legislation, and the President exerted strong
pressure on the Congress to secure their adoption. This practice was bitterly
attacked by those who were opposed to the New Deal, and was resented by
many members of Congress.

The various executive departments also propose legislation to Congress
from time to time. Departmental drafts are sent to the chairmen of the
committees concerned. Congress has been a willing tool in this exercise of
the legislative function by the executive departments. Administrative problems have become more and more complicated and technical, and naturally
Congress looks to the administrative agencies for assistance in shaping and
planning legislation to deal with these problems. Many of the committees
refer bills to the appropriate departments for advice and guidance, and a
bill is rarely reported favorably unless the department has given it the
green light.

In order to prevent confusion, as well as to secure better results, a Division of Legislative Reference was set up in the Bureau of the Budget during the administration of Franklin Roosevelt. It acted as a clearing house
for proposed measures from the various departments in an effort to bring
them into harmony with the President's program. Committee chairmen
often consult this agency about legislative proposals.

These various practices are resented in some quarters of Congress.
Members dislike being relegated to the role of "rubber stamps" who merely
review and approve or disapprove of proposals by the Executive. It is one
thing, these critics reason, to make suggestions to Congress, but it is improper to send ready-made measures down to Congress. The function of
drafting laws belongs to members of Congress, not to departments and
bureaus, the dissenters reason. According to this view, the chief reason why
Congress has suffered this indignity is that it has had inadequate bill-
drafting assistance, while the Executive has had ample legal assistance for
this purpose.

Still Congress has not entirely yielded up its right to draft legislation.
Reports of legislative counsel in both houses indicate that a large portion
of bill drafting is now done by their staffs. For instance, in the Seventy-
eighth Congress, 50 per cent of all bills and joint resolutions introduced in
the Senate had been drafted by the Senate Legislative Counsel, while the
Legislative Counsel of the House drafted 23 per cent of the public bills and

resolutions, 21 per cent of the private bills, 36 per cent of the concurrent resolutions, and 14 per cent of the simple resolutions." [9]

The increasing delegation of sublegislative powers to executive departments and regulatory commissions has led some critics to deplore this trend as a derogation of the legislative function. This complaint has been voiced by such outstanding leaders as the late Senator Robert M. LaFollette, Jr., and Representative Howard Smith of Virginia. Nevertheless, this is an inevitable trend in view of the increasing volume and complexity of legislation.

The assertions that the President and the executive departments have usurped the legislative function are obviously exaggerated. After all, the President was expressly given important legislative powers by the Constitution. The President is the only Federal official who is elected by the entire country, the only possible spokesman for everyone. If he proves to be a good leader the President, in consultation with his party leaders in Congress, will develop a constructive program of legislation in the national interest which, as a rule, should be assured of generally favorable action by Congress. Since members of Congress represent at most only small segments of the population, they often cannot see the forest for the trees.

Furthermore, there is something to be said for the practice of sending legislative proposals from executive departments to Congress for acceptance or rejection. Heads of departments are often in a better position to judge legislative needs than members of Congress. There is no danger of usurped authority so long as Congress has the power freely to accept, reject, or revise departmental measures. The final decision after all rests with Congress, and if proposals are put into the hopper and hastily passed, the fault lies with Congress and not with department heads.

The Powers of Congress

Some, but by no means all, of the powers of Congress are expressly granted, in so many words, by the Constitution. But certain important powers are merely implied in the Constitution; or they result from other powers. Some congressional powers are exclusive, while some are shared with the states. A number of these implied or resultant powers were "discovered" years after the establishment of the Constitution, found by congressional explorers in response to some pressing legislative need of the times. In the determination of whether or not these were, indeed, legitimate powers the Supreme Court has played a key role. Almost invariably, congressional experimentation with "new" powers has been subjected to Court scrutiny in the form of a test case. Sometimes the Court, having de-

[9] George B. Galloway, *Congress at the Crossroads*, p. 9, The Thomas Y. Crowell Company, New York, 1946.

livered a negative opinion, has been asked again to pass on Federal use of the same power. In some instances, the passage of time or a change in Court personnel has had the desired effect and the Court has reversed itself, declaring valid the use of a power which once it had declared invalid. Some of the newer powers are immensely significant in dealing with the problems which modern times have thrown upon the national government.

Express Powers. In Article I, Section 8, of the Constitution, a number of powers are expressly conferred on Congress. These include the power to tax, regulate interstate and foreign commerce, borrow money on the credit of the United States, "establish a uniform rule of naturalization, and uniform laws on the subject of bankruptcies throughout the United States," coin money and fix the standard of weights and measures, provide for the punishment of counterfeiting, establish post offices and post roads, regulate patents and copyrights, create courts, declare war, raise and support armies, provide and maintain a navy, and legislate for the District of Columbia and other Federal territories. Some of these powers are capable of considerable expansion by interpretation of the courts. Particularly is this true of the spending power, the taxing power, and the commerce power.

The Taxing and Spending Powers. Article I of the Constitution provides: "The Congress shall have power to lay and collect taxes, duties, imposts, and excises, to pay the debts and provide for the common defense and general welfare of the United States." The last clause was long a subject of controversy. James Madison held to the narrow view, insisting that it merely referred to the powers enumerated in the subsequent clauses of the same section. In contrast, Hamilton believed that the clause conferred a power separate and distinct from those later enumerated, and that Congress was thus given a substantive power to tax and to appropriate, limited only by the requirement that when the power is exercised it must be for the general welfare of the United States. Justice Story held to the Hamiltonian view. Professor Edward S. Corwin contends that the power of Congress over expenditures is unlimited.[10] In *United States v. Butler,* the Supreme Court upheld the views of Hamilton and Justice Story.[11] The validity of the tax imposed by the Social Security Act on employers of eight or more was challenged by an Alabama corporation in *Steward Machine Company v. Davis.*[12] Insisting that the problem of unemployment came under the general-welfare clause, the Court upheld the tax:

To draw the line intelligently between duress and inducement, there is need to remind ourselves of facts as to the problem of unemployment. . . . The

[10] Edward S. Corwin, "Spending Power of Congress," *Harvard Law Review,* Vol. 36, p. 548, 1923.
[11] 297 U.S. 1 (1936).
[12] 301 U.S. 548 (1937).

problem had became national in area and dimensions. There was need of help from the nation if the people were not to starve. It is too late today for the argument to be heard with tolerance that in a crisis so extreme the use of the moneys of the nation to relieve the unemployed and their dependents is a use for any purpose narrower than the promotion of the general welfare.

In *Helvering v. Davis*,[13] second social-security case, the Court underlined the same view.

The question of what measures will promote the general welfare is, as a rule, determined by Congress and not by the courts. Thus, as we understand it today the power of Congress to levy taxes and to spend money to promote the general welfare is very broad. New national powers hitherto untapped are opened up here.

Broad powers to regulate through the use of Congress' taxing power have also been upheld by the Supreme Court in a number of cases. The taxing power and the commerce power are the basis of what has been called "Federal police powers."

In *McCray v. United States*[14] the Court upheld an act of Congress which provided for a tax of 10 cents per pound on yellow oleomargarine. This tax virtually prevented the sale of yellow oleomargarine, but it was justified by the Court on the ground that it eliminated fraud, since oleomargarine could be colored to look like butter. And in *United States v. Doremus*[15] the Supreme Court declared valid a tax levied on narcotics. Here the Court said that the act could not be declared invalid merely because another motive than taxation, not shown on the face of the act, might have contributed to its passage. In both these cases, the purpose of Congress in levying taxes was not merely to raise revenue, but to regulate the sale of oleomargarine and narcotics.

These are limits, however, beyond which the Supreme Court will not sanction regulation in the guise of taxation. When Congress attempted to regulate child labor by taxing the profits of manufacturing concerns employing children, the Court held the act null and void on the ground that Congress was exercising the power to regulate manufacture under the guise of a tax.[16] Still, regulation through use of the taxing power offers many possibilities for expansion of the powers of Congress.

The Commerce Power. In the earlier days of our history, when our economy was highly localized, the power of Congress to regulate commerce was unexploited. Congress legislated only with regard to trade and intercourse across state boundaries and not with regard to intrastate commerce

[13] 301 U.S. 619 (1937).
[14] 195 U.S. 27 (1904).
[15] 249 U.S. 86 (1919).
[16] But Congress *may*, as will be seen below, regulate manufacture under its commerce power.

or regulation of manufacture. As our economy expanded and became national in scope, Congress discovered more facts in its power to regulate commerce. So we find the Supreme Court holding in the Shreveport Case that the power to regulate interstate commerce carries the power to regulate intrastate commerce, where the latter bears a substantial relation to the former. And although in 1918 the Supreme Court was not ready to declare that the power to regulate commerce included the power to regulate manufacture,[17] by 1937 this authority was upheld.[18] Today the power to regulate commerce includes the power to regulate manufacture as well as labor relations where the products are destined for interstate commerce.

Most of the recent Federal legislation dealing with industry, business, finance, agriculture, and labor has been grounded in the power granted to Congress to regulate commerce. Under the New Deal, Congress went beyond even the fondest hopes of Chief Justice Marshall in the exercise of this power; with only a few major exceptions, the courts have upheld Congress. Several cases will bear out this point. In *National Labor Relations Board v. Jones and Laughlin Steel Co.*,[19] the constitutionality of the National Labor Relations Act of 1935 guaranteeing collective bargaining was challenged. It was contended that the act invaded the reserved powers of the states, in that it attempted to regulate all industry, and that industrial relations and activities in manufacturing are not subject to federal regulation. In upholding the act the Court justified Congress by pointing out: "The steel industry is one of the great basic industries of the United States, with ramifying activities affecting interstate commerce at every point."

In a similar case, *United States v. Darby Lumber Co.*,[20] the constitutionality of the Fair Labor Standards Act of 1938, prescribing minimum wages and maximum hours in business engaged in commerce, was challenged. No concern covered by the act could ship goods beyond the state's bounds unless it abided by the act. The main question was whether Congress had the constitutional power to prohibit the shipment in interstate commerce of lumber manufactured by employees who were not receiving the benefits prescribed by the act. Reversing an earlier decision, the Court held that goods produced under substandard labor conditions could be barred from interstate commerce.

"While manufacture is not of itself interstate commerce," said the Court, "the shipment of manufactured goods interstate is such commerce and the prohibition of such shipment by Congress is indubitably a regulation of commerce. . . .

"Congress, having by the present Act adopted the policy of excluding from in-

---

[17] *Hammer v. Dagenhart*, 247 U.S. 251 (1918).
[18] *National Labor Relations Board v. Jones & Laughlin Steel Co.*, 301 U.S. 1 (1937).
[19] *Ibid.*
[20] 312 U.S. 100 (1941).

terstate commerce all goods produced for the commerce which do not conform to the specified labor standards, it may choose the means reasonably adapted to the attainment of the permitted end, even though they involve control of intrastate activities."

And the Court went on to say that Congress has full power "to exclude any article from interstate commerce subject only to the specific prohibition of the Constitution." It is now clear that the power of Congress to regulate commerce includes the power to regulate the incidents of commerce.[21]

Implied Powers. Article I, Section 8, of the Constitution, which provides that Congress shall have the power "to make all Laws which shall be necessary and proper for carrying into execution the foregoing powers," has been held to grant what have become known as implied powers. These powers are second only in importance to the express or delegated powers. It was Chief Justice Marshall, a broad constructionist, who discovered the great possibilities of the necessary-and-proper clause of the Constitution and made them available to future Congresses by his judgment in the case of *McCulloch vs. Maryland.*[22]

Opposed to this broad view were the strict constructionists, foremost among whom was Thomas Jefferson. Holding to the narrow view of the necessary-and-proper clause, Jefferson said:

I consider the foundation of the Constitution as laid on this ground: That all powers not delegated to the United States, by the Constitution, nor prohibited by it to the States, are reserved to the States or to the people. To take a single step beyond the boundaries thus specially drawn around the powers of Congress, is to take possession of a boundless field of power, no longer susceptible of any definition.

This is the states' rights or strict constructionist view of the implied powers, as opposed to the nationalist or broad constructionist view of Marshall and the Federalists. For good or ill, events have shown that Jefferson was wrong. The personal prestige of Marshall and his long tenure of office conspired with the needs of a growing economy to make broad construction the dominant rule in our constitutional law. Charles A. Beard expressed it vividly when he referred to the necessary-and-proper clause

---

[21] There are a few other cases that show how broad and inclusive the commerce power is. In *United States v. South Eastern Underwriters Association,* 322 U.S. 533 (1944), a decision of 75 years standing, *Paul v. Virginia,* 8 Wall. 168 (1869), was overturned; thus the fire-insurance business has now been declared to be commerce. And in *United States v. Appalachian Electric Co.,* 311 U.S. 377 (1940), the power of Congress to regulate watershed developments and flood control was asserted. Furthermore, the power to regulate agriculture, denied under the taxing and spending power in *United States v. Butler,* was upheld in *Mulford v. Smith,* 307 U.S. 38 (1939), as a proper exercise of the commerce power.

[22] 4 Wheat. 316 (1819).

as "a Pandora's box of wonders under the light shed by the expansive imagination of Chief Justice Marshall."

Resultant Power. Of far less importance is the resultant power of Congress. This may best be described as plural implied power, since it results from the implications of a number of enumerated powers. This power was upheld in *United States v. Gettysburg Electric Co.*[23] when the Court held that Congress had the right to pass a law providing for acquisition of land at Gettysburg for the purpose of establishing monuments and the like. This power the Court found by implication under the war and taxing powers, saying, "Any number of these powers may be grouped together, and an inference from them all may be drawn that the power claimed has been conferred."

Although the Supreme Court has given a broad interpretation of the powers granted to Congress, it has never held that there is an emergency power apart from those contained in the Constitution. "Emergency does not create power," said the Court in *Home Building and Loan Association v. Blaisdell;*[24] neither does an emergency add to the powers granted in the Constitution, nor does it curtail the limitations on the exercise of power. It is true that Congress can find the powers necessary to meet an emergency, but they must be clearly inferred from the Constitution.

References on Congress will be found at the end of Chap. 14.

[23] 160 U.S. 668 (1896).
[24] 290 U.S. 398 (1934).

CHAPTER 14 *Congress: A Going Concern*

The Legislative Process

Before a bill introduced in Congress becomes a law it must traverse a long and complicated route. Most of the thousands of bills introduced at each session never make it. They are lost at some point or other of the tortuous way. Some emerge, but so transformed that their progenitors can hardly recognize them. Some start the journey session after session, and only come to the finish line years or even decades after they made the original attempt.

Some of the bills that fail to pass are of great importance; but because of strong opposition they are sidetracked and killed. Some good bills are so amended and watered down in the legislative mill that they are worthless when finally enacted. The large majority are pigeonholed by the committees to which they are referred. Naturally many of the bills proposed deserve little or no consideration.

The Stages of a Bill

The fact that it is so difficult to get a bill through to passage, in its original or any other form, is not entirely a liability to good government. There is much to be said for the trial by democratic fire which proposed legislation must survive. Many people believe that we have too many laws as it is, that our citizens suffer from an inability to find their way through the maze of congressional directives and pronunciamentos. The months or years which it takes for someone's good idea to become transmuted into a law of the land can provide an opportunity for the idea to become refined, popularized, and tested by public opinion.

On the other hand, the process is maddeningly deliberate when an emergency seems to be at hand. However, it has been shown that strong leaders in the Presidency and in Congress usually know how to expedite legislation when they feel that haste is sufficiently important.

Initiation. Let us suppose that a bill is introduced by Representative

John Smith in the House of Representatives, providing for a 3 per cent tax on the sale of all cosmetics. The bill is dropped into the "hopper" (actually a basket) at the clerk's desk. While the power to refer bills is vested in the Speaker, the Parliamentarian normally makes the assignment; if there is an issue, however, the Speaker decides.[1] Before the bill goes to the committee it is given a number (H.R. 100, let us say), a record is made of its introduction and of the date submitted, and then it is printed. The title of the bill is printed in the *Journal* and *Congressional Record* and this satisfies the requirements of Rule 21 for a first reading.[2]

If a bill is introduced in the Senate, the person who introduces it rises and gets recognition of the chair and then sends the bill to the Secretary's desk.[3] If there is no objection the bill is read by the legislative clerk by title only. The bill must lie over for a day if there is objection to an immediate second reading. No bill can be referred to a committee until after the second reading. The Senator introducing the bill usually indicates his preference as to the committee to which the bill is to be referred; the presiding officer actually designates the committee. After a bill has been referred to a Senate committee it is given a number (S. 150, for example) and is entered in the bill book and in the Senate Journal for the day. On the day following, printed copies of the bill are delivered to the office of the Secretary, and to the document rooms of both houses.[4]

Committee Consideration. When printed copies of H.R. 100 come to the clerk of the Committee on Ways and Means, it is placed on the list of bills pending before that committee and is then ready for consideration. Because of the great number of bills introduced, it is impossible for all of them to be considered, and unless H.R. 100 is highly regarded by the chairman of the committee or has strong support, the chances are it will never be taken up. As a bill of considerable importance, it would be referred to a subcommittee designated by the chairman, and public hearings would be conducted. If a majority of the committee decide in favor of the bill, it is reported out with a recommendation that it be passed. Ordinarily it is accompanied by a printed report giving an account of the bill, its history, purposes, and the arguments in its favor. It is not uncommon for majority and minority reports to be submitted. Before the bill is acted

[1] The introducer of a bill is always eager to have it referred to a committee which will be friendly, and often there is a neat bit of strategy in drawing the bill so that it can be referred to a favorable committee. The most favorable situation obtains when the bill is introduced by the chairman of the committee to which it is referred, thus almost assuring favorable consideration.

[2] Every bill must be read three times in both houses before passage.

[3] A money bill cannot originate in the Senate.

[4] Even though a bill originates in the President's office or in a government department, a member of the House or of the Senate must introduce it. Usually bills coming from an executive department go directly to the committee concerned and are introduced by the chairman or a member of the committee.

on by the committee, however, it is carefully reviewed to see that it has been properly prepared, and in most cases it will be considerably revised by the committee, with the aid of its own staff and the Legislative Counsel. If the decision is negative, the bill is not reported out by the committee, but is laid on the table or pigeonholed. In rare instances a bill may be reported to the legislative body with a negative report. The amended bill and the report are now printed.

After a bill has been assigned to a committee for 30 days or more without action, a member of the House may file a petition to discharge the committee from further consideration. This requires the signatures of 218 members.[5] Such petitions may be presented before the House on specified days, and if a majority of those present vote favorably, the bill is taken up. In such a case the bill may be given a privileged position and be brought to the House floor for consideration at once, or it may be placed on the proper calendar.

Bill Placed on Calendar. H.R. 100, having been favorably reported by the Ways and Means Committee, is now placed on the calendar to await its turn, provided it is not given a special order for immediate consideration. Under the Rules of the House (Rule 13, House Manual, 1953) there are five calendars:

"First. A calendar of the Committee of the Whole House on the State of the Union, to which shall be referred bills raising revenue, general appropriation bills, and bills of a public character directly or indirectly appropriating money or property.

"Second. A House calendar, to which shall be referred all bills of a public character not raising revenue nor directly or indirectly appropriating money or property.

"Third. A calendar of the Committee of the Whole House, to which shall be referred all bills of a private character."

The other calendars are the Consent Calendar and the Discharge Calendar. Bills placed on the Consent Calendar may be called up on the first and third Mondays of each month by unanimous consent. The Discharge Calendar is the one where motions to discharge a committee from consideration of a bill are placed.

Since H.R. 100 is a revenue measure, it would be placed on the Calendar of the Committee of the Whole House on the State of the Union. A revenue bill enjoys precedence and may be taken up out of turn. Should the Rules Committee consider the bill of great importance and deserving of immediate consideration, the committee could obtain a special rule to that effect. Such a rule would prescribe the terms under which the bill is to be

[5] The discharge rule is rarely used. It is difficult to secure the signatures of 218 members to such a petition, for there is a strong tradition against taking a bill away from a committee to which it has been assigned.

considered and a time limit for debate. Suppose H.R. 100 is given a special rule and the limit for debate is fixed at six hours.

Consideration by Committee of the Whole House. In considering a revenue bill, the House resolves itself into the Committee of the Whole House; the Speaker names a chairman to preside, and withdraws from the chair. Here the procedure is more informal than in a plenary session of the House. A quorum is only 100, whereas a plenary session requires 218.

General debate on H.R. 100 [6] now takes place. The rule usually divides the time equally between the chairman of the Ways and Means Committee and the ranking minority member of the committee who leads the opposition. Each of the two leaders allots time to other members as he sees fit. After the expiration of the time allotted for general debate, the bill is read for amendments under the five-minute rule. The sponsor of an amendment has five minutes to discuss his amendment, and the first person to get recognition may speak for the same length of time in opposition. This is the procedure for consideration: the Committee of the Whole House rises and reports to the Speaker, who now resumes the chair.

The Speaker then puts the question: Shall the bill be passed to a third reading and engrossment? Usually at this time each side is permitted to offer one of two motions, either to amend or to refer the bill back to the standing committee for further consideration. The adoption of either motion in effect kills the bill. On such motions, the roll call, which is not permitted in the Committee of the Whole House, may be demanded. In some instances, members reverse their votes when a roll-call vote is taken, as they then have to go on record. If the vote is in the affirmative, the bill is read by title only. The Speaker then puts the question of final passage of H.R. 100.

H.R. 100 may now be debated and amended further, unless the previous question is ordered, in which event the bill is voted on immediately. The Speaker, rising, says: "As many as are in favor say 'Aye,'" and when those in the affirmative have expressed themselves, the Speaker says, "As many as are opposed say 'No.'" If a division is called for, the Speaker may ask those who favor to rise and stand until counted. Should tellers be ordered, the members favoring as well as those opposing will be requested to file up the aisles between tellers and be counted. One-fifth of the membership may order a roll call, in which case those who favor say "Yea" when their names are called by the Clerk, while those opposing say "Nay."

About 90 per cent of the bills in the House go through the Committee of the Whole. Those bills not requiring consideration by the Committee of the Whole are read the second time in full and are then debated and amended. The third reading is by title only. Actually bills are never read,

[6] The reading actually is by title only.

as required by the rules, even in the amendment stage, except when demanded as an obstructionist tactic. Since they are printed, reading by a clerk in a dreary monotone would be a waste of time.

Consideration by the Senate. H.R. 100 is then sent to the Senate with a message. Here it is referred to the Committee on Finance, which may hold hearings, amend, and report it back to the Senate. Suppose the committee reports and recommends passage with amendments. It is given the required three readings, is again debated, and may be amended further by the Senate. As its membership is much smaller, the Senate does not utilize a Committee of the Whole in considering legislation. If the bill is finally passed with amendment, it goes back to the Speaker's table.

Consideration of Amendments by the House. If any of the Senate amendments require consideration in Committee of the Whole, the bill is referred to the standing committee having jurisdiction, and when this committee reports the bill with its recommendations, H.R. 100 is referred to the Committee of the Whole House on the State of the Union. Here it is considered and is then reported back to the House. Should consideration by the Committee of the Whole not be necessary, the bill goes before the House directly from the Speaker's table.

Each Senate amendment is considered separately by the House, which may vote to agree to it, agree to it with amendment, or disagree to it. Should the House disagree to an amendment or amendments to H.R. 100, it may then ask for a conference with the Senate or send notice of disagreement and leave to the Senate the matter of receding or of requesting a conference.

Consideration by Conference Committee. If a conference is agreed to, an equal number of managers are appointed by the presiding officer of each house and they meet to compromise the differences. When an agreement is reached, a report is made to the houses by their respective managers. Ordinarily both houses then agree to the report, the bill is finally passed, and is enrolled for signature. In this case, the enrollment is on parchment in the House of Representatives.

Examination by Committee on House Administration. The chairman of the Committee on House Administration now certifies that H.R. 100 has been properly enrolled. The bill is then signed by the Speaker and the President of the Senate, and is transmitted to the President.

Consideration by the President. If the President approves H.R. 100, he signs it and it then becomes a law. But if the President disapproves of the bill, he returns it to the House with his reasons for disapproval. In order to become a law, H.R. 100 must be repassed by a two-thirds vote of both houses. The President may elect to take no action on a bill. If Congress is still in session at the expiration of 10 days, the bill becomes law without his signature, but if Congress has adjourned, the failure of the President to sign a bill kills it, and is known as a "pocket veto." [7]

Determining Congress' Agenda

It might be supposed that when a committee reports a bill to the House of Representatives and it is placed on one of the regular calendars, in due course it will be considered, but in actual practice this is not the case. Relatively few bills of importance are ever taken up in the regular order from the calendars. Appropriations and revenue measures have privileged status, and may be considered whenever the chairman of the committee can secure recognition by the Speaker, provided some other measure is not before the House. Noncontroversial measures may be brought up under unanimous consent and quickly disposed of at specified periods. Generally, however, other legislative measures about which there are differences of opinion can be brought before the House for action only by securing a special rule which must be proposed by the Rules Committee. Thus the Rules Committee occupies a special position in the legislative process, for it has the power of life and death over legislation. It can give the green light to measures which it approves and can hold up, sidetrack, or kill those which it opposes. Its sway begins after a committee has passed favorably upon a bill and has recommended its passage. The Rules Committee may even require a bill to be amended to meet its wishes before it will agree to bring in a special rule permitting consideration by the House.

During the Roosevelt and Truman administrations, the Rules Committee was dominated by conservatives of both parties, with the result that liberal measures were frequently blocked. In 1947 a bill providing for universal military training was bottled up because the Republican chairman of the Rules Committee was opposed to it.

When the Democrats were returned to office in 1949, one of the first acts of the Democratic majority in the House was to adopt a rule curbing the power of the Rules Committee so that it could not block the legislative program of the President. This was accomplished by providing that after a bill has been before the Rules Committee for 21 days without action, the chairman of the legislative committee reporting the bill, upon securing recognition of the Speaker, could make a motion on the floor of the House to take up the measure without the benefit of a special rule. Such a motion could be offered only on the second Monday of each month.

Hardly had this change taken place, however, before many members of the House began to regret their action. The Rules Committee had per-

Reprinted with the permission of the National Education Association.

How A Bill Becomes A Law

League of Women Voters of the U.S.
1026 - 17th Street, N.W.
Washington 6, D.C.

August 1951

Price 5¢

FIG. 1. How a bill becomes a law. Source: National Education Association.

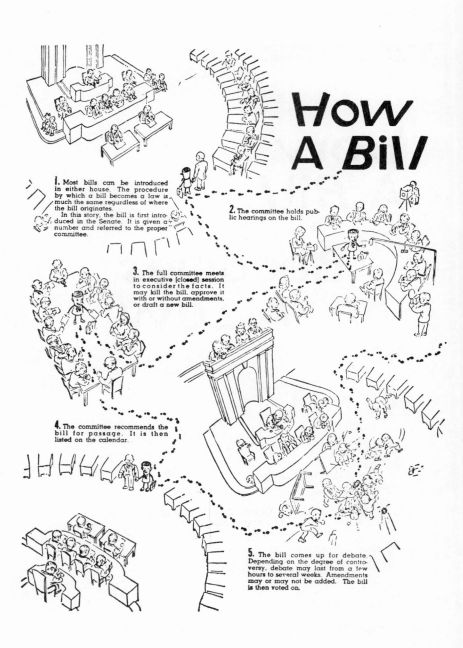

HOW A BILL

1. Most bills can be introduced in either house. The procedure by which a bill becomes a law is much the same regardless of where the bill originates.

In this story, the bill is first introduced in the Senate. It is given a number and referred to the proper committee.

2. The committee holds public hearings on the bill.

3. The full committee meets in executive [closed] session to consider the facts. It may kill the bill, approve it with or without amendments, or draft a new bill.

4. The committee recommends the bill for passage. It is then listed on the calendar.

5. The bill comes up for debate. Depending on the degree of controversy, debate may last from a few hours to several weeks. Amendments may or may not be added. The bill is then voted on.

234

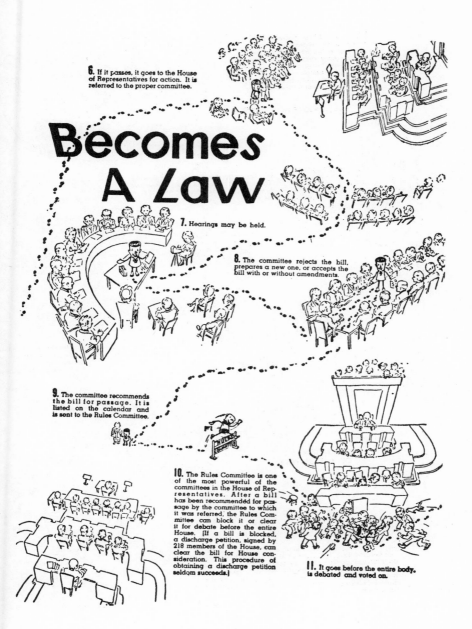

6. If it passes, it goes to the House of Representatives for action. It is referred to the proper committee.

Becomes A Law

7. Hearings may be held.

8. The committee rejects the bill, prepares a new one, or accepts the bill with or without amendments.

9. The committee recommends the bill for passage. It is listed on the calendar and is sent to the Rules Committee.

10. The Rules Committee is one of the most powerful of the committees in the House of Representatives. After a bill has been recommended for passage by the committee to which it was referred, the Rules Committee can block it or clear it for debate before the entire House. [If a bill is blocked, a discharge petition, signed by 218 members of the House, can clear the bill for House consideration. This procedure of obtaining a discharge petition seldom succeeds.]

11. It goes before the entire body, is debated and voted on.

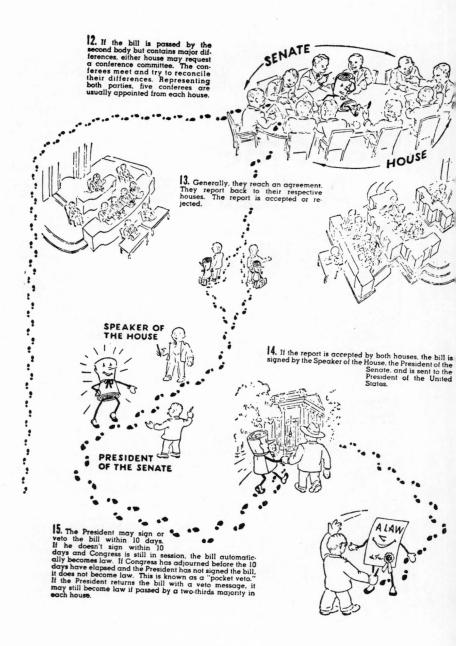

12. If the bill is passed by the second body but contains major differences, either house may request a conference committee. The conferees meet and try to reconcile their differences. Representing both parties, five conferees are usually appointed from each house.

SENATE

HOUSE

13. Generally, they reach an agreement. They report back to their respective houses. The report is accepted or rejected.

SPEAKER OF THE HOUSE

14. If the report is accepted by both houses, the bill is signed by the Speaker of the House, the President of the Senate, and is sent to the President of the United States.

PRESIDENT OF THE SENATE

15. The President may sign or veto the bill within 10 days. If he doesn't sign within 10 days and Congress is still in session, the bill automatically becomes law. If Congress has adjourned before the 10 days have elapsed and the President has not signed the bill, it does not become law. This is known as a "pocket veto." If the President returns the bill with a veto message, it may still become law if passed by a two-thirds majority in each house.

A LAW

formed a useful function by refusing to bring out undesirable measures. If such bills come before the House for action, it frequently happens that many members feel impelled to vote for them because of the political and pressure-group support behind them, even though they regard the bills as unsound and hope they will be defeated in the Senate. In 1949, Representative Rankin of Mississippi, then Chairman of the Committee on Veterans' Affairs, was able under the new rules to call up a bill providing a huge increase in veterans' pensions, which the Rules Committee had blocked. When this legislation came before the House for a vote, it was carried by an overwhelming majority. Fortunately the worst features of it were defeated in the Senate. No better illustration could be cited of the need for the screening of bills, and this is the function of the Rules Committee.

While the Rules Committee has been criticized for blocking certain kinds of legislation and for occasionally substituting its own ideas for those of committees, there is much to be said for allowing it very substantial powers. The committee's task is by no means an easy one. In addition to screening proposed bills and determining the order in which measures are to be considered, the Rules Committee is called upon to consider and propose new rules from time to time. The purpose of these rules is to make it possible to carry on the people's business in an orderly and efficient manner. As much deliberation as possible is desirable, but in such an unwieldy body as the House of Representatives, time is of the essence. Since such a large number of bills are thrown into the hopper at each legislative session, the more important measures must be given first consideration. It is up to the Rules Committee to see that such bills are given precedence.

Limitations on Debate

The House. The House of Representatives necessarily provides for limitation on debate, for otherwise it would not be able to dispose of its business. There are several ways of limiting debate in the lower chamber. In the first place, when the Rules Committee proposes a special rule for consideration of a bill it usually specifies a limit on debate. In the second place, under Rule 17 there may be a motion for the previous question, "which being ordered by a majority of members voting, if a quorum be present, shall have the effect to cut off all debate, and bring the House to a direct vote upon the immediate question or questions on which it has been asked and ordered." And in the third place, debate on a proposed bill may be limited by unanimous consent. Rarely is even the most important bill debated more than two days, and usually it is less than that.

The Senate. The Senate has resisted all efforts at effective limitation on debate. It prides itself on the fact that the Senators are not shackled by rules limiting debate as are the members of the House. The method commonly used in the Senate to end debate and bring a measure to a vote is a unanimous-consent agreement that the vote will be taken at a specific hour. Such motions are usually made by the majority floor leader, but the objection of a single Senator will block such an agreement. In 1917, after a small group of Senators had held up President Wilson's proposal for arming American merchant ships, the Senate adopted a cloture rule. This rule provided that when 16 Senators petition to close debate on "any measure, motion or other matter pending before the Senate," the presiding officer shall state the motion at once to the Senate. The motion must be put one hour after the Senate convenes "on the following calendar day but one," and if carried by a two-thirds vote, no Senator thereafter may speak for more than one hour on the measure, motion, or other matter pending. When the rule has been applied, debate has always ended within a short time and the vote has been taken. However, although 17 attempts have been made to apply the cloture rule, in only four instances has it been adopted. Even though rarely used, the threat of its adoption has at times been used to prevent filibusters.

The Southern Senators, however, have discovered a way of beating the cloture rule by starting a filibuster before a motion is made to take up legislation to which they are opposed. For instance, in 1948 they filibustered for days on the reading of the *Journal*, on the form of the *Congressional Record* of the previous day, and on a motion to consider the proposed legislation—all of this taking place before any legislation was actually before the Senate. The presiding officer at the time, Senator Vandenberg, ruled that cloture did not apply to these dilatory tactics. The next year, Vice-President Barkley ruled to the contrary, but the majority reversed his ruling. The effect was actually to nullify the cloture rule altogether. The Democratic Senators from the South, with the support of most of the Northern Republicans, then amended the rules to permit the application of the cloture rule to motions to take up legislation, as well as to the measure itself, but changed the rules so as to make it more difficult to invoke. A two-thirds majority of all members of the Senate, not merely of those present and voting, is now required to adopt the cloture rule, and it may not be applied at all to a debate on changing the rules of the Senate. Under these revised rules, a determined minority will be able hereafter to filibuster indefinitely, and it seems unlikely that cloture can be applied at all under the rules.

Still, there are some things to be said for the filibuster. In the first place, it enables minorities to protect themselves against legislation which they consider harmful to their interests and at least to prevent the hasty passage of such legislation and bring it to public attention. In the second place, it preserves the Senate as a free forum for debate and thus serves as an effective weapon against too much concentration of power in the executive department. Finally, it must be admitted that, surprisingly enough, very few important measures are defeated by the filibuster.

Forces behind Legislation

As holders of great power, members of Congress do their work under a variety of pressures. No account of our national legislature as a going concern can ignore the sources of these pressures. The groups which seek most steadily to influence legislation may be classified broadly as the political parties, the pressure groups, and the executive agencies. The pressure groups speaking for private interests are dealt with extensively in Chapter 17. Here we limit ourselves to a brief discussion of the influence of the parties and of the executive agencies.

Political Pressures. Members of Congress are politicians. They may seek office on the strength of business or professional success, but whether or not they retain office depends almost absolutely upon their acquiring political skill and wisdom. This sort of skill is tested most frequently in connection with the member's relations to the political organization "back home" and to the national leadership of his party. With respect to the former, it is clear that in most cases the member of Congress becomes and remains a member by keeping his fences in good repair in his own state or district. Even safe seats in one-party areas are kept safe by a multitude of favors and services to constituents. These are rendered quite willingly because politicians are a gregarious lot and genuinely interested in people; but never far from the member's mind is the fact that if he does not perform them acceptably, some ambitious rival will be eager to unseat him. Even greater foresight, acumen, and industry are needed in districts where the opposition party is well organized and well financed.

Also, because the member quite often owes his seat very largely to the efforts of the local "organization"—to the "machine," if one dare use a harsher word—he must keep on good terms with that little oligarchy of kingmakers. These local leaders are influential not only because in one way or another they direct the traffic in local political appointments, but also because they are normally in close touch with the important economic interests of the district. These interests are, of course, also part of nationally organized pressure groups whose lobbyists in Washington are not slow to make the acquaintance of the member. His official and much of his personal life is lived in the center of the pressures implied by the very existence of such persons and groups. In the midst of these how is he to find the *national* interest?

The bearing of national party leadership on the conduct of individual members of Congress is most significant when the President and Congress are of the same party. If this is not the case, there is ordinarily no party leadership in Congress capable of influencing members on any question upon which the people and the party at home have strong views. This is true because the former can impose no effectual penalties if the member gets "off the reservation," while the latter have it in their power to retire him to private life.

Executive Pressures. When a party first comes into power, the new President is usually able for a time to secure the necessary support in Congress for his legislative program. With a mandate from the voters, he is at the height of his popularity and prestige, and the men of all parties wish him well; many members of Congress owe their election to his popularity. The country expects him to exercise leadership in proposing a legislative program, for unless he does so, little legislation of importance will be passed. If he is wise, he will consult with the leaders of his party in Congress, and with their assistance and advice determine his program. At the outset he will have a large number of patronage appointments at his command which will help him in securing the support of members of his party, but the jobs will soon give out and then the "honeymoon" period will be over. Thereafter the President will need great skill as a political leader to maintain the unified support of his party in Congress and to secure the adoption of his legislative program.

In addition to the measures which are incorporated in a President's legislative program, most of the executive departments and agencies have less important bills which they are anxious to have passed by Congress. Most of these bills are of a corrective nature, devised to remove difficulties which have been encountered in administering existing laws. The departments also watch closely any bills affecting their operations, opposing those which they regard as potentially harmful. Bills relating to public health, for example, are likely to originate in the U.S. Public Health Service. Health bills introduced without the backing of the Service are certain to be referred to it for comments and criticisms by the committee chairman before any action is taken. It has become customary in recent years for most departments and agencies to maintain close contacts, usually through liaison officials, with the committees on Capitol Hill which pass on legislation affecting them.

Reorganization of Congress

Despite the tremendous increase in the responsibilities of Congress, the growing importance of the subjects, domestic and international, on which it legislates, and the greatly increased size and complexity of the Federal government, until recently Congress operated with the same organization and substantially in the same manner as in the early days of the country. Because Congress recognized the need to streamline its organization and to provide greater staff facilities to enable it to cope with its much larger tasks of today, in 1944 it established a Joint Committee on the Organization of Congress to inquire into its own operations and to recommend improvements. It should be noted, however, that the joint committee was not authorized to inquire into the procedures which Congress uses, or into such subjects as the seniority rule. Extensive hearings were held and studies made by the committee and a report was submitted in 1946. Among important recommendations of the committee were:

1. That the number of Senate standing committees be reduced from 33 to 16 and House committees from 48 to 18.

2. That committee chairmen be required to report promptly all bills approved by their committees and seek a rule to bring them to the floor for consideration.

3. That each reorganized committee be authorized to employ four staff experts to be chosen under prescribed standards.

4. That appropriations for Legislative Counsel be increased from $90,000 a year to $150,000 a year for the ensuing two-year period.

5. That the appropriation for the Legislative Reference Service in the Library of Congress be increased from $500,000 annually to $550,000 for 1948, and $750,000 annually thereafter.

6. That a merit system be adopted for recruitment of congressional employees.

7. That Congress divest itself of the duty of governing the District of Columbia, and provide for a referendum on the adoption of home rule.

8. That the Court of Claims be empowered to hear and settle major claims against the Federal government, and that lesser claims be adjusted by heads of agencies involved.

9. That there be provision for adjournment (or recess) by the end of each fiscal year.

10. That salaries of members of Congress be increased to $15,000 annually.

11. That there be provision for retirement of members of Congress.

12. That each Senator and Representative be authorized to employ a high-caliber administrative assistant at an annual salary of $8,000 to assist in handling nonlegislative functions, thus enabling the member to devote more time to his legislative duties.

Most of these recommendations were incorporated into the Legislative Reorganization Act of 1946. The Senate committees were reduced from 33 to 15 and House committees from 48 to 19; each standing committee, with the exception of the appropriations committees, was authorized to employ four experts; the appropriations for the Legislative Reference Service in the Library of Congress and for the Office of Legislative Counsel were substantially increased; registration of lobbyists was required; it was provided that claims cases involving over $1,000 may be brought in the

United States district court where the plaintiff resides or where the tort occurred and may be appealed to either the Circuit Courts of Appeal, or to the Court of Claims, while claims of $1,000 or less may be settled by the head of the Federal agency involved; and retirement for members of Congress and salaries of $12,500 plus $2,500 for expenses free of taxes, were provided. Recommendations for application of the merit system for congressional employees and divestment of Congress of its control over the District of Columbia were defeated.

Although the House failed to follow the suggestion for majority and minority policy committees, the Senate did act on this matter. Likewise, the Senate has provided for administrative assistants to perform nonlegislative functions, but the House has failed to follow suit.

In spite of the widespread publicity given to the Reorganization Act of 1946, the results have been disappointing. In 1948, just two years after the act went into effect, President Truman attacked the record of the Eightieth Congress just past as the worst in the history of the nation, and the vote in the 1948 elections seemed to indicate that many of the voters agreed. The worst faults of Congress—the seniority system, the irresponsible chairmen of committees, the filibuster, the autocratic power of the House Rules Committee, the lack of responsible leadership, the low level of debate— all these have been left untouched, although the committee system has been streamlined, and Congress has a larger staff.

Senator Estes Kefauver and Dr. Jack Levin have come forward with a number of suggestions for the improvement of Congress which merit consideration. They suggest, among other things, that Senate rules be amended to provide that debate may be closed by a majority, rather than a two-thirds, vote. To eliminate the time lost by executive officials who must repeatedly appear before committees, they recommend provision of a two-hour question period in Congress once every two weeks, where departmental and agency heads would appear to answer written and oral questions. Besides, they suggest regular liaison between the President and Congress, and between departments and congressional committees, by means of specially assigned executive representatives. Other proposals are use of an electrical voting machine by the House of Representatives, to save time; abolition of District of Columbia committees; election of the chairmen of standing committees by the majority members and of the minority leader by minority members; and automatically placing bills on the calendar if reported by a unanimous committee vote.[8]

The members of Congress are, on the whole, able and honest men. They try to do a good job and are conscientious and hard-working. The faults of Congress are to be attributed largely to outmoded rules, traditions, and

[8] Estes Kefauver and Jack Levin, *A Twentieth-century Congress*, Duell, Sloan and Pearce, Inc., New York, 1947.

procedures. Congressmen are hard-pressed in the performance of their duties and they must often take the short cuts. They need information as a basis for legislation and they turn to those who have it to offer. This is where pressure groups come in. It is the group that gets there "fustest with the mostest" that has the greatest influence. More organizations devoted to the advancement of the public interest, like the League of Women Voters and the National Planning Association, are needed.

Political parties should play a larger and more responsible role in developing legislative programs. There should be some way to discipline party members who frequently wander off the reservation. Loss of committee assignments and loss of seniority might be ways of disciplining recalcitrant members. More frequent use of caucus action, even binding majority members to support the party program on major legislation, might also bring results. A degree of independence by members of Congress is desirable and should always be retained, but carried to the extreme it defeats responsible leadership of Congress and strengthens the hands of pressure groups to the point where they are able to dictate the policies of the country.

REFERENCES

Stephen K. Bailey, *Congress Makes a Law* (1949).
——— and Howard D. Samuel, *Congress at Work* (1952).
James Bryce, *The American Commonwealth*, Vol. I (1889).
F. L. Burdette, *Filibustering in the Senate* (1940).
James M. Burns, *Congress on Trial* (1949).
E. J. Eberling, *Congressional Investigations* (1928).
The Federalist.
George B. Galloway, *The Legislative Process in Congress* (1953).
Ernest S. Griffith, *Congress: Its Contemporary Roles* (1951).
Bertram M. Gross, *The Legislative Struggle* (1953).
George H. Haynes, *The Senate of the United States,* 2 vols. (1938).
Estes Kefauver and Jack Levin, *A Twentieth-century Congress* (1947).
Floyd M. Riddick, *The United States Congress: Organization and Procedure* (1949).
Lindsay Rogers, *The American Senate* (1926).
Rules and Manual, United States House of Representatives (1951).
G. H. E. Smith and F. M. Riddick, *Congress in Action* (1949).
Roland Young, *This Is Congress* (1943).

CHAPTER 15   *The Office of the President:*
Nomination and Election

The selection of the executive head of the government of the United States is not only a vital part of the democratic process but is also one of the most interesting procedures in the great game of politics. Forty-two elections have been held, and 35 men have occupied the Presidency for periods ranging from William Henry Harrison's one month to the extended term of Franklin D. Roosevelt, who served as President from March, 1933, until his death on April 12, 1945. Once in four years the voters go to the polls to select a President. This process now begins as early as February of the election year and is not over until the election which occurs on the first Tuesday after the first Monday in November. During the entire period the interest of the citizenry is centered on this, the greatest of all political contests.

Nominating Methods

In the early history of the United States, Presidents were chosen by congressional caucus. Members of each party in Congress held closed meetings and selected the Presidential nominees. Though today this system appears undemocratic it was a necessary part of our formative political history. Not only was the franchise limited in those days but so also were means of transportation and communication. It seemed natural for the chosen representatives of the people to select the men to contest the Presidency. Washington, the unanimous choice of all citizens, was not nominated by caucus, but the succeeding nominees through 1820, and Crawford in 1824, were nominated in that manner.

In 1831 the Anti-Masonic party held the first national convention of a political party. Locally selected delegates gathered in convention to nominate a candidate for the Presidency. Other parties adopted this plan of making nominations and it remains today the system used by all important political parties. The Republican party as a rule holds its convention late in June or early in July of the election year, while the Democrats meet several weeks later. Only once, in 1888, has the Democratic National Convention been held first. Minor parties generally hold their conventions prior to those of the two major parties.

Selection of Convention Delegates

Convention delegates are chosen in each state and territory by one of three methods: by the state executive committee of the party, by the state convention of the party, or by a primary. In some states, a particular method is not required by the law of the state but is followed by the parties through custom. In only four states is the committee system used.[1] Selection by convention is the most popular mode, used in 28 states. In addition, delegates of both parties from the territories are selected by convention, as are the Republican delegates from the District of Columbia. The Democrats hold a primary in the District of Columbia. The remainder of the states use the primary for the selection of all or most of their delegates. Included in this last group are the five states with the largest delegations in the conventions: California, Illinois, New York, Ohio, and Pennsylvania. For every official delegate there is an alternate who serves if the official delegate is not able to attend the convention. In many instances, these alternates attend the convention as interested spectators.

In the four states where the state committee of the party chooses the delegates, the committee itself has, as a rule, been chosen by a previous state party convention. In those states where the state convention selects the delegates, the members of that convention are chosen either by local conventions or by a primary. The Presidential primary, because of its use in the populous states and because of the national attention given to it, deserves special attention.

In 1905, Wisconsin enacted the first law providing that delegates to the national conventions should be elected by the voters in primary elections. Five years later Oregon added the provision that voters might cast a preferential vote for the Presidential candidate of their choice. Other states have adopted laws having a similar effect by providing that delegates to the national convention could be pledged to vote for a particular candidate. Today there is much variation in state laws on the subject. Ten states provide for a preferential vote on Presidential candidates, accompanied usually by the election of delegates to the convention at primary elections. Other states provide for the primary election of delegates, but without a preferential vote, except in states where delegates are pledged. In none of these states, however, is the preference of the voters absolutely binding on the delegates. The state law generally specifies that the delegates must vote for the preferred candidate until it is reasonably certain that the

[1] In addition, Alabama permits the Democratic party the choice of selection by executive committee or primary; the Republican party uses the convention method.

candidate will not be the choice of the convention. Minnesota and Wisconsin have perhaps the strongest law binding the delegates. Those states require that the popular choice be supported until release by the candidate himself or until the candidate receives less than 10 per cent of the votes on any one ballot. The dates on which Presidential primaries are held vary from early March until June.[2]

Critics of the primary put forth a strong case against it. It is, they say, an extra expense for the state and an overwhelming financial burden for some candidates. In addition, when the candidate is a member of Congress or an officer of the government, the time required for campaigning interferes with the performance of his official duties. Moreover, the primary is not binding, and for this reason some candidates do not choose to enter each primary.

Nevertheless, there has been a growing demand to institute a nationwide primary for the purpose of instructing convention delegates how to vote. Senator Paul Douglas of Illinois and Senator George Smathers of Florida are the present leaders of this movement in Congress. Senator Smathers would abolish the national convention and let the primary be the final nominating machinery. If a candidate should not receive a majority of the votes in the first primary there would be a second primary between the two high men. The amendment, of course, if adopted, would be binding on all states. This proposal, if perfected, would perhaps do a great deal to take the confusion out of the nominating process. In addition, it would eliminate sectional candidates, "dark horses," and "favorite sons." But a tremendous financial burden would be placed on the candidates.

Opponents of the primary have pointed out that the most popular candidates in the primary elections have frequently failed to capture the nomination in convention. Harold Stassen, for example, ran very well in a number of states in 1948, though he later lost the Oregon primary to Dewey, who was nominated by the Republican party. In 1952 Senator Kefauver led in the Democratic primaries by a wide margin, but failed to win the nomination. Though both Taft and Eisenhower ran well in certain states, it may be doubted whether the final choice of the convention was greatly influenced by the primary votes. In several instances the person nominated was not even entered in the primary elections. This was true of Hughes in 1916, Willkie in 1940, and Stevenson in 1952.

The Convention Call and Voting Formulae

The national committees of both major parties issue a call to convention and select the convention sites in January or February of the election year.

---

[2] For a compilation of state and territorial laws on this subject, see the hearings entitled *Preference Primaries for Nomination of Candidates for President and Vice-President,* S. 2570, 82d Cong., 2d sess., 1952.

These committees, composed of one man and one woman from each state and territory, are chosen by the party organization within each geographical area.[3] The committee members serve for four years and are the most important single units in the party hierarchy.

The site of the convention is important. In the early years of the country, Baltimore was the popular choice of all parties mainly because of its central location at that time. Now the choice of a city is made with two major conditions in mind: is the city within a doubtful state with a large electoral vote, and is the city willing to pay handsomely for the privilege of being the host? In addition, the city must have an assembly hall to hold at least 10,000 persons; it must have adequate hotel facilities and should be easily accessible to delegates from all points in the nation. In recent years Chicago and Philadelphia have been the most frequent choices of each major party.

Along with its call to convention, the national committee informs each state how many votes it may have in the forthcoming convention. This is a very important matter for the states concerned, and it is therefore necessary to examine the formulae by which the parties parcel out votes. Originally the Democrats gave a state one vote in convention for each of its electoral votes. Later this was increased to two convention votes per electoral vote. After the abolition of the two-thirds rule for nomination in 1936, the party granted a bonus of two convention votes to any state that went Democratic in the previous Presidential election. This rule, later changed to a bonus of four votes, was instigated to compensate partially for the position lost by the solid South when the two-thirds rule was dropped. Hence today a state with 20 electoral votes, which went Democratic in the last election, would be given 44 votes at the next Democratic convention. This rule applies to all states. Alaska, the District of Columbia, Hawaii, and Puerto Rico each have six votes, whereas the Canal Zone and the Virgin Islands have only two votes each. In 1952 there were 1,230 votes in the Democratic National Convention in Chicago. The voting strength of the states ranged from six votes each for Delaware and Vermont to 94 votes for New York.

In contrast with the comparatively simple Democratic formula is the system used by the Grand Old Party. Until 1916 the Republicans allotted votes proportionally among the states according to the electoral vote. In time, however, the Southern states achieved a position in the GOP convention all out of proportion to the vote cast by the party in these states. As a result, the party altered its rules, the change becoming effective in 1916. At present, states are given Republican convention votes in this manner: four votes at large to each state, one vote for each congressional

---

[3] The Republicans have no members from the Canal Zone or the Virgin Islands. Both parties have members from the District of Columbia.

district in the state that polled over 1,000 Republican votes at the last Presidential election, an extra vote for each congressional district that polled over 10,000 Republican votes, and a bonus of three votes if the state went Republican in the last Presidential election. If the state did not go Republican in the last Presidential election but did elect a Republican Senator two years later, it gets the three-vote bonus. This has proved to be a satisfactory system. Regarding the territories: eight votes go to Hawaii, six votes to the District of Columbia, three votes each to Alaska and Puerto Rico, and one vote to the Virgin Islands. In 1952 at the Republican National Convention in Chicago there were 1,205 votes. The voting strength of the states ranged from Mississippi's four votes to New York's 96.

The Keynoter

As the day for the opening of the convention approaches, the host city dresses itself in patriotic bunting. Advance guards for the potential candidates establish local headquarters in hotels, usually renting a suite or a whole floor for offices. Campaign literature smothers the city. Billboards are adorned with slogans and with candidates' pictures. A campaign button is on every lapel.

Following the customary opening ceremonies, the national committee chairman calls for the selection of the temporary chairman of the convention. The latter, called the keynoter, has generally been selected beforehand by the national committee and his acceptance by the convention is a matter of form. It is the duty of the keynoter to fire the political passions of the delegates. If the particular party controls the Presidency at the time, the keynoter defends the President's policies. If the party is hoping to regain the office of President, the administration and its actions during the past four years are vehemently criticized. The following is a typical passage from a keynote speech from the peroration of Claude Bowers at the 1928 Democratic National Convention:

We shall win because our cause is just. The predatory forces before us seek a triumph for the sake of the sacking. Their shock troops are the Black Horse Cavalry whose hoof beats have made hideous music on Pennsylvania Avenue during the last eight years. They are led by the money-mad cynics and scoffers— and we go forth to battle for the cause of man. In the presence of such a foe "he who dallies is a dastard and he who doubts is damned." In this convention we close debate and grasp our sword. The time has come. The battle hour has struck. Then to your tents, O, Israel! [4]

Convention Committees

When order is restored after the keynote address, the business of organizing the convention is considered. The four important committees of

[4] *The New York Times,* June 27, 1928.

the convention are those on permanent organization, credentials, rules and order of business, and platform and resolutions. The committees comprise a man and woman from each state and territory, named by each delegation as the secretary reads the temporary roll of the convention.

The committee on permanent organization selects the permanent officers of the convention. Nominally, the permanent chairman is chosen by this group. Actually he has been selected beforehand by the national committee. Nevertheless, when the committee reports to the convention there may be disagreement on its choice. If so, the convention votes on the rival contenders for the chairmanship. Generally the permanent chairman is an able and experienced parliamentarian.

The committee on credentials examines the credentials of the various delegations to ascertain whether or not they officially represent the party in their respective states. The committee then draws up a permanent roll of the convention, to take the place of the temporary roll prepared by the national committee before the convention met. Occasionally more than one delegation from a state seeks official recognition from the committee. Both delegations may be accepted and given a divided vote, or one delegation may be completely rejected.

The work of the committee on rules and order of business deals primarily with the adoption of rules which will govern the procedure of the convention. This committee can do valuable work in criticizing current procedures and recommending to the national committee changes for future conventions. Time limits for nominating and seconding speeches and desirable restrictions for the benefit of the immediate audience and for radio and television spectators are adopted by this committee. Delegates are very much aware of the radio and television audiences that now follow a national convention and they are apt to give minor performances when a mike or a television camera is near. Instead of merely announcing his state's vote the Louisiana delegation chairman in the 1952 Republican National Convention loudly declaimed "Louisiana casts 13 hard-earned votes for General Eisenhower." In the same year's Democratic National Convention, one delegate, when polled, declaimed: "I am happy to cast my vote for the man of destiny from the mountains of Tennessee, Estes Kefauver."

The Platform. The duty of the platform and resolutions committee is to draw up the platform. It is not uncommon for a subcommittee picked by the national committee to meet in advance of the convention to begin outlining the platform. At times sharp controversy develops in the committee over a particular plank, and this fight is generally not settled until the majority and minority committee reports have been made to the convention and the convention has voted upon which report to accept. The civil-rights issue in the Democratic National Convention of 1948 resulted in the walkout of all of the Mississippi and part of the Alabama delegations.

The platform itself is a formal statement of the philosophy of the party and the party's stand on past and future issues. As a rule the platform is vague and very general. However, new issues may bring new planks. For instance, it was the pledge of Senator Douglas before the 1952 Democratic convention that he would seek Democratic approval of a constitutional amendment to abolish the national convention. He failed to accomplish this purpose. The platform is the birthplace of many great programs that someday may become the law of the land. In the past the Democrats have been able to be more specific in their platform than the Republicans by virtue of the fact that the Republicans make their platform first. It is also true that third parties and minority parties that have little chance of coming to power can draw up more specific platforms than can the major parties. From these minority-party platforms come many of the major parties' future legislative programs.

The final decisions are made by the convention itself. Should there be sharp division in the committees, particularly over the adoption of rules or the seating of delegates, majority and minority reports are made to the convention and the matter is finally determined by a vote of the entire membership of the convention.

Credentials

In the Republican National Convention of 1952 two delegations each from the states of Texas, Louisiana, and Georgia made their appearance. This was done in spite of the fact that, in making up the temporary roll for the convention, the Republican National Committee had selected the pro-Taft groups as the delegates to be seated. Had these names been placed on the temporary roll it would have made it possible for the Taft forces to determine rules and, in all probability, to have determined the party's nominee for the Presidency. In each instance, the pro-Eisenhower group contested the seating of the Taft groups. They succeeded in getting the matter before the convention when a new rule was proposed which provided that state delegations, against whose seating one-third or more of the Republican National Committee had voted, could not vote on other contests. After fiery debate this rule was adopted. Thus enough Taft supporters were prevented from voting to assure the seating of pro-Eisenhower delegations.

During the early hours of the Democratic National Convention of 1952 a resolution was adopted by the convention requiring all delegates to sign a "loyalty pledge" promising to use all honorable means to get the convention's nominees on the ballots in their states. This rule was to apply for that convention only and was not binding if it was contrary to state laws. Virginia, South Carolina, and Louisiana refused to sign. Later, in the convention, however, these states were allowed to take their seats notwithstanding this refusal.

Nominating the President

Once the delegations are seated, the platform adopted, and the permanent chairman assumes the chair, the convention is ready for its most important business, the nomination of a President. Today the roll is called alphabetically by states. Formerly it was called geographically, beginning with Maine. States at the top of the roll may, and usually do, by prior agreement, defer to some other state wishing to nominate a favorite son or the popular primary choice. Nominating speeches are not extemporaneous affairs. All important ones are carefully written; and at their conclusion the followers of each candidate put on a demonstration of marching, noise, and music to impress upon the convention the popularity of the candidate.

Nominating speeches have at times led to future good fortune for the speechmaker. Garfield's nomination of John Sherman in 1880 caught the fancy of the convention and was later a factor in Garfield's own nomination. The same was true when William Jennings Bryan made his famous "Cross of Gold" speech in the 1896 Democratic convention. Franklin D. Roosevelt's nomination of Al Smith in 1924 and 1928 also had important political implications.

When the nominations for President are completed, the balloting begins. In each convention it takes a majority to nominate, that is, 616 votes in the 1952 Democratic convention and 603 votes in the 1952 Republican convention. The Democrats still use the so-called unit rule. Under this rule a state can send its delegation to the convention bound to cast its votes in a block, with the majority of the delegation deciding how all the votes will be cast. Actually the unit rule is declining in importance because states are choosing not to put their delegations under such a restriction. The convention, however, honors the wishes of those states which bind their delegations by enforcing the unit rule in such cases.

The voting is done by alphabetical roll call of the states. The chairman of each delegation announces the vote of the delegation. Occasionally a member of a delegation will challenge the vote as announced. In such a case each member of the delegation is polled to ascertain his vote. Such a procedure is time-consuming yet necessary where there is division within a delegation.

A candidate may receive a majority of votes on the first ballot. Especially is this true of an incumbent President who is renominated. Some conventions, however, have taken 30 and 40 ballots before a candidate received the necessary votes for nomination. The record for the number of ballots to nominate was set by the Democrats in 1924. After 102 ballots the convention was still deadlocked between Al Smith and William Gibbs

McAdoo. On the next ballot a dark horse, John W. Davis, received the nomination.

In the 1952 Republican National Convention, at the end of the first ballot, General Eisenhower lacked but four votes of securing the nomination. But a second ballot was unnecessary. Minnesota asked that its vote be shifted to Eisenhower. Other states followed this lead and as a result Eisenhower received 845 votes and the nomination. Later the vote was made unanimous. The Democrats the same year were deadlocked after two ballots. On the third ballot there was unmistakable evidence of a swing to Governor Adlai Stevenson of Illinois. The final count showed that Stevenson lacked two and one-half votes of being nominated. Immediately there was a grand rush to get on the Stevenson bandwagon and he was easily nominated without another roll call of the states.

When the Presidential nominee has been selected, the convention proceeds to choose his running mate. By this time the convention delegates are tired and generally ready to go home. Consequently the choice of a Vice-President is seldom a lively affair although the procedure is the same as that for choosing the Presidential nominee. The Vice-Presidential nomination is frequently the result of deals and political expediency. In recent years the Presidential nominee has had much influence over the selection of the Vice-Presidential candidate. This second man as a rule is selected primarily because the choice will help to carry a doubtful state or region or because it will satisfy a disgruntled faction of the party.

The Candidates

Upon what grounds is a Presidential nominee selected? Is it his personal ability as a potential Chief Executive or is it his ability to get votes, to harmonize the factions of the party, and win the independent vote in November? Actually, the most important factor is "availability," a quality all successful candidates must possess.

Several considerations enter into the determination of a candidate's availability. It is desirable that he be in his fifties or early sixties and in good health. It is important that a candidate be from a doubtful state with a large population in order to win the electoral vote of that state. For this reason New York, Illinois, and Ohio are states where Presidential candidates are nurtured. A candidate should be a loyal party man and preferably one who is acceptable to the leaders of the party. Wendell Willkie was an exception to this rule, and so was General Eisenhower, but both had great personal popularity. Senator Estes Kefauver's campaign for the Democratic Presidential nomination in 1952 was made difficult because of the opposition of party leaders. There should be nothing in a candidate's record to alienate a section of the party or a distinct element of the voting populace. For this reason Senator Russell was never seriously considered for the Democratic nomination in 1952, and Senator Taft was regarded by many as a weak candidate.

Political astuteness of a candidate is naturally a requirement. He should also be an able public speaker and willing to conduct a vigorous campaign. Party leaders prefer the man with the fewest political liabilities. They have the opinion that voters vote against one candidate as much as they vote for another. Doubtless this is true, although it may not be important enough to allow this negative factor to be the primary one upon which the selection of a nominee is made. All these factors unite to determine a candidate's availability.

The Campaign

After the candidate has accepted the nomination, either at the convention or at a later date, the machinery is set up for the campaign. The top party men decide on the campaign strategy. Generally the campaign manager is the new head of the national committee. On him most of the planning falls. However, the two Roosevelts and Wendell Willkie directed their own campaigns. Campaigns take one of two forms; one is for the nominee to remain at home or in the White House and make a few carefully planned speeches over a nation-wide radio and television hookup. The other is to carry the campaign to the people.

The strategy involved in the "front porch" campaign is for the candidate to make few speeches but to issue statements and possibly hold press conferences. Generally a candidate who does not make a good personal appearance, or who is unfamiliar with the basic issues, prefers this sort of campaign. This strategy is also used on occasion by White House incumbents who feel confident of victory. McKinley and Harding won by this "stay home" strategy. On the other hand, Hoover used it in 1932 and lost. It is said that Harding's managers feared that he would confuse many issues if he stumped the country and answered queries from the public. Calvin Coolidge and Franklin Roosevelt enjoyed success on occasion by completely ignoring the opposition and going about the Presidential chores almost as if there were no campaign in progress, although Roosevelt took to the stump before the campaign ended.

Most candidates, however, stump the country, generally on a special train. Hundreds of speeches are made at whistle stops and, of course, in the big cities too. Such a campaign is especially desirable for a candidate who is not well known and who has speaking ability and the knack of meeting the public. But the strategy has its faults. It requires careful planning with reliance upon numerous local party groups. When those groups for any reason do not whip up enthusiasm for the speaker's appearance he is apt to find himself talking to sparse gatherings. He makes friends by speaking in certain localities but gains ill-will by not including other cities and towns on his speaking itinerary. Some candidates speak so often that towards the end of their campaign their remarks are old and are worn thin. Furthermore, the candidate himself may become physically exhausted. It is thought that Hughes in 1916, Cox in 1920, and Willkie in 1940 overdid their campaigns to their own detriment. On the other hand some feel that Truman's tour through the Middle West in 1948 saved the day for the Democrats.

The candidate's personal speaking abilities cannot do the whole job of winning an election. A vast organization of party workers is needed as well. Although the permanent headquarters of a party is usually in Washington, D.C., a temporary headquarters is also established for the campaign, most likely in New York City. In 1952 the Democratic campaign was directed from Springfield, Illinois, the home town of the candidate.

Campaign Costs. Obviously, such an organization requires vast sums of money to make its effects felt throughout the country. If only one postal card were mailed to each of the 97 million potential voters in the United States, the postage alone would be almost $2 million. The price of nation-wide radio and television broadcasts may be as high as $200,000. Radio and television are perhaps the major expense. Other aids, such as pamphlets, buttons, posters, and billboard space cost heavily. Newspaper advertising is also expensive although a friendly newspaper can lighten the party's financial burden if it chooses. Contributions from party members big and small are the major sources of finance for a party. Jackson- or Jefferson-day dinners at $50 or $100 a plate add to the Democratic fund. So do the Republicans' Lincoln-day feasts.

The campaign of 1952 illustrates not only the tremendous cost of Presidential elections but also the woeful inadequacy of Federal laws regulating campaign expenditures.[5] These rules were widely evaded in the 1952 campaign, for possibly never before was so much money spent in an election. No one will ever know how much it was. For the 1952 Presidential campaign, reports filed with the Clerk of the House show expenditures of nearly $18 million. Of this amount the Republicans spent approximately $10 million while the Democrats spent only half that amount. The remainder was spent by Labor and thirty-four other political organizations.[6] *The New York Times*, early in December, 1952, had already discovered the expenditure of over $32 million. This is by no means the total. Even the *Times* stated that it was a "rock bottom" figure. Other estimates have been as high as $100 million. How are these huge sums spent within the law? That neither party has been charged with exceeding the legal limits arises

[5] For a full discussion of the problems of regulating campaign expenditures see Chap. 10.

[6] See *Congressional Quarterly Almanac*, 1953, p. 51.

from the fact that very large sums are spent by so-called "independent groups,"—citizens' and volunteer organizations and various local groups—which are not technically elements of a political party.

How is this money used? A tremendous amount goes to broadcasting, particularly to television broadcasts. Our Corrupt Practices Acts were passed before the television era. Both national committees earmarked at least one-half of their respective $3 million funds for television and radio broadcasts. But the total amount paid for these telecasts and broadcasts was much larger. Both committees depended upon "citizen organizations" to take care of the needed extra funds. Representative Hale Boggs, chairman of a special House committee to investigate campaign expenditures, stated that "the recent campaign added 'jet stops' to the 'whistle stops' and expensive T.V. rhetoric to the 'fireside chats.' The enactors of laws passed in 1925 and 1939 could not possibly have foreseen these drastic changes in campaign techniques and the alarming costs of these techniques." [7]

In each of a dozen states over a million dollars were spent during the 1952 campaign. Although complete returns have not been made at the time of the writing, the first report shows that in Pennsylvania the Republican organization alone spent over $2,300,000. Presidential elections have become an expensive democratic procedure. In doubtful states the amounts spent are staggering. Money plays too great a part in determining the winners of contests for the Presidency.

The whole problem of financing a campaign is a pressing one for the nation, both materially and morally. Some of the suggested solutions were discussed earlier in Chap. 10. Certainly it is desirable that winning an office should depend upon campaign issues and the quality of the candidates rather than upon the amount of money that may be raised in support of a particular candidate.

The Election

In order to be elected President of the United States a candidate must receive a majority of the votes in the electoral college. A majority of the popular vote is not necessary for election. John Quincy Adams, James Buchanan, Abraham Lincoln in 1860, Rutherford B. Hayes, James A. Garfield, Grover Cleveland in 1884 and in 1892, Benjamin Harrison, and Woodrow Wilson in 1912 each received less than a majority of the popular vote. Only John Quincy Adams, Hayes, and Benjamin Harrison, however, are considered minority Presidents since each received fewer votes than his chief opponent. In 1912 Wilson had only 42 per cent of the popular vote but he captured 82 per cent of the electoral vote. In 1944, in New York State, Roosevelt received the entire electoral vote although 2,997,586 per-

[7] *The New York Times,* Dec. 1, 1952.

sons voted for Dewey. In 1952, Stevenson garnered a popular vote of 27,311,316, but only 89 electoral votes. Eisenhower received 55.1 per cent of the popular vote but that proved sufficient to win a little over 83 per cent of the electoral vote. With only a slightly larger proportion of the popular vote in 1956 President Eisenhower won nearly 88 per cent of the electoral vote—459 out of 531.

The Presidential election of 1952 was noteworthy because a record number of votes were cast: 61,574,861. Sixty-three per cent of the adult population participated in this election. This has been estimated to represent 81 per cent of the eligible voters and is nearly 12 million more votes than were ever before cast in a Presidential election.

The Electoral College

Usually one candidate receives a majority of the electoral vote and immediately after the November election it is known who the next President will be. Notwithstanding this fact, the electoral college must go through the procedure of casting ballots and of sending the returns to Washington. Who are these electors and what is the electoral college? Voters cast their ballots for electors rather than for a candidate for President. The constitutional fathers provided that the people should select individuals who in turn should use their own judgment in choosing a President. Due to the fact that nowadays electors state in advance that they are Democratic or Republican and will vote for the nominee of their particular party, the meeting of the electoral college is a mere formality to carry out the constitutional requirements.

Because the list of electors in the populous states is very long, various procedures are used to shorten the length of the ballot. In 26 states, in fact, the electors' names do not even appear on the ballot; only the names of the Presidential candidates appear. In 12 states the names of the electors are on the ballot beneath the name of the nominee they are pledged to support, but voters are allowed to vote a straight party ticket by marking the ballot at the head of the column. In other states, the electors are voted upon directly.

In a few instances electors have refused to cast their votes for the candidates of their party, but such cases are extremely rare. In 1952 a test case went to the United States Supreme Court on whether a political party could exact a pledge of its electors that they would vote for the candidates of the party. The Court held that [8]

The Twelfth Amendment does not bar a political party from requiring the pledge to support the nominees of the National Convention. When a state authorizes a

[8] *Ray v. Blair*, 343 U.S. 214, 231 (1952).

party to choose its nominees for elector in a party primary and to fix the qualifications for the candidates, we see no federal constitutional objection to the requirement of this pledge.

On the first Monday after the second Wednesday in December, the
electors meet in their respective state capitols to cast their votes. Some
states have an elaborate voting procedure; others permit voice votes. The
results are sent to the President of the Senate where, according to constitutional mandate, he must count the votes in the presence of both houses.

Close Elections

When no Presidential candidate receives a majority of the electoral
vote, the election is thrown into the House of Representatives. The names
of the three candidates receiving the highest electoral vote are placed before the members of the House. The balloting is by states and each state
casts one vote. A majority is needed to elect. Twice in the history of the
United States has the election been thrown into the House. The first occurred after the Election of 1800 and before the passage of the Twelfth
Amendment. According to the Constitution, each Presidential elector was
to vote for two persons. The one who got the highest number of votes was
to be President, the other, Vice-President. The vote resulted in a tie between Jefferson and Burr. The election was therefore thrown into the
House where Jefferson was elected on the thirty-sixth ballot. This contest
led to the passage of the Twelfth Amendment which provides for voting
for the office of President and of Vice-President separately.

In the election of 1824 Jackson received 99 electoral votes, John Q.
Adams 84, William Crawford 41, and Henry Clay 37. As no candidate
received a majority, the three highest names went to the House where
Henry Clay was the Speaker. He became a President-maker. When Clay
threw his support to Adams, 13 states voted for Adams, while only 7 voted
for Jackson and 4 for Crawford.

If no candidate for the office of Vice-President receives a majority of
the electoral vote, the election is thrown into the Senate where only the
two highest candidates are voted on. No matter how close or complicated
the election, this is supposed to take care of any eventuality. Only once
has the Senate elected the Vice-President. In 1836 Martin Van Buren's
electors refused to vote for Richard M. Johnson as Vice-President, and he
was elected by the Senate by a vote of 33 to 16.

In one close election it proved impractical to have the decision made
in Congress. This was the famous Hayes-Tilden election dispute of 1876.
Tilden had 184 votes, Hayes 165, and 20 electoral votes were in dispute.
The number required for election was 185. The House was Democratic
while the Republicans controlled the Senate. It was finally agreed to refer

the matter to a special election commission composed of five Senators, five Representatives, and five members of the Supreme Court. The House selected three Democrats and two Republicans; the Senate, three Republicans and two Democrats; two Republican and two Democratic justices were indirectly selected by the act establishing the commission and it became their duty to select the fifth justice. The man selected was a Republican who was the least obnoxious to the Democrats. In each instance, by a party vote of eight to seven, all votes in dispute were given to Hayes and he became President by an electoral count of 185 to 184. Tilden's popular vote was a quarter of a million greater than Hayes'.

The near-revolution that resulted from this disputed election was responsible for an Electoral Count Act which places upon the state the burden of determining the correct returns but leaves to Congress the final decision. It is indeed fortunate that this law has never been tested, for it is not an example of careful and meticulous lawmaking.

Proposed Electoral Reforms

It is obvious that the electoral college is not a thoroughly democratic institution. The criticisms made against it are many, the most important of which are that it is an open invitation to fraud since electors are not bound to follow the popular mandate; that campaigns are restricted to pivotal states in which large sums of money are spent; and that candidates tend to be drawn exclusively from large, closely divided states.

It has often been proposed that the electoral college be abolished entirely and the direct election of President and Vice-President be established in its place. This proposal finds no favor in the South, because of the light vote cast and the consequent lessening which would follow of the South's voice in the election of President. It is also unpopular in the smallest states, which now have a minimum of three electoral votes and would suffer a similar reduction of their effective strength in Presidential elections. There is, accordingly, no prospect for the adoption of an amendment to the Constitution to provide for a direct election, since it would require a two-thirds vote of each house of Congress and the approval of three-fourths of the states.

The leading recent proposal to revise the electoral-college system is the Lodge-Gossett Amendment, introduced by Senator Lodge of Massachusetts and Representative Gossett of Texas in 1950. It passed the Senate in that year by a vote of 64 to 27, but lost in the House. The Lodge-Gossett resolution would abolish the electoral college but retain the electoral votes of the states. Electoral votes in each state would be apportioned according to the percentage of the popular vote which each party received in the November general election. At present the party which polls the highest vote is given the entire electoral vote of a state, but under the

Lodge-Gossett Amendment, it would receive only its proportionate share, as would other parties.

The proposed amendment also carries with it a change in the vote needed to elect the President. Instead of the majority now required, it would take a plurality of 40 per cent of the electoral vote to elect. If no candidate received 40 per cent, the election would be thrown into Congress, the choice to be made between the two candidates having the largest electoral count. Congress would vote by members and not by states. Each member would have one vote.

The Lodge-Gossett resolution appears to be an improvement on the old system. It is feared by many, however, and with some justification, that such an amendment might destroy the two-party system at both the national and state levels, although its backers claim that it would have just the opposite effect. In any case, should this amendment be approved by both houses of Congress, it is likely to find rough sledding when submitted to the states.

The Twentieth Amendment takes care of other situations that might deprive the country of a President. It provides that if, at the beginning of a Presidential term, the President-elect shall have died, the Vice-President-elect shall become President. If the President is not chosen by Inauguration Day, the Vice-President-elect shall act as President until the President qualifies. If neither qualifies, Congress shall decide by law who shall act as President until a President or a Vice-President qualifies.

Title and Qualifications

The President of the United States has become the most powerful figure which a democracy can produce without sacrificing the basic characteristics that make a government democratic. At the time the government was established the monarchical concept of the Presidency was very strong. The Constitutional Convention debated what to call the Chief Executive. In Pinckney's plan the term "President" was used and this was accepted by the committees on style and detail in the Convention. In the First Congress committees were appointed to determine how the President should be addressed. "His Excellency" was suggested, also "His Highness, the President of the United States, and Protector of their Liberties." It has been said that Washington favored "His High Mightiness." No agreement could be reached and since then the Executive has been referred to as "Mr. President."

The qualifications for holding the office of President are few and simple. The President must be a "natural-born citizen," thirty-five years of age, and for 14 years a resident of the United States. The 14 years' residence does not have to be immediately preceding his inauguration. The same requirements apply to the office of Vice-President.

Compensation

Benjamin Franklin argued in the Constitutional Convention that, since wealth and power are the corrupting forces that men find hardest to resist, the President should be paid nothing beyond his expenses. His advice was not followed and George Washington as President received $25,000 a year. The amount was raised to $50,000 when Grant became President. Several times since then it has been raised until, today, the President receives a salary of $100,000 a year and an expense allowance of $50,000, both subject to tax. It is the honor, prestige, and power of the office which attract men, not the salary. A large number of business executives as well as actors receive higher salaries. But the office of the President carries with it perquisites befitting the highest office of the nation.[9] Most Presidents have left office poorer men than when they entered, but Taft, Coolidge, and Truman are reported to have saved money while in office.

Eligibility for Reelection

The question of whether the President should be eligible for reelection was left out of the Constitution although at that time there was considerable support for a single term of seven years with the incumbent unable to succeed himself. The term of four years was agreed upon with no mention of any limitations on running again. Washington very reluctantly accepted a second term and refused a third term. He did this for private reasons. Jefferson could, in all probability, have been reelected for a third term but declined, not for private reasons but for the public interest. He thought that the best interests of a democratic people would be served if a President remained in office no longer than eight years. It was Jefferson, therefore, who actually started the two-term tradition. Jackson could have been elected for a third term but did not desire it. Grant tried but failed to secure the Republican nomination for a third term. Theodore Roosevelt failed also when running on the Bull Moose ticket in 1912. Coolidge, who most people thought could have been elected for a third term, "did not choose to run." It was President Franklin D. Roosevelt who shattered the two-term tradition. In doing so, he had the approval of the American people, for traditions may be broken as well as adhered to.

The reaction to the broad exercise of executive power during crises and

[9] In the *United States News and World Report*, Jan. 28, 1948, p. 11, it was stated: "As it stands, whatever the Chief Executive might need or want for his travel, security, comfort, recreation, health and pleasure is within easy reach. The President has a private Pullman car, a yacht, an airplane and a fleet of automobiles. He has a squad of Secret Service men and a private police force. He has a house and a 16-acre estate, a retinue of servants, a barber, a library. He has a private swimming pool, tennis courts, horseshoe pits, horses to ride when he wants them. He and his family have free medical and dental care. He has free bands, movies, the pick of singers, dancers and artists of all kinds and his choice of athletic events."

wars occurred, not unexpectedly, after the close of World War II. As a part of this reaction a movement was started to amend the Constitution in order to limit a President to two terms. Some of the amendment's sponsors objected to having one man hold office for a long period of time in a democracy. The claim was made that a President of long tenure would appoint so many Federal officeholders that his supporters would make it practically impossible to secure a change except through a declination by a President to run for another term or by his death. Other sponsors of the term limitation were political enemies of President Roosevelt who chose this method of showing their opposition to anything that smacked of Rooseveltian principles. One member of the House said in the debate that the amendment was an attack on the memory of a great statesman who was lying sleeping on the banks of the Hudson. It was called the Anti-Roosevelt Amendment. The amendment was approved by both houses of Congress, and the thirty-sixth state, Nevada, ratified on February 26, 1951. Two other states approved later. Included in the number were many Southern states that had strongly supported President Roosevelt as the standard bearer of the Democratic party. This amendment, while limiting the President to two terms, specifically exempted President Truman and provided that a Vice-President who has served no more than two years of a predecessor's unexpired term may be reelected for two complete terms. What the effect of the amendment will be remains to be seen. Those who were opposed to it fear that it will weaken the leadership of a President during his second term, since he cannot be a candidate again to succeed himself.

The Vice-President

The office of Vice-President was established to provide a successor to the office of President in case of death or disability. By the Constitution, he is given only one duty to perform while serving as Vice-President—to preside over the Senate. He has no vote, except in case of a tie, may not participate in debate, and his influence on legislation is ordinarily slight. When he is absent from the Senate, which is not uncommon, the president pro tem or another Senator takes the chair. One of the anomalies of the Constitution is that the second-highest executive officer is given so little to do, although some Presidents have invited the Vice-President to attend Cabinet meetings and to join in the formation of administrative policy.

Too little attention has been given to the selection of Vice-Presidents. As has been mentioned, the person who is nominated for this office receives the nomination not because he will make an outstanding President if called upon to assume the office, but because he will strengthen the party ticket in the November election and because his nomination will promote harmony in party ranks.

Only seven Vice-Presidents have, in the history of the United States, assumed the office of President. But the possibility is always there, particularly in this age of hovering violence. It has been suggested that the Vice-President be given additional responsibilities, to make the office a more important one and thus to attract to it weightier personalities. Some Presidents have given their Vice-Presidents additional duties of significance. For example, Franklin Roosevelt gave Henry Wallace important assignments in promoting the war efforts of the country and President Eisenhower has made even greater use of Vice-President Nixon, who presides at Cabinet meetings in the absence of the President. But it may be that a constitutional amendment would be a more effective way of aggrandizing the Vice-Presidency. There seems no question but that some means needs to be found to assure that the Vice-President will be worthy to be President of the United States, should he be called by fate to the highest office in the land.

Succession to the Office. One of the most unsatisfactory provisions of the Constitution concerns the succession to the office of President in the event the President becomes unable to perform his duties. The question first arose when President Garfield was shot and lingered between life and death for many days. Who decides when the President is unable to carry out the duties of his office? The Congress has never given a definite answer to this question. Some authorities claim that Congress should designate the Vice-President to exercise the duties of the office. Others say that the Vice-President himself should step in when the President is clearly unfit to remain in office. Still others would prefer that either the Supreme Court or the Cabinet make this grave decision. During President Woodrow Wilson's second term the question of inability arose first when he was away from Washington attending the Peace Conference in Paris and later in connection with his protracted illness. In the first instance certain members of Congress hoped to have a 24-hour absence from the country declared inability in the constitutional sense of the term. In the latter case, a Republican measure sought to define inability in such a way as to leave no doubt that the condition of the President constituted inability. It has been suggested that the best solution is for the Supreme Court to be given the duty of determining when disability exists and when it comes to an end, but nothing has come of the suggestion.

Presidential Succession

One very remarkable fact of American constitutional history is that while seven Presidents and seven Vice-Presidents have died in office no other officer has been called upon to fill the office of President.[10] The framers of the Constitution left to Congress the duty of determining the line of

[10] In addition to the above, John C. Calhoun resigned as Vice-President.

succession. Congress has passed three measures concerning succession.[11] The first act, passed in 1792, provided that after the President and the Vice-President, the officer next in the line of succession should be the president pro tem of the Senate and after him the Speaker of the House. Objections were raised to this act on the grounds that it violated the doctrine of separation of powers by making it possible for high legislative officers to take over the head of the executive branch, that neither officer might meet the constitutional requirements for President, and that a difficult situation could develop if a new Congress had not been organized or its officers selected. Also it might happen that a member of an opposition party would succeed to the office of President. This possibility arose in 1885 during the first term of Cleveland, who was the first Democratic President since James Buchanan. After the death of Vice-President Hendricks, succession would have devolved upon the president pro tem of the Senate, John Sherman, a Republican. This situation was largely responsible for the passage of the Presidential Succession Act of 1886 which established a line of succession in the Cabinet in the order of the establishment of the offices. The chief merits of this act were that it contained succession in the executive branch within the same party, and that it provided a long line of succession.

In 1945 President Truman sent a special message to Congress proposing a new succession act under which the presiding officers of the House and Senate would be next in line. He justified his request on the grounds that the President should not be allowed to select his successor and that the office should be filled by an elected official, although his real reason probably was that he did not regard Secretary of State Stettinius as a suitable successor. He recommended that the Speaker of the House should be next in line of succession. Thus a line of succession was suggested from the Vice-President to the Speaker of the House followed by the president pro tem of the Senate and then the Cabinet officers in the order of the establishment of their offices. After considerable debate the measure was finally passed in 1947, two years later.

This measure leaves much to be desired. It is subject to the same criticisms as the first succession act. On the whole, the Secretaries of State have throughout history been more nearly of the caliber that is desired for President than Speakers of the House. It is well, however, that a long line of succession is established to provide for any contingency that might develop in this atomic age.

[11] Stat. L. 240 (Mar. 1, 1792), 24 Stat. L. 1 (Jan. 19, 1886), 61 Stat. L. 380 (July 18, 1947).

REFERENCES

Hugh A. Bone, *American Politics and the Party System* (1949).
Edward S. Corwin, *The President: Office and Powers* (1948).
James A. Farley, *Behind the Ballots* (1938).
————, *Jim Farley's Story: The Roosevelt Years* (1948).
Sidney Hyman, *The American President* (1954).
Paul F. Lazarsfeld, Bernard Berelson, and Hazel Gandet, *The People's Choice: How the Voter Makes Up His Mind in a Presidential Campaign* (1944).
Stefan Lorant, *The Presidency: A Pictorial History of Presidential Elections* (1951).
Louise Overacker, *Presidential Campaign Funds* (1946).
————, *The Presidential Primary* (1926).
Howard R. Penniman, *Sait's American Parties and Elections* (1952).
Ruth C. Silva, *Presidential Succession* (1951).

CHAPTER 16   *The President and His Powers*

It is an axiom of modern business and politics alike that no organization can flourish without a vigorous executive head. But when the Constitution was framed that was a recent and hard-won truth. The Articles of Confederation had been doomed to failure by the lack of an executive; it was one of the chief missions of the Constitutional Convention to supply one to the fledgling nation. In spite of the fact that the governors of the several states were given few powers in the original constitutions, the framers of the Federal Constitution purposely created a strong Chief Executive with real powers. As Woodrow Wilson put it, the President "is at liberty, both in law and in conscience, to be as big a man as he can." [1]

Power in an executive is important, yet how powerful can he become before there is danger of despotism? The founders inserted controls by the national legislature and the judiciary, to prevent the President from becoming a king. But they could not foretell the exigencies of modern times, and the need for swift, vigorous action in the face of economic crisis or military threats perpetrated by less democratic nations than our own. The leeway which they so carefully allowed the Executive in their original document has been used in recent years, with the aid and comfort of both Congress and the Supreme Court, to make of the President a far more powerful official than most of the founders could possibly have envisaged. Has this development been for better or for worse? Are we building up a dictatorship or merely an adequate Presidency? About this question bitter controversy raged particularly during the tenure of Franklin D. Roosevelt.

There is no doubt but that all Presidents have at their disposal the same powers of office but some exercise power in a more circumspect and careful manner than others. A few of our Presidents, including those who are more commonly considered our great Presidents, were fortunate in that the time in which they served afforded a better opportunity for a full exercise of

[1] *Constitutional Government in the United States,* p. 70, Columbia University Press, New York, 1921.

executive power. Under any circumstances, as Justice Frankfurter has said, "a constitutional democracy like ours is perhaps the most difficult of man's social arrangements to manage successfully." [2]

In a recent rating of Presidents by 50 outstanding historians, six were rated as great, three as near great, 11 were considered average, six below average, and two were rated as failures. George Fort Milton lists eight Presidents as outstanding, including Washington, Jefferson, Jackson, Lincoln, Cleveland, Theodore Roosevelt, Wilson, and Franklin D. Roosevelt.[3] While many people differ with this list, they usually agree on six out of eight names. All these men were forceful leaders; each dealt with some great crisis in American history. Six out of the eight were lawyers, although only one, Lincoln, made his living from the law. Two of our Presidents came from a college campus. It might be thought that the give-and-take existence of public life is a far cry from the quiet life on a campus; yet George Fort Milton, in speaking of Woodrow Wilson's departure from Princeton to enter political life, remarked, "In a short while he turned from the bitter politics of the college to the comparative honesty of party politics." [4]

Increasing Strength of the Presidency

In spite of the fluctuating ability among the holders of this office, the Presidency down through the years has unquestionably grown in power and prestige. Many factors are responsible for this development: the emergence of the President as the leader of his political party; the transition to the administrative type of state where the President, or his agents, affect the every-day life of each citizen; the delegation of power by Congress; and the use of emergency powers. It is, however, with respect to military affairs and in the field of foreign relations that the President's power has had its greatest development.

The danger in this growth of power is that too strong an executive in a democratic state could impair popular government and the American concept of individual liberty. Professor Corwin also sees a hazard in granting a President personalized powers which he is permitted to exercise without popular advice or control. This is particularly dangerous when Presidents are selected in a grab-bag type of procedure, and when the President is permitted to exercise extraordinary power without popular advice. The Supreme Court, however, has recently comforted those greatly concerned over the too-broad exercise of Presidential power by acting as a brake to slow down unlimited expansion.[5]

[2] *Youngstown Sheet & Tube Co. v. Sawyer,* 343 U.S. 579, 593 (1952).
[3] *The Use of Presidential Powers,* pp. 311 ff., Little, Brown & Company, Boston, 1944.
[4] *Ibid.,* p. 202.
[5] *Youngstown Sheet and Tube Co. v. Sawyer,* 343 U.S. 579 (1952).

The Appointment and Removal Power

One of the most important of the powers granted to the President by the Constitution is that of appointment and removal. Certainly it is the one that is the most political; through it, the President can reward his friends and punish his enemies. The administration of government depends to a large degree upon the ability of its personnel. When poor appointments are made for political reasons the government suffers. On the other hand, if the President should fill the highest offices without regard to political beliefs and party loyalty, his party leadership would be impaired and he would lose much of the support that is necessary to secure the adoption of his program and to win elections. The result is usually a compromise in which the President appoints to office the best possible "available" candidate. Happy is the President who finds qualifications, proper political affiliation, and loyalty in the same person.

The Power of Appointment. According to Article II, Section 2, of the Constitution, the President:

. . . . shall nominate, and by and with the advice and consent of the Senate, shall appoint ambassadors, other public ministers and consuls, judges of the Supreme Court, and all other officers of the United States, whose appointments are not herein otherwise provided for, and which shall be established by law: but the Congress may by law vest the appointment of such inferior officers, as they think proper, in the President alone, in the courts of law, or in the heads of departments.

The President shall have power to fill up all vacancies that may happen during the recess of the Senate, by granting commissions which shall expire at the end of their next Session.

Besides the well over two million government positions now filled under civil-service rules, as of 1954, 26,000 of the more important civilian officers were nominated by the President.[6]

There are three stages to an appointment to office: the nomination by the President, the assent of the Senate, and last, the final appointment and commission. The power to nominate, wrote Alexander Hamilton in No. 76 of *The Federalist,* was given to the President because it was believed that a single executive could be held responsible for his selections of persons for office. The framers of the Constitution, aware of the poor appointments made by state legislatures as a result of political deals, did not favor vesting the appointing power in a legislative body because then the responsibility for poor appointments could not be fixed.

In making an appointment the President is guided by many considerations: the ability of the man, his party affiliation, who his sponsors are,

6 Federal Personnel Council, *Facts on File,* June 15–July 1, 1954, p. 218.

where he lives, his economic principles, and a host of others. Geographical considerations are often as important as the qualifications of the nominee. Persons outside the career Foreign Service are frequently appointed to represent the United States at important diplomatic posts as a reward for services and contributions to the party. In making judicial appointments, economic and social beliefs are carefully scrutinized.

Of the thousands of civilian positions which are filled by nominees of the President, many are local in character and the President ordinarily follows the advice of others in filling these offices. Senatorial courtesy usually controls; that is, the President nominates the person suggested by the Senator from the state where the office is located, provided that the Senator is of the same political party as the President. Whenever the President follows such senatorial advice there is usually little difficulty in securing Senate confirmation. However, when the President disregards a Senator's recommendation, the Senator may counter by asserting that the nominee is "personally obnoxious" and ask that the committee to which the nomination has been referred not report it to the Senate. Many recommendations made by Senators are actually the work of party leaders within the state and the offices are regarded strictly as party patronage. These appointees hold key political positions.[7]

It is Congress that creates all offices not provided for in the Constitution. In establishing an office Congress may set up qualifications respecting age, party affiliation, technical training, and other considerations. However, no matter what the limitations some choice must be left to the appointing officer. Congress also may increase the powers and duties of a particular officer without necessitating a new appointment to that office.

Recess appointments are made by the President to fill vacancies that happen to exist when the Senate is not in session. Whenever the Senate reconvenes, the name must be sent to it for confirmation. Then the matter is referred to an appropriate committee.

Usually the President is given a free hand in the selection of his Cabinet. But occasionally the Senate balks. When President Eisenhower proposed Charles E. Wilson's name for Secretary of Defense, the confirmation was in serious doubt because of the objection of many Senators to Mr. Wilson's stock holdings in companies which had, or might in the future receive, government contracts. The confirmation came through only after the nominee agreed to sell his stock. Earlier, the Senate had refused outright to confirm the nomination by President Coolidge of Charles Warren as Attorney General, because it was believed his earlier connections with the

---

[7] For an excellent study of the use of senatorial courtesy see Joseph P. Harris, *The Advice and Consent of the Senate,* Chap. 13, The University of California Press, Berkeley, 1953.

"Sugar Trust" would prevent vigorous prosecution of anti-trust suits. However, this was an unusual case; the Cabinet nominations of only four Presidents have been rejected.

Nominations to important diplomatic, judicial, and administrative positions, however, are more carefully scrutinized by the Senate. Most contests in the Senate over nominations are not due to the nominee's lack of the necessary qualifications, but are based largely on political considerations. Senators who are opposed to the President and who wish to embarrass his administration are quick to oppose his nominations, often on grounds which have little merit. Chief Justice Taney, twice rejected by the Senate, later confirmed, became one of the greatest Chief Justices in our history. Similarly, Chief Justice Hughes and Chief Justice Stone were opposed in the Senate. The contest over the nomination of Justice Brandeis by Wilson in 1916 rocked the country; he was confirmed by a strictly party vote, and was later to become one of the most distinguished Justices to sit on the Court. In recent years the fights in the Senate over the nominations of David Lilienthal as chairman of the Atomic Energy Commission, Gordon Clapp to the chairmanship of the Tennessee Valley Authority, Philip Jessup to the United Nations Assembly, and Charles E. Bohlen as Ambassador to Russia illustrate the partisan or factional considerations which are often present. When the Senate is not controlled by the President's own party, confirmation sometimes becomes a difficult problem unless the nominee is extremely popular and has an excellent record in public life.

The Removal Power. While the Constitution sets up specific rules regarding the power to appoint, nothing is said about the removal power. In the famous debate over the removal power in the first session of Congress several different interpretations were advanced. Some thought that it belonged to the President because it was not given to any other governmental agency. A few at that time considered an office a vested right, but the American view is that there is no property right in public office. Others maintained that Congress had the removal power and could place it wherever it desired because of the "necessary-and-proper" clause in the Constitution. Lastly the removal power was considered as incident to the power to appoint and therefore as resting in the President. This last interpretation has been the one accepted by the Supreme Court and most constitutional lawyers.

Congress has made many attempts to limit the power of the President to remove Cabinet officers. In 1867 the Tenure of Office Act fixed the tenure of Cabinet officers and permitted no removal without consent of the Senate. This act was repealed before its constitutionality could be tested. An act of 1876 provided that the President could not remove postmasters without the consent of the Senate. The constitutionality of this act was not questioned until 1920 when President Woodrow Wilson removed a postmaster before the expiration of his term. A suit brought by the discharged postmaster came before the Supreme Court in the famous case of *Myers v. United States.* Chief Justic Taft, speaking for the Court, held that the law was unconstitutional, for the President could not faithfully execute the law if his removal power were abridged.[8]

A number of earlier acts creating independent boards and commissions restricted the President's power of removal. For instance, members of the Federal Trade Commission, by act of Congress, could be removed by the President only for inefficiency, neglect of duty, or malfeasance in office. Were these provisions constitutional? In 1935 a case came before the Supreme Court dealing with President Roosevelt's removal of a member of the Federal Trade Commission without giving any reasons other than that the incumbent did not see eye to eye with the President on the policies to be followed. The removal was challenged in the courts as unconstitutional, and in the case of *Rathbun v. United States* the Supreme Court held that the commissioner in question had been wrongfully removed from office. The Court reasoned that while Congress could not limit or regulate the President's power to remove an executive officer, such as a postmaster, the same rule did not apply to an independent regulatory commission which performs quasi-legislative and quasi-judicial duties.[9]

The authority of Congress, in creating quasi-legislative or quasi-judicial agencies, to require them to act in discharge of their duties independently of executive control cannot well be doubted; and that authority includes, as an appropriate incident, power to fix the period during which they shall continue in office, and to forbid their removal except for cause in the meantime.

This decision limits the unrestricted removal power of the President to purely executive officers and permits Congress to regulate the removal of other officers.

At times the President has kept in office persons who have lost the confidence of Congress. Can Congress force the removal of such officers without impeaching them? The matter was debated at length when the Senate passed a resolution requesting President Coolidge to remove Secretary Denby from the Cabinet. President Coolidge stoutly maintained that this was an executive function and denied any right of the Senate to interfere. Shortly afterwards Denby resigned.

The President as a Legislative Leader

The President of the United States is not only the nation's highest executive officer but also participates actively in the legislative process. This

[8] *Myers v. United States,* 272 U.S. 52 (1926).
[9] *Rathbun v. United States,* 295 U.S. 602, 629 (1935).

participation is provided for by the Constitution, which vests in the President the message power, the power to call special sessions of Congress, the power to adjourn Congress when that body is unable to agree upon a time for adjournment, and, last but not least, the power to veto acts and joint resolutions of Congress. The legislative leadership of the President depends not only on the powers granted to him in the Constitution, but also upon the fact that he is the head of his party; upon his personal and political abilities; upon whether the times call for strong executive leadership, and whether the same political party controls both the executive and the legislative branches of government.

A President can exert considerable influence over legislation by working closely with the Congressional party leaders, by consulting with them, and through them securing the introduction of measures in Congress that are called administrative measures. The President may also appeal to the people in an attempt to arouse public opinion in favor of his legislative program.

A President who does not exercise the requisite legislative leadership may be considered at least a partial failure. The need is very great for someone to guide Congress through the welter of proposals through which the legislative bark tosses during every session. The pull of the opposing party aims and the stresses and strains of conflicting political personalities which prevail in Congress are not conducive to the formulation of a unified program for the welfare of the nation. While the President may not always be right, at least it is within his power, as a single individual who has a single political philosophy and the support of a large part (if not all) of the voting populace, to chart a reasonably straight legislative course. A strong President can get Congress to adhere in large measure to such a course, and the result is bound at the very least to reduce national confusion; at best, it can immeasurably enhance the national welfare.

The Message Power. The President, by Article II, Section 3, of the Constitution, is required periodically to give Congress "information of the state of the Union, and recommend to their consideration such measures as he shall judge necessary and expedient." Upon the opening of each session of Congress, the members of the Senate cross over to the House of Representatives to sit in joint session and listen to the message of the President on the State of the Union. This is usually a carefully prepared document in which the President not only gives his interpretation of current affairs, both foreign and domestic, but also outlines a legislative program that he wants the Congress to follow in the session just beginning. Obviously the degree of acceptance by Congress of these Presidential proposals depends not only upon their quality but also upon whether Congress is controlled by the President's own political party. The legislative program of a President is given to Congress, not only in his State of the

Union message, but also in his budget message and a third message accompanying his "Economic Report to the Congress." Other matters are presented in a series of special messages.

Both George Washington and John Adams delivered their State of the Union messages to Congress in person. Thomas Jefferson, who was a better writer than a speaker, discontinued the practice and sent his message to Congress to be read in the joint session by the Clerk of the House. The Jeffersonian precedent was followed by subsequent Presidents until Woodrow Wilson restored the early practice by delivering his major messages. The Presidents who followed Wilson have continued this practice but messages concerning particular legislative programs are usually submitted in writing to be read by the clerks of the two houses.

The preparation of these messages requires much thought and labor. At times they represent the written opinion of the President himself. Otherwise, the President gathers together the work of experts to whom he has assigned the duty of helping prepare the message. The American Political Science Association was asked several times by President Truman to make unbiased studies of particular problems and to furnish him with reports to be incorporated in his messages. The report of a committee of this Association which studied congressional reapportionment became the basis of a Truman message to Congress in 1951. Also, in his message to Congress requesting legislation on the subject of voting in the armed services, the President stated, "I requested the American Political Science Association . . . to make a special study of voting in the Armed Forces . . . The results of their study and their recommendations are embodied in their report to me, which I am transmitting, with this message, to the Congress." [10]

The President's message to Congress is also a report to all citizens. By press, by radio, and now by television, people in all sections of the country learn the contents of the message. All Presidents are aware of this large unseen audience and are keenly concerned with the reaction of citizens to their recommendations. In the future it is only reasonable to expect that Presidents will more and more direct their messages to the American people rather than to Congress alone.

Power to Call Special Sessions. The power to call Congress into extraordinary session was formerly much more important than it is today. Before the adoption of the Twentieth Amendment, the newly elected Congress did not meet until December of the following year. For this reason special sessions were frequently called during the year following the election to enact needed legislation. The Twentieth Amendment changed this system and today sessions of Congress are held each year, beginning in January, and last from seven to nine months of each year.

Presidents are loath to call special sessions unless absolutely necessary,

[10] H. Doc. 407, 82d Cong., 2d sess., p. III.

for in reality they enjoy the periods when congressmen are away from Washington and peace and quiet descend upon Capitol Hill. Whenever a special session is called Congress is not limited to the subjects mentioned in the call. In contrast, the business considered during a special session of state legislatures is usually limited to that mentioned in the call of the governor.

The President is also given the power to adjourn Congress when there is disagreement between House and Senate as to time of adjournment. This power has never been exercised, for Congress has always been able to agree on that subject.

The Signing of a Bill. All bills and joint resolutions, when passed by both houses of Congress, must be presented to the President for his signature. The President has 10 days in which to consider the matter. Several alternatives are open to him. In the first place, he may sign the measure whereupon it becomes law. Usually no statement is made as to the reasons for signing except when the President protests certain sections of the bill. When the bill is a popular or important one the signing becomes a ceremony and the pen or pens used by the President are given to the principal sponsors of the legislation as souvenirs.

Second, if the President fails to take any action within the 10 days allotted to him by the Constitution for signing, the bill becomes law without his signature. This procedure is followed when the President, having recommended legislation upon a particular subject, secures the passage of a bill through Congress but does not approve of its final form. Thirdly, he may veto the measure or, near the close of the session, make use of the pocket veto.

The Veto Power. In describing the veto power of the President a recent writer declared, "It is almost impossible to overevaluate or exaggerate the importance of the Presidential veto power in our political economy." [11] Woodrow Wilson considered it beyond all comparison his most formidable prerogative. It was his opinion that the President is no greater than his prerogative of veto makes him.

The members of the Constitutional Convention differed greatly as to the nature and use of the veto power. The Virginia plan suggested a Council of Revision. Alexander Hamilton was willing that the President have an absolute veto over all legislation. It was Elbridge Gerry who suggested the general idea of the veto power that was incorporated in the Constitution. Whenever the President disapproves a measure he may veto it. This kills the bill unless Congress, by a two-thirds vote, passes the measure over the President's veto. The bill then becomes law without the President's signature.

[11] Charles J. Zinn, *The Veto Power of the President*, p. 5, House Committee on the Judiciary, 1952.

The veto power has been used more vigorously in recent years than formerly. Eight Presidents, John Adams, Jefferson, J. Q. Adams, Van Buren, W. H. Harrison, Taylor, Fillmore, and Garfield did not veto any bills. The first six Presidents vetoed only three bills. In contrast, during his long term of office Franklin D. Roosevelt vetoed 631 bills. During the first session of the Eighty-second Congress, President Truman signed 253 bills of a public nature and 411 private bills. He vetoed 13 bills, two of which became law over his veto. Four of the vetoes were pocket vetoes. President Eisenhower during the two years of the 83rd Congress vetoed 52 bills; 21 of these were regular vetoes while 31 were pocket vetoes.

Washington and other early Presidents vetoed only bills which they regarded as unconstitutional. Jackson was the first President to use this power to defend the executive branch from legislative encroachment. Today Presidents veto bills which they regard as inexpedient, contrary to public policy, or for any other reason that is considered compelling.[12]

The Supreme Court has overruled many technical objections that have been raised against full use of the veto power. The President may exercise the veto power during a temporary recess, after a session, and after a final adjournment of Congress, provided his veto is used within the prescribed 10-day limit.

Formerly, the duty of signing and vetoing bills made it necessary for the President to remain in the vicinity of Washington. Today, rapid means of transportation make it possible for the President to be reached in the remote corners of the world within the allotted 10-day period; thus the mobility of the Chief Executive has been greatly increased.

Whenever a bill passes Congress within the last 10 days of the session the President may sign the measure or, if he disapproves, pocket-veto the measure. This is done by simply not returning the bill. Obviously he can hold the bill until Congress has adjourned and then no chamber would be in session to receive the vetoed bill and veto message. The President does not have to give any explanation of a pocket veto, although President Franklin D. Roosevelt wrote a short memorandum to accompany each measure that received his pocket veto.

Whenever a bill is vetoed and is returned to the house of its origin it may become law over the President's veto if passed by a two-thirds vote in both Houses, a quorum being present. Tyler was the first President to have a veto overridden. Andrew Johnson was particularly unfortunate in having his vetoes overridden by a hostile Congress. Woodrow Wilson was reversed six times whereas Franklin D. Roosevelt had nine vetoes overridden.

[12] Proposed amendments to the Constitution, which have been approved by both houses of Congress, are not sent to the President for his signature. However, the Thirteenth Amendment was sent although the Senate later said it was done "inadvertently" and that the signature was unnecessary.

It is usually very difficult to secure the necessary two-thirds vote that is required to pass a bill over the President's veto.

It has frequently been proposed that the President should be granted an item veto, which the large majority of state governors possess. At the present time he must accept an entire bill or nothing at all. Particularly with respect to appropriation measures is there a need for the item veto. If this power were given to the President by constitutional amendment, it would sound the death knell to many "riders" that merit a quick and complete demise.

The Power to Pardon

For crimes committed against the state, the power of clemency has existed since the beginning of organized government. Originally, in England, the King exercised this power. However, it is not an inherent executive power and in a democracy may be placed anywhere. There was little debate in the Constitutional Convention over the power to pardon and what debate did take place was over the power to pardon for treason. It was given to the President, who exercises that right by himself or through appropriate agents.

Pardons may be granted for many reasons, the most common of which is to prevent a miscarriage of justice. The pardoning power is also used to reduce a sentence when the punishment is not in proportion to the offense, or when the part of the sentence already served is considered adequate. At times pardons are promised to certain persons who are under indictment and who agree to testify against more serious offenders. When the power to pardon is properly used, justice is secured without any loss to society.

The definition of a pardon, once given by the Supreme Court, is "an act of grace, proceeding from the power intrusted with the execution of the laws, which exempts the individual on whom it is bestowed from the punishment the law inflicts for a crime he has committed." [13] It does not wipe out the offense as if it had never been committed. All that it provides is an exemption from punishment.

The exercise of the power of granting clemency takes various forms. The pardon may be absolute or conditional. A commutation, which is a lessening of punishment, is another form of pardon. Also there is the reprieve, which is only a stay of execution of punishment, and an amnesty, which is a general pardon. Probation and parole do not stem from the pardoning power but rather from the power of the legislative branch to maintain and establish rules governing penitentiaries.

The President, acting through proper agents, has complete liberty in

---

[13] *United States v. Wilson*, 7 Pet. 150 (1833).

determining when clemency shall be exercised. Congress cannot change the effect of such clemency any more than the Executive can change a law. However, Congress may grant amnesties or group pardons for political offenses as was done after the close of the War Between the States. The judiciary also cannot grant pardons. The Supreme Court even forbade a court to grant an indefinite suspended sentence for it would be, in effect, a pardon.[14] Federal courts can, however, temporarily suspend judgment and may shorten a sentence during the same term of court in which the original sentence was handed down.[15] What might be considered as two possible limitations on the power to pardon are the power of subordinate officials to remit fines and forfeitures and the fact that the pardoning power does not extend to those found guilty by a Court of Impeachment. The President's power extends to persons who have been found guilty [16] of contempt of court in criminal but not in civil cases.[17] This is because in criminal cases only the person and the state are involved, while in civil cases a pardon would relieve a person of doing what the court has ordered him to do or not do with respect to other persons.

Pardons may be granted any time after the crime has been committed, even before trial, but may not be granted before the crime has been committed. Formerly pardons were considered private acts and had to be brought forward in court by the person to whom they were granted. This is not true today for they are considered public acts and can be granted whether the prisoner wants to accept the pardon or not.[18]

The granting of a pardon is at best a poor remedy when innocent persons have been convicted. A pardon can give freedom but cannot restore years. It is well that the power to pardon exists even though it can never return to an innocent person the years of his life spent in prison for a crime that he never committed.

The Head of National Administration

Upon the President rests the overwhelming responsibility for the administration of the national government. The Constitution vests in him the duty of seeing to it that all the laws of the United States are properly executed. The awesome significance of this responsibility was well stated in the report of the Hoover Commission on Organization of the Executive Branch of the Government: [19]

The critical state of world affairs requires the Government of the United States to speak and act with unity of purpose, firmness, and restraint in dealing with

[14] *Ex parte United States,* 242 U.S. 27 (1916).
[15] *United States v. Benz,* 282 U.S. 304 (1931).
[16] *Ex parte Grossman,* 267 U.S. 87 (1925).
[17] *In re Nevitt,* 117 Fed. 448 (1902).
[18] *Biddle v. Perovich,* 274 U.S. 480 (1927).
[19] *General Management of the Executive Branch* p. 2, 1949.

other nations. It must act decisively to preserve its human and material resources. It must develop strong machinery for the national defense, while seeking to construct an enduring world peace. It cannot perform these tasks if its organization for development and execution of policy is confused and disorderly, or if the Chief Executive is handicapped in providing firm direction to the departments and agencies.

A law passed by Congress is only a piece of paper until life is breathed into it by the President, acting usually through his administrative agents.

But the responsibility goes further even than that. For this is the age of general law, and to a large extent the President now has the task of shaping the details of the law itself. Instead of prescribing all the minute particulars of a given piece of legislation, Congress usually sets forth the broad policies, purposes, and limits of the law, then delegates to the President and to his agents the duty of filling in the rest. An example of this procedure is the present tariff policy. For many years Congress passed successive tariff measures embodying specific tariff schedules. Then, in 1922, the flexible-tariff policy was inaugurated whereby the President was given power to alter tariff rates within certain limits without specific authorization by Congress. The 1934 Trade Agreements Act permits the President to negotiate reciprocal trade agrements with foreign states under limitations set up by Congress in the grant of power. Thus Congress retains ultimate control over tariff policy but leaves to the President and to his agents the duty of filling in the minute regulations. This gives flexibility to the law and relief to Congress.

The ordinance power that the President exercises has been delegated to him by Congress. The issuance of specific regulations to fill in the acts of Congress has become more common today until it has been said that the average citizen is more closely regulated by these administrative rulings or ordinances than by the law itself. Members of Congress often condemn the continued delegation of power to the President and administrative agents and urge that the legislative body take back many grants of power. However, as the work of Congress continues to increase it is indeed doubtful that there can be any decrease in the exercise of such legislative power by administrative agencies.

In the process of administering the law, it also becomes the duty of the President and his assistants to construe the law that is being administered. Whenever alternate constructions are possible, the administrator exercises a quasi-legislative function in determining the particular interpretation of the law that shall be followed by his agency.

The executive responsibility of officials is of three general types: First, there is the political responsibility to the party in power. Cabinet officers, the heads of independent executive agencies, and to a lesser extent, subordinate officials feel a political responsibility to the President as the head of a political party. The second type of responsibility is administrative in nature and is that responsibility that a subordinate has for his superior officer. This responsibility is sustained by the power of removal. Lastly, there is legal responsibility that is maintained through the doctrine of judicial review and by personal liability of officers when they act in excess of their power.

The personal liability of officers is an outgrowth of the old maxim that the king can do no wrong, from which it follows that the officer himself is liable. The United States government cannot be sued without its consent, although in the Court of Claims and in certain other courts it has consented to be sued for contracts either expressed or implied. The President himself cannot be held legally for acts done in his official capacity and some writers would say that this immunity from suit extends to acts of a criminal nature.

Subordinate officials have a civil liability in that a writ of mandamus may be issued by the proper court to compel the performance of a ministerial duty. For criminal acts, Federal officers are liable in actions which may be brought before state courts, although under Section 25 of the Judiciary Act, it is possible to secure the removal of the trial to a Federal court.

The President and the Conduct of Foreign Relations

The emergence of the United States as a great world power has made the conduct of foreign relations increasingly important. No more can the United States maintain a foreign policy based on isolation, for a riot in Burma or a revolution in Greece today is *ipso facto* a matter of grave concern to the United States. New means of communication have made the world smaller. New methods of warfare have made the successful conduct of foreign relations a necessity for the very existence of a nation. The United States has accepted the responsibility of world leadership and it is the President who is the spokesman for the United States in foreign affairs.

The conduct of foreign affairs is similar in many respects to driving an automobile on a highway. Safety on the highway is promoted by good driving, proper driving rules, and mechanical excellence of the automobile. But accidents still may occur because of the carelessness of the driver in the car ahead or other errors over which the driver of the first car has no control. Similarly, the success of the conduct of foreign relations depends not alone on the ability of United States officials and the excellence of this country's policy but also upon the actions and reactions of other powers.

The President, as the agent for the conduct of foreign relations, is the repository for inherent powers as well. He receives his powers by direct grant in Article II of the Constitution and in addition has certain inherent powers as the head of the state. The Supreme Court speaks of the President's control of foreign affairs as the "plenary and exclusive power of the President as the sole organ of the federal government in the field of international relations." [20] Possible interference by Congress through the non-appropriation of funds necessary to do the work could occur but it has never taken place.

Recognition of Foreign Governments. The President, as executive head of the government, receives diplomatic envoys from foreign states. This is a ceremony that, at times, can be very important, for by his reception of a representative he recognizes the government that sent him. Actual recognition depends not only upon the credentials that the representative presents but also upon political considerations. When the United States was eager to build the Panama Canal but could not obtain the consent of Colombia for the proposed project, the independence of Panama was recognized after a three-day revolution; a satisfactory agreement for building the canal followed in short order.

The recognition of Israel was even more precipitate. President Truman was notified that an independent republic was being declared and that a provisional government had been established that would discharge the obligations of Israel to the other nations of the world. The Act of Independence was to become effective "one minute after six o'clock on the evening of May 14, 1948, Washington time." On the same day a release was made to the press from the White House that stated,[21]

This Government has been informed that a Jewish state has been proclaimed in Palestine, and recognition has been requested by the provisional government thereof.

The United States recognizes the provisional government as the *de facto* authority of the new State of Israel.

President Truman promised that when a permanent government was established *de jure* recognition would be given. On Feb. 13, 1949, pursuant to this promise, another White House statement was issued to the effect that [22]

Election for such a government was held on January 25. The votes have now been counted, and this Government has been officially informed of the results. The United States Government is therefore pleased to extend *de jure* recognition to the Government of Israel as of January 31.

[20] *United States v. Curtiss-Wright Corp.*, 299 U.S. 304, 320 (1936).

[21] *Department of State Bulletin*, Vol. 18, No. 464, p. 673, May 23, 1948. *De jure* recognition would have committed the United States to a finding that the provisional government was permanent. *De facto* recognition avoids the question of permanence but requires the new nation to observe all international obligations. Usually when doubt exists on this point recognition is withheld and when this assumption proves false, recognition is withdrawn.

[22] *Department of State Bulletin*, Vol. 20, No. 502, p. 205.

The "unseemly haste" of this action was responsible for much criticism. Thomas Jefferson, while Secretary of State, wrote to Gouverneur Morris, then in Paris, that "it accords with our principles to acknowledge any government to be rightful, which is formed by the will of the nation, substantially declared." [23] This, according to one commentator means: "The regime is accepted by the inhabitants of the area and that there is no evidence this regime cannot take care of its immediate obligations." [24] Whether these two obligations were met at the time of the recognition of Israel has been questioned.[25] Because of the failure of the USSR to meet its obligations with respect to United States citizens, recognition of the Soviet state was delayed for over 16 years.

Whenever a diplomatic representative of a foreign state acts so as to offend the United States, the President may ask for his recall and if this does not occur he may be handed his passport. When Cleveland was President, Sackville-West, the British ambassador, became *persona non grata* because of some comments upon the Presidential election then taking place and he was recalled at Cleveland's suggestion. Whenever relations between the United States and a foreign power become strained, diplomatic relations may be severed and the diplomatic agents of both nations return home. This is a step that quite frequently leads to war.

Appointments. The President nominates and with the advice and consent of the Senate appoints ambassadors, other public ministers, and consuls. Diplomats at the lower level are career men in the foreign service but the President at times goes outside the foreign service for the appointment of some of the high ranking diplomats. This policy enables him to pay off political debts but is not always advantageous to the United States.

Treaties and Agreements. The authority to make treaties is given to the President with the advice and consent of the Senate. Consent is secured by a favorable two-thirds vote. Treaties are contracts between nations. The President in person, or working through agents, usually within the State Department, negotiates the treaty. If it is an important one and the approval of the Senate is doubtful, a Senator or two may be included in the diplomatic mission. Senate approval is not always easy to secure, particularly because of the requirement of a two-thirds vote.

Another form of international contract is the executive agreement. This is an agreement made by the President with the foreign state and does not require Senate approval. An executive agreement has the same force as a treaty and therefore it is possible for the President to get what he wants without running the risk of not securing Senate approval. Should an

[23] H. A. Washington (ed.), *The Writings of Thomas Jefferson,* Vol. III, p. 489, Washington, 1853.

[24] Arthur Krock, *The New York Times,* May 20, 1948.

[25] See editorial in *The Catholic World,* Vol. 167, pp. 289–297, 1948.

executive agreement require legislative support this can be done through a joint resolution, thereby bypassing the two-thirds requirement. Although originally it was thought that these agreements could be of a temporary character only, they now approach the scope of treaties. Congress also may authorize the President to make trade agreements, which are similar in their effect to an act of Congress.

To provide a check on the power of the President to make executive agreements and to prevent the transfer of power to world government, Senator Bricker of Ohio became the sponsor of a proposed constitutional amendment bearing his name that would curb the power to make and implement treaties and international agreements. The debate in the Senate over this resolution, that occurred early in 1954, was bitter and brilliant and has been described as "a crossfire of legal arguments (the experts disagree) and conflicting philosophies of government and foreign relations." [26]

The proposed amendment would have required Congressional legislation before an international treaty or agreement could have the effect of international law. The requirement for implementation, however, could have been waived by a two-thirds vote of the Senate. This proposal was amended several times and when finally voted upon by the Senate provided that:

1. A provision of a treaty or other international agreements in conflict with the Constitution shall be of no force or effect.

2. A non-treaty agreement shall take no effect as international law unless implemented by Congressional action.

3. Senate consent to ratification by roll-call vote.

4. The amendment to be inoperative unless ratified by three-fourths of the states within seven years of submission. [27]

A two-thirds majority is necessary in both houses to propose a constitutional amendment. By one vote the proposal was lost, for by a vote of 60 to 31 the Senate on February 26, 1954, rejected the modified version of the proposed Bricker amendment. It was reintroduced in 1955.

In exercising his control over foreign affairs the President makes use of many governmental agencies. The Department of State, in which is the foreign service, is his right arm in this field. The Department of Defense, in periods of extreme military tension, is next in importance. Other departments and commissions are also concerned with foreign relations.

The military power of the President is used primarily in the field of foreign affairs. In fact, all the different powers bestowed on the President by the Constitution may be used to a varying degree to influence the conduct of foreign affairs. The President's foreign policy today is usually a

[26] *Congressional Quarterly*, Vol. 12, No. 3, p. 47.
[27] *Congressional Quarterly*, Vol. 12, No. 10, p. 282.

pivotal issue in Presidential elections. The moulding of public opinion in order to secure popular support for his policies is the last but not the least of the President's responsibilities.

The Military Power of the President

There are two constitutional provisions which are the bases of the President's military powers, (1) that he shall be Commander in Chief of the armed forces, and (2) that "he shall take care that the laws be faithfully executed." [28] Broad as these powers are, the President is by no means unlimited in his power to wage war. On the contrary, the large substantive war powers are in the hands of Congress.

The power of waging war is not dependent alone on constitutional authorization for it is indeed an inherent national power. The highest right that a state has is to preserve its own existence. For this purpose it may go into debt, may exhaust all the national wealth and physical resources, and may demand the lives of its citizens. In this day of total war, armed conflicts cannot be entered into lightly. Even the most localized military action may easily develop into a world conflict. With atomic weapons, hydrogen bombs, jet planes, biological warfare, and other equally destructive forces, war may mean not only death and destruction on an unprecedented scale but the possible extinction of the human race. The location of the power to wage war in a democratic state is, therefore, of great importance.

The war powers are divided between Congress and the President. It is Congress that declares war, governs territories, sets up military law to govern the armed forces, appropriates money, and takes all appropriate action that might be necessary and proper for winning a war. During World War I, prohibition was adopted as a war measure. The rationing of gasoline, the issuance of food stamps, in fact, the close regulation of all phases of civilian life during World War II stemmed from the war powers of Congress.

The President is the supreme military commander over all branches of the armed forces of the United States and the state militia when called into the active service of the United States. Although it was not contemplated that he command troops in actual campaigns, he consults with the general staff as to strategy and policy. All persons in the Armed Forces think of him as the chief.

Duties as Commander in Chief

The President's war powers are instrumental. Whenever Congress declares war (and according to that body it has never declared an aggressive

[28] Art. II, Sec. 3.

war) the President is authorized to use the Armed Forces to conduct the war. While the President cannot declare war, he can bring about a state of armed conflict and then it becomes the moral obligation of Congress to support the President in his actions. Actual hostilities may occur, as in the War Between the States, before the formal declaration of war by Congress.

The extent to which the President participates in military planning and military decisions depends to a considerable extent on his experience and qualifications. A President who has had a military background and training is likely to play a key role in the coordination of political and military policies and the actual determination of military strategy, while one drawn from civilian life is apt to leave all but the major policy decisions to the military.

The power that the President exercises as Commander in Chief cannot be limited by Congress although such attempts have been made at various times. After his retirement from the Presidency, Washington was made Commander in Chief and during the Presidency of Andrew Johnson, General Grant was also made Commander in Chief. Both actions, although never tested in the courts, were patently unconstitutional.

In waging a foreign war the President's power over prisoners and property of the enemy is limited only by the laws of war. Treatment of prisoners of war in the Korean War, although governed by the laws of war, became a serious problem chiefly because the North Koreans refused to be bound by accepted rules.

Military Law. As Commander in Chief, the President, acting through appropriate agents, is responsible for the execution of the military law that Congress has enacted to govern the Armed Forces. These enactments of Congress were formerly called the Articles of War, but after World War II they were extensively revised and are now known as the Uniform Code of Military Justice. This revision tempered some of the harshness of previous Articles and eliminated others found by the experience of World War II to be undesirable. Persons who violate military law are tried by military courts and are permitted to have counsel. An appeal may be taken to the United States Court of Military Appeals in Washington and eventually to the President himself.

Military law extends to all persons in the Armed Forces, even to camp followers. In the last war, it extended to members of the merchant marine when the vessel on which they were serving was part of a military convoy. Also, enemy spies who entered the United States to commit acts of sabotage were tried and convicted by a military court, although at least one of them maintained he was an American citizen.[29] Military personnel are not only bound by military law, but must also obey the civil law. When there

[29] *Ex parte Quirin,* 317 U.S. 1 (1942).

is conflict in jurisdiction, custody of a prisoner may hinge upon whether the United States is at war and whether the crime was committed within the continental United States or abroad.

The President may establish military government in conquered territory and in territory acquired through cession, subject to the acts of Congress. During the Reconstruction period Congress set aside the government established by President Johnson in the South. After World War II, military governments were set up by the United States in Italy, Japan, and in certain sections of Korea, Germany, Austria. These military governments were to continue until the signing of the peace treaty and were administered by a combination of American and local personnel.

Military Force in Domestic Affairs. In domestic affairs the President enforces the constitutional guarantee that each state is guaranteed a republican form of government. The question of what is a republican form of government is a political one and is left to Congress to determine in the final analysis. However, the President, by statute, is authorized to use the military might of the nation to enforce this constitutional guarantee.

Except in the most unusual cases military forces are unnecessary to secure the enforcement of law within the United States. Local and state law is enforced by local police officers. If they are unable to restore order, the governor of the state may be asked to make use of the state police or to call out the state militia. If this is not sufficient, the governor may request military assistance of the President of the United States. But the President may send troops into a state without waiting for such a request if he believes that this action is necessary to carry out the functions of the Federal government, as, for example, the carrying of the mails. Today, due to the number and variety of Federal instrumentalities it is difficult to conceive of any sizeable disturbance that would not interfere with some Federal agency.

It is easy to understand that military force may be used to secure the enforcement of Federal law and, under certain conditions, state law. However, it is also permissible for the Federal government to use force against a state. The theory of the nullificationists held that this power was to protect the states and not to be used against them. In the Prize Cases the Supreme Court was of the opinion that the Court must be governed by what the political department of the government thinks is the necessary action and that the President must determine what degree of force the crisis demands.[30]

Whenever military forces are called out to secure obedience to law and to suppress riot and insurrection, they may be used as auxiliaries to the civil police, or martial law may be declared. Martial law differs from military law; it is the law that governs civilians in the area affected when the

[30] 2 Black 635 (1863).

civil courts are not functioning properly. It is in reality no law at all for once martial law has been declared by the President or his agents the military may establish courts for the trial of civilians and may inflict any punishment that the court thinks best. Naturally its use is not welcomed by civilians and when used improperly it is the very essence of tyranny. The following general rules should govern its use.

Martial law is an emergency measure and may be used when necessary as a means of last resort. It is incident to the war power and is a means of the executive to see that the laws are faithfully executed. Certain restrictions have grown up respecting its use. It cannot be used outside the war zone. In time of civil disturbance it can be used only when the courts are not functioning in the proper manner. Whenever a governor declares martial law, during times of riot and domestic violence, his decision is reviewable by the courts, a procedure which has never been applied to declarations of martial law by the President. Finally it is well to remember that martial law is not suspensory in nature but is restorative. It does not supplant the Constitution but is the means used to restore it to full operation.

The President and Emergencies

All states have the fundamental right of preserving their own existence. The use of martial law has long been justified as an emergency power to be exercised only at a time of great stress to restore law and order. During the past two decades emergencies have been used as a reason for the exercise of other governmental powers as well, chiefly in order to combat economic emergencies that seemed to threaten the life of the nation. In recent years, crisis has followed crisis; emergencies have appeared to create new emergencies. One wonders if the United States will ever return to what was formerly considered normal times.

Both Congress and the President may use emergency powers. Those exercised by the Chief Executive are based either on his military power, his responsibility to see that the laws are faithfully executed, or on emergency power delegated to him by Congress. Stringent and severe may be the measures required to restore normal conditions. In times of military emergency it has long been customary for the President to resort to extraordinary means. However, it was not until 1933 that the President first made use of emergency powers to meet an economic crisis. Since that date Presidents have issued proclamations declaring both "limited" and "unlimited" national emergencies.

There is little uniformity in the laws passed by Congress concerning actions which may be taken in the case of emergencies. Under a few such laws the President may act only after Congress itself has declared that an emergency exists, but ordinarily the President himself is authorized to determine whether there is an emergency. The use of emergency powers is both salutary and dangerous. Properly used they are restorative; improperly used, they may become a prelude to dictatorship.

The President's emergency power is not unlimited. The Supreme Court, in a recent famous decision,[31] refused to uphold President Truman when he issued an order directing the Secretary of Commerce to take possession of and operate most of the nation's steel mills. The President's justification for his action was that to avert national catastrophe it was necessary. The Supreme Court, speaking through Justice Black, could find no source of authority for the President's action either in the Constitution or in any act of Congress. On the contrary, Congress had refused to give such power to the President in 1947 when it rejected an amendment to the Taft-Hartley Act authorizing such action. It could not be a valid exercise of the military power for, according to Justice Black, the Commander in Chief does not have the power "to take possession of private property in order to keep labor disputes from stopping production. This is a job for the Nation's lawmakers, not for its military authorities . . . The Constitution does not subject this law-making power of Congress to presidential or military supervision or control." [32]

In a concurring opinion Justice Douglas emphasized the danger of permitting the President such freedom of action: "Today a kindly President uses the seizure power" but once granted it could be used "to regiment labor as oppressively as industry thinks it has been regimented by this seizure." [33] Justice Douglas reiterated the statement made by the Court in 1934 that an emergency does not create power, and pointed out that Congress had by legislation set up procedure for handling situations similar to that created by the steel strike. Justice Frankfurter doubted that any emergency existed that made such drastic action necessary. It was his opinion that the case did not arise suddenly but was a long time in the making.

From this decision it would appear that the President may act without the authorization of law only under certain contingencies: there must be a real emergency; it must be of a type for which Congress has not already legislated; and it must be one which has arisen suddenly, not affording sufficient time for action by Congress. These are certainly valid and necessary limits to the exercise of emergency power by the Chief Executive.

Yet, the President may still act in time of emergency. It is true that limits are set to the exercise of this power but there will be many times when these limits are obscure. Justice Clark, in agreeing with the majority, stated "In my view . . . the Constitution does grant to the President ex-

[31] *Youngstown Sheet & Tube Co. v. Sawyer*, 343 U.S. 579 (1952).
[32] *Ibid.*, pp. 587–588.
[33] *Ibid.*, pp. 633–634.

clusive authority in times of grave and imperative national emergency. In fact, to my thinking, such a grant may well be necessary to the very existence of the Constitution itself." [34] This is but a substantiation of the doctrine that when emergency power is used properly, it is restorative in nature.

Presidential Agencies

The Executive Office of the President. Under authority of the Reorganization Act of 1939 and by various acts of Congress and Executive orders, a number of staff and coordinating agencies have been placed in the Executive Office of the President and under his direct supervision. Among these are the White House Office, the Bureau of the Budget, the Council of Economic Advisers, the National Security Council, the Central Intelligence Agency, the Operations Coordinating Board, and the Office of Defense Mobilization. The White House Office carries out the many minute duties incident to the office of President. The Bureau of the Budget, in addition to assisting the President in the preparation of the budget, acts as a staff agency. The other offices and boards, which also have administrative duties, serve as well in an advisory and consultative capacity to the President. For instance, the Council of Economic Advisers

assists the President in the preparation of his annual Economic Report to Congress; studies national economic development and trends; appraises activities of the Federal Government bearing upon the Nation's economy and the advancement thereof; develops and recommends to the President national economic policies to foster economic growth and stability; and furnishes the President with such other studies and reports relating to Federal economic policy and legislation as the President may request.[35]

The Cabinet.[36] The Cabinet serves the President in a dual capacity. It is a source of consultation, within the President's own political family, on matters of importance. It is also the nucleus for the administration of the national government, for its members comprise the heads of the major government agencies. In selecting his Cabinet, the President must take into account many factors: the qualifications of persons under consideration, their political backing, the sections of the country from which they come, their personal and party loyalties, what they stand for, and with what groups they are identified. Cabinet rank is determined by the order of the establishment of the different departments. A few Cabinet officers like Andrew Mellon have served under different Presidents but this is unusual.

[34] *Ibid.*, p. 662.
[35] *United States Government Organization Manual, 1951–52*, p. 62.
[36] The origins of the Cabinet are discussed in Chap. 8.

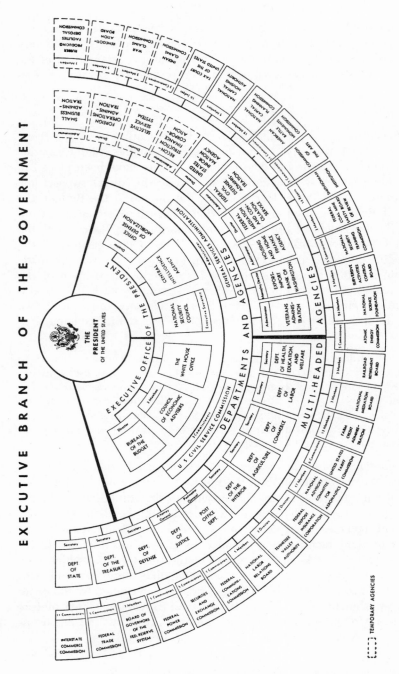

EXECUTIVE BRANCH OF THE GOVERNMENT

FIG. 2. Executive branch of the government.

288

Whenever a Cabinet meeting is held the President may ask for a vote or may ask the opinion of each member of the Cabinet. But he is not bound by Cabinet opinion and can make his own decision. Some Presidents have been more inclined to follow the advice of unofficial advisors rather than of members of the Cabinet. At times disputes and disagreements have marred the harmony of Cabinet meetings and caused the President to consult with individual Cabinet officers rather than with the Cabinet as a body. Woodrow Wilson requested the resignation of Secretary of State Robert Lansing, justifying his action by the fact that Lansing called Cabinet meetings without Presidential authorization when Wilson was ill.

All Presidents have utilized the advice of persons who are not members of the Cabinet. Colonel House was a close advisor to President Wilson, as was Harry Hopkins to Franklin Roosevelt, and Bernard Baruch to several Presidents. While the practice of using unofficial Presidential advisors has been criticized, a President is entitled to consult with anyone he selects, and to give greatest weight to advice from persons in whom he has most confidence.

Within recent years the Cabinet has declined in importance, particularly under President Franklin D. Roosevelt. It has been said that strong Presidents are inclined to have weak Cabinets while weak Presidents have strong Cabinets, a statement that has some truth in it but not enough to justify the generalization. Composed of vigorous, able men, the Cabinet can become a useful instrument in the consideration of policies and the coordination of the government. Paradoxically, the concentration of power in the hands of the President has tended to weaken rather than strengthen the position of the Cabinet. This is doubtless explained by the fact that ambitious and able men would not long be content with a merely advisory role.[37]

REFERENCES

C. A. Berdahl, *War Powers of the Executive in the United States* (1921).
Wilfred E. Binkley, *President and Congress* (1947).
L. H. Chamberlain, *The President, Congress and Legislation* (1946).
E. S. Corwin, *The President: Office and Powers* (1948).
———, *The President's Control of Foreign Relations* (1917).
James Hart, *The American Presidency in Action, 1789* (1948).
E. P. Herring, *Presidential Leadership* (1940).
Sidney Hyman, *The American President* (1954).

[37] Due to world tension, the threat of war, and the need of defensive measures to preserve the position of the United States, the Joint Chiefs of Staff, actually an agency of the Department of Defense, has become one of the most important policy-determining agencies and an advisory body to the President of the first importance. Composed of top men in the different branches of the armed services, they are the principal military advisors to the President, the National Security Council, and the Secretary of Defense.

H. J. Laski, *The American Presidency* (1940).

G. F. Milton, *The Use of Presidential Power* (1944).

C. P. Patterson, *Presidential Government in the United States* (1947).

Robert S. Rankin (ed.), *The Presidency in Transition* (1949).

C. L. Rossiter, *Constitutional Dictatorship* (1948).

————, *The Supreme Court and the Commander in Chief* (1951).

H. M. Somers, *Presidential Agency: OWMR* (1950).

William Howard Taft, *Our Chief Magistrate and His Powers* (1916).

CHAPTER 17 *The Federal Judiciary*

Independence of the Courts

The more government grows, the more functions it undertakes, the more agencies it creates to perform these functions, the more disputes between citizens and individual governmental agencies come into the courts. Rigid and severe tax laws have the same effect. And an independent judiciary is necessary if these individual rights are to be secure against arbitrary governmental action. In 1913, while lecturing at Yale University, William Howard Taft, who later was to become Chief Justice of the Supreme Court, remarked [1]

Judges to fulfill their functions properly in our popular government must be more independent than in any other form of government and that need of independence is greatest when the individual is one litigant, and the State, guided by the successful and governing majority, is another.

The judiciary, as one of the three main branches of the government, has important relations with the other two branches. Both the executive and the legislative divisions of government exercise some control over the judiciary. Indeed, its continued existence is dependent upon action that must be taken by Congress and the President. The control by Congress is extensive and will be discussed later, as will the power of the President to determine the personnel of the judicial branch. In spite of this control and the interrelations that exist, the courts have indeed remained independent in the performance of their functions, a condition vital to a healthy judiciary.

Through the years certain customs and rules have developed which have aided the judiciary in repelling outside influences and in maintaining its independence and at times even its isolation. In the first place, while many decisions of the courts have political significance, the courts will not

[1] William Howard Taft, *Popular Government,* p. 170, Yale University Press, New Haven, 1913.

determine questions of a purely political nature. The recognition of one of the two governments set up in Rhode Island during Dorr's Rebellion, said the Supreme Court, was a political question and must be left to political divisions of government rather than to the judiciary.

Secondly, the courts will not exercise other nonjudicial functions. During Washington's administration the Supreme Court refused to determine who should receive pensions for fighting in the Revolutionary War for this again was considered a political rather than a judicial matter. Individual justices, however, at times have performed specific duties that have been placed upon them by the President. Justice Jackson helped conduct the Nuremberg trials while Justice Roberts served on the committee appointed by the President to investigate the Pearl Harbor disaster.

Independence of the judiciary is also maintained because of the fact that all judges in the Federal system of courts are appointed for life, as long as good behavior is maintained. Indeed it is most difficult to remove even an incompetent judge. Also, even if a particular justice, when appointed to the Supreme Court, might have the same economic and social philosophy as the President who appointed him, it does not follow that he will not change his beliefs. On the contrary, the history of the Supreme Court shows that independence of thought develops with service on the bench and that this independence is frequently incorporated in specific court decisions. The constitutional guarantee that the compensation of Federal judges shall not be diminished during their terms of office is a further guarantee of independent thinking.

Independence of the judiciary is promoted by the fact that a court is never directly responsible for enforcing its decisions. At first glance this would not appear to be advantageous, for the possibility of the nullification of court action by the inaction of the enforcing bodies would destroy the effectiveness of a court. Yet, today, all decisions are accepted and are enforced without any action by the judiciary. In the famous case of *Virginia v. West Virginia*,[2] when it was doubtful whether one state would abide by the decision, the Supreme Court left to Congress the responsibility of taking the proper procedure for the enforcement of the finding of the Court.

It is difficult to maintain an independent judiciary and, at the same time, to have judges and courts that always perform in a satisfactory manner. Whenever judges are appointed for the duration of good behavior there always arises the problem of how to get rid of judges who are undesirable and should not be kept upon the bench. For many years there was no system of retirement with pay, and, therefore, many judges remained on the bench long after their usefulness had ended simply as a matter of dollars and cents. Today, any judge or justice of the United States appointed to hold office during good behavior may resign after attaining the

[2] 246 U.S. 565 (1918).

age of seventy and after serving 10 years continuously on the bench. During the remainder of his lifetime, he will continue to receive the same salary as when he resigned. Should a circuit or district court judge become physically or mentally disabled and unable to perform his work, but refuse to resign, the President may appoint an additional judge to the bench. Later, when the vacancy does occur through death or resignation, it is not filled. If a lower-court judge becomes permanently disabled and resigns after he has served on the bench for 10 years he receives full pay; if he has served less than 10 years, he receives one-half of the pay that he was receiving at the time of his resignation. Many judges today are far more willing to retire because of this generous retirement policy of the Federal government.

Impeachment is also a remedy by which judges may be removed from office. And yet, either because of the high quality of the persons selected for the bench or because of the cumbersome machinery of impeachment, or both, the impeachment of judges has occurred only in a few isolated instances. Nine Federal judges have been impeached and of this number only four have been removed from office. It would appear, therefore, that members of the judiciary are relatively safe in office unless their conduct is obviously of a highly undesirable character.

Origin of the Courts

Judicial power is the power to try and determine cases. The courts must exercise this power in conformity with law and by the methods established by usage. The Constitution stresses the importance of such legally constituted judicial power, as distinguished from any inherent authority of the courts. It gives Congress the duty of establishing the Federal courts necessary for the impartial exercise of the judicial function. Cases and controversies brought to the courts for determination vary from the simple to the complex; from a minor violation of a revenue statute to a suit that involves large corporations and millions of dollars; from a person asking redress for a fancied wrong to a case involving the civil liberties of thousands of persons.

Within the term "judicial power" are also included functions not commonly associated with a court trial. Among these are the power to admit attorneys to practice before the courts or debar them from it, to grant injunctions, to issue writs of mandamus, habeas corpus and other writs, to punish for contempt of court, and to interpret the law through the exercise of the power of judicial review.

During colonial days each colony had its own courts but at that time the judiciary was the least developed of the three branches of government. In no instance was there an established system of courts. Most of the judicial work of that day was done in the courts of the justices of the peace. Usually there was a higher court in each colony but grounds of appeal were vague and the colonial legislative bodies themselves exercised certain judicial powers. One of the great weaknesses of the Articles of Confederation was that it failed to provide for a system of national courts.

By the time of the Constitutional Convention the need for the establishment of a Federal system of courts was apparent to many citizens. The convincing reasons leading to the creation of the Federal court system have been stated as follows: [3]

1. The new government was to pass laws binding on individuals.

2. There was a great need for the uniform application of law.

3. There was an equally important need for an umpire of disputes between the states and the Federal government.

4. A need existed for a court where the rights of foreigners could be adjudicated.

5. An umpire to determine disputes between states was imperative.

6. A tribunal was required to settle controversies between citizens of different states.

There were differences of opinion among the members of the Convention as to the number and type of Federal courts that should be established. As a result, Article III of the Constitution, dealing with the judiciary, provided simply for one Supreme Court and for Congress to establish by law inferior courts as needed. To these courts was given the jurisdiction of determining all judicial questions of a Federal nature and the responsibility of acting as umpire of the Federal government. It was implied in the Constitution that the Supreme Court was to pass on the constitutionality of laws passed by Congress. Indeed, it was even suggested in the Constitutional Convention that the Supreme Court be permitted to veto acts of Congress. This idea, though strongly urged, was rejected by a very close vote. There was little objection to the judiciary article during the debates over ratification in the state conventions.

Congress took its responsibility seriously and in the Judiciary Act of 1789 established a system of courts that in form and essence remains in existence today.

Congressional Control of the Courts

The control that Congress exercises over the judicial branch is extensive. Without congressional action there would be no Federal judiciary. Congress has created all Federal courts that are in existence today. Even the Supreme Court was established by Congress, subject to the constitutional restriction that there be only *one* Supreme Court. All courts established under the authority of Article III of the Constitution are called constitu-

[3] Samuel P. Orth and Robert E. Cushman, *American National Government*, pp. 489–491, Appleton-Century-Crofts, Inc., New York, 1931.

tional courts; other courts created by Congress are called legislative courts.

Article III is not the only source of authority for the establishment of courts. This power is implied when Congress is given the responsibility of regulating commerce, of granting patents, of appropriating money to pay claims, of governing the District of Columbia and the territories, and of making treaties effective. One difference between these two types of courts is that the judges of the legislative courts hold office either for a definite term or during good behavior, as Congress determines, while all other Federal judges hold office during good behavior. Legislative-court judges also are subject to removal by the President under the terms of the act of Congress. Impeachment is the only method of removing other Federal judges.

It is Congress that determines the number of Federal judges and also the number of judges that shall sit on each court. Because of the growth of population, new activities undertaken by the Federal government, and for other reasons, the business of the courts has increased year by year. There are today approximately 230 district judges, 68 courts-of-appeals judges and nine Supreme Court justices.

Originally the Supreme Court was composed of a Chief Justice and five Associate Justices. Congress has altered the number from time to time; once there were 10 members. In order to keep Andrew Johnson from making appointments to the Court, Congress reduced the size of the Court during his term from 10 to 7, providing that vacancies occurring either from death or resignation should not be filled until the number of justices dropped to the lower figure. Actually the number never dropped below eight and when Grant became President the size of the Court was increased by Congress to nine.

The last attempt to alter the size of the Supreme Court occurred in 1937 when President F. D. Roosevelt, in a message to Congress, urged the enactment of the "court packing" plan under which as many as six additional justices could be appointed. This recommendation, coming after the Supreme Court had stricken down the NRA, AAA, and other New Deal legislation, was generally regarded as designed to secure a more liberal-minded Court. The proposal was advanced on the ground that new blood was needed, and it provided that for each Justice who was over the retirement age of seventy years, an additional Justice could be appointed, but not to exceed a total of 15. The bill was bitterly debated in the halls of Congress and by citizens everywhere. The Senate Judiciary Committee reported the measure unfavorably and it never became law. Later, through death and by resignation, the President was able to place new men on the Supreme Court bench and thus gain his original objective.

Congress may abolish courts. When the Antifederalists gained control of Congress and the executive branch in 1801, they promptly abolished the courts that had previously been created under Federalist leadership and which had been filled by the "midnight appointments." The circuit courts in 1911 and the Commerce Court in 1913 were also abolished by Congress. Whenever this action is taken the question of what to do with the judges of the defunct court always is raised. In 1801 nothing was done and the judges lost their jobs although Marshall urged that they be transferred to other Federal courts where the pay was either the same as or more than they received while members of the courts that had been eliminated. This is the accepted practice today, a correct one if the independence of the judiciary is to be maintained.

Congress has extensive control over the jurisdiction of all Federal courts. The Constitution provides that Federal jurisdiction shall be determined either by the nature of a controversy or by the identity of the parties to a suit. For example, a case arising under the Harrison Narcotics Act would be tried in the Federal district court because the subject matter of the suit is of a Federal nature. Or, should a United States marshal kill someone in the performance of his duty, the trial could take place in the Federal court because of the person on trial being a Federal officer.

The original jurisdiction of the Supreme Court is specified in the Constitution and cannot be altered, save by amendment. Other jurisdictional matters are determined by statute. No other Federal court has exclusive jurisdiction of a matter unless Congress bestows it upon that court. Congress determines all appellate jurisdiction. This control, which is an important one, has been exercised by Congress in a circumspect manner with one important exception. During Reconstruction days Congress altered the appellate jurisdiction of the Supreme Court in order to prevent that body from rendering a decision that Congress thought would be contrary to what it desired. In the case of *Ex parte McCardle* [4] the Supreme Court upheld this control of jurisdiction and refused to consider Congress' motives in taking such an action. It is doubtful that the Supreme Court today would take the same position.[5]

Indirectly, through its power to fix punishment for crimes, which includes probation, Congress may grant the courts such discretion as will enable them to vary the punishment to suit the individual case. Congress, therefore, enacts the laws which define crimes and fix the nature and

[4] 7 Wall. 506 (1869). In this case, the Court said, "It is quite clear, therefore, that this court cannot proceed to pronounce judgment in this case, for it has no longer jurisdiction of the appeal; and judicial duty is not the less fitly performed by declining ungranted jurisdiction than in exercising firmly that which the Constitution and the laws confer."

[5] The Supreme Court maintains, however, that it limits its field of activity to interpreting and applying laws "in cases properly brought before the Courts." *Massachusetts v. Mellon*, 262 U.S. 447 (1923).

degree of punishment. The judiciary tries offenses under these laws and imposes punishment within the limits and according to the methods specified.

The judiciary is at the mercy of Congress in still another respect. It is Congress that appropriates all money necessary for the operation of all Federal courts and for the salaries of the judges. In theory, this could result in the destruction of all courts. In practice, Congress has been loath even to consider the use of this method of controlling the judiciary.

The Federal Court System

In 1789 Congress passed the Judiciary Act which established a federal system of courts. There was created a Supreme Court of six justices, three circuit courts each consisting of two Supreme Court justices sitting with a district judge, and 13 district courts each with a judge. Although the number of inferior courts has been increased and the circuit courts were abolished in favor of the courts of appeals, the Federal court system today is basically the same as when it was originally established.

Supreme Court. The Supreme Court of the United States is the highest and most important body in our judicial system. It is composed of a Chief Justice and eight Associate Justices appointed for duration of good behavior by the President with the advice and consent of the Senate. The Court sits in Washington in a very beautiful and impressive marble building. It holds annual sessions beginning on the first Monday in October and extending until late spring or early summer of the next year. Special and adjourned terms may be held whenever necessary. The salary of the Chief Justice is $35,500 while the Associate Justices receive an annual salary of $35,000.

The Supreme Court has both original and appellate jurisdiction. The Constitution states: "In all cases affecting ambassadors, other public ministers, and consuls, and those in which a State shall be party, the Supreme Court shall have original jurisdiction. In all the other cases before mentioned, the Supreme Court shall have appellate jurisdiction, both as to law and fact, with such exceptions, and under such regulations, as the Congress shall make."

The amount of business before the Supreme Court increases yearly. There were no cases before the Court during its first three semiannual terms and from 1793 to 1803 the Supreme Court determined only 64 cases. From 1809 to 1815 the Court sat for only 30 days a year. In 1818 the judges lived together but this experiment did not work out to good advantage.[6] The Court disposes of approximately 1,202 cases a year and usually about

[6] See James M. Beck, *May It Please the Court*, p. 7, The Macmillan Company, New York, 1930.

one hundred of these have written opinions.[7] In 1950, 673 petitions for a writ of certiorari were directed to the Court. Oral argument before the Supreme Court today is severely limited and justices rely upon printed briefs rather than upon the argument of counsel. This was not true of the early days of the Court and for many years there was no time limit set for lawyers. On three occasions counsel consumed 11 days. In the famous case of *Gibbons v. Ogden,* Daniel Webster opened with a two-and-a-half-hour statement as to the nature of the case. Oakley then spoke for two days, Emmet for two days more, and William Wirt closed the argument with a two-day summary.[8]

The Chief Justice presides over sessions of the Court and his office is one of great honor. William Howard Taft, the only American who has served both as President of the United States and as Chief Justice, is reported to have considered the second office of greater prestige. The pay of the Chief Justice is only $500 more than that received by the Associate Justices but this to no extent measures the extra duties he performs. However, in so far as decisions are concerned, his vote counts the same as any Associate Justice's vote. After a case has been heard and all discussions among the Justices concerning the evidence and the law have been concluded, the Justices vote as individuals upon the determination of the case. It is customary for the most recent appointee to the bench to vote first; the others then vote according to seniority, except the Chief Justice, who votes last. All 5-to-4 decisions are, in the last analysis, determined by the vote of the Chief Justice. Six Justices are necessary for the Court to consider a case and four of these must vote together to secure the required majority. If, because of absence, the vote happens to be a tie, either a rehearing is scheduled or else the finding of the lower court stands.

For important cases, one of the Justices is designated to prepare the opinion of the Court. This opinion consists of a statement, sometimes a lengthy one, of the reasoning of the Court and the basic law upon which the decision is based. This is called the opinion of the Court and, of course, is the majority opinion. Justices who agree with the decision but not the argument may write concurring opinions. The Justices who do not agree with the decision of the Court are listed as dissenting and have the opportunity of writing dissenting opinions. These dissenting opinions are carefully prepared to explain why the Justice or Justices do not agree with the majority. Many dissenting opinions, especially those of Justice Oliver Wendell Holmes, have been quoted more widely than even the majority opinion of the Court, and in some instances have been instrumental in securing a subsequent reversal by the Supreme Court of its decision. Much

---

[7] David Fellman, "Constitutional Law in 1950–1951," *The American Political Science Review,* Vol. 46, March, 1952.

[8] Beck, *op. cit.,* pp. 11–14.

of the reasoning in the dissenting opinions of Justice Holmes was later used by the Court in formulating majority opinion.

A growing individualism among the Justices of the Court is reflected in the unwillingness of a particular Justice to accept the legal argument of another Justice. As a result the number of concurring and dissenting opinions have increased greatly. In the Dennis case,[9] concerning communism and its control under the Smith Act, three Justices joined Chief Justice Vinson in his announcement of the opinion of the Court. Justice Jackson and Justice Frankfurter each wrote a separate concurring opinion while Justice Black and Justice Douglas each wrote dissenting opinions. In a recent term of Court, of a total of 181 separate written opinions, 98 were those of the Court, 23 were concurring, while 60 were dissenting. Justice Douglas and Justice Frankfurter have been frequent dissenters while Justice Jackson and also Justice Frankfurter have been prone to make use of the concurring opinion. Although it is interesting to the constitutional lawyer to compare these different opinions it is also true that the failure of the Justices to agree on any common ground in their reasoning has shaken the confidence of citizens in the Court. Also, the time expended in the preparation of concurring and dissenting opinions is indeed great and has resulted in a decrease in the number of cases heard and determined by the Court. For lack of time the Court has declined to review a number of important cases that it should have considered.[10]

Courts of Appeals. Between the district courts and the Supreme Court of the United States there are 10 courts of appeals and an additional one for the District of Columbia. These courts were established to hear appeals from the district courts and from the important regulatory commissions, such as the Federal Trade Commission, and the Interstate Commerce Commission, and thereby to relieve the Supreme Court of some of its work.

Nine out of 10 cases are determined finally in the courts of appeals. Matters involving the constitutionality of a statute may always be appealed to the Supreme Court and, by a writ of certiorari, the Supreme Court may bring up any case from a court of appeals. Also, a court of appeals may certify a case to the Supreme Court for instructions. The Supreme Court

[9] 341 U.S. 494 (1951).

[10] The decisions and opinions of the Supreme Court are published in a series of volumes entitled the *United States Reports.* After the name of a case, usually there is found the citation of the volume and page of the *Reports* where that particular case may be found. For instance, *Dennis v. United States* has the following citation: 341 U.S. 494 (1951). By this citation the reader knows that he will find the Dennis case in volume 341 of the *United States Reports,* that it begins on page 494, and that the year the decision was rendered was 1951.

There are two other editions of the Supreme Court reports; the *Lawyers Edition* and the *United States Supreme Court Reporter.* The first 90 volumes of these reports are known by the name of the court reporter and are cited by the reporter's name: Dallas (1789–1800), Cranch (1801–1815), Wheaton (1816–1827), Peters (1828–1842), Howard (1843–1860), Black (1861–1862), and Wallace (1863–1874).

may give binding instructions or require the entire record to be sent up to decide the matter in controversy.

The courts of appeals have no original jurisdiction. At present the number of appeals-court judges is approximately 68. All are appointed by the President with the advice and consent of the Senate. The number of judges assigned to each circuit is determined by the amount of judicial business it has. Usually three judges sit together in hearing cases, the judge who is senior in service acting as chief judge.

Appeals from territorial courts are made to particular courts of appeals. Puerto Rico is in the first circuit, the Virgin Islands are in the third, the Canal Zone is in the fifth, and appeals from Alaska and Hawaii are heard in the ninth court of appeals. Except with respect to the District of Columbia, each appeals-court judge is a resident of the circuit to which he is appointed and while in service must remain a resident of that area. The salary of all appeals-court judges is $25,500 a year. Annual terms of court are held at designated cities but the court may sit at other places within its district. The number of cases filed in the courts of appeals for one year is approximately 3,000. About one-fifth of this number come from the Tax Court of the United States and from the National Labor Relations Board. The median time interval from the filing of a complete record to final disposition is approximately seven months.

A judicial council composed of all appeals-court judges within a circuit meets twice a year for the purpose of making a comprehensive survey of the condition of business and other matters of common interest. Under present rules and regulations, the Chief Justice of the United States may designate and assign temporarily any appeals-court judge to act as circuit judge in another district when necessity demands. The senior chief judge of a circuit may designate and assign temporarily a circuit judge to act as a district judge and may also assign one or more district judges within the circuit to sit on a court of appeals. Supreme Court justices are assigned to particular circuits in a supervisory capacity but none ride the circuit as formerly.

There was created in 1942 an Emergency Court of Appeals to hear and determine cases that arose under the Price Control Act of 1942. The personnel of the court is made up of appeals-court and district judges designated by the Chief Justice of the United States to serve in the Emergency Court of Appeals. Instead of having a general type of jurisdiction, it is in effect a special court for the determination of a particular variety of cases. The life of the court was extended by the Housing and Rent Control Act of 1948 and the Defense Production Act of 1950.

District Courts. At the lowest level of the federal court system are the Federal district courts. These courts have original jurisdiction only. There are approximately 84 district courts and, in addition, Federal district courts have been established in the District of Columbia, Hawaii, and Puerto Rico.[11] Court may be held at several designated places within a district and there are approximately 230 Federal district judges. A district may consist of an entire state or of a division within a state.

District judges are appointed by the President with the advice and consent of the Senate for the duration of good behavior. The salary of district judges is $22,500 a year. In districts having more than one judge, the one senior in commission is designated as chief judge of the district.

Much of the time of the courts is taken up with cases concerning antitrust laws, bankruptcy, copyright, patents, interstate-commerce suits, and suits that arise under the Harrison Narcotics Act, the Mann Act and other Federal criminal statutes. As the population of the United States has increased so has the business of these courts. Should you file a civil case in a Federal district court, it would be necessary to wait over a year on the average for the disposition of the case. In the southern district of New York where business is excessive the average time between filing and disposition is $35\frac{4}{10}$ months. From 50,000 to 55,000 cases are usually pending before the district courts.

Judges may be transferred from one district to another by action of the chief judge of a circuit but even this action has failed to relieve congestion. Recently 11,148 civil cases were pending in the southern district of New York which, at that time, had 16 judges. This was more civil cases than were pending at that date in all the district courts of the first, fourth, seventh, and eighth circuits, with a total of 58 district judges. There is a constant need for an increase in the number of district and circuit-court judges. Judicial business increases far more rapidly than additional judges are appointed to handle this business. During a period of time, where the number of judges in the courts had increased 5 per cent, the number of cases before the same courts had increased from one-fifth to one-third. Much of this great increase in business has been attributed to the number of antitrust suits that have been started by the government within recent years and to a 1946 law that permits citizens to sue for injury when the Federal government is thought to be responsible.

Any comparison between Federal district courts and the usual state superior or circuit court brings into bold relief the superior manner in which the business of the district court is conducted. The district judge sees that business is handled in a dignified and respectful manner. He controls the courtroom, even the lawyers. Grand juries are used for the preparation of indictments and a trial jury may be requested in all criminal

[11] The district courts of Puerto Rico and Hawaii are in the same classification as other district courts and are "courts of the United States." Territorial district courts exist in Puerto Rico, Hawaii, Alaska, the Virgin Islands, and the Canal Zone. These territorial district courts are in a different category for they also have jurisdiction over controversies that within the states would be determined in the state courts.

cases and all important civil cases. Many persons plead guilty. When this occurs there is no trial and the judge determines, within the law, the extent of the punishment. Usually he is inclined to be more lenient with the young lawbreaker and more severe with the hardened criminal. When a case does come to trial, the judge passes upon all questions concerning the admission of evidence. In doing this he must not act in a biased or arbitrary manner but according to well-developed rules of evidence. At the conclusion of the presentation of evidence and cross examination, the judge charges the jury, showing how the law applies to the case. If the verdict of the jury is "not guilty" the prisoner is immediately set free; if the verdict is "guilty," it is the judge who determines the nature and extent of punishment within the law. In civil cases the judge issues the orders of the court according to the facts agreed upon by the jury.

The development of a body of Federal criminal law within recent years has increased the importance of the work of the district courts. The Lindbergh Act, the Fugitive Felon Act, the Mann Act, and the Harrison Narcotics Act are but illustrations of Federal law enforced by the Federal district courts. Federal penitentiaries, the most famous of which is the one at Alcatraz in San Francisco Bay, are maintained for the care and restraint of prisoners who have been found guilty of breaking Federal law.

Legislative Courts

In addition to the courts established under the authority of Article III of the Constitution, Congress has provided for certain special or legislative courts under authority implied from other sections of the Constitution. These courts are the Court of Claims, the Court of Customs and Patent Appeals, the United States Customs Court, United States Court of Military Appeals, and the courts for the territories and the District of Columbia.

The United States Court of Claims. Many citizens desire to sue the United States government for real or fancied wrongs. However, no person has the right to bring such a suit in any of the regular courts without the consent of the government. The maxim "The King can do no wrong" has become in this way a part of our legal system. Also, the Eleventh Amendment to the Constitution makes it impossible for a citizen of one state or of a foreign state to bring suit against a state of the Union. Although claims made by citizens for damages were often valid, for many years the only means of securing redress was through a special act of Congress. This was most unsatisfactory. In 1855, therefore, Congress established a Court of Claims to hear and pass on claims brought against the United States which an ordinary court would consider if the United States were suable in that court, and claims referred by Congress or an executive department. Appeal may be taken directly to the Supreme Court. The Court of Claims is made up of a chief judge and four associate judges who hold office for the duration of good behavior, at a salary of $25,500 a year. This court is open to aliens whose home government offers the same privilege to our citizens. Congress frequently alters the jurisdiction of this court. Members of Congress are forbidden to practice before it. The Court of Claims makes out an annual report to Congress of judgments rendered, for money must be appropriated to pay all claims held to be valid.

The United States Customs Court. This court is composed of nine judges and sits in New York City. Not more than five members of this court can be from the same political party. They receive an annual salary of $22,500 and the term of office is good behavior. Should an importer object to the appraisal of imported goods, a single judge is assigned to the matter and appeal from his findings may be made to a panel of three judges. A single judge or a panel may be sent to any port of entry in the United States to conduct hearings. Appeal is to the Court of Customs and Patent Appeals.

The Court of Customs and Patent Appeals. This court sits in Washington and is composed of five judges who receive an annual salary of $25,500, It has appellate jurisdiction only, reviewing cases that have been appealed from the Customs Court, the Tariff Commission, and the Commissioner of Patents. This court handles cases that are extremely technical in nature and gives considerable relief to the Federal district courts.

The Tax Court was established in 1942 to hear and determine cases arising under the internal-revenue laws. It is a court of 16 judges appointed by the President with the advice and consent of the Senate for a term of 12 years, at an annual salary of $22,500. The principal office of the court is in Washington but the court works in divisions and a division may sit anywhere within the United States. Appeals may be made to a court of appeals. By statute the President may remove any member of this court after notice and a hearing for neglect of duty or malfeasance in office but for no other cause.

The United States Court of Military Appeals. This court was established because of the need of a court to review courts-martial. It is composed of three judges appointed from civilian life by the President with the consent of the Senate for a term of fifteen years. The salary is $25,500 annually. This court is located for administrative purposes in the Department of Defense.

The Courts of the District of Columbia and the Territories. By virtue of its authority to govern the District of Columbia, Congress has established for the District a system of courts having at its lower level the usual municipal and police courts found in most American cities. There is also a court of appeals for the District and a district Court which not only hears appeals from lower District of Columbia courts but also acts as a court to hear appeals from certain administrative regulatory agencies such as the Securities and Exchange Commission.

Through its power to provide for the government of territories Congress has established courts in the different territories. Not only are territorial courts established as a part of the territorial government but Federal district courts have been set up in Alaska, Hawaii, Guam, Puerto Rico, the Canal Zone, and the Virgin Islands. Some of the important cases relative to the use of martial law in Hawaii arose in the Federal District Court for that territory. Appeals may be taken, under the rules provided by statute, to courts of appeals in the United States proper and eventually to the Supreme Court of the United States.

The Administration of the Federal Judicial System

Although the judiciary is a main branch of government, for many years it was unorganized. Judges in one Federal district court might easily be unaware of what was going on in another district. Many of the Supreme Court judges knew little of what occurred in the lower courts. In 1922, through statutory authorization, the Chief Justice of the United States assumed a position as directing head of the federal judicial system. In order to aid in carrying out this new assignment, Congress in 1939 provided for the Administrative Office of the United States Courts. This office acts as the housekeeping unit for the judicial system. It maintains records of the different courts, makes studies of the amount of business and types of business, and is responsible for making recommendations concerning the improvement of the entire system. The administrative office is maintained in the Supreme Court Building in Washington with a director and assistant director.

To expedite the work of the Chief Justice and of the business office the Chief Justice of the United States annually calls together the ranking appeals-court judges of each circuit for the purpose of surveying the business pending in the Federal courts and to prepare recommendations for expediting business. In each circuit a conference composed of the appeals-court judges within the circuit meets twice a year. This council makes plans for the improvement of the work of the judiciary in that particular circuit. In addition, there is a judicial conference of both appeals-court and district-court judges within each circuit that meets annually for the disposition of problems and to consider methods of improving judicial administration. While good results of the work of these councils are not clearly evident because of the tremendous increase of court business, it is doubtful whether the courts could do the volume of work they are now doing without the organization and planning of the councils and the administrative office.

The Appointment of Judges

All Federal judges are appointed by the President with the advice and consent of the Senate. The term of office, except for some legislative courts, is during good behavior. Because of the honor, the security, the increased salaries, and retirement provisions, most lawyers consider a Federal-court appointment desirable and few object to having their names proposed for a judgeship. Particularly pleasing is appointment as a Justice of the Supreme Court. This prestige has not always existed, for Washington had some difficulty in making his first appointments to the Supreme Court. Robert Harrison even declined the nomination as a Supreme Court Justice, preferring instead to be Chancellor of Maryland. Today, an appointment to the Supreme Court is considered a fitting climax to a lawyer's successful career. While appointments are not openly sought, the availability of certain men is brought strongly to the attention of the President whenever a vacancy occurs.

The original appointments made by Washington to the Supreme Court were considered good ones. Since then many distinguished persons have served on the bench of the Supreme Court. Justices Story, Cardozo, Holmes, and Brandeis have rendered particularly distinguished service as Associate Justices. Altogether there have been a total of 14 Chief Justices since the Court's creation in 1789 with an average term of nearly 12 years. John Jay, the first Chief Justice, served six years. John Marshall and Roger B. Taney, the fourth and fifth respectively, served a total of over 60 years. In recent years the average term served by Chief Justices has declined.

In making an appointment to the Supreme Court, the President is governed by a host of considerations. The record of the nominee on the bench or in public life must be good. His social and economic viewpoint is considered. Geography plays a part for it is not advisable to have all justices from the same section of the country. Personal friendship, the recommendations of common friends, and many other factors are considered by the President in sending a nomination to the Senate for approval.

Not least among these other factors is the probable attitude of the Senate toward confirmation. Whenever a nomination comes to the Senate it is referred to the Judiciary Committee, whose recommendation is usually followed. However, 21 nominees to the Supreme Court, or approximately one out of every five, have been rejected by the Senate, although within the last 60 years only one nomination (Judge J. Parker in 1930) was not confirmed. The nomination of Chief Justice Stone was considered for 31 days; the name of Brandeis, one of the most distinguished justices, was before the Senate 124 days before final confirmation.

Usually debates in the Senate over confirmation bring out not only the political background of the appointment but also the nominee's position with respect to current economic and social problems. Much depends upon whether a friendly political party is in control of the Senate. To a distinguished public servant or an able lawyer, these debates are an ordeal that must be endured. But they do have some value. The debates in the

Senate over the nomination first of Mr. Hughes and then of Mr. Parker showed the essentially political character of much of the work done by the Supreme Court. Regarding the Hughes nomination Frank Kent remarked: [12]

Mr. Hughes will be a better Chief Justice for the experience. He has lost practically all of his tail feathers and reaches this highest and most secure perch on our governmental tree a badly battered and bedraggled bird, so peppered with shot that it will be some time before he can comfortably assume a sitting position.

In recent years there has been a growing tendency for the President to nominate Senators or ex-Senators to judgeships, for the Senate is far more prone to confirm a member or a former member of that body than a nominee from the bench or from private life. Of the present Supreme Court (1954) Justices Black, Burton, and Minton all served in the United States Senate. Oddly enough, few judges from the inferior Federal courts are promoted to membership on the Supreme Court.

In making appointments to lower Federal courts, particularly to the district courts, the President receives much advice from local political leaders and groups. Some of this advice is solicited but much is not. Although there is no requirement in the Constitution that judges must be admitted to the bar, it would be most difficult to secure the confirmation of any one who is not a lawyer. In 1951 the American Bar Association requested that each political party include in its platform a policy plank stating that (1) only the best-qualified persons available shall be selected for appointment for judicial offices; and (2) the President before nomination, and the Senate before confirming, shall request the report and recommendation of the judiciary committee of the American Bar Association.[13] Usually the President follows the well-established tradition of nominating the persons recommended to him by Senators of his own party for vacancies in the states. If he rejects their nominees, the Senators are able to prevent the confirmation of other nominees, appealing to the "courtesy" of the Senate. It is impossible for the President to know all nominees first-hand. Unfortunately many recommendations are made to him for the purpose of paying off political debts and because of personal friendship rather than judicial ability. In a very critical analysis of recent lower-court appointments, Joseph E. Finley [14] places most of the blame for poor nominations upon these recommendations rather than upon the President for following them. He states:

[12] From his column in the *Baltimore Sun;* see *The South Atlantic Quarterly,* Vol. 30, p. 429, 1931.
[13] *The New York Times,* Sept. 21, 1951.
[14] Joseph E. Finley, "Truman's Judges," *The New Republic,* p. 11, Mar. 10, 1952.

Appointments to the District Court benches, where trials and jury cases are held, are logically the most politics-ridden of all. The President cannot be held personally responsible for these choices because of the distance in political echelons from the White House.

Occasionally, however, the President has declined to accept the recommendation of Senators in making a nomination to lower courts. A famous case arose in 1938 when Franklin D. Roosevelt declined to nominate one of the persons recommended by the two Virginia Senators and nominated instead a Virginia judge recommended by the Representative from the district where the vacancy occurred. The two Virginia Senators had often opposed the President's legislative program. They entered a personal objection to the President's nominee, though admitting he was well qualified, and the Senate rejected the nomination. Both Virginia Senators stated that the nomination was personally obnoxious to them and they requested that Senate confirmation be refused. Their request was granted by their colleagues.

The most recent dispute over the confirmation of appointments and the place of "senatorial courtesy" occurred when Congress created two vacancies in the Federal District Court of Northern Illinois. Senator Douglas of Illinois, after consultation with state party leaders of the Democratic Party, suggested two nominees. President Truman, six months later, sent to the Senate the names of two other persons who were also within the Democratic organization. Senator Douglas contended that the President had not consulted him. He also maintained that his selections were better than the President's. In an informal poll conducted among Chicago lawyers, the persons selected by the Senator ran far ahead. Douglas therefore announced that he would take advantage of the Senate tradition and declare the method of appointing the nominees to be personally obnoxious to him.[15]

In registering his objections before the Senate Judiciary Committee, Douglas argued that the constitutional requirement for Senate "advice" as well as "consent" in appointments should be real and not nominal. The Senate Judiciary Committee acted unfavorably upon the President's nominations and later the Senate sustained the committee's action. By the time this action was taken there were 4,149 cases on the docket for the Federal District Court of Northern Illinois and some of the civil cases were running as much as two years behind.

It is possible to write either a defense or a criticism of the use of senatorial courtesy in making judicial appointments. Obviously the President needs aid in finding the proper person. Sometimes the help he gets is good; at other times he makes mistakes by following recommendations. One

[15] See Joseph P. Harris, *The Advice and Consent of the Senate,* pp. 215–217.

substitute that has been suggested is that a judicial commission composed of three Senators, three laymen, and three lawyers be established to survey the field and to submit three names to the President to fill vacancies on the bench at both the appeals-court and district-court level. The President would then select one of the three as his nominee. It is maintained that this would result in a better judiciary and in certain confirmation by the Senate.[16] But it is hard to imagine that either the President or the Senate would approve any system that would limit the control that they both now exercise over the appointment of Federal judges.

Relation of State Courts to the Federal Court System

In the United States there is a dual court system, for each state has its own courts to try all cases not handled by the Federal courts. Most civil and criminal cases are determined in the various state courts. The average citizen is better acquainted with the work and practices of state courts than he is with Federal courts. It is in the state courts where offenses committed against the state are tried. The Federal courts' criminal jurisdiction is limited to the trial of cases arising under the limited number of federal criminal laws or to those cases involving a United States officer. The civil jurisdiction of state courts is also very broad and includes not only controversies arising under the state civil law but also civil actions involving certain Federal statutes such as housing laws and rent control measures. Authorization for the state courts to exercise jurisdiction in these cases is provided in the specific Federal acts. Within each state, therefore, these two court systems exist and operate side by side. Although it is confusing to many citizens, jurisdictional lines have been drawn reasonably well, and in most instances the two systems work together rather than in competition with each other. Unfortunately, there is more than enough business for both.

Any decision of a state supreme court involving the Federal Constitution, Federal statutes, or treaties may be appealed from that court directly to the Supreme Court of the United States. Such appeals *do not* go to the lower national courts. Many cases come to the Supreme Court in this way and, in acting as a court of review, the Court has in many instances protected the rights of the individual citizens from arbitrary state action. Illustrative of this type of protection are those cases which arise under the due-process clause of the Fourteenth Amendment, which reads: "nor shall any State deprive any person of life, liberty, or property, without due process of law." This provision is zealously enforced by the Supreme Court, for it is the "basis for protection under the national Constitution against state infringement of civil liberties and for the enforcement of the 'rudiments of fair play.' In short, in this single phrase is included the potentiali-

[16] Finley, *op. cit.*, pp. 10–11.

ties of all the protection against government which the individual may need." [17] State statutes concerned with segregation, the rights of minorities, taxation, criminal proceedings, administrative procedure, and other subjects that affect individual rights are subject to the review of the Supreme Court to insure the individual the protection guaranteed by the Constitution of the United States.

Reform of the Judiciary

A case or controversy brought before a tribunal means that one party wins while another loses. Many losers are not good losers and are prone to criticize the umpire who makes the decision. When the courts make their rulings and decisions with care, most criticism falls of its own weight and the prestige of the courts is high. But at times the criticism is deserved. Recent suggestions to improve the quality of judicial work and the machinery of the courtroom include the following:

1. Judges should be more carefully selected. Judicial appointments should not be made to pay off political debts or because the nominee is a Senator and therefore his confirmation in the Senate will not be difficult.

2. The cost of litigation, which has increased greatly in recent years, should be reduced. Citizens often put up with injustices rather than take their cases to court.

3. The time consumed in court actions is frequently excessive and works a real hardship upon the litigants. Court procedure, in many respects, is archaic and outworn and needs speeding up.

4. Courts should be more careful to avoid political questions.

5. Appointees to the highest courts must be those who will render unbiased interpretations of the Constitution and the laws, without borrowing from their own political or social philosophies. It has been said that a Justice's vote in a particular case may depend more on what he had for breakfast than on legal precedent.

In spite of this criticism, the courts are to be commended for their good work. Improved organization of the court system, the creation of judicial administrative officers to expedite the work of the courts, the use of judicial councils, have all resulted in improved court procedure, efficient court administration, and better all around performance by both the Federal and state judiciaries.

REFERENCES

F. R. Aumann, *The Changing American Legal System* (1940).
A. J. Beveridge, *The Life of John Marshall,* 4 vols. (1916–1919).
Fred V. Cahill, *Judicial Legislation: A Study in American Legal Theory* (1952).

[17] Virginia Wood, *Due Process of Law,* p. vii, Louisiana State University Press, 1951.

Clarence N. Callender, *American Courts: Their Organization and Procedure* (1927).

B. N. Cardozo, *The Nature of the Judicial Process* (1921).

Jerome Frank, *Law and the Modern Mind* (1930).

Felix Frankfurter and James M. Landis, *The Business of the Supreme Court* (1928).

C. G. Haines, *The Role of the Supreme Court in American Government and Politics, 1789–1835* (1944).

Robert J. Harris, *The Judicial Power of the United States* (1940).

J. W. Hurst, *The Growth of American Law* (1950).

Robert H. Jackson, *The Struggle for Judicial Supremacy* (1940).

Roscoe Pound, *Organization of Courts* (1940).

C. H. Pritchett, *The Roosevelt Court* (1948).

Max Radin, *The Law and Mr. Smith* (1938).

O. J. Roberts, *The Court and the Constitution* (1951).

Charles Warren, *The Supreme Court in United States History,* 3 vols. (1923).

CHAPTER 18　*The Administration: Theory and Practice*

Government at all levels within the United States has become big business. In the past the American community generally coped with its social and economic problems through local and private effort. Today a complete change has occurred. If a flood destroys life and property, government is expected to offer relief. If production of wheat results in a bumper crop, government must withhold the surplus wheat from the market and thereby keep up prices. In short, whenever anything goes wrong or when something very necessary or something expensive is needed, citizens turn to government.

Government has grown big both through the expansion of its regulatory function and by an increase in the number of services offered to citizens. Each decade sees the creation of new agencies, new functions, and the addition of personnel. The variety of services has widened greatly. The Mutual Security Agency was not created until late in 1951 but when its functions were transferred in 1953 to the Foreign Operations Administration it had over 5,000 employees. Included in its duties is the responsibility of giving attention, in backward areas, to the exploration and production of basic materials needed for defense. The Federal Communications Commission has recently been made responsible for setting up rules, regulations, and engineering standards for TV. All this has resulted in a spectacular growth in the number of governmental agencies, in the number of persons necessary to perform these functions, and—inevitably—in a huge annual Federal budget.

Does government have to be so big and so expensive? While there is considerable legitimate concern about the high cost of the Federal government, the difficulties of reducing these costs are almost insurmountable. There are powerful groups which not only bring pressure to bear against cutting the costs of services in which they have a special interest, but who constantly press for increases. And they are backed up by many members of Congress who see eye to eye with them. The chief reasons for a swollen budget are the tremendous costs of defense and of the Veterans' Administration. If these costs could be eliminated or considerably curtailed, the budget would not be stupendous. But who would be willing to eliminate the defense program at the risk of losing our liberties? And if Congress should attempt to reduce the appropriations for veterans, the organized pressures from the powerful veterans' organizations would be so great that Congress would very likely be compelled to back down.[1]

Similarly, any attempt to reduce substantially the federal expenditures for agriculture, public works, conservation, highways and other state aids, welfare, the merchant marine, or other activities would be strongly opposed. It should be noted that, aside from defense and the operation of the Post Office Department, administrative costs constitute a very small part of the total budget. The widely held notion that the high cost of government is for the salaries of bureaucrats is contrary to the facts; the largest expenditures are for defense, foreign aid (at present), veterans, interest payments on public debt, grants to the states, subsidies to agriculture and other sectors of the economy, and public works.

Big government is often referred to as the "bureaucracy," particularly by its critics. This term is often used to condemn governmental red tape, bungling, arbitrariness, and wastefulness. Strictly speaking, however, bureaucracy is a word which merely describes the total personnel, organization, rules, and procedures which comprise the living governmental organism of today. Actually, bureaucracies have been found necessary to the effectuation of all sorts of human endeavor. The comments concerning the government bureaucracy in this chapter, with a few minor changes, could be applied equally to purely business and social organizations. For example, such vast enterprises as United States Steel and the American Telephone and Telegraph Company can be carried on only by what really amounts to a bureaucracy. The detailed procedures and records which in government are derisively called "red tape" are present also in business, but there they are called "system."

The Functions and Organization of the Federal Administration

Woodrow Wilson defined public administration as [2] the

. . . detailed and systematic execution of public law. Every particular application of general law is an act of administration. The assessment and raising of taxes, for instance, the hanging of a criminal, the transportation and delivery of the mails, the equipping and recruiting of the army and navy, . . . are all obviously acts of administration. . . .

[1] See Paul H. Douglas, "Colossus on the Potomac," *Harper's Magazine*, Vol. 207, pp. 21–27, July, 1953.
[2] "The Study of Administration," *Political Science Quarterly*, Vol. 2, p. 212, 1887.

Or, to put it another way, public administration specifically furthers the ultimate ends of government by maintaining peace and order, instructing the young, equalizing opportunity for the nation's citizens, protecting citizens against disease and insecurity, and adjusting and compromising the differences between conflicting groups and interests.

The development of the theory and practice of administrative management has gone hand in hand with the growth of the administrative function. Evidence of this comes first from the increasing recognition of the importance of the executive at all levels. Governmental administrative officers are not lackeys of Congress but are proficient executive officers engaged in functions that require training and technical competence. Second, because of the importance of the jobs performed the science of administrative management has developed, through the use of research units, systematic attempts to analyze and improve administration. Many departments and agencies have research units that are on the alert for new ways of doing business. Reports showing improved techniques of administrative management have been issued by these agencies and have been of value not only to the agencies concerned but to other Federal agencies having similar aims and conditions.

There have grown up also the new professions of administrator and administrative analyst. College and university catalogues of two decades ago listed few courses in public administration. Today public administration is a recognized discipline and at various universities there are departments or schools of public administration.

Another important trend in the development of administrative management has been the creation of staff agencies and the acceptance of the principle that it is advantageous for an executive to have a managerial staff.

The President as Chief Administrator

Under the Constitution the executive power is vested in the President, who is the head of the executive branch and the chief administrative officer of the Federal government. A distinction needs to be made at the outset between the President as an individual and the Presidency as an institution which embraces an elaborate organization and many officials and employees. It is with the Presidency as an institution that we are concerned here. The first of a series of reports issued by the Hoover Commission in 1949 dealt with the Executive Office of the President under the title, *The General Management of the Executive Branch.*[3] Declaring that the President, and under him the department heads, was responsible to the people and to the Congress for the conduct of the executive branch, the Commission found that his authority to direct and control the many agencies within

[3] Commission on the Organization of the Executive Branch of the Government, 1949.

the executive branch had been weakened by a faulty organization, by detailed and rigid laws which removed subordinates from clear-cut responsibility to their administrative superiors, and by the lack of an adequate staff. It made a number of important recommendations for strengthening and improving the management of the government which are summarized later in this chapter.

To assist the President in his duties as chief administrator, as well as in other activities which lie outside the field of administration, the President has several agencies, which together constitute the Executive Office of the President. These include the White House Office, consisting of his immediate staff of advisors and assistants and a considerable records and clerical staff; the Bureau of the Budget, which has a staff of approximately 500 persons—budget analysts, specialists in finance, attorneys, engineers, administrators, and other experts; the Council of Economic Advisers; the National Security Council; and the Office of Defense Mobilization. In addition to these staff organizations, the President creates from time to time many special advisory and planning committees, to which are assigned important problems.

The purpose of these elaborate staff organizations is to see to it that problems which require the President's determination have been carefully considered before they come to him; many lesser decisions must necessarily be made by subordinates in his name. It would be a mistake to assume that the President's role as chief administrator can be separated from his role as legislative leader, as the head of his party, as the head of the government in its international relations, as ceremonial head of the state, and as Commander in Chief of the Armed Forces. The decisions he makes usually have many implications which must be considered—administrative, political, public-relations, financial, and international implications.

With the assistance of the staff organizations in his own office, and the heads of departments, the President directs, controls, and coordinates the activities of the vast executive organization. One of his most important powers is that of appointment and removal of the chief officers of the government. No executive can be held responsible unless he is able to select his principal assistants, and to remove them if he becomes dissatisfied with their performance. The President's power of appointment is shared with the Senate, for he must secure its approval, but by tradition he is given a free hand in the selection of members of his Cabinet. In the appointment of minor officials, however, the President does not have the same discretion, but must often name those pressed on him by members of the Senate or party organizations. And his power to remove members of regulatory commissions is subject to regulation by acts of Congress, for these officers are not regarded as executive but rather as quasi-legislative and quasi-judicial. The President's direct appointing power obviously does not extend to the thousands of civil-service employees, who are appointed by the heads of departments and other officers under civil-service rules and regulations. Such employees may be removed only "for such cause as will promote the efficiency of such service and for reasons given in writing." [4]

Departmental plans, programs and policies of major importance usually require the President's approval. This is due in part to the fact that legislation is usually necessary to put them into effect, and departments are required to submit legislative proposals to the President for his consideration before transmitting them to committees of Congress. The President's support is ordinarily essential to the passage of any measure of first-rate importance. Acting in behalf of the President, the Office of Legislative Reference of the Bureau of the Budget sees to it that all interested departments and agencies are informed of any proposed legislation which might affect them, and differences of opinion and conflicts within the administration are ordinarily cleared up before proposed legislative measures are submitted to Congress.

Even when no new legislation is required, all programs and new policies ordinarily require funds, and the President through his control over the budget exercises control over the departments. As described in Chap. 20, all departments and agencies are required by law to submit their budget requests to the President for review and revision, which is done for him and under his direction by the Bureau of Budget. Aside from this Presidential control through review and revision of legislative proposals and budget requests, the heads of departments keep the President and his staff aides advised of major developments and seek his approval of any new policies of major importance. Most decisions, however, must be made by the responsible departmental officers rather than the President, though he must be responsible for their decisions.

Another control exercised by the President over the executive branch is through his power over administrative organization. Although Congress is extremely jealous of its power to determine the administrative organization, it has found it impracticable to make the necessary changes by legislation, and from time to time has granted a limited power of reorganization to the President. He is authorized to submit plans for reorganization to Congress, and unless they are set aside by the action of either House, such plans go into effect. In addition, the President is usually given very wide powers in periods of national emergency or war to create agencies to carry on emergency activities authorized by Congress.

In the exercise of his power as chief administrator, the President issues orders and communications of various types for the guidance of executive departments and agencies. The most formal of these are the Executive orders, many of which are authorized by acts of Congress, and when

[4] 5 U.S.C. 652.

officially promulgated have the effect of law. In addition, the President issues directives, instructions, circulars, memoranda, letters, and oral communications in all the shades of the imperative from a formal command to a veiled wish. The quality and content of these acts are a measure of the effectiveness and energy of administration, for it is through them that the Chief Executive reveals his abilities or weaknesses as administrator.

Regardless of ability, however, the President is restricted by time and the limitations of the human body. Since it is physically impossible for the President to exercise close supervision over the 40-odd major agencies reporting directly to him, he delegates authority to departmental and agency heads who act in his name and use his directional power indirectly to accomplish routine administrative objectives.[5] These officers in turn delegate authority to their immediate subordinates and so it continues down the chain of command. Like the President, their tools of administration are letters, directives, circulars, memoranda, and verbal orders. In addition, Presidential subordinates formulate rules and regulations which, when promulgated over authorized signature, have the force of law. This, of course, is the ideal picture. Actually, "The line of authority from departmental heads through subordinates is often abridged by independent authorities granted to bureau or divisional heads, sometimes through congressional act or stipulations in appropriations." [6]

Presidential directional power is normally exercised in direct or indirect accord with some congressional act, although there are also precedents which permit him to exercise direction without prior statutory authorization.[7] Through this power he must satisfy the requirements of the thousand-and-one demands of day-to-day administration. But it must be realized that the American President must also be a politician, and his administrative activities can never be completely divorced from political considerations, nor would this be desirable.

Keeping in mind the fact that political activities and obligations form an ever-present backdrop to the stage of administrative operations, one sees the President as chief administrator exercising his directional and appointive powers to keep the form and function of the administration as closely in harmony with his political goals as constitutional and congressional limitations will permit. In case recalcitrant subordinates fail to work in furtherance of his plans the President has at his disposal all sorts of coercive devices ranging from a mild reprimand up to the sine qua non of administrative control, the power of removal.

[5] *The Hoover Commission Report,* McGraw-Hill Book Company, Inc., New York, 1949, on p. 25 reveals that 65 agencies and departments reported to the President. However, according to the *United States Government Organization Manual 1954–55,* p. 556, only 41 major agencies now report directly to the Chief Executive.

[6] *Ibid.,* p. 23.

[7] See *In re Neagle,* 135 U.S. 1 (1890) and *In re Debs,* 158 U.S. 564 (1895).

Federal Administrative Organization

The construction of an administrative organization is like the construction of a building. First, the plans must be drawn and the contract let before one brick can be laid. Similarly, the agencies of the Federal government are planned and authorized by Congress which in turn appropriates the funds and directs the President to undertake the construction of the new administrative unit.

Generally, after describing organizational purposes and goals, Congress provides a rough sketch of the proposed structural form and it is up to the President and subordinate executive officers to design and execute the more intricate organizational details.

New organizations are usually constructed from the top down. The President first appoints the chief and assistant administrators who will plan the organizational details in keeping with congressional and Presidential purposes and within the amount of money appropriated or promised to carry out these purposes. At this point, unless the chief administrator insists on running a one-man show, staff units will be formed to provide technical advice and aid in the planning and budgeting. As the agency's major purpose or line units are established, auxiliary units must begin functioning to install personnel, provide communications and transportation, and establish files and records. Ideally, the organizational units growing into hierarchical form would be designated in descending order—first bureaus, then divisions, then branches, then sections and units.[8] Each unit is made up of a number of positions, to which individual employees are assigned.

Thus the chain of command in the administrative hierarchy reaches from the head of the department through the heads of each lower administrative echelon to the lowest employee, and each employee and administrative official is responsible in turn to his administrative superior. Speaking in defense of the President's power of removal, James Madison stated in the famous debate on the removal power in the first session of Congress: " . . . one of the most prominent features of the Constitution, a principle that pervades the whole system, (is) that there should be the highest degree of responsibility in all the Executive officers thereof." He urged that the "chain of dependence" be preserved, under which "the lowest officers, the middle grade, and the highest, will depend, as they ought on the President, and the President on the community." [9]

The Executive Department. Since the original three, State, Treasury, and War, were set up in 1789, the department has been the standard line agency through which the government has carried out its major policies. Today there are 10 departments; the largest and the smallest are the De-

[8] *The Hoover Commission Report,* p. 28.
[9] Quoted in Leonard D. White, *The Federalists,* pp. 22–23, New York, 1948.

partments of Defense and Labor, respectively. The National Security Act Amendments of 1949 established the Department of Defense and made provision for the inclusion therein of the Department of the Army, the Department of the Navy, and the Department of the Air Force as military departments. Departments have always been established to carry on activities which were well understood and widely accepted in the nation as a whole.

The executive branch of the government is made up of the following types of administrative organizations: (1) executive departments, each headed by an officer with the title of Secretary; (2) executive agencies outside of the ten regular departments headed by single administrators; (3) boards and commissions, which may be further divided into regulatory, nonregulatory and advisory; and finally, (4) the government corporation. Agencies outside the 10 regular departments are usually termed "independent," in the sense that they are not responsible to the head of any department. Some of these enjoy a large degree of independence of the President, while others do not; all are subject to legislative control by Congress. Executive organizations may also be classified as "line" or "staff." Line organizations render services or carry on regulatory functions, dealing directly with the general public, while "staff" organizations serve the line departments. Agriculture, Defense, Post Office, and Interior are good illustrations of line departments, while the Civil Service Commission, General Services Administration, and the Bureau of the Budget are examples of staff units. Treasury and Justice have both line and staff functions. Staff units are sometimes further divided into those which exercise planning, direction, and control activities, and those which only render services or perform "housekeeping" activities. It should be noted, moreover, that within each executive department there are both line and staff units.

Although experimental functions have, from time to time, been assigned to the executive departments, no department has ever been created until its major activities were authorized and well established as a continuing function of the government. Although official commissioners urged the creation of a Department of Health, Education and Welfare as early as 1925, it was not until 1953 that Congress was convinced that welfare was a permanent function which warranted the establishment of such a department.

Most of the Federal departments are organized to work in a particular field such as agriculture, commerce, defense, or foreign affairs. For purposes of classification, commentators and public administrators have attempted to designate departments as primarily functional, clientele, process or geographic on the basis of the principal activity or spatial jurisdiction. But there probably is no realistic way to classify them because they all participate, to a greater or smaller extent, in all of these classifications.

Federal department heads are called "Secretary of ———" with the exceptions of the Postmaster General and the Attorney General. While their duties are primarily executive, department heads have frequently been assigned functions which are both legislative and judicial in nature. Secretaries, undersecretaries, assistant secretaries, and deputy secretaries are all appointed by their chief, the President; their selection is usually based upon political considerations. There has long been a movement to establish in each department the office of permanent undersecretary, to serve our Federal departments in a manner similar to that of their counterparts in Great Britain. The undersecretary would be a nonpolitical civil servant who would provide continuity to departmental operations, regardless of political changes. On the recommendation of the Hoover Commission, Congress has created in a number of departments the office of administrative assistant secretary, to be appointed from the ranks of career civil servants. This is a step in the right direction and should materially improve departmental administration.

Organizational charts of the Federal government give one the impression that an unbroken chain of command extends from the President to the lowliest employee. Such an ideal state of affairs does not exist. There are many exceptions where legislative acts make bureau chiefs and other subordinate officers responsible to Congress or to some officer other than the department head. For example, the Comptroller of the Currency, although two levels below the Secretary of the Treasury, is appointed directly by the President and is required by law to make annual reports to Congress independently of his department head.[10] Another example is the Corps of Engineers of the Army, which is given the civilian functions of improving rivers and harbors and erecting public works to control floods. This agency has always regarded itself as the agent of Congress, and although nominally under the Secretary of the Army, the Secretary of Defense, and the President, its ties with Congress are so close that it accepts little direction and control from executive officers. This relationship has been the subject of much criticism, but little can be done about it because of the strong support which the corps has in Congress.

Single-headed Administrative Agencies. Today there are approximately 12 major single-headed administrative agencies in the executive branch. The most familiar are the Veterans' Administration, the General Services Administration, and the Selective Service System. Judged by organizational standards, these agencies have many of the characteristics of the typical line department. All are headed by an administrator, nominated and appointed by the President with Senate advice and consent. The internal organizational characteristics of the single-headed agency are similar to the departmental pattern. And, like the department, each agency has developed its own nomenclature so that some are divided into bureaus,

[10] *United States Government Organization Manual 1953–54,* p. 96.

others into offices, and still others into services. With the exception of the Veterans' Administration and the General Services Administration, most of these agencies were established during a period of war or depression to carry on special activities which were not regarded as necessarily permanent functions. The life expectancy of this type of organization is usually for the duration of the emergency or special condition which brought it into existence. An exception is the Veterans' Administration which seems to have achieved immortality and to have an excellent chance of being transformed into a department.

Boards and Commissions. It is a well-accepted principle of organization in government as well as in business and industry that departments and agencies should, as a rule, have a single head rather than a board or commission. In the case of a single-headed organization responsibility can be definitely fixed; while if there is a board it is divided between the several members, and if things go wrong no one can be held responsible. A single head can better provide the vigor, initiative, leadership, prompt decision, and control which are needed in any large organization. Administrative departments and units in business and industry are rarely placed under a board, but this form of organization has been widely adopted in government, due in large part to the fear of placing too much authority and power in the hands of a single person. Many states and local units of government are plagued by the use of boards in charge of operations which are essentially administrative in character. Fortunately, there has been much less use of this form of organization in the Federal government.

There are certain types of activities or situations for which a board or commission is suitable. To Napoleon is attributed the maxim that single heads should be used for administration and boards for deliberation. If the primary functions of an organization are quasi-legislative or quasi-judicial, a board or commission is a suitable form of organization. If the function is new, controversial, and one in which public policies must be evolved on the basis of further experience, a board will provide the needed deliberation, and may greatly facilitate public acceptance of the new function. The board type of organization permits the representation of each of the two major parties, different sections of the country, or different interest groups in the population, where such representation is deemed essential or at least desirable. Students of public administration, however, are somewhat dubious about the wisdom of such representation in the head of an agency. What is usually needed is nonpartisan rather than bipartisan administration. The requirement that a board be bipartisan often fails to secure bona fide representation of the minority party, but may result in the appointment of politicians of no great ability—often defeated members of Congress. The requirement of geographical representation often prevents the appointment of the best-qualified person, and leads instead to these offices being regarded as political perquisites to be awarded on the basis of service to the party.

Boards and commissions in the Federal government may be classified into three types, depending essentially on the character of their functions: regulatory bodies, which usually enjoy a large degree of independence, nonregulatory agencies which carry on large-scale enterprises, and advisory and staff agencies.

THE INDEPENDENT REGULATORY COMMISSION. Within this group are such agencies as the Interstate Commerce Commission, the Federal Trade Commission, the Federal Communications Commission, the Securities and Exchange Commission, and the National Labor Relations Board. Their functions are regulatory, and they have been accorded almost complete freedom from executive direction and control. Professor White has stated that, to be independent, a commission should have the following characteristics: [11]

First, the term of office of commissioners is longer than that of the President.

Second, under the doctrine of the Rathbun case, Congress may prescribe the causes for the removal of commissioners of these bodies.

Third, the decisions of the commissions are final so far as the Chief Executive is concerned. Decisions are not submitted to or discussed with the White House; nor are they subject to review or veto by the President.

Fourth, there is no legal or formal liaison between the President and these independent regulatory commissions.

These agencies violate the concept of the separation of powers. They have legislative, judicial, and executive functions, all in the same agency. In the first place, they were originally created to regulate economic activities, a legislative task which Congress did not feel itself able to undertake. The ICC, for example, regulates freight and passenger rates for bus, truck, and rail lines and prescribes materiel and personnel standards. In the second place, all these agencies hear cases and hand down decisions. Examples of this would be the NLRB in settling a labor dispute or the FTC in enjoining an unfair trade practice. In the third place, they administer certain activities which are essentially executive in nature. From a functional standpoint they are, therefore, quasi-legislative, quasi-judicial, and administrative. However, they are not independent of Congress and can be altered or abolished at the legislative will.

There are two other regulatory commissions which although independent of the departments, do not possess the same degree of independence of executive control as the five commissions mentioned above. These are the Federal Power Commission and the Board of Governors of the Federal Re-

[11] Leonard D. White, *Introduction to the Study of Public Administration* rev. ed., p. 113, The Macmillan Company, New York, 1945.

serve System. Some direct Presidential control is exercised over the Federal Power Commission but the bulk of its work, such as licensing hydroelectrical projects and regulating the sale of natural gas, is of a quasi-legislative and quasi-judicial nature, and in the exercise of these functions the Commission is independent. The last of these agencies, the Board of Governors of the Federal Reserve System, is quite independent of the President, but its activity in controlling credit and distributing currency depends to some extent upon Treasury Department operations.

These independent regulatory commissions are headed by a multi-member board composed of from three to eleven members selected by the President with Senate advice and consent. The terms of office of commissioners are, in all cases, staggered and for a duration of more than four years.

NONREGULATORY COMMISSIONS. A number of commissions have been created to carry on large-scale governmental programs which are not regulatory in character, but for which Congress considered a multiheaded agency desirable. The leading examples are the Tennessee Valley Authority, the Atomic Energy Commission, the Civil Service Commission, and the United States Tariff Commission. These and several other multiheaded agencies in the same category are subject in varying degree to executive direction, control, and coordination. The TVA and the AEC are both extremely large-scale operations in fields where a board was needed to develop new policies; the Tariff Commission is essentially a research agency, whose function is to conduct scientific studies of the effects of various tariff provisions on American industry and trade with other countries. The Civil Service Commission is a staff agency and is directly responsible to the President. Recently under a plan approved by Congress its chairman has been given charge of its administration, and the duties of the other members are limited to policy matters, and to quasi-legislative and quasi-judicial determinations. This arrangement, which was recommended by the Hoover Commission, has also been applied to a number of other commissions.

ADVISORY (STAFF) BOARDS. This category comprises those miscellaneous thinking, advising, planning, and consulting bodies like the Council of Economic Advisers, the National Security Council, and the National Advisory Committee for Aeronautics. These particular agencies seem to have acquired permanent status, but most other staff agencies of this type lead a precarious life and have relatively small staffs. The National Advisory Committee for Aeronautics, however, has a staff of over 7,000 persons and carries on an extensive research and testing program. While the majority of these staff agencies work primarily with the President and the executive branch, congressional committees call upon them from time to time for information and advice.

THE GOVERNMENT CORPORATION. The corporate form of organization was first used by the Federal government in the early days of the Republic, but after the demise of the quasi-official Bank of the United States government corporations fell into disuse until acquisition of the Panama Railroad Company in 1903. Government corporations have been used for two broad, major purposes: first, to extend credit to agriculture, banking, insurance, transportation, manufacturing and other commercial enterprises, especially during periods of war or depression and, second, to carry on activities of a commercial or industrial nature. In order to give management a free hand to accomplish these goals, these enterprises were deliberately placed outside of the sway of civil service, the executive chain of command, and the General Accounting Office.

Government corporations, like private corporations, are set up with a policy-forming board of directors, an executive chairman of the board, and a general manager. Some deviations from this pattern have been found in the past, but the standard organizational features are the norm. In general, government corporations may sue and be sued, borrow money, operate on a profit or loss basis, and make changes in internal structure and procedure without new executive or legislative authorization. Since the 1930s, more and more exceptions to these operational features are to be noted. For example, the Government Corporation Act of 1945 [12] provides for an annual audit of all corporation accounts by the General Accounting Office and the presentation of a business-type budget through the Bureau of the Budget to the President and Congress. Another blow was struck at corporate independence by the Supreme Court in 1941 when it upheld the removal of one of the board members of TVA by the President. By this decision the Court practically moved that corporation into the executive hierarchy.[13]

There seems to have been a trend since the reorganization movement in 1939 toward weakening the policy-making position of the corporation boards and standardizing these bodies on the basis of executive-line departmental operating practice. The paradox is that Congress presumably established these agencies in the corporate form to achieve fiscal independence and managerial autonomy. Then, after a very short breathing spell, it began to do all that was possible to *prevent* fiscal independence and managerial autonomy. Some students of government corporations believe that the existing legislative restrictions and executive controls have largely nullified the special advantages of this form of organization, and urge that Congress revise its policy, drawing upon the British experience, where government corporations enjoy a large degree of autonomy and freedom from ordinary bureaucratic controls.[14]

[12] 31 U.S.C.A. 841 ff.

[13] *Morgan v. Tennessee Valley Authority,* 28 F. Supp. 732 (1939), writ of certiorari denied, 312 U.S. 701 (1941).

[14] For an authoritative treatment of this subject, see Marshall E. Dimock, "These Government Corporations," *Harper's Magazine,* Vol. 190, pp. 569 ff., May, 1945.

Reorganization of the Federal Government

Merely setting up an administrative organization does not necessarily mean that public policy will indeed be translated into action with the greatest efficiency, economy, and service, and in a manner consonant with democratic ideals. Whether or not the executive branch of the government does its work well depends in large part on the tools given it by the legislative agency.

During the nineteenth century the administrative structure of the Federal government was founded upon a series of unrelated, piecemeal legislative acts which generally strove to achieve selected, short-range objectives. By 1900 the result of this lack of administrative planning had become apparent. Waste, duplication of functions, authority not commensurate with responsibility, random grouping of unrelated functions under the same agency, and the absence of clear channels of command became the features of a disintegrated administrative organization which has plagued every President from Theodore Roosevelt to Dwight D. Eisenhower.

As a result, since 1887, 10 different investigating commissions have been created for the purpose of studying the Federal administrative organization and making recommendations for its improvement.

One of the first comprehensive attempts to cope with the problem was made by President Taft's Efficiency and Economy Commission in 1911. Soon after the commission reported, however, Taft retired from office and Congress took no action. Other attempts to reorganize the executive branch were made during the Harding, Coolidge, and Hoover administrations, but without success.

When Franklin D. Roosevelt became President in 1933, Congress passed an act authorizing the President to transfer, consolidate, or abolish government agencies and functions or parts thereof through the use of executive orders. Utilizing this power, the President issued a number of executive orders, one of the most notable being the merging of the several agencies engaged in extending agricultural credit into a single Farm Credit Administration. During this period, however, the government created numerous new agencies to deal with emergency problems arising out of the depression, and very soon the number of independent executive agencies reporting directly to the President had substantially increased.

In 1936 President Roosevelt appointed a Committee on Administrative Management, headed by one of the country's outstanding public administrators, Louis D. Brownlow, to conduct an investigation not only of the organization, but also of the management of the executive branch and to prepare recommendations. The committee's report in 1937 called for sweeping changes in the organization and administrative management of the government.[15] It recommended that all executive agencies be placed

[15] *Administrative Management in the Government of the United States*, 1937.

within one of the regular executive departments, but advocated the creation of two new departments—public works and social welfare. It urged the enactment of legislation authorizing the President to assign agencies to executive departments, and to transfer, merge, or abolish agencies in the interest of administrative efficiency.

Another important recommendation was to strengthen the staff serving the President, and particularly to strengthen the Bureau of the Budget and to move it from the Treasury Department to become a part of the Executive Office of the President. This was the most important Committee recommendation to be adopted. Concerning personnel management, it recommended a complete overhaul of the civil-service system to attract and retain in the service well-qualified officers and employees, the extension of the civil service "upward, outward, and downward," to include all but a few of the highest policy-determining officers, and the substitution of a single head, a director of personnel with an advisory board, in the place of the present Civil Service Commission.

One of the most controversial recommendations of the committee was that the Comptroller General should be changed to an Auditor General, and limited to the functions of conducting a post-audit of Federal financial transactions. At present the Comptroller General prescribes accounting systems, conducts pre-audits of expenditures, interprets the statutes with regard to expenditures, and settles accounts, all of which the committee deemed to be executive functions. Congress, however, which regards the Comptroller General as its agent, saw little merit in these recommendations and no change has been made. Another recommendation which attracted strong opposition was that the administrative functions of independent regulatory commissions should be placed within one of the regular executive departments, thus placing such activities within the control of the President. The committee also urged that the practice of creating independent commissions outside of the executive branch be stopped, referring to such agencies as a "headless fourth branch" of the government.

Shortly after the President submitted the report of the Committee on Administrative Management to Congress, urging its adoption, he dropped into the lap of Congress his explosive proposal to increase the size of the Supreme Court; and the administrative-management and reorganization proposals were sidetracked for two years. When Congress got around to enacting legislation it was only a pale reflection of the original proposals. The Reorganization Act of 1939 authorized the President to submit plans for the reorganization of executive departments and agencies to Congress, which would become effective unless set aside by both houses of Congress within 60 days. Many of the recommendations of the committee, however, were carried out, particularly those relating to personnel, budgeting, and the strengthening of the White House staff. And it may be noted that the recommendations of the President's Committee on Administrative Management in 1937 bear a striking similarity to those made 12 years later by the Hoover Commission.

The most recent and successful reorganization movement centered about the creation of the Hoover Commission in 1947. Headed by former President Hoover, this group organized into 18 task forces, swept through the Federal bureaucracy, gathered its information and data, and reported to Congress in 1949. The Hoover Commission made many recommendations concerning the reorganization and management of the Federal government. Among them the following are of particular importance.

Findings. First, the executive branch is not organized into a workable number of major departments and agencies which the President can effectively direct, but is cut up into a large number of agencies which divide responsibility and which are too great in number for effective direction from the top.

Second, the line of command and supervision from the President down through his department heads to every employee, and the line of responsibility from each employee of the executive branch up to the President, has been weakened, or actually broken, in many places and in many ways.

Third, the President and the heads of departments lack the tools to frame programs and policies and to supervise their execution.

Fourth, the Federal government has not taken aggressive steps to build a corps of administrators of the highest level of ability with an interest in the program of the government as a whole.

Fifth, many of the statutes and regulations that control the administrative practices and procedures of the government are unduly detailed and rigid.

Sixth, likewise the budgetary processes of the government need improvement, in order to express the objectives of the government in terms of the work to be done rather than in mere classifications of expenditures.

Recommendations. 1. The 65 departments, administrations, agencies, boards, and commissions which engage in executive work should be grouped into about one-third of this number, consisting principally of major-purpose departments. To accomplish this, the President should be granted authority to submit reorganization plans to Congress which would become effective unless disapproved.

2. Executive departments should be the main organizational divisions of the executive branch of government and, although independent regulatory commissions were not condemned, the creation of new commissions was discouraged. Government corporations should be utilized for the conduct of business enterprises carried on under authorization of Congress.

3. Under the President, the heads of departments should hold full responsibility for the conduct of their departments. There should be a clear line of authority reaching down through every step of the organization and

no subordinate should have authority independent from that of his superior.

4. Department heads should be authorized, with Presidential approval, to reorganize their departments. The internal-organization structure of executive agencies should not be prescribed by legislation.

5. The President and department heads should be provided with adequate staff assistance to enable them to exercise effective direction, coordination, and control over the executive agencies for which they are responsible. The Bureau of the Budget should be strengthened as a staff agency of the President, and he should be granted broader discretion in the organization of the Executive Office. Department heads should be assisted by an undersecretary, several assistant secretaries, an administrative assistant secretary, and staff units in charge of finance, personnel, legal information, management research, and similar activities.

6. A number of recommendations were designed to improve the personnel of the Federal government. Among these were the following: an Office of Personnel should be created in the President's Office, headed by the Chairman of the Civil Service Commission; the government should develop an aggressive program for building a corps of departmental administrators of the highest level of ability; and the quality of the entire service should be improved through more effective recruitment procedures, adequate salary scales, and well designed rating and promotion systems.

7. Budgeting should be strengthened and improved through the adoption of a "performance" budget which shows the cost of the various programs, functions, and activities of the government, in the place of a budget based on organizational units and itemized objects of expenditure.

8. An Office of General Services should be created to handle central purchasing and supplies, to coordinate such activities carried on by the several departments, and to be in charge of the construction and maintenance of public buildings and other general services. This was one of the first recommendations to be carried into effect with the creation of the General Services Administration.

The recommendations of the Hoover Commission received strong support throughout the country, and Congress passed the Reorganization Act of 1949 which authorized the President to reexamine the organization of all agencies in the executive branch and determine what changes would be necessary to promote more economical and efficient administration. Having made such determinations, he was authorized to submit to Congress reorganization plans which, if not rejected by either house within 60 days, became effective.[16] This law expired on April 1, 1953, but was extended to give President Eisenhower the same power.[17] A number of

[16] 63 Stat. L. 203.
[17] While he was President, Harry S. Truman (as of January, 1952) submitted 36

such reorganization plans were submitted in 1953 and were approved by Congress.[18]

Keeping Bureaucracy Responsible

A government organization is like that familiar natural phenomenon, fire. It has immense powers for good or for evil, depending on whether or not it is kept under proper control. Government must have administrative organization, sometimes a huge administrative organization, to carry out the multifarious activities so necessary to a peaceful, prosperous and orderly society in our complex civilization. Because of its magnitude, this vast bureaucracy must be subject to effective controls, for otherwise there is always the danger that it will become arrogant, inefficient, and even corrupt. An uncontrolled bureaucracy, as history has often indicated, can easily come to be regarded by its members as an end in itself, rather than as the servant of the people.

One of the most common faults in large governmental organizations is for the administrative officers at all levels to be unwilling to accept responsibility for their actions, to develop a "don't blame me" attitude and point to statutes, rules, regulations, central controls, political interference, and other factors which make it difficult if not impossible for them to accomplish the desired results. They are, alas, often truly not to be blamed for the miscarriages of their administrative efforts. Sometimes the fault lies with the compartmentalization and division of labor which naturally characterizes a large organization. When so many hands each have a small part in a total job, it is difficult indeed to lay the responsibility for good or poor work at any one door. Sometimes the fault belongs with Congress for legislative meddling in matters of pure administrative procedure. By attaching riders to bills, which are swept into permanent law along with the laudable objectives of the body of a bill, Congress often tries to dictate to administrators as to whom they shall employ to do the job, how they shall organize their work, how they shall dole out the money they have to spend, or other details which are administrative rather than legislative.

Nothing is more discouraging to a governmental official who desires to promote economy and efficiency in his organization than to find himself unable to do so because of restrictive legislation. To do a good job, he must have control over his organization. While it is the duty of Congress to

reorganizational proposals, and Congress approved 28 of these plans. "Of the eight rejected, two were duplicates and six failed in important particulars either to conform to the Hoover reports or to long-standing congressional policy." See *Reorganization of the Federal Government*, S. Doc. 91, 82d Cong., 2d sess., 1952, p. 1.

[18] To keep up with changes in governmental organization, in January of each year the Senate Committee on Government Operations publishes a chart outlining the current Federal administrative organization with an explanatory statement. Information concerning personnel changes as well as organizational changes that occurred during the past year are set forth.

make appropriations and determine the amount to be spent, Congress should leave the executive sufficient discretion to determine the organizational machinery necessary for doing the job. The *Hoover Commission Report* states that department heads must have four kinds of discretion if they are to be held responsible for the work of the department. "They need organizational discretion, budgetary discretion, personnel (appointing and firing) discretion, and the discretion to arrange with top management assistance as they require." [19]

Responsibility of administration is not an end in itself, but merely the means of assuring sound administration, efficiency, faithful discharge of duties, avoidance of bad practices, and a spirit of true service. And by far the principal obstacle in the way of securing responsible administration is that executive officers are denied the authority which they must have if they are to be held responsible. Authority not commensurate with responsibility is a perennial complaint of administrators, much stressed in the Hoover Commission reports. Neither Congress nor the public can hold an administrator responsible for the conduct of his department if he is hamstrung by legislative restrictions, rulings of the Comptroller General, excessive central control by the Budget Bureau and other central agencies, a rigid organization which he cannot change, or inability to choose his principal assistants. Civil-service restrictions and red tape are also at the bottom of much executive frustration. All these restrictions are based on the old distrust of the executive, which is part of the American tradition. Such distrust is only slowly giving way to a realization that there can be no real responsibility without giving executive officials the necessary authority and discretion to manage their organizations. If they are so empowered, they can be held responsible for results and detailed administration, but not otherwise.

Controlling Bureaucracy

How can government administration be prevented from acting like a bureaucracy in the invidious sense of the term? How can red tape be kept to a minimum, administrative delay be reduced, high-handedness and petty tyranny in dealing with individuals be eliminated, and spending be controlled by economy?

Internal Administrative Control. Although less spectacular than other devices, the most important controls and corrective measures are those normally taken within an administrative organization as safeguards against incompetence and abuse of authority. A citizen who believes that he has not received the service or treatment to which he is entitled, or has been dealt with unfairly, illegally, or discourteously by a government official, may always make an appeal to his administrative superior and thus seek

[19] *Task Force on Departmental Management,* pp. 5–6.

to have the subordinate official overruled. Arrogance, incompetence, discourtesy, and abuse of authority are normally discovered in this manner, and the necessary disciplinary actions are taken. Occasionally, however, the citizen cannot secure any satisfaction from the administrative officials, and his only recourse is to turn to his member in Congress or to the courts. In the vast majority of cases, it should be noted, the administrative officials are courteous and cooperative in their dealings with citizens, and appeals to Congress often are made when the citizen is seeking some special treatment or favor to which he is not entitled.

Individual citizens often protest against certain policies which are adopted by government departments. Individual protests of this kind are likely to have little effect, unless they are very numerous, but the objections of large organizations of citizens (usually called pressure groups) are likely to carry great weight. The representations of the Farm Bureau Federation, for example, are extremely effective with the Department of Agriculture as are those of veterans' organizations with the Veterans' Administration. Organized interest groups often come to look upon a particular agency or department as their own, and virtually dictate its policies and programs. When this happens the particular group often benefits at the expense of the general public.

Executive Control. Unlike monarchical or dictatorial governments, ours is headed by a President who must bow to the verdict of the voter every four years. The President determines the major administrative policies, and through the choice of the principal officers sets the tone and general character of his administration. As the head of his party, which to stay in office must retain public confidence and support, he and his assistants are highly sensitive to public opinion and particularly to criticisms of his administration. No President today can escape for long the consequences of chronic and persistent Federal administrative irresponsibility. Thus the President in the dual role of chief administrator and elected representative of all the people must, if he would remain in office, use every means at his disposal to keep his administration responsible and responsive to public opinion. Any serious criticism of the operation of any part of the vast Federal government executive organization is certain, sooner or later, to be brought to the personal attention of the President. If orders, directives, instructions and conferences fail to correct the situation, the President may be forced to shake up the organization concerned and replace those in charge. Department and agency heads in turn bend every effort to avoid public criticisms and scandals.

Control by Congress. One of the most important controls is that exercised by Congress. Legislative bodies have been the traditional stronghold of popular liberty in Anglo-American governments since 1688. Congress has four major weapons it can wield. It may, by general legislation, create, alter, abolish, or reform any agency of the government. Congress also has the power of the purse strings, the power to investigate, and the power to conduct post-audits.

The controversial Administrative Procedure Act of 1946 is the most recent and far-reaching piece of legislation by which Congress has tried to limit the activities of the Federal Administration. This act requires Federal agencies to publish in the *Federal Register* a description of the line of authority and its distribution, show the "established places at which, and methods whereby the public may secure information or make submittals or requests. . . . ," give notice of contemplated rules so that the parties affected can appear before such agencies and protest, separate the function of investigation from that of adjudication, permit attendance of parties concerned at hearings, permit counsel or other representatives to appear before the agency, and make decisions on the basis of the facts submitted in the case.[20] These are just the highlights of the law, but they illustrate a congressional concern for individual rights and their protection.

Congress may, at any time, restrain the activities of any government agency simply by refusing to appropriate money for that agency's needs. The most handy weapon in the congressional arsenal, however, is the power of investigation. The mere threat of a congressional investigation often has a salutary effect. It is unfortunate that this power has been seriously abused in recent years, and that many investigations have been conducted for obvious political purposes and to capture newspaper headlines rather than to expose administrative mismanagement. Instead of leading to improvements in administration, certain congressional investigations have been used principally to ventilate reckless and unsupported charges, to malign and smear public employees with little regard as to whether they are guilty or innocent, and to impair seriously the work of some departments. These bad examples, however, should not obscure the fact that through its investigative role Congress often exposes faulty administration and abuses and forces the adoption of corrective measures.

In passing on the requests of the departments for funds the Appropriations Committees of both houses of Congress conduct a detailed review of their programs, administrations, and results. If there are criticisms of the work of any agency, it is certain to be brought to the attention of these committees, and the departmental officials will be called upon to defend their actions. In many instances funds have been curtailed as a result of these criticisms, and administrative policies and practices are often revised to meet such objections.

Another review by Congress of administration occurs when departments seek new legislation affecting their operations or authorizing new activities. In considering such legislative proposals, which are constantly

[20] 60 Stat. L. 237.

before Congress, the committees concerned will necessarily inquire into the administration of the department. This brings these committees into continuous contact with the departments and affords them the means whereby they exert great influence over departmental operations and policies.

Another control exercised by Congress is that conducted in its behalf by the General Accounting Office, which audits and settles all accounts of the government. Its powers are much stronger than those customarily given to an auditing officer, for it has the power to disallow expenditures, to prescribe the form of accounting records, and to determine whether a given activity is authorized by Congress. For certain expenditures this office conducts a pre-audit as well as a post-audit. Ordinarily the auditing officer is given only the function of conducting a post-audit, and reporting his findings to the legislative body, which in turn calls administrative officers to account for any improper or unauthorized expenditures or faulty accounts. The Federal system, which vests controlling, accounting, and auditing functions in the same official, has been criticized by public administrators and by leading authorities in the field of accounting as being contrary to sound practice, but Congress has not looked with favor on proposals to reduce the powers of its own agent—the Comptroller General who heads this office.

Control by the Judiciary. Dicey's rule of law that "no man is above the law, but . . . every man, whatever be his rank or condition, is subject to the ordinary law of the realm. . . ." [21] is the basis for judicial review of administrative acts. The judiciary will set aside acts of agencies, when these acts violate due process or deviate from prescribed procedures. The citizen may also claim protection of the courts if the administrator intervenes in cases where he has no jurisdiction, when he abuses his discretion, when he violates or misinterprets the law. Generally, however, administrative findings of fact will not be disturbed by the courts.

Until recent decades public administration was generally regarded as unimportant; the great questions of state were debated and decided in the halls of Congress, by the President and the courts, while the details of carrying them into effect could be left to clerks. And for the first hundred years the public employees of the government consisted largely of clerks. But today with the vast growth of governmental functions since the opening of the twentieth century the situation has greatly changed. Administration has taken its place along with the executive, the legislative body, and the courts as a major part of government. The key to the spectacular rise of business and industry in this country may be attributed in large part to the development of management. This is also true of government, and

[21] A. V. Dicey, *Introduction to the Study of the Law of the Constitution,* 8th ed., p. 189, 1915.

will be increasingly true in the future. The wisest of laws and public policies are of no avail without a competent administration to carry them into effect. No longer is administration confined to the detailed execution of policies and laws, but it is looked to for initiative, expert advice, and the preparation of major programs and policies for consideration by the political officers of the government. Without an able staff and a strong administration, no government today can hope to cope with the highly complex problems of an industrial society.

REFERENCES

Paul H. Appleby, *Big Democracy* (1945).
———, *Policy and Administration* (1949).
James C. Charlesworth, *Governmental Administration* (1951).
Robert E. Cushman, *The Independent Regulatory Commissions* (1941).
James Fesler, *Area and Administration* (1949).
W. Brooke Graves, *Public Administration in a Democratic Society* (1950).
Luther Gulick, *Administrative Reflections from World War II* (1948).
——— and Lyndall Urwick (eds.), *Papers on the Science of Administration* (1937).
Edward H. Hobbs, *Executive Reorganization in the National Government* (1953).
The Hoover Commission Report (selections from the official reports prepared by McGraw-Hill Book Company, Inc.) (1949).
Charles S. Hyneman, *Bureaucracy in a Democracy* (1950).
Albert Lepawsky, *Administration: The Art and Science of Organization and Management* (1949).
Arthur Maas, *Muddy Waters: The Army Engineers and the Nation's Rivers* (1951).
Fritz Morstein Marx (ed.), *Elements of Public Administration* (1946).
———, *The President and His Staff Services* (1947).
Robert K. Merton, Ailsa P. Gray, *et al.* (eds.), *Reader in Bureaucracy* (1952).
Felix A. Nigro, *Public Administration* (1952).
Herbert A. Simon, Donald W. Smithburg, and Victor A. Thompson, *Public Administration* (1950).
Harold Stein (ed.), *Public Administration and Policy Development* (1952).
United States Government Organization Manual, Washington, D.C. (issued annually).
Max Weber (Talcott Parson and A. M. Henderson, eds.), *The Theory of Social and Economic Organization* (1947).
Leonard D. White, *The Federalists: A Study in Administrative History* (1948).
———, *Introduction to the Study of Public Administration,* 3d ed. (1948).
———, *The Jeffersonians: A Study in Administrative History* (1951).

CHAPTER 19 *The Federal Civil Service*

The greatness of any government and the quality of its administration depend in large measure on the ability, loyalty, and devotion of the men and women who constitute its staff and carry on its activities. This basic fact was fully recognized by the Hoover Commission, which placed great emphasis on needed improvements in the Federal personnel system. Earlier commissions which surveyed the organization and management of the government made similar recommendations.

Even wise laws, sound organizations, and well-designed procedures will work badly without competent employees. The motto of the Wisconsin civil service, "the best shall serve the state," is one which all public agencies should follow. But it is not enough merely to recruit qualified persons as public employees. They must be trained and given opportunities for advancement and for creative and satisfying careers; salary scales must be high enough to attract and retain competent personnel in competition with private employers; and public service must be looked upon not as a passing job, but as a lifetime career.

A well-rounded personnel program includes far more than the giving of entrance examinations. It must be equally concerned with the highest and most effective utilization of the abilities of employees under conditions of work which will elicit their best efforts. Personnel administration includes many types of activities: placement, training, promotions, transfers, service ratings, classification, salary scales, human relations, supervision, discipline, health and safety, employee relations, and retirement. Of especial importance in any personnel system is the development of skilled administrators who are able to plan, direct, supervise, coordinate the work of the staff and provide imagination, drive, and leadership.

For many years the Federal service was greatly handicapped by the tradition of patronage appointments and a high rate of turnover of employees after each change of administration. Under the spurious slogan that "to the victor belong the spoils," the winning party demanded the discharge of the employees of the preceding administration and the appointment of party workers as a reward for their services. Under this system, persons with little or no qualifications were appointed to the public service, only to be turned out of office a few years later after they had acquired a measure of competence. Such a wasteful and incompetent system was tolerated for years partly because the functions of government were relatively few and inexpensive and did not require persons of ability and training. Most government employees, at least it was so thought, were merely clerks, and continuity of service was not regarded as necessary.

When the civil-service-reform movement finally swept the country after the War Between the States, it was designed primarily to purify politics by combatting the spoilsman and the political machines which thrived on patronage rather than as a means of selecting qualified persons. It was not until fifty years ago that a new affirmative concept of personnel management overcame the older idea of civil-service reform. Under the earlier concept of civil-service reform the Civil Service Commission served as a police agency to prevent patronage appointments; its functions were limited largely to giving entrance examinations. With the rise of personnel management, it has become instead a central personnel agency whose function is to assist the departments in maintaining high personnel standards. Within recent years many of the entrance examinations formerly given by the Civil Service Commission have been delegated to the departments, and the great bulk of the personnel work in the Federal service is now carried on not by the Civil Service Commission, but by the operating departments and agencies. Great progress has been made in the direction of a true career service, but further improvements are still needed.

The two major characteristics of the Federal civil service today are: first, its vast size, totaling well over two million civilian employees, and second, the extremely wide range of occupations and professions represented in its ranks. Approximately one-half of its civilian employees, it may be noted, are in the Defense Department, and roughly one-fourth are in the Post Office Department, leaving only one-fourth in all the other departments and agencies. Instead of the service consisting largely of clerks, as is commonly supposed, the government employs thousands of engineers, lawyers, physicians, foresters, agriculturists, scientists of all types, administrators, economists, public-health officers, nurses, accountants, statisticians, and many other kinds of specialists and experts. In its military and naval installations and munitions yards are to be found also hundreds of thousands of blue-collar workers, representing practically all crafts and skilled trades.

Despite the immense strides taken in recent decades toward the development of a great civil service, the Federal personnel system still operates under a number of handicaps. The first of these is the hang-over of patronage appointments to certain administrative positions which should be filled by promotions from the career service. The largest block of such positions are the postmasters of all except the smallest offices, numbering about 20,000. Although placed under a form of civil service before 1940, the actual selections are made by members of Congress or the party organizations. United States marshals, district attorneys, collectors of customs, and certain other field officers continue to be subject to political appointment, although President Truman attempted unsuccessfully in 1952 to place most of these under the civil service.

In recent years the Federal service has also suffered because of the indiscriminate attacks which have been made on its employees as being subversive or disloyal, and for association with Communist-front organizations. The rank and file of its employees has unquestionably been loyal, and the number found to be disloyal or poor security risks has been extremely small, but the morale of the whole service has suffered. It is hardly to be doubted that such charges have often been made for political reasons rather than the safety of the country, but they have served to discredit the public service and to lower its morale.

A third handicap of the Federal service is that it does not pay as high salaries for top administrative and professional positions as are paid in business and industry, and as a result loses many of its ablest employees when they are of greatest value to the service. It is hardly to be expected, however, that the government will ever be able to match the top salaries paid in private industry; it must rely instead upon prestige, opportunities for public service, security, and other rewards to hold its able men and women. Although a career in the public service does not offer the lure of high salaries, it has many other attractions. Today, along with a more liberal salary scale in the higher brackets, there is a recognized need for the development of a corps of able administrators.

A fourth handicap is the common notion that all public agencies are greatly overstaffed, and that the same work could be done at much less expense by fewer employees. Doubtless there will always be some units in any large governmental organization which are overstaffed, due to changes in the volume of work, poor supervision, inefficient employees, or for other reasons. But any blanket indictment of the public service generally as overstaffed is not only untrue, but harms its prestige and standing. Many government agencies are, in fact, seriously understaffed. Reductions in the number of public employees are often possible as the result of more efficient management, improved procedures, and better selection and training of employees. Better personnel administration will produce true economies and may at times make reductions in staff possible, but in the long run, it is more likely to bring about an increase in governmental services. The mere fact that the Federal government employs more than two million civilian employees is not in itself proof that it is overstaffed or inefficient.

Development of the Civil Service

During the administrations of Washington and John Adams, employment in the Federal civil service was largely based on merit, although political considerations were not absent by any means. With the development of political parties, the spoils system began to evolve.

The Spoils System. Although Jefferson did not resort to wholesale firing of Federalists when he came into power, he did favor Republicans for appointment as positions became vacant by resignation or death or as new jobs opened up. Jefferson was moved to remark: "How are vacancies obtained? Those by death are few, by resignation none."

An act of 1810 provided that terms of district attorneys, collectors, surveyors of customs, navy agents, paymasters, and certain other officeholders should henceforth be limited to four years. It paved the way for rotation in office with the change in administration. William H. Crawford, Secretary of the Treasury, was chiefly responsible for this act. He saw in it an opportunity to build up a political machine and become President.[1]

The spoils system is the practice, resorted to by political parties as well as factions, of filling appointive offices with their supporters when they come into power. "To the victor belong the spoils of the enemy," said Senator Marcy in a debate in the United States Senate in 1832. While Andrew Jackson did not inaugurate the spoils system, he gave it considerable impetus during his administration. In his first year as President, it is estimated, Jackson removed between 690 and 734 employees in the executive departments. Still he did not make a clean sweep, and Senator Benton insisted that a majority of the offices were left in the hands of political enemies.[2] Jackson attempted to rationalize his position on the spoils system in his first annual message to Congress when he said: [3]

The duties of all public officers are, or at least admit of being, made so plain and simple that men of intelligence may readily qualify themselves for their performance; and I can not but believe that more is lost by the long continuance of men in office than is generally to be gained by their experience. I submit, therefore, to your consideration whether the efficiency of the Government would not be promoted, and official industry and integrity better secured, by a general extension of the law which limits appointments to four years.

---

[1] R. C. Brooks, *Political Parties and Electoral Problems,* 3d ed., p. 543, Harper & Brothers, New York, 1933.

[2] *Ibid.,* p. 544.

[3] James D. Richardson, *Messages and Papers of the Presidents, 1789–1891,* Government Printing Office, Washington, 1896, Vol. 2, p. 449.

Jackson voiced the popular demand of the common man for a chance to share in holding public office, and also the wide-spread disapproval of a permanent bureaucracy. It reflected the democratic movement of the time. Perhaps no more plausible statement was ever made in defense of the system of patronage appointments to reward the party workers.

It became the custom after Jackson's time to make a clean sweep of employees after a victory at the polls over an opposing party, and even when a different faction of the same party came into power. "Turn the rascals out" became the slogan of the victors.

Throughout history Presidents have made use of patronage in order to bring about party unity and to secure the adoption of their programs by Congress. Abraham Lincoln did it and so did Franklin Roosevelt in the early days of his administration. James Farley points out that Roosevelt held up judicial appointments in states where the congressional delegation failed to support the administration's program. In states where the delegation went along, appointments were put through promptly.[4]

In spite of the apparent plausibility of Jackson's arguments, and in spite of the demonstrated effectiveness of patronage as a weapon for securing party unity, history has revealed that the price of the spoils systems is too high. The spoils system and political patronage have always produced incompetent and inexperienced public servants, and sometimes grafting or corrupt ones. By the time of the War Between the States, the standards of the Federal service were at such a low ebb that civil-service reform had become the aim of a popular political crusade.

Progress of the Merit System. The goal of the civil-service reformers was to establish a merit system, under which appointments to the public service would be based on ability, experience, knowledge, and training rather than on party loyalty. While there were protests against the baneful effects of patronage as early as the middle 1830s, by prominent men like John C. Calhoun, not until the late 1860s did the public become aroused. Clamor for civil-service reform increased as a result of the fraud and corruption of the Grant administration. In 1868 the Democratic party urged in its platform that corrupt men be expelled from office and that useless offices be abolished. In 1872 both major political parties advocated civil-service reform.[5]

The assassination of President James A. Garfield in 1881 by a disappointed office-seeker crystallized the sentiment for reform. While Garfield's life was ebbing away, the National Civil Service League was formed; and in 1883 Congress passed the Pendleton Act which is the basis of our present civil-service system.

[4] James A. Farley, *Jim Farley's Story: The Roosevelt Years,* p. 74, McGraw-Hill Book Company, Inc., New York, 1948.
[5] Brooks, *op. cit.,* p. 551.

The act called for the establishment of a bipartisan Civil Service Commission composed of three persons. The members of the Commission were to be appointed by the President by and with the consent of the Senate and were to hold no other office under the United States. Section 2 of the act set forth the duties of the Commission, among which was the formulation of rules for making the act effective. These rules were to provide "for open competitive examinations for testing the fitness of applicants for the public service now classified or to be classified," and to specify that positions in the classified service were to be filled from among those who made the highest grades. Furthermore, positions in the classified service were to be allotted on a geographical basis. No person in the service was to be penalized for failure to contribute to a political fund or to perform political service. Also, all classified employees were required to abstain from using their official authority or influence "to coerce the political action of any person or body." The Hatch Act of 1939 went even further.

Under President Arthur, 15,573 positions were put under the "classified" civil service, hence to be filled by competitive examination. Those positions placed under the jurisdiction of the Civil Service Commission have long been known as the classified service, while other positions not subject to its control are called the unclassified service. These terms do not refer to the classification of positions according to duties and responsibilities, which is described in a later section of this chapter. In each succeeding administration additional positions were brought under the classified service. Cleveland added over 60,000 in his two administrations, Theodore Roosevelt over 128,000, Taft 47,657, Wilson 165,515, and Hoover over 35,000. Harrison, McKinley, and Coolidge also transferred substantial numbers to the classified service.

Although Woodrow Wilson placed postmasters of the first, second, and third class under the merit system in 1917, these positions were again to become "political plums" in later administrations. The Executive order issued by Wilson provided that the person who stood at the top of the list after an examination should receive the appointment. However, political appointees who were giving satisfactory service were allowed to continue in office. In 1921 Harding revised the order to provide that any one of the top three candidates in an examination could be appointed, and once more patronage appointments became the rule. When a vacancy occurred in a postmastership, the local congressman belonging to the party in power was permitted to select a temporary appointee. The examination which was subsequently given consisted only of an oral test and a general check-up of the reputation of the candidates, hence it was not difficult for the temporary appointee to stand among the first three and thus to receive a permanent position. This system was continued under Coolidge, Hoover, and for a while under Franklin Roosevelt. In 1936, however, Roosevelt returned to the Wilsonian rule of appointing only the top person on the list. Then, in 1938, Congress passed the Ramspeck-O'Mahoney Act, which placed the postmasters under civil service, but reinstated the rule of three. The result was that postmasters are again political appointees, in spite of the pseudo-merit-system examination. Once in office, however, they have life or indefinite terms, and are required to abstain from political activities.

A large number of new agencies was set up after Franklin D. Roosevelt came into power, and the employees in most of them were not put under the civil service. Thus patronage appointments became the general rule for these agencies. However, at the insistence of Senator George W. Norris, the TVA set up a rigid merit system of its own, and the Farm Credit Administration also made use of the merit system in selecting its employees. But the merit system had another setback when the President withdrew the Bureau of Foreign and Domestic Commerce from civil-service rules.

In spite of these changes, a high-water mark was reached by the classified service during the Roosevelt administration. In 1937 the President's Committee on Administrative Management called for the extension of the classified service downward as well as upward and outward. In the same year, President Roosevelt urged Congress to extend the classified system to cover all positions except those of a policy-determining nature. The following year the President, by Executive order, provided that all positions of a nonpolicy-making nature over which he had control should be placed under the merit system. Two years later the Ramspeck Act authorized the President to bring into the classified service almost all jobs other than those requiring appointment by the President with the consent of the Senate. A 1941 Executive order transferred some 182,000 to the merit system. While only 10.5 per cent of the employees in the executive civil service were included in the classified service in 1884, 88.3 per cent were so classified in 1950.[6]

Has the merit system fulfilled all the expectations of its advocates in the past 75 years? The reply cannot be an unqualified affirmative. Critics of modern civil service—and there are more than a few—make the point that the same legal walls which keep political appointees out of the service also serve to keep inside many incompetents and misfits, as well as political appointees who acquired their jobs before classification. These critics single out cases in which civil-service examinations have not resulted in the selection of qualified employees. They legitimately object to the cumbersome processes of civil-service appointment, its frequent inflexibility and slowness at times when quick action is important.

There is truth in all these criticisms but they do not by any means impeach the merit system as a useful, operating principle of good govern-

[6] W. E. Mosher, J. D. Kingsley, and O. G. Stahl, *Public Personnel Administration*, 3d ed., p. 27, Harper & Brothers, New York, 1950.

ment. Time will heal some of the defects; the political appointees and the incompetents will die off or resign, and be replaced by candidates of merit. Improved civil-service techniques, also a matter of time and experience, will take care of other merit-system problems. Any enterprise operated by human beings is bound to have its chinks and its weaknesses. But to the impartial observer, there seems no question but that the merit system is so much superior to the old spoils method of filling public positions that there is no choice between them at all.

Classification and Compensation

There is more to a good civil-service system than the mere process of appointment. Once an employee has been hired, his conditions of employment must be such that he is encouraged and helped to do his best. In the past several decades, big advances have been made in the Federal administration toward providing a system of job classification and a compensation plan—essentials in an effective civil-service system.

Classification and Pay. The 1923 Classification Act laid the groundwork. Under this act, which was administered for a number of years by a special board, and then assigned to the Civil Service Commission, positions in the Federal service were classified according to their duties and responsibilities. A basic feature of the plan and of classification today is that the position—not the employee—is classified. Positions which involve substantially similar duties and the same level of responsibilities are placed in the same class, regardless of the fact that they are located in different departments and agencies. The description of each class includes a title, which should indicate the general character of the work performed, and contains also a general statement of duties and responsibilities followed by examples of typical tasks performed, a statement of the education and experience required, the salary range, and finally, the lines of promotion.

Positions may be classified only after detailed information is secured about the character of the work performed by employees who occupy them. A fundamental principle of classification is that all employees engaged in the same work and having the same responsibilities shall be treated alike and shall receive the same rate of pay. Classification makes it possible to provide "equal pay for equal work," but this is only one of its purposes. A good classification system is essential to effective recruitment and examination, for unless the civil-service examiner knows what are the duties and responsibilities of the positions to be filled, he will be unable to design suitable examinations. Without a classification plan, the titles given to positions often have no relation to the actual work performed, and employees engaged in the same work may be paid widely differing rates, with the resultant lowered morale due to the feeling of many employees that they are being treated unfairly. Classification is also essential to a sound promotion plan, to the development of in-service training, to transfers, to the most effective utilization of employees, and to almost every aspect of personnel administration.

In 1949 Congress passed another Classification Act which superseded the act of 1923 as well as amendments to that act. A position-classification plan was established, as well as a pay plan for approximately 900,000 positions. The chief feature of the new law is an operating method for classifying and reclassifying positions on a day-by-day basis. Briefly summarized, this method calls for the Commission to establish and publish standards for placing positions in their proper classes and grades in individual cases (except for the three higher grades) on its own responsibility. The Commission then checks up on compliance by the departments, and corrects erroneous classifications. In the event a department is found not to be observing classification standards, its authority to classify may be revoked. The pay plan of the act consolidates the four former pay schedules of 41 grades into two pay schedules of 18 and 10 grades, respectively, establishing a floor and ceiling for adults of $2,120 and $14,000, respectively. Provision is also made for increases for long and satisfactory service over and above the scheduled maximum for each grade.

Recruitment

The Civil Service Commission was at first concerned only with the administration of examinations and certification of lists of eligibles, but now it has many other duties. These include: classification of civil-service employees, formulation of rules and regulations concerning in-service training, looking into charges of political activity against classified employees, administering the loyalty program, seeing to it that the fair-employment-practices program is carried out, keeping service records, supervising the efficiency-rating system, as well as the retirement law, and many other things. The Commission employs upwards of 4,000 people.

Recruitment is the promotional work that is done in attracting applicants to take examinations. While this is chiefly the task of the Civil Service Commission, the various operating departments assist. The 14 regional offices of the Commission, each headed by a director, as well as branch offices, are also concerned with recruitment. Special appeals are made to young men and young women through the schools and colleges. While the Civil Service Commission, as well as the various departments, generally prefer people with at least minimum educational qualifications, there has been considerable opposition in Congress to imposing any educational qualifications as a condition of taking civil-service examinations.

Today the task of recruitment has been made much more difficult as a result of the indiscriminate charges that have been made against Federal employees. (So many innocent public servants have been charged with disloyalty that some of our best talent has left the public service, and it has become more difficult to induce qualified young men and women to enter.[7]

Examinations. Examinations are conducted by the 14 regional offices and their branches, as well as by hundreds of examining boards. Approximately 700 boards composed of Federal officials conduct assembled or group examinations at post offices or in other Federal buildings in their respective cities. In addition, there are approximately 700 rating boards which hold unassembled or individual examinations for all classifications of the civil service.

While the examinations in the early days of our civil-service system were concerned more with knowledge of subject matter, the trend in more recent times has been toward a more "practical" test. Instead of laying emphasis on spelling, geography, arithmetic, and the use of good English, the tests now are pointed in the direction of the duties to be performed in the particular job for which the examination is being held. The politicians insist on practical rather than intelligence tests, and the Civil Service Commission must listen to them. However, in an effort to attract better-qualified, college-trained young people to the service, the Commission has provided for junior-grade administrative and management positions, for which the examinations stress general knowledge.

Appointment. The names of all persons who have passed an examination with a grade of 70 or more are kept by the Commission on registers from which appointments are made. When a vacancy occurs, the appointing officer requests the Commission to certify the names of persons at the top of the list of eligibles. As a rule, the three highest are certified, and the appointing officer either selects one of the three or else asks for more names.) If he does ask for additional names, he must give a good reason for his action.

From the beginning, veterans of wars have had preference. After World War II Congress passed an act which gives veterans a virtual monopoly in certain minor jobs. It gives disabled veterans, unmarried widows of such veterans, as well as wives, a bonus of 10 points on competitive examinations, and places all such persons who have made grades of 70 or above (including the extra 10 points) at the head of the lists of eligibles. The only exceptions to this rule are professional and scientific positions where the beginning pay is $3,000 or more. In addition, all honorably discharged able-bodied veterans are given five extra points on competitive examinations. As a result of these preference provisions, a large percentage of those persons now in the classified service are veterans.

The Civil Service Commission is required to take note of geography in the certification of employees for appointment. In so far as possible, posi-

[7] For further discussion of the loyalty program, see section on Loyalty, later in this chapter.

tions are to be distributed among the states according to population, but this does not mean that the bars are to be let down as to qualifications. If the quota of a state is not filled, applicants from the state will be preferred over those from other states provided they can qualify.

Promotions. For a long while there was no well-defined policy for promotion of classified employees. It is true that the Pendleton Act provided that no person in the classified service could be promoted unless he had passed an examination or unless it was shown that he was exempt from such an examination. Furthermore, a directive by the President provided that competitive examinations should be given in so far as practicable "to test fitness for promotion in the classified service." Both the law and the Executive order left loopholes and resulted in a lack of uniform promotion policy in the various departments. Competitive examinations were used, but only in a limited way. Promotion was left to administrative heads, and politics often entered. It was left to the administrator's discretion whether or not to use competitive examinations.

In 1938, however, President Roosevelt directed the Civil Service Commission to set up and put into effect a uniform promotional system for all services. The Commission holds competitive examinations for promotion in positions that cut across departments and supervises examinations within the various departments. Provision is made for transfers, from one department or agency to another, which may result in promotion.

In its plan for reorganization of the Civil Service Commission, the Hoover Commission under Recommendation 4 [8] suggested that:

a. Departments and agencies should be required, under the direction of the Civil Service Commission, to work out specific programs for promoting career employees.

b. The Civil Service Commission should be given the authority and resources for developing a program which will open up promotion opportunities across agency lines . . .

e. The efficiency rating system should be simplified and should be used solely to develop a better understanding between supervisors and employees.

The Classification Act of 1949 as outlined elsewhere carried out some of these recommendations. Certainly today the employee is given a clearer understanding of what is necessary to receive promotion. This assurance should serve as an inducement for better-qualified persons to enter the service. The opportunities for advancement in rank and pay are excellent for able and efficient civil servants.

The Right to Organize

The Federal government guarantees the right of employees in private business to organize and to bargain collectively with their employers, as

[8] The Commission on Organization of the Executive Branch of Government, *Personnel Management: A Report to the Congress,* pp. 12–13, February, 1949.

well as the right to strike; but the right to strike is not recognized in the civil service. President Franklin D. Roosevelt clearly stated the position of the government in 1937 when he upheld the civil servants' right to organize but denied the right to strike. On this last point, he said: [9]

Since their own services have to do with the functioning of the government, a strike of public employees manifests nothing less than an attempt on their part to prevent or obstruct the operations of government until their demands are satisfied. Such action looking toward the paralysis of government by those who have sworn to support it is unthinkable and intolerable.

Government employees are permitted to affiliate with such labor groups as the American Federation of Labor. Generally the organizations of civil servants have been used to improve the public service, thus achieving wholesome results.

While Theodore Roosevelt permitted employees to use pressure for favorable legislation only through the heads of departments, government employees' organizations are now free to have their own officers appear before the committees of Congress. Government unions are fully recognized by the TVA and carry on collective bargaining with the administration. The management of the TVA has found that the unions of their employees contribute much to the improvement of administration.

Conduct and Discipline

Political Activity. While there were restrictions on political activity of government employees long before 1939, the Hatch Acts of that year and the year following went much further. A number of Presidents, including Jefferson, issued orders prohibiting political activity of Federal employees. The earliest civil-service order was issued in the 1880s after the passage of the Pendleton Act. In 1907 a rule based on an Executive order forbade employees in the classified service to take any active part in political management or in political campaigns. Although the Civil Service Commission interpreted this to mean that a civil-service employee could not be a delegate to a political convention, address political gatherings, serve on party committees, and the like, still he might attend political meetings and contribute to party funds, providing the person soliciting funds was not connected with the Federal government. Of course a classified employee could vote. But since the Commission could only make an investigation and report its findings and had no power to remove for infractions, there continued to be considerable activity of the forbidden sort. Most of this political activity was traceable to unclassified employees, however, who were beyond the reach of the rule.

[9] From a letter of Franklin D. Roosevelt to Luther D. Steward, Aug. 16, 1937, as cited by Sterling Spero in *Government as Employer*, pp. 1–2, Remsen Press, New York, 1948.

In 1938 it was widely charged that persons on Federal relief and those employed by the Federal WPA were actively engaged in politics. An investigation by the Senate confirmed these charges, and led shortly thereafter to the passage of the Hatch Act of 1939. This act restricted the political activities of unclassified as well as classified employees with the exception of those holding policy-making positions. Under the act, classified and unclassified employees are forbidden to participate in politically organized campaigns or in political management. While those in the unclassified service may voice their opinions publicly on issues and candidates, they must refrain from taking part in organized campaigns or using the prestige of their offices to influence the election of any person running for Federal office.

In 1940 a second Hatch Act was passed upon the recommendation of President Roosevelt. This amending act extended the provisions of the act of 1939 to cover state and local government employees who were employed in departments or agencies financed in whole or in part by Federal funds. It is estimated that about 2,600,000 employees are affected by this act. Curiously enough, state-highway departments do not come under the act.

Loyalty. All civil-service employees are required to take an oath when they enter upon the duties of their office. In addition, the records of all prospective civil-service employees are now thoroughly scrutinized in order to be certain of the applicants' loyalty to the government. The Hatch Act of 1939 declared it unlawful for any person employed by the Federal government to be a member of "any political party or organization which advocates the overthrow of our constitutional form of government in the United States." So many charges were made that there were Communists in the employ of the Federal government that President Truman directed in 1947 that all Federal employees be screened for loyalty. Loyalty boards were set up in every department and the screening was eventually completed. More than 10,000 were given a thorough investigation by the FBI. All but a few were cleared, but a larger number resigned during the course of the investigation, some to take other jobs and some doubtless to avoid the investigation.

Shortly after he took office, President Eisenhower issued Executive Order 10450, establishing a new and stricter federal security program. An investigation is required not only of new appointees, but of all employees who were not previously investigated and, in addition, the cases of approximately 19,000 employees who had been cleared previously after a full investigation were ordered to be reviewed. The order lists twelve grounds for dismissal, including, among others, unreliability, immorality, dishonesty, mental disorder, falsification, and unauthorized disclosure of restricted information, as well as membership in or association with communist groups and organizations. All of these grounds, to be sure, are in addition to removal for unsatisfactory performance. The Loyalty Review Board, which previously served as an appeals body, was abolished, and final authority was granted to the heads of departments and agencies with respect to their employees. The Civil Service Commission was placed in charge of investigations of new employees, but if any derogatory information about a prospective employee is discovered, the case must be referred to the FBI.

Some authorities, including the late Professor Mosher, have doubted the wisdom of the program as it has been carried out, especially in view of the high cost, since extremely few were found to be disloyal. Many innocent people among the suspects were accused simply because of some past or present associations. Guilt by association is an unfair test of loyalty. The approach has been largely negative and appears to have done irreparable damage to the public service. Some well-informed persons have contended that a security program should be limited, as in Great Britain, to sensitive positions, and that it was a mistake to apply it to all employees. Only a few persons were found disloyal, but the cloud of suspicion hangs over many more employees. The vast majority of public employees are loyal, honest, and hard-working, and the number who are disloyal or dishonest is not proportionally greater than would be found in any large organization. If we are to have efficient and honest public servants, the prestige of the public service must be maintained. Nothing can undermine our democratic system so quickly as the indiscriminate distrust of our civil servants.

Removal. The regulations for both the classified and unclassified service provide that employees may be disciplined or removed for sufficient cause other than "religious and political reasons." The disciplinary action which may be taken by a superior varies from reprimand to suspension for a period not to exceed 70 days, reduction of an offending employee's rank and pay, and, for more serious offenses, removal from the service.

The Supreme Court decided in the case of *Myers v. United States* [10] that the power to appoint an executive official carries the power to remove and that this rule applies to those in the classified service. An employee is, however, protected against unreasonable removal. Under the act of 1912 a classified employee may be removed if the efficiency of the service requires it, but he is entitled to a notice in writing of the grounds on which he is being removed, and must be given an opportunity to reply in writing. At the discretion of the officer making the removal, he may be given a hearing, but this is not required. Contrary to the practice in a number of states and cities, the discharged employee may not appeal his case to the Civil Service Commission, except on the technical ground that he was not given

[10] 272 U.S. 252 (1926).

the required notice, or that his removal was for political or religious reasons, which is prohibited by law.

Retirement

A sound retirement system is another important factor in good morale. A man works better when he is not beset by worries and feelings of insecurity. Also, he is more likely to stay on the job if safe retirement is in view. But not until 1920 was there any provision for retirement of persons in the Federal civil service. That year's Civil Service Retirement Act has been amended several times and has now been superseded by a 1948 law. Under this law, 6 per cent is deducted from each employee's salary; the government adds 3 per cent interest compounded annually to the fund as it accumulates and also pays the additional amount needed to keep the fund solvent. No person may receive annuity benefits unless he has had at least five years of service. An employee must retire at the age of seventy. But he may retire earlier, at the age of sixty-two, if he has had 15 years of service, or at sixty, with 30 years or more of service. An immediate annuity is available for those who retire after 25 years of service provided they are retired through no fault of their own.

Improvement of the Career Service

As a result of the study made by the President's Committee on Administrative Management, a number of recommendations for improvement of the classified service were made, including the following:

1. Extension of the merit system upward, outward, and downward.
2. Replacement of the Civil Service Commission by a single personnel administrator. All duties, functions, powers, and authority vested in the Civil Service Commission were to be transferred to the Administrator. There was also to be a nonsalaried Civil Service Board, consisting of seven members, which was to act largely in an advisory capacity.
3. An increase in compensation in the highest grades of the career service.
4. Extension of the Classification Act to the field service and to exempted positions in the departmental service and in some of the governmental corporations.

The first recommendation was carried out by President Roosevelt and Congress. While the Senate went along with recommendation 2, the bill was defeated by the House of Representatives.

The Hoover Commission listed a number of deficiencies of the career civilian service. Among these were: (1) overcentralization of personnel transactions in the Civil Service Commission and in central personnel offices of departments; (2) slow and cumbersome machinery for recruiting personnel; (3) failure often to get "the right man for the job or the job for the man"; (4) insufficient time spent in recruiting young men and young women for junior professional and other jobs; (5) lack of a comprehensive administration pay policy for the entire executive branch; (6) low salary ceilings for professional, scientific, technical, and administrative personnel; (7) inadequate opportunities for employees to give suggestions for improvement of practices and procedures; (8) a complicated rating system; (9) low morale due to poor supervisory practices; (10) too much red tape in removal of inefficient and unnecessary employees; (11) failure of the civil service to attract more of the nation's best talent; (12) overstaffing of some personnel offices; and (13) the lack of proper organization of the Civil Service Commission so as to be able to handle personnel problems promptly or to render effective over-all leadership in the personnel field.

In order to cure these deficiencies, the Hoover Commission made several recommendations. They asked, among other things, that steps be taken to (1) reorganize the Civil Service Commission so as to centralize administration in the Chairman; (2) provide a director of personnel in every department and agency; (3) place primary responsibility for examination and recruitment of employees on the departments and agencies; (4) give appointment officers more leeway than the "rule of three" permits; (5) place more emphasis on programs designed to attract talented youth; (6) enact a law embodying a comprehensive pay policy for the entire executive branch; (7) require departments and agencies to work out specific programs for promotion of career employees; (8) amend existing directives dealing with dismissals so as to provide a more workable method for firing inefficient employees.

Several of these recommendations have been put into effect, notably in the Classification Act of 1949. Most important has been the adoption of the single-administrator plan for the Civil Service Commission.

Future of Civil Service

The public service is not looked upon with much favor as a career for our youth today. A poll of parents as to whether they would like their sons to enter the government service resulted in a "no" answer from three-fourths of those questioned. Senator Paul Douglas lists the following reasons why good men are not attracted to the public service: "too much indiscriminate smearing and hounding of men who were just trying to do a good job," low pay in the higher and more responsible ranks of the service, lack of a vigorous recruitment program to seek out the best talent, failure to encourage good public servants by giving them "a pat on the back when they do a good job," and, finally, the hesitation of people of stature to enter public service because of the "black eye" it has received from the evidence of scandal and corruption brought out by congressional investigating committees. To correct these handicaps, Senator Douglas suggests the following steps: (1) end the indiscriminate harassment and smearing of public servants; (2) increase the pay of administrators, especially those at the top; (3) search more diligently for the people who will make good public servants; (4) press for universal public service, whereby every person will get some experience in the public service; (5) build up "the prestige of being a public servant," and finally, (6) set up standards "of proper conduct for public servants" and see to it that they are met.[11]

If the Federal government is to perform effectively and efficiently the vast and complex functions placed on it by a highly industrialized society, if it is to discharge its responsibilities in an atomic age, it must build and maintain a personnel staff of high quality. This requires that the Federal service be made a true career system and that it attract its share of able and qualified persons drawn from many professions and occupations. It must offer to its employees not only salaries and conditions of work comparable to those of the best private employers, but also opportunities for training, advancement, and most important of all, a sense of achievement. Greater recognition needs to be accorded to public servants who have served their country well, and the prestige of the service must be elevated. No government, regardless of which party may be in office, can be strong unless it has an able staff of men and women as its employees.

REFERENCES

W. Brooke Graves, *Public Administration in a Democratic Society* (1950).
The Hoover Commission Report (1949).
Charles S. Hyneman, *Bureaucracy in a Democracy* (1950).
William E. Mosher, J. Donald Kingsley, and O. Glenn Stahl: *Public Personnel Administration* (1950).
Sterling Spero, *Government as Employer* (1948).
William G. Torpey, *Public Personnel Management* (1953).
Leonard D. White, *Introduction to the Study of Public Administration* (1948).

[11] "Help Wanted in Washington," *American Magazine,* October, 1951.

Taxation

Raising money to defray the expenses of the government has always been a difficult and at times an unhappy task. Although citizens demand services from their government, they dislike any rise in tax rates or the adoption of a new tax. The problem of the government is threefold: to collect the money necessary to pay the expenses of government as painlessly and as equitably as possible under the law, to spend it wisely and economically, and to establish machinery that will accomplish these objectives efficiently and effectively.

Prior to World War I the cost of the Federal government was relatively small. The necessary revenue was raised through customs duties and other indirect taxes which caused no great financial burdens to the taxpayer. Today, however, Federal taxes take approximately 20 per cent of the national income, and many wealthy individuals are required to pay the major portion of their annual income in taxes. It is an understatement to say that this causes tremendous interest in certain quarters in how the money is raised and how it is expended by the government.

When national income increases more rapidly than taxation the sharp bite of the added tax is not keenly felt. Therefore the government must try to keep up a high national income; for, should taxation increase and the national income decrease, taxation would become an intolerable burden. Besides, the huge national debt bears correspondingly huge interest that would become much harder to pay should the national income decrease sharply. The indirect effect upon our economy of a high level of taxation is also most important. Standards of living, expansion of industry, allocation of money for research, and many more aspects of our complex modern life are influenced by the rate of taxation.

Where does the money come from that the government collects in taxes? [1] The 1955 Federal budget estimated receipts at $62.7 billion. The

---

[1] For a brief but excellent picture of income and expenditures see the annual publication of the Bureau of the Budget, *The Federal Budget in Brief.*

main source of this sum is the direct taxes placed on the income of individuals and corporations: it amounts to 77 per cent of total tax receipts. Seventeen per cent, or $10.2 billion, is derived from excise taxes on liquor, tobacco, gasoline, and other commodities and services. Six per cent, or $4.3 billion, comes from customs and other receipts. It is significant that customs, once a major source of Federal revenue, has become only a minor one today.[2]

Is this a good tax system? Probably no one can answer the question without provoking dispute. Every taxpayer is either an active or a potential tax critic and tax questions have always provided the liveliest and most ubiquitous of political issues. However, there are certain criteria which may be applied to taxes, as a rough measure, at least, of their desirability. Everyone can assess a given tax for himself by asking questions such as these:

Is it truly based on ability to pay?

Has it some relationship to benefits received—that is, is the taxpayer getting something in return?

Is it hidden, or is the taxpayer always aware that he is paying the tax?

Are costs of administration excessive?

Is the tax flexible as to its yield, and also as to its provisions?

Does the tax system as a whole have a broad base, or is it limited to just a small group of taxpayers?

Is it easily administered, and is the cost of collecting the tax low?

With these standards in mind, it becomes possible to make a more meaningful survey of the sources from which the United States government derives its support.

The Income Tax. The most lucrative, and certainly the most widely publicized, Federal tax is the income tax, the only direct tax which is imposed by the Federal government. A direct tax is a head or capitation tax or a tax on property, while excise levies, license fees, and tariffs are the principal examples of indirect taxes. The Constitution requires that direct taxes be apportioned among the states in proportion to their populations. Thus it has been impractical for the Federal government to levy direct taxes, for the criteria of ability to pay and other important considerations are ruled out by the constitutional limitation. During the early days of the United States certain direct taxes were levied but, for nearly a century, no direct tax, except an income tax, has been used by the national government.

The first income tax was levied during the War Between the States but was later abandoned as a source of revenue. The second income tax, which was enacted in 1894, placed a flat tax rate of 2 per cent on all incomes of more than $4,000. When the constitutionality of the tax was challenged,

[2] *Ibid.*, p. 4.

the Supreme Court in a 5-to-4 decision held that an income tax was a direct tax, and that since the tax was not apportioned among the states according to population, it was unconstitutional.[3] In order to get around this decision the Sixteenth Amendment to the Constitution was adopted in 1913. It gives Congress the power "to lay and collect taxes on incomes, from whatever source derived, without apportionment among the several States, and without regard to any census or enumeration."

The income tax, which is levied both on individuals and on corporations, has become by far the largest source of revenue of the Federal government, yielding at present 77 per cent of the total tax receipts. Based primarily on ability to pay, it is regarded by economists as an equitable tax. The principal criticism voiced against it is directed at the very high tax rate of nearly 90 per cent on persons with the largest incomes; a concerted movement has been made to secure a constitutional amendment which would establish a ceiling rate of 25 per cent, except during wartime. About half of the states have passed resolutions calling for a constitutional convention to propose such an amendment, but several states have rescinded these resolutions. A limitation of this type would substantially reduce the revenue from income taxes and probably force the levying of other less progressive forms of taxes. During recent years employers have been required to withhold income taxes from salaries and wages and to pay them directly to the government, thus spreading the tax burden over the entire year.

Excise Taxes. Excise taxes levied on tobacco, gasoline, jewelry, and many other items constitute the second largest source of Federal revenue. The only constitutional restrictions are that they must be uniform throughout the United States, giving no preference to one state over another. (Taxes on exports are forbidden.)

The Federal tax of 6 cents on each package of cigarettes may be cited as an example of an excise tax. Stamps are sold by the government to the manufacturer who places the tax stamp upon each package of cigarettes; the consumer pays the tax when he buys the cigarettes. The tax money is collected in the state where the manufacturing plants are located, but is eventually paid by consumers throughout the country.

A high excise tax is levied on liquor, not only as a revenue producer but also to discourage its use. The problem is to determine the rate that will accomplish both of these purposes, and at the same time avoid the growth of illicit manufacture and sale. Excise taxes are also placed upon the manufacture and sale of such consumer goods as radios, television sets, phonograph records, cosmetics, and luggage, and upon telephone service, travel, amusements, and other items.

Like other taxes, excise taxes are the target of much criticism. Consumers object to high levies on such items as gasoline and cigarettes, claim-

[3] *Pollock v. Farmers' Loan and Trust Co.*, 158 U.S. 601 (1895).

ing that they are not luxuries but daily necessities and that the impact of these taxes is heaviest on the lower-income groups since a larger proportion of their incomes goes for such commodities. Another criticism is that excise taxes are, for the most part, hidden. The consumer isn't really aware that he is paying them, for they are lost in the total cost of the item. This, it is claimed, is an unsound situation from the standpoint of true democracy. The taxpayer ought to be aware of the taxes he pays, so that he can voice his approval or disapproval to the legislators who impose the taxes. In an attempt to remedy this, and thus to institute a subtle propaganda against the taxes, certain utilities advertise on their bills the proportion of the total which may be attributed to Federal taxes.

Taxation for Regulation. Although the primary purpose of taxation is to raise revenue, the taxing power may be used for the purpose of regulation. Any tax measure has certain regulatory effects, but many taxes have been levied primarily for regulatory ends rather than as sources of revenue. An early example was a 10 per cent tax on state bank notes levied by Congress to drive the notes out of circulation. Congress could probably have accomplished this end directly by legislation, since it is given the power by the Constitution to coin money and to regulate its value, but it chose to utilize instead the taxing power, and the tax was upheld by the Supreme Court.[4] Other illustrations of taxes for regulatory purposes are those levied on matches made with poisonous phosphorus, on narcotics, oleomargarine, sawed-off shotguns, and alcoholic beverages, all of which have been upheld by the Supreme Court as legitimate uses of the power of taxation. High customs duties have often been levied not to produce revenue, but rather to protect home industry against foreign competition.

With few exceptions, the Supreme Court has upheld the power of Congress to levy taxes, and has not looked behind the tax to ascertain whether it may have regulatory effects. In a few instances, however, it has held tax laws unconstitutional. An early law enacted by Congress to regulate child labor was based on the taxing power. Congress enacted a child-labor code and provided penalties for noncompliance in the form of taxes, but the Supreme Court held that this was not a tax measure at all, but was a labor law, and held it unconstitutional.[5] Years later Congress enacted a child-labor law under its power to regulate commerce, which was upheld. The first AAA law, which provided payment to farmers for limiting the crops according to a plan, levied a processing tax to cover the cost of such payments. The Court held the tax unconstitutional on the ground that it taxed one group for the benefit of another.[6] Subsequently

[4] *Veazie Bank v. Fenno,* 8 Wall. 533 (1869).

[5] *Bailey v. Drexel Furniture Co.,* 259 U.S. 20 (1922). See also Chap. 11 for further discussion of the taxing power.

[6] *United States v. Butler,* 297 U.S. 1 (1936).

Congress reenacted the law omitting the processing tax, and this act was upheld.

It may be concluded that the Supreme Court has construed very broadly the power granted to Congress to levy taxes. This power may not be used for a private purpose or for the taxation of one group to benefit another. "But if taxes are collected for a public purpose, there is no limit to the taxing power, regardless of whether it is exercised for the purpose of revenue, regulation or even destruction of the thing taxed." [7] In *Sonzinsky v. United States*,[8] Justice Stone said, in speaking of the heavy tax on sawed-off shotguns:

Here the annual tax of $200 is productive of some revenue. We are not free to speculate as to the motives which moved Congress to impose it, or as to the extent to which it may operate to restrict the activities taxed. As it is not attended by an offensive regulation, and since it operates as a tax, it is within the national taxing power.

Intergovernmental Immunity from Taxation. With both the national government and the states engaged in various activities and businesses, and with both having broad powers of taxation, the question might well be asked: how has "an indestructible union of indestructible states" been maintained? May the Federal government levy a tax on state governments or state activities of which it does not approve, and do the states have a corresponding power to tax the Federal government? The issue arose in the famous case of *McCulloch v. Maryland*[9] in 1819, when the State of Maryland levied a tax on a Federal branch bank located in Baltimore. Chief Justice Marshall, who delivered the opinion of the Supreme Court, held the act invalid, for the power to tax, he declared, is the power to destroy. If the states were permitted to tax Federal instrumentalities, they could drive them out of existence by levying prohibitive taxes. Out of this case has developed the basic constitutional doctrine under which the instrumentalities of both the Federal government and the states are exempt from taxation by the other.

Intergovernmental immunity from taxation continues today, but the definition of "governmental instrumentality" has been severely restricted. In *South Carolina v. United States*[10] it was held that immunity of state agencies from Federal taxation extended only to those engaged in the performance of a governmental function. Should a state engage in a business, that business could be taxed by the same method and to the same degree that similar businesses were taxed. More recently, a Federal tax

[7] Dean Alfange, *The Supreme Court and the National Will*, p. 175, Doubleday & Company, New York, 1937.
[8] 300 U.S. 506, 514 (1937).
[9] 4 Wheat. 316 (1819).
[10] 199 U.S. 437 (1905). See also, *New York v. United States*, 326, U.S. 572 (1946).

upon admissions to football games of a state university was upheld by the Supreme Court.[11] The Court thought football was a business rather than a governmental activity; also, the tax was paid by the holders of tickets rather than by the state university.

For many years the salaries received by state officials and employees were exempt from Federal income taxes, while the salaries of Federal employees were exempt from similar state taxes. A change in the attitude of the Court toward these exemptions was first evinced in the Panhandle Oil Company case.[12] Here, in his dissent, Justice Holmes raised objections to the broad interpretation of the power to tax as the power to destroy. He could see no bad results if a tax was uniform and extended to everyone alike. He also made the statement that "the power to tax is not the power to destroy while this Court sits." Thus he reiterated the doctrine that the Supreme Court is the umpire of the federal system and will maintain proper relationship between the states and the national government.

In the 1930s Congress amended the Federal personal income tax law so that it became applicable to the salaries of state employees. The states, in turn, amended their laws to tax the salaries of Federal employees. In a test case,[13] the state of New York imposed an income tax on the salary of an employee of a Federal agency, the Home Owners' Loan Corporation. In upholding this tax Justice Stone said,

The present tax is a non-discriminatory tax on income applied to salaries at a specific rate. It is not in form or substance a tax upon the Home Owners' Loan Corporation or its property or income, nor is it paid by the corporation or the government from their funds. It is measured by income which becomes the property of the taxpayer when received as compensation for his services; and the tax laid upon the privilege of receiving it is paid from his private funds and not from the funds of the government, either directly or indirectly.

By this decision the income-tax laws became applicable to all United States citizens and a new source of income was opened for both the states and the Federal government. It should be noted, however, that neither the Federal government nor the states have amended their laws to tax income derived from bonds issued by the other governmental units, though this has often been proposed. The principle of intergovernmental tax immunity still exists, although it has been greatly modified by recent laws and court decisions.

Where the Money Goes

Of the huge sum of money raised by the national government the major portion is used today for the Armed Forces and to strengthen friendly nations. The staggering cost of modern warfare is evident when a com-

11 *Allen v. Regents of the University System of Georgia*, 304 U.S. 439 (1938).
12 *Panhandle Oil Co. v. Mississippi*, 277 U.S. 218, 223 (1928).
13 *Graves v. New York*, 306 U.S. 466, 480 (1939).

parison is made of the sums allocated for military purposes and those allotted for the ordinary functions of government. The budget for the fiscal year 1955 contemplated expenditures of $78.6 billion. Of this sum approximately $56 billion was allocated to military purposes. Included in the classification "military purposes" are military assistance to allies, interest on money spent for past wars, veterans' benefits, and money allocated to the armed services. The price of security is a tremendous one.

The expenditures included in the budget for 1955 are as follows: [14]

Purposes	*Billions of dollars*
National security	$44.9
International	1.2
Interest	6.9
Veterans	4.2
Natural resources	1.1
Social security, welfare and health	1.8
Transportation and communication	1.4
Agriculture	2.4
General government	1.2
Housing, education, labor and commerce	0.5

Thanks to the high cost of modern military equipment, 33 per cent of the money set aside for the military services goes for equipment alone. As the Budget Bureau points out, the electronic gear in some types of aircraft costs more than an entire World War II plane designed for the same purpose. Procurement costs fluctuate greatly from year to year, depending on the outlook for war or peace. Expenditures for pay of military personnel, operational costs, research, stockpiling, and other military purposes are usually more stable.

In 1913 the total expenditures for all levels of government were $3 billion. Over twice that amount is expended today for international security in the form of military, economic, and technical assistance to our allies and to friendly nations. Most of it goes to the NATO countries of Western Europe but nations in the Near East, the Far East, and Latin America also receive help. The sums designated for Europe are largely intended for building up the military forces of friendly nations, although some direct economic aid is included. In the other sections of the world United States financial aid is primarily for economic and technical purposes. Expenditures for the conduct of foreign affairs, the operation of the Voice of America, and information services take a little more than $200 million.

In the domestic field the Federal government spends significant amounts for the expansion of the productive capacity of the nation, particularly with reference to those activities which have a direct relationship to national defense. Large expenditures are made for building highways and for aiding and regulating navigation and aviation. Expenditures for highways

[14] *Federal Budget in Brief,* 1955, p. 4.

take the form largely of grants-in-aid to the states but some money is used for road building in the territories and in the national parks and forests.

The post office has become a financial liability to the United States government. The extensive use of the franking privilege, the increased cost of operations, and the low rates charged for second class mail (newspapers and magazines) and third class mail (circulars) account for the deficit of over half-a-billion dollars annually. Postal rates will have to be sharply increased if the service is to be made self-supporting, but Congress is reluctant to raise the rates on newspapers and magazines, thus in effect reducing the Federal subsidy which they now receive. The press, which generally demands greater economy in government and a balanced budget, has an effective lobby to oppose any increase in the postal rates affecting newspapers and magazines.

Approximately 3.6 per cent of the budget goes for agricultural purposes. Of this amount price support and related programs take nearly half. The other half supports conservation, rural electrification, farm loans, the control of pests, and other such functions. Other appropriations pay for labor statistics, mediation of labor disputes, and the Federal Employment Service. Unemployment compensation and general administration of the Labor Department and other services connected with labor programs take only 0.4 per cent of the total budget. Housing activities and civil defense account for only 0.4 per cent and education 3 per cent. Social security, welfare, and health require 2.8 per cent of the budget. The major portion of the latter item is used for payments to the states for public assistance to the needy.

Less than 2 per cent of the budget is required for running Federal governmental machinery. Today the cost of operating many of the regulatory activities is greater than the cost of Congress and the judiciary. For instance, nearly twice the sum required for the operation of Congress and the courts is needed for the FBI, alien control, and related programs. Nevertheless, even though such expenses increase year by year, they are the least of the reasons for the size of contemporary budgets.

When revenues from taxes, and other receipts, fall short of expenditures the government is forced to borrow money and thus to increase the public debt. Wars and the economic depression have been chiefly responsible for the rise of national indebtedness. During World War I Congress borrowed heavily to meet the staggering cost of fighting a modern war. Before the debt could be repaid the depression of the thirties and World War II brought about new and even greater obligations. As of Sept. 30, 1954, the United States government owed bondholders $274 billion. While much of this spending is justified, some is not. In 1945 the deficit for that one year alone was $53.9 billion. Since 1945 the Federal government has had a deficit in all years but two. The interest paid annually on Federal bonds amounts to $6.9 billion, a sum approximately the size of the entire Federal budget 20 years ago. This is a reflection not only of the great size of the national debt but also of the higher interest rates now being paid. Bonds issued during World War II are now maturing but in order to encourage bond holders not to cash them, they may be held beyond maturity at a higher rate of interest. American families own about 40 per cent of these savings bonds. Banks, insurance companies, and trust funds hold most of the rest.

The return to power of the Republican party in 1953 brought into sharp relief the different opinions regarding the huge national debt. The Republicans promised to stop deficit spending, to lower the national debt and to establish a pay-as-you-go policy. A further increase in the national debt, they contended, would threaten the financial security of the nation. But some economists maintain that the size of the present debt is not serious in view of the greatly increased national income, and that an effort to reduce the debt sharply would be deflationary and would lead to another depression. Congress has fixed the national debt limit at $275 billion, but will undoubtedly have to raise it if deficits continue. Indeed in August, 1954, this debt limit was temporarily increased by Congress to $281 billion until June 30, 1955.

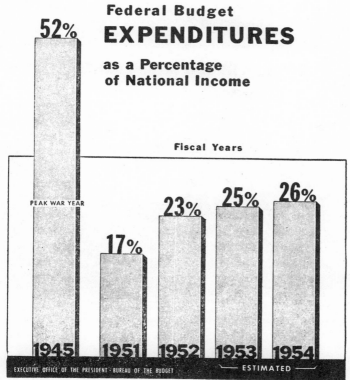

Federal Budget
EXPENDITURES
as a Percentage
of National Income

Fiscal Years

52%
PEAK WAR YEAR
17%
23%
25%
26%

1945 1951 1952 1953 1954

EXECUTIVE OFFICE OF THE PRESIDENT · BUREAU OF THE BUDGET   ESTIMATED

Fig. 3

The Budget

The budget of the Federal government, like that of a person or a family, is a financial plan for a specific period. Within a single document, called the budget, there are brought together the estimates of revenues, fixed charges, capital outlays, and expenditures which will be required to carry on the work of the government. The budget is based on the work program or plan proposed for the coming fiscal year; it is essential, as it provides both President and Congress with an over-all view of Federal finance, enabling them to consider expenditure needs against estimated revenues and weigh the relative claims of each governmental program against others. Because of the jealousy of Congress over control of the purse, however, the United States was the last major country to adopt a national budget system.

When a government official works under specific budget provisions he knows pretty well how he can conduct his work and within what limits he must operate. The general public has information available as to the sums of money allocated and, if interested, can ascertain how the money is spent and if to good advantage. The fiscal year begins on July 1 and extends to June 30 of the next year. The fiscal year 1954, therefore, began on July 1, 1953, and extended to June 30, 1954.

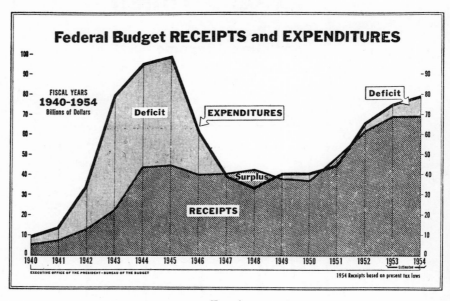

FIG. 4

During the greater part of the history of the United States there was neither budget bureau nor executive budget. Congress decided how the money was to be raised and how it should be spent. The President participated to some extent in the making of these decisions. The first act creating a budget system was vetoed in 1919 by President Wilson. He opposed it because the act created the office of Comptroller General, who was placed beyond the removal power of the President. Later, President Harding approved the Budget and Accounting Act of 1921 and the executive budget became a reality.

By the provisions of this act the President is made responsible for the preparation of the budget, which contains estimates of expenditures and appropriations for the coming fiscal year with comparative information concerning appropriations and expenditures during the current and past fiscal years. The budget document itself is an immense volume of over 1,000 pages. Obviously the President himself cannot do the actual preparation. The Budget Bureau serves as a staff agency which prepares the budget under the direction of the President, and, after Congress votes the funds, supervises the execution of the budget. The President determines the general fiscal policy which guides the Bureau in its review of the departmental requests, and he reviews the most important decisions. In 1939 the Bureau of the Budget was placed in the Executive Office of the President and given additional powers, which has made it a staff arm of the President to assist him not only in preparing the budget but also in a wide variety of activities affecting the management of the entire government.

Budget preparation involves several stages. Each year, usually in June, the Bureau of the Budget issues a call to the spending agencies to submit estimates. Instructions are given as to the form in which they shall be submitted. At the same time the departments receive the President's statement concerning his fiscal policies. Already the departments will have been given ceiling figures by the Bureau. Although these limits are not binding, administrators are expected to observe them. The departmental budget officers, under the direction of the head of the department, review and amend the estimates submitted by the subdivisions of the agency, to make them conform with general policy. During this period of revision, there are intradepartmental hearings and conferences to iron out differences.

When the departmental estimates are finally submitted to the Budget Bureau they are critically examined by an estimates staff which by long experience has become highly expert on the operations and programs of the particular departments whose figures it reviews. The recommendations of the estimates staff are reviewed and may be revised by the Director of the Budget, but it is the responsibility of the President finally to determine the budget which he submits to Congress.

One of the basic problems inherent in the budget system is that when a change of administration occurs, as in 1953, the budget which has been prepared under the direction of the outgoing President does not reflect the policies and program of the incoming President. After the election of 1952, President Truman invited President-elect Eisenhower to send a representative to take part in the final conferences on the budget before its submission to Congress, and the President-elect designated Joseph W. Dodge, later appointed as Director of the Budget, to represent him. The budget which was submitted to Congress early in January, as required by law, however, was the budget of the outgoing President, and the new administration subsequently submitted recommended revisions. One of the first steps of President Eisenhower was to issue instructions to his department heads through the Director of the Budget to reexamine their requests and to make substantial reductions. Among the revised estimates submitted to Congress about two months later, the largest reduction was made in the Air Force budget, which was reduced by approximately $5 billion. Substantial cuts were made all along the line, reflecting the fiscal policy of the new administration.

Within 15 days after Congress meets each January the President sends the budget to Congress with an explanatory message and a statement of fiscal policy. He usually estimates the revenues that the government will receive under existing taxes and states the amounts necessary to carry out the functions of government. If the estimates of expenditures exceed expected revenues, it is his responsibility to recommend additional measures to finance the proposed expense.

While the President recommends the fiscal program of the government in his budget, the final decision rests with Congress. Appropriation bills are prepared by the Committee on Appropriations in each house. Subcommittees are used, hearings are conducted, and critics and proponents of various budget allocations are heard. It is a difficult task to cut appropriations. If a cut in appropriations to the Department of Agriculture is contemplated, various farm organizations protest. If the proposed cut is in military appropriations, the cry is raised that the safety of the nation is imperiled. Frequently there is a tug of war between Congress and the President. President Eisenhower differed with members of his own party in Congress in 1953 over the size of proposed reductions and the repeal of the excess-profits tax.

After the appropriation bills have been passed by Congress and signed by the President there is the task of seeing that their provisions are carried out. Under the direction of the President the Budget Bureau exercises control by a system of quarterly allotments to departments and agencies, requiring each group to live within its apportionment during each quarter of the fiscal year. The Bureau may also require that reserve funds be set aside for emergencies and may make other requirements intended to bulwark budgetary policy. Still other controls are exercised by the General Accounting Office.

One of the most important recommendations of the Hoover Commission in 1949 was that the government should adopt a "performance" budget. By this it was meant that the budget document should be so arranged that it would be possible to ascertain exactly the cost of each program and activity of the government, and that with the estimates for each activity— for example, a hospital—there should be submitted an account of the work program proposed including statistics and unit costs. This would require administrators to justify their requests by submitting in detail their work plans, which would enable Congress and the President to allocate public funds more wisely between competing claims. This plan was not new; several departments were already following the practice. Since 1949 performance budgeting has been widely adopted throughout the Federal government, and has been installed also in many states and cities.

The greatest weakness in the Federal budget system today would appear to be the procedures in Congress rather than those in the executive branch. When the President's budget is received by Congress, it is immediately divided into 10 parts, each of which is considered by a separate subcommittee of the Appropriations Committees of the two houses. To some extent this defeats the purpose of an over-all budget. More than a dozen separate appropriations acts are enacted each year, and taxation is considered by another set of committees in each house. Furthermore, all the standing committees in each house have a voice in fiscal affairs, for they recommend legislation authorizing expenditures, and in effect commit the government to future expenditures. Responsibility for passing on the fiscal policies is so divided between these numerous committees and subcommittees in each house that it is largely lost. Proposals for reform include the adoption of a single or omnibus appropriation act, and granting the President an item veto, which is given to the governor in 38 states. But these proposals have not found much favor in Congress; the omnibus appropriation act was used in 1950, but abandoned the following year.

The General Accounting Office

To serve as a financial watchdog over the administration, Congress in 1921 established the General Accounting Office headed by the Comptroller General of the United States. Although this officer is appointed by the President for a term of 15 years, Congress alone has the power to remove him from office and then only for specific causes.

The General Accounting Office audits the accounts of governmental departments and agencies, sets up accounting rules, helps the agencies to perfect their accounting systems, settles claims by or against the United States, issues rulings on fiscal matters, conducts investigations, and makes reports with its recommendations to Congress. In one year its activities included a review of the whole field of military procurement, the settling

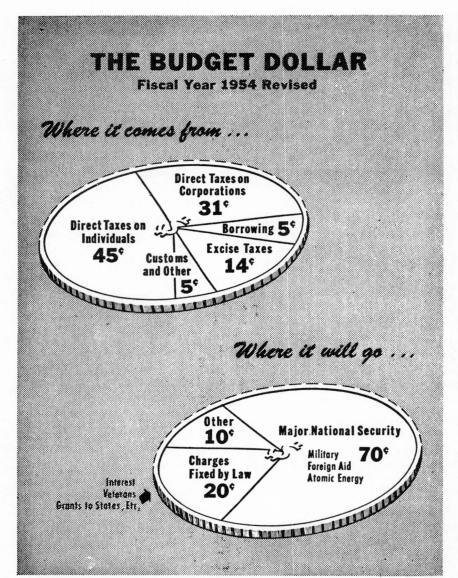

THE BUDGET DOLLAR
Fiscal Year 1954 Revised

Where it comes from ...

Direct Taxes on Corporations **31¢**

Direct Taxes on Individuals **45¢**

Borrowing **5¢**

Excise Taxes **14¢**

Customs and Other **5¢**

Where it will go ...

Other **10¢**

Major National Security **70¢**
Military
Foreign Aid
Atomic Energy

Charges Fixed by Law **20¢**

Interest
Veterans
Grants to States, Etc.

EXECUTIVE OFFICE OF THE PRESIDENT • BUREAU OF THE BUDGET

Fig. 5

of nearly half-a-million claims, and the disposition of 11,997 legal matters, including the case relative to the sale of the liner S.S. *United States*.[16]

Before any agency may receive funds the General Accounting Office must see that the proposed expenditures are in conformity with the appropriation acts. This preexamination coupled with a post-audit check, provides a close watch over the spending agencies. The vesting of accounting and control functions in the same office which is charged with the auditing responsibility has often been criticized. The Hoover Commission in 1949 and the Brownlow committee in 1937 both stated that accounting and day-to-day financial control were executive functions and urged that they be placed in an agency responsible to the President. According to their findings, the present system results in an excessive amount of red tape and delays. But Congress favors the present system and has turned a deaf ear to suggestions for change.

There is a truly close relationship between the Accounting Office and Congress. In one year over 800 special reports were made to Congress. Lindsey Warren, as Comptroller General, has written: [17]

Having been a member of Congress for 16 years, I have been keenly aware during my 12 years as Comptroller General of the absolute necessity for Congress to be fully informed on the financial operations of the Government and the import of proposed legislation . . . While the duty of the Comptroller General in the legislative field ends with reporting facts and making recommendations, the consideration given by the Congress and its committees to General Accounting Office reports and the adoption of many of the recommendations made—the test of their real value—have been a source of great satisfaction to me.

Money

In colonial days and during the period of the Articles of Confederation there was no uniform system of currency in this country. Business suffered as a result. Both the states and the Confederation issued coins. Private firms were licensed by the states to coin money. British, Spanish, French, Dutch coins and the money of other foreign nations were used freely. Both the states and the banks issued paper money. The relative value of these different forms of money fluctuated from year to year and from state to state. The very term "dollar" has a Spanish rather than an English origin. It is no wonder then that the constitutional fathers had little difficulty in securing agreement that the national government should determine and regulate the medium of exchange.

In Article I of the Constitution Congress is given power to coin money and regulate its value. The same article forbids the states to "coin money; emit bills of credit; make anything but gold and silver coin a tender in payment of debts." Congress's power over the monetary system stems not

[16] *Annual Report of the Comptroller General of the United States, 1952*, pp. iii–vi.
[17] *Ibid.*, pp. iv–v.

alone from this particular constitutional grant but is implied also in other related powers granted to Congress by the Constitution. The power to regulate commerce and the power to borrow money, plus all the powers necessary and proper for carrying into execution those powers, imply congressional control over money. Thus Congress has unquestionable authority to establish a uniform currency having a uniform value. Chief Justice Hughes stated that, in order to accomplish this purpose, the Federal government may even attach to the ownership of gold and silver "those limitations which public policy may require by reason of their quality as legal tender and as a medium of exchange." [18]

By the Coinage Act of 1792 Congress provided for a system of money based on the decimal system. Both silver and gold were to be used in the coinage of money at a ratio of 15 to 1. This means that 15 ounces of coined silver were considered equal to one ounce of coined gold. This ratio was difficult to maintain. It was changed later to 16 to 1, but as the supply of gold and silver fluctuated with the discovery of new sources of each the scarcer metal would be driven from circulation. The system, however, continued until the War between the States when due to war conditions the banks refused to redeem their issues of money in specie and the nation went upon an inconvertible paper standard. This situation prevailed until 1879 when the government adopted the gold standard.

Silver continued to be used in coinage but it was no longer a standard. Then additional discoveries of silver occurred in the West and pressure was exerted upon Congress to do something for silver. Instead, in 1900 the Gold Standards Act stopped inflationary tendencies and made paper money redeemable in gold on demand. There was no change in policy until 1933 when President Franklin Roosevelt, under authorization of Congress, issued an Executive order taking the country off the gold standard and outlawing the possession of gold. Later the exportation of gold was also forbidden. For the requirement that the government must redeem in gold on demand Congress substituted the proviso that any obligation to do so should be fulfilled "upon payment, dollar for dollar, in any coin or currency which at the time of payment is legal tender for public and private debts." [19] Later President Roosevelt reduced the weight of the gold dollar. This devaluation led to the present managed monetary policy and to the inflationary tendencies that have continued to the present day.

These policies were challenged before the Supreme Court on the ground that they impaired the obligation of contracts, but the Court upheld the management of the currency: [20]

Contracts, however express, cannot fetter the constitutional authority of the Congress. Contracts may create rights of property, but when contracts deal with a

[18] *Norman v. Baltimore & Ohio R.R. Co.*, 294 U.S. 240, 304 (1935).
[19] 48 Stat. L. 112.
[20] *Norman v. Baltimore & Ohio R.R. Co.*, 294 U.S. 240, 307–308 (1935).

subject matter which lies within the control of the Congress they have a congenital infirmity. Parties cannot remove their transactions from the reach of dominant constitutional powers by making contracts above them.

Money, as the term is currently used, includes not only coin and currency but also both time and demand deposits in banks. These deposits represent the greater share of the money supply. Ordinarily currency and coin in circulation represent less than 15 per cent of the total supply of money. Thus, in order to regulate the supply of money it is necessary to regulate bank deposits. The Federal Reserve System was created to perform that task.

The Federal Reserve System

In 1789 banks were chartered by the several states. This fact, along with the rejection by the Constitutional Convention of certain specific proposals to give the national government control over banking, led many people to take the position that there could be no centralized banking system. There was also a fear of abuse of power should financial power be centralized. In spite of this feeling, Alexander Hamilton was able to secure a charter for the first United States bank which worked well but lasted only from 1791 to 1811. Financial difficulties resulting from the irresponsible issuance of paper money by state banks led to the chartering of the second United States bank. This institution engendered the animosity of President Jackson and when he withdrew all deposits of Federal money in 1833 the bank was given a death blow which eventually forced it to discontinue operations in 1836. The first and second United States banks functioned both as commercial banks and as central banking institutions. In the latter capacity they were depositories for government funds, served as fiscal agents for the government, and exercised regulatory functions over state banks. The opposition that developed was based upon the alleged unconstitutionality of the United States bank, plus the fear of the concentration of financial power. It was also claimed that there was mismanagement and that bank officials were engaged in political activities.

Until the War between the States made changes imperative, the banking system was composed exclusively of private banks and those chartered by the various states. In 1864 Congress passed the National Banking Act establishing federally chartered banks to help with the financing of the War between the States. There was no change until 1914, when the Federal Reserve System was established. During this period of over a half century state banks continued to operate due to the fact that state regulations were not so strict as Federal rules. Because this banking system did not avert financial panic and also because of the lack of elasticity of national bank notes and an unsatisfactory reserve system, agitation for reform continued until Congress passed the Federal Reserve Act of 1914.

By this act the United States was divided into 12 Federal Reserve districts, in each of which there is a Federal Reserve bank. No change in number has been made since their establishment. The Reserve banks bear the names of the cities in which they are located and are referred to as the New York Reserve Bank or the Dallas Reserve Bank. There are branches in other cities to expedite business. For example, the San Francisco Bank has branches in Portland, Seattle, Salt Lake City, and Los Angeles. The banks vary in size and in the amount of influence they exercise. The largest bank by far is the New York Bank.[21]

At the head of the Federal Reserve System is a Board of Governors composed of seven men appointed by the President with Senate confirmation. It is customary to have different sections of the United States represented on the Board as well as the various segments of our economic life, such as industry, agriculture, and banking. Assisting the Board of Governors are the Federal Open Market Committee, composed of officers of the Reserve System, and a Federal Advisory Council, comprising one banker from each of the Reserve districts. Each Reserve bank has a chairman; altogether there are approximately 20,000 officers and employees in the system.

Commercial banks within a district which have met certain requirements may become members of the Federal Reserve System if approved by the bank. But after so doing the banks must obey the rules, submit to periodic investigations, maintain the reserves demanded, and subscribe to stock in the System. However, a member bank may borrow money from the Reserve bank and utilize the other advantages that accrue to membership.

The activities of the Federal Reserve System are clearly revealed in the Annual Report of the Board of Governors. By regulating the supply, availability, and cost of money the System exerts great influence. By determining discount rates, by open-market purchases and sales of government securities, and by altering the ratio of reserves which banks must carry as against their deposits, it maintains effective control of finance and banking. (Other Federal credit regulations affect the quantity but not the type of credit. For example, during the war consumer credit was controlled; at the present time margin requirements on listed stock purchases are regulated.)

Federal Reserve banks have been called "banker's banks." A member bank can secure money during a financial crisis from the Reserve bank through loans, using its assets as security, including the paper by which loans have been made to individuals and corporations. Reserve banks may also advance money to member banks for short terms with satisfactory security.

[21] For a description of work of the Board of Governors and the framework of the Federal Reserve System, see the Annual Reports of the Board of Governors of the Federal Reserve System.

Through careful and periodic examination of member banks, through the close watch that is maintained not only upon member banks but on others as well, the Federal Reserve System has weathered periods of financial storm. Economic stability has been sought through increases in reserve requirements and rediscount rates, by the sale of government securities, and by curbs on consumer credit. One member of the Board of Governors states [22] that

. . . our problem as a nation is to prevent the development of inflationary or deflationary tendencies which might upset this stability. Many factors contribute to the maintenance of economic stability, one of the most important being the supply, availability and cost of money in accordance with the needs of the economy and the objectives of economic stability.

Guaranteeing of bank deposits, first used as government procedure in 1933, became a settled policy in 1935. An independent agency, the Federal Deposit Insurance Corporation, insures deposits in banks up to $10,000. Not only may member banks take advantage of the services offered by this insurance but so also may nonmember banks who meet certain designated requirements. This legislation grew out of the dark days of the depression when depositors, fearful of the safety of funds deposited in banks, withdrew them and thus added to the financial crisis. It is hoped that a recurrence of such runs on banks will be avoided in the future should another crisis develop.

REFERENCES

Annual Report of the Board of Governors of the Federal Reserve System.
Annual Report of the Comptroller General of the United States.
George L. Bach, *Federal Reserve Policy-making* (1950).
Roy Blough, *The Federal Taxing Process* (1952).
Bureau of the Budget, *The Budget of the United States Government* (annual).
———, *Federal Budget in Brief, Fiscal Year 1954* (1953).
Committee on Public Debt Policy, *Our National Debt: Its History and Its Meaning Today* (1949).
Merle Fainsod and Lincoln Gordon, *Government and the American Economy*, 2d ed. (1949).
Federal Reserve System, *The Federal Reserve System: Its Purposes and Functions*, 2d ed. (1947).
Harold M. Groves, *Financing Government* (1945).
Alvin H. Hansen, *Monetary Theory and Fiscal Policy* (1949).
Seymour E. Harris, *The National Debt and the New Economies* (1947).
Edwin W. Kemmerer and Donald L. Kemmerer, *The ABC of the Federal Reserve System*, rev. ed. (1950).
Harvey Mansfield, *The Comptroller-General* (1939).
Tax Foundation, *Facts and Figures on Government Finance*, 7th ed. (1952).

[22] From a speech made in Philadelphia on Apr. 30, 1950, by M. S. Szymczak, member of the Board of Governors of the Federal Reserve System.

CHAPTER 21 *Government and Business*

The Regulation of Business

At the time of the making of the Constitution the framers were keenly aware of the need for governmental regulation of commerce and business. Under the Articles of Confederation the government had been unable to make foreign nations live up to their agreements, and in domestic affairs the trade barriers between states had seriously crippled trade and commerce. According to Justice Jackson: [1]

The desire of the Forefathers to federalize regulation of foreign and interstate commerce stands in sharp contrast to their jealous preservation of the state's power over its internal affairs. No other federal power was so universally assumed to be necessary, no other state power was so readily relinquished.

In Article I of the Constitution Congress is given power to regulate foreign and interstate commerce and to make all laws "necessary and proper" for carrying these regulations into execution. In the field of foreign commerce little difficulty or conflict has arisen over federal regulation. In the field of interstate commerce much of the time of the Supreme Court in the past has been occupied in attempting to distinguish between intrastate and interstate commerce. Today, however, Congress regulates not only interstate commerce but through the necessary-and-proper clause is permitted to regulate intrastate commerce when it affects interstate commerce. Needless to say there is little commerce today that does not affect interstate commerce to some degree. State regulation still exists but is restricted to commerce that is purely intrastate in character or to fields where Congress has enacted no regulatory measures.

Little use was made of the commerce clause to regulate business practices until late in the nineteenth century. The spectacular development of American business, after the effects of the War between the States were

[1] *Hood and Sons v. DuMond,* 336 U.S. 525, 533–534 (1949).

overcome, not only made the United States an industrial giant among nations but also brought some undesirable business practices. Through the concentration of power in the hands of certain business organizations, monopolies were created that controlled production and regulated the price of commodities. Big business in the minds of many became synonymous with bad business.

In 1890 Congress, sensing the feeling of the people, enacted the Sherman Antitrust Act [2] to protect citizens from contracts, combinations, and conspiracies in restraint of trade. At first the effect of the Sherman Act was negligible, for the Supreme Court relieved large business concerns from the regulatory provisions of the act by holding that manufacturing was not a part of interstate commerce and therefore was subject only to state regulation.[3] Later the Supreme Court modified its position to permit Federal regulation of those businesses that "unreasonably" restrained trade.[4]

The need for more explicit legislation and for a supervisory body like the Interstate Commerce Commission resulted in the passage by Congress in 1914 of the Clayton Act [5] and the Federal Trade Commission Act.[6] Since that day the power of Congress to control business has been an expanding one. The Supreme Court, it is true, has at times curtailed this power as when its decision in the Schechter case held the National Recovery Act unconstitutional, but much legislation providing for the regulation of particular types of business and creating regulatory agencies has been sustained by the Supreme Court. The next few pages will describe the activities of the most important of these boards and commissions.

The Federal Trade Commission. Dissatisfaction with the administration of the Sherman Act was largely responsible for the creation of the Federal Trade Commission in 1914. Some agency to serve as an "interstate trade commission" was desired, first, to prevent the creation of monopolies and, second, to protect competition from practices which might prove detrimental to business. According to the Commission: [7]

The underlying principle which governs the American economy is competition. It is the free play of competitive forces, the haggling in the market-place, the unseen hand of competition which protects the public interest. It is the constant rivalry among numerous firms for a greater share of the market which, over the long run, protects the consumer from high and extortionate prices. It is free and open markets which safeguard the independent producers in their efforts to offer new and better products.

[2] 26 Stat. L. 209.
[3] *United States v. E. C. Knight Co.,* 156 U.S. 1 (1895).
[4] *United States v. American Tobacco Co.,* 221 U.S. 106 (1911).
[5] 38 Stat. L. 730 (1914).
[6] 38 Stat. L. 717 (1914).
[7] *Annual Report of the Federal Trade Commission, 1952,* p. 1.

It then is the purpose of the Trade Commission to foster and protect free competition, subject to certain exceptions. Some industries, notably public utilities, are necessarily monopolistic in nature, and are regulated by other governmental agencies. And in times of war or national emergency regulations designed to promote free competition may be suspended to encourage production.

The Federal Trade Commission is an independent regulatory agency consisting of five members appointed by the President, with Senate confirmation, for terms of seven years. No more than three members may be of the same political party. The chairman not only presides but also acts as the administrative officer and is responsible for the proper functioning of the Commission.

Basically the Commission engages in two types of activities. The first, which is legal in nature, is to issue cease-and-desist orders in instances of the use of unfair trade practices. The second is to make studies and investigations of certain businesses or business conditions and issue reports for the use of both the government and the citizens.

The complaints of unfair trade practices may be made by other governmental agencies, by a competitor, or by a consumer. Or else the Commission on its own initiative may start an investigation. Broadly speaking the complaints may be placed in two categories: first, cases which involve restraint of trade or violations of the Clayton Act, and second, instances of false and misleading advertising. Members of the staff are assigned the duty of collecting the facts for presentation to the Commission. Field trips are made and interviews held with competitors. The examiner prepares a factual report and recommends the action to be taken. This report, after being reviewed by higher administrative officers, is submitted to the Commission for its decision. The Commission in turn may decide to issue a formal complaint, may initiate negotiations with the interested parties leading to an agreement to cease and desist the practice complained of, or may decide to drop the matter.

When a formal complaint is issued a respondent has twenty days to answer. He may admit or deny the complaint, or make an offer of settlement. Hearings are held before an examiner who makes an initial decision. This decision may be appealed to the Commission. Appeals from the decisions of the Commission are to the courts of appeals and the matter may finally be determined by the Supreme Court of the United States should that body grant a writ of certiorari.

The work of the Commission has been enlarged by several different acts of Congress. In addition to the Clayton and Federal Trade Commission Acts, it now administers the Export Trade Act, the Wool and Fur Products Labeling Act and certain sections of the Trade Mark Act. In spite of this increase in functions and the growth of American business, the number of employees under the Commission was smaller in 1952 than in 1918. In 1915 the total output of goods and services of business firms was valued at $39.5 billion. Today it is about $341 billion. Advertising—and it is the duty of the Commission to stop false and misleading advertising—cost American business about $200 million in 1949 but only $6.5 million in 1915.

In carrying out its antimonopoly work the Commission during a typical year will make over three hundred investigations resulting in the issuance of about forty cease-and-desist orders. In its effort to stop unfair and misleading advertising, the Commission has prohibited certain practices, including "various methods to create the impression that the customer is being offered an opportunity to make purchases under unusually favorable conditions when such is not the case." [8] Truly the Commission has much work to do here.

While it is true that monopolistic practices continue and advertising is often misleading, the Commission, within its powers and appropriations, is doing an acceptable job and merits a broader scope of operations.

The Securities and Exchange Commission. After the stock-market collapse in the late twenties, much blame was placed upon the unregulated sale of securities and the inability of the average investor to protect himself from salesmen and promoters using unethical if not downright dishonest means of selling securities. To correct abuses and excesses the Securities and Exchange Commission was created in 1934 as a supervisory agency over the entire security market. Members of the five-member commission are appointed by the President with the approval of the Senate for terms of five years. No more than three may be of the same political party. The President designates the chairman. The Commission is located in Washington but there are ten regional offices scattered over the United States. The work of the Commission is to administer acts of Congress providing for regulation of the issuance and sale of securities and the control of holding companies. The three principal acts outlining duties and functions are the Securities Act of 1934, the Securities and Exchange Act of 1935, and the Public Utility Holding Company Act of 1935.

In protecting investors in the security markets the Commission carries on varied types of activity. Whenever listed securities are to be issued, approval must be secured from the Commission and public disclosures of pertinent facts must be made. It also regulates investment companies and the trading in securities. With respect to holding companies, it supervises the purchase and sale of securities, utility property, and other assets and is responsible for their simplification. As an advisory body it gives assistance to those courts engaged in reorganization proceedings.

No completely satisfactory protection can be given to the reckless and unwary investor, but the Commission has done much to eliminate many

[8] *Ibid.*, p. 114.

practices and procedures that previously not only hurt the investor but also the reputation and standing of security markets.

The Interstate Commerce Commission. Although who deserves the honor of building the first railroad is still a matter of dispute, the Baltimore and Ohio Railroad had 23 miles of track in operation by. 1831. The nearly one hundred years thereafter was a period of growth for the railroad industry. The pattern of growth was for short lines to be built and then joined together into trunk lines. The War between the States made clear the need of transcontinental lines linking the Pacific coast with the East, and at the war's conclusion a period of railroad construction began that by 1916 resulted in the completion of 254,037 miles of railroad track. Since that date there has been a gradual decrease in mileage as new methods of transportation have competed with the railroads for business and forced the abandonment of certain lines. The railroads continue vital to the economic welfare of the nation, however, and are particularly essential in time of war.

The railroads have undergone three stages in their relations with government: a period of no regulation, one of state regulation, and now one of Federal regulation. Not only was the first period one of no regulation but the states and the Federal government encouraged the building of railroads by giving them financial aid and thousands of acres of the public domain. Grants of land in twenty years amounted to nearly 1,500,000 acres. Settlers were lured to the West by fabulous tales of the fertility of the soil and the wealth of natural resources. Much of what was said proved to be true. However, overproduction occurred and this along with high freight rates left little or no profit for the farmer. The railroads were largely blamed for these economic ills. Citizens, unable to protect themselves, turned to the government. Help came from the states in the form of state laws regulating the railroads. The railroads fought state regulation by contesting its legality and by corrupting many of the legislatures. At first the courts upheld state laws,[9] but in the Wabash case [10] the Supreme Court held that state regulation could not apply to railroads that were interstate in character. It then became necessary for the Federal government to act if regulation was to be maintained. Congress in 1887 passed the Interstate Commerce Act regulating railroads and creating the Interstate Commerce Commission, the first Federal independent regulatory commission.

The Interstate Commerce Commission is composed of 11 members with terms of seven years. Its functions include the regulation not only of railroads, but also interstate trucking, water and pipe-line transportation, Pullman service, and express companies. Because of the increased duties and responsibilities assigned to the Commission by Congress it requires a staff numbering over two thousand.

[9] *Munn v. Illinois,* 94 U.S. 113 (1877).
[10] *Wabash, St. Louis, and Pacific R.R. v. Illinois* 118 U.S. 557 (1886).

One of the major functions of the Commission is determination of the rates to be charged by railroads. In attempting to prescribe just and reasonable rates the Commission takes into consideration the effect of the rates on the movement of traffic, on adequate and efficient transportation at lowest cost, and on revenue sufficient to enable carriers under honest and efficient management to give satisfactory service. A fluctuating amount of business and the difficulty of determining a proper valuation of the railroads cause rate making to be the most difficult duty of the Commission.

The Commission is responsible for the enforcement of safety regulations, the promotion of safety programs, and the maintenance of accident statistics. Railroads today have excellent safety records owing to some extent to the work of the Commission.

Another responsibility is to see to it that the railroads offer proper service. This has proven to be difficult with respect to passenger service on local lines, which is often insufficient to pay the cost. The Commission may authorize the construction or abandonment of particular lines, the curtailment of train service, the joint use of terminal facilities, or may take other action for the improvement of service.

Since 1887 Congress has passed many laws concerning railroads and transportation. Some are regulatory while others have sought to aid the railroads. Public carriers have had both fat and lean years. Other means of transportation have cut into the business and profits of the roads. The Transportation Act of 1920 permitted the consolidation of lines and the pooling of traffic under the watchful eye of the Commission. Although advocated at times by certain groups, government ownership has never received support worth considering. Claims of the elimination of ruinous competition, the advantages of integration, and the putting of service before profit have been more than offset by a desire to keep government out of business and to maintain this source of taxation.

The Interstate Commerce Commission regulates motor transportation in the same manner as rail. Unfair practices like rebates and other discriminations are forbidden. Licenses to operate must be secured, rates are set, and standards of service are provided. Due to the fact that the building and maintenance of highways are state functions and that speed limits and other traffic rules are made by the states, a close working relationship must always be maintained between the Commission and the states.

The Federal Communications Commission. The Federal Communications Commission was created by an act of Congress in 1934 to regulate communications by wire and radio in interstate and foreign commerce. Its jurisdiction includes telephone, telegraph, submarine cable, radio and television. The regulation of these forms of communication assigned to the Commission by Congress is intended to secure adequate facilities, assure reasonable charges, promote safety measures, and advance the national defense. The Commission consists of seven members appointed by the President with the approval of the Senate. The term of office is seven years and the President designates the member to serve as chairman.

The Commission exercises general oversight over telegraph and telephone companies and can require extension of services and maintenance of reasonable rates or forbid special benefits or favors. In doing its work the Commission makes investigations, conducts hearings, makes rules, and can issue cease-and-desist orders to enforce compliance with these rules.

In the field of radio the Commission regulates not only broadcasting but also public and private communication by radio. There are less than 3,000 radio stations engaged in broadcasting programs but there are more than one million radio authorizations held by individuals and public and private corporations.[11] Many agencies using radio frequencies are engaged in the promotion of safety in land, sea, and air transportation. Municipal fire and police departments have found the use of radio particularly advantageous.

The Commission awards licenses to broadcasting stations, assigns frequencies, determines the location of stations and their power, provides the regulations respecting the actual operation of stations, participates in the making of international agreements relative to broadcasting and, while freedom of speech cannot be abridged, can forbid the use of profane and obscene language over the air and require that advertising meet certain broad standards. In refusing to renew a license to a broadcasting station the Commission found "misrepresentation of facts" as well as the use during broadcasts of "intemperate language," and concluded that the applicant "lacked the character to be a licensee." [12]

As television has developed rapidly the duties of the Commission have greatly increased. Generally speaking the Commission regulates television in the same manner and with the same power that it controls radio. The large number of requests for licenses and the many contests for station authorization necessitating hearings keep the Commission busy. Already Americans own over 25 million television sets and the popularity of TV continues to grow.

The national-defense activities of the Commission include all fields of electrical communications. Of particular importance to this defense program are "measures to control electromagnetic radiations both from communication and noncommunication sources, which could be used as 'beams to guide enemy aircraft and flying missiles.' 'Conelrad' (abbreviation of control of electromagnetic radiation) is the short name applied to this project." [13]

---

[11] See *Annual Report of the Federal Communications Commission, 1952.*

[12] See *Independent Broadcasting Co. v. Federal Communications Commission*, 193 F.2d 900 (1951).

[13] *Annual Report, 1952*, p. 2.

In the international field, agreements are constantly being made in allocating spectrum space. Cases of interference may also be handled by the Commission.

Civil Aviation. Air transportation, like rail and motor-carrier transportation, went through a period of state and local regulation before the Federal government began to control and supervise all aviation and air commerce of an interstate nature. All foreign commerce is exclusively under Federal control. Two agencies, the Civil Aeronautics Administration and the Civil Aeronautics Board, supervise civil aviation and administer regulations. The former is in the Department of Commerce, but the latter is an independent regulatory board, which reports to Congress and the President directly.

The Civil Aeronautics Administration is executive in character and enforces the rules of the Civil Aeronautics Board.[14] It directs the Federal Aid Airport Program with the ultimate purpose of providing a national airport system. It also administers the Washington National Airport.

The Civil Aeronautics Board is an independent board of five members who are appointed by the President with the approval of the Senate. It makes civil-aviation rules and regulations, determines rates, adjudicates differences, makes investigations, and performs other functions essential to the promotion of air transportation, the postal service, and national defense. It issues certificates of convenience and necessity and furnishes "permits" to foreign carriers. With respect to international civil aviation the Board consults with and advises the Department of State. One additional function of the Board should be mentioned. This is the safety program. Each civil-aircraft accident is investigated to ascertain as far as possible the probable cause of the accident. According to the 1953 report of the Board, passenger fatalities in 1953 were 1.3 persons per 100 million passenger-miles flown.[15]

Patents and Copyrights. In order to promote science and the arts the Constitution authorizes Congress to give to authors and inventors for a limited time the exclusive right to their writings or inventions. By this grant of power Congress established the Patent Office in the Department of Commerce. A patent gives the inventor an exclusive grant of the use of his invention for a period of time—usually seventeen years. If a patent is denied, an appeal may be taken to the Court of Customs and Patent Appeals. Once a patent is granted the United States does not protect the grantee from infringement. The inventor must protect his invention.

The practice of granting patents has been of great value to the United States in encouraging inventive genius but there has also been criticism of the system by which patents are granted. One criticism is that large corporations have benefited more from the patent system than has the

[14] Ross H. McFarland, *Human Factors in Air Transportation,* p. 29.
[15] *Annual Report of the Civil Aeronautics Board,* 1953, p. 60.

individual inventor. Also it has been claimed that the suppression of patents by large corporations is not unknown. The length of time between the application for and the granting of a patent is discouraging, though actually the classification "patent pending" gives an extension of the time that the patent is in force. Some chemical firms, relying on their own "know-how," prefer not to apply for a patent, choosing to run the risk of another firm duplicating a complex formula rather than make known the formula through the securing of a patent.

By copyrights similar privileges are granted to authors, composers, artists, and photographers. Copyrights are granted for twenty-eight years with privilege of renewal for a similar number of years. They are obtained from the Copyright Office, and authors and composers, like the inventor, must protect their own works from infringement.

The Tennessee Valley Authority

The United States now operates approximately one hundred types of business organizations, large and small, in which the people have invested about $40 billion. According to *Time,* "the Government has become the nation's largest insurer, electric-power producer, lender, landlord, grain owner, warehouse operator and shipowner. It monopolizes the world's biggest potential new industry: atomic energy." [16] Many of these enterprises are old but most are of recent vintage. The Boston Rope Walk, operated by the Navy, had its beginning during the Presidential term of Andrew Jackson, while the production of atomic energy is the government's most recent large-scale undertaking. "The Government is engaged in everything from tire recapping to coffee roasting, from binding books to freezing ice cream." [17]

Today the participation of the United States government in the business field is a subject of much debate by individual citizens and between rival political parties. Generally speaking, the Democratic party defends the TVA and other government enterprises as beneficial to citizens, business, and the nation, particularly in times of national emergency. The Republicans are prone to characterize these undertakings as "creeping socialism" and advocate getting the government out of business. Former President Herbert Hoover, in a critical vein, voiced the following opinion of the TVA, "Above all we must rescue free men from this variety of creeping socialism. The American people have fought off socialized medicine but here is a hole in the dike of free men that is bringing a flood." [18] The defenders of the TVA are numerous, and a recent poll is reported to have shown the American people as being against socialism but very much in favor of the program and activities of the TVA.

[16] *Time Magazine,* July 13, 1953, p. 84.
[17] *Ibid.*
[18] From a speech made at Case Institute of Technology, Apr. 11, 1953.

The 1933 act which created the Tennessee Valley Authority specifically directed the construction of the Norris, Wheeler, and Pickwick dams and the renovation of the Wilson dam that had been constructed during World War I. Since then nine major dams have been constructed on the Tennessee River alone while over twice this number have been built across neighboring streams and the tributaries of the Tennessee. Steam power plants also have been erected to generate more power and to afford a steady flow of current during droughts. According to the law, the purposes of these dams and other installations were to prevent floods, to improve navigation, to combat erosion, and to produce electric power. The objectives of the TVA, however, are broader, for they comprehend the unified development of a particular region for the benefit of the nation as a whole.

The Tennessee Valley Authority is headed by a board of three members with overlapping terms of six years. The members are appointed by the President with Senate approval and are subject to removal by the President. The Authority has a corporate name and seal, may sue and be sued, may make contracts, and has the power of eminent domain. Originally $116 million were allocated for this agency but each session of Congress appropriates additional sums. The Kentucky Dam alone cost approximately $100 million, not including the power system.

The TVA now employs 23,933 people, but the number fluctuates, depending upon the amount of construction under way. The Authority has been complimented frequently on the quality of its personnel. Rates of pay are based upon prevailing rates for similar work, the difficulty of the job, and performance. Annual pay rates have been standardized for trades and labor employees.

The production of electric power has increased yearly. In the steam plants 7 million tons of coal are used annually in the production of electric current. The United States government uses 12 billion kilowatt-hours of TVA power each year. Consumption by cities and industries continues to grow. Industry has expanded more rapidly in the Tennessee Valley than in the nation as a whole both as a source of income and of employment. Friends of the TVA urge that it has become essential to national defense as a supplier of power to the Oak Ridge plant and to chemical and other basic industries.

TVA is not only a producer of electric power but is engaged in other activities that have for their purpose the development of the valley. The prevention of soil erosion and floods and the improvement of navigation have already been mentioned. Indirectly the interests of the TVA include also fertilizers, food processing, research in minerals and forest products, power machinery for farming, and many others. One by-product of the TVA is the number of visitors who come to the valley. Some come to see the TVA in action. A visitor from India said, "The essentials of the TVA approach, though first tried out in the world's richest country, have even greater and no less relevance to an old heavily populated, resource-poor country like ours." [19] Other visitors flock to the valley for recreational purposes. It is ideal for those who love fishing, boating, and other outdoor sports. The lakes, particularly those located in the mountains, make the area a scenic wonderland, and an ever-growing tourist trade has become a valuable source of income to the inhabitants of the area.

The TVA, although attacked by critics, is a going concern. The sale of power during the last fiscal year gave a 4.7 per cent return to the government. To be sure, this is the return estimated by the TVA itself and so it is subject to criticism. However, irrespective of its critics, the TVA remains the most important example of government planning and operation in the field of business today.

The Post Office

The Constitution gives to Congress the power to establish post offices and post roads. From this authorization stems the power that has been used to create the gigantic postal system that is administered by the Post Office Department. In the early days mail was carried by pony, by stagecoach, and by sailing vessels. Today the bulk of the mail is transported by train, by motor transport, and by airplane. More and more use is being made of air and motor transport; in fact, during the past quarter of a century 65 per cent of the trains carrying mail have been eliminated by the railroads.

The Post Office Department is a business that employs over one-half million persons. No other Department is larger except the Department of Defense. The revenues of the Department amount to $2 billion annually and the pieces of mail handled reach astronomical figures. Yet, during the last fiscal year, the postal deficit amounted to over $662 million. It is nothing new for the postal service to end the year in the red; for a century the Post Office has had annual deficits in all but thirteen years. It is the size of recent deficits that gives concern. Before 1946 it seldom reached $100 million, but for the past four years the deficit has been over the half-billion mark each year.

The reasons offered for these deficits vary greatly. Opponents of government operation of business say that it is the usual government inefficiency plus the injection of politics into a business operation. The Postmaster General gives other reasons: "first, the unprecedented but unavoidable increases . . . since 1945 in the costs of operating the service; and second, the fact that during the same period the rates for postage and the fees for the special services were not correspondingly adjusted." [20] His solution of the difficulty is to revise upward those postage rates that are out of line

19 *Annual Report, 1952*, p. 76.
20 *Annual Report of the Postmaster General, 1952*, p. 2.

with the cost of the service. First-class mail as a whole has paid its way save in the handling of post cards where there is still a deficit despite the two-cents postage. The handling of fourth-class mail nearly pays its way. Two-thirds of the entire deficit comes from the handling of second- and third-class mail. The present rates act as a subsidy to those who send newspapers, magazines, circulars, and advertising matter through the mail. In requesting permission from Congress to raise rates, the Postmaster General stated, "I am especially concerned about the fact that in this rate matter the postal service is in an ambiguous position—neither a social service nor a business—and that it carries unfairly the onus of an excessive deficit over which it has no control on either the revenue or expense side, and which is too generally attributed to mismanagement." [21] He might have added that government penalty mail, franked mail, and mail in the classification of "free for the blind" amounted to nearly 18 per cent of all mail handled. This of course is nonrevenue mail.

In 1949 an Advisory Board for the Post Office Department was established. In the initial report of this Board there were two recommendations [22]

1. Congress should accept full responsibility . . . for the deficit by reason of the fact that it enacted legislation fixing rates and costs out of all relationship to each other and through the lack of a definite subsidy policy.

2. It is our best judgment that Congress should consider the creation of a Board within the Post Office Department, with power adequate for the fixation of rates under policies, as to standards of pay, etc., and subsidies as deemed wise and laid down by Congress.

REFERENCES

W. E. Atkins, G. W. Edwards, and H. G. Moulton, *The Regulation of the Security Markets* (1946).

Thomas C. Cochran and William Miller, *The Age of Enterprise* (1943).

J. R. Craf, *Economic Development of the United States* (1952).

Robert Cushman, *The Independent Regulatory Commissions* (1941).

Merle Fainsod and Lincoln Gordon, *Government and the American Economy* (1948).

D. Lynch, *The Concentration of Economic Power* (1946).

Ross McFarland, *Human Factors in Air Transportation* (1953).

Vernon A. Mund, *Government and Business* (1950).

United States Government Organization Manual.

See also the annual reports of the Civil Aeronautics Board, Securities and Exchange Commission, Federal Communications Commission, Federal Trade Commission, Interstate Commerce Commission, Postmaster General, and the Tennessee Valley Authority.

[21] *Ibid.*, p. 14.
[22] *Ibid.*, p. 30.

CHAPTER 22   *Agriculture and Conservation*

Agriculture in American Life

When George Washington took office in 1789 nearly all Americans were farmers; in 1950 six out of ten lived in cities and only one out of seven of those employed was engaged in farming.[1] If we translate these figures into terms of political power, we may well wonder why the needs of such a minority are heeded in national policy. It would seem reasonable to expect the majority to ignore the wishes of the farm population and devote its attention to the interests of industry and trade. Actually, however, it is well known that Congress and the Executive give anxious attention to the demands of agriculture and that the administration of the national farm policy involves widely ramifying and costly machinery and very large expenditures of public funds. Looked at realistically, this is a way of saying that the American farmer is the most successful of politicians. In terms of what he gets from government he has probably outdistanced labor and business and all other sectors of our economy.

The reasons for this are not hard to find. The first is the general recognition of the basic character of farming as a human activity. Even "city slickers" know that the food they eat and some at least of the clothing they wear comes from farms and for this reason they are willing to support policies intended to keep agriculture productive and reasonably prosperous. In the second place, the mass of folklore about the importance of the land and the greater "naturalness" of life in the country is still persuasive even with city dwellers. For most of us the tie with the land is not yet completely severed. If we are not immediately related to farmers

[1] Although the Bureau of the Census reports 40 per cent of our population as living in rural territory, only a minority of these are engaged in farming. Rural territory contains many small towns and villages, the inhabitants of which are employed in mining, lumbering, retail merchandising, the service trades, and in such enterprises as running motels and recreation resorts. These facts account for what may at first sight seem a discrepancy in the figures in the text.

we at least sense the importance of their role in our lives. Thirdly, in both Congress and the state legislatures the farmer is represented out of all proportion to his numbers and is thus assured of a respectful hearing. And, fourthly, in spite of the alleged individualism of farmers, as a group

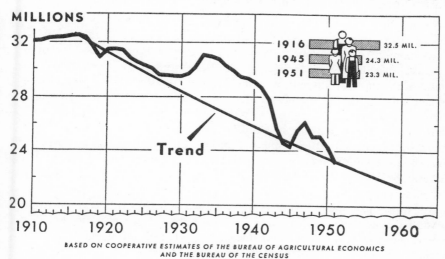

BASED ON COOPERATIVE ESTIMATES OF THE BUREAU OF AGRICULTURAL ECONOMICS
AND THE BUREAU OF THE CENSUS

FIG. 6. Decline in farm population 1910 to 1951 and projected decline 1951 to 1960. SOURCE: U.S. Bureau of Agricultural Economics.

they have been notably successful in creating pressure organizations led by able and skilful men and women.

The result of these factors is a vast mass of laws conferring favors or advantages on agriculture. Homestead and other land laws encouraging the rapid exploitation of our soil and water resources were produced by our legislatures almost from the beginning of settlement. In more recent years legislation providing farmers with such services as scientific research, marketing and weather reports, disease and pest control, and favorable credit arrangements, has grown steadily in bulk. Of even more direct value has been government assistance in the improvement of highways and the extension of electrical and telephone service. In 1945 the Census of Agriculture reported that two out of three farms were on all-weather roads and 20 per cent more were within 2 miles of such roads. The extension of electrical service in rural areas has been phenomenal. In 1935 only 11 per cent of our 6 million farms had central-station service. In 1950 nearly nine farms out of ten were electrified. Such improvements obviously have incalculable effects in making farm and village life psychologically more attractive and economically more profitable. National policy has now moved beyond such aids to guarantee the support of farm commodity prices. Since farmers are in control of most of our state legislatures, additional favors are forthcoming from those bodies. In terms of what he "gets out of" government, the farmer has done very well indeed.

Agriculture and the National Government

By a strict construction of the Constitution agriculture would seem to be a matter subject to state and local control. As a matter of fact it has always been of national concern as well. Land legislation was a preoccupation even of our colonial legislatures. In the early national period the disposal of the national domain was never out of "politics." The special place of agriculture always deeply influenced national tariff policy. In short, farming and farmers in one way or another have always been an important part of the stuff of legislation. Until fairly recently, however, *laissez faire* has been the official attitude toward agriculture as toward labor, business, and other economic interests, however much it might be departed from in practice from time to time. The Department of Agriculture began as an independent establishment as early as 1862, but it did not gain Cabinet status until 1889 and for many years its chief function was the collection of statistics and the dissemination of information. Research and advisory functions were added later, but an active policy of *aiding* and *directing* agriculture was not adopted until quite recent years.

The abandonment of *laissez faire* in agriculture in favor of something very like economic planning under government auspices is a chapter in the general development by which every organized interest powerful enough to do so has secured favors and advantages from government. In principle, farmers, perhaps more than any other occupational group, have been individualists, preferring to make their own plans and take their chances in the market. Their recent insistence on direct aid from government is justified by the argument that business, labor, and other groups have long enjoyed special favors and that, if the "game" is to be played that way, farmers are entitled to share more equitably in its gains. This may seem to be a purely selfish point of view but it is supported by the contention that farm prosperity is basic to the national welfare. Farm income in recent years has averaged between $13 and $17 billion and the 60 million persons who live on the land constitute a vast market for the products of industry which, as the farm leaders see it, has long enjoyed such favors as tariff protection and other government aids. Conservation measures, while of immediate benefit to farmers, are justified as guarantees of continual national production of foods and fibers. Furthermore, agriculture is obviously a national and not merely a local interest because in recent years such products as grain, meat, and cotton have become potent weapons of foreign policy. The more general argument is offered that farm living standards, in the form of cash income and such amenities as good roads, cheap power, "reasonable" freight rates, and easy credit, must be kept high in the interest of national power.

The National Agricultural Policy

The objective of the present farm policy of the national government is to preserve for the farmer an equitable proportion of the total national income on which he can depend. This is usually referred to as the guarantee of farm price parity, and means the securing, by methods described below, of a price that will enable the farmer to buy what he needs at an actual cost no greater than he paid during the "base" period of 1909 to 1914, a period in which, according to farm spokesmen, a just balance existed between the incomes of industrial workers, management, investors, and other segments of the economy. This means, of course, that with respect to what the program calls the basic commodities—cotton, corn, rice, tobacco, and peanuts—prices, instead of finding their own level on the so-called free market, are supported by the national government at a figure calculated to make the farmer as well off, *in terms of actual purchasing power,* as receivers of income from sources other than agriculture. Special provisions exist for other than the "basic" commodities.

Now this program is in reality not merely an economic one. It is true that it puts behind agriculture the enormous financial power of the national government, but in terms of realistic practical politics farm price parity stands for what the farm pressure groups call "simple economic justice." Such a phrase, frequently repeated, becomes a potent slogan about which cluster all the major and minor myths which tend to exalt the tillers of the soil as the basic contributors to national productivity and virility. It is because these myths confront others constructed to give significance to other groups that farm policy involves "politics" of the most practical kind. For obviously what seems "simple economic justice" to farmers strikes other interests as mere favoritism. It is hard indeed to cast the beam out of one's own eye!

The road to "parity" has been a long one, dating back to the days of the "farm bloc" in Congress in the years following World War I. It was during those years that the farmer acquired his reputation as a "radical," at least with the industrial population. The farm states' representatives in Congress were once referred to by Senator Moses of New Hampshire as "the sons of the wild jackass." It is well to remember, however, that farmers everywhere are conservatives and that American farmers are no exception to this rule. Only reluctantly and after many years of baffling misfortune have they accepted the stringent measures of regulation and control now in effect. At the end of World War I there occurred a sharp fall in farm prices at the very time when the farmer was burdened with debt, some of it incurred in meeting the huge demand of the war years, and when there had not been anything like a comparable drop in the prices of the things he had to buy.

Throughout the 1920s representatives of the farm states were able to compel unwilling executives to take various measures intended to increase farm prices. Many of these were costly to the treasury and none was successful, or at least not successful enough to please the farmer. Yet even greater disaster was in store for him. The depression which began late in 1929 seriously reduced the buying power of the industrial population both here and among our customers in foreign lands. Following this calamity were years of drought and crop failure which piled upon the farmer the woes of foreclosure and bankruptcy, the growth of tax delinquency in his local governments, and the deterioration of such capital assets as farm homes and equipment and even the land itself. Rural life generally lost its boasted satisfactions.

From this situation the so-called New Deal attempted to rescue the farmer. The theory of the New Deal program was a simple one and, in spite of hysterical charges of "socialism" or even "communism," operated strictly within the confines of orthodox "capitalist" ideology. It was assumed that if production of farm products were curtailed, the smaller supply would bring higher prices. Farmers were to be paid therefore to hold land out of production, payments to be made from the proceeds of a tax laid upon the processors of farm products, for example, flour millers. These tax provisions were put into the law on the theory that to make payments directly from the Treasury would be resented by the general taxpayers. Three years after the passage of the Agricultural Adjustment Act, it was held unconstitutional by the Supreme Court on the ground that the processing tax was not a tax for the support of government but was rather a levy upon one class for the benefit of another.[2] Even before this decision, however, Congress, aware of the unpopularity of the Agricultural Adjustment Act in many quarters, passed in 1935 the Soil Conservation Act as a means of accomplishing the same objectives. Under this act also land was to be held out of production, but the payments to farmers who complied with its provisions were to be made out of the general funds in the Treasury. This sort of act may not be challenged in the courts for the technical reason that no individual taxpayer can show such a separable interest in the sums expended as to give him a claim to judicial relief.

Under both the Agricultural Adjustment and the Soil Conservation Acts considerable areas of land were removed from cultivation, and improved farming practices were more generally introduced than had been the case in the past. The New Deal, however, did not stop with these measures, so that it is hard to say how much they had to do with the improvement in the condition of the farmer which took place in the years just before

[2] *United States v. Butler*, 297 U.S. 1 (1936).

World War II. Beginning about 1937 or 1938 an extensive program was instituted to halt wind-and-water erosion and to rebuild wornout land by the use of soil-building crops and new methods of cultivation. In some cases marginal land was bought by the government and taken out of cultivation for farm crops, the families on it being resettled and, with government assistance, given a new start on better land. At the same time credit facilities were extended for land purchase and crop loans, and public assistance was forthcoming for extending electric service to farm homes. During the same period the work of the Tennessee Valley Authority was steadily pushed ahead—a great deal of it being of direct value to the agriculture of the area or serving in any case as an example elsewhere in the country.

The Present Farm Program

The conservation program formally begun by the Soil Conservation Act of 1935 has remained in effect and has been systematized since that date, so that it may now be regarded as a permanent part of any future farm policy. In this program, as was generally true of farm measures adopted under the New Deal, payments to farmers were less direct subsidies than compensation for the restriction of supply believed necessary in a period of surpluses. There was at least no overt acknowledgment of any obligation to support farm income directly, the assumption being that temporary government assistance would help restore the working of the law of supply and demand. The conception of farm price "parity" was indeed implied in payments for restricting tilled acreage, but the demand for "parity" as something like a "right" had not yet appeared. Perhaps it is not even yet so regarded except by a few doctrinaires, but it has become an important slogan of the farm propagandists. When described as only "economic justice," it is bound to make a powerful appeal and keep the farm problem a political issue of first consequence, no matter what the precise machinery may be by which "parity" is sought.

Most of the devices by which the national government tries to support farm prices still involve the restriction of supply. This restriction may be brought about in various ways. The simplest is for the government to buy up and store surplus commodities, and everyone is familiar with the fact that vast amounts of such products as butter and eggs and potatoes have at various times been in storage to keep their prices up. As this is written it is estimated that more than $7 billion are tied up in food and cotton. Waste through spoilage and corruption through illegal speculation have also been accompaniments of this policy. It would be possible theoretically to get rid of embarrassing surpluses by selling them abroad for whatever they would bring, but this is likely to get us into trouble with foreign nations, some of them at the moment political allies.

The principal difficulty of attempting to support prices by buying up surpluses is that it obviously does nothing to prevent the recurrence of surpluses. For this reason it is necessary to devise some direct or indirect means of limiting production. Under existing laws the chief means is the establishment of marketing quotas. The Secretary of Agriculture has authority to fix such quotas with respect to products like grain and cotton which normally move in large quantities in interstate commerce. Each farmer, having been assigned an acreage, can ship in interstate commerce only the product of that acreage. Indeed, if he exceeds the quota the government may forbid him to ship *any* of his crop. As a result, he cannot realize cash from his produce, since the crops to which quotas are applied are ordinarily sold and not consumed entirely on the farm. Drastic though this procedure may seem, it has been upheld by the Supreme Court. The Court held that although the quota device is primarily a way of protecting the farmer's prices, it is valid as an indirect way of balancing the national economy and hence is in the interest of the general welfare.[3]

It is far too early to say whether public regulation of agriculture will be successful. Perhaps more than any other calling farming is subject to unpredictable hazards. The best-founded prediction as to total probable production may be belied by such uncontrollable factors as the weather or the incidence of plant or animal diseases. There is also the enormous difficulty of enforcing restrictions on more than 6 million farms. In attempting to regulate the manufacture and marketing of industrial products government would need to deal with far fewer persons and could proceed with far more accurate information as to production. In the case of farming there is also the danger that the guarantee of prices will disturb the entire agricultural economy by affecting land values, encouraging farm indebtedness, and in other ways raising production costs—thus leading to demands for new guarantees at higher levels. It is hard to see, in fact, how farm-price parity can be achieved and preserved unless substantially every aspect of planning and carrying out the individual farm enterprise is supervised by government—a development scarcely consistent with traditional ideas of individual initiative and freedom.

On the other hand, without some sort of government control the farmer seems almost completely unable to control production and therefore influence prices. If prices fall his natural tendency is to produce more, not less, whereas industries are usually in a position to produce in line with demand.

Conservation

Of immediate interest to the farmer but vital to the welfare of all of us is the problem of conserving our natural resources. Until the beginning

[3] *Wickard v. Filburn*, 317 U.S. 111 (1942).

of the present century these resources were exploited as if they were unlimited. There is now, however, a lively appreciation of the fact that actual disaster will be our lot if we do not make better use of our land, water, and forest wealth. Our basic wealth, of course, is the land itself. Until very recent years public policy toward the use of land aimed at getting under the plow, or at any rate into private hands, as much of the public domain as possible as rapidly as this could be accomplished. The general theory of our land laws was that the public good would be best served by building up a class of small owners, each free to use his land as seemed best to him. This policy was in line, of course, with prevalent individualistic economic theories. Some of its results, however, have been unfortunate. As a leading authority puts it, Americans in practice have not learned to love the land but have, for the most part, regarded it as something to exploit and as a source of immediate financial return. Even if this harsh judgment does not apply to all farmers, it is true that, without external stimulus, few have been willing or able to apply measures to prevent depletion of the land by natural forces.

Erosion of land by wind and water, often aggravated by unwise management of crop land and by overgrazing, is estimated to cause an annual monetary loss of $400 million and to have been responsible already for a total damage of $10 billion.[4] Soil scientists tell us that nature requires from three hundred to a thousand years to build one inch of topsoil, which by the millions of tons is annually washed or blown from American crop and grazing land. Methods by which this loss can be prevented are well known to conservationists. Although progressive farmers were here and there applying these methods many years ago, there was no national policy of soil conservation until the mid-thirties of the present century.[5]

The Soil Conservation Act of 1935 was passed both as a way of restricting farm output and as a means of introducing better methods of using the soil. With the adoption of the device of marketing quotas, the first of these purposes has grown less important and emphasis is now on the latter. The Soil Conservation Service in the Department of Agriculture operates through seven regional offices and soil-conservation committees organized under the laws of the individual states. Farmers desiring to form a soil-conservation district petition the state committee which then holds a referendum among the owners of land in the proposed district. If the referendum is favorable, a district is set up under a board composed of a majority of elected members in the district. Individual farmers then enter into

---

[4] The experts do not agree on the figures of loss but they are very high by any reckoning. See the Yearbook of Agriculture for 1938, entitled *Soils and Men*, U.S. Department of Agriculture.

[5] This paragraph and the preceding one have been adapted from the second edition of Lane W. Lancaster's *Government in Rural America*, D. Van Nostrand Company, Inc., 1952, with the permission of the publishers.

agreements with the district to use their land according to its capabilities as determined by a survey conducted by the Soil Conservation Service. They may then receive the technical assistance of the specialists of the Service, some soil-building plants, and quite often the use of machinery belonging to the district. Methods of conservation include the planting of crops to rebuild the soil or to hold the topsoil in place, the filling in of gulleys, the building of dams, and the diversion of streams.

As this is written, there are more than 2,300 organized soil-conservation districts covering a billion and a quarter of the nearly two billion acres classed as land in farms. It is estimated that conservation practices have been applied to 150 million acres and that about twice that area is planned. The annual appropriation for the Soil Conservation Service has in recent years run to between $50 and $60 million. Soil conservation, however, makes a strong popular appeal and there is heavy pressure to increase these sums. For example, the local districts are organized into a National Association of Soil Conservation Districts and that body is constantly agitating for larger expenditures. Since a good deal of honest sentiment is attached to plans to save the soil, pressures of this sort are hard to resist. As to concrete achievements, Dr. Hugh Bennett, former Chief of the Soil Conservation Service, estimated in 1952 that one-fifth of the job was done and that at the present rate of progress conservation practices would cover all agricultural land in about thirty-five years. Incidentally, the administration of the program is an interesting illustration of how the cooperation of local self-government with respect to an important function can be stimulated by central authorities. Many farmers require educating in the value of sound soil management and the Soil Conservation Service has been very successful in promoting this sort of education.

The Problem of Dry Land

Whereas millions of acres of cultivable land are subject to serious erosion by water, other millions lack moisture entirely. All the minerals needed to produce crops are present, if only water could be brought to the land. The problem of bringing the soil and the water together is a tremendous one which the national government has been attacking for many years. Most of the work, consisting largely of the building of dams and the subsequent allocation of water to the land needing it, is under the direction of the Bureau of Reclamation in the Department of the Interior. Other dams, conceived primarily as flood-control projects, are constructed by the Corps of Engineers of the Army. Whatever the primary purpose of such dams, whether to supply water to otherwise unproductive acres or to prevent disastrous floods, they produce vast amounts of electrical energy, the use of which has meant much to the people in the areas nearby.

Reclamation of dry land was recognized formally as a public function by the passage of the Reclamation Act of 1902. Between that date and 1931 the Bureau of Reclamation spent about a quarter of a billion dollars in building and operating projects which irrigated nearly three million acres of land in the 17 western states. By the end of 1948 the government's investment in such works was about $1¼ billion, and a program was under way to spend $2 billion during the next seven years for the irrigation of 7 million additional acres. Government projects are now capable of irrigating about thirty million acres, and the Bureau of Reclamation believes that with complete storage of water a total of fifty million acres could be made productive.

Much of the "politics" of reclamation centers about the rivalry between the Corps of Engineers and the Bureau of Reclamation. Both services are competently staffed, but the Army has in recent years generally enjoyed a greater popularity with Congress, whereas the Bureau has been suspected of "socialistic" leanings, perhaps because of the very zeal of its personnel in planning and executing projects which affect in quite different ways various economic interests in the areas where it operates. Critics of the Bureau's policies believe that the government should get out of the business of building dams and leave the field to private capital. Enthusiasts for the Bureau's program, on the other hand, feel that such a move would make possible "exploitation" of individual power and water users by the private utility companies. Since each of the opposing groups has powerful allies in Congress and in the public at large, neither is likely to win a complete victory, so that reclamation projects of the future are likely to be carried on by both public and private agencies.

The whole water-conservation-and-control program has given rise to an almost ferocious kind of "politics." The policy of government in the United States has been to favor the family-size farm—say, of 160 acres—in the allocation of water. This runs counter to what seems a recent decided tendency toward much larger farming units, managed in some cases by corporations. Our farm folklore is built around the quarter section tilled by a single family; that corporations should engage in farming seems somehow unnatural, if not actually sinister, so that the allotment of water from government dams involves the same sort of bitter struggles once called forth by the alleged crimes of the "money power" or the "trusts." Subsidiary scuffles occur between the various national agencies concerned in the water question—the Bureau of Reclamation, the Corps of Engineers, the Soil Conservation Service, and so on—and between state and sectional interests on the one hand and national programs on the other. This bickering, of course, eventually reaches Congress. In general, the compromises made in that body satisfy none of the protagonists and end in a policy which restricts output by marketing quotas and, on the other hand, increases it by increasing the quantity and improving the quality of farm land. All one can say of this inconsistency is that it is the sort of result to be expected in a political and social order as complicated as our own and in which every interest is free to present its case.

The Public Domain

Although few Americans are aware of it, more than 20 per cent of the area of the United States is owned by the national government. That is, it belongs to all of us. These holdings amount to more than 450 million acres and are found for the most part in the 17 states west of the eastern boundaries of North Dakota in the north and Texas in the south. These figures do not include land still owned by the individual states or the very substantial amounts owned for highway, airport, park, and other state and municipal purposes. To the casual observer, much of this land, consisting as it does of mountains or deserts, would seem to have little value; but it is obvious on reflection that in water, minerals, forests, and grazing lands it constitutes a vast treasure, the proper management of which affects everyone. These lands are also important from the point of view of recreation and the preservation of wild life, as everyone knows who has lived in or visited a national park.

Perhaps the two most important problems of the public domain continue to be the proper use of the grazing lands and the wise exploitation of the forests. Overgrazing is certain to remove the natural soil cover and end in destructive wind-and-water erosion, while excessive cutting of timber not only depletes a valuable resource but also exposes the land to destruction by wind and water. The two national agencies primarily responsible for the execution of policy—the Bureau of Land Management in the Department of the Interior in the case of grazing lands, and the Forest Service of the Department of Agriculture—are under great pressure from private interests eager to profit from the use of these resources at an excessive rate. Public regulation of the use of these resources is often stigmatized as "socialistic" and "bureaucratic" and the demand is often made for its relaxation in the interest of "private enterprise." Another approach now being made is to urge that the national government turn back to the states the public lands within their borders—this in the name of "states' rights" or "local self-government." Probably neither demand is sound in terms of the true public interest nor even quite honest from the point of view of political doctrine.

There would seem to be nothing specially "socialistic" about the wise and frugal planning of the exploitation of such irreplaceable wealth as grasslands and forests any more than it is "socialistic" to look ahead with reference to the use of privately owned wealth of any other sort. As to the question of "states' rights" it is probably true that the real basis of the appeal to that historic "issue" is found in the desire of interested persons to escape regulation altogether, a result which may be expected to follow the return of such resources to state control. Such words as "socialistic" and "bureaucratic" and "states' rights" ought to be looked at for what they are—terms of uncritical denunciation and praise—and assessed at their correct value. They ought not to be accepted as justifying policies which might lead to the waste of wealth which cannot be recreated. It may well be that the regulatory agencies of the national government are guilty from time to time of bureaucratic tactics, but there is no persuasive evidence that they have not been careful trustees for the people who are the ultimate owners of our natural treasure in the land.

The "Politics" of Agriculture and Conservation

The formation of a policy on any but the simplest issues is a matter of extreme difficulty. This is true because politics is at bottom a contest for power. There are a dozen possible solutions to any public problem, but each will involve the interests, perhaps even the prosperity or the very existence of important persons, groups, or sections. Any solution that is finally adopted is sure to involve compromise in the course of which these groups will contend bitterly for as much of their own solution as can be extorted from their determined antagonists. Statesmen may talk eloquently of the public purposes they have in mind, but it is obvious that they can realize no purposes at all *unless they achieve power.* And the price of power is compromise.

Agricultural policy is no exception to this rule, and it may be useful to pass in review the interests that have to be compromised in order to attain a program that will be supported with more or less willingness by those who are affected by it in quite different ways. The first thing that strikes us here is the vast extent of the United States and the correspondingly great variety of crop interests, some of them in sharp conflict with others. Farmers are no more a unit than are business men or workers and it will not do to think of them so. Consider, for example, the conflict of interest between the growers of cotton and peanuts on the one hand and dairy farmers on the other—a conflict highlighted by the long controversy over the taxation of colored oleo. New England farmers have not the same interest in high price supports for grain that is found among western farmers. Because of their relatively greater efficiency, large farmers benefit more from government payments than small farmers and this fact, in the early days of the New Deal, threatened to widen dangerously an already existing social cleavage. Other differences in interests will readily occur to the observer—between truck farmers, wheat farmers, ranchers, stock feeders, fruit farmers, and so on. The very fact that lively controversy flared up over the definition of what should be called "basic" crops for price support indicates the different valuations placed upon commodities by those engaged in producing them. Corn, rice, tobacco, peanuts, and cotton are officially "basic" in part at least because their producers were politically powerful enough to have them declared so by law.

Cutting across these crop differences are other and more general ones. Farmers, as is true of all other groups, are divided with respect to the desirability of preserving the "free market" or supporting more "liberal" policies—that is, government planning. Even now it may be assumed that many a farmer who accepts government payments does so reluctantly, justifying his abandonment of *laissez faire* by arguing that subsidies are only temporary expedients. It is also true that farmers have the same traditional party loyalties that other groups have and find themselves as Republicans or Democrats experiencing mixed feelings with respect to official farm policies. Moreover, quite apart from crop differences, farmers in one section of the country may still harbor suspicions about farmers elsewhere, since a kind of psychological sectionalism persists in the United States. Finally, of course, the interests of farmers clash, or at least seem to clash, with the demands of union labor, with the interests of city dwellers, with transportation concerns, with bankers, and so on.

Even these conflicts do not complete the picture, for within the ranks of farm politicians and governmental agencies are other tensions and hostilities. The three big farm lobbying organizations—the Grange, the American Farm Bureau Federation, and the Farmers' Union—represent somewhat different constituencies and hence want different things from government. This fact makes for clashes not only before Congress but on the state and local level where these groups come into contact with the state colleges of agriculture, the local soil-conservation administrators, and other agencies serving farm needs. Nor is cooperation always the rule even between national agencies, conflicts occurring between the Bureau of Reclamation and the Soil Conservation Service and the Corps of Engineers, and between the advocates of "big" and "little" dams in the soil-conservation program and in the various schemes for river-basin development. In this setting it is noteworthy not that farm policy is full of inconsistencies and wastefulness, but that any workable policy is possible at all.

REFERENCES

Hugh H. Bennett, *This Land We Defend* (1942).
John D. Black and Maxine Kiefer, *Future Food and Agricultural Policy* (1948).
Marion Clawson, *Uncle Sam's Acres* (1951).
A. Whitney Griswold, *Farming and Democracy* (1948).
Luther Gulick, *American Forestry Policy* (1951).
Charles M. Hardin, *The Politics of Agriculture* (1952).
Russell Lord, *To Hold This Land* (1938).
U.S. Department of Agriculture, *Soils and Men* (1938).

The New Philosophy of Security

The creation of the Department of Health, Education, and Welfare early in 1953 marked the formal completion in the United States of a revolution in thinking and practice with respect to a whole series of governmental functions. The new department is responsible for what is inaccurately but significantly called "social security." This is inaccurate because, strictly speaking, "social security" is only a part of the new department's work; it is significant in that the phrase marks the acceptance of a new attitude toward poverty and misfortune. Public policy is no longer directed to the "relief" of the poor; it aims at nothing less than the provision of a minimum of well-being for substantially the entire population. In the land of "rugged individualism" the welfare state, for good or ill, has become a reality.

In every society there will be found a certain number of individuals who for one reason or another are unable to "pay their way." Among these are the chronically ill, the crippled, the feeble-minded and insane, the aged infirm, those out of work, and the improvident and indolent. In primitive societies where the margin between comfort and want is a narrow one, the physically unfit and in some cases the aged unable to work are eliminated by exposure to the elements or to wild beasts, while the merely lazy are brought by severe social discipline to do their share of work on pain of banishment. In so-called civilized countries what is done with or for such persons depends largely upon popular views as to the cause of their plight. These views have undergone great changes in the last four or five centuries.

Traditional Attitudes toward the Unfortunate

When the entire Western world was ostensibly Catholic the Church taught that the poor were the proper objects of the charity of the more fortunate. Since the state could scarcely be said to exist much before the

395

seventeenth century, the Church was the agency most active in relieving the needs of the poor, the ill, the crippled, and other afflicted persons. The object of alms, however, aside from the salvation of the charitable, was largely to relieve suffering; there was no attempt to get at the causes of distress. Actually few explanations which we should call rational were offered for dependency, since the modern phrase "maladjustment" could not have been coined until men came to distinguish between the personal and environmental causes of poverty and suffering. In practice what we now call social ills were regarded as the result of human wickedness or explained as the working of the inscrutable will of God.

The modern state came into being when such ideas were dominant. Even though the English government acknowledged in the Elizabethan poor law of 1601 some responsibility for the unfortunate, the interests of the dominant social classes favored the holding of assistance to a minimum. As late as the eighteenth century a "catechism" held that it was "the purpose of the laws to confirm the rich in their possessions, and to restrain the vicious poor." Here was implicit the ancient idea, so pleasing to those already comfortable, that wealth was the reward of virtue and suffering the inevitable and just punishment of wickedness. It would have been hard, of course, to demonstrate that Providence so divided the population, but the fact remained that the rich made the secular laws and there was no gainsaying their power to make their own views prevail.

These ideas were if anything stronger among the American colonists than in the mother country. Nearly everyone lived on the land and it seemed reasonable to argue that the land would yield a living to all willing to work. Only in such cases as catastrophic crop failure could one plead that he was the victim of hard luck. For the most part it was assumed that poverty was the penalty of sin and that the poor could at best claim a charity whose coldness has become proverbial. The Reverend Thomas R. Malthus was not a cruel man, yet he could speak words which the present age no doubt finds shocking. The pauper, he wrote in 1798 [1]

. . . should be taught that the laws of nature which are the laws of God, had doomed him and his family to suffer . . . that he had no claim of *right* on society for the smallest portion of food beyond that which his labor would fairly produce; and that if he and his family were saved from feeling the natural consequence of his improvidence, he would owe it to the pity of some kind benefactor, to whom, therefore, he ought to be bound by the strongest ties of gratitude.

Men and women who believed this were not unkind. Especially in America, the land of promise, such beliefs seemed only the most obvious inferences from observation and experience. Where land could be had

[1] *Essay on Population* (Everyman edition), Vol. II,. p. 201.

almost for the asking, everyone could reasonably be held responsible for making his own living and even for accumulating an inheritance for his children. If he failed, let him not look to the provident and industrious to do for him what he should do for himself. Society would at best, and that grudgingly, relieve his most pressing wants, but it would see to it that his lot was not such as to put a premium upon laziness and lack of foresight in others. As a transgressor against the "natural law" of self-help, he could expect his way to be hard. In an individualistic society even the poor acquiesced in such views.

"Poor Relief" as a Local Function. Hence "poor relief" and the arrangements for administering it. Charity was a local affair. The national government had nothing to do with it and the state governments very little more. The latter quite early assumed some responsibility for the insane, the feeble-minded, and the blind, but the problem with respect to all other dependents was one for the towns, townships, or counties. "Relief" was of two sorts—indoor and outdoor. Indoor relief was furnished in local almshouses or on "poor farms." Little attempt was made to discriminate among recipients, so that until nearly the twentieth century it was not unusual to find in the poorhouse all the unfortunates in the community—orphans, hoboes, the unemployable aged, the chronically ill, the crippled, and misfits generally. Supervision was unprofessional and care haphazard. The almshouse itself was often located in a remote part of the township or county and here the inmates lived out their bleak lives, largely ignored by local officialdom and forgotten even by relatives only too happy to be rid of them.

Outdoor relief consisted of the support of the poor and unfortunate in their own homes. This type of relief normally involved supplying the recipients with food and other elementary necessities. The decision to aid was commonly made by the local governing body and took the form of "grocery orders" to the clients or delivery of the needed supplies either by a member of that body or by some petty functionary appointed by it. It is perhaps significant of ingrained public attitudes that the latter official in some parts of the country was called the "poormaster." In any case the persons in charge were untrained, and investigation of need, if made at all, was quite perfunctory. This policy, if indeed it can be called a policy, made no attempt to get at the causes of dependency. At its best, traditional "poor relief" was charity of the coldest sort; at its worst, a fine example of crass inhumanity.

Changing Attitudes

By the opening of the present century it was becoming evident here and there that the common assumptions about poverty and misfortune could not stand examination. The urbanization and industrialization of

American society meant that men and women were more and more divorced from the soil and increasingly dependent for their livelihood upon a complicated and impersonal economic system in the working of which individual industriousness, honesty, and foresight were of relatively little significance. An individual's prosperity no longer depended wholly on his own efforts as could once be persuasively argued; on the contrary, decisions made by persons whom he had never seen, hundreds or even thousands of miles distant, might take away his job and leave him with no resources except scanty savings soon exhausted. A retreat to farming was actually not open to most city workers even if they had the necessary skill to "make a go of it." Under these circumstances few could by their own efforts accumulate enough for their own old age, so retirement meant an unwilling but inescapable dependency on the grudging support of relatives or acceptance of the cold charity of the local government.

The great depression which began at the end of 1929 struck a society so closely knit in its economic relationships that scarcely any class escaped its devastation. The farmers facing foreclosure with corn at 10 cents a bushel, the 12 million workers suddenly cast adrift from their jobs, the country bankers embarrassed by worthless "investments," and the brokers who hurled themselves from the windows of skyscrapers—all were victims of an insecurity which most Americans fondly believed would never be a part of their lives in this favored land. After three years of patient endurance the mood of the public was one of such chastened desperation as to make feasible some bold experiments. By the time this mood had passed, the first steps had been taken toward a comprehensive system of social security. This system concerned itself at the outset with the principal types of insecurity—those attributable to old age, loss of employment, and the loss or incapacity of the family breadwinner. The new system repudiated the two leading ideas underlying traditional "poor relief." It abandoned very largely the notion that insecurity resulted from individual wickedness or inadequacy, and it proceeded on the assumption that security was a responsibility of the national government, the magnitude of the problem being obviously beyond the resources of both private charity and local government.

Old-age Assistance and Insurance

The proportion of our population over the age of sixty-five is steadily increasing. A hundred years ago it was about 2.5 per cent of the total, or about one person in forty; in 1950 it was approximately 7.7 per cent, or one person in every thirteen. Projecting this trend into the future, it is estimated that the proportion in 1980 will be one person in eight. It is well known that age is a distinct bar to employment in large sectors of the modern economy; perhaps half the working force of the nation is employed in occupations where the doors are pretty well closed to persons beyond fifty. Cold statistics do not, of course, reveal the personal tragedy suffered by those who reach the age of sixty-five with inadequate resources. Their only recourse is to seek the support of their families, where, it may as well be said, they are frequently not welcome, or accept help from the local relief authorities.

The social-security program of the national government makes provision for the aged in two ways. The short-run plan is called old-age assistance, known officially as OAA. This is charity pure and simple and is intended to meet the immediate problem of caring for that large proportion of those over the age of sixty-five who need assistance. The national and state governments cooperate in financing and administering the program. Under present laws the national government contributes from 50 to 75 per cent of the individual payments up to a maximum of $50 per month and pays one-half the cost of state administration. To qualify under national laws the states must extend benefits to all citizens over sixty-five who are dependent on public support except inmates of public institutions, and set up administrative agencies acceptable to the Social Security Administration in the Department of Health, Education, and Welfare. If a state wishes to exceed the $50 maximum it must use its own funds. Determination of need is made by local assistance authorities and payment is made to recipients in cash. No special taxes are levied to defray the cost of the program and no contributions are made by persons receiving aid. In short the system is one of relief, intended to take the place of traditional forms of assistance and, although it has in many places put the poorhouse out of business, it still involves the stigma associated with charity.

At the present time about 2,750,000 persons receive OAA, or about 214 out of every 1,000 persons over the age of sixty-five. The total annual cost is about $1.5 billion and the average monthly payment is about $43—a few states paying considerably more than the average sum and a few others falling far below it. It is the expectation of administrators that the number of recipients will grow smaller as more persons become eligible for old-age pensions, but, since large numbers will probably never qualify for the latter, it is likely that many will always be on the assistance rolls.

The long-range plan for dealing with the aged is old-age and survivors' insurance, or OASI as it is usually called. This is a strictly national program, the state governments having nothing to do with it. It is financed by taxes laid upon the payrolls of industries whose workers are covered, plus contributions of the same amount deducted from the workers' earnings. These sums are paid into a trust fund administered by the Social Security Administration. As the law stands now 4 per cent of wages up to $4,200 a year is paid to the account of the insured worker, half from the payroll tax, half from the payroll deductions. Out of the fund thus accumulated benefits of three sorts are paid—an annuity to the insured upon his attaining the age of sixty-five, a lump-sum payment upon his death, and annuities paid to his survivors. The annuity paid at the age of sixty-five is based upon the length of covered employment and the average earnings of the insured, and varies at present from $30 to $108 per month. The annuitant's wife, if aged sixty-five or over, receives in addition up to 50 per cent of the sum paid to her husband. Upon his death the widow is entitled to an annuity up to one-half of their combined benefits. Each dependent child may receive up to 50 per cent of the father's annuity. The lump-sum death benefit is three times the annuitant's monthly benefit and may thus reach $324. The annuitant, if still employable after sixty-five, may earn up to $1,200 a year, and there is no limitation on the income that he may receive from other sources.

The intent of this scheme is clear. The workers covered are to receive not charity but the proceeds of a publicly administered fund to which they have themselves contributed. They are entitled to their annuities as a matter of *right*. In other words this is a plan whereby the earnings during active employment are spread over all of one's life, instead of coming to an end upon retirement. The law today covers between 70 and 80 per cent of the total labor force of the country, or about 45 million persons. The effect of 1954 legislation will be to add a large number of farmers, some professional people, and many of the self-employed—categories previously not covered. The principal categories of workers still excluded are farmers, members of the professions, and persons already covered by Federal, state, and local retirement systems. Railway workers are covered by the Railroad Retirement Act of 1934. About four million persons are now receiving benefits, the average monthly payments for single annuitants being about $41 and for families about $70. The system has not been in effect long enough for many of those covered to receive the maximum benefits. The trust fund out of which payments are made amounts now to something more than $13 billion, all of it invested in government securities. It seems altogether likely that, as obligations increase, the fund will be exhausted, and benefit payments under the various programs will be met by annual appropriations out of current taxes.

Unemployment Compensation

Undoubtedly the principal threat to security for the bulk of the working population is involuntary unemployment. In times of what is called full employment it is estimated that about 3 per cent of the labor force are out of work. In the catastrophe of 1930 to 1935 probably twelve million workers or nearly 20 per cent of the gainfully employed had no jobs. Accumulated savings could lighten the blow only to a small degree; after their exhaustion public or private charity was the only available recourse for the majority.

Public works programs could be regarded as only a stopgap which the public could not be expected to support indefinitely. A new policy was needed, one that would, if possible, make unemployment relief a part of the normal cost of doing business and therefore of the cost of living.

The administration of the unemployment-compensation system—often called "insurance"—is in the hands of the state governments. The national government makes no payments under it and does not dictate details as to coverage or state operation of the various systems. Theoretically the states are free to have a system or not as they see fit. All have been "induced" to accept the program by the device of the tax offset. This works as follows: The national government levies an excise tax of three per cent on the total payroll of all employers of more than eight workers, whether the state in which they operate has a compensation system or not. If a state comes into the program the employer need pay the national Treasury only ten per cent of the total owed under the three per cent tax, being credited with 90 per cent of the tax which is paid to the state government. Since if the state had no system the tax would be collected anyhow and used by the national government elsewhere, it is easy to understand why all the states have fallen in line. Funds collected within the states are kept in a national Unemployment Trust Fund, each state having its separate account. The national government pays all the expenses of administering the plan on the state level. The states are free to adopt whatever provisions they see fit as to the size of compensation payments, length of the period covered, and so forth. In view of this freedom of action there is considerable variety in the benefits permitted. Most states however provide for payments of at least $20 per week during involuntary unemployment, benefits running for at least 20 weeks. Workers covered are commonly required to accept suitable employment if available. They are disqualified if they leave their jobs without good cause, are discharged for sufficient reasons, or engage in labor disputes which cause work to cease. Although crooked practices have by no means been eliminated, the system seems to have been generally satisfactory. It must be said, however, that there has been no really adequate tests of its merits, employment having been at a high level almost ever since the introduction of the scheme.

Aid to Dependent Children

The death or incapacity of the breadwinner, especially when there are minor children, is an important aspect of modern family insecurity. The traditional way of caring for this situation was to send the children affected to orphanages or "boarding homes." There was often very little that was homelike about such institutions. By 1933 almost all the states had widows' or mothers' pension laws providing for various kinds of assistance to broken families, but provisions were often inadequate. A solution on a national

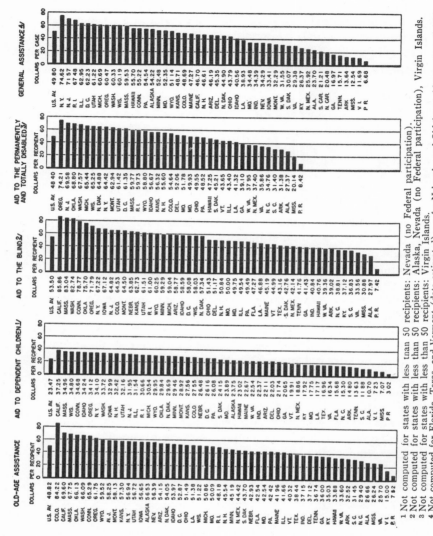

Fig. 7. Public assistance: average monthly payment, December, 1952 (exclusive of vendor payments for medical care and cases receiving only such payments). SOURCE: Social Security Administration, Bureau of Public Assistance, Division of Program Statistics and Analysis.

1 Not computed for states with less than 50 recipients: Nevada (no Federal participation).
2 Not computed for states with less than 50 recipients: Alaska, Nevada (no Federal participation), Virgin Islands.
3 Not computed for states with less than 50 recipients: Virgin Islands.
4 Not computed for Florida, Texas, and Vermont (data estimated) nor for Nebraska and Oklahoma (data not available).

scale was provided by the original Social Security Act of 1935. The national program allows payments to the states of three-quarters the amount paid up to $12 per month for each dependent child up to age sixteen (or eighteen if in school) and half of any additional amount up to $27 monthly. Children to the number of 1,600,000 in 630,000 families were being assisted in 1952. Average payments per family were nearly $75 per month and the total annual cost of the program exceeded half a billion dollars. The Social Security Act provided also for grants-in-aid to the states for a wide variety of services connected with maternal and child welfare. Benefits of this sort available under the act do not take the form of cash payments but consist of such assistance as the care of crippled and otherwise handicapped children, home nursing, treatment of infantile paralysis, and clinics for mothers and children. The administration of all the programs for mothers and dependent children is by local health and welfare agencies which are required to comply with rules and regulations imposed by the national government.

Aid to the Blind

People generally fear blindness so much that its victims have always called forth great public sympathy, and the various states have for many years made special provisions for their care and rehabilitation. Most of the state programs involve institutional care and occupational training. The Social Security Act introduced on a national scale the system of direct cash payments to the blind. The national government assists the states on a fifty-fifty basis up to a limit of $50 a month. Three states have elected to retain their own system for blind assistance. Of the other forty-five some go beyond the limit of $50, paying the excess from state funds. At present more than 97,000 persons are receiving benefits under the national act—about 40 per cent of all the blind in the country. Annual expenditures under the program total about $54 million and the average monthly payment to each recipient is about $47.

Aid to Permanently and Totally Disabled

The latest of the so-called "categorical" aids under "social security" was added late in 1950 with the inauguration of payments to the permanently and totally disabled. Probably a majority of the persons eligible for relief under this program had theretofore been receiving "general assistance"—that is, traditional "poor relief"—since they could not qualify for any of the other types of aid. "General assistance" is supplied almost wholly by local authorities, with no Federal and little state aid, and therefore provides only minimum relief. Federal payments for assistance to the permanently and totally disabled follow the same scheme as that in effect for old-age assistance. Latest available figures show that thirty-eight states have adopted the program and that slightly over 100,000 recipients are on the rolls. The average monthly payment is about $44.

The Administration of Social Security

The national program of social security is now administered by various bureaus and divisions within the Department of Health, Education, and Welfare. Supervision for all the programs except old age and survivors' insurance, which is wholly national, consists in the approval of state plans for each specialized program, as a necessary prerequisite for the allocation of Federal funds, and the routine oversight of state operations. Actual administration of benefits is in the hands of state and local officials. County and other agencies operate under the supervision of the state authority which has been approved by the appropriate supervising officials in Washington. State and local personnel must be chosen by some sort of merit system approved by the national department and are forbidden by national law to engage in political activity. While the national government has not hesitated to enforce its regulations in dealing with recalcitrant states, even to threatening to withdraw financial aid, the general policy has been to give the states the greatest possible latitude in developing programs fitted to their own needs and desires.

National Health Services

Under our constitutional system the national government has few direct responsibilities in the area of public health. Under the power to regulate foreign and interstate commerce and immigration Congress may institute measures to prevent the introduction and spread of disease, but beyond this it may enter the field only through its power to tax and spend for the general welfare. By virtue of this authority, however, the U.S. Public Health Service in the Department of Health, Education, and Welfare is responsible for a significant program of research in critical areas and for assistance to the states in disease-control programs and in the planning and construction of hospitals and health centers. Extensive programs of research in cancer control, tuberculosis, heart disease, and mental health are conducted at the National Institute of Health at Bethesda, Maryland, and their results are made available to the medical profession and local health authorities. Under the so-called Hill-Burton Act of 1946, nearly $150 million have been obligated or expended for the construction of hospitals and health centers intended primarily to extend medical and hospital services to areas hitherto lacking them. The U.S. Public Health Service supervises this program in cooperation with state and local hospital "authorities."

The most lively issue in the general field of public health is presented by the demand made in some quarters for a national health-insurance program to guarantee medical service to those now unable to pay for it. Many such schemes have been suggested, but they have in common national financial support and presumably some degree of control by the national government over the conduct of the medical profession. The appeal of such schemes is an obvious one not only to those with strong humanitarian impulses but also to those who on principle would extend farther the social services. On the other hand, it arouses the bitter opposition of a large section of the medical profession who quite naturally fear political control of their practice. Such schemes are labelled "socialistic" by their opponents and, while there is considerable vagueness about such adjectives, they are handy weapons in arguments of this sort.[2] It is not necessary to assume, as some do, that physicians are interested wholly in large fees, to know that modern medical care is costly and beyond the reach of many people. The cost of equipping and operating an efficient office or hospital and laboratory is very large and someone must pay for it. The doctors are not very different from other professional men in wishing to prevent the invasion of their "mystery" by uninformed laymen. It is, in fact, a marked development of our age that all occupational groups seek self-government and the protection of their vested interests.

Probably some extension of health services under public auspices is to be expected but in the current controversy it would seem the part of discretion for both sides to abate their extreme claims. That the public generally leans to moderation seems to be indicated by the rapid growth of private insurance schemes and the increase of medical and hospital benefits under labor contracts. The number of persons now partially protected by such schemes has been estimated to run as high as seventy million. The doctors would do well to support this tendency more vigorously, while the doctrinaire believers in the "welfare state" should consider that there may be a middle way. In any case, plans under private auspices would seem to fit best into our tradition of self-help, even though it must be remembered that many wage earners cannot be covered by such schemes.

The National Government and Education

The provision of formal instruction has always been regarded as a local and state responsibility and there has not been to date any significant national participation in it. There is, however, an Office of Education in the Department of Health, Education, and Welfare with certain functions of a promotional, consultative, and advisory nature. The Office supervises the expenditure of national and state funds in connection with programs

[2] In behalf of the official point of view of the organized medical profession, it should be said that the government's hospital program amounts to a public-health subsidy and that some 20 million veterans are now eligible for care at public expense. The doctors may reasonably argue that such things constitute a considerable installment of "socialism."

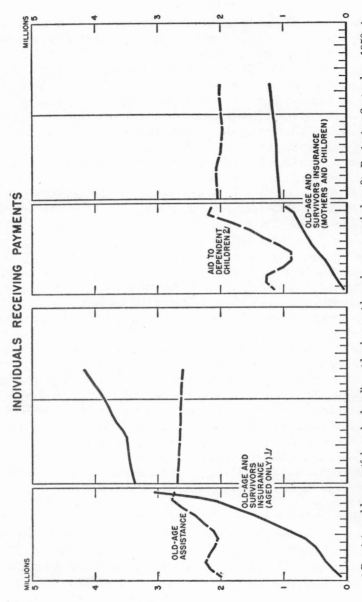

INDIVIDUALS RECEIVING PAYMENTS

¹ Receiving old-age, wife's or husband's, widow's or widower's, or parent's benefit. Beginning September, 1950, includes a small proportion of wife beneficiaries under age 65 with child beneficiaries in their care.

² Children plus one adult per family when adults are included in assistance group; before October, 1950, partly estimated.

406

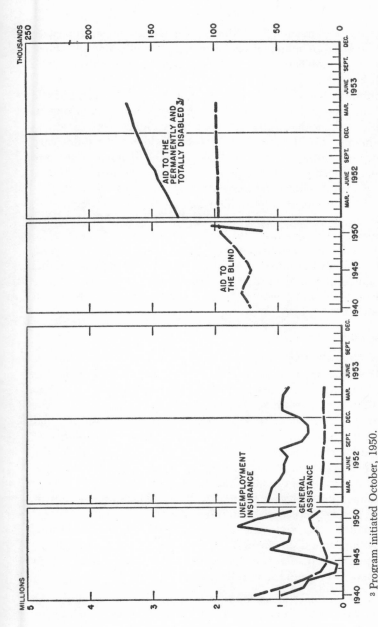

[3] Program initiated October, 1950.

FIG. 8. Individuals receiving payments. Old-age and survivors insurance: beneficiaries receiving monthly benefits (current-payment status), estimated for August, 1952; annual data represent average monthly number. Public assistance: monthly number of recipients under all state programs; annual data, average monthly number. Unemployment insurance: average weekly number of beneficiaries for the month under all state laws; annual data, average weekly number for the year.

SOURCE: *Social Security Bulletin*, July, 1953, Social Security Administration.

of vocational education and rehabilitation conducted in cooperation with the states, but otherwise confines itself largely to the collection of educational statistics and to advising state and local authorities with respect to educational problems.

Although national influence on education is now small, there can be little doubt that it will increase. For some years pressure has been strong to secure national grants for the support of elementary and secondary education. The argument here is that the local districts and even the states vary so widely in taxable resources that only by national financial assistance can educational opportunities be equalized among the nearly 100,000 districts now operating schools. The Senate has twice passed a bill providing for the distribution of $300 million among the states. Opposition growing out of religious and racial issues has so far prevented the adoption of such a scheme, but when ways to compromise these differences are found some such scheme is certain to be adopted. The national government will then have wide opportunities to mold in subtle ways the educational system of the entire nation, even though formal controls are likely to be few and weak in view of the well-organized opposition of teachers and school administrators.

Social Security and the Courts

The first question asked of all novel legislation in the United States is not whether it is wise or desirable but whether it is constitutional. The social-security program involved such apparently sharp departures from settled policy that this question seemed a particularly touchy one at the time the original act was passed in 1935. It was feared, for example, that the special payroll taxes might be outlawed by the same reasoning that had cast doubt upon the validity of the processing taxes levied under the Agricultural Adjustment Act. It was also argued in some quarters that the national government was coercing the states in fields traditionally "belonging" to those units, and that the "general welfare" clause of the Constitution could not justify such coercion and invasion.

These fears and doubts were set at rest, however, in two decisions rendered by the Supreme Court in 1937. In upholding the unemployment-compensation program, Justice Cardozo, after stating that from 1929 to 1936 the unemployed averaged ten million, said: [3]

Disaster to the breadwinner meant disaster to dependents. Accordingly the roll of the unemployed, itself formidable enough, was only a partial roll of the destitute and needy. The fact developed quickly that the states were unable to give the requisite relief. The problem had become national in area and dimensions. There was need of help from the nation if the people were not to starve. It is too late today for the argument to be heard with tolerance that in a crisis

[3] *Steward Machine Co. v. Davis,* 301 U.S. 548 (1937).

so extreme the use of the moneys of the nation to relieve the unemployed and their dependents is a use for any purpose narrower than the promotion of the general welfare.

That portion of the social-security program having to do with assistance to the aged was sustained by much the same reasoning. The Court held that unemployment and indigence might be caused by the disabilities of age as well as by the absence of work to do: "Rescue becomes necessary," it said, "irrespective of the cause. The hope behind this statute is to save men and women from the rigors of the poorhouse as well as from the haunting fear that such a lot awaits them. . . ." To the argument that the national statute invaded the legitimate preserves of the states the answer of the Court was decisive: [4]

"The issue is a closed one. It was fought out long ago. When money is spent to promote the general welfare, the concept of welfare or the opposite is shaped by Congress, not the states. So the concept be not arbitrary the locality must yield."

Although it is clear that the reasoning of the Court was to some extent based upon the existence of a crisis, there is no doubt that these decisions place beyond question the national power to institute and maintain a system of social security generally.

Social Security and the American Tradition

The adoption of the social-security program marks a new epoch in the development of American ideas about the proper role of government in human affairs. To a new interest in the more adequate care of the ill, the aged, the blind, and the orphan has been added a widespread conviction that government should guarantee a minimum of security to all citizens who have not been able to acquire it through their own efforts. This is a far cry from the traditional creed of individualism which assumed quite bluntly that "every tub should stand on its own bottom" and that men had only themselves to blame if they failed to acquire financial independence. This was a gambler's "psychology" and, as we see it now, it produced millionaires and paupers without reference to the deserts of its victims and its darlings. Although this individualism, on any showing, was responsible for much that was callous in human relations, it may even now not be out of place to recall the comment of a distinguished English student of political thought: "Energy, self-reliance, and independence, a strong conviction that a man's fate should depend upon his own character and conduct, are qualities without which no nation can be great." [5] A hu-

[4] *Helvering v. Davis*, 301 U.S. 619 (1937).
[5] Leslie Stephen, *The English Utilitarians*, Vol. I, p. 131.

manitarianism which attributes every misfortune to "social" causes needs to be reminded of the truth contained in this statement. Even though it be admitted that, in a world full of impersonal forces, misfortune is less and less predictable, the question as to whether a population centering its attention on security has not lost some of its virtue is a fair one. Life, to have zest and interest, must have some elements of danger.

The historian Gibbon believed that the happiest and most prosperous period in human history was the second century of the Christan era when the world was under the benevolent autocracy of the Antonines. But even from the point of view of social efficiency there was something lacking. "The long peace and uniform government of the Romans," wrote Gibbon,[6] "introduced a slow poison into the vitals of the empire, the minds of men were gradually reduced to the same level, the fire of genius was extinguished, and even the military spirit evaporated," and, finally, "the rich and polite Italians, who had almost universally embraced the philosophy of Epicurus, enjoyed the present blessings of ease and tranquillity, and suffered not the pleasant dream to be interrupted by the memory of their old tumultuous freedom."

It would be both fanciful and alarmist to argue that the American system of social security as so far developed is liberal enough to remove the need or desire for individual effort. Such a system is in fact the logical product of an industrialization which has so completely divorced men from the soil as to make them wholly dependent upon forces which they have no real possibility of bending to their own advantage. The industrial worker and the propertyless man of our great cities simply cannot fend for themselves in the world which mechanical power has created for them. More practically, the demand for *some* shelter against the hazards of indigent old age, catastrophic illness, and unemployment is now so insistent that no party or politician can successfully ignore it. The dangers to individual liberty which many see in a program of social security are, however, not yet imminent. No one can live either affluently or irresponsibly on an old age pension or an assistance check of $45 a month, nor will the unemployed be tempted to extend the period of idleness in order to receive compensation at the rate of $20 a week.

On the other hand, one need not be a "mossback" to suggest that all schemes aimed at increasing payments beyond a modest scale should be scrutinized with care. Something can and should be done by government to soften the most cruel blows of chance and circumstance; but the only real security available to man lies in those areas of faith and serenity of mind where runs the writ of no earthly king. A wise public policy, and one in line with our tradition, would lay stress upon private and semiprivate

[6] Edward Gibbon, *Decline and Fall of the Roman Empire* (Modern Library edition), Vol. I, pp. 50–51, 53.

schemes under which individual incentive may be preserved and men may feel that they are in some real sense in charge of their own lives.

Some final reflections may not be out of place. A conception of the general welfare which requires the state to guarantee a national minimum of security below which no one is to fall is undoubtedly in part the result of the growth in humanitarian sentiment. Even more important, however, have been the parts played by democracy and nationalism. In countries where all adults may vote, those public policies are most widely popular which seem to guarantee material benefits. This is true because the emphasis in a democracy is certain to be upon those things which the "average" citizen can understand. And nothing is so universally understood as money! There are many critics, however, who feel that the desire for security, far from being the result of the growth of democracy, is evidence of a weakening of our faith in it. Such people argue that democracy can do no more than guarantee freedom to the individual in seeking ends which seem worthwhile to him. This sort of freedom, the argument runs, necessarily involves our making wrong and even disastrous choices, from the consequences of which no government can rescue us. If, then, no government can guarantee anything beyond a risky freedom in the adventure of living, it follows that all attempts to guarantee more will mean giving our rulers power enough to crush even *that* freedom, and thus to put an end to democracy itself. The "security" offered to citizens in Germany and Italy by their recent dictators or, at present, by the rulers of Russia, is surely bought at an exorbitant price.

After full allowance has been made for the influence of humanitarianism and democracy, the fact remains that social-security legislation is one aspect of our growing nationalism, evidences of which are to be found in every part of our community life. It is a commonplace to say that we live in a dangerous world in which genuine internationalism has a precarious existence. Our present difficulties with the Soviet Union are frequently described as stemming from different ideologies—communism on the one hand and what is called the "American way" on the other. This is at best an oversimplification, for surely it is of more than passing significance that in the minds of many the best defense of our free institutions seems to lie in the adoption of social policies which, it is alleged, can do better for us what the Russians say communism can do for them! If this were all there was to the struggle, one would have to admit that we are assailing the enemy with his own weapons. But the real parties to the conflict are, as of old, nations, not simply creeds, except as creeds serve the usual purpose of strengthening the sinews of a nation. To a nation struggling for survival victory seems to depend upon military and industrial efficiency. That sort of efficiency seems to be promoted by a contented labor force and by a population convinced, by the promise of security, of the beneficence of its rulers' purposes. In short, nationalism seems everywhere to end in something like "socialism" no matter what the official creed may be.

Humane sentiments and a livelier sense of interdependence among classes and individuals are thus harnessed to the ends of the state—ends which may or may not be consistent with the highest human goals. Now the legitimate goals of living are as various as the individuals who pursue them, and democracy as we have known it in the past assumes that no ruler or group of rulers is wise enough to set those goals once and for all. The provision of the social services described here requires a powerful government, and it may well be that such a government may come to have ends hostile to the citizens' deepest aspirations. This is no argument for a do-nothing state any more than it it an apology for the misdeeds of corporate wealth or of ambitious political and labor leaders. It is only to suggest that all power is suspect and to be granted to no one on the ground that such a grant is the necessary price for a security which, in an uncertain world, is at best but an illusion.

REFERENCES

Grace Abbott, *From Relief to Social Security* (1941).

H. P. Allen, *The Federal Government and Education* (1950).

George W. Bachman and Lewis Meriam, *The Issue of Compulsory Health Insurance* (1948).

Charles A. Beard, *Public Policy and the General Welfare* (1941).

Eveline M. Burns, *The American Social Security System* (1949).

Karl De Schweinitz, *People and Process in Social Security* (1948).

Paul H. Douglas, *Social Security in the United States* (1939).

Abraham Epstein, *Insecurity: A Challenge to America* (1938).

Lewis Meriam, *The Cost and Financing of Social Security* (1950).

CHAPTER 24

The Role of the United States in World Affairs

The Policy of "Isolation"

For more than a century after the establishment of the American Republic, the official policy of our government was one of aloofness from the affairs of other nations. There were a number of reasons for this attitude. In the first place, a republic in a world of kingdoms and empires was something new and precarious and the United States had all it could do to demonstrate that such a state deserved to survive. The energies of our public men were completely absorbed in the work of converting republican government into a going concern and they had little time or taste for international adventures in the familiar pattern of European diplomacy.

In the second place, the people of the United States had ample outlet for their energy in the conquest of a continent and in the "politics" which that conquest involved. The affairs of Europe were far away and seemed to have little bearing upon our own future. The politics of internal expansion, involving, as they did, the creation of new states, relations with the Indians, the construction of public improvements, and the management of the vast public domain, were difficult enough to keep busy several generations of politicians. Furthermore, Europe *was* a long way off, in view of the modes of communication prevailing until the mid-nineteenth century, and what came to be called "isolationism" was more or less dictated by the factor of distance alone.

Finally, it may as well be admitted that a policy of isolation· accorded well with the concepts Americans had both of themselves and öf Europeans. As to our view of ourselves, the myth had rapidly taken form that America stood for the time-honored virtues of republican simplicity, honesty, forthrightness, and purity; Europeans, or at any rate European politicians, were believed to be oversuave in their manners, devious in their methods, and corrupt in character. There are echoes of this historic view in the scorn with which the "average" American even now speaks of the "striped pants" of the diplomat, the implication being that formal wear of this sort, obviously a fashion that originated abroad, is somehow sinister. The fact that this view was a gross oversimplification of both politics and morals did not keep it from being effective among the people and eventually with officials.

As a matter of fact, those portions of Washington's Farewell Address dealing with foreign affairs, the first statement of something like "isolationism," are in a sense rationalizations of this attitude:

> The great rule of conduct for us in regard to foreign nations is in extending our commercial relations to have with them as little *political* connection as possible. So far as we have already formed engagements let them be fulfilled with perfect good faith. Here let us stop.
>
> Europe has a set of primary interests which to us have none or a very remote relation. Hence she must be engaged in frequent controversies, the causes of which are essentially foreign to our concerns. Hence, therefore, it must be unwise in us to implicate ourselves by artificial ties in the ordinary vicissitudes of her politics or the ordinary combinations and collisions of her friendships or enmities. . . .

This policy of isolation did not, of course, preserve us from all contacts with foreign nations or even from conflicts. We came close to war with France only a year after Washington retired from office and we actually fought a war with Great Britain in 1812. As an official policy, isolation may be said to date from the publication of the Monroe Doctrine in 1823, and for three-quarters of a century thereafter we were actually little involved in international politics. Victory in the Spanish War of 1898, however, revealed us as too powerful to be ignored by other nations while, it must be admitted, it tempted us to "play a role" in world affairs. We were inevitably involved in World War I, and, although Woodrow Wilson's activities in founding the League of Nations seemed likely for a time to usher in a period of internationalism, the failure of the Senate to support him meant a relapse into isolationism which did not end until our participation in World War II.

In this chapter a brief synopsis will be given of the control of foreign policy in the United States, a matter which has been touched upon in the chapters dealing with Congress and the executive department, and attention will be given to the content of our foreign policies. It is important for the student to have some knowledge of our past policies in order that he may understand the present. Most emphasis, however, will be given to United States foreign policy since 1900, for in this period a revolution has occurred in American diplomacy. From a weak and secondary role in world affairs, the United States has been catapulted into the role of leadership.

Control and Shaping of Foreign Policy

The President. Many agencies of the Federal government have a hand in controlling and shaping foreign policy. The President is made responsible by the Constitution for the conduct of our relations with foreign nations. The late President William Howard Taft held that the President has the sole power to negotiate. He made this important point after certain leaders had challenged the right of Woodrow Wilson to initiate the Versailles Treaty, which included the Covenant of the League of Nations. It is true, however, that all treaties and agreements within the meaning of the Constitution of the United States must be ratified by the Senate.

In 1799 John Marshall said, "The President is the sole organ of the nation in its external relations, and its sole representative with foreign nations." That the President is the agent through whom all communications with foreign nations are to go was what Marshall had in mind. Thomas Jefferson took the same position in a letter to the French diplomat Genet:

As the President is the only channel of communications between the United States and foreign nations, it is from him alone that foreign nations or their agents are to learn what is or has been the will of the nation, and whatever he communicates as such they have a right and are bound to consider as the expression of the nation, and no foreign agent can be allowed to question it.

Not only does the President initiate treaties but he also carries them out when approved. He may also enter into executive agreements which do not require the approval of the Senate. In recent years extensive use has been made of executive agreements, often for matters of great importance which formerly were the subject of formal treaties. The Open Door policy of 1900 was an executive pronouncement. Indeed, our Far Eastern policy up to World War II was built up on executive agreements. Before the United States entered World War II, President Franklin D. Roosevelt made an agreement with Great Britain whereby fifty American destroyers were exchanged for air bases in British territory. Several other notable agreements, including Teheran and Yalta, were made by President Roosevelt. The latter agreement has resulted in a bitter controversy, the Roosevelt critics charging that he yielded concessions to Russia in Southern Sakhalin, Mongolia, and Manchuria which led directly to Russian domination of China.

The Secretary of State. Communications with foreign countries are carried on by the State Department. The Secretary of State and the Department of State constitute "the right arm of the President in the conduct of international relations." The roles of Congress, the President, the Department of State, and other executive agencies were described very aptly and concisely by Secretary of State Dean Acheson when he said: [1]

---

[1] *Our Foreign Policy*, Department of State Publication 3972, pp. 20–21.

The President lays down what the policy shall be. In many cases the Congress lays down what the policy shall be. The President may propose and the Congress dispose but the State Department has the job of foreseeing a problem before it arises. It gets all the other agencies in the Executive Branch together to make a proposal. It gets the President's approval, or modification, and then takes it up with the Congress through the House and Senate committees, and moves it forward to some final action in the government. Therefore, the State Department is a sort of activator in the center of the government.

The State Department serves as "the eyes and ears" of the government. It is represented abroad by 300 missions in 75 countries and the routine reports from these missions supply the Department with information essential to the formulation of a realistic policy. In some administrations the Secretary of State has played a very important part in the initiation and shaping of foreign policy. This was true of such men as Thomas Jefferson, Hamilton Fish, John Hay, and Charles Evans Hughes, all of whom were outstanding secretaries. The President, however, usually gives close attention to foreign affairs, and in some instances has taken the direction of foreign policies into his own hands, as did Wilson when Lansing was Secretary of State.

Other Executive and Administrative Agencies. Most of the agencies of the Federal government are involved to some extent in foreign relations. They work together through a number of joint committees and subcommittees that study and advise on matters of foreign policy. Defense, Treasury, Commerce, and Agriculture, to name only a few, play a conspicuous part in foreign relations.

Congress. Both houses of Congress play a part in determining the foreign policies of the country by passing laws affecting foreign relations and by voting the necessary funds. The role of the Senate, however, is far greater than that of the House. The framers of the Constitution evidently expected that the Senate would act as a council to the President in the conduct of foreign relations. He was given the power to make treaties "by and with the advice and consent of the Senate," and the concurrence of two-thirds of the Senators present was required. When Washington attempted to consult with the Senate as a body over some Indian treaties, however, the Senate insisted on referring the matter to a committee, and Washington angrily strode out of the chamber, declaring that he would never return on a similar mission. He found it preferable instead to consult informally with the leaders. This practice has been followed ever since. If the President fails to consult with the leaders of the Senate about an important treaty which is being negotiated, the treaty stands in danger of being subsequently rejected. Occasionally the Senate has added crippling reservations to treaties, as, for example, the provisions for compulsory arbitration added to the Hay treaties.[2] In this instance, as well as in some others, the Senate reservations caused the treaties to be set aside. Profiting by Woodrow Wilson's experience with the League of Nations treaty in 1919, Franklin D. Roosevelt appointed the ranking members of both parties on the Foreign Relations Committee of the Senate and the Foreign Affairs Committee of the House to serve on our delegation at San Francisco in 1945, when the United Nations Charter was framed.[3] As a result, the Charter was ratified with little opposition in the Senate.

The appointments of ambassadors and other diplomatic agents must be confirmed by the Senate. This is another important role that the Senate plays in foreign affairs.

The Senate Foreign Relations Committee exerts considerable influence in shaping our foreign policies. Occasionally a strong chairman of this powerful committee may be almost as, if not more, important than the Secretary of State. William E. Borah and Arthur H. Vandenberg were chairmen of this type.

Both houses of Congress may initiate foreign policies by joint resolution. Notable examples are the Fulbright and Connally Resolutions in 1943. The Fulbright Resolution was introduced in the House by Representative Fulbright of Arkansas, and was concurred in by the Senate. Senator Connally, the chairman of the Senate Committee on Foreign Relations, sponsored the second resolution, which was passed by the Senate only. These resolutions put Congress on record as favoring participation of the United States in an international organization designed to outlaw war.

The control of the purse also gives Congress control over foreign policy. Money can be appropriated only by Congress. In order to implement the Truman Doctrine, the Marshall Plan, the Point Four program, and the North Atlantic Treaty Organization, many billions of dollars were required and Congress had to approve of the policies involved in order for the money to be made available.

The People. In the last place, the people have much to do with the formulation and control of foreign policy. When rejection of the Treaty of Versailles, including the covenant of the League of Nations, appeared imminent in 1919, President Wilson decided to tour the West to secure public support for his program. It was on this tour that the President's health broke down and the last speaking engagements had to be canceled. Had the President been in robust health, his appeal to the people over the heads of the Senate might have been successful. Although Wilson said the elec-

[2] The Hay treaties, between the United States and a number of nations, including England and France, were concluded in 1903.

[3] While negotiations were under way on the treaty with Japan, concluded in 1951, Mr. Dulles, our special ambassador, consulted frequently with members of the Senate.

tion of 1920 would be a solemn referendum on the Covenant of the League, it is very doubtful whether that issue played much of a part in the landslide victory of Warren Harding, whose position on the League was not very clear.

The people may make themselves heard on foreign policy in many ways. Through telegrams and letters to members of Congress, as well as to the State Department, the people may exert a direct influence on foreign policy. Through civic, educational, and religious organizations and the media of radio and newspapers, the people may communicate indirectly with the government and bring pressure to bear on those responsible for foreign policy. Certainly the people were given an opportunity to express themselves when plans were being made for a United Nations organization and they responded.

Internal Expansion and Foreign Policy

While during most of our history we Americans have proclaimed devotion to an aloofness from international politics, we have never been averse to using diplomacy in order to enlarge our territory. In fact, successive additions to our national holdings gave rise to one of our distinctive patriotic slogans, that of "manifest destiny." By this was meant that the United States was destined by nature or by the Almighty's own purpose to occupy the entire continent, thus spreading the blessings of self-government among the subjects of less-favored nations on our borders. The Revolution, while successful in ousting Great Britain from the area east of the Mississippi River, left us hemmed in to the west and south by the territories of the Spanish monarchy. As an incident of the Napoleonic Wars the vast and ill-defined territory known as Louisiana passed into the hands of the French. Napoleon, finding it difficult to defend such distant possessions and in need of cash, suddenly offered to sell all of Louisiana to the United States. Although President Jefferson had doubts at first about his constitutional authority to acquire territory by treaty, he overcame them, and the treaty of cession was approved both by the Senate and by the public. The area of the United States was more than doubled by this purchase. A few years later in 1819, President Monroe acquired by treaty the remaining Spanish possessions in Florida.

The chief official propagandist of manifest destiny was President James K. Polk. Polk had been elected in 1844 partly because of his demand for the annexation of Texas, formerly a province of Mexico but since 1836 an independent republic. His success in accomplishing this annexation led in time to the war with Mexico, and the spoils of victory for the United States were California, Arizona, New Mexico, and parts of half a dozen other Western states. It was in connection with Polk's advocacy of the annexation of Texas and the acquisition of the Oregon Territory (the latter in spite of the claims of the British) that he elaborated the theory of manifest destiny. Defending the expansion of the United States, he said:

Our Union is a confederation of independent states, whose policy is peace with each other and all the world. To enlarge its limits is to extend the dominion of peace over additional territories and increasing millions.

In regard to Oregon he spoke these words in his Inaugural Address:

Nor will it become in a less degree my duty to assert and maintain by all constitutional means the right of the United States to that portion of our territory which lies beyond the Rocky Mountains. Our title to the country of the Oregon is "clear and unquestionable" and already are our people preparing to effect that title by occupying it with their wives and children. But eight years ago our population was confined on the west by the ridge of the Alleghenies. Within that period—within the lifetime, I might say, of some of my hearers—our people, increasing to many millions, have filled the eastern valley of the Mississippi, adventurously ascended the Missouri to its headsprings, and are already engaged in establishing the blessings of self-government in valleys of which the rivers flow to the Pacific.

A few months later, in his first annual message to Congress, he announced that the people of the United States cannot view with indifference attempts of European powers "to interfere with the independent action of the nations of this continent" and went on to say that any nation of the North American continent was free to join the American Union.

Development of the Monroe Doctrine

While the views expressed by Polk in these utterances merely supplied the official reasons for internal expansion, they were not without significance in our future relations with nations across the Atlantic. One of their important effects was to prepare the public mind for later forceful interpretations of the Monroe Doctrine. That doctrine, proclaimed by Monroe in his annual message to Congress in 1823, was our government's reaction to Spain's plan to recover her lost possessions in this hemisphere. It was not aggressive in tone but expressed rather a policy of defense. Monroe's statement set forth three principles as controlling American policy toward the states of Latin America: (1) from this time on the American continents were no longer "to be considered as subjects for future colonization by any European powers"; (2) any attempt on the part of European powers to extend their system to any portion of this hemisphere would be considered as "dangerous to our peace and safety"; (3) the United States itself would neither interfere with the existing situation in the states of the Western Hemisphere nor meddle in European affairs.

The Monroe Doctrine, in short, was issued from the highest of motives and was almost universally popular. It stated simply that, while we had no designs for expansion in the territories once owned by Spain, we would not stand idly by and see the new states of Latin America reduced again to the status of colonies. It can only be regarded as unfortunate that Polk, in furtherance of his aim of "rounding out" our continental possessions, used the sort of smug language which would keep alive an expansionist psychology capable of justifying adventures *beyond* our borders. For arguments which could be used with reasonableness to extend our authority over immediately adjacent territory stand on a different footing when used to justify adventures elsewhere.

One incident may serve to illustrate the possibilities inherent in the attitude expressed by Polk. In 1895 Great Britain and Venezuela became involved in a boundary dispute in the course of which Venezuela asked for the protection of the United States, alleging that the British were attempting to expand their holdings in South America. The American Secretary of State, Richard T. Olney, compelled the British to submit the matter to arbitration. Said Olney,[4] with a memorable truculence,

Today the United States is practically sovereign on this continent, and its fiat is law upon the subjects to which it confines its interposition. Why? It is not because of the pure friendship or good will felt for it. It is not simply by reason of its high character as a civilized state, nor because wisdom and justice and equity are the invariable characteristics of the dealings of the United States. It is because, in addition to all other grounds, its infinite resources combined with its isolated position render it master of the situation and practically invulnerable against any or all other powers.

The new status attained by the United States as a result of the successful war with Spain in 1898 tempted us as a new great power to make our influence felt in the councils of the nations. President Theodore Roosevelt proclaimed in 1904 and 1905 what came to be known as the Roosevelt Corollary to the Monroe Doctrine. In 1902 Great Britain, Germany, and Italy had blockaded the coast of Venezuela in order to force that country to meet obligations owed to their citizens. By a show of force Roosevelt compelled arbitration of the claims against Venezuela. The gist of the Roosevelt Corollary was that, while the United States would not tolerate intervention by European nations in the affairs of Latin America, it would itself intervene if necessary to protect the lives and property of citizens of other countries if they were threatened by turbulence in Latin America. At the same time Roosevelt disavowed any imperialistic intentions, saying,

It must be understood that under no circumstances will the United States use the Monroe Doctrine as a cloak for territorial aggression. We desire peace with all the world, but perhaps most of all with the other peoples of the American continent.

[4] Samuel F. Bemis, *The American Secretaries of State*, Vol. VIII, p. 306, 1928.

Notwithstanding this disavowal, concurrently with the announcement of the Roosevelt Corollary the United States set up what amounted to protectorates over two Latin American nations. By the Platt Amendment to a treaty with Cuba in 1903 that nation conceded to the United States the right "to intervene for the preservation of Cuban independence, the maintenance of a government adequate for the protection of life, property, and individual liberty." In the same year the new Republic of Panama, whose revolt from its parent state of Colombia we had encouraged, entered into a treaty which made it a virtual protectorate of the United States, so serious were the limitations on its sovereignty thought necessary to protect the Panama Canal.

During the next generation American intervention in Latin American affairs was frequent and often drastic. For one reason or another we imposed our will upon Santo Domingo, Haiti, and Nicaragua, and, during the administration of Woodrow Wilson, military action only formally short of war was taken against Mexico. General Smedley Butler of the Marine Corps was on one occasion during this period moved to say that he was tired of these expeditions "to collect the bad debts of Wall Street" and many Americans by no means "radical" in their customary outlook deplored what came to be called "dollar diplomacy." It is little wonder that Latin American leaders made "Yankee imperialism" a perennial issue in local politics or that popular resentment was deep-seated and strong against the "Colossus of the North." In the United States itself, while minorities opposed our policy, it may as well be admitted that it was strongly supported by business and agricultural interests eager for new markets and investment opportunities.

The trend in the direction of imposing our will upon our weaker neighbors to the south was not to be reversed until the adoption of the so-called Good Neighbor policy—first announced by President Hoover but carried into effect by Franklin D. Roosevelt and his Secretary of State, Cordell Hull. At the Pan-American Conference held in Montevideo in December, 1933, the United States agreed to put an end to intervention. In 1934 the restrictions embodied in the Platt Amendment were dropped from a new treaty with Cuba, while the sovereignty of Panama was formally recognized the same year. Finally, at a special Pan-American Conference held in Buenos Aires in December, 1936, the Monroe Doctrine was formally made multilateral, all the American nations agreeing to uphold it. Although these belated acts of justice have by no means healed old wounds, we are now probably as little suspected as could be the case considering the differences in resources and power which set us apart from the smaller nations of the hemisphere.

The United States and the Far East

The defeat of Spain and our acquisition of the Philippine Islands made us a power to be reckoned with in the Far East. Long before the end of the nineteenth century we had had, of course, trade relations with both China and Japan, and for that reason were involved in the politics of commerce along with European nations long active in eastern and southeastern Asia. Our first important diplomatic move in the Orient in the new century was the promulgation of the so-called Open Door policy in 1900. This has often been thought of as embodying strictly idealistic purposes, whereas its objectives were quite materialistic. The author of the policy was Secretary of State John Hay, a man deeply disillusioned about politics and human nature in general and not likely to be greatly influenced by humanitarian motives. Both Great Britain and the United States were concerned about the carving up of China into spheres of political influence and preferential trade areas by the various European powers. Among these were France, Germany, and Russia—besides those powers, such as Great Britain herself, Portugal, and Japan, who had already long enjoyed special privileges in China. At the urging of the British government Hay dispatched a circular letter to Great Britain, Russia, France, and Japan containing three principles on which he sought agreement among the powers:

1. [That each power] will in no way interfere with any treaty port or any vested interest within any so-called "sphere of interest" or leased territory it may have in China.
2. That the Chinese treaty tariff of the time being shall apply to all merchandise landed or shipped to all such ports as are within said "sphere of interest" (unless they be "free ports"), no matter to what nationality it may belong, and that duties so leviable shall be collected by the Chinese government.
3. That it will levy no higher harbor dues on vessels of another nationality frequenting any port in such "sphere" than shall be levied on vessels of its own nationality, and no higher railroad charges over lines built, controlled, or operated within its "sphere" on merchandise belonging to citizens or subjects of other nationalities transported through such "sphere" than shall be levied on similar merchandise belonging to its own nationals.

These proposals were agreed to by Great Britain and Germany and were accepted by Japan and Italy on condition that other powers did so. Russia remained silent. In a note issued in March, 1900, Hay took it for granted that all the powers had agreed, in spite of the continued silence of Russia. While one purpose of the Open Door policy was undoubtedly the highly moral one of preserving the territorial integrity and administrative freedom of China, surely an equally important one was to ensure equal access by all nations to the trade opportunities of that ancient land. Actually the policy was a mere statement of these purposes, no power promising to do anything to see that they were enforced.

That trade interests rather than concern for Chinese independence were of first importance to the powers involved was made evident by the later history of the Open Door policy. Thus in 1908 Japan confirmed her acceptance of the policy in the Root-Takahira Agreement with the United States. That agreement guaranteed "equal opportunity for commerce and industry in China" and the "integrity and independence" of that country. It is vital to note, however, that this confirmation came only after Japan had gained recognition of her special interests in Manchuria and China by secret agreement with Russia. A few years later China was compelled to accede to the famous Twenty-one Demands of Japan—one of them involving control over certain Chinese provinces—no other power being willing to back her in resisting them. Two years later Japan and the United States joined in reaffirming the Open Door policy, the United States on its part, however, recognizing the "special interests" of Japan in China. The recognition of these "special interests" on our part amounted to acknowledging the legitimacy of a Japanese Monroe Doctrine for eastern Asia.

Critics of our foreign policy have insisted that we were unrealistic in our grudging and delayed recognition of the "special interests" of Japan in China and Manchuria. The argument is that in view of our comparatively unimportant interests in eastern Asia, it was unwise to risk the enmity of Japan by blocking, allegedly in the name of high moral principles, her efforts to develop China. George Kennan, for example, contends that a more realistic attitude could have avoided war with Japan and that a strong Japan would have been an effective bulwark against rising communism in the Far East.[5] A part of such criticism is based perhaps on the superior wisdom of hindsight; in any case it may not give weight enough to the fact that the American public likes to think that its officials are moved by high moral notions, even though those officials themselves realize that diplomacy must deal with considerations of physical power. In any event the Open Door policy was pretty effectively abandoned by the Yalta Agreement in 1945 by which we in our turn recognized the "special interests" of Russia in Mongolia and Manchuria.[6]

The End of Isolation

Complete isolation had never, of course, been the actual policy of the United States. Even when we were a second-rate power in comparison with the great nations of Europe, some degree of involvement in their affairs was from time to time acknowledged by those in charge of our foreign policy. It is beyond doubt true, however, that most of our people, if they thought about the matter at all, approved of "going it alone." Our own

[5] *American Diplomacy, 1900–1950*, pp. 46–54, University of Chicago Press, Chicago, 1951.

[6] Felix Morley, *The Foreign Policy of the United States*, Alfred A. Knopf, Inc., New York, 1950.

internal affairs were continental in scope and sufficient in their persistent urgency and difficulty to occupy our attention and energies. Although our own internal problems were comparable in difficulty and importance to those that plagued the various chancelleries of Europe, we did not look upon them as diplomatic in character, reserving the word "diplomacy" to describe operations conducted by scheming foreigners corrupted by living in a society morally inferior to our own. Our public men were more sophisticated than this, of course, but did their best to pretend that successive international involvements were somehow temporary and unfortunate departures from the sound policy of self-sufficiency.

After the beginning of the twentieth century only perverseness could preserve this comforting view of the facts of international life. The easy victory over a weak but gallant enemy in 1898 revealed not only that we had significant military power but, even more important, that that power rested upon an industrial system fast reaching maturity. The resulting power to make war successfully marked the United States as one of the great powers—a great power being by definition one capable of fighting. It was inevitable that in any future European or Asiatic war the power that dominated the Western Hemisphere and was in a position to block the sea lanes of the Pacific would be cultivated by both sides. And so came about American participation in two world wars. Whatever the issues at stake in these conflicts, it was assumed on all sides that they could be settled by the application of sufficient force. Since we were on the winning side in both wars and emerged with our military and industrial power largely unimpaired in a world incredibly impoverished and weakened, leadership seemed to be our destiny.

The first effort to exercise this leadership was marked by a recrudescence of American idealism. As spokesman for the Allied and Associated Powers at the end of World War I President Wilson led the fight for a League of Nations which he hoped would be the instrument through which order might be brought into a world of sovereign states. The League idea reflected the notion of the average American that the same kind of overarching law that has mastered anarchy here should and could be made effective among the nations. Wilson was successful at the Versailles Peace Conference and the unwary came to believe that an era of internationalism was about to open. The United States Senate, however, expressed decisively the other side of American thinking—fear and distrust of the foreigner, and prevented our joining the League. Without our participation—and this is a measure of our importance as a power—the League had few triumphs in preserving peace, and came to concern itself for the most part with matters which did not affect the prestige or the "national honor" of its members.

The lapse into isolationism which followed rejection of League membership was short-lived. Within three years after the repudiation of the League, a belligerent dictatorship was installed in Italy, and ten years later an even more belligerent and vastly more efficient one came to power in Germany. These regimes posed such threats to the whole way of life of Western Europe that armed resistance by France and Great Britain ushered in a second world war in 1939.

The United States and the Second World War

Almost immediately after the outbreak of World War II the United States began to move away from the policy of neutrality which it had proclaimed a few years earlier. Before the end of 1939 our neutrality acts were amended so as to permit the sale of war materials to any nation that would pay for them and carry them away in their own vessels. In practice this favored Great Britain, which still was strong enough to control the Atlantic and prevent her enemies from taking advantage of our laws. About a year later President Franklin Roosevelt entered into an executive agreement with Great Britain under which we gave to the British fifty destroyers in exchange for leases on British territories on this side of the Atlantic. Within a few months of this agreement, Great Britain and her allies having exhausted their credits in this country, Congress passed the Lend-Lease Act under the terms of which we agreed to provide military supplies without any definite commitment as to payment, the President simply being authorized to allocate such supplies to any nation whose war efforts could be construed as protecting the essential interests of this country. All these acts made the United States virtually a belligerent throughout 1940. The Japanese attack on our fleet in Pearl Harbor on December 7, 1941, brought us into the war as a full-fledged, and senior, partner.

Prior to our formal entry into the war President Roosevelt and Prime Minister Churchill announced the war aims of the two countries in a document known as the Atlantic Charter. Since this agreement outlines policies which we have presumably not even yet entirely abandoned, its provisions are worth setting forth. The Charter contained the following eight points: (1) both powers renounced all desire for national aggrandizement, territorial or otherwise; (2) no territorial changes were to result from the war without the consent of the peoples involved; (3) the right of self-determination was to be guaranteed; (4) all states were to have free access to the raw materials and trade of the world; (5) collaboration was urged among all nations to secure improved labor relations, economic advancement, and social security; (6) after the destruction of the Nazi tyranny both powers were to work for the establishment of a peace which would guarantee freedom from fear and freedom from want; (7) freedom of the seas was to be guaranteed; and (8) the use of force in international affairs was ultimately to be abandoned. It was further agreed that, pending the establishment of a system of general security, all aggressive nations which threatened peace would be disarmed.

The United States and the United Nations

As the defeat of Japan and the Axis powers became imminent, the victorious nations accepted the leadership of President Roosevelt in setting up the United Nations, the organization of which was completed shortly after his death. Although the Charter of the new organization was adopted in June, 1945, its origins are to be found in the association of 26 nations whose representatives had previously subscribed to the Atlantic Charter and pledged themselves not to make a separate peace or armistice with the enemy. The United States Senate ratified the Charter at the end of July, 1945. Since then the United States has played a leading part in the work of the United Nations. The UN headquarters have been established in New York City and we have regularly sent to its deliberations some of our ablest men and women in public life.

The primary aim of the United Nations is to keep the peace through collective action by its members. Its chief organs are the Security Council on which eleven powers are represented, five of them with permanent seats, the Assembly with members from all cooperating nations, a Social and Economic Council having responsibilities with respect to matters indicated by its title, and the Permanent Court of International Justice. The principal weakness of the United Nations is that while it can deal adequately with small aggressors, it cannot do so in the case of the great powers, each of which has an absolute veto in the Security Council, the more important of the two "legislative" bodies. Although it has to its credit some minor triumphs in forestalling aggressive action, its most dramatic intervention occurred when it took action against the invasion of South Korea by a North Korean—and later a Chinese—army. For the first time in history an international body attempted by force to stop an aggressor. Although the United States furnished most of the troops and supplies for fighting the resulting war, more than thirty nations assisted either with troops or materials. The result of this sort of intervention is by no means clear, yet the fact that any action at all was taken under such auspices is a landmark. So far as the United States is concerned, it is hard to see how we can retreat from this sort of involvement into our historic isolation.

The United States and Soviet Russia

The most dramatic result of World War II was the reducing of the great powers from five to two—the Soviet Union and the United States. In Europe Germany was devastated and for the time being, at least, impotent; France was reduced—probably permanently—to the level of a

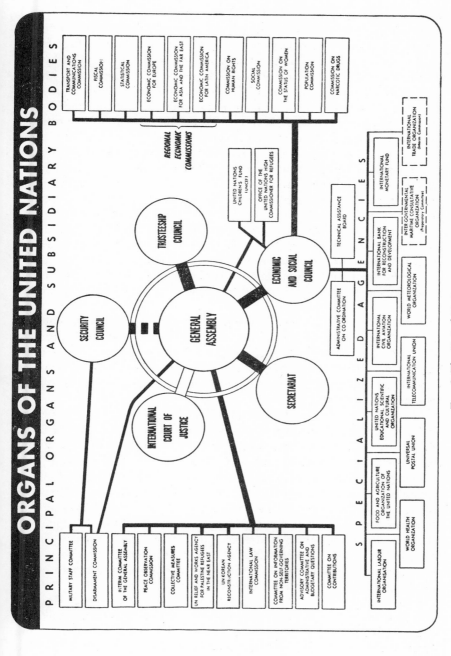

ORGANS OF THE UNITED NATIONS

PRINCIPAL ORGANS AND SUBSIDIARY BODIES

MILITARY STAFF COMMITTEE

DISARMAMENT COMMISSION

IN-TERIM COMMITTEE OF THE GENERAL ASSEMBLY

PEACE OBSERVATION COMMISSION

COLLECTIVE MEASURES COMMITTEE

UN RELIEF AND WORKS AGENCY FOR PALESTINE REFUGEES IN THE NEAR EAST

UN KOREAN RECONSTRUCTION AGENCY

INTERNATIONAL LAW COMMISSION

COMMITTEE ON INFORMATION FROM NON-SELF-GOVERNING TERRITORIES

ADVISORY COMMITTEE ON ADMINISTRATIVE AND BUDGETARY QUESTIONS

COMMITTEE ON CONTRIBUTIONS

TRANSPORT AND COMMUNICATIONS COMMISSION

FISCAL COMMISSION

STATISTICAL COMMISSION

ECONOMIC COMMISSION FOR EUROPE

ECONOMIC COMMISSION FOR ASIA AND THE FAR EAST

ECONOMIC COMMISSION FOR LATIN AMERICA

COMMISSION ON HUMAN RIGHTS

SOCIAL COMMISSION

COMMISSION ON THE STATUS OF WOMEN

POPULATION COMMISSION

COMMISSION ON NARCOTIC DRUGS

REGIONAL ECONOMIC COMMISSIONS

SECURITY COUNCIL

TRUSTEESHIP COUNCIL

INTERNATIONAL COURT OF JUSTICE

GENERAL ASSEMBLY

SECRETARIAT

ECONOMIC AND SOCIAL COUNCIL

UNITED NATIONS CHILDREN'S FUND (UNICEF)

OFFICE OF THE UNITED NATIONS HIGH COMMISSIONER FOR REFUGEES

ADMINISTRATIVE COMMITTEE ON CO-ORDINATION

TECHNICAL ASSISTANCE BOARD

SPECIALIZED AGENCIES

INTERNATIONAL LABOUR ORGANISATION

WORLD HEALTH ORGANIZATION

FOOD AND AGRICULTURE ORGANIZATION OF THE UNITED NATIONS

UNIVERSAL POSTAL UNION

UNITED NATIONS EDUCATIONAL, SCIENTIFIC AND CULTURAL ORGANIZATION

INTERNATIONAL TELECOMMUNICATION UNION

INTERNATIONAL CIVIL AVIATION ORGANIZATION

WORLD METEOROLOGICAL ORGANIZATION

INTERNATIONAL BANK FOR RECONSTRUCTION AND DEVELOPMENT

INTERNATIONAL MONETARY FUND

INTER-GOVERNMENTAL MARITIME CONSULTATIVE ORGANIZATION (Preparatory Committee)

INTERNATIONAL TRADE ORGANIZATION (Interim Commission)

Fig. 9. The United Nations system.

427

third-rate power; and even Britain, deprived of her balances abroad and bereft of large parts of her prewar empire, faced perhaps generations of austere living and a secondary role in world affairs. In the Far East Japan was crushed and the resulting vacuum of power had to be filled by the United States. The "game" of international politics would be played henceforth by two giants; in the foreseeable future other nations could be little more than makeweights in the impending struggle for dominance.

From the point of view of the United States, the postwar policy of Russia was one of militant and ruthless aggression. In eastern and central Europe the small Baltic states were annexed outright to Russia, Poland was placed under Russian control, and Hungary, Romania, Bulgaria, Yugoslavia, Albania, Czechoslovakia, and half of Germany became satellites of the Soviet Union, their native rulers being the willing tools of Russian policy. From the Russian official point of view this territorial expansion was justified as a way of escaping "capitalist encirclement," although it has to be said that the Communist leaders have never given up the grandiose plan of reorganizing the entire world along Marxist lines. In any case, statesmen of the West must assume that both policies are in the minds of Russian rulers, whatever devious twists and turns they may execute in the conduct of affairs.

As stated by the State Department, "the policy of the United States in meeting the threat of Soviet Communist expansion has been to help promote situations of strength." [7] This remains the leading policy of the United States today. To this end the Truman Doctrine, the Marshall Plan, the Point Four program, and military assistance to Western Europe have been put into effect.

What became known as the Truman Doctrine was enunciated by President Truman in an address to a joint session of Congress in March, 1947, when he called for military and economic aid to Greece and Turkey. But the new policy was broader than that, for the President asked for support to "free people who are resisting attempted subjugation by armed minorities or by outside pressures." The independence of both Greece and Turkey had been threatened by Russia and some of her satellites. Two months after President Truman's proposal, Congress authorized the aid requested. Undoubtedly the aid given to Greece and Turkey, at an estimated cost in the first three years of $1,800,000,000, put those countries on their feet. Both held free elections in 1950 and voted new governments into office. The Communists had been beaten back.

In June, 1947, Secretary of State Marshall made an address at Harvard University in which he advocated economic aid to bolster the weak and sagging governments of Western Europe. What became known as the Marshall Plan was thus born. This proposal called for the allotment by the

[7] See *Our Foreign Policy*, Department of State Publication 3972, p. 11.

United States of several billion dollars to the free nations of Western Europe in order to stimulate economic recovery and prevent the spread of communism. The fact that economic conditions had so improved by 1952 in the countries aided by the Marshall Plan that they were all able to bear a substantial share of the rearmament program of NATO would appear to bear out the wisdom of the Marshall Plan.

Russia from the beginning deeply resented the Marshall Plan and countered with the establishment of the Cominform to lead the attack on recovery. In February, 1948, the Communists took over Czechoslovakia. Alarmed by the danger to their independence unless common action were taken, five nations signed a Brussels treaty in March 1948, calling for a Western Union and a fifty-year mutual-defense alliance of the United Kingdom, France, Belgium, the Netherlands, and Luxembourg. Military forces were to be pooled under a joint command. On the same day that the treaty was concluded, President Truman called upon Congress to extend military assistance to the Western Union on the same basis as aid was given to Greece, Turkey, and China.

In June, 1948, the Vandenberg Resolution authorizing the government to negotiate defense pacts for the collective defense of the North Atlantic was approved by the United States Senate. Immediately after the passage of this resolution, discussions with countries which signed the Brussels treaty began and the result was the North Atlantic Treaty, which was concluded in March, 1949, and ratified by the Senate in July of the same year. Article 5, the heart of the treaty, provided that an attack on one party to the treaty would amount to an attack on all, and that each nation would assist the victim of attack by "such action as it deems necessary, including the use of armed force, to restore and maintain the security of the North Atlantic area." Seven other nations joined with the five Brussels treaty nations in concluding the North Atlantic Treaty. They include the United States, Iceland, Canada, Denmark, Norway, Italy, and Portugal. Later on, Greece and Turkey came in. The North Atlantic Treaty Organization was finally set up in order to implement the agreement. There is a North Atlantic Council, consisting of the foreign ministers of the fourteen member countries, there is a committee of deputies meeting continuously, and there are various other committees.

Congress voted substantial funds for the rearmament of NATO members.[8] A unified command with General Eisenhower at the head took over in 1951. The United States has now doubled the size of its force in Western Europe, augmenting the first five divisions with five more.

Another device for developing strength of free nations is the Point Four

[8] In September, 1949, a broader program of military aid was authorized by the Mutual Defense Assistance Act. In addition to Western Europe, military aid was to be provided for Iran, Korea, the Philippines, Greece, Turkey, and China.

program announced by President Truman in 1949. Under this program, aid is to be extended to underdeveloped regions in order to provide a better standard of living by giving them the results of scientific and technological development. India is one of the nations receiving aid under this program, and this aid may help to keep that country from going communistic. One of the most serious problems of India is the backwardness of her agriculture because of the continued use of primitive methods. Under the Point Four program, the U.S. Department of Agriculture has made available experts in various fields to enable this great country to improve her agriculture and increase production. In 1952, under the Point Four program, the United States and Iran signed an agreement whereby $11 million was earmarked by the former for three new projects. The three projects involved technical aid to Iran in the fields of agriculture, public health, and education. But so far Congress has been unwilling to vote any substantial amount to carry out the challenging Point Four program.

Since the beginning of World War II the foreign policy of the United States has undergone a decided change. It has been nothing short of a revolution. From isolation or semi-isolation this country has advanced to leadership of the free nations in world affairs. Our country has thus been cast in a new role, and one which by its past history of isolation it has been ill equipped to carry out. If the United States is to meet this great responsibility of leadership of the free world in the years ahead, the government must meantime be able to act wisely and vigorously and pursue a consistent course in international affairs with the support of an informed and intelligent public opinion.

It must not be supposed that the policies now being pursued by the United States enjoy unanimous support by Americans. They are, in fact, widely and acutely criticized. Since they involve us in constant contact with foreign officialdom, it is always easy for those disposed to do so to arouse the suspicions latent in large numbers of people toward all foreigners as persons eager to "sell us a bill of goods." More open-minded critics raise the question of our ability, in spite of our great wealth, to continue indefinitely to extend financial and military assistance to most of the rest of the world. There are even more fundamental criticisms. As for our economic aid in raising living standards among backward peoples and thus offsetting the appeal of communism, there are many who believe that since men do not live by bread alone, something additional must be offered, which may or may not go along with our economic aid. These critics point out that the impact of American aid on ancient social and economic systems may ultimately be so disastrous in disrupting accustomed ways of doing things as to be really self-defeating. Some even go so far as to say that American attempts to provide our aid and introduce our modern ways to less advanced peoples constitute a mistaken kindness, since all nations, even poor ones, have a justifiable pride in their own cultural accomplishments and may be affronted by too confidently being offered the cultures and ideals of those who are better off materially. It will indeed require humility as well as skill, in such a setting, to fulfill wisely the role of world leadership into which we have been thrust.

REFERENCES

Samuel F. Bemis, *The United States as a World Power* (1950).
Henry S. Commager, *Documents of American History* (1943).
George F. Kennan, *American Diplomacy 1900–1950* (1951).
Felix Morley, *The Foreign Policy of the United States* (1951).
Dexter Perkins, *The Evolution of American Foreign Policy* (1948).

CHAPTER 25   *State Constitutions*

Probably the most serious brake on the progress and the efficiency of the 48 state governments is the fact that, almost without exception, each has an outmoded or an inappropriate written constitution. These state constitutions are also considered by many serious authorities to be one of the chief reasons for the headlong increase in federal activities during recent years.

"Most of the circumstances," says United States Senator Richard L. Neuberger, who has seen service in his state government as well, "which have put state government on the toboggan slide can be rectified through a wholesale overhauling of state constitutions." [1]

Some of the reasons for this situation which affects not only the governmental life of the people of the United States, but in large measure their social and economic life as well, have their beginnings in the circumstances surrounding the framing of the original state constitutions. Even the constitutions framed later (that is to say, in the nineteenth, rather than in the eighteenth century) reflect the prejudices of those earlier times, for in many essentials they were copied from the early state charters. In particular they embody distrust of the executive and a distrust of government in general. Such constitutions, hedged about with limitations, leave modern governments, which must cope with complex economic conditions and sophisticated demands for governmental service, at worst impotent, at best bridled and hampered.

What Is a State Constitution?

A state constitution has been defined as "a body of limitations on a state legislature, or sometimes a grant of power from the people to the government." [2] In the Western world generally it has been customary to

---

[1] *Adventures in Politics*, p. 26, Oxford University Press, New York, 1954.

[2] E. C. Smith and A. J. Zurcher, eds., *A Dictionary of American Politics*, p. 77, Barnes & Noble, Inc., New York, 1944.

emphasize limits on power rather than grants of power. The reason for this is that people have been more interested in protecting themselves against powerful rulers than in constructing efficient governments. In state matters the constitution is the fundamental law, setting limits to the action of all authorities and officials within the state. It is inferior, however, to the Constitution of the United States, to the laws enacted by Congress in pursuance of powers granted it by the Constitution, and to treaties concluded under the authority of the United States. Whether or not state action is consistent with the national Constitution as "the supreme law of the land" is a question finally determined by the Supreme Court of the United States. The decisions of that court in umpiring the federal system are binding on all other courts, national and state, and must be enforced by all executive officers at every level of government.

Leading Ideas in State Constitutions

The fundamental principles on which American government is based, discussed in Chaps. 1 to 4, have been embodied in all state constitutions as a matter of course. First of all, the eighteenth-century doctrine of natural rights is given specific content in the bills of rights found in all constitutions. Here are found limitations on state and local government with respect to the customary freedoms of speech, press, assembly, and religious beliefs. The usual procedural guarantees are also provided— trial by jury, prohibition of excessive bail and fines and unusual and cruel punishments, the requirement that accusation of crime be by some orderly process such as grand jury indictment or sworn information, and the preservation of the writ of habeas corpus. And in one form or another the guarantees in the Fourteenth Amendment of the national Constitution also appear—no deprivation of life, liberty, or property without due process of law and no denial to any person of the equal protection of the laws. A novel addition to these familiar "rights" is a provision found in some recent constitutions safeguarding the privilege of collective bargaining.

Underlying every state constitution also is the concept of the separation of powers. While a state constitution may not expressly state this principle, most of them imply its operation, since in every case there is a description of the three departments of government and an enumeration of their respective functions. The constitution of Massachusetts, however, expressly states that there shall be a separation of powers. In each state the system of checks and balances accompanies the separation of powers. In every state except North Carolina, the executive has the veto power; through the power of impeachment the legislature may hold the governor accountable for his acts, and the judiciary has the final say as to what the constitution means. As with the national government, however, the separation of powers is not absolute, for governors share in the legislative function and legislatures share in the exercise of executive and administrative powers.

Finally, the doctrine of judicial review is deeply embedded in all state constitutions. Everywhere the courts have the duty of interpreting the state constitution and state laws. Indeed, it was in the states that judicial review was first practiced. This power was exercised by the highest courts in Rhode Island and other states soon after the first state constitutions were established. Not only is it the duty of the state judges to determine whether laws are in accord with the state constitution, but also whether they are in conflict with the national Constitution and acts of Congress. Where such a conflict occurs the decision of the state's highest court may be reviewed and the question determined by the Supreme Court of the United States. It is clear that only by preserving such an opportunity for review can the public law of the nation be made a harmonious whole.

Establishment of First Constitutions

By a resolution of the Continental Congress of 1776 the states were called upon to set up provisional governments and frame constitutions as soon as possible. Accordingly, all the thirteen original states adopted constitutions between 1776 and 1780. Two of the states, Connecticut and Rhode Island, merely converted their colonial charters into constitutions.

All the original constitutions were very brief. The framers contented themselves with the adoption of a bill of rights, the establishment of the framework of government, and the definition of the powers and duties of the three departments of government. The details were left for the legislature to work out. In most cases the governor's powers were very limited and he was subject to election by the legislature. This system did not work well, for legislative abuses soon arose.

Practically all the early constitutions set up property qualifications for voting, and in some states religious tests were also required. For instance, in South Carolina no one could vote unless he believed in God and also in a future state of rewards and punishments. Failure to vote in Georgia made the offender subject to a fine of five pounds.

Provision for amendment and revision was made in all state constitutions of the early period, by implication if not expressly, but in some cases it was made very difficult to change the constitution after it had been adopted. Thus many of the outmoded limitations and specifications embodied in fundamental state law years ago still hobble some of our states today.

Contemporary State Constitutions

The brief state charters of early times have for the most part given way to long documents encrusted with detail. New York's is typical, though it is by no means the longest. Article 1 contains a Bill of Rights, while Article 2 deals with the suffrage, listing qualifications for voting as well as disabilities. Articles 3 through 6 have to do with the framework of state government, providing for three major departments—legislative, executive, and judicial. Article 7 is concerned with state finances, budgeting and borrowing, while Article 8 covers local finances, prescribing limits on local indebtedness. Articles 9 through 12 cover local government, corporations, education, and the military, while Article 13 deals with public officers and prescribes an oath of office and certain provisions as to the conduct of such officers. Articles 14 through 18 relate to conservation, canals, taxation, social welfare, and housing. Finally, Article 19 prescribes methods of amendment and revision. While state constitutions vary, of course, they nevertheless follow the general pattern of New York's constitution.

The New York constitution, like the vast majority of the state constitutions now in force, is much too long and detailed. The New York document contains 19,036 words and has been amended 127 times since its adoption in 1894. This is about par for the constitutional course, not only as to the period of origin but also as to length and multiplicity of amendment. But the extremes are infinitely worse. The Constitution of California contains over 70,000 words, Louisiana's over 200,000. California's has been amended 372 times, Louisiana's 326.[3] In nine other states the constitution exceeds 20,000 words and in only seven states is it under 10,000 words. These facts are presented in summary form in the table on pages 438 and 439.

Most of this wordiness stems from the fact that many constitutions are full of material better handled by ordinary legislation. Such matters are not only out of place in the fundamental law but their inclusion in it seriously hampers efficient governmental operation. On this point Senator Neuberger pungently observes: [4]

By attaining the length of a detective novel, a constitution inevitably will include many needless and absurd inhibitions on state government.

The constitution of Oregon restricts the location of all new state institutions such as colleges and mental hospitals to just one out of the state's thirty-six counties . . . West Virginia's constitution bars officials of railroads from serving in the legislature. The constitution of Texas forces the state to maintain five times the number of courts and judges as serve the infinitely larger population

[3] *Book of the States, 1956–57*, p. 70, Council of State Governments.
[4] *Adventures in Politics*, p. 16.

of the United Kingdom. California's constitution goes into endless detail regarding such trivialities as the duration of wrestling matches and the breeding of mollusks and crustaceans.

But a multiplicity of detail is not the only fault of most constitutions. Old-fashioned provisions like the legislative sessions that are two years apart, or arbitrarily brief sessions when legislatures do convene, are responsible for haste and lack of adequate consideration for many pressing state problems. Moreover, the heavy reliance of state constitutions

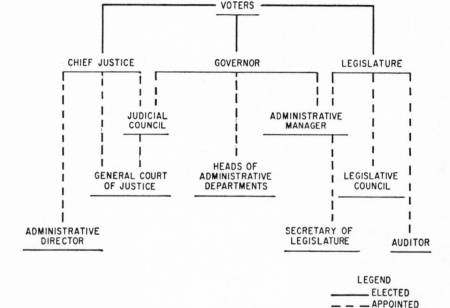

Fig. 10. Government under the Model State Constitution.

on the county as a basis for legislative representation has resulted in a disproportionately heavy representation for rural areas, underrepresentation for cities. Thus state governments often have not faced up to peculiarly urban needs for service. "Many state constitutions restrict the scope, effectiveness, and adaptability of state and local action," the Commission on Intergovernmental Relations found. "These self-imposed constitutional limitations make it difficult for many states to perform all of the services their citizens require, and consequently have frequently been the underlying cause of state and municipal pleas for federal assistance." [5]

Confronted with the necessity of picking his way through such a littered constitutional field, even the most forward-looking governor or

[5] *Report*, pp. 37–38.

legislator finds his task hopelessly complex. The result in many states has been virtual paralysis of the body politic at times when swift action might have averted trouble of one kind or another. Often, by the time enough public energy is mustered to get a state constitution amended so that the legislature or officials may act (and the amending process often takes years) the Federal government has had to step into some state crisis or else the crisis has been allowed to take its toll by default.

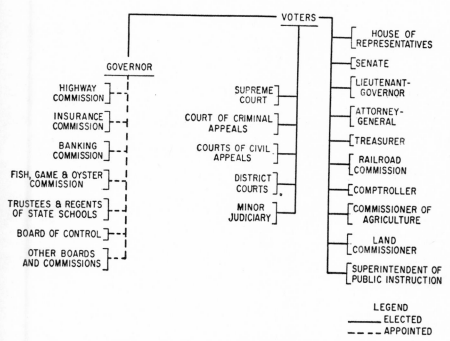

Fig. 11. Government under a typical state constitution.

There is no question but that a constitution must place limitations on governmental authority to protect the individual, but authorities agree that those limits must be broad to be workable. The niggling details frozen into most of our present state constitutions do not fall in that category. Hence the considerable movement for constitutional reform which in recent years has been sweeping the states with varying degrees of success.

Methods of Changing State Constitutions

Most state constitutions specify such cumbersome or difficult procedures for amendment or revision that it may take many years to throw off the dead hand of the past from the basic law. On the other hand, in some states like California, change is regrettably easy so that pressure groups have used the constitutional revision process as a means for writing their desires into the state's fundamental charter. Once such amendments are in the constitution, it takes an opposing pressure group to apply equal zeal to get them eradicated, and such a group often does not exist.

State Constitutions

	No. of conventions	Date of adoption of present constitution	Estimated no. words	No. of amendments adopted
Alabama	6	1901	39,899	110
Arizona	1	1912	15,369	36
Arkansas	6	1874	21,500	42
California		1879	72,000	372
Colorado	1	1876	23,095	56
Connecticut	2	1818	6,741	48
Delaware	5	1897	13,409	21
Florida	5	1887	30,000	102
Georgia	9	1945	25,000	18 °
Idaho	1	1890	13,492	53
Illinois	5	1870	13,838	8
Indiana	2	1851	7,816	18
Iowa	1	1857	7,997	19
Kansas	4	1861	8,052	42
Kentucky	6	1891	21,500	16
Louisiana	10	1921	201,423	326
Maine	1	1820	10,302	77
Maryland	4	1867	23,300	79
Massachusetts	5	1780	28,760	81
Michigan	5	1909	15,290	59
Minnesota	1	1858	15,465	80
Mississippi	7	1890	15,302	32
Missouri	6	1945	30,000	4
Montana	1	1889	17,409	23

State constitutions generally prescribe two alternative methods of change: either piecemeal amendment, upon the initiative of the legislature or popular petition, usually with ratification by popular vote, or wholesale revision, by constitutional convention or commission, followed again by ratification.

Amendment. In all states except New Hampshire the legislature is free to propose amendments to the state constitution. While in most states a proposed amendment must be passed by a two-thirds vote of the legislature, in some states a three-fifths vote of the entire membership is required. Other states amend by a majority vote either of the entire legislative membership or, as in Arizona, by simple majority. In some states an amendment must be passed twice, by two successive legislative sessions. In New Hampshire the legislature may offer amendments to the people only once every seven years.

Constitutional amendments may be proposed by the people in 14 states. The number of signers required varies widely. For example, in South Dakota a petition must be signed by 5 per cent of the voters, while

State Constitutions (*Continued*)

	No. of conventions	Date of adoption of present constitution	Estimated no. words	No. of amendments adopted
Nebraska	4	1875	16,555	69
Nevada	2	1864	16,657	56
New Hampshire	14	1784	10,900	94
New Jersey	4	1948	12,500	None
New Mexico	1	1912	15,150	36
New York	8	1894	19,036	127
North Carolina	6	1876	8,861	28
North Dakota	1	1889	17,797	64
Ohio	4	1851	15,417	72
Oklahoma	1	1907	35,360	37
Oregon	2	1859	18,100	94
Pennsylvania	5	1874	15,092	54
Rhode Island	7	1843	6,650	33
South Carolina	7	1895	30,063	220
South Dakota	1	1896	24,545	60
Tennessee	4	1870	9,460	8
Texas	5	1876	39,000	121
Utah	1	1896	13,261	29
Vermont	11	1793	5,759	40
Virginia	9	1902	23,101	87
Washington	1	1889	14,650	28
West Virginia	2	1872	14,928	27
Wisconsin	1	1848	10,517	59
Wyoming	1	1890	14,603	13

* This figure does not include amendments of a local nature.

SOURCE: *Book of the States, 1956–57,* pp. 70–74, Council of State Governments, Chicago, 1956.

in Massachusetts the number of signatures must equal 3 per cent of the vote for governor in the previous biennial election. In Illinois an amendment must be passed by a two-thirds popular vote, though in the greatest number of the states only a majority is necessary. In some states a majority of all votes cast at the election is required—an extremely difficult proviso, since many of those who vote in a general election do not vote on proposed constitutional amendments. In New Hampshire and Connecticut amendments must be ratified by town meetings. In some of the states, as in Georgia, amendments must be voted upon separately, while in other states a group of amendments may be submitted in a block.

Constitutional Revision. In most states the legislature may propose a constitutional convention (or commission, as the case may be) generally either by a two-thirds vote of the entire membership or a majority. However, in several states the question of whether a constitutional convention should be held must be submitted to the voters at specified periods: in New York every twenty years and in New Hampshire every seven years.

There is much to be said for periodically submitting to the voters the question of holding a constitutional convention, for state legislatures often fail to act until long after the need for revision has arisen. A major reason for such legislative inertia is the "rotten borough" composition of many state lawmaking bodies. Frozen into many state constitutions is an apportionment of legislative seats based upon a geographical-population balance which has long since changed. The result is that an area of the state which has become urbanized and heavily populated may have the same number of representatives as an area which has only a fraction as many inhabitants. Hence the legislature becomes dominated by rural interests who fear that constitutional change will bring reapportionment and upset their control. These interests are in a position to block constitutional revision perhaps indefinitely.

Should constitutional revision actually be achieved—and it does infrequently occur—the new constitution must usually be approved by a majority vote in a referendum. Some states, such as Indiana and Texas, make no provision for the legislature to call a convention to revise the constitution. In Oregon 8 per cent of the voters may initiate a measure to call a constitutional convention. While most constitutions call for ratification by the people (usually a majority vote on proposals), a number of states do not specify the method for ratification. In New Hampshire ratification must be by a two-thirds vote of annual town meetings.

The Convention vs. Commission Method of Change. The constitutional revision commission is not an innovation—it has been used for nearly a hundred years. In more recent times it has been utilized by Georgia, California, Louisiana, New Jersey, Michigan, Minnesota, South Carolina, and Virginia. Proposals worked out by commissions in several of these states failed to be approved either by the legislature or by the people. It may be that the failure of the proposed constitutions was due in some cases to distrust of the members of the commission. In Georgia practically all the commission members were legislators, administrative officials, and judges, and their proposals were acceptable both to the legislature and to the people.

The commission plan enjoys several advantages over the convention method. Chief among these are that it is inexpensive, makes more use of experts (for much research is required to frame a good constitution), permits informal discussion since it is small, saves time, provides more opportunity for reflection on vital problems, and can draw more effectively on the experience of other states. But the convention system has its own advantages. The elected convention is more democratic and representative and thus may inspire confidence that the people's interests will be protected. Since the convention is more widely used its very familiarity renders it more acceptable. Probably the commission plan is actually the better system where only limited revision is being undertaken.

Model State Constitution

In 1921 the first edition of the Model State Constitution was published by the National Municipal League. It was prepared by a committee of experts. The fifth edition was published in 1948. The last edition was the work of a committee of 23 under the chairmanship of W. Brooke Graves. Included among the committee besides Graves were John E. Bebout of the National Municipal League, Frank Bane, A. E. Buck, J. A. Burdine, Frederick H. Guild, Arthur N. Holcombe, Rodney L. Mott, Frank M. Stewart, Lloyd M. Short, Robert S. Rankin, and others. The list included the most notable scholars in the field.

The Model State Constitution calls for a simplified organization of state government. Among several of the novel features of the constitution are the provision for a unicameral legislature, a short ballot whereby the governor is given the power to appoint and remove all 20 department heads, appointment of an administrative manager to serve at the pleasure of the governor, and a general court of justice consisting of a supreme court and inferior courts headed by a chief justice. In addition, a judicial council would be set up under this scheme of government.

Undoubtedly, many states now planning revision of their constitutions will follow some of the features recommended by the committee. Certainly traces of the influence of the model constitution can be found in the new constitutions of Missouri and New Jersey where the short ballot was applied. The principal differences between a "typical" state constitution and the model constitution are shown in Figures 10 and 11.

New Constitutions

The requirements which constitutions lay down for their own revision are in many cases extremely difficult to meet in actual practice. The size of the petition and the popular vote required for both initiation of revision and ratification, the frequent requirement of legislative assent at either or both ends of the process, have all acted effectively to block direly needed constitutional revision in most states. It is considered a hopeful sign that in recent years the agitation for constitutional modernization in many states has spread from the progressive civic groups, such as the League of Women Voters, to governors and officials themselves. It is significant that strong governors played an important part when Georgia, Tennessee, Missouri, and New Jersey finally revised or broadly amended their constitutions during the last 10 years.

Amended Constitutions

The constitutions of Georgia and of Tennessee are styled "amended" since the new constitutions which resulted were not complete revisions. In both cases while several important amendments were proposed and adopted, the constitution remained essentially the same.

The movement for revision in Georgia began in 1930 when the *Atlanta Constitution* pointed out that the constitution of Georgia was like "Grandpa's pants" because it was such a patched-up document. But the small counties objected to the revision proposal because the membership of the convention would be based on population and they feared the result might bring a reapportionment of the legislature on the basis of population.

In 1931 the chancellor of the University of Georgia appointed a committee of outstanding citizens to prepare a new constitution. This body prepared a draft based upon the Model State Constitution of the National Municipal League. This proposal, however, was never seriously considered. Later a resolution passed the Georgia Legislature calling for a commission to prepare a new constitution but the governor failed to take the necessary action. Agitation continued; in 1943 Governor Ellis Arnall proposed the creation of a constitutional revision commission which the general assembly approved. The commission had 23 members, including the speaker of the house, the president of the senate, and several other members of the legislature, as well as the governor, the state auditor, and several judges. The commission's task was completed in December, 1944, and its proposals went to the legislature, where some changes were made. In August, 1945, the people finally ratified the proposed constitution as a whole by a two-to-one vote.

Chief among the 48 major changes in the old constitution were: elimination of the tax exemption of the Georgia Railroad; removal of the veto power of the governor on constitutional proposals; increase in the governor's salary; consolidation of all school districts into county school systems; provision for home rule for cities; empowering of counties and cities to contract with one another for services; and provision for a state merit system. While actually the constitution of 1877 was merely revised, the Georgia supreme court later ruled that this was a new constitution.

In Tennessee a convention was used to accomplish the same result. So difficult was the procedure to amend or revise the Tennessee constitution that it had not been changed since its adoption in 1871, despite 13 earlier efforts at revision. The movement for revision which eventually succeeded was started in the 1940s by the state League of Women Voters, who received press backing. In 1949 the question of revision was submitted to the voters, but was rejected by a small majority. It remained for Governor Frank Clement to secure constitutional change. He called a convention early in 1953 and assigned it six subjects to consider. There were 99 delegates, under the chairmanship of a well-known political leader. The delegates assembled at Nashville on April 21, 1953, labored for 33 days, and finally proposed eight amendments to the constitution of 1871. At a special election on November 3, 1953, all the proposals were adopted by the people.

Of the eight changes made in the Tennessee constitution in 1953, the most important was undoubtedly the power given to the legislature to call future limited constitutional conventions. Other changes increased the compensation of legislators, lengthened the governor's term to four years and gave him an item veto on appropriation bills, eliminated the poll tax, and provided for local home rule and county consolidation. But the most important change of all was a by-product of those written on the ballot, according to an observer.[6]

The document had remained unamended for so long—over 75 years—that the idea of changing it had become suspect. . . . When the people voted to call the convention this fearful attitude was reflected in that it was a "limited convention" to consider certain named items and no others. . . . During the convention sessions this attitude, this fear of change, began to melt. . . . The discussion and debate was the best Tennessee had had in generations. And it was well reported by press and radio. For the citizens of Tennessee it was a much needed course in constitutional government. . . . They began to see the constitution with new eyes. They saw its place in our scheme of government and began to lose the "venerable document under a glass cover" attitude.

The new attitude remains. . . . This new attitude toward the constitution— that it belongs to the people and is a living part of our government—is the most important gain from the 1953 convention—more important than the amendments secured.

Revised New Constitutions

In two other states, Missouri and New Jersey, new and substantially revised constitutions have recently been adopted. In both states constitutional revision conventions were employed.

After several attempts at revision, Missouri advocates of constitutional

[6] Martha Ragland, "Constitutional Climate Improves in Tennessee," *National Municipal Review*, Vol. 4, No. 4, p. 203, April, 1955.

change finally met with success in 1945. In the fall of 1942 the people approved the calling of a convention and in April of the next year delegates were elected, 68 from senatorial districts and 15 from the state at large. The convention began its work in September, 1943, and completed its task in a little over a year. The convention voted to submit a complete revision rather than a series of amendments.

The new constitution was shorter by about 11,000 words than the old one. Changes of considerable importance were: (1) revision of the bill of rights to accord full political and civil rights to women, to add freedom of the air waves to freedom of the press, and to safeguard the privilege of collective bargaining; (2) provision for a legislative committee on research and for senatorial redistricting; (3) reduction of the 70 state boards, departments, and offices to 14; (4) empowering the supreme court to make rules of practice and procedure for all courts and the abolition of justice of the peace courts; (5) provision of home rule for counties of 85,000 people and over, county consolidation and county-city consolidation; (6) authorization to abolish segregation in the schools; (7) authorization of a classified property tax.

New Jersey operated under the constitution of 1844 for over a hundred years. This constitution had been amended 32 times, but only 4 times since 1875. A new constitution was obviously more than overdue. The movement for revision started around 1900 but made no appreciable headway until the early 1940s. Then the New Jersey Constitutional Foundation was established to educate the voters on the urgent need for revision. The eminently respectable backers of the movement were the New Jersey League of Women Voters, the State Chamber of Commerce, and the State Bar Association, as well as leaders of both the Republican and Democratic parties.

Finally, the New Jersey legislature passed a resolution creating a constitutional revision commission to draft a proposed constitution. The commission submitted its proposals to the legislature in May, 1942, but the new constitution, which was submitted to the people in November, 1943, was defeated largely because of the opposition of Mayor Hague of Jersey City.

Efforts toward revision continued, however, and with the backing of Governor Driscoll, in June, 1947, the people of New Jersey selected delegates to a constitutional convention. The convention met at Rutgers University the following month and finished its work in September. In November the people overwhelmingly approved the new constitution which went into effect on January 1, 1948. Among the chief changes were the liberalization of the state's Bill of Rights to guarantee civil rights without regard to race, sex, religion, and national origin, and to guarantee labor the right to organize and bargain collectively; the lengthening of the terms of senators from two to four years and of representatives from one to two years; reorganization of the executive department so as to centralize control in the governor and increase his term of office from three to four years; provision for a simplified and unified system of courts; and finally simplification of the procedure for constitutional amendment by providing that by a three-fifths vote of both houses of the legislature an amendment could be sent to the people for approval or disapproval.

Whether they be styled amendment or revision, the changes made in the constitutions of Georgia, Tennessee, New Jersey, and Missouri were of great significance. They indicated, as the Tennessee observer pointed out, that the people had become, at long last, educated to the need for modernization of state government, that ideas once confined to the minds of political scientists had become common coin. And the changes themselves were in most cases vital to state governmental efficiency and ability to cope with current problems. Raising legislative salaries, increasing officials' terms of office, bestowing home rule on local governments, installing a merit system, centralizing state government administration, and reducing the number of independent agencies, all these are cardinal principles of modern governmental practice. Now the states in which they were installed are equipped to do an efficient job.

Proposed Constitutional Change in Other States

The constitutional change movement is alive in many other states as well. The latest *Book of the States* [7] found significant activity in nine states and one territory, and in seven others noted the adoption of basically important constitutional changes such as lengthening of the governor's term and establishment of annual legislative sessions. Many authorities believe that limited revision of a constitution can accomplish most of what is needed in most states, and with far less objection from apprehensive conservative citizens who might fear "revolution" of some sort if it were proposed to scrap the old constitution and write a new one.

Here is what was going on in the states, constitutionally speaking, at latest reports:

Alabama. Governor James Folsom's proposal for constitutional revision is still pending. The state supreme court has ruled that a limited constitutional convention, as in Tennessee, is not possible. The governor has repeatedly urged legislative reapportionment but so far his efforts have been thwarted by representatives of the small counties. However, at this writing constitutional amendments providing for reapportionment are soon to be voted upon by the people.

Florida. Early in 1955 Governor Collins appointed a citizens' committee

[7] 1956–57, p. 67.

to draft proposals for constitutional revision and present them to the legislature. Later the governor recommended that a commission be set up to study revision and in June, 1955, a 37-member commission was named, with instructions to report to the legislature at its 1957 session and recommend revisions article by article. Any such recommendations must receive at least a three-fourths vote in both houses of the legislature before going to the people in 1958.

Illinois. The outmoded condition of Illinois' constitution is evidenced by the fact that no more than nine amendments have been added to the Illinois constitution of 1870, only three of these since 1890. In 1919 a new constitution drafted by a convention was rejected at the polls and the proposal to hold a convention in 1934 met with the same fate. After repeated failures to revise or amend, a constitutional commission was established in 1949 under Governor Adlai Stevenson's leadership. This commission proposed the "gateway amendment," which became the first constitutional change in 42 years when the voters approved it in 1950.

The amendment became, in effect, a gateway to change. Prior to its adoption it was not possible to propose more than one amendment at an election and it was necessary to secure approval by no less than a majority of all those voting in the election. Repeatedly in the past amendments had received a majority of those actually voting on the amendment, but less than half the total vote cast, since many uninformed or uninterested voters failed to ballot on constitutional amendments. Under the "gateway amendment" this massive majority is no longer required; an amendment is approved if twice as many voters cast their votes for it as vote against it. A most important result has been adoption, after 50 years of deadlock between urban Cook County and rural "downstate," of an amendment providing for an effective way to reapportion the legislature now and every ten years hereafter.

Kentucky. A Constitutional Research Commission was created in 1953. The state assembly rejected its recommendations in 1954 but submitted proposals of its own, which were approved by the voters in 1955. One of the amendments gives 18-year-olds the right to vote. The other exempts from taxation all household goods of any person if in use in his home. In 1956 the functions that had been performed by the Kentucky Constitutional Research Commission were assigned to the Legislative Research Commission.

Louisiana. Prospects for a constitutional convention have increased as a result of considerable civic agitation. In the meantime, annual legislative sessions have been instituted.

New Hampshire. The limited convention to consider amendments to the constitution was held from May 15 to June 13, 1956. The convention approved six amendments. The three that were submitted to and approved by the voters in 1956 will allow: (1) absentee voting in primary elections; (2) the right of trial by jury in civil cases in which the full value in controversy exceeds $500; and (3) the governor to exercise full powers when out of the state. The three others, to be voted on in 1958, would (1) change the title of county solicitors to county attorneys; (2) eliminate a provision that limits voting to male residents; and (3) delete obsolete provisions as to parishes and plantations and the list of state offices declared to be incompatible with federal employment, and clarify the provision for advisory opinions by the supreme court.

Oregon. A constitutional study committee was authorized in 1953 but its recommendation for a convention died in the legislature.

Pennsylvania. The proposal to set up a constitutional convention died in 1953 though it was supported by both major parties.

Rhode Island. A limited constitutional convention held in 1955 resulted in three proposals, of which the electorate adopted one providing for urban redevelopment.

Alaska. The constitutional convention finished its work in February, 1956, and the constitution was submitted to the people on April 24 and was adopted. It is now before Congress.

Future Revision

The evidence is abundant that state constitutional change is in the air and it is obviously only a matter of time, albeit years, perhaps, before it arrives. Certainly home rule for local governments, increased services for urban areas, state administrative reorganization, financial modernization, and merit systems for state employees are among the "musts" for many of the states, if they are to meet the requirements of the twentieth century. The most serious obstacle in the way of constitutional change is the rural control which prevails in the legislatures of even some of the most industrialized and urbanized states. Reapportionment must come first if vital reforms are to follow. This is the challenge to civic groups and enlightened leaders everywhere.

REFERENCES

Clarence N. Callender *et al.* (eds.), "The State Constitution of the Future," *Annals of the American Academy of Political and Social Science,* September, 1935, entire issue.

Committee on State Government, National Municipal League, *Model State Constitution,* 5th ed. (1948).

Council of State Governments, *Book of the States,* 1956–57 (1956).

John P. Keith, *Methods of Constitutional Revision,* Bureau of Municipal Research, University of Texas (1949).

New York State Constitutional Convention Committee, Report, Vol. 3, *Constitutions of the States and the United States* (1938).

Oklahoma State Legislative Council, *Oklahoma Constitutional Studies* (1950).

Albert L. Sturm, *Methods of State Constitutional Reform*, University of Michigan Press (1954).

Raymond Uhl *et al.*, *Constitutional Conventions*, Bureau of Public Administration, University of South Carolina (1951).

CHAPTER 26 *The State Legislature*

The men and women who comprise our state legislatures could be, and sometimes are, the most important single influence on the lives of the people in the state. It is they who have the power to tell us what taxes we shall pay, what sort of schools we shall have, what kinds of roads; to lay down the rules for the operation of our banks, our physicians, our barber shops, and, indeed, every phase of our economic lives; and even, in decreeing capital punishment for crimes, to tell us whether we shall live or die.

True, because of the fact that the members of the legislature are elected by the qualified voters for the purpose of translating their wishes into governmental action, it may be said that these vast powers lie in the voters themselves. As our legislative system actually operates, however, the legislators are not always as representative of the electorate as in theory they ought to be. It is also true that as our legislative system really functions in many of our states, constitutional limitations, some of them seriously outmoded, keep our lawmakers from exercising all the power they otherwise might wield. Some of these limitations are for the best; some are not so felicitous.

What do our state lawmaking bodies actually do? And how can their work be improved for the general good?

Functions of State Legislatures

The primary function of a legislature is to legislate. The product of legislation is variously referred to as a statute, law, resolution, or enactment. Each state legislature passes hundreds of laws at each session and considers and rejects hundreds more. A good many deal with matters affecting particular cities or towns and would be eliminated if more state constitutions gave their localities home rule.

Financial matters comprise an important part of the work of a state legislature. While the governor may take a strong lead in formulating the state budget, it is up to the state legislature to find sources of revenue and to appropriate money. State constitutions usually provide that no money may be drawn from the treasury except through legislative action in the form of an appropriation law. In recent years a number of states have increased the governor's control over the budget. This trend is to the good, within limits, but the legislature should never surrender its power over finance, which is basic to democratic government.

The legislature's power to investigate is of great importance. Woodrow Wilson has said that "it is the proper duty of a representative body to look diligently into every affair of government and to talk much about what it sees." [1] Through its investigatory function the legislature becomes a watchdog over the treasury, to make sure that money appropriated is properly spent. The recent increasing frequency of legislative investigations has been in large part a result of the augmented powers of the governor, for legislatures feel that they must keep a close watch on the spending of public money.

State legislatures also exercise a number of other nonlegislative functions, including approval of appointments, which is generally vested in the upper house; election of certain officials, such as auditor; and the power of impeachment. In cases of impeachment the lower house draws up articles of impeachment and prosecutes before the upper house which sits as a court.

Evolution of State Legislatures

Since the time when English lawmaking bodies, predecessors of our American legislatures, were first established, legislatures have had successive periods of power and weakness, of popular favor and disfavor. The more immediate origin of our own state legislatures was in the colonial assemblies, most of which were weak until they learned how to manage dictatorial royal governors by getting control of the purse.

As a reaction, the original state legislatures were all-powerful. Bitter experience had taught the people to distrust strong executives. Thus they conferred great powers on the legislatures of the newly formed states. In time these powers were abused and the role of the governors was enhanced at the expense of the legislatures. Governors were eventually made elective by the people and were given the power of veto. Legislative abuses also led to the placing of constitutional limitations upon legislatures.

Today state legislatures are regaining some of their lost prestige. Legislation has been considerably improved through the use of expert

---

[1] *Congressional Government,* p. 303, Houghton Mifflin Company, Boston, 1887. The student should also read Chap. V of John Stuart Mill's *Considerations on Representative Government,* 1861.

bill-drafting services, legislative reference bureaus, interim committees, and legislative councils, all of which will be considered below. Nevertheless, the factor which continues to keep down the quality of legislative output, in the opinion of many authorities, is the two-house system and the scheme of legislative apportionment which is usually part of bicameralism.

The Bicameral Legislature

The two-house, or bicameral, legislature is our heritage from England. This system was generally used in colonial assemblies and was the model for the national Congress when the Constitution was drawn up. Three of the original thirteen states, Georgia, Pennsylvania, and Vermont, departed from the two-house pattern at first and used one legislative body but only Vermont retained it for any length of time and even Vermont eventually returned to bicameralism.

American cities also followed the congressional lead and adopted bicameral legislative bodies but, except in rare instances, this form of city council has now been discarded as cumbersome and full of faults, and unicameralism prevails. Still the states cling to bicameralism. Only Nebraska now has a one-house legislature, adopted in 1934 under the leadership of the late Senator George Norris.

As it usually operates in the 47 states, the bicameral legislature consists of an upper house which often, like the United States Senate, gives representation to various areas of the state more or less irrespective of population, and a lower house which purports to represent the various parts of the state on a population basis, like the Federal House of Representatives.

Proponents of bicameralism advance five major arguments for its retention: (1) two houses are a preventive against hasty and careless legislation; (2) a second chamber serves as a check against popular passions and impulses; (3) there is a danger that a one-house legislature will usurp the powers of other departments and thus take away the rights of the people; (4) a bicameral legislature is good insurance against corruption and control by vested interests; (5) the bicameral legislature is a tradition in America, while the unicameral idea is foreign to our institutions.

Almost all authorities on political organization disagree with these arguments. They maintain that two houses, in actual practice, promote hasty and careless legislation, rather than prevent it. The cumbersome processes involved in duplicated committees and hearings, the need for passing every bill twice, and then sending it through a conference committee, create legislative log jams at the end of every session and send many hasty and ill-considered bills into the statute books.

Next, it is pointed out that a second chamber has checked, not popular passions and impulses, but legitimate popular wishes. Important or desirable legislation is often stalled, sometimes for years, in the crannies of complicated legislative processes, or stymied behind the closed doors of conference committees by the maneuvering of special interests.

Opponents of bicameralism point to the public record of the state legislatures everywhere as evidence aplenty that bicameral legislatures are often rife with corruption and a prey to the control of vested interests. The exposé a few years ago of the extralegal control wielded over the California legislature by a powerful liquor lobbyist (later jailed) is a case in point.

That the bicameral legislature is a tradition in this country is unquestionable, but examination of this tradition shows that it has its roots in English history when two legislative houses were created to give representation to two distinct social classes. The opponents of two houses point out that the absence of a nobility in this country removes all reason for giving anyone separate representation in an upper house.

The fears regarding unicameralism are dissipated by the experience with unicameral legislatures in most American cities, in Nebraska, and in the many foreign countries which have adopted the one-house system, including Canada, Finland, Turkey, Iceland, Norway, and Denmark.

The proponents of unicameralism advance these arguments: (1) membership in a unicameral body lends more prestige and dignity to legislators and thus attracts better talent; (2) a single chamber is more efficient and considers legislation more thoroughly; (3) stalemate which often occurs in bicameral bodies due to jealousy, friction, and rivalry is eliminated; (4) responsibility for failure or success is more easily established and pinpointed; (5) legislative leadership is concentrated in one house, not dissipated as it is in a two-house system; (6) relations between the legislature and the executive departments are simplified and thus improved by reducing the houses to one; (7) far from being a prey to vested interests, the one-house legislature holds selfish interests in check; (8) the unicameral legislature makes reporting more complete and enables the public to get full information on what is going on in the legislature, whereas reporting of debates and discussions in bicameral state legislatures is very incomplete and sketchy; (9) a one-house legislature is more economical to run.

Authorities on political organization almost unanimously condemn the two-house legislature and recommend unicameralism. The Model State Constitution (framed by an expert Committee on State Government of the National Municipal League) calls for a unicameral assembly. The Committee on American State Legislatures of the American Political Science Association has also recommended it. "States with bicameral legislatures," says the report, "might well re-examine the traditional arguments and claims for bicameralism in the light of the facts of its actual operation. It may be found that some of the original justifications for two houses are now obsolete and that many of the supposed advantages cannot be demonstrated in practice. Many of the supposed checks and safeguards provided by a bifurcated legislature are more or less illusory. Other checks, notably the executive veto, judicial review, and public opinion, are more effective." [2] The committee goes on to point out that unicameralism in Nebraska has been successful and that none of the anticipated evils have developed. Even though the unicameral legislature is no panacea for legislative ills, the committee admits, still "a single house seems a more logical framework upon which to hang these changes. It facilitates in many respects the effectiveness and responsibility of the legislature as the 'board of directors' state government."

Professor Richard C. Spencer, reporting on Nebraska's experience after 15 years of unicameralism, found that the people now seem well satisfied with the system and there is no demand for a return to the two-house system. "A lieutenant governor who presided over the new legislature is numbered among the converts," he relates. "Election records show that voters are fully aware of their legislature and are interested in their representatives. . . . Between 80 and 90 per cent of those voting at primary elections vote for legislative candidates even though they are not on partisan sections of the ballot.

"More than that, candidates elected are usually persons who have already won some local distinction. . . .

"Until now, at least, no member seems to have his district sewed up through local machine politics."

Summing up the factors that have contributed to the success of the system in Nebraska, Dr. Spencer finds: "(1) knowledge of what goes on, that is, absence of the uncertainty so common under bicameral systems caused by not knowing what another chamber, its standing committees or committee chairmen or conference committees may do; (2) a bill procedure that is deliberate and democratic; (3) procedure that is clear, understandable, observable, and easily reportable by the newspapers; (4) committee structure that promotes some degree of internal leadership and coordination; (5) a session that is not limited as to duration."

Finally, the quality of legislation, in terms of thorough consideration, is found to be high in Nebraska, without a diminution of ultimate legislative output.

"The preliminary examining or drafting of bills is real and not per-

[2] *American State Legislatures*, Report of the Committee on American Legislatures, pp. 59–60, American Political Science Association, Belle Zeller, ed., Crowell, New York, 1954.

functory. . . . The legislature itself has an adequate opportunity to debate each bill. Technical safeguards are provided so that there seems to be little opportunity to railroad a bill through, as so frequently happens in bicameral legislatures.

"Perhaps one of the greatest assets of the Nebraska system," Dr. Spencer concludes, "is that operations, including those of lobbyists and members alike, are out in the open where newspapers may report them and keep the people of the state currently informed." [3]

Legislative Composition and Apportionment

If unicameralism has been so successful in Nebraska, why then is there so much opposition to its adoption in the other states? The answer lies in the peculiarities of legislative apportionment in most of the state legislatures, and in the vested interest which many pressure groups, political parties, and politicians themselves have in keeping those peculiarities intact.

Composition. As they are now constituted, most state legislatures have an upper house, usually called the senate, which ranges in size from 17 to 67 members, and a lower house with from 35 to 399 members. Lawyers and farmers are now outnumbered by businessmen among the members of both houses. Of a total of 7,475 legislators in 1949 1,728 listed themselves as in business of some sort, while lawyers numbered 1,674 and farmers 1,468. There were only 145 laborers and 222 craftsmen. Professional people were not very well represented either, doctors numbering 80, teachers 188, and undertakers 40. [4]

Apportionment. It is in the basis of legislative apportionment in the two houses that most criticisms of our bicameral legislatures have their roots. In most state legislatures both houses derive their membership from some variant of the single-member district system. That is, the state is divided into districts, each of which may elect one representative to the legislature. Differentiation between the two houses results from the different way in which districts are determined. For example, in California the district for the upper house is the county; except for the smallest counties, each county, regardless of population, is entitled to elect one senator; the only exception is that some of the smallest counties are merged for senatorial purposes. The lower house in California derives from districts supposedly equal in population; each of these elects an assemblyman.

The crux of the apportionment problem is that the end result of the single-member district system usually is that population growth takes

[3] Richard C. Spencer, "Nebraska Idea 15 Years Old," *National Municipal Review,* Vol. 39, No. 2, pp. 83–86, February, 1950.

[4] Report of the Committee on American Legislatures, *op. cit.,* p. 71.

place without corresponding redistricting. Since most constitutions leave it to the state legislature to undertake periodic redistricting, reapportionment seldom happens. The sitting legislators do not care to disturb the status quo at their own expense. Thus the large cities find themselves with far fewer representatives than their actual population warrants, and the balance of power comes to rest with the rural areas which keep the same number of representatives even though their population may be much less, proportionately, than the cities. Such small overrepresented districts have been called "rotten boroughs."

Bicameralism aggravates the rural hold on the legislature. Even though the house which is apportioned according to population may actually be fairly representative of the populous areas, the other house, based on counties or some other such geographical, unchangeable unit, retains its rural cast. In California, for example, three cities with more than half the state's population have only three senators out of 40. Thus, bills favored by the urban areas may pass one house repeatedly, but fail to be passed in the other. From the standpoint of the urban areas, the result is a reactionary state government which neglects problems of pressing moment to the majority of the people. A further result, in the view of many, is Federal intervention to solve whatever urban problems the rural-dominated legislatures will not attack.

A further bar toward realistic reapportionment is often the political complexion of the existing legislature. A legislature may recognize population growth while being unwilling so to redistrict that another party might come into power. The result is the same sort of gerrymandering which has resulted in such peculiar congressional districts. The legislative apportioners carve out districts of a shape and size to suit their own political ends, and the legislature is no more representative than before.

An interesting recent study shows that the "representativeness" of legislatures declined in more than three-quarters of the states from 1937 to 1955. A statistical scheme was devised, based on the assumption that "a measure of the representative character of the legislatures can be achieved by determining the smallest percentage of a state's population which could theoretically elect a majority of the lower house and a corresponding figure for the upper house under present district boundaries." Two tables showing the representativeness of upper and lower houses in all the states were compiled. It was found that in Georgia 5.96 per cent of the population could theoretically elect a majority of the upper house; in Connecticut 9.59 per cent of the population could theoretically elect a majority of the lower house. In 1955, 9.6 per cent of the population actually did elect the majority of the lower house in Connecticut. The researchers found that "the worst situations exist in those states where a constitutional or statutory limitation sets a rigid system

which recognizes some unit of local government as the basis of representation, such as the town or county . . . Many of the states near the top
of the rankings are found there because of frequent legislative action in
making changes in district boundaries in order to adjust to population
movements." [5]

1955 Apportionment of Upper Houses of State Legislatures [a]

Rank order	State	Minimum percentage of population needed to elect majority	Average population per senator	Smallest population per senator	Largest population per senator
1	Massachusetts	48.76	117,263	92,216	164,334
2	Wisconsin	47.53	104,078	73,301	128,970
3	Missouri	47.37	116,313	87,559	148,999
4	Arkansas	46.95	54,557	43,114	65,562
5	West Virginia	45.68	62,672	30,646	119,814
6	Vermont	45.67	12,592	3,406	17,027
7	Kentucky	45.19	77,495	51,992	104,254
8	New Hampshire	44.75	22,218	12,051	34,368
9	Virginia	43.93	82,967	55,637	135,449
10	Oregon	42.18	50,711	26,317	67,362
11	Nebraska	41.88	30,826	21,579	40,998
12	New York	40.91	244,887	146,666	344,547
13	South Dakota	40.85	19,198	10,450	35,455
14	North Carolina	40.09	81,239	48,375	191,057
15	Maine	39.71	27,690	16,052	42,300
16	Indiana	39.25	78,684	39,592	122,717
17	Texas	36.80	248,748	136,756	806,701
18	Connecticut	36.50	55,758	24,309	122,931
19	Colorado	36.12	37,860	15,931	59,194
20	Louisiana	36.00	68,808	25,326	158,236
21	Minnesota	35.93	44,513	16,878	153,455
22	Pennsylvania	35.44	209,960	78,181	442,516
23	Washington	35.44	51,717	18,839	130,635
24	North Dakota	35.36	12,909	5,405	39,933
25	Mississippi	34.59	44,468	17,869	96,910

Whether gerrymandered or not, it is usually very difficult to get any
reapportionment at all in most of our state legislatures. This is so because
the constitutions of 42 states provide for the legislature to reapportion
itself; 39 of these make the legislature the sole agency for performance
of this function. The result is that reapportionment is far overdue in many

[5] Manning J. Dauer and Robert G. Kelsay, "Unrepresentative States," *National
Municipal Review*, Vol. 44, No. 11, pp. 571–75, Dec., 1955. Reprinted by permission.

of these states, especially in those where there is a considerable rural population. In 1926 the supreme court of Illinois ruled in *Fergus v. Marks*⁶ that the legislature could not be mandamused to perform its duty of legislative reapportionment. Thus, even though the constitution of a state may call for reapportionment by the legislature, there is no way

1955 Apportionment of Upper Houses of State Legislatures (*Continued*)

Rank order	State	Minimum percentage of population needed to elect majority	Average population per senator	Smallest population per senator	Largest population per senator
26	Iowa	33.94	52,421	21,173	226,010
27	Kansas	33.67	47,631	20,381	240,785
28	Tennessee	33.26	99,748	43,392	208,255
29	Michigan	32.34	187,405	61,008	396,001
30	Oklahoma	29.45	50,758	15,898	251,286
31	Illinois	29.42	150,210	17,063	383,803
32	Wyoming	28.77	11,174	2,481	23,831
33	Alabama	28.26	87,478	18,018	558,928
34	Georgia	26.89	63,788	16,237	473,572
35	Utah	26.75	27,554	9,642	45,815
36	South Carolina	26.57	46,022	9,577	168,152
37	Delaware	22.70	18,711	3,496	57,179
38	Ohio	20.68	240,807	52,455	1,389,532
39	New Mexico	20.07	21,974	3,013	145,673
40	Arizona	19.30	26,735	8,510	330,770
41	Idaho	19.05	13,379	918	70,649
42	Montana	18.40	10,554	1,026	55,875
43	Florida	17.67	72,929	10,413	495,084
44	New Jersey	17.01	230,254	34,423	905,949
45	Maryland	15.52	80,793	12,272	269,362
46	Rhode Island	13.53	19,315	732	55,060
47	Nevada	12.36	9,417	614	50,205
48	California	11.88	264,656	14,014	4,151,687
49	Georgia (Primary)	5.96			

ᵃ Populations of legislative districts are taken from the 1950 Federal census. District data are latest available in state statutes or obtainable from state officials.

SOURCE: Manning J. Dauer and Robert G. Kelsay in *National Municipal Review*, Vol. 44, p. 572. Reprinted by permission.

to compel that body to carry out the mandate. A solution, as in Missouri and Illinois, is to vest the power to reapportion in a board which can

⁶ 311 Ill. 510.

be mandamused if it fails to act. Arizona gets the job done by providing for automatic reapportionment every two years by the secretary of state. California, Texas, and South Dakota require action by boards in the event the legislature fails to do its duty.

A four-point program to meet the problem of apportionment has been suggested by the Committee on American State Legislatures:

1955 Apportionment of Lower Houses of State Legislatures

Rank order	State [a]	Minimum percentage of population in districts needed to elect majority	Average population per representative	Smallest population per representative	Largest population per representative
1	South Carolina ..	46.72	17,073	9,577	23,173
2	Illinois	46.02	49,221	39,809	68,665
3	Oregon	45.42	26,230	12,740	48,313
4	California	44.70	132,327	62,512	
5	New Jersey	43.95	80,589	34,423	135,910
6	Virginia	43.69	33,187	14,057	82,233
7	Michigan	42.29	57,925	32,469	94,994
8	Massachusetts ...	42.15	19,544	2,870	28,675
9	Pennsylvania ...	41.63	49,991	4,944	77,106
10	Idaho	41.53	5,401	918	14,629
11	Montana	40.80	6,287	1,026	10,366
12	Wyoming	39.92	5,188	2,481	7,943
13	Texas	39.85	51,408	29,192	100,850
14	Maine	39.12	6,051	2,372	11,090
15	North Dakota ...	39.02	5,484	3,180	16,609
16	Utah	38.99	10,934	364	16,768
17	Wisconsin	38.87	34,346	14,355	56,554
18	West Virginia ..	38.87	21,335	5,119	37,540
19	South Dakota ..	38.73	8,703	3,319	21,044
20	Kentucky	37.59	29,448	12,890	104,254
21	Arkansas	37.52	19,095	6,680	36,614
22	New Hampshire .	37.40	1,336	16	2,179
23	New York	37.06	95,374	14,182	167,226

1. Divide the state into districts for election of members of the legislature. In bicameral bodies enlarge districts for the upper house. Each district should be equal in population, gerrymandering should be eliminated, and district lines should be so drawn as to provide for wide representation of interests.

2. Provide for administrative agencies to reapportion after each decennial census in the event the legislature fails in its duty.

3. Avoid use of counties and other local government areas in setting up units for representation.

4. Where bicameralism prevails use a different base of representation for each house. In the event single-member districts are used for election of members of the upper house, provide for multiple districts for lower house or vice versa, taking into account regional economic interests in so doing.

The plan suggested by the Committee on State Government, which

1955 Apportionment of Lower Houses of State Legislatures (*Continued*)

Rank order	State	Minimum percentage of population in districts needed to elect majority	Average population per representative	Smallest population per representative	Largest population per representative
24	Indiana	36.95	39,342	15,674	68,353
25	New Mexico	35.67	12,385	4,360	63,413
26	Colorado	34.67	20,386	7,520	55,687
27	Rhode Island ...	34.17	7,919	732	14,810
28	Washington	33.87	24,030	9,419	65,317
29	Oklahoma	33.38	18,457	4,589	46,479
30	Mississippi	32.67	16,383	4,966	57,737
31	Louisiana	31.94	26,569	6,244	79,118
32	Minnesota	31.56	22,767	7,290	107,246
33	North Carolina ..	30.16	33,849	5,048	71,220
34	Tennessee	30.13	33,250	3,948	75,134
35	Iowa	29.34	24,269	8,753	56,502
36	Ohio	29.19	59,303	10,759	99,610
37	Nevada	28.82	3,406	614	5,991
38	Maryland	27.57	19,049	6,136	44,894
39	Alabama	27.15	28,884	8,027	79,846
40	Georgia	26.30	16,803	2,494	157,857
41	Missouri	23.71	25,189	4,777	47,599
42	Kansas	22.59	15,242	1,925	80,262
43	Delaware	19.40	9,088	1,321	35,762
44	Florida	17.19	29,171	2,199	165,028
45	Vermont	12.58	1,505	1	33,155
46	Connecticut	9.59	7,195	130	88,699

[a] Arizona is omitted from this table because apportionment is by separate county boards based on votes cast in preceding gubernatorial elections. Population figures of electoral districts were not available. Nebraska, having a unicameral legislature, is represented only in table on page 456.

SOURCE: Manning J. Dauer and Robert G. Kelsay in *National Municipal Review*, Vol 44, p. 574. Reprinted by permission.

formulated the Model State Constitution, is multiple-member districts based on population and a unicameral legislature.

Terms, Compensation, and Privileges of Legislators

Except in two states with longer terms, members of lower houses serve two years, while senators serve four years in 32 of the states. Fifteen states provide for terms of two years for members of the upper house. In Nebraska the term for its one house is also two years.

Although 25 states have raised salaries of legislators since 1946, in most states they are still too low—so low, it is argued, that able men are discouraged from legislative service and some legislators are prey to the blandishments of well-heeled lobbyists. Members of the state legislature are paid on a per diem basis in 16 states, ranging from $4 in Tennessee to $20 in Louisiana. The remaining states pay either by the biennium or by the year. New York salaries are the highest, $5,000 annually; the lowest paid legislators are in New Hampshire, where they receive only $200 a year. Members receive additional allowances for travel in many states; in some states allowances are paid for expenses during the session. Some states provide weekly allowances for travel, some daily allowances for members within commuting distance of the capital.

The Committee on State Legislatures of the American Political Science Association has recommended that legislators be paid enough to "offset personal sacrifice as measured by average income." Furthermore, for the sake of flexibility, compensation should be fixed by statute rather than frozen into the constitution. Extra compensation for officers and members of interim committees and legislative councils is also urged.

Sessions of State Legislatures

How long a legislative session is, and whether or not the legislature is meeting at a time when there are pressing public problems to be solved, can have a great deal to do with the quality of the laws that are passed, and the efficiency of state government in general. In this respect, many states are handicapped by the provisions of their constitutions.

There are four different kinds of legislative sessions: regular, special, split, and adjourned.

Regular. All state constitutions provide for regular sessions. Ten states now have annual sessions but in the others the legislature meets regularly only every second year. The trend is toward annual sessions since the business of legislatures is rapidly increasing. In nearly half of the states, the legislative session is arbitrarily limited—36 days in Alabama, 5 months in Connecticut, 60 days in a number of states, 120 days in California. Some states either stop or reduce the pay of legislators after a fixed number of days, which is another way of limiting the length of sessions. The result of such limitations is often either a rush of ill-considered legislative business at the end of a session, or failure to meet certain problems at all because of lack of time.

Special. While in most of the states only the governor may call special sessions of the legislature, in several the legislature may convene itself upon a petition signed by anywhere from a majority to two-thirds of the membership. As a rule, when the governor calls a special session he may limit the subjects on which the legislature may legislate to those mentioned in his call. The frequent use of special sessions indicates the need for annual sessions. Nineteen states have limitations on the number of days of special sessions—for example, 36 in Alabama, 15 in Arizona.

Adjourned Sessions. In order to circumvent the limitations of biennial sessions, some states use what is known as an adjourned session, *i.e.,* the legislature uses only part of the allotted period for a regular session, then adjourns to meet again the following year. Georgia, Tennessee, Alabama, Ohio, and Pennsylvania use variations of this scheme.

Split Sessions. California is the only state that uses the split session, whereby the legislature meets at a short session of about a month, chiefly for introduction of bills, following which the legislature is recessed for about six weeks. It then reconvenes and continues for the remainder of the 120 days allotted. Although designed to allow time for study of bills and consultation with groups interested in legislation, and to avoid hasty consideration of bills, the split session has not been entirely successful. It has been used in California since 1911.

Organization of Legislatures: Officers. Often the kinds of laws passed by a legislature, and the laws which are bypassed as well, depend on who is chosen presiding officer. The speaker of the lower house of any state legislature is particularly powerful. His right to recognize members and to decide parliamentary questions may turn the whole course of a legislative battle, often to great partisan or factional advantage. Perhaps even more important is the speaker's power to appoint committees. In many states the members of committees are actually picked by party leaders and appointment by the speaker is a mere formality. However, in one-party states the speaker's power of appointment is very great.

Usually the speaker is hand-picked in advance by the majority party or faction and the house only goes through the motions of electing. Other officers who are elected by the house include the clerk, speaker pro tem, doorkeeper, messenger, and postmaster.

In upper houses the lieutenant governor is usually the presiding officer. He has less power than the speaker of the lower house, particularly with regard to appointment of committees. In many states the committees in the upper house are appointed by a committee on committees or by resolution, as in Colorado. In Connecticut, Delaware, New York, and other states the committees are named by the president pro tem.

The Committee System. Since both the upper and lower houses of state legislatures are too large to grind out legislation in plenary session, committees are essential. It would be impossible for either house to act upon the hundreds and thousands of measures proposed at each legislative session without committees. It is in committee that the more important part of a legislature's work is done. Actually, what goes on in plenary session is, as a rule, just window dressing. The committees do most of the work of preparing, considering, revising, and screening proposals in both houses. There are several kinds of committees—standing, special, interim, and joint.

STANDING COMMITTEES. Standing committees are more or less permanent and are divided according to the subject matter with which they deal. For example, a committee on ways and means deals with ways of raising money.

As a rule, there are entirely too many standing committees. For example, the lower house of Georgia has 63 standing committees, Michigan, 69, and Tennessee, 46, while the upper house of Arkansas has 53 committees, Mississippi, 49, and North Carolina, 52. Duplication of effort and dissipation of legislative leadership results. Some members are overburdened with important committee assignments, while others assigned to unimportant committees have little or nothing to do. A legislator who has as many as half a dozen or more committee assignments cannot do justice to any one of them. Often several committees may be meeting simultaneously and then the legislator must choose which one he will attend.

Following the reorganization of Congress in 1946, state legislatures began to follow suit and reduce the number of their committees. In Oklahoma the number in the lower house was cut from 69 to 27, in South Carolina from 35 to 8, and in Nevada from 42 to 24; in the upper houses Oklahoma reduced its committees from 33 to 25, South Carolina from 36 to 15, and Nevada from 26 to 15. In 1956 the Georgia senate cut its committees from 33 to 15 and the house from 63 to 20. Similar reductions have been made in other states.

Not only are legislative committees too numerous but they are generally too large to do efficient work; sometimes they have over 60 members. Following the lead of Congress, several state legislatures have cut down the size of standing committees and limited membership of each legislator to a maximum of from one to three committees.

OTHER COMMITTEES. Special committees are temporary and are appointed to perform a certain specific task and then terminate. Interim committees are appointed also to do a particular job between sessions of the legislature. For example, they may be assigned to look into governmental economies or to investigate some administrative abuse. Joint committees, composed of members of both houses, deal with matters of common concern. In Massachusetts, Maine, and Connecticut practically all standing committees are joint. Joint committees have many advantages, eliminating much needless duplication and providing better coordination of the work of both houses.

The Committee on American Legislatures of the American Political Science Association has made the following recommendations with respect to a sound committee system:

1. Substantially reduce the number of standing committees.

2. Utilize joint committees so as to avoid duplication and bring about more coordination.

3. Reduce the number of committee assignments of each legislator, preferably to one, to increase the efficiency of committee work.

4. Select able leaders for chairmen of committees and assign members to committees for which they are specially qualified.

5. Adopt rules requiring adequate notice of hearings as well as complete records of proceedings; also, provide for prompt consideration of proposals referred to committees.

6. Establish either a legislative council or some similar legislative service to look into most important legislative matters and to recommend appropriate action.

7. Employ competent staffs to carry on research and to assist committees in the performance of their tasks.

Legislative Procedure

While the procedure in making laws is similar in all the states, there are some significant variations. Generally, three readings of bills on separate days are required. Although a simple majority vote in both houses is all that is necessary to pass a measure in most states, a constitutional majority (majority of the total membership) is necessary in a few. As a rule, money bills must originate in the lower house, but there are some exceptions, as in New York.

There are several steps in the making of a law. As an example let us take a bill which calls for reorganization of the state administrative system. Either a member of the house or possibly the governor may have an appropriate bill drafted. Nowadays, most states have expert drafting services which draw up bills after they have been outlined. The proposed measure is introduced in the house by dropping it in the hopper at the clerk's desk (actually giving it to the clerk) who assigns it a number— HR 150. The bill is now read by title only and referred to a standing committee.

Since this is a very important measure and is likely to be controversial, public hearings are held, at which both proponents and opponents are given an opportunity to discuss the bill before the committee. After this the committee may go into executive session and debate the bill among themselves, possibly to propose and make changes. Finally, a vote is taken and if a majority favor the proposed measure, a favorable report is made to the house.

The bill is now put on the house calendar and a second reading takes place. Then the bill is passed on to a third reading or, as in some states, the debate and amendment stage of the bill may occur on the second reading. In the debate and amendment stage the bill is considered section by section and amendments are now in order. Although the bill is required to be read, it is highly unusual for a bill to be actually read throughout, and such a reading would serve little or no purpose, for printed copies are on the desk of each member. Usually the actual reading is dispensed with after a few lines are read and only a token compliance is made with the constitutional requirement of three readings.

After debate and discussion is ended, the bill is put to a final vote. The speaker puts the motion and asks all those who favor to say aye and those who oppose to say no. If a division is called for, the speaker then may ask all who favor to rise and stand until counted which simply means to hold up their hands. After the affirmative count is taken, the speaker asks for the negative votes. A roll-call vote may be requested by a certain portion of the membership, usually one-fifth.

The bill now goes to the upper house where it follows through the same stages as in the house. (Sometimes, however, an identical bill has already been introduced in the upper house by a member so that consideration of the same proposal has taken place simultaneously by both houses.) If amendments are made the bill goes back to the originating house for approval. Should the lower house fail to concur on all amendments, a conference committee is necessary. The presiding officer of each house appoints a certain number (the same number from each house) who meet to iron out the differences. A report is now made to the respective houses and is voted upon by their membership. Usually such reports are accepted. HR 150 is now signed by the presiding officer of each house and is sent to the governor for his signature. The latter is allowed so many days in which to consider the bill. If he vetoes it, the bill returns to the legislature and must pass by a two-thirds vote in order to become a law.

When a bill comes to either house for consideration, it may be killed in either of two ways. If a member moves indefinite postponement of the measure and the house votes favorably on the motion it is dead. A motion to table, if passed, will also kill the bill.

In some states a committee of the whole house is used for consideration of more important bills. The procedure is more informal than in a plenary session. The speaker withdraws and appoints a chairman who presides. The bill is read by sections, amended, debated, and finally passed or rejected. After this, formal approval in the house is all that is necessary.

Forces behind Legislation

Political parties or political factions may play an important role in the shaping of legislation. A party may adopt a legislative program either in a state convention or at a caucus of members. A candidate for governor may run on a specific platform and if elected will then attempt to carry out his program by making recommendations to the legislature. In two-party states candidates for governor run on platforms framed by their respective party conventions or conferences and the successful candidate is expected to submit a legislative program to the legislature.

Nowadays, pressure groups actually exert more influence over legislation than political parties do. While political parties are chiefly interested in patronage and personnel, pressure groups are concerned only with policy determination. There are numerous pressure groups in the various states—railroads, trucking interests, education groups, insurance agents, retail merchants, doctors, banking concerns, liquor interests, manufacturers, farmers' associations, labor organizations, horse-racing interests, petroleum dealers, utilities such as power and natural-gas companies, temperance organizations, League of Women Voters, and many, many others.

All pressure groups use similar methods. At meetings held far in advance of legislative sessions, a plan of action is determined. In the preliminary stage such a group may consist of an executive committee which encourages all members to send in suggestions. The committee then works out proposed legislation which may later be approved by a more representative group of the organization. Not only does the organization press for positive legislation, but it is prepared to fight bills which it regards as inimical to its interests.

In their efforts to get a bill passed or defeated, moneyed groups employ special agents as lobbyists, while organizations such as the League of Women Voters use their own members to appear before legislators. Legislators are interviewed both individually and collectively. At public hearings on bills which concern an organization, representatives appear to speak. Legislators may be bombarded with telegrams, letters, and telephone messages, or may be buttonholed by personal representatives. Threats of defeat in the next election may be hurled both at individual legislators and at whole parties. It is, indeed, very difficult for a legislator to lend a deaf ear to pressure groups, nor should he do so, for pressure groups are a voice of at least a segment of the people he represents.

While most pressure groups have selfish ends which they pursue, the contribution they make to the legislative process is often real and valuable. They and their lobbyist-representatives serve as expert bill-drafters and legislative researchers, sometimes even as errand boys for legislators who are without such resources, and they are the funnel through which the desires of a legislator's many constituents are poured. In a very real sense, they are the voice of the people. The problem, of course, is that they are not the voice of all the people. Many important parts of the population are unorganized and thus legislatively voiceless. A few groups, such as the League of Women Voters, speak for the general welfare, but even in such cases there can be an honest difference of opinion.

Thus, it is the legislator's problem critically to weigh the arguments and materials presented by pressure groups and their lobbyists, to use them for what they are worth and to seek further where they are misleading or lacking. It is also the legislator's responsibility to resist the blandishments of those lobbyists who employ methods which are considered unethical. Legislative committees could not function if lobbyists were not present to offer relevant arguments concerning proposed legislation. But when lobbyists offer bribes to committee members in the form of meals, drinks, entertainment, money, stock, jobs, or clients, then the honest legislator must recognize these forms of persuasion for what they are and, of course, refuse them. Popular impressions to the contrary notwithstanding, most lobbyists are honest practitioners of an important democratic art. It is to the dishonest members of the profession that most of the current regulatory attempts are directed.

The usually unjustified odium attaching to the lobbyist is evidenced by the provision of some state constitutions, inserted by well-meaning but naive framers, that defines lobbying as a crime. Most states have statutes on their books which attempt, more or less realistically, to control the abuses to which lobbying is subject. Most such laws are intended to provide public reporting and publicity for lobbyists and lobbying. A common requirement is that each lobbyist must register, give the names of his clients, the legislation which he favors or opposes, his compensation, and other details. Unfortunately, such laws are seldom enforced, or they are circumvented. These are the recommendations of the Committee on American State Legislatures on the subject of lobbying:

1. Every state should provide by statute for lobby regulation and publicity, realistically taking into account the part played by pressure groups in the legislative process. Paid and unpaid lobbyists should be required to register and to file periodic as well as final expense accounts in cases where they appear before legislative agencies to influence legislation.

2. Employers of pressure agents and those resorting to the "indirect lobby," who strive to influence legislation by appealing to the public by

means of mass media, should also be required to file periodic statements of sources of income as well as detailed expenditures.

3. An enforcement agency should be set up either in the form of a legislative committee or in the attorney general's office. Such an agency should have adequate sanctions to carry out the law with respect to registration. Such matters as revocation of registration certificates, hearing complaints, reports on violations of the law should be among their functions.

4. Since corrupt-practices legislation is related to lobby laws, revamping of either should take into consideration the effect on the other.

5. Reorganization of state legislatures is also related to lobby regulation. Wherever modernization takes place, it is a step toward regulation and control of lobbying.[7]

Legislative Service Agencies

So complex and varied are the problems of state government nowadays that it is impossible for amateur legislators, in the brief time they have to consider these problems, to do justice to them in legislation. Legislatures are increasingly utilizing the services of experts. At least two-thirds of the states now make use of legislative councils, while some of those which have not adopted this plan employ legislative reference bureaus and interim committees. Some legislators are prejudiced against experts as "theorists," but gradually this narrow view is disappearing.

Legislative Councils. Legislative councils might be styled super interim committees in that they conduct a wide variety of inquiries into legislative issues and prepare reports and proposed measures for the next legislative session. Membership in the council consists of members from both houses of the legislature. Size of the council varies from 3 to 27 members, although one or two states have provided that all members of both houses are *ipso facto* members of the legislative council. The council is usually assisted by a research staff, and its effectiveness will depend upon the ability of its staff. In many instances the staff director is a political scientist. The council performs an invaluable service in planning legislation well ahead of a legislative session and in publishing research reports on matters of great interest to legislators. Some of these councils prepare a legislative program for the coming session of the legislature and make recommendations, while others merely prepare reports and draft bills with no recommendation. It is probably best for a council to limit itself to the functions requested by the legislature. In ten states the legislative council also has the job of continuously reviewing state revenues and

[7] *Report,* pp. 238–39.

expenditures and analyzing the budget before the session begins. In other states this function is given to a specialized staff.

That legislative councils are highly regarded is attested by the fact that a large portion of their recommendations are often approved—for example, 80 per cent in Kansas and 72 per cent in Pennsylvania. States with legislative councils, and the year of adoption, are:

Kansas 1933	Alabama 1945	South Carolina 1949
Virginia 1935	Indiana 1945	Texas 1949
Connecticut 1937	North Dakota 1945	New Hampshire 1951
Illinois 1937	Arkansas 1947	New Mexico 1951
Nebraska 1937	Minnesota 1947	South Dakota 1951
Pennsylvania 1937	Utah 1947	Louisiana 1952
Maryland 1939	Washington 1947	Arizona 1953
Oklahoma 1939	Wisconsin 1947	Colorado 1953
Maine 1940 °	Wyoming 1947	Montana 1953
California 1941	Florida 1949	Tennessee 1953 †
Missouri 1945	Ohio 1949	

° In Maine the agency is called a legislative research committee and in several other states the title of committee or commission or something similar has been adopted.

† Kentucky abolished its council in 1948 and replaced it with a research commission having the powers of a legislative council.

Legislative councils answer three important needs. First, they make possible effective and continuing legislative participation in policy formation. Second, they provide lawmakers with impartially gathered facts on which to base their decisions, thus relieving them of the need for relying entirely on the biased materials provided by pressure groups. Third, they also serve to educate the electorate, through the hearings they hold and the research reports they distribute.

Interim Committees. While legislative councils are comparatively new devices, interim committees go back to the beginnings of state legislatures. An interim committee is a temporary agency composed of selected legislators, set up to gather information on a particular problem, while legislative councils are permanent and not so restricted in their functions. Interim committees do not make as wide use of research staffs as councils. Still, interim committees are invaluable to legislatures. Even if there is also a legislative council, this is true. When both are used their work should, of course, be coordinated.

Legislative Reference Bureaus. The oldest of the agencies established to aid legislators is the legislative reference bureau, which is now to be found in 40 states. The bureau employs experts who do needed research and assemble information on behalf of the lawmakers. In some states the bureau even prepares legislative programs.

Bill Drafting. Practically all the states now have some form of bill-drafting service. In some cases the legislative council is given this function, while in others there may be a special drafting agency which in some states is placed in the attorney general's department. The result has been great improvement in the quality of legislation generally.

Reorganization of State Legislatures

Like state government in general, most state legislatures are greatly in need of reorganization and modernization. Much has been done in recent years, but much more is required. The increased and increasing number and complexity of the problems which legislators must solve, the rapidly rising cost of state government, all underline the need for state lawmaking bodies which can attack their jobs with efficiency, honesty, and dispatch.

Unfortunately, the constitutional equipment of most state legislatures is still antiquated. Spurred on by the reorganization of Congress in 1946, several states have reorganized their legislatures in recent years. Some of them have drastically cut the number and size of their legislative committees. Other improvements, constitutional and otherwise, have been made here and there. These are the fields in which improvement is still needed in most states:

1. *Annual Sessions.* There is now too much legislative business for biennial sessions alone. Several states already have instituted annual sessions but the larger number meet regularly only every two years. The fact that some states now make use of adjourned sessions illustrates the need for annual sessions.

2. *Legislative Services.* Some sort of legislative agency comparable to the legislative council should be adopted in every state. These agencies should be able to help the legislature regain its lost prestige and reassert its policy-determining powers, especially in states where the governor has become too dominant in such matters.

3. *Reduction of Legislative Committees.* State legislatures should reduce the number of committees in both houses, as several states have already done. Drastic reduction of committees should make for greater efficiency and better utilization of leadership.

4. *Reduction of Size of Committees.* The size of the committees should also be sharply reduced, and the number of comittees a legislator may serve on should be not more than two and preferably one.

5. *Compensation and Allowances of Legislators.* In order to attract better talent to the legislature, compensation for members should be substantially increased in most states. Those men and women who serve in the legislature are called upon to do so at a considerable sacrifice and they should be rewarded accordingly. Annual salaries rather than per diem compensation would be preferable. In addition, travel allowances for more frequent trips home should be provided.

6. *Lobbying.* Legislation to cover lobbying should be more realistic. Certainly lobbying is so well established and often so useful that its normal practice should not be considered a crime. Legislation calling for full publicity with regard to lobbying activities should be enacted. Paid as well as unpaid agents should be required to register and file periodic reports of expenditures. Employers and others who use mass media to influence public opinion should also be required to make periodic reports on sources of income and on expenditures.

7. *Adoption of Timesaving Devices.* A number of states now use electric voting machines. These devices save a great deal of time on roll calls, especially in large legislative halls. All states would do well to install similar systems.

8. *Apportionment and Reapportionment.* In order to do away with the evil of gerrymandered legislatures, automatic provision for reapportionment of members of legislatures should be made, preferably in state constitutions. Urban populations are discriminated against in practically all the states. States should follow the lead of Illinois and Missouri and set up commissions to perform the task of reapportionment. Such boards can be mandamused. Arizona has the only really automatic provision for reapportionment. In that state the secretary of state must reapportion memberships every two years. The county and town should be abolished as units of representation and legislative districts should be substituted.

9. *Unlimited Sessions.* Limitations on the number of days that a legislature is allowed for its sessions should be removed, so that legislators may be allowed sufficient time for deliberation.

10. *Reduction of Membership.* Some state legislatures, especially the lower houses, are too large and unwieldy for efficient work, and should be reduced in size.

11. *Revision of Rules.* Rules of both houses should undergo frequent revision. Many unnecessary or unfair rules are still retained in some states. Means should be provided for bringing a proposed measure to a vote when it is being needlessly held up by a committee.

12. *Adequate Provision for Public Hearings.* State legislative committees should be required to hold public hearings on all controversial bills. Advance public notice should be given and sufficient time should be allotted for such hearings.

13. *Allow Legislature to Convene Itself.* The legislature should be permitted to convene itself, provided a certain percentage of the legislators petition the governor to do so. It is probably better to require that two-thirds or three-fifths of the legislators shall sign such a petition. There are times when the governor is reluctant to call a special session of the legislature, even though one is urgently needed. A number of states now provide for their legislatures to convene themselves.

14. *Provision for Unicameral Legislature.* States with bicameral legislatures should seriously consider adoption of the unicameral system following the lead of Nebraska. Not only is the unicameral legislature a timesaver, since legislation must run the gauntlet of only one house, but it also provides more opportunity for deliberation. Moreover, as the late Senator George Norris insisted, the one-house system cuts out the conference committee where vested interests get in their deadly work behind closed doors. Nebraska has found that the unicameral plan works well—that legislation is carefully considered, that all interests are well represented, and that the cost is less.

A Judgment about Legislatures

Considering the conditions under which they work it must be admitted that our state legislatures do not serve us badly. They are limited in scores of ways by constitutional prohibitions and judicial decisions; the problems with which they wrestle are often of extreme complexity; they are continually subject to pressures of all sorts; and they do not always have the information required to act promptly or intelligently. Some of these limiting factors could be offset by better organization and by the provision of better research staffs. Legislatures have perhaps not moved as rapidly as they might with respect to these latter although there is encouraging progress to be reported. When legislatures are criticized for crookedness or lack of seriousness it must be remembered that every large body of men is likely to contain both rogues and clowns. These "make the headlines" while their less spectacular colleagues labor fruitfully in obscurity. By and large our state legislators reflect with reasonable accuracy the various currents of opinion held by their constituents; when supplied with the facts they are not lacking in judgment; and their sense of responsibility is at least as high as that found in the business community and in some of the professions.

REFERENCES

American State Legislatures, Report of the Committee on American State Legislatures of the American Political Science Association, 1954.

Armand B. Coigne, *Statute Making* (1948).

Council of State Governments, *The Book of the States* (Biennial).

Council of State Governments, *Our State Legislatures,* Report of Committee on Legislative Processes (1948).

Hallie Farmer, *The Legislative Process in Alabama,* University of Alabama, Bureau of Public Administration (1949).

CHAPTER 27 *The Office of Governor*

Except possibly in those states where his powers have been recently enlarged, the governor as head of a state has never had power commensurate with his responsibility. Alexis de Tocqueville, writing about conditions that existed at the time of President Jackson's administration, said "The executive power of the state is represented by the governor . . . although he enjoys but a portion of his rights." [1] J. A. Corry, the distinguished Canadian observer of American government, recently observed that when the states "established the office of Governor, they denied to him any substantial authority, dispersing executive power into many hands. The result was a weak executive and a very low level of efficiency in state government. The efficiency of state government did not begin to rise until the movement to reorganize the state executive power was launched in 1917." [2] Even today, the Kestnbaum Commission was forced to conclude that "few states have an adequate executive branch headed by a governor who can be held generally accountable for executing and administering the laws of the State." [3] History provides the chief reasons why this situation prevails.

History of the Office

The office of governor has had a long and eventful history in the United States for it dates not from the time of the making of the Federal Constitution but from the very beginning of colonial government in America. Although most colonies were started as private enterprises, by the time of the Revolution the royal colony had become the norm and a fairly uniform system of government existed. The governor, appointed from the

[1] Alexis de Tocqueville, *Democracy in America*, Vol. 1, pp. 84–85, Knopf, New York, 1945.

[2] J. A. Corry, *Elements of Democratic Government*, new ed., p. 136, Oxford University Press, New York, 1951.

[3] The Commission on Intergovernmental Relations, *A Report to the President*, p. 42, Washington, 1955.

mother country, became the instrument of royal authority. In all colonies he was first at all social functions, was referred to as "his excellency," and might receive a salute of 17 guns. His powers, outlined in his instructions and commission, were broad and numerous. Until late in colonial history the legislative and judicial branches were subordinate to the executive. A governor's commission usually gave him power "to make, constitute and ordain laws" with the advice and consent of the assembly and council. He had an absolute veto over all legislation.[4]

Still, his office was not a bed of roses. It was difficult simultaneously to act as an agent binding the colony to the mother country and as the head of the local government seeking the best interests of the colonists. The loss of prestige sustained by these governors at the time of the Revolution was due largely to the fact that many of them put first their responsibility to the mother country and neglected or ignored the desires of the citizens. For this reason they were thought of more as tyrants than as champions of the people.

It was unfortunate that at the time of the making of the early state constitutions this distrust of executive power was incorporated into the state constitutions themselves and that the powers of the executive were drastically curtailed. In 1787 James Madison remarked, "The executives of the states are in general little more than ciphers; the legislatures omnipotent." After the North Carolina constitutional convention in 1776 one delegate reported that the governor was given "just enough power to sign the receipt for his salary."

During the nineteenth century power began to accrue to the governorship but even during this period the office lacked both the power and the prestige that would have placed the executive on an equal standing with the other two branches of government. When a state was asked to perform new services, the legislature, instead of making the governor responsible for their execution, would create new officers, boards, and commissions and would frequently put them beyond the supervisory power of the governor. Even when the governor was given some authority to supervise, the duties and powers of the new agencies were so minutely defined in the statute that little was left to executive discretion. In so far as the states were concerned, the nineteenth century was a hundred years of legislative dominance over state affairs.

It was not until the early years of the twentieth century that the office of governor began to assume its proper place in state government. There were six contributing factors: (1) a growing realization that the states had suffered from the lack of a strong executive to check the legislature, (2) a broadening concept of the executive responsibilities placed upon

[4] Leonard Woods Labaree, *Royal Government in America*, pp. ix ff. Yale Press, New Haven, 1930.

the chief executive, (3) the grant of additional powers by statute and constitutional amendment, (4) the reorganization of the state's administrative machinery whereby the governor became the head of the organization, (5) the replacement of the legislative budget with the executive budget, and (6) the recognition of the governor as the head of his political party within the state.

States today vary in the amount of power granted to the chief executive. In some instances his authority is still too limited. In addition to any grant of power in the constitution and statutes of a particular state, much also depends upon the personality of a particular governor, the strength of his political organization, and his philosophy of government. In general, however, the past 57 years have been a period of growth and development in the office of governor, although there is still plenty of room for future expansion. In spite of the limitations placed on the office the governorship carries great prestige and, except for the Presidency, engages the attention of the citizens of the United States more than any other elective office.

Qualifications for Office

The usual constitutional requirements for eligibility for the governorship are very simple; age, residence, and citizenship. A typical statement of qualifications is in the Virginia constitution: "No person except a citizen of the United States shall be eligible to the office of Governor; and if such person be of foreign birth, he must have been a citizen of the United States for ten years next preceding his election; nor shall any person be eligible to that office unless he shall have attained the age of thirty years, and have been a resident of the State for five years next preceding his election."

In addition to these customary requirements, others exist in particular states. Until recently in Maine the governor had to be a native-born citizen. In Arizona women are ineligible. In five Southern states there is a requirement that to be eligible for the governorship a person must believe in a Supreme Being. But if a candidate hopes to be elected, he must meet many extralegal qualifications as well. In the one-party states, the gubernatorial aspirant must be a faithful member of a particular party. In certain states, the geographical location of the home of the person desiring office plays an important part and, while women are eligible for office in all states but one, men are usually elected to the governorship. In all states the governor is elected by a vote of the people.

Salary

Even though the state government is often the biggest of all the businesses in a state, the salary paid to the governor who is the head of this huge enterprise is insignificant compared to the emoluments of presidents of comparable private business organizations. Today salaries are being raised considerably but most governors are still decidedly underpaid. In 1956 salaries varied from the $50,000 paid to the governor of New York to the $9,000 received by the governor of North Dakota. One must not conclude that all that a governor receives for his services is his salary. In addition to his stated compensation it is customary to furnish a governor with a mansion in which to live, servants, a sum for operating expenses, a car, and various other allowances. A governor, therefore, frequently receives total emoluments several times the amount of his nominal pay.

Term of Office and Succession

In most states the realization has come that no executive can do a good job if his term is so short that he barely has time to learn his work before he is out of office. In early state constitutions the term of office for the governor was either one or two years. Today the term has been lengthened so that 19 states have a two-year term and the other 29 have a four-year term. While the term of office has been made longer, other provisions have been adopted in several states that limit the number of terms a governor may serve or make it impossible for an incumbent to succeed himself. Such limitations have both critics and defenders. On the one hand such provisions are held to be undemocratic and to lose to the state the continued services of an experienced governor. On the other hand they are said to make it difficult to perfect a political machine. They also afford many governors a graceful way of retiring from office. Actually, however, political machines are as powerful in those states having these limitations as in those having none.

There is no uniform line of succession to office should a vacancy occur in the office of governor. Of the 48 states, 38 make constitutional provision for a lieutenant governor. In those states where there is no lieutenant governor, succession usually goes to the presiding officer of the senate. The Model State Constitution provides for no lieutenant governor and merely states that "the powers and duties of office shall devolve upon the presiding officer of the legislature." In some states the line of succession is short, in others it extends to the seventh degree. Virginia makes no provision for succession beyond the lieutenant governor while in New Mexico it extends first to the lieutenant governor, then to the secretary of state, to the president *pro tempore* of the senate, and to the speaker of the house in that order. Quite frequently the lieutenant governor serves not only after the death, disability, or resignation of the governor, but also when the governor is absent from the state or is "unable to perform his duties." In one state a lieutenant governor serving while the governor was away on vacation, made use of the pardoning power as a means of building up a political following. When Huey Long was governor of Louisiana he wanted to attend a meeting outside the state but was unwilling to turn the reins of government over to his lieutenant governor. The latter solved the problem by suggesting that they both make the trip together.

"Fine," said Huey, "that's the only way to go and keep my promise not to let you become Governor of Louisiana."

"And I think," added Huey, "that it would be best if we 'bunked' together, we don't want to get out of each other's sight." [5]

The Governor as First Citizen of the State

The duties and powers of the governor are detailed in the constitution and statutes of a state just as the regulations that govern the conduct of a baseball game are set down in an official rules book. Certainly a foreigner unacquainted with baseball would get a distorted picture of the game simply by reading the official rules. A similarly inaccurate picture of the governorship would come from simply reading the grants of power in the constitution and statutes. Today, powers accrue to the governor just by virtue of the fact that he is the governor and the first citizen of the state. When the legislature is in session the governor falls heir to many legislative and advisory jobs. When the legislature adjourns he breathes a sigh of relief and turns to the other gubernatorial duties discussed later in this chapter. However, as first citizen of the state, the governor at all times leads a very busy life. Receiving visitors, some on legitimate business, others who merely want to shake his hand, laying cornerstones, dedicating buildings, visiting state institutions, attending commencements of various state educational institutions, preparing addresses, delivering impromptu speeches, answering mail, all consume time and energy and make the job of being governor an interesting but a killing one. As one governor has stated, "The governorship gives a man great distinction, great honor, great glory, great happiness for himself and his family, but he has to pay." [6]

In certain large and politically doubtful states the governorship has become a stepping stone to the Presidency. Rare indeed is the Presidential nominating convention that does not have more than one governor as a strong candidate for nomination. In recent years, Dewey and Harriman of New York, Stevenson of Illinois, and Lausche of Ohio have illustrated the significance of the governorship as a developer of candidates for the Presidency.

[5] Webster Smith, *The Kingfish*, pp. 218–219, G. P. Putnam's Sons, New York, 1933.
[6] Alfred E. Smith, *Up to Now*, p. 306, The Viking Press, New York, 1929.

The Power of Appointment and Removal

It is not remarkable that all governors give time and thought to the use of the power to appoint. It is at once a political power and the means by which efficient administration may be secured. While at times it is difficult to secure desirable personnel there never seems to be a lack of applicants for any position. After some months spent in office, Governor John S. Battle of Virginia remarked that "It is trite to say it is remarkable how many people wish to serve the Commonwealth." [7]

Actually the appointment power of most governors is considerably limited. It is indeed a rare occasion when a governor has complete freedom of choice in the selection of administrative officials. Many high administrative officers are elected and have a responsibility to the people rather than to the governor. Another limitation that exists in certain states is that executive appointments are made with the consent of the senate, or the council, or, as in Virginia, with the consent of both houses. Another common brake on a governor's freedom of choice is for the legislature to require that a board be bipartisan or that its membership be distributed according to some geographical plan. Civil service rules in the most progressive states also may limit the governor's appointive power. Political considerations too must not be ignored. All in all, it is easy to see that this power of the governor is exercised subject to many curbs.

The President of the United States has the removal power because he makes appointments and the Supreme Court of the United States has held that the removal power is incident to the power to appoint.[8] No such rule is applied to the states. On the contrary there has been a continuing reluctance to give a governor the power to remove officers. Obviously the governor does not have power to remove elective officers. Civil service rules have put many persons beyond any removal power that the governor might exercise. Frequently, when appointments are made with the consent of the senate or general assembly, the consent of the same body must be secured to make a removal effective. Yet, within recent years, several factors have arisen to strengthen the removal power of the governor. Constitution makers have become aware that the governor as chief administrator must have the power to remove in order to make supervision effective. Administrative reorganization with the governor at the apex of the administrative structure has included a broader removal power for the governor. Finally, the control of the budget has enabled the governor to threaten to reduce and at times to withhold

[7] John S. Battle, "The Work of the Governor's Office," *Proceedings of the Virginia State Bar Association,* Vol. 65, p. 233, Richmond, 1954.

[8] *Ex parte Hennen,* 13 Peters 225, 258–259 (1839).

salaries and thereby accomplish the same purpose that would have been secured by using the removal power.

Legislative Powers

In each state the governor is an integral part of the legislative process and, to a varying degree, the bills that are enacted into law have been influenced by the state's chief executive. The governor, of course, does not have the right to legislate and much of his legislative power is negative in character, yet, through his power to call special sessions, to deliver messages, to veto bills, and to consult and recommend, he exerts a profound influence on the legislative program of any state. It is well to examine both the nature and the use of these legislative powers.

Power to Call Special Sessions

Whenever there is need for immediate legislative action, particularly in time of emergency, and when the governor deems it best not to wait until the next regular session of the legislature, the governor of each state has the power to call special sessions. In seven states it becomes the duty of the governor to call a special session when asked to do so by a specific vote of the legislature. In Nebraska he must do so when requested by a two-thirds vote of the legislature. In three states the legislature may assemble on its own call, while in two states, should the governor fail to issue a call when asked to do so by the legislature, the legislature may convene itself. The supreme court of Oklahoma has held that when this power is not mentioned in the constitution, the legislature has no inherent right to convene itself.[9]

During crisis periods of war or depression frequent special sessions of state legislatures have been necessary, and in a number of states more than one session has been held within the same year. Special sessions were either called or urged in certain Southern states immediately after the Supreme Court decision on desegregation. Today, with the trend toward annual sessions, there is less need for special sessions.

In his call for a special session, the governor lists the purpose for convening the legislature. He is the sole judge of the necessity for calling such a session and his exercise of power is not reviewable by the courts. There is one important difference between the operation of a special session of Congress and that of a state legislature. During a special session, Congress may consider any matter that it desires. In practically all the states, consideration may be given by the legislature only to those matters mentioned in the governor's call.[10]

    9 *Simpson v. Hill*, 128 Okla. 269, 263 Pac. 635 (1927).
    10 Impeachment charges brought against Huey Long during a special session of the Louisiana legislature were not considered by the senate acting as a court of impeach-

Message Power

Through the message power a governor has the constitutional responsibility of giving information to the legislature and the opportunity of suggesting a program of work to that body. It is at the same time a public relations tool, for the message generally receives wide publicity. At the beginning of a legislative session the governor's message informs the legislature concerning the status of governmental affairs and tells them what new laws are needed. In his message the governor may praise and he may condemn. Later he sends to the legislature his budget message describing the broad principles upon which the budget has been prepared. During a session he may send any number of special messages. Trends in state government may be easily plotted by the content of governors' messages.

In addition to messages the governor issues many proclamations. Proclamations are sometimes used like the ordinance power of the President. A proclamation cannot change existing law but it may be used to supplement and to fill out existing legislation. Proclamations are also used by the governor to designate various types of activities and purposes as Hay Fever Prevention Month, Noise Abatement Week, Brotherhood Week, and hundreds of others. Rare is the day that has not been designated in some state for a particular purpose mentioned in a governor's proclamation.

Veto Power

Of all the legislative powers of the governor the most important is the veto. While negative in character, it not only prevents certain bills from becoming law but the threat of veto is frequently enough for the governor to secure desired changes in proposed legislation or even its abandonment. Of the state constitutions that were adopted when the national government went into operation, only two gave the governor the power to veto. By 1812 over half the state constitutions gave this authority to the governor. Save West Virginia, all new states have included the veto power in their state constitutions when admitted to the Union. Today, only North Carolina denies the governor this power.

The veto has been extensively used only since the beginning of the twentieth century. According to Professor Frank Prescott more than half the total number of vetoes have occurred during these years. Also it has become more difficult to override the governor's veto. Prescott points out that for 50 years only 28 vetoes were overridden in California, 3 in Illinois in 80 years, 4 in Iowa in over 100 years, and none in Kansas in 30

---

ment because the matter of impeachment was not mentioned in the call for the special session.

years.[11] To override a veto a two-thirds vote of both houses is usually required. In some states this is a two-thirds vote of those present, in others it is a two-thirds vote provided a majority is present, while in still others a two-thirds vote of the entire membership is necessary to override. Miss Hallie Farmer writes, "The fact that the Legislature rarely over-rides a veto gives the Governor tremendous power if he chooses to exercise it, and Governors have not been unaware of that power. As one of them has said, 'I get the last vote. The Constitution gives it to me. And when I vote, my vote is more powerful than all the votes of the Legislature.'" [12]

In 39 states the governor is given the item veto which permits him to veto any item in an appropriation bill without vetoing the entire measure. In one state he has the power to veto an item in any type of bill. The desirability of this type of veto has been recognized and recently both the new constitutions of New Jersey and of Georgia have given the governor the item veto.

Whenever a measure is presented to a governor for his approval, he may sign, veto, or permit the measure to become law without his signature. Should the legislature adjourn before the measure is signed, some states permit the pocket veto, which means that the measure is killed unless signed by the governor. Other states follow the simple rule that all measures, after the number of days for signing has elapsed, become law unless vetoed. The number of days the governor has for consideration of a measure varies from state to state but most frequently is limited to five days. Because of the great number of measures that pass a legislature during the closing days of a legislative session certain states have extended the period for consideration after adjournment. New York provides 30 days, New Jersey 45. When a bill is vetoed before adjournment, the governor returns it to the house of its origin with a message giving detailed reasons for his veto or a simple statement that it is contrary to the public interest.

The Governor as Chief Administrator

Theoretically the power of administrative supervision should rest wholly with the governor. Actual practice with respect to this varies from state to state. Few governors have power comparable to the President's control over Federal administration. In each state the governor has the responsibility of seeing that various state agencies are performing their functions as directed by law. But the typical governor does not have

[11] See Frank W. Prescott, "The Executive Veto in American States," *The Western Political Quarterly*, Vol. 3, pp. 98–112, 1950.

[12] Hallie Farmer, *The Legislative Process in Alabama*, p. 182, Bureau of Public Administration, University, Ala., 1949.

sufficient and proper tools to do a top-flight job. In the performance of his administrative duties the governor possesses no inherent powers but has only those given him by the state constitution and statutes.

Possibly the most damaging factor relative to the governor's position as chief administrator and executive exists in his relationship to departmental heads. Usually seven or eight of these high administrative officers are elected, in some cases for a longer term than the governor's. In addition there are the many independent boards and commissions. Obviously these men do not have a strong feeling of responsibility to the governor. Many other officers do not come under the appointment and removal power of the governor and this seriously limits the governor in making effective his power of supervision.

Legislative enactments too limit the governor's control. In essence, his supervisory power actually depends upon the breadth of his appointment and removal power, the political power he wields as a leader of his political party within the state, and his control of the budget. To make his administrative organization function properly one governor has stated that conferring with state officials takes more time than any other gubernatorial activity.

The leadership of the governor as chief administrator is also adversely affected in those states having a two-year term of office. He hardly gets the feel of office and becomes acquainted with his assistants before he must run for reelection.

On the positive side, the governor does have the prerogative of instigating investigations concerned with the management of any department or of any state activity. He may require reports and apply other controls, especially financial controls, over departments under him.

There are also ameliorative tendencies in many states. The trend toward increasing the governor's term of office to four years has already been noted. The appointment and removal power of the governor is being broadened so that programs placed under his supervision must be carried out by assistants in a manner pleasing to the governor. Governors have been greatly aided by the creation of executive staffs to help in executing the law and supervising administration. Every governor today has an executive assistant. In general, whenever a state administration has been reorganized it has resulted in the strengthening of the governor as chief administrator. As Professor Fesler has said, "He must not merely sit at the peak of an organizational pyramid; he must have the managerial tools and the personal assistants that will enable him to be effective as chief executive." [13]

It should be noted that with respect to the duties placed upon the

[13] James W. Fesler, "The Challenge to the States," in *The Forty-eight States*, p. 11, Columbia University, New York, 1955.

governor, a writ of mandamus may be secured from the courts to require the performance of his ministerial duties but not for the performance of a discretionary one in which he is responsible only to the people.

Power to Enforce Law

A constitutional duty placed upon all governors is to see that the laws are faithfully executed. But the enforcement of criminal law in this country is carried on largely by local police and other law-enforcement officers who are not directly responsible to the governor. The multiplicity of state laws makes most citizens lawbreakers, albeit many laws are broken unintentionally and unknowingly. Under ordinary circumstances local law-enforcement officers are sufficient to apprehend lawbreakers and to enforce state law as well as municipal and county rules and ordinances. At the governor's call in most states is the state police, an organization established primarily for the promotion of highway safety but frequently with sufficient authority to make arrests for breaches of the peace.

During times of emergency, riot, and rebellion the governor plays a more important role in enforcing the law. If the sheriff of a particular county with his deputies is unable to maintain the peace he may call upon the governor for assistance. This aid may take the form of a group of state policemen, a company of the National Guard, or even personnel from the United States military force when asked by the governor to intervene. The favorite instrument today is the state police. There have been fewer instances of the use of the National Guard. This has stemmed in part from a growing reluctance on the part of governors to use the militia during industrial disputes, in part from the fact that the state police in many states are better trained in riot and mob control. When the National Guard is called out it has been found more effective to use a company from another locality.

Seldom have governors found it necessary to call upon the President of the United States to send troops into a state to preserve order. Yet it has been done and could happen again. Federal troops may be sent into a state under two conditions: first, when the governor asks for them and, second, when Federal functions and activities are interfered with, as the collection and delivery of mail and the operation of the Federal Reserve System. Indeed, it is hard to visualize a disturbance of any magnitude that would not affect the performance of some Federal function.

In cases of serious disturbance, the governor may declare martial law. There are two forms of martial law: preventive and punitive. When preventive martial law is used arrests are made by the military, and when order is restored, the offenders are turned over to the ordinary courts of the state for trial. When punitive martial law is used, civilian offenders are brought to trial before military commissions which determine the punishment for specific offenses. Martial law may be compared to the drug morphine. When used properly, morphine is one of the most effective of drugs, but when used improperly it becomes exceedingly dangerous. The same is true of martial law. When used properly and as a last resort, it is a most effective remedy for the restoration of constitutional government. When used improperly, it is the essence of tyranny.

For many years a governor's decision to use martial law was not subject to review by the courts. But this immunity to review ended in 1932, after Governor Sterling of Texas declared martial law. The Supreme Court of the United States held then that if such action interferes with the people's rights under the Federal Constitution the Federal courts may review the facts to determine whether the declaration of martial law was justified.[14] In that particular case the declaration was disallowed because the Court found that there was no insurrection in Texas and that the civil courts had remained open, their jurisdiction unobstructed. Martial law was again disallowed when a governor of South Carolina used it to oust an unfriendly highway commission. Its use was upheld when a governor of Indiana declared martial law at the request of a sheriff who was unable to preserve the peace in a particular locality. While it is desirable always to have sufficient force for the execution of the law it is to be hoped that instances requiring the use of military force for law enforcement will become less and less frequent.

The Power to Pardon

As the President of the United States may grant pardons to persons who have committed offenses against Federal law, so the governor of each state may pardon those who have broken state law. In most states the governor has a pardon board or commission to investigate and recommend and even share with him the responsibility of determining whether a pardon shall be granted or denied. It is right that he should have this aid, for as one governor has said, "I say unto you, my friends, the most trying duty that any chief executive has to perform is in the realm of pardon applications." [15] Alfred E. Smith wrote in a similar vein when he stated, "Nothing is so distressing as the attention the governor is compelled to give to applications for executive clemency when the prisoner is to be put to death. It is impossible for a man to escape the thought that no power in the world except himself can prevent a human being from going over the brink of eternity. . . . I had very many unhappy nights when executions took place." [16]

---

[14] *Sterling v. Constantin*, 287 U.S. 378 (1932).
[15] John S. Battle, *op. cit.*, p. 235.
[16] Alfred E. Smith, *op. cit.*, p. 306.

In many instances a conviction has barely been made before machinery is started to secure a pardon from the governor. If possible, recommendations are secured from the trial judge, members of the jury, the prosecuting attorney, members of the family of the person injured, and the signatures of all citizens who are willing to sign a petition for pardon. An interesting recent discovery was a pardon request signed by Abraham Lincoln long before he became President of the United States and himself the recipient of many pardon requests. This one was directed to the governor of Missouri because the person seeking pardon "has been more imprudent than guilty, and more unfortunate than criminal, but if guilty he has suffered a long confinement, and we most respectfully suggest that he be considered, by the uncertainty of his guilt and the certainty of his punishment, a fit subject for the exercise of that clemency which your Excellency is so happy as to be able to apply." [17] The pardon was granted.

Varied are the reasons given by governors for the exercise of clemency. Those most frequently cited are doubt of guilt, the first offense, excessive punishment, a good prison record, the care of dependents, and because the ends of justice have already been met. Pardons are also used to make a person eligible for parole or to secure evidence against a more dangerous criminal. Even after completion of a sentence a pardon is sometimes granted to prevent deportation of an alien or to remove disability or restrictions upon the privileges of citizenship. LaFollette, when governor of Wisconsin, thought an important function of the power to pardon was to equalize sentences imposed by various courts in the state for the same crime.[18] Politically motivated pardons are also not unknown.

A pardon which is to remove or decrease punishment inflicted for a crime which a person has committed may be absolute or conditional. A reprieve, which is a stay of execution, and a commutation, which is a lessening of punishment, are outgrowths of the pardoning power. Amnesties, or general pardons, may be granted in most states by both the governor and the legislature. Parole and probation stem from the power of the state legislature to operate prisons rather than from the governor's power to pardon.

It has already been pointed out that pardon at best is not a satisfactory remedy. Nothing can restore to an innocent man the years spent in prison as punishment for a crime he has never committed. It is also true that the issuance or denial of a pardon depends to some extent upon the man who happens to occupy the governor's chair. Some governors issue only

[17] Hugh P. Williamson, "Lincoln's Part in a Plea for Clemency to the Governor of Missouri," *Case and Comment*, p. 30, July–August, 1955.

[18] See J. L. Gillin, "Executive Clemency in Wisconsin," *Journal of Criminal Law and Criminology*, Vol. 42, pp. 755–765, 1952.

four or five pardons a year while one governor of Georgia pardoned 1,012 persons during his last 24 hours in office.

Impeachment

In a democratic state there is no satisfactory method of removing a faithless and corrupt official from office before the ordinary expiration of his term. Various methods have at times been used: forced resignation, recall, impeachment, even (unofficially!) assassination. All the states save one provide for the impeachment process, while Oregon uses the recall. Actually few governors have been impeached and fewer still have been removed from office. State constitution makers have been uncertain where to place the impeachment provisions. In some constitutions they are in the article devoted to the judiciary, in others they are placed under legislative powers, while in one they are under "Administration" and still another places them under "Elections and Officers." To impeach is to charge with a crime, and the actions which constitute impeachable offenses are sometimes constitutionally specified. Usually these offenses are called "high crimes and misdemeanors" but some constitutions, as in Alabama, may list actions extending from malfeasance in office to intemperance and moral turpitude. In each state the senate acts as the impeachment court save in Nebraska, where the supreme court acts in this capacity, and New York, where the impeached official is tried before a joint session of the senate and the court of appeals.

If the accused is found guilty the punishment in 42 states is removal from office and disqualification from holding any other public office within the state. Three state constitutions limit punishment to removal from office, while two make no reference to punishment. The pardoning power does not extend to persons found guilty by a court of impeachment and in Texas, where the legislature may grant an amnesty, the state supreme court has held that only through a constitutional amendment can the disability be removed.[19]

Impeachment is based more frequently upon political reasons than upon misconduct. Usually when it occurs the state legislature is controlled by a political party hostile to the governor or by an opposing faction within a party. When the vote is recorded it is apt to follow party lines rather than objective determination of innocence or guilt.

There have been 16 instances of the impeachment of governors or lieutenant governors. Seven of these were removed from office. Impeachment extends not only to the governor but to other state officials as listed within the state constitutions. A study of the instances of impeachment suggests several conclusions. First, there is a general reluctance on the part of the judiciary to interfere in any way with an impeach-

[19] *Ferguson v. Wilcox*, 119 Texas 280, 28 S.W. 2d 526 (1930).

ment trial. Second, although it is customary to have a long list of impeachment charges, the charge upon which the impeached official is most vulnerable is voted upon first. All that is necessary to secure removal is for the incumbent to be found guilty of one of the charges. Third, a person may be impeached during his second term for acts committed during the first term or even before election to office, as was Governor Sulzer of New York. Last, the predominant reasons for impeachments have been political.

The recall, as used in certain states and in many municipalities, provides that upon petition by a sufficient number of registered voters, an election shall be held to determine whether the officer shall be removed. Eight states provide that every public officer is subject to recall, while three more state constitutions grant power to the legislature to make provision for the recall if desired. According to the Oregon constitution, the legislature may require that the petition be signed by up to 25 per cent of those voting in the preceding election. The petition must set forth the reasons for recall. Should the incumbent then resign, the vacancy is filled according to law. If a recall election is held in Oregon, each side is allowed 200 words on the sample ballot to explain its position.

The recall transfers to the people the responsibility of ousting undesirable officers. Like impeachment, the outcome of a recall is often determined by political conditions. But since the recall does not necessarily have the criminal implications of impeachment, the political tinge is probably more defensible.

REFERENCES

Roma S. Cheek, *The Pardoning Power of the Governor of North Carolina* (1934).
J. H. Finley and J. F. Sanderson, *The American Executive and Executive Methods* (1908).
W. Brooke Graves, ed., *The American Commonwealth Series,* 1 (1953–).
Christen Jensen, *The Pardoning Power in the American States* (1922).
Leslie Lipson, *American Governor from Figurehead to Leader* (1939).
George H. Mayer, *The Political Career of Floyd B. Olson* (1951).
Coleman B. Ransome, Jr., *The Office of Governor in the South* (1951).
Charles J. Rohr, *The Governor of Maryland* (1932).
Alfred E. Smith, *Up to Now, an Autobiography* (1929).
W. C. Williams, *Smut of Colorado* (1943).

CHAPTER 28 *State Administration*

An observer in Washington might think, as he watches the afternoon exodus of thousands of Federal employees from hundreds of office buildings, that most governmental activities have been transferred to the Federal government, leaving little for the states to do. But this is certainly not so. In most states today the state government and its subdivisions conduct the largest business, handle more money, and employ more people than any single private business organization. Indeed, there are actually fewer Federal employees than there are employees of states and local units of government.

Government at the state level is truly big business. Established activities in which the states have been engaged for many years have been expanded, and new services demanded by citizens have been added. The trend is for the people to demand more services all the time. Some activities previously considered functions of the county and municipality have also been taken over by the state.

Contrary to popular impression, the expansion of Federal activities has not reduced the functions of the states but has often increased them. The social-security program of the Federal government, for example, has enormously increased the number of employees and the budgets required by state and local governments, and at the same time has increased the importance and scope of the states' job. Since 1915 there has been a continuing demand by citizens that the states regulate and promote the economic and social life of all those within their boundaries.

The legal basis for the creation of the administrative agencies which perform these services is found in the constitution and statutes of each state. Most state constitutions establish only the general framework of the government and authorize the legislature to set up by statute the agencies needed to perform state functions. Many of these state agencies, such as state utility commissions, exercise legislative, judicial, and administrative powers. In the delegation of legislative power the state legislatures are faced with the same problem as the Congress of the United States: to give the agency enough independence to do a good job but at the same time to retain the agency's responsibility to the legislature for the satisfactory performance of its work. There is one important difference between the situation in Washington and that in the states. Congress is in session most of the time while some state legislatures meet only two months out of two years. This takes a little of the pressure off state employees although it does not relieve them of responsibility.

While health, welfare, education, and highways continue to be the main fields of state administration, this is the day of state orchestras, state museums, organized recreation, planned conservation, and many more new state functions. The creation of new state agencies occurs during practically all the sessions of the state legislatures. Unfortunately, these new agencies are usually set up more or less haphazardly, without regard to the state's over-all administrative structure. As a result, the administrative machinery by which a state carries out its many and varied duties does not make up an organization in the strict sense of the term. As will be shown later, much is being done at the present time, and with considerable success, to perfect state organization.

Certainly no private business of any size would imitate the organizational pattern followed by many states. A typical state's administrative structure consists of the governor as the head; various elective and appointive officers, each of whom is responsible for the performance of a particular phase of administration; a large administrative structure made up of departments, boards, commissions, divisions, and independent agencies, and, finally, a vast army of people to do all the work and to supervise the workers.

How does this peculiar administrative aggregation work? Except for the office of governor, which is of such importance that a separate chapter is devoted to it, let us consider each component part.

The Secretary of State

All states have a secretary of state. He is elected in all except seven, where he is appointed by the governor, and three, where he is chosen by the legislature. This office, while one of the oldest of state executive offices, has little similarity to the office of Secretary of State of the United States. Obviously the entire field of foreign relations is of little concern to a state secretary of state. His office performs many and varied duties, some of which are relatively unimportant. When the office was established in the older states there were few state executive officers. As new functions accrued to the state and some officer had to be designated to oversee their execution, the secretary of state received many responsibilities and duties having little connection with the office and no connection with one another. In the early days of the states the secretary of state served as a superintendent of education. Later, as specific offices were set up, many of these duties were transferred to the proper officer.

Today the secretary of state is usually the keeper of the state seal and must authenticate certain types of documents. He maintains state records and is responsible for their publication when authorized by law. He also publishes the session laws. In many states he issues certificates of incorporation, has general oversight of elections, regulates the sale of securities, and performs many duties of a similar nature. He is, therefore, largely a clerical officer. One of his usual duties is to serve as custodian of the state house and sometimes he must even determine who is to have a telephone. He is an ex officio member of many state boards and frequently ranks high in the line of gubernatorial succession.

The Attorney General

Although the attorney general is a technical officer and must in practice be a trained lawyer, he is elected in 43 states, appointed by the governor in four states, elected by the legislature in Maine, and selected by the judges of the supreme court in Tennessee. The attorney general is the legal advisor to the governor and other state officials and renders legal opinions to state officials and local officers. For example, recently in North Carolina it was found that the great seal of the state did not conform in all particulars to the description of the seal as contained in the general statutes. An opinion of the attorney general of the state held that it conformed generally to the law and that those documents which had been authenticated by the seal were indeed properly executed. While an opinion of the attorney general is not law, his interpretation has great weight and in effect is followed until set aside by the supreme court of the state. The attorney general also represents the state as legal counsel in certain suits brought either against or by the state. Generally speaking, he has little or no control over the district attorneys, although there is some tendency today to give him more supervisory power. He is an ex officio member of many state boards.

The Treasurer

All states have a treasurer. He is elected in 42 states, appointed by the governor in three, and selected by the legislature in the remaining three. This is not a policy-determining office. His particular duty is to maintain custody of state funds under bond and strict accountability. Income from taxes and other sources is in his care and money may be paid out by him only in a manner prescribed by law. He is limited by law as to the selection of banks for the deposit of state monies. However, even within these limits the treasurer must exercise great care that the banks to which he entrusts state funds have no link to his own personal finances. Such a case developed in California in 1956 and gave rise to many a newspaper headline.

The Auditor

This officer should be neither a servant of the legislature nor a tool of the chief executive. At all times he is the peoples' representative to see that the state's financial affairs are handled in a proper manner and according to law. Elected in 32 states, he is appointed by the governor in three and selected by the legislature in seven. In California he is appointed by a joint legislative committee. In South Carolina he is appointed by the state budget and control board. Four states do not have an officer designated as an auditor.

Typically, the auditor's duties were redefined in North Carolina in 1951, in this manner: "his major responsibilities are: keeping a record of financial matters of each state agency, the issuance of all warrants for the payment of money upon the state treasurer, the conduct of annual audits and special investigations, and the reporting of all fiscal irregularities to the governor."

The Superintendent of Public Instruction

When the state entered the field of public education, the superintendent, assisted usually by a board of education, became one of the most important administrative officers in the state. As the scope of public education has broadened to include the educative process from nursery school to graduate and professional education, so has the responsibility of all officers concerned with education increased. While the superintendent's duties are usually limited to secondary schools, he is able profoundly to influence the entire educational policy of a state.

Secretary of state, attorney general, treasurer, auditor, and education superintendent are the usual state constitutional officers although some constitutions also require commissioners of labor, agriculture, insurance, and mines, to name a few typical ones.

The Departments

Speaking generally, there does not exist in state government a cabinet in the accepted meaning of the term. New York, California, and a few more states have used the cabinet idea with respect to certain high executive officers. North Carolina has a council of state. Still, it is difficult to find in the states a body with the same relationship to the governor as the Cabinet of the United States has to the President. The fact that many of these executive officers are elected rather than appointed by the governor prevents the creation of the intimate advisory body which is a cabinet in the federal sense.

Some state departments are headed by individuals, others by boards or commissions. The usual number is from 10 to 15 but Texas has 54 and Oregon has 78. The term "department" is often used loosely. In some states it describes what might be a division or a bureau in another state. The departments common to most states are:

Department of Revenue
Department of State
Department of Labor and Industrial Relations
Department of Public Health
Department of Welfare
Department of Education
Department of Agriculture
Department of Conservation
Department of Justice
Department of Commerce
Department of Banking
State Highway Department
Department of Mines and Mining

Naturally, not all of these are found in all states. The departments also vary from state to state in number of personnel and importance.

Within a department may be found an astonishing number of divisions, bureaus, commissions, and other agencies. Outside the departments most states have a large number of independent boards and commissions. All together, they form what has been referred to as "a wonderland of bureaucracy." This is the state's administrative structure.

Administrative Reorganization

One of the most interesting and valuable trends in state administration has been the extensive reorganization of administrative structure that has taken place in most states during the past 30 or 40 years. The purpose of reorganization, which has been both piecemeal and over-all, has been to secure an efficient organization for executing the duties placed upon state administrative officers. It has already been pointed out that, due to the tremendous but haphazard development of state agencies, little attention had been paid to sound principles of organization, lines of responsibility, unifunctional departmentalization, and integration. By the time of World War I it became apparent that the states were seriously handicapped by antiquated administrative machinery. Starting with Illinois in 1917 many states have reorganized their administrative structures with excellent results. A second reorganization movement has taken place within the last decade and nearly three-fourths of the states have made substantial alterations and improvements in their organizations. Some of the recent states to accomplish reform were Georgia, Missouri, and New Jersey. North Carolina has recently established a commission to recommend to its general assembly proposals for improvement.

All evidence seems to indicate that at times wholesale reorganization is necessary in order to keep administrative machinery in the best possible working order. There continues also an unremitting need for lesser alteration to meet new conditions. Only thus can we overcome a criticism recently voiced that "State administration organization continues to be governed by chance rather than by conscious attempt to implement particular principles of administrative organization." [1]

Reorganization may take place through constitutional amendment or by statute. If it is by statute it is obvious that no alterations can be made in that part of the administrative machinery outlined in the constitution, nor any changes made in the duties of executive offices mentioned in the constitution. Statutory authorization, while less advantageous, is much easier to secure. Each state has its own reasons for wanting to reorganize and a different set of conditions to improve but, speaking generally, the usual goals of reorganization are:

1. Increased power to the governor so that his authority will be commensurate with his responsibility, thus making him chief administrator in fact and as well as at law. This is secured by broadening his power to appoint and remove, by increasing his power of supervision, and by establishing lines of administrative responsibility directly to the governor. The establishment of the executive budget and administrative reorganization as a whole have also strengthened the position of the governor.

2. Extension of the term of office for the governor and other elected administrative officials, which increases their efficiency.

3. Coordination of the terms of office of executive officers.

4. Definition of lines of responsibility. It is a cardinal principle of administration that there must be clear-cut lines of responsibility between subordinates and their superior officers.

5. Functional departmentalization so that each department is assigned all activities relating to a major function of government, such as health or welfare or agriculture, and can thus coordinate the work of the several divisions operating in the same field.

6. Abolition of many boards and commissions. Some agencies remain in existence after their usefulness has disappeared, others have little work to do, and some duplicate functions performed by other agencies. Many of these boards and commissions could be abolished. It must be admitted, however, that one of the most difficult undertakings in modern

---

[1] Robert T. Daland, *Government and Health,* p. vii, Bureau of Public Administration, University, Ala., 1955.

government is to secure the demise of any governmental agency whether it is needed or not.

Reorganization, to be effective, must go deep into the administrative structure. As one writer has said, "reorganization must be more than the reshuffling and consolidation of departments at the top; there must be continuing attention to the problem at all levels." [2]

Personnel

No one can deny the importance of qualified and efficient people to do any given job. Even the most experienced bridge player will tell you that while systems are important you cannot win without good cards. Administrative work is done by individuals and the quality of the work depends largely upon the quality of the personnel. Although that truth is undisputable, most states have been slow to adopt proper civil-service rules and satisfactory merit systems. At the present writing only one-half of the states have fairly comprehensive civil-service laws that cover most departments while one of even these states has been unable to put its law into effect because the legislature failed to appropriate the necessary funds. It has been estimated that of the nearly 900,000 state employees in the 48 states approximately one-half are covered by civil-service regulations. The requirement of the Federal government that those state employees whose salaries are partly paid out of Federal funds must secure their appointment through merit has helped raise the quality of personnel.

For many years a battle has been going on in the states between the spoils system and the merit system. To those interested in the promotion of merit as the basis of employment, the fray is only half won. It is indeed a continuing struggle marked by both advances and forced retreats along with a gradual extension of the merit system. Obstacles in the way of broader extension are many, but two comments should be made with respect to present conditions. First, the prevailing low esteem in which state employees are held by the citizenry is not deserved. The majority of state employees are faithful and work hard to give honest service to the state. Second, employment by the state does not appeal to many able and qualified persons. Rewards for service are greater elsewhere. As one writer has said,[3]

More or less externally imposed requirements do not get at the need for state governments themselves to show initiative and concern for getting their fair share of the cream of classes graduating from educational institutions— many of them state supported. Nor do they get at the need for the states to make service to the state a rewarding experience. Salaries are but a part of the

---

[2] James W. Fesler, *op. cit.*, p. 11.
[3] James W. Fesler, *op. cit.*, p. 11.

reward. More important may be the conviction of administrative and professional people that they are sharing in important and creative work on behalf of the public interest.

One beneficial development has been the adoption of regulations requiring professional training before a person is able to qualify for a technical or specialized position, stemming from the entrance into such fields as highway construction, public health, welfare, and education. Job requirements have been established to good effect, but sometimes professional requirements set too high have made it difficult for the state to fill vacant positions. Inflation has also worked hardships on technical employees of the states, whose salaries are not comparable to those offered in private industry.

Adoption of a civil-service plan is only the first step. A personnel system needs constant improvement and must be altered at times in order to meet new conditions. There is always the danger that a strong civil service can become an autocratic bureaucracy which, while entirely different from the spoils system, is equally undesirable. Professor James K. Pollock has stated, "we must stop acting as though personnel administration is something different from and not part of the main stream of executive management. I think personnel administration should be a positive force rather than predominantly a protective mechanism. I should like the career service to be flexible enough to identify and reward genuine merit at the same time that it conducts a constant war on dry rot and extravagance." [4]

To achieve good personnel administration, the legislature should arrange for proper methods of recruitment, a merit system, opportunities for advancement, satisfactory rates of pay, desirable working conditions, a retirement plan, and other provisions that make working for the state profitable and pleasant. Much of this has been done by those states with civil-service regulations. What can be done in those states where the legislature is unwilling to make these reforms? The citizenry must be told the cost of the spoils system and the importance of good administration. Only then will they demand that their elected lawmakers take the needed action.

Fiscal Administration

The state budget is a vital part of state administration, for only through planned expenditure can governmental spending ultimately be democratically controlled. During the early history of the states, budgets were prepared by the state legislatures. Sums of money appropriated were small and the states were engaged in few activities. When state government became big business, the budgetary function was transferred to

[4] James K. Pollock, "The Michigan Civil Service," *Good Government*, p. 8, Jan.–Feb., 1955.

the executive branch and there it remains today. The Kestnbaum Commission concludes that "probably the greatest progress in State administration has been in the field of budgeting and fiscal management, although the usefulness of these tools is often seriously impaired by constitutional limitations and by the existence of officials independent of the chief executive." [5] Irrespective of how or by whom the budget is prepared, it must have legislative approval before going into effect.

State budgets have three essential elements: a financial plan, a governmental authority responsible for each step of procedure and control, and last, provision for the audit of all financial proceedings. Actually there are two phases to any budget; budget making and budget control. Let us examine each of these briefly.

Budget making requires first an estimate of expected revenue from both existing and new sources. Next come surveys by the budget office of the need for money, the filing of requests by the different state agencies, hearings, analyses of reports, and a careful examination of the relationship of a particular request or need to the budget as a whole. Last, the budget authority recommends appropriations by function and object.

Budget control consists primarily of the revision of estimates and the establishment of allotments of funds at regular intervals so that the funds appropriated to various agencies will be sufficient to last through the fiscal year. Provision must also be made for transfers and an amount of money must be set aside for possible contingencies. These last two provisions are to keep the budget flexible enough to meet unexpected situations and emergencies.

In sum, the budgetary process gives each department, bureau, and agency the opportunity to present its financial needs and to prove its case to the budgetary agency, but it is the governor, aided by his budget officers, who determines how much each agency shall actually request. When the budget is presented to the legislature for approval, that body is at first prone to increase appropriations for pet agencies or at the demand of interested parties. However, when the time for final adoption arrives and new taxes or an increase in tax rates become necessary to provide funds for the increased appropriations, the legislature nearly always returns to the amounts stipulated in the budget.

A fear frequently expressed is that the budget authority will usurp the administrative function and will exert more power over administration than contemplated by the legislature. Certainly the control of the purse strings is an important power and by using his control of the budget the governor has been able to strengthen his position as chief administrator of the state. This is beneficial, rather than dangerous—provided, of course, that the governor is held to strict accountability.

Essential to an effective budgetary system is the audit which keeps the

[5] *Report of the Commission on Intergovernmental Relations*, p. 44.

executive posted on the spending of the various agencies so that he may call a halt when any administrator is in danger of exceeding his allotment. This audit is to be distinguished from the post-audit exercised by many legislatures. The purpose of the post-audit is to make sure that the executive and his subordinates have adhered to the spending plan laid down in the budget. It is, however, a check after the fact whereas the governor's pre-audit can control the course of spending in time to prevent excesses.

The Relationship between State and Federal Administration

Sometimes state administration is made or marred by the relationship between the Federal government and the state, notably when both the states and the Federal government are working in the same field, such as health, roads, or welfare.

The Federal government has the choice of using Federal employees exclusively or it may combine a given job with a related state activity and make use of state employees. Whenever the Federal government gives financial aid to the states and utilizes state employees it is customary for Washington to set up requirements regarding employment and general supervisory control. This extension of Federal control is opposed by those who champion states' rights and who object to the "creeping" enlargement of Federal power at the expense of the states. Also, as has been said, "Federal supervision weakens state administration in by-passing administrative supervision and coordination at the state level through the governor's office, thus perpetuating the existing disintegration of state administration." [6] This "encroachment" is defended on the grounds that Federal supervision is desirable and that the Federal requirements of the merit system and proper financial procedure are beneficial. It is further maintained that by permitting this type of Federal control, state employees continue to do work that otherwise would be done by Federal employees. Thus the states retain their responsibilities. Persons acquainted with the outcome of these Federal-state relationships agree that the Federal requirement of a merit system for those state employees whose pay comes partly from the Federal government has proved to be advantageous to both the states and the Federal government.

The Relationship of State to Local Administration

The relationship between a state and its counties and municipalities is quite different. All counties and cities are creatures of the state. They exist only because state law gave them life. This means that the state legislature can at will set up requirements that must be met by the var-

[6] Robert T. Daland, *Government and Health,* p. vii, Bureau of Public Administration, University, Ala., 1955.

ious subdivisions, provided, of course, that the matter is not already covered by the state constitution. Some states closely supervise local government administration; others grant home rule and virtual independence in handling purely local administrative matters. In either case it is well to remember that whatever powers are exercised by local units come as grants either from the state constitution or from state law. The option is the state's.

Administration and "Politics"

The reforms described in this chapter—in the machinery of administration, in personnel selection and supervision, and in fiscal control—have nearly all been based upon the view that state government is "big business" and that the devices used by private enterprises in their search for efficiency and profits are applicable to state affairs. They illustrate the fact that in a business civilization the thinking of businessmen permeates thinking about *all* subjects. Now there can be little doubt that these reforms have increased the efficiency of state administration. The contrast between the greater alertness of state governments today and the easygoing hit-or-miss methods of fifty years ago is a striking one. Beyond much doubt we now get more for our money in both the quantity and the quality of state services and the tone of administration is definitely higher. This is all to the good and it behooves us to keep these gains.

On the other hand it is well not to be naive about the progress that has been made or complacent about the difficulties to be surmounted. State government may indeed be "big business," but it is something more. Those who rule possess *legal power* which is something different from business efficiency. The governor and legislature who adopt a budget, by the very act of increasing some items and decreasing others, determine the prosperity or the poverty of individuals or even communities; the power to appoint, supervise, and remove officials involves the opportunity to increase or decrease the importance and self-esteem of those persons affected, while the opportunities for rewarding one's friends or punishing one's enemies that are inherent in the power to award contracts and make purchases are too obvious to require illustration. There is actually no way in a democracy such as ours to take government "out of politics" and conduct it on "business principles" so long as men lust after power. All schemes of reform must accept the fact that this lust is a permanent part of the human endowment and proceed accordingly.

REFERENCES

The American Assembly, *The Forty-eight States: Their Tasks as Policy Makers and Administrators* (1955).

Paul H. Appleby, *Morality and Administration* (1952).

J. C. Bollens, *Reorganization in the States since 1939* (1947).
A. E. Buck, *The Reorganization of State Government in the United States* (1938).
W. S. Carpenter, *The Unfinished Business of Civil Service Reform* (1952).
James C. Charlesworth, *Governmental Administration* (1951).
The Commission on Intergovernmental Relations, *A Report to the President* (1955).
Council of State Governments, *Reorganizing State Government* (1950).
Robert T. Daland, *Government and Health* (1955).
W. Brooke Graves, *Public Administration in a Democratic Society* (1950).
W. E. Mosher, J. D. Kingsley, and O. G. Stahl, *Public Personnel Administration,* 3rd ed. (1950).
Albert L. Sturm, *State Administrative Organization in West Virginia* (1952).

CHAPTER 29   *The State Judicial System*

The Functions of Courts

The plain man will normally say that it is the business of the courts to "try cases." By this he means that they settle disputes and he is not far wrong. In any society at all complicated the occasions on which men differ about their "rights" will be numerous. Some of these differences affect only private individuals and fall under the general category known as the civil law. In the interest of uniformity and orderliness the state provides courts for the impartial consideration of such disputes. Two men, for example, may differ as to the meaning of an agreement into which they have entered; a court is a device by which its exact meaning may be authoritatively decided, and thus the respective rights of the opposing parties determined.

When differences between individuals tempt one of the parties to use violent or fraudulent means to enforce what he regards as his rights, his action may amount to an implicit threat to peace and good order so serious as to make it a crime, that is, a potential attack on the rights of people in general. In the case of crimes (or less serious offenses called misdemeanors) the state not only provides a court for determining guilt but intervenes itself through its prosecuting officers. Penalties then follow to discourage others from enforcing their rights by violence; *force for such purposes must be the monopoly of the state.* In the area of civil law, then, the parties are private persons and their dispute is recorded in the law reports as *Jones v. Smith*, etc.; at criminal law, the state itself is a party and the case is reported as *The State v. Brown.*

In both kinds of cases the court is doing three things. In the first place, it must determine exactly what the facts are in the dispute about the agreement or the offense charged. This involves the taking of the testimony of witnesses and their examination by the opposing lawyers in accordance with the rules of evidence worked out over the centuries. The facts once established, it is next the duty of the court to apply the

499

law to these facts—that is, to decide whether or not the facts amount to a breach of the contract as alleged by the aggrieved party in the civil case or to the crime charged by the prosecuting officer. If the court finds that a breach of contract has actually occurred it may award appropriate damages; if, in the criminal case, the facts constitute the crime charged, the court imposes the penalty provided by the law and turns the offender over to the proper authorities—the chief of police, the sheriff, or the warden of the state prison—for the carrying out of its judgment.

But a third duty is involved in these first two—what *is* the law applicable to the facts disclosed by the trial? Actually the law is not always as clear as it might be since conflicts are possible between different acts of the legislature, between such acts and the rules of the common law, or between acts of the legislature and the state or national constitution. It is the duty of the court to decide which law is to be applied to the facts. The law is, in fact, a pretty complicated matter, and it is well to keep this in mind when thinking of such things as the qualifications of judges and the methods of choosing them.

The work of the courts does not end, however, with the settlement of disputes. A fourth function has to do with the prevention of wrongs as distinct from providing compensation for them *after* they have occurred. This is accomplished by the courts in the exercise of their equitable jurisdiction. The difference between law and equity may best be explained by a glance at the historical development of judicial processes. The remedies available to injured persons in the common-law courts of England were sought through various so-called *writs* which the court issued to petitioners and which set in motion the procedure for determining the rights of the parties. As time went on new situations arose for which no adequate writ had been developed so that actually no remedy existed. In such cases it became usual for persons threatened by loss to petition the King for relief. The theory here was that the King in creating the common-law courts had not exhausted his power or will to do justice. Such petitions were ordinarily referred by the King to his chancellor, frequently a churchman, with the command that justice be done in accordance with "equity and good conscience." The court of chancery in time developed a body of rules quite as complicated as those of the common law but differing from the latter in affording relief from threatened loss, whereas the common law provided a remedy only *after* loss had occurred. Equity, then, is prospective while law is retrospective.

One example will suffice to illustrate the nature of equity procedure. Let us suppose that one's neighbor begins the construction of a wall which will have the effect of diverting water onto one's property. At common law one could only wait until the damage had been done and then bring the proper action for compensation. The remedy here is obviously inadequate—what is wanted is to prevent the loss. On a proper showing of the likelihood of damage, a court, in the exercise of its equitable jurisdiction, may issue an injunction forbidding the construction of the wall. Violation of this injunction would be contempt of court and punishable as a crime. Injunctions may also be issued against labor unions threatening to damage the property of employers or against corporation officers believed to be about to take action contrary to the interests of stockholders. Equity may also intervene to compel, again under contempt penalties, the specific performance of an agreement where noncompliance would do irreparable damage to the other party.

The Courts as Property Managers

A final important function of the courts has to do with the management of property. When a corporation goes bankrupt it is the duty of the court to appoint a receiver to conserve the assets and even to conduct the business either until its affairs are wound up or it is again solvent. As is well known, many large corporations have been managed for long periods of years by court-appointed receivers. Likewise trusts which are created by will or by trust agreement are managed by trustees named by the court and held responsible to it in the interests of the beneficiary. Administrators of estates are in the same manner required to carry out the intent of the will, to deal with the property involved in accordance with the law. Finally, the property of minors or of insane or otherwise incompetent persons is usually controlled by a guardian named by the court. It is easy to see from these two sets of examples that the courts are always administrators of very considerable property interests and that the safety of these interests depends upon the honesty and competence of our judges and their staffs.

The Nature of Law

The rules, principles, and precedents followed by the courts in the settlement of disputes are known collectively as the law. The nature of American law is complicated by two things: the federal organization of the American nation and the inherited system of the common law. It follows from federalism that the states possess and administer a body of law quite different in many ways from the law applied in the national courts. The highest category of law is, of course, the national Constitution. By its own terms it and acts of Congress "made in pursuance thereof, and all treaties made, or which shall be made, under the authority of the United States, shall be the supreme law of the land, and the judges in every state shall be bound thereby, anything in the Constitution or laws of any state to the contrary notwithstanding." [1] This means that any law

[1] *Constitution of the U.S.*, Article VI, Par. 2.

or treaty adopted by the appropriate national authority pursuant to powers delegated to it (as interpreted by the Supreme Court) is of greater binding force than any law in conflict with it adopted by an individual state, the fact of such conflict again being in the end determined by the United States Supreme Court. It follows from this that state constitutions, while fundamental in terms of state power, are of secondary importance in contrast to the Constitution of the United States. This fact must be recognized by state courts and decisions at variance with it would be reversed by the United States Supreme Court.

The constitution of a state is, then, its fundamental law, but it is fundamental only with reference to powers not recognized by the United States Supreme Court as belonging solely to the national government. Thus the power which Congress has of regulating interstate and foreign commerce takes precedence over commercial regulations of a state unless it can be shown that such regulations apply solely to transactions beginning and ending within the boundaries of a state. As was pointed out earlier in this book, many regulations of trade that would seem to be of local importance only have been interpreted by the Supreme Court as having been passed "pursuant to" congressional power over interstate commerce and are thus withdrawn from state control. A similarly liberal interpretation of other delegated powers of Congress has had the effect of reducing the area of state action with respect to many matters once considered as of primarily local importance. At the same time it must be recognized that government generally has widened its scope and that the states have shared in the resulting greater activity. This means that the state constitutions, while in a sense subordinate law, are still the fundamental basis of a growing state power.

State Statutes

Next in the hierarchy of law administered by the courts come the statutes enacted by the state legislatures. In this connection it must be remembered that the legislatures are the sole lawmaking bodies in the states. With the exception of those communities enjoying "home rule" powers, all local units—cities, counties, townships, school districts, and so on—exercise only such powers as are conferred upon them by state statutes. These powers may be restricted or broadened or even abolished by the state legislature. Even when the constitution confers "home rule" powers on local units, the tendency of the courts has been to construe these narrowly so as to confine local freedom to those few matters of strictly local concern. Our states, in short, are unitary and not federal in their organization.

Our state legislatures every session turn out many hundreds of enactments. Most of these, however, have nothing to do with the conduct of private individuals and are therefore not really an important part of the law which the courts administer. They are rather in the nature of administrative "directives," ordering certain procedures to be followed by executive agencies, setting salaries, shifting bureaus, prescribing accounting methods, and so on. The number of statutes dealing with contracts, property, sales, crimes, wills, domestic relations, and other matters of individual conduct is quite small. Some of the states have tried to sum up the law regarding such basic concerns in comprehensive codes but these are rarely completely successful since the variety of situations to be covered—to say nothing of those to be anticipated in a dynamic society—is so great as to make complete and exact statements almost impossible. No matter how carefully such codes are drawn there is almost always need for judicial interpretation to fit them to the facts of actual situations.[2]

The Common Law

The second complicating factor in American law is the final category, the common law. The common law may be regarded even now as the basic law of the American states since, while it may be changed by statutes, the latter are properly to be regarded as principally amendatory of the common law. Even the codes referred to in the preceding paragraph are for the most part attempts to put in systematic order principles of the common law. The common law itself is not easy to define briefly. It is both a body of rules and a way of thinking about legal principles. As a body of rules it may be described as those customs of the English people which in the course of time received the approval of the royal judges. These judges, speaking with the authority of the holders of the King's commission, lent the weight of their office to the enforcement of such local customs as seemed already to be most generally obeyed. Most of these customs quite naturally were concerned with such matters as property, crimes, and personal relations of various sorts. Over the course of centuries the royal judges sitting on circuit in various parts of the kingdom tended to reach much the same conclusions about desirable customs so that the law which they created by their decisions eventually became common to the whole of England. It was this law which the colonists brought with them to the New World to become the basis of the law effective everywhere except in those parts of the nation where French and Spanish influences predominated.[3]

The common law is often referred to as unwritten law. This is correct

[2] Statute law as used here includes the orders and regulations issued by various state and local officers since such regulations to be valid must be authorized by statute.

[3] In Louisiana and in the states made from the territory ceded by Mexico large parts of the law are derived ultimately from Roman law.

only in the sense that there is no one place in which it is set forth completely and formally as is the case with statutes and constitutions. It *is* written, however, in the sense that its principles are to be found in the recorded decisions of the judges. For several centuries the decisions of the most important English and American courts have been preserved in written form and by consulting these a trained student can discover the established rules. Such a study will also reveal the meaning of the common law as a way of thinking. In the earliest days the judges discovered that the people in their communal life had worked out satisfactory customs with respect to individual conduct—such things as that men should pay their just debts, keep their contracts, refrain from trespassing on the property of others, and so forth. Judicial approval of such ways of acting converted custom into law. In the course of this process—which must be understood as extending over many years and involving the work of many judges—the courts worked out certain general principles and definitions applicable to various sets of facts. When succeeding disputes before them involved the same pattern of facts it was natural to apply the same rule of law. In this way was built up the doctrine of precedents, which means simply that similar cases will be decided by the same rule. This way of reasoning ensured that within broad limits the law would be a stable affair, with the result that men could plan their enterprises with considerable assurance that what they proposed to do would be legal. Life does not stand still, however, and situations are constantly arising which do not fit neatly into any of the traditional rules of the common law. In such cases the judges are faced with the problem of doing justice to the new pattern of facts without overturning the established rule. Usually, by reasoning from analogy between the new facts and those out of which the traditional rule was wrought, they are able to modify the latter without fatally weakening it. This is normally possible because no situation is ever *totally* unlike all previous ones. What the judges here face is the problem of deciding the case before them justly without at the same time contradicting those rules whose permanence men take for granted.

In other words the common law has grown by more or less gradual modifications of accepted principles, a process in which the courts are aware of the need of both stability and change. No one could conduct his business with any feeling of security unless he could have reasonable certainty that the accepted rule would continue to be applied; on the other hand a too rigid adherence to the rule would in time hamper his business. It is precisely because judges must constantly keep in mind the need of both stability *and* change that their task is a delicate one and also that they are so often criticized as either too "liberal" or too "conservative." A wise and creative judge is a bit of both and is for that very reason not completely satisfactory either to "progressives" or tradi-tionalists. Whether a man has the rare combination of intellectual and temperamental qualities needed to discharge such a function wisely is the question that should be in the minds of those who choose judges.

The State Court System

The constitutions of the states provide in greater or less detail for a series of courts and outline their respective jurisdictions. In general the system consists of three grades of courts: minor tribunals, widely dis-tributed, for the settlement of civil controversies and the trial of petty offenders; general trial courts, with unlimited jurisdiction as to subject matter; and a supreme court exercising final authority in matters of law. In a few states—principally the more populous ones—a fourth grade of courts has been provided between the general trial courts and the su-preme court. Such appellate courts are designed to relieve the highest court of a mass of business that might otherwise go to it on appeal from the general trial courts and are normally given final jurisdiction over a considerable variety of matters.

The Justice of the Peace

The lowest court in the judicial hierarchy is that of the justice of the peace. The office is a very old one, originating in England at least as early as the middle of the fourteenth century as a convenient means by which the King's justice was made available in minor criminal matters to the mass of the population. The justices of the peace were originally appointed largely from the ranks of local landowners or squires and to this day are frequently referred to as squires. As time went on the central administration added to their duties such func-tions as the care of roads, the licensing of taverns, and the oversight of local police functions, so that by the nineteenth century the "bench" of justices in an English county was responsible for the general supervi-sion of local government outside incorporated boroughs.[4] Most of these duties were taken from them and transferred to elective county councils in 1888, but they still retain the power to try petty offenders and to "bind over" more serious wrongdoers to the higher courts. Some of these administrative powers are still exercised by the justices in a few Southern states but in most of the country only the functions of trying minor cases or acting as examining magistrates in more serious cases belong to them.[5]

---

[4] They had the powers, that is, now exercised in the United States by boards of county commissioners.

[5] As presiding officer of the county "court" of Jackson County, Missouri, former President Truman was often referred to as "judge." The "court" in Missouri retains

In rural areas the court of the justice of the peace is the only one available for the settlement of minor civil disputes and for the trial of misdemeanors and is therefore the court with which people are most familiar. In civil matters the justice is limited to the consideration of disputes involving small amounts of money and he is generally not permitted to deal with the title to real property. On the criminal side he may impose small fines or short jail sentences and, in accusations of serious offenses, hold the accused for trial before the general trial court. Appeals from the justice go to the general trial court which ignores the proceedings below and tries the case anew.

Although his jurisdiction is commonly county-wide the justice of the peace is usually elected by the voters of the township or similar small area. The law does not require justices to have any legal training and most of them have only a little formal education of any sort. Compensation is in the form of fees set by statute and, since in criminal cases the fee is a part of the fine imposed, the temptation is strong to find the accused guilty. Because of numerous scandals arising from the abuse of the fee system the entire system of justice courts has been widely criticized. In some states statutes permit the abolition of the office and the substitution of salaried magistrates trained in the law, but these have been little used and the system continues much as it has always been. A notable exception is New Jersey where the constitution adopted in 1947 abolished the office and transferred the cases formerly heard by the justice to 487 municipal courts. In 1956 more than a third of the municipal judges were trained lawyers.

In towns and villages justice in petty cases is administered by courts called variously magistrates' courts, police courts, mayors' courts, or municipal courts. The presiding officer is almost always elected. In larger towns he may be a lawyer but in the smaller places he is little if at all better equipped professionally than the rural justice. In sizable cities the jurisdiction of the municipal court may be considerably greater than that of the justice, in some cases being largely concurrent with that of the general trial court, so that litigants may begin action—except possibly in the most important cases—in either court. The record of these city courts is very spotty and in general the criticisms made of the justice courts apply to them as well.

In view of the fact that these minor courts handle each year many thousands of cases and are the only courts with which most people are familiar, they are in many ways the most important part of our judicial system. The typical court in action, meeting in bleak quarters, presided over by an ignorant and uncouth magistrate, managed without dignity,

---

many of the administrative duties long exercised by the English justices and is not to be looked upon as a judicial body.

and staffed by uninspiring and insensitive party hacks, is not an edifying spectacle. Its offhand and unfeeling disposal of most of the business that comes before it is beyond doubt responsible for the undesirable cynical attitude toward judicial administration generally. There is scarcely any reform in the area of local government more pressing than the improvement of these courts.

General Trial Courts

Every state has a system of courts for the trial of cases more important than those within the jurisdiction of the justice and municipal courts. These courts have unlimited jurisdiction in both civil and criminal cases and act also on appeals from the lowest grade of courts. Their name varies from state to state—common pleas, superior, circuit, and district being the most common designations, although in New York State the general trial court is called the supreme court, the highest court in that state being the court of appeals. In sparsely settled areas several counties may be combined in a judicial district or circuit, the judge sitting in turn in each of the counties in his district. Where population is more dense the county constitutes the judicial district and there may be more than one judge if business justifies it. In all but a few states the judge is elected by the voters of the county or district, the most usual term being four years. General trial courts are known as courts of record, each having attached to it a clerk with the duty of recording its proceedings. Also attached to the court is the prosecuting officer, known variously as the state's attorney, county attorney, prosecuting attorney, or solicitor. The executive officer of the court is normally the sheriff of the county where it is sitting. Although appeals may be taken from them to the state's highest court, or to an intermediate appeals court, if one exists, the great bulk of civil and criminal business begins and ends in the general trial courts. Here are tried the more serious criminal charges and here a great majority of civil disputes—over contracts, personal injuries, and property rights. In most states both equitable relief and legal remedies are available, the older system of separate chancery courts having been almost everywhere abandoned. The general trial court is the one in which most frequent use of the trial (or petit) jury is made. Civil actions are begun by a complaint filed by the party claiming injury, while criminal charges are made either by grand jury indictment or, more frequently at present, by an information filed by the prosecuting officer.

In a few states the general trial court has charge of probate matters, that is, the supervision of the administration of the estates of decedents, but generally separate probate courts have been created for this specialized business—known variously as probate, surrogate, and orphans' courts. Mention should be made also of certain administrative duties still performed here and there by general trial courts—such as a share in the supervision of the election machinery and the appointment of minor officials. There has been a tendency in recent years to reduce the number of these miscellaneous nonjudicial functions, thus leaving the judges free from the political entanglements which they sometimes involve.

Considering the relatively low salaries paid judges in most states, their comparatively short terms of office, and the necessity of periodically "running" for office, the quality of the personnel of the general trial courts is higher than might be expected. It is true that many trial judges are inferior in legal learning to some of the lawyers who practice before them, but the tendency of the voters to reelect sitting judges offsets the apparent evil of short terms and affords an intelligent judge an opportunity to acquire the requisite expertness and to cultivate a judicious temperament. On the whole they compare favorably with officials in the administrative branches of our state and local governments.

State Supreme Courts

The highest court in most of the states is called simply the supreme court although, as was indicated above, that of New York is called the court of appeals. With the exception of New Hampshire, where the supreme court was created by statute, every constitution makes specific provision for such a court. In the great majority of states the members of the supreme court are elected by the people, in some cases from the state at large, in others by districts. The number of justices varies from three to sixteen, the most frequent number being seven. The head of the court is the chief justice, appointed as such in the few states where popular election is not the method of choice, chosen by all the voters of the state, elected by the members of the court itself, or held either by the senior member or the member whose commission first expires.[6] Although the chief justice is the administrator of the court's business he has only one vote in the decision of cases argued before it.

The supreme court has both original and appellate jurisdiction. Cases may be begun in it on a limited range of matters—such as where the state itself is a party or those involving the issuance of certain writs. The supreme courts themselves discourage the use of their original jurisdiction and the tendency has been to reduce its scope in view of the increase in appeals from lower courts. In the case of the latter it is the court of last resort, its judgments being final except when the interpretation of the Constitution of the United States is involved. In such cases appeals go directly to the Supreme Court of the United States. This means that in

---

[6] Details on these matters may be found in *The Book of the States* and, for the student's own state, in the annual or biennial "Blue Book."

all cases involving only the interpretation of the state constitution and statutes the decision of the state supreme court is the last word.

The appellate business of the supreme court does not involve the trial or determination of facts. It makes, therefore, no use of the jury and does not hear witnesses. It confines itself almost exclusively to ruling on points of law, to the construction of statutes, and to the determination of the constitutionality of laws and administrative actions. Even so its burden is often so heavy as to make it necessary for it to sit in sections or to associate with itself certain inferior-court judges for the consideration of appeals. The court both hears the oral argument of lawyers and considers their printed briefs. It reaches its decisions, as does the Supreme Court of the United States, at periodic conferences after which the chief justice appoints a member of the majority to write the court's opinion. Justices who reach the majority decision by different reasoning and justices who differ from the majority may write concurring and dissenting opinions respectively which are printed along with the majority opinion in the official court reports.

Specialized Courts

What may be called the "standard" court system thus briefly described was developed at a time when legal relationships were not specially complicated and when lawyers and judges could be expected to know and apply the law with reasonable skill and efficiency. Most contacts among men fell more or less accurately under the limited number of headings worked out by the architects of the old common law—master and servant, husband and wife, contracts, torts, bailments, agency, trusts, and the rest. But just as specialization has arisen in other human concerns so it has been bound to occur in the law. The day has gone when even judges can claim the universality of legal knowledge attainable by their professional ancestors of less complex times. Just as lawyers tend to specialize in their practice, confining themselves largely to probate work, criminal or corporation law, or the law of real property, so we often find, especially in our appellate courts, one judge who has taken public utility law as his special province, another tax law, another corporations, and so on. The official opinion may appear as that of the entire court, but it reflects the expert touch of the specialist.

The clearest examples of court specialization are found today in the inferior courts. In many of these it has been found desirable, for instance, to devise special machinery for dealing with juvenile delinquency since it is thought undesirable to deal with young offenders by procedures applied to adults. In some cases this specialization is achieved by giving juvenile cases to one of the judges of the general trial court. In others a special juvenile court may be created distinct from the general trial court.

In still others young offenders may be tried by the judge of the probate court. In any case, it is the intention of these special arrangements, by informal conference to get at the causes, personal and environmental, of the offense charged, and to prevent its repetition, rather than to punish as is the case with adults. The hope is that the child may be saved from a criminal career. Such a specialized court is usually supplied with investigators trained in social work, probation officers, and persons fitted to act as guardians of the child in cases where it is found necessary to remove him from the custody of unfit parents. The informal procedure followed in such courts is intended to prevent the child from thinking of himself as a criminal, and punishment in the usual sense is avoided except in extreme cases. Although the handling of such offenders is admittedly a difficult problem, the idea underlying the juvenile court movement is to provide a sympathetic treatment of those young people who have taken the first steps in the wrong direction, and thus save them from criminal careers.

The relatively high cost of "going to law" in the standard courts has led in a good many states to the creation of small-claims courts, either as branches of the municipal courts or as special tribunals. Before these courts come large numbers of disputes regarding rent, tradesmen's bills, and neighborhood squabbles generally. Individually these disputes are petty but in the aggregate they may involve very considerable sums of money and, in any case, they are important to the parties. Procedure is informal, fees are small, and, in some cases, lawyers are barred from appearing in such cases so that costs may be kept low. The small-claims court is an example of a widespread movement to make justice more readily available to the poor and humble who cannot afford the cost of proceeding in the general trial courts and whose view of the law and of justice generally is based all too frequently on what amounts to a denial of justice when court fees are prohibitive.

Another device for avoiding the delays and the high cost of justice is illustrated by the use of what is called conciliation. Where this is permitted, either a special conciliation court or a judge empowered by statute to act as conciliator attempts simply to bring together the parties to a dispute in order to find, if possible, a basis for settlement. The technicalities followed in the usual court are dispensed with, fees are small, and the parties may state their cases without retaining a lawyer. If a basis for agreement can be found in this informal way it has the binding force of a court judgment when approved by the conciliator.

Actions against the State

As the range of public functions grows so grows also the number of instances in which citizens are injured in person or property by negligent action of public officials. It is an established principle of our law that the state may not be sued in its own courts without its consent.[7] The plain man, especially if his property has been damaged, say by the action of the state highway department, can take little comfort from the old maxim that the "King can do no wrong" on which this principle is based, and common sense would seem to indicate that where an injury has occurred an effective remedy should be provided. To some extent our states have recognized the justice of this view. Frequently the only recourse of the injured party is to present his claim to the legislature which may grant it and appropriate money to satisfy it. The difficulty with this is that the legislature is seldom a fit body to audit such claims and, if it were, the consideration of any large number of them would require time better spent on legislative functions. Some states permit suit in certain specified courts, the judgments against the state being satisfied by a legislative appropriation. A few states have taken the matter out of the legislature and put it under the jurisdiction of a court or commission of claims, a specialized tribunal patterned after the Court of Claims in the national government. The judgments of such a court or commission still have to be satisfied by an appropriation, but injured persons have at least the satisfaction of knowing that their case has been considered by an expert body. This scheme has been adopted in only a few states but there is urgent need that it be more extensively used, especially in populous states where contacts between state agencies and citizens are frequent and the chances of injuries numerous. Where fault or negligence has been established there is no good reason why the state should escape the liability which must be borne by private individuals in similar cases.

Judicial Personnel: Selection

The office of judge involves ideally not only considerable learning in the law, but also a judicious temperament, unusual insight into human nature, familiarity with public affairs, and a willingness to resist popular and partisan pressure. This combination of qualities is, of course, a rare one, but it is important to secure it especially in a society where so much depends upon the efficiency and honesty of judges. For in the United States the courts are not only responsible for the settlement of thousands of disputes and for the vindication of the criminal law—they are also to a high degree the actual *makers* of law since ultimately the law is what they say it is. All these considerations have a direct bearing upon the method by which they are chosen.

In our early history the choice of judges was everywhere in the hands either of the executive, frequently with the requirement of confirmation

[7] The Eleventh Amendment to the Constitution of the United States makes the states immune to suits in the national courts by citizens of other and of foreign states.

by his council or the legislature, or of the legislature itself. Beginning as early as 1812, however, popular election of some or all judges was introduced and spread rapidly among the states during the era of "Jacksonian democracy." The older states tended to retain the traditional methods but on the frontier these smacked of "aristocracy" and it seemed reasonable to subject to popular election those who applied and interpreted the law as well as those who made it. Although popular election has been under fire in recent years it still remains the principal method of choice for some or all judges in 37 of the states. The United States, in fact, is the only nation in which judges are so selected, appointment by the chief executive being the universal rule elsewhere. Even in the United States the judges of the national courts are named by the President.

Since choice by the legislature is the rule in only three states and there is no interest in extending this method to others it is the respective merits of popular election and appointment by the governor that are now argued. Academic students tend to believe that executive appointment is superior to choice by the people, on the grounds that a governor is more likely to be informed about the qualifications of appointees and to act with a greater sense of responsibility. On the other hand it is held that the voters are not able to pass upon the technical fitness of judges and that they are likely to be swayed by partisan considerations, in which case those chosen will be lacking in both ability and independence. Before trying to evaluate these arguments it is well to see what happens under the two systems.

In most states where popular election is the method used judges continue to be chosen on a party ballot and to be nominated in primaries or conventions. As is the case with respect to other elective officers what frequently happens is that the real choice of nominees is made by party officials instead of by the rank and file. The voters in other words do not really choose at all except as between two men named by their leaders. In this case everything obviously depends upon the caliber of the leaders and their willingness to take their responsibilities seriously. To some extent the evils that might be expected from the partisan choice of judges are mitigated by the part played by the local bar in endorsing aspirants for the bench. The lawyers themselves, because of their constant contact with the judges, are in a better position than any other group to have an informed opinion as to their ability. If the bar itself has high professional standards its endorsement will carry weight both with the voters and the party leaders. It may also be said that the voters and party leaders have shown a tendency to reelect judges as long as they wish to serve and thus have given the bench more stability and in effect more independence than the system of popular election might seem to make likely. Actually the voters regard judges as in a higher category than the common run of administrative officers and are usually willing to follow the lead of the bar. It is, in fact, a tribute to their common sense that they do not normally think of themselves as competent to choose such officials. It is for these reasons that many elective courts are quite as able and in some cases abler than appointive courts.

Where the governor appoints, everything depends upon his character and ability. He has perhaps more ready access to expert opinion than do the people at large but it does not follow that he will avail himself of such advice. If he is a narrow partisan he will look upon judgeships as a species of patronage and use his appointing power to further his personal ambitions. The effect is not likely to be any better than when choice is by the voters. In those states where the appointive judiciary is demonstrably of high quality it will usually be found that there is a tradition of choosing able and upright governors. Such a tradition would give us good judges even in those states where the people do the choosing. As in many other governmental problems it is the imponderable factors that count. No clear verdict can be given for the appointive system. And it must finally be remembered that so long as judges have the authority to pass upon the constitutionality of laws a good case can be made for allowing the voters an influence in the choice of the persons who make such judgments.[8]

Problems of Court Reform

The enormous growth in the variety, importance, and complexity of state and local functions has of course added to the work of the courts. Each new statute and administrative ruling creates new rights and obligations and requires prompt interpretation if the public business is to go on smoothly. Along with this purely legal work has gone a vast growth in what may be called the judge's administrative work—the keeping of records, the oversight of clerical help, and the supervision of receivers, trustees, probation officers, and other specialized personnel. The judge is expected to be both a scholar and a businessman. The burden is in many cases too great with the result that dockets are crowded and the law's delays further prolonged.

Perhaps because of the traditional conservatism of the legal profession reform of the courts lagged behind that of the other branches of govern-

---

[8] An interesting modification of executive appointment is in force in Missouri. There certain judges are named by the governor from a list of nominations made by a nonpartisan commission. At the end of their terms these judges run for office on their record, the voters simply deciding whether they shall serve a new term. If a judge is repudiated by the voters, the governor makes an appointment from a new list. Judges thus do not run *against* another aspirant but on their own record in office. In New Jersey judges of the supreme and superior courts are appointed by the governor for an initial term of seven years; if reappointed they serve during good behavior.

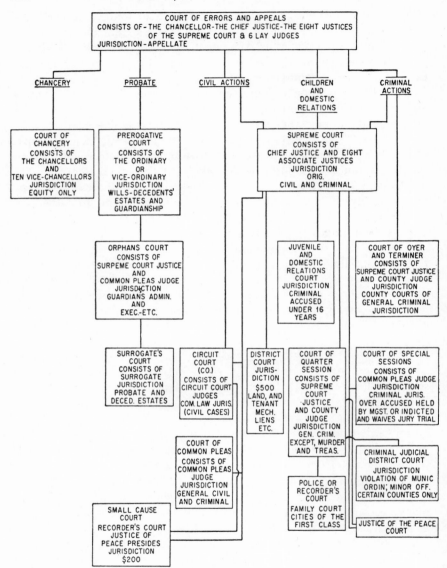

Fɪɢ. 12. New Jersey court system under constitution of 1844. Courtesy of New Jersey Constitution Foundation.

ment. Until a generation ago the outline of the judicial system remained much as it was originally and attempts to meet the rush of business consisted principally either of some specialization in the lower courts or in the addition of judges to the general trial and appellate courts. Unfortunately, as new courts and judges were added no attention was paid to the working of the system as a whole. As a result some courts fell far behind in disposing of cases while others had little or nothing to do. In the absence of any scheme for managing the business of the courts *in general,* all the evils of congestion and delay were simply compounded. There was not even in most cases any responsible person who knew the facts with respect to the amount of pending business.

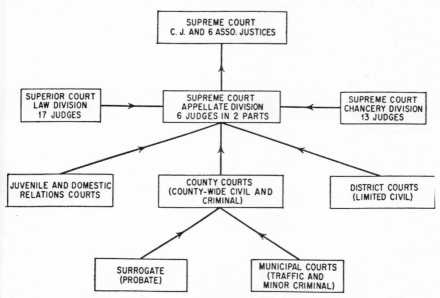

FIG. 13. New Jersey court system under constitution of 1947. Courtesy of Edward B. McConnell, Administrative Director of the New Jersey Courts.

Two things were clearly needed. The first was some authority with power to supervise the entire judicial system. The second was to make provision for the constant study of the pending business of the courts and the working of existing procedures with a view to suggesting needed changes. In line with these needs two hopeful developments have taken place. One is the movement toward a unified court system, the other the creation of judicial councils and the office of administrative director of the courts.

Understood literally a unified court system would be one in which all the courts of the state would be regarded as a single body, each local court being considered as a branch, and all operating under the administrative supervision of the chief justice of the state. Under such a scheme the chief justice would have authority to transfer inferior judges from districts with little business to those with crowded dockets, thus keeping the courts abreast of their work. As a member of the judicial council the chief justice would be in a position to know the needs in various local communities as well as the general state of judicial business. Some reformers would go as far as to give the chief justice power to appoint all subordinate judges, but local feeling is too strong to make such a development at all likely. No state, in fact, has yet a completely unified system, although a number have approached it in varying degrees. A very high degree of centralized control is provided, for example, in the New Jersey constitution of 1947. In that state "the Chief Justice of the Supreme Court shall be the administrative head of all the courts in the state. He shall appoint an Administrative Director to serve at his pleasure." The chief justice "shall assign Judges of the Superior Court to the Divisions and Parts of the Superior Court, and may from time to time transfer Judges from one assignment to another, as need appears." [9] Even though most states have not gone as far as New Jersey, there is at least considerably more oversight by the state's highest court than was true a generation ago. There are clear advantages in an arrangement which assumes that the court system is a unit, and the movement toward unification is one to be encouraged.

The Supervision of Court Business

Where, as is usually the case, the court system has grown up without much attention to its parts, it is quite often true that there is no way of knowing how it is actually working in terms of the volume of business transacted and the distribution of that business among the various courts. In recent years two devices have been more or less widely adopted for the purpose of studying and in some cases exercising some oversight of judicial business. The first of these is the judicial council which now exists in more than two-thirds of the states. The judicial council has as its object the continuous and systematic study of judicial statistics and of the working of the rules of procedure in effect in the various courts. It is also its duty to discover outmoded provisions of the law. With respect to such matters it has the authority to recommend to the courts or to the legislature such changes as will bring about greater promptness and efficiency in the work of the courts. While some of the councils are relatively inactive the energetic ones prove that the device can be most useful. They always consist of representative judges from the different grades of courts, plus members of the bar association and even representatives of the public. The chief justice of the state is frequently the chairman.

Of perhaps greater significance is the administrative officer of the

---

[9] Article VI, Section VII. The difference between the traditional court system and a modern one is illustrated in the two charts of the New Jersey courts, Figures 12 and 13.

courts. An official bearing this or a similar title now exists in 16 states, as well as in the national court system and in that of Puerto Rico. It is his duty, subject to the direction of the state's highest court (or the chief justice), to conduct a continuous study of the business of the courts of the state, to advise the chief justice concerning the more efficient distribution of cases among the various courts, to advise with inferior courts with respect to pending business before them, and, in general, to look after the business aspects of judicial work—the provision of quarters, the ordering of supplies, and so on. The importance of such an officer in enabling judges to keep abreast of their work and thus preventing those delays which so often amount to a denial of justice, is difficult to overestimate. The value of such an officer is greatest where, as in New Jersey, the chief justice is made the administrative head of the entire judicial system with power to assign inferior judges where they are most needed, but even where there is no such centralization, the office has proved its worth. In 1956 a National Conference of Court Administrative Officers was organized for the purpose "of facilitating the exchange of information among those persons and offices directly concerned with the administration of the courts, of fostering the application of the principles and techniques of modern business management to the work of the courts . . . and to increase the efficiency and effectiveness of the judiciary in the various jurisdictions." [10]

The Role of Lawyers

No discussion of law and the courts would be complete that did not emphasize the vital importance of the legal profession. This is true not only because the judges of the more important courts are invariably lawyers but also because lawyers are in effect a part of the court in the settlement of disputes. It is a rare judge who is experienced and learned enough that he does not profit from the arguments of the lawyers before him. It is the latter in fact who do the research for which he has insufficient time. Moreover much of the tone of the court is set by the bar. In short the judicial process cannot be better than the lawyers who conduct it. It is no mere technicality to speak of these as officers of the court obligated as much as is the judge to see that justice is done.

In criticizing the French Estates-General which carried through the early stages of the Revolution, Edmund Burke paid his compliments to the lawyer members in language which all too frequently describes a

[10] From an address before the Conference on Judicial Administration delivered at the University of Chicago School of Law, November 8, 1956, by Mr. Edward B. McConnell, Administrative Director of the Courts of New Jersey. The author is deeply indebted to Mr. McConnell for the opportunity to read this address before its publication as well as for much information about the working of the New Jersey court system since the constitutional changes of 1948.

large section of the modern bar. The legal contingent of the assembly was composed, he said, "not of distinguished magistrates who had given pledges to their country of their science, prudence, and integrity; not of leading advocates, the glory of the bar; not of renowned professors in universities; but for far the greater part . . . of the inferior, unlearned, mechanical, merely instrumental members of the profession; . . . the general composition was of obscure provincial advocates, of stewards of petty local jurisdictions, country attorneys, notaries, and the whole train of the ministers of municipal litigation, the fomenters and conductors of the petty war of village vexation."

Access to the practice of the law in the United States has been on the whole so easy as to attract far too many of what Burke called the "unlearned, mechanical, merely instrumental." Law schools have too often been merely trade schools with the result that their graduates have tended to regard the practice as little more than a trial in the skills of deception and mere cleverness. When members of a calling have no higher conception of it, it is little wonder that the profession as a whole is looked upon by many with suspicion. What is needed are stricter standards of admission and a prelegal training in the liberal studies. The latter might be expected to give the lawyer an awareness of his responsibilities as an integral part of a serious process the end of which is not merely victory for the clever but the maintenance of high standards of justice. For it must be repeated that lawyers are a part of what we call the court and in the end their standards tend to be those of judicial administration.

A bar constituted of broadly educated men might well be given powers of disciplining its own members, thus holding them to higher standards and eliminating the "merely instrumental," the tradesmen. It is admitted that a bar so organized might develop some of the undesirable features of the medieval guilds—exclusiveness and a tendency unduly to restrict the opportunities for entrance to the profession—but these are worth risking in view of the benefits that would accrue to the public. It is encouraging to record that these views are coming to be shared by a growing number of lawyers. Bar associations and associations of law schools are more and more interesting themselves in professional and preprofessional education and are coming to regard themselves as quasi-public bodies with the responsibility which such recognition entails. It is scarcely too much to say that the improvement of the bar is the most fundamental aspect of legal and judicial reform.

REFERENCES

Benjamin N. Cardozo, *The Nature of the Judicial Process* (1921).
Jerome Frank, *Courts on Trial* (1949).

William E. Hannan and Mildred Csontos, *State Court Systems,* Council of State Governments (1940).

Evan Haynes, *The Selection and Tenure of Judges* (1944).

J. W. Hurst, *The Growth of American Law* (1950).

Raymond Moley, *Our Criminal Courts* (1930).

Gail M. Morris, *Justices of the Peace Courts* (1942).

Roscoe Pound, *Criminal Justice in America* (1945).

————, *Organization of the Courts* (1940).

Arthur T. Vanderbilt (Chief Justice of New Jersey), "The First Five Years of the New Jersey Courts under the Constitution of 1947," *VIII Rutgers Law Review,* 289–315 (Spring 1954).

————, "The Municipal Court—The Most Important Court in New Jersey; Its Remarkable Progress and Its Unsolved Problems," *X Rutgers Law Review* (Summer 1956).

W. F. Willoughby, *Principles of Judicial Administration* (1929).

CHAPTER 30 *Local Government*

No matter how centralized a state may be as a matter of law, use is everywhere made of local districts either for the detailed performance of state functions or for dealing with those matters regarded as of purely local interest. There is no reason *in theory* why all the functions of government might not be performed by agents of the central power; yet even such highly centralized nations as France find it convenient to maintain a more or less complicated system of local authorities. These, though without what we should call powers of local self-government, do manage to attach to themselves the loyalty of the local population and to cultivate and perpetuate regional and local differences. The federal organization of the United States emphasizes the traditional belief that some things "belong" to local government and others to the central government. While everyone knows that no hard and fast line can be drawn between local and national functions and that the respective jurisdictions of each authority vary from time to time and are in fact blended in baffling ways at any given period, the fact remains that we are committed to what we call local self-government, no matter how its content may be defined at various epochs. It is for this reason important to examine the ways in which functions are distributed and to pass in review the devices by which they are performed.

While the nation is organized on the federal system each American state is unitary in its structure. This means that there is but *one* authority —the state—and that local units are its creatures, having only such powers as the state may see fit to confer upon them and discharging them only in such ways as the state may determine.[1] So far as the letter of the law is concerned every local unit in an American state could be abolished and its powers transferred to appointees of the state government. The

[1] Municipal "home rule" may seem an exception to this and yet it must be noted that "home rule" is granted by the *state* constitution and that its limits are finally set by the *state's* courts.

state legislature, in short, is quite as sovereign in these matters as, say, the British Parliament. Aside from the obvious difficulties involved in governing the affairs of a whole state from its capital, the degree of centralization theoretically possible is made practically impossible by the fact that local officials are everywhere chosen by the local voters. This means that local officeholders owe their first allegiance to those who elect them no matter what their legal status may be. It would be a rash state administration that would exert its technically supreme legal power against popular local officials. It is not too much to say that the heart of what we call local self-government consists in the right of local voters to choose their immediate rulers.

The Value of Local Self-government

Great and sometimes extravagant values have been assigned to local self-government and, after all reasonable allowances have been made, its importance in a democratic system must be granted. It is no doubt true that apathy quite often characterizes the local electorate and that over large areas and for long periods affairs are in the hands of bosses, machines, and cliques; yet the voter is there to punish and rebuke and the occasions on which he is aroused are frequent enough to give real substance to the claim that he is the ultimate and, on the whole, the most satisfactory repository of power. He may not always be enlightened and he is often wrongheaded, but he knows what he does *not* want well enough to call a halt on occasion to the "unending audacity of elected persons." On the balance no better way has been found to enlist the services of so many people in public affairs than the decentralized system of rule adopted in countries like the United States and those others whose political forms and ideals are English in origin. The thousands of local government units in the United States with their hundreds of thousands of offices are the training ground of men and women who go on to higher posts, and invaluable nurseries for whatever public spirit the political process is able to generate. No better way has been found for giving citizens a "feel" for affairs than their access to the many posts, often unpaid, in local units of government.

Local Rural Government

For this necessarily brief discussion we divide the units of government into the two broad categories of rural and urban. Aside from the greater density of population in urban areas the principal difference between the two classes is that rural units for the most part are set up with a view to the more convenient performance of functions regarded as belonging to the state—such as the recording of land titles, the administration of justice, and the preservation of peace—whereas urban units, such as incorporated cities and boroughs, are, in a sense, more "natural" areas, representing the voluntary grouping of the people and created, at their own request, in order to supply services of special interest to the local inhabitants—such as the provision of parks and public recreation, the supply of water, the regulation of construction, the fighting of fire, and so on. Legally the city is as much a creation of the state as the county or rural township but in practice its local patriotism is more likely to be respected by the state authorities. Many cities have, in fact, been granted "home rule" powers which, though perhaps narrowly construed by the courts, have at least given them far more freedom than is commonly enjoyed by typical rural units.

Rural Units: The County

Outside New England, where it has had relatively little significance, the most important unit of rural government is the county. The great majority of the 3,049 counties are purely rural areas but about 200 are so built up that they might well be given the apparatus of city government. The average county is nearly 1,000 square miles in area but the median is nearer 600 square miles. The average population is about 50,000 but the median is somewhat under 20,000 and one-sixth of all counties have populations between 10 and 15 thousand.

County Functions. Counties in many states have political significance as the areas used in the choice of state legislators but they are primarily agents for the performance of the state functions referred to above. As newer functions such as parks and recreation areas, airports, hospitals, and libraries are adopted by rural people, counties grow more important as areas for the performance of duties of interest to local people and thus tend to approximate the status of true municipal corporations. The laws of many states permit counties to perform such functions but they do not seem to have been widely adopted by rural counties, the vast majority of which remain essentially state agents.

The County Board. The governing body of the county is almost everywhere a board of commissioners or supervisors, elected by the voters at large or by districts for terms of two or four years. In sparsely populated counties the salaries paid are almost nominal and in only a few cases are they large enough to attract very able persons. As a matter of law the county board has general oversight over the business of the county; in fact, this overstates the board's powers since it has relatively little control over the long list of elective officers who discharge the administrative functions of the unit. The duties and the salaries of these officials are commonly prescribed by statute, and board control is in fact often limited to denying them assistants and supplies and in other petty ways limiting their effectiveness. Politically, however, the board is of

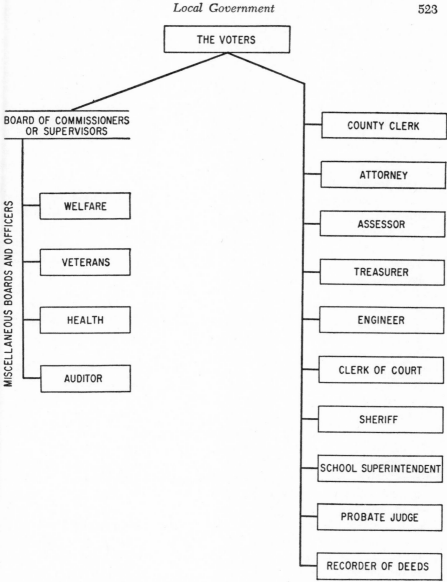

Fig. 14. The organization of a typical county.

great significance since it not only determines the extent of county expenditures and controls considerable patronage but also has authority to make many decisions affecting property rights, such as the location of highways, the awarding of contracts, the purchase of supplies, and the approval of claims.

County boards are not particularly effective bodies. Numerous surveys have shown that, while outright corruption is not widespread, careless business practices are followed and a good deal of money is lost by the general unawareness of efficient administrative procedures. There are numerous and shining exceptions but, generally speaking, county boards have not taken advantage of modern improvements in such matters as budgeting, purchasing, personnel administration, and record keeping. It is true, on the other hand, that large numbers of counties are too small and too poor to do these things well. Nevertheless even these could do better if the boards made any serious attempt to keep abreast of developments.

County Administrative Officers. Subject to an ill-defined and haphazard supervision by the board the county functions are performed by a long list of elected officers—a clerk, sheriff, recorder of wills and deeds, assessor, treasurer, highway engineer, a clerk of the local trial court, and a superintendent of schools. On the whole the most important of these is the clerk. He acts not only as secretary of the county board but performs a large variety of recording functions not committed by law to other officers. To a very great degree his work is central to county administration since he has come to be the custodian of the various precedents with respect to the handling of county business. He issues various permits and licenses, certifies many documents, advertises for bids for county purchases and contracts, supervises the machinery of elections, and keeps the agenda and records of board meetings. In less populous counties he may carry out also the functions of certain other officers such as assessor, or clerk of the court, or recorder of deeds and wills. He is by all odds the best informed county officer and his command of tradition and precedent is confirmed by the established practice of frequent reelection.

A county office of great historical importance but of declining significance is that of sheriff. As the chief peace officer of the county the sheriff, at least in the most rural areas, enjoys high visibility, since he has practically a monopoly of police work, being expected to patrol the county roads and apprehend offenders. He is also usually the county jailer. In addition to his police duties he is the principal officer of the local courts and the county board in the service of legal processes of various sorts. He is everywhere elected and is paid a fixed salary plus fees for the service of process and, in many cases, for the feeding of prisoners. In spite of his distinguished origin in the local peace administration of England the sheriff in the United States is of declining importance as a police officer. Many sheriffs take little interest in that part of their duties, confining themselves to their civil functions. As state police and highway patrols have grown more efficient the population has come to rely more upon them for law enforcement with the result that the sheriff has receded into the background. On the other hand the office nearly everywhere has constitutional status and will long continue to exist in spite of its growing ineffectiveness. It is also true that the fee system makes it in many counties the most lucrative office and this gives it considerable importance in local politics.

In many ways the most important of all county officers is the county attorney, or, as he is variously called, the state's attorney, district attorney, or prosecuting attorney. He is not only responsible for the prosecution of those accused of crimes but is also adviser in legal matters to the county board and other county officers. The wide discretion which he enjoys in deciding whether or not to prosecute those suspected as wrongdoers makes it possible for him to be a key figure in local politics—a fact emphasized by the large number of politicians who have obtained national reputations and high office as a result of having made a record as prosecutors. Unofficially the prosecutor is looked to by many citizens to arbitrate neighborhood quarrels and in general to keep an eye on community morals.

The other county officers merit little discussion, their duties being largely routine and sufficiently indicated by their titles. Many of them, as, for example, the county engineer and the superintendent of schools, have tended to become less important as the state government has grown more active in its oversight of road building and school administration. It is the function of the county assessor to value property for taxation and this makes him important. Few rural assessors, however, are trained for their jobs and the fact that they are elective subjects them to undesirable personal and political pressures. The office of treasurer is largely ministerial, consisting almost wholly of the custody of county funds. He often has discretion with respect to the deposit of these moneys in local banks and this discretion has often been marked by favoritism which at the very least approaches corrupt conduct.

Forty years ago the county was referred to as the "dark continent of American politics," not only because its operations largely escaped the attention of the public but also because investigation showed that it was the least efficient governmental unit and the happy hunting ground of grafters. With the passage of the years it has not entirely escaped the reform movement but on the whole it has been successful in resisting change. There are counties that are almost models of good and honest administration but they are relatively few even now. Considerable improvement has taken place with respect to the administration of those services financed by the national government, such as highways and "social security," for central supervision has had the paradoxical effect of putting new life into the county; but the older functions are managed much as always. There is relatively little corruption of the grosser sort but a great deal of careless administration.

The New England Town

In the six New England states and in New York the town continues to be the most significant unit of local government in rural areas. In contrast with the Middle Western township which was often laid out by surveyors in advance of actual settlement as an area six miles square, the New England town is an area of irregular shape and varying size corresponding to the limits of actual settlement. Some of the earlier towns were coterminous with the parish and the town government might be looked upon as the civil aspect of the religious congregation. In any case it was a "natural" area to a degree seldom attained farther west. Essentially the town was both an urban and a rural area, consisting of one or more village centers and the outlying farm lands. The entire territory, however, was governed as a unit.

It may be said in general that traditional town government is today confined to the purely rural parts of New England and New York State. In densely populated towns it has been found necessary to introduce various modifications. Thus, where the village center or centers need services not desired by the outlying rural population, resort is had to the special district—for water supply, fire protection, sanitation, and so on. The special district may have authority to levy special taxes for these services but in other respects remains a part of the town government. In the many cases where the area of a town is completely urbanized a city charter may be granted and the town organization to all intents and purposes disappears.

The Town Meeting. The distinctive feature of town government is the town meeting. This is held annually, or more frequently at the call of the selectmen, and consists of the entire body of voters. It meets under the presidency of a "moderator," often a distinguished citizen or "elder statesman" of the town, and is the ultimate authority in matters of policy and finance. All town officers are chosen by it and are responsible to it. The agenda for the meeting is prepared by the board of selectmen on their own authority or from suggestions which may be submitted by individuals or groups and is published in advance in a "warning." The selectmen also present their recommendations with respect to appropriations and tax levies, although in many towns the budget is now prepared by a finance committee of unpaid citizens, or, as is the case in many Maine towns, by the town manager. In any event the final decision in financial as well as in all other questions of policy is made by the meeting. Questions concerning desirable town improvements or even what might appear to be minor administrative matters often give rise to spirited debate. The town meeting also listens to the reports of the town officers who are thus subject to questioning and criticism of the voters.

It is easy, of course, to grow sentimental about town-meeting government, forgetting that, like all government, it may often have its seamy side; but when all allowance has been made its contribution to democracy has been an imposing one. It has trained thousands of men and women in the technique of debate and discussion and has taught generations the essentials of responsible citizenship. No small part of the contribution that New England has made to orderly popular government is traceable to a device which periodically brings rulers and ruled together and teaches each his share in the enterprise of self-government.

Town Officers. Under the final authority and direction of the town meeting the selectmen supervise the affairs of the town. There may be as many as nine selectmen but the most frequent number is three. In some states one is designated as first selectman and enjoys a vague primacy among his colleagues. The board of selectmen is in reality an executive committee acting for the town in the intervals between meetings. It has power to appoint such functionaries as are not elected by the voters, to authorize expenditures, buy equipment, and, in general, carry out the mandates of the voters. It occupies in the town, in fact, the same place filled by the county board in the county so far as oversight of administrative functions is concerned.

Little need be said about the other town officers since their duties are clearly enough indicated by their titles—assessor, treasurer or collector, constable, justice of the peace, and clerk. Unless the town has a manager —and often when it does—the clerk is the central figure. Although he is chosen annually by the town meeting, reelection is so common that the clerk is usually the one official with a complete command of the town's business. Selectmen come and go but the clerk stays on to become in time the custodian of the town's governmental tradition, unofficial information center of the community, and keeper of the selectmen's conscience. Since the county has had only a slight development in New England the clerk is also the chief local government recording officer. Besides being responsible for vital statistics in the town, he issues marriage and other licenses and permits, and records wills, deeds, mortgages, and a great variety of other documents.

In rural areas the town continues to be a surprisingly vigorous unit in spite of the growth of stricter state supervision in such matters as highway administration and public assistance. Matters of purely local interest are still numerous and important enough to command the attention of the voters and to attract to its service many public-spirited persons. No doubt the fact that it is still the unit for the selection of members of the lower house of the state legislature has had much to do not only with its ability to preserve its identity but also with the prevention of the least desirable kinds of centralization. In urban areas where the population exceeds ten thousand the original pattern has been more or less seriously altered. Representative town meetings not greatly different from large city councils have replaced the general town meeting of the past. The increasingly technical character of some town functions has in many cases led to the adoption of a modified form of the manager plan and to a wide use of finance committees charged with the preparation of the annual budget and of long-range plans for public improvements and debt management. Even in these cases, however, old habits are strong and town-meeting government has not entirely disappeared.

The Township

The success of the New England town as an area of democratic self-government was persuasive with those who were responsible for the organization of the Northwest Territory. Because of this there exist in the states north of the Ohio and as far west as North Dakota and Nebraska modified forms of the town known as townships. The modification is to be attributed to the fact that settlement followed the creation of the townships instead of preceding it as had been the case farther east. Because of this the township is seldom a natural area whose boundaries correspond with the community. It is simply an area six miles square. Moreover the Western population did not reside in villages whence they went out to cultivate their fields; on the contrary, the isolated farm home was the rule. Under these circumstances, little sense of community was developed. The greater distances involved made frequent assembly of the voters difficult so that, although a town meeting was provided by law, it has never had any real substance.

Township government shows considerable variation from one section to another. A township meeting is found in some states with power to levy taxes and choose officers but west of New York it seldom amounts to much more than a device for electing the township officers, and consists frequently of none but the officials in office and a scattering of curious voters. In some states authority is vested in an elective board of three trustees; in others in a single trustee or supervisor who, with the clerk and the justice of the peace, constitutes the governing body.

Township functions were never extensive, consisting largely of the care of local highways, the administration of "out-door relief," and, in a few cases, of the care of schools. Where cities and villages are excluded from the jurisdiction of township authorities they are left with power over only purely rural or suburban areas with a resulting severe shrinkage in their tax base. In recent years the care of roads and the administration of welfare laws and of elementary and secondary instruction have all been passing rapidly to the county or state level with the result that the township has ceased to be a significant unit of local government. As a matter of fact it has recently been abolished in Iowa and Oklahoma and it may be surmised that in many other states it has been kept alive largely by the inertia of the voters and by the political influence of the thousands of township officers who have a vested interest in perpetuating the petty perquisites attached to their posts. Occasionally persons are found to defend it as a means of preserving local self-rule but there seems to be little real substance to this argument. After all, most of our states never had townships and, under modern conditions, they would seem to be useless, if not parasitic.

School Districts

In addition to what may be called the standard units of local government in rural areas, there are at present in the United States something like 60,000 school districts existing independently of the counties or other units of general governmental powers. Most of these districts actually manage schools although an undetermined number exist only as legal entities in order to raise taxes sufficient to pay the tuition of students attending schools in neighboring districts better equipped to supply instruction. There is no good reason in theory why the schools should not be administered by the general government of the community as one of its functions, taking their chances, in the matter of financial support, for example, with highways, welfare, police, health and the other services provided.

Special treatment of the schools seems to be explained by two facts. In the first place, the instruction of the young has always been specially close to Americans and it has seemed to be giving it less than its due to make it a mere department of the general government. Closely connected with this has been the belief that the device of a separate district is a good way to keep a vital function "out of politics." In the second place, the average rural school district was quite small, being designed to serve a dozen or so farm families and having a school building readily accessible by early means of travel. Built as it was around a function calling forth much honest sentiment it may be looked upon as the one unit which best institutionalized community feeling. Because of this fact it resisted centralizing tendencies longer than any other local unit. Country people, seeing the care of roads and the administration of "poor relief" transferred to the county or the state, clung to the local management of the schools because it seemed to them to be the last vestige of local self-government.

The affairs of the school district are in the hands of an elective board, usually unpaid and chosen without reference to party membership. The board has power to levy a school tax, borrow money, manage the school property, employ a superintendent and teachers, and, in the early days, largely determine the curriculum subject to an ill-defined authority in the hands of a state superintendent. The board's policy and budget are not subject to review by the authorities of the county or other local unit within which it operates. In small districts the board members may directly concern themselves with the details of administration, but the general rule is to leave these in charge of the superintendent, the board contenting itself with general oversight.

In recent years the school district system has yielded, as have other units, to the modern forces of centralization and standardization. The causes have been largely financial in nature, and the principal changes have been two in number—the creation of larger districts and the tightening of central controls.

If accurate figures were available they would show beyond doubt that there are now only half as many districts as were operating 25 years ago. This reduction has been accomplished by the consolidation of many small districts. Surveys in practically every state have shown that many thousands of rural districts maintained a school for fewer than ten pupils; in many cases, in fact, there were fewer than five with the result that in hundreds of districts the number of board members exceeded that of pupils. It is obvious that the per capita cost of instruction in such tiny schools is unjustifiable. With the coming of modern means of transportation larger districts maintaining larger schools became feasible. A larger district means a larger tax base and the wherewithal to supply not only a better school building but a better curriculum, a better library, and better trained teachers. Whether the product of these modern schools is superior has in recent years been widely questioned but in any case consolidation goes on and, at least in terms of statistics, has been a success. There is a definite limit to this movement, however, since in sparsely populated states there will always be areas in which small districts will have to be maintained because of the great distances involved.

The local and largely amateur management of the schools has also been greatly affected by the appearance of various devices of state control. When the local school's curriculum was confined to the "three R's," it required no special competence to install it and employ teachers. A local board of farmers and villagers served well enough. The modern curriculum, however, goes far beyond the "tool" subjects and requires the setting of uniform standards of teacher preparation in a variety of specialties. Power to certify teachers has been lodged with the state department of public instruction and local boards may employ only those who meet the department's prerequisites. Failure to do so would entail loss of accredited status by the local school and the withdrawal of state aid, which, in many states, constitutes a large portion of the local budget. Even in such matters as school construction state suggestion or advice or even control is persuasive.

Miscellaneous Special Districts

The school district is the special district par excellence in rural local government but it is only one of many in a bewildering mosaic. Something like 12,000 districts for other specialized functions now exist in the United States, many of them in the open country. These have been created from time to time under permissive statutes to provide some service required by some but not all of the inhabitants of a county or town or other local authority with general governmental powers, or to cope with a problem affecting a population living within the boundaries of several such units. Examples are the special districts for fire fighting, police protection, sanitation, and water supply found in many New England towns and, farther west, for soil conservation, drainage, irrigation, the generation of electric power, or the eradication of noxious weeds. Such special districts are governed by elective boards or committees and, although they normally have power to levy taxes and borrow money, may be subject to some degree of oversight by the state or by the local authorities within the boundaries of which they operate. There is no doubt that the existence of such districts complicates the local government picture and offends persons who want a more "rational" scheme; on the other hand, they are flexible instruments for dealing with problems which the standard governmental units could handle only with great difficulty.

Urban Government

Whenever the density of population passes a certain point common needs arise which can best be met by governmental machinery more elaborate than that which suffices for the open country. Smaller built-up areas may be called villages or boroughs and are generally simpler in their organization than cities. There is, however, no uniformity in usage since in some states a "city" may be as small as 1,000 in population, legislatures normally using population as the basis of classification. The term "city" will be used here to include all such places as are separately constituted for the performance of local government functions, the fact being kept in mind that the organization in the larger ones is more extensive.

In the eyes of the law cities are creatures of the state legislature, deriving their powers and their organization from state law and being subject to such control and direction as may seem wise to the legislature.

They exist in part to act as agents of the state in performing functions of general interest, and in part as devices for doing things of interest primarily to the local inhabitants. The general rule of our courts has been to construe the powers of cities strictly and to infer nothing from a grant unless necessary to give it effect.

Three methods have been followed during our history in creating city governments. The act by which the people are created a corporation is known generally as its charter. The charter may be actually a special act of the legislature, it may be simply that portion of the statutes of the state applicable to the population group to which the city belongs, or it may be locally drawn under "home rule" provisions of the state's constitution.

In the colonial and early national periods cities and other urban governments were usually created by special acts of the legislature. Such charters were normally granted at the request of local citizens and provided for the organization and the range of powers felt by the latter to be desirable. This was not necessarily the case, however, special charters having often been the occasion for a good deal of jockeying and horse trading among legislators, most of whom, of course, had no direct interest in the community seeking the charter. Much of this was prompted by the desire to secure partisan advantage or to control the lucrative business of city contracts and patronage, so that the record of special legislation for cities is not an edifying chapter in our history.[2]

The abuses of special charter legislation were so serious that in time the constitutions of many states—though not yet all—were amended so as to prohibit it and to require cities to be chartered by general law. Since this sort of provision, strictly applied, would not fit the needs of all cities, resort was had to the device of classifying cities, on the basis of population, so that a city might adopt that portion of the statutes most closely meeting its needs. Another method in effect in some states is the enactment of alternative forms of city government,—mayor-council, commission, or council-manager,—each city being free to choose among these. In all of these cases, it is to be remembered, the statute is an act of the legislature which can be altered or repealed as that body sees fit.

The most recent method of acquiring a charter is provided in 20 states by a "home rule" provision in the state's constitution. Where such a

[2] Thus, the Connecticut public expenditure council reported in the spring of 1956 that "the legislative hopper in the 1955 sessions included over 500 local bills, many of them dealing with such local matters as the changing of the hour of a town meeting, the conferring of power on a tree warden, the vesting in a town of the control of its own sidewalks, the provision of traffic lights at street intersections, the awarding of pensions to deserving policemen and their widows, and so on." It is clear that if such bills did not have to be discussed the state legislature would be free to consider matters of state-wide concern.

provision exists any city may draw up its own charter and put it into effect by popular vote.[3] It is to be noted, however, that home rule charters may concern themselves only with "local and municipal affairs" and may introduce no changes with respect to those matters regarded by the courts as of state-wide importance. But such terms as "local" and "municipal" are in fact quite vague so that the adoption of home rule has everywhere put upon the courts the heavy burden of deciding where to draw the line between state and local matters. The general tendency of the courts has been to cut down the range of "home rule" powers for the simple reason that, as population grows more dense and agencies of transportation and communication more efficient, more and more problems take on state-wide importance.

A review of judicial decisions interpreting home rule grants indicates that there is little agreement among the state courts. There is some reason to regard the choice of the form of city government to be of primarily local concern and this seems generally to be true with respect to the adoption of the merit system and the administration of personnel regulations, the management of the local police force, the care and construction of streets and sidewalks (except possibly through streets) and the enactment and administration of zoning ordinances. On the other hand, there is something like general agreement that educational and judicial functions, the regulation of public utilities, large parts of the process of taxation, and the annexation of adjacent territory are matters of state-wide concern and hence beyond local control. Finally, there are a good many matters on which the state supreme courts are in complete disagreement. Among these are certain aspects of local finance, the settlement of claims against the city, health and sanitary regulations, parks and recreation facilities, and city planning. As a matter of fact, it is one of the strongest arguments against home rule that, in the nature of the case, no unanimous consensus on the legitimate area of local freedom is likely ever to be achieved.

Home rule is one of those reforms certain to be popular in local units which have long suffered from the intervention of meddlesome and perhaps corrupt state legislatures. It capitalizes on a large fund of honest sentiment in favor of local self-rule and when uncritically accepted as a battle cry has the effectiveness of all slogans. Powerful arguments may also be made for it as a way of freeing legislatures from work for which they are not well equipped, thus releasing their energies for consideration of matters of general concern. The fundamental question, however,

[3] There is frequently a provision restricting this privilege to cities of a certain minimum population. It is also possible for a city heretofore operating under the general statutes to adopt the applicable laws by local vote, thus acquiring in effect a "home rule" charter.

is, what are matters of general concern? The American state is organized in a unitary fashion and its government has the inescapable duty of protecting individual rights and providing for the general well-being of its inhabitants. So long as it does not attempt to do these things directly the various local units must act as its agents. Moreover, the state contributes to the support of many functions of value to the local citizenry and it can scarcely be argued that it may not supervise the expenditure of such funds as the ultimate guardian of the wealth of the state from which these payments are drawn. There is no evidence that there is discontent with this arrangement or that anyone seriously believes in complete local freedom. So long as this continues to be true, home rule will probably be of uncertain content and, perhaps, of declining importance.

Forms of City Government

The plain citizen, if he thinks about it at all, is likely to dismiss the question of municipal organization as of little importance, holding that much if not everything depends upon the character and ability of those in office. Although bound to have sympathy with this point of view, the serious student will not so readily minimize the importance of the form of government. An organization which confers power and fixes responsibility will normally have the effect of encouraging and rewarding able men and making it possible for them to do efficient work; one which does not have these merits will make it hard even for good officeholders to render service and is more likely to attract those who wish to conceal their inefficiency in its obscurities. The form of government is a tool and poor tools are likely to produce poor work.

The search for good forms of local government has been a preoccupation of the American people for a century. As one surveys the various reform movements of the late nineteenth and early twentieth centuries one is tempted to believe that men thought that there existed a type of organization which, once discovered and installed, would automatically produce good—or at least democratic—government. We are perhaps more sophisticated now and yet the tinkering has not come to an end. It can be said, however, that three "standard" forms have been developed, although there is within each considerable variation as to details of organization. These forms are: (1) the mayor-and-council; (2) the commission; and, (3) the council-manager types.

Mayor-Council Government. The oldest of these three principal types involves a rough division of authority between an executive, usually called the mayor, and a representative body, called the council, both elective by the voters. Two types are distinguishable, the so-called weak and strong executive types. In the "weak" executive form the mayor has relatively little power over administrative functions either by way of appointing officials or directing their work. He may name a few such officers but as a rule the appointive power of the council is substantially greater. The mayor's appointees are furthermore subject to confirmation by the council. In short, his functions are confined largely to presiding over meetings of the council and acting as ceremonial head of the community. The weak-executive type is still in use in a very considerable number of smaller cities but the tendency is all against such diffusion of power in places where municipal functions are at all complicated and expensive. Where it persists it is defended by the argument that it prevents an undesirable concentration of power, and, by allowing the election of many officials, keeps the government close to the people. It may be surmised, however, that the real reason for its continued existence is inertia. Where problems are not complex it probably does well enough and, if community standards are high, it may give a good account of itself.

The "Strong-mayor" Plan. For several decades now the principal object of municipal reform has been to provide for a better *administrative* machinery. This has meant in practice the strengthening of the executive power and a more distinct separation of the functions of policy formation and execution. Where the actual head of the city administration continues to be popularly chosen, this form of organization is called the strong-mayor form; where the direction of administration is vested in an appointive officer, the typical form is that of city-manager government. The latter is described briefly below.

In the so-called strong-mayor plan the distinguishing feature is the dominant position occupied by the mayor. He has substantially complete control over the administrative departments of the city with power to appoint and remove their officials. The latter name their subordinates subject to civil-service rules if the merit system exists. The mayor also prepares the budget and may veto items in appropriation ordinances as well as other acts of the council. All of these powers he exercises in addition to those functions of a ceremonial nature normally discharged by the chief executive. The council, for its part, is expected to keep its hands off administration and confine itself to policy.

Those who believe that a city should be governed as if it were a business object to the fact that the strong-mayor form places an elective official—a politician—at the head of the administrative services. This, it is feared, opens the way to the political manipulation of those services. But there really is no way by which administration can be clearly separated from politics. It is desirable, of course, that corruption be prevented and high standards be reached in the performance of municipal functions, but it does not follow that these objectives are impossible under a political executive. A politician is by definition an expert in human relations. If he possesses common sense and sound judgment he may in fact provide precisely those qualities of balance and flexibility often lamentably lacking in experts. City government is more than just a business. The

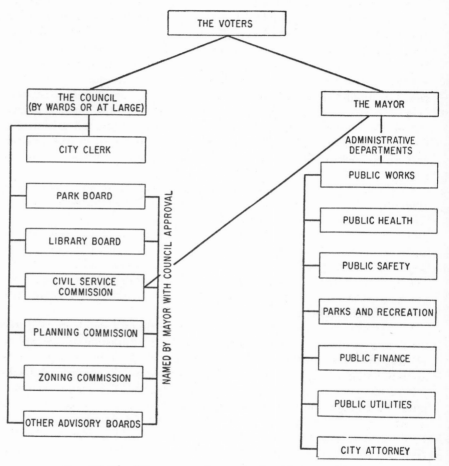

FIG. 15. The "Strong-mayor" organization of city government.

very word "government" means many things beyond careful buying, honest contracting, and technical administrative skill—essential as these are. It is the tendency of experts to emphasize government *for* the people and to forget that democracy means also government *by* the people— stupid and wrong-headed people as well as wise ones. It is the business of political leaders to tell the administrators what the people will not stand for, and no government can remain free unless it finds a place for such leaders. The publicized pillaging of men like Frank Hague should not cause us to withhold our recognition of many mayors who have quietly given unselfish and devoted leadership to hundreds of other cities.

City Government by Commission. Few influences have been so pervasive in city government in the last half-century as that of the business community. To businessmen, especially those acting through corporate forms, traditional arrangements of governmental machinery have seemed irrational, inefficient, and wasteful in contrast with the apparently more simple and direct structure of the corporation. Looking upon the city as primarily engaged in employing labor, buying materials, and constructing public works, it has seemed to such men only sensible that local units should adopt machinery which has had such conspicuous success in doing these things for private concerns. It was the application of this line of thought that led to the introduction of the commission form of government. Although it was introduced in Galveston, Texas, under crisis conditions, its rapid spread between 1901 and about 1920 showed how responsive the public was to the arguments used to support it. Since the latter date about one-fourth of the cities adopting it in the heyday of its popularity have abandoned it, in most cases in favor of the manager plan.

The principal features of commission government are: (1) the placing of all the powers of local government in the hands of an elective commission of from three to seven members; (2) the commission as a body exercises the policy-making powers usually vested in a city council; (3) the commissioners as individuals act as heads of administrative departments; (4) the usual power to appoint and remove officials is vested in the commissioners as a body; (5) one member is designated as mayor with power to vote but with no veto or appointive power. The mayor presides over commission meetings, is responsible for general law enforcement, and serves as ceremonial head of the city government. This is the general type but there are numerous variations in detail.

It cannot be denied that on paper at least the commission plan has definite merits. The voter's task is limited to voting for a short list of officials. Since all the corporate powers of the city are concentrated in the commission the plan in theory permits the fixing of responsibility for the conduct of the city's business. Finally, for what it may be worth, the plan has at least a superficial resemblance to corporate organization.

For a time after its introduction the plan seemed to give good results— probably, as is the case with many reforms, the energy required to adopt it carried over into other improvements not necessarily connected with it organically. In fact, only a few years' experience was required to demonstrate the weaknesses which have accounted for its rapid loss of popularity. In the first place, it was discovered that while election might produce a reasonably efficient legislative body it did not do so well as a way of choosing administrators. Men chosen because of their appeal to the voters turned out often to be indifferent or even incompetent administrators. The original promoters of the plan apparently expected the commissioners to leave the active conduct of their departments to experts, but it did not work out that way. In many if not most cases the commissioners showed themselves definitely interested in their departmental duties for which they were usually not fitted. This is not surprising since the rewards in local politics are to be found in manipulating such things as purchases, contracts, and appointments. In any case two undesirable results followed from this mingling of politics and administration. City commissioners were tempted to do a good deal of back-scratching and log-rolling with respect to the departments which they headed, often to the detriment of the city as a whole. Again this preoccupation led to a neglect of the legislative functions with which the commissioners were collectively charged.

In the second place, if it be argued that three, five, or seven administrative heads are better than the diffusion of management among numerous department heads, as under traditional forms, a stronger argument can be made for still greater concentration. At its best the mayor-council form did provide in the "strong" mayor a focal point of administration totally lacking in commission government. Moreover, at least when a city passes a certain size, its activities are too numerous to be compressed into the limited number of departments provided by the plan, while greatly to exceed the usual number would destroy the advantages of the short ballot. Closely connected with this is the fact that in a populous city the small number of commissioners is probably inadequately representative.

On the credit side it will probably be found that the chief service performed by the commission form was to accustom people to a break with some of the less desirable features of the older types of organization—such as the too strict application of the doctrine of the separation of powers with its typical resulting conflicts between mayor and council. It showed also the possibilities of a clearer and more compact organization of municipal functions. And finally it did put a desirable emphasis on administration and encourage the introduction of more efficient methods of management.

The Council-Manager Plan. At the close of 1955 nearly 1,400 cities of all sizes in the United States were operating under the council-manager plan or, as it is more frequently called, the city-manager plan. This plan, which was introduced in its classic form in Dayton, Ohio, in 1914, carries more nearly to its logical conclusion the principal idea embodied in the

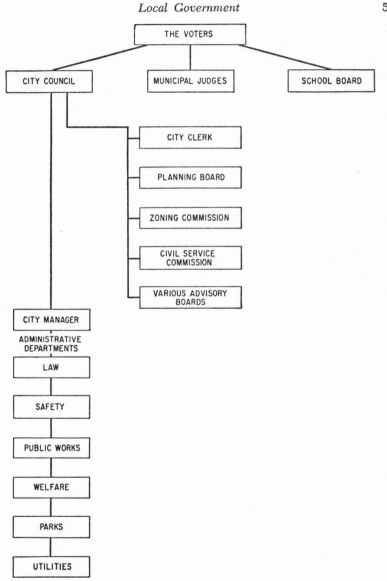

Fig. 16. Council-manager government.

commission form. First of all it places all the powers of the city in the hands of a popularly elected council which, since its authority is entirely legislative, need not be restricted in number to the three, five, or seven found in commission cities. Once the voters have chosen the council—either at large or by districts—their task is done. One of the council is designated mayor, either by the council itself, or by the voters, and has the duty of providing the political and public leadership which all units of general government require.

Once elected, the council proceeds to choose a manager to exercise supervisory power over the administrative departments, appointing, removing, and directing them in their work and naming their subordinates subject to controlling civil-service rules. The spirit of the plan requires that the council be free to choose the manager from outside the community and best results are obtained when this is done, not only because the field of choice is widened in a desirable way but also because an outsider is less likely to be involved in local squabbles. Since the principal functions of a modern city involve planning and construction, engineers are the most numerous category of managers. However, as time has gone on something like a profession of management has come into being involving other than engineering skills—accounting, budgeting, purchasing, and personnel work—so that a great variety of professions is found among the ranks of active managers.

It is evident that there is a close resemblance between the manager form and corporate organization. In a general way the voters are analogous to the stockholders, the council to the board of directors, and the manager to the president. Certain conditions must be met by citizens and council, however, before the plan works as it is supposed to do. It is necessary of course that the council confine itself to the field of legislation and refrain from interfering with the details of departmental management. Unless this rule is observed the city is certain to lose the benefits arising from the professional skill and discretion of the manager. On his part it is incumbent on the manager to remain aloof with respect to policy decisions. The spirit of the plan requires that political leadership be supplied by the council and especially by the mayor. It is often hard to observe this rule because an energetic manager is likely to be the most conspicuous figure in the city government and quite superior in stature to council members. If this fact leads the community to expect statements of policy from him he is certain to become involved in local politics in undesirable ways. No manager, of course, can be completely indifferent to questions of policy; the fact that he is responsible for budget-making entails important decisions as to what it is desirable for the city to do. The point is that his recommendations must be as unobtrusive as the nature of the case admits. If he is too vigorous in urging his views and allows himself to assume the community leadership reserved to the mayor and council the entire plan is jeopardized. On the other hand, if both council and manager respect the subtle requirements of the plan and if the voters have the will to make it work, the proper relationship will pay dividends in terms of efficient and economical government.

It goes without saying that the long American experiment has produced no ideal form of city government. On the whole, however, probably the manager plan has been the most successful scheme so far evolved. To a greater extent than any other it has achieved a clear-cut concentration of responsibility. Although the council is confined to policy control, it is also ultimately responsible for administration since the manager serves at its pleasure and may be removed if the quality of administration is poor. Another distinct advantage of the plan is that it emphasizes professional skill in administration. The fact that a career may be found anywhere in the country has encouraged well-trained men to seek employment as managers and has almost literally created a new profession. Managers as a rule have been well-trained and well-qualified men in spite of numerous exceptions where politicians have been chosen or where managers, impatient with their councils, have yielded to the temptation to assume political leadership. Finally, just because managers have been professional men they have kept abreast of developments in the various areas of expert public administration and have introduced into city government better methods of budgeting, accounting, purchasing, and physical planning. Since good city government consists precisely in improvement in these areas indebtedness to the manager plan is very great.

The Future of Local Government

Two quite contrary tendencies are observable in the development of our thinking about local government. On the one hand, there is the traditional belief in the virtue of keeping affairs in the hands of the local citizens; on the other there is the steady growth of the habit of looking to the state or the national government for the performance of more and more functions. If the latter tendency continues it may confidently be predicted that local government will be drained of its content and will cease to hold the interest or arouse the public spirit of citizens. As centers of decision and control grow more remote the habit of self-determination will be replaced by a formal efficiency devoid of that vital principle of action which depends upon the immediacy of responsibility possible only within small and manageable areas. Only by insistence upon more efficient administration and a jealous watchfulness over local liberties can these recent tendencies be halted. Here as elsewhere in democratic society vigilance is the price of independence.

REFERENCES

William Anderson, *Units of Government in the United States* (1942 and supplements in 1945 and 1949).

Council of State Governments, *The Forty-eight State School Systems* (1949).
————, *State-Local Relations* (1946).
Jefferson B. Fordham, *Local Government Law* (1949).
International City Managers' Association, *The Technique of Municipal Administration* (1947).
Lane W. Lancaster, *Government in Rural America*, 2nd ed. (1952).
Joseph D. McGoldrick, *The Law and Practice of Municipal Home Rule* (1933).
National Municipal League, *Model City Charter* (1941).
————, *Model County Charter* (1956).
New York State Regents' Inquiry, *Education for American Life* (1938).
Harold A. Stone, Don K. Price, and Kathryn H. Stone, *City Manager Government in the United States* (1940).
Paul Wager, ed., *County Government across the Nation* (1950).
Roger H. Wells, *American Local Government* (1939).

CHAPTER 31 *The American Political Achievement*

An American, simply because he *is* an American, cannot be expected to be entirely objective when he tries to estimate the nature and importance of his country's political achievements. What makes a man a patriot is the sense, however dim, of being somehow a participant in, and a product of, his country's history. We are what we are in part because men called Washington and Jefferson and Lincoln lived and wrought. Thus, we talk of "one world" and yet preserve a respect for Washington's advice to steer clear of the quarrels of Europe; many who do not know who said it, assert their belief in Jefferson's demand that there be equal rights for all and special privileges for none; and the dullest spirit is stirred by the simple but lofty language of the Gettysburg Address. Just so are Englishmen what they are because of Henry II and the common law, Cranmer and the Book of Common Prayer, Cromwell and the Bill of Rights. French political institutions and practices are explicable only in terms of the work and words of Richelieu, Louis XIV, Robespierre, and the two Napoleons.

No patriot, by the most strenuous effort of the imagination, can *really* be a citizen of the world; much less can he transcend the boundaries of time and space and look upon his country and its institutions as if he were the famed man from Mars. But if such complete detachment is impossible, the sober patriot has certain advantages in studying his own institutions not possible in the case of foreigners. He has at least a feeling for them, especially for the more subtle political adjustments, rarely attained by outsiders. Few foreigners, for example, have shown a real understanding of our baffling party system or of the intricacies of federalism. These, indeed, are often enough puzzles to Americans, but if one makes the effort to put himself outside that of which he is inevitably a part, his interpretations may not be without value. The United States, however reluctantly, has been forced by events into the role of leadership in the free world, while at home it faces novel domestic problems of great difficulty. It is of more than academic interest for us to examine our fitness to discharge these new

543

responsibilities. This involves among other things an estimate of our success in meeting our political problems of the past.

Government and Physical Factors

In surveying our political accomplishments, the first thing that strikes one is the scale on which government in the United States has been forced to act. Next to the Soviet Union, China, Brazil, and the Dominion of Canada, the United States is by long odds the largest area under unified political control. Confining ourselves to the continental United States, we discover an area of more than 3 million square miles. By contrast the United Kingdom of Great Britain and Northern Ireland covers only 94,278 square miles, or roughly the area of Wyoming. The area of the United States is more than a dozen times that of France or Germany and twenty times as great as such countries as Sweden and Finland. Among the more significant smaller countries, the Netherlands and Belgium are each only a little larger than the state of Maryland and together are about the size of West Virginia.

Some idea of the comparative size of the United States and other nations and, by inference, of the variety of climatic and other differences within our borders, is supplied by some figures on distances. It is 2,547 miles by air from New York City to San Francisco. This is only a little greater than the distance between Lisbon, Portugal, and Istanbul, Turkey. Chicago and Denver are almost as close together as Oslo and Moscow. The air traveler between Berlin and Port Said would traverse a dozen countries and cover 1,747 miles; in the United States the same trip would take him from Los Angeles to Chicago, all of the distance being within the same political unit, although in the latter case as many kinds of geographic conditions are found as in the former. Although many of the conditions making it possible have been accidental, the relatively peaceful extension of orderly government over such a truly imperial domain has been itself a significant achievement. It is not wholly fanciful to attribute our success in accomplishing this to a very considerable degree of political wisdom, inventiveness, and adaptability. Only a small part of this vast territory has ever passed through a colonial status and no significant portion of its citizens has for long been without the institutions of free government constructed and enjoyed by the settlers of the original colonies. The problem of imperial organization which baffled British officials in the eighteenth century was solved by "backwoods" politicians on the very fringes of civilization.

Successful Federalism

Chief among the factors making possible the orderly exercise of political power over such a vast and varied society as that of the United States must be placed the federal principle of organization. This principle was adopted, as was pointed out earlier, not in deference to any mere theory, but because no other would have been acceptable to Americans of the late eighteenth century. This fact, however, does not detract from its importance. The problem of reconciling multiplicity and unity, diversity and uniformity, is quite as difficult in politics as it is in philosophy, and requires an ingenuity and adaptability not always encountered. Certainly no closet philosopher, impressed by the apparent need for decisive central control in a dangerous modern world, would recommend federalism today. It is apparently much easier to argue that economic unity should be accompanied by political unity. To support forty-nine governments even over such a vast area as that of the United States inevitably makes for the sort of duplication, inefficiency, and quarrelsomeness that offends tidy minds. System makers, with a limited number of molds into which to compress the facts of political life, must find intolerable disorder in the American federal system. But the life of politics as of law is not logic but experience, and our experience has made a theoretically unpromising system work with considerable efficiency.

The federal system as it works in practice exhibits great complexities, the surmounting of which has required much subtlety on the part of public men and great adaptability on the part of our people. The problem consists of dividing the power to rule in such a way that matters of truly national interest shall not be jeopardized by the activities of local and sectional groups, or truly local interests be subjected to a rigid control from the center. Since local and national interests are not fixed for all time but are, on the contrary, in a state of constant flux, great skill and forbearance are required to preserve the delicate balance which is implicit in the system. Ways and means have had to be found to avoid the undesirable extremes of centralization on the one hand and something like local anarchy on the other.

The problem of making federalism "work" is complicated by the fact that in our complex modern world few actual problems are purely national or entirely local. Traditionally such functions as public health, assistance, and education have "belonged" to the state and local governments, but it would be difficult now to hold to this view. These and many other functions, when studied realistically, are seen to have both local and national aspects. The concrete problem is to devise methods of supporting and administering these services in such a way as to give proper emphasis to both aspects. The federal system as we have developed it has gone far toward solving these problems. Through such devices as the grant-in-aid and interstate agreements a practicable balance between local demands for independence and the national necessity for uniformity has been worked out or, rather, is in constant process of being worked out.

In practice the endless adjustment of national and local interests, required by a federal system, has involved action by all branches of government at both the state and national levels. For example, such a device as the national grant-in-aid is worked out in Congress which, from this point of view, is in reality a kind of diplomatic gathering. While members of Congress are legally *national* officers, they cannot forget that they owe their seats to *local* electorates. This means, with respect to all legislation in which the state governments have an interest, that the members must balance state and national needs. Even though they might prefer a centralized solution of a problem, elementary political prudence tells them that some combination of national and state administration is best if they are to be reelected. National laws in such areas, then, are something like treaties among sovereign powers. If they seem less neat and tidy than the ideal, they have at least the merit of being workable.

The Vitality of Local Government

Federalism is still a reality in the United States because of the persistence of a strong feeling of attachment to local institutions. It is true, of course, that the balance has long seemed to tip in favor of national as against state power and that this has led many to assume that local self-government is on its way to extinction. If this were true it would be evidence of a decline in the quality of our citizenship and of a growing willingness to evade responsibility for government in general. But no one familiar with the actual working of local and state government can hold such views. Not only are these units assuming more functions and spending more money than ever before; but it is clear that most of the devices for keeping government close to the people are still vigorously alive. Our state legislatures are still constituted by a system which preserves the identity of such units as the county and the township; and anyone who has been concerned with the question of legislative apportionment knows how tenaciously this identity is defended. Whether or not home rule as technically understood exists for villages and cities, it is clear that these units have by no means become mere administrative areas of the state government. Even where the paramount position of the state is recognized with respect to certain functions, ways and means are usually found to modify state policy so as to meet local demands in their administration. Local officials continue to be locally elected, nor can state officers, whatever their *legal* powers, entirely ignore local wishes.

In theory these factors might seem to make for inefficient management; in practice the record of local government during the past generation is not a bad one. Our cities and counties can no longer be described as the one conspicuous failure of American democracy. Even our smallest local units are no longer total strangers to newer methods of administration. After every allowance has been made for "official sinning," improvements in the conduct of public business have been very real. Much of this progress is traceable to the fact that local self-government has enlisted in the public service the interest and the activity of more individuals than is probably the case in any other country.

It would be difficult to overestimate the importance of such facts. That local service is the best training for state and national political and administrative careers is still true. Men and women who have the feel of affairs on the local level do not look to central authorities for suggestions and directions, but are themselves the source of new ideas. The fact that many thousands of them are in touch with local government means, almost as a matter of course, that experimentation in political and administrative devices will be the normal thing and that centrally determined policy will be adjusted to local conditions. Government is thus kept close to the people who pay the bills and a more vital sense of responsibility is preserved. It may not require as high a degree of imagination and resourcefulness to manage the affairs of a village or county as it does to direct those of the state or nation; but a system of self-government in small units probably calls forth as many of these qualities as are to be found in the common run of men and women. The modern national state is a pretty impersonal and abstract sort of thing, and those who, like the citizen of the modern dictatorships, are carried away by the illusion that they share in its government are more than likely, by that very experience, to be tricked into a passive surrender of any effective part in its actual conduct. At any rate it is the American view that the selectman or the county commissioner, unromantic though he may be, is somehow a more desirable political type than the indistinguishable members of a "leader's" cheering section.

Liberty and Authority

The most persistent governmental tradition in the United States is that government shall be a servant of the people, not their master. We have ordinarily looked upon it with suspicion, not expecting it to be a beneficent force, and have granted it powers only reluctantly. No philosopher has gained prestige amongst us by exalting the state and those from abroad who do so have few convinced disciples. Hegel's oft-quoted remark that "the State is the march of God in the world" would strike most Americans as mystical nonsense. Even when, under stress of circumstances, new and strange powers are vested in government, we are more likely than not to make their exercise difficult by congressional investigations, writs of injunction, or various ingenious if informal kinds of resistance. We have created a powerful executive office which we fill from time to time with able and determined men, but we send to our legislatures other men to obstruct their programs by every device which personal ambition or fertile imagination can suggest. We have national party organizations charged with the task of nominating and electing a President and announcing a party platform, but between these and the voters we allow to exist powerful state machines capable of challenging or even thwarting the national leadership if it seems in their interest to do so. These are aspects of our old friends, the separation of powers and checks and balances, not discussed in the court decisions but nevertheless significant parts of the machinery by which government is resisted. Only grudgingly do we admit the legitimacy of government at all, and then we defy it to govern except with respect to the most essential functions.

Freedom and Group Life

If all this is true, and we think it is in spite of the recent increase in governmental functions, how do we manage to get governed at all? It is here that we encounter a distinctive thing about our society. We restrict formal government in order that we may *govern ourselves,* and we govern ourselves paradoxically largely through nongovernmental agencies. The United States is not only a nation of "joiners" but in no other country do private associations play such a significant part in ruling. When formal treatises on political science distinguish between state and society, what they are doing is pointing out that behind the official machinery of the state, the government, stand the organizations of the people—formed for nonpolitical purposes but exerting nevertheless a profound influence upon what the formal government does. We are a pluralistic society in which a good share of governing is done by private groups.

It is difficult to overestimate the importance of this fact which we may now illustrate. Every human interest, as we know from casual observation, is organized in its appropriate association. These range from such relatively uninfluential groups as stamp-collectors' clubs and bowling leagues on up through federations of women's clubs and local medical, dental, engineering, and other professional societies to such imposing organizations as the Congress of Industrial Organizations, the American Medical Association, and the American Farm Bureau Federation. It is a rare American indeed who does not belong to two or three such associations.

The fact that American society is thus an infinitely complicated series of intertwining associations has important consequences. In the first place, mere citizenship is not enough to exhaust the social impulses of man. His contacts with the State through voting and attending party or other political meetings are too rare to be significant in his life. The State itself is too remote and impersonal to give him, except in times of great crisis, that sense of "belonging" which seems to be essential to human self-realization. Further than this, the things with which formal government concerns itself rarely touch him closely—or at least not with the immediacy felt in his contacts with smaller face-to-face organizations. If he is to express himself adequately it must be in some more personal and intimate way than is afforded by membership in the larger society of his state, province, or fatherland. Surely it is more important to one's self-esteem to be president of one's lodge when his turn comes around than to be a rank-and-file member of a political party.

Of special significance to the student of politics is the fact that membership in nonpolitical bodies initiates one into the procedures and traditions of self-government. Few persons can be legislators or even school-board members, but hundreds and thousands of persons can get something of the feel of political management as a member and officer of some private organization existing to advance the interests of its members. The bearing of this upon free government is important and immediate. Nearly a century ago the English philosopher, John Stuart Mill, wrote words that are still true: [1]

In France, a large part of the people, having been engaged in military service, many of whom have held at least the rank of non-commissioned officers, there are in every popular insurrection several persons competent to take the lead, and improvise some tolerable plan of action. What the French are in military affairs, the Americans are in every kind of civil business; let them be left without a government, every body of Americans is able to improvise one, and to carry on that or any other public business with a sufficient amount of intelligence, order, and decision. That is what every free people ought to be; and a people capable of this is certain to be free; it will never let itself be enslaved by any man or body of men because they are able to seize and pull the reins of the central administration.

In short, where the freedom of association is preserved, there will always be available a reservoir of governing talent, trained in nonpolitical matters but capable of being turned to the discharge of public duties. When Mr. Truman unexpectedly assumed the Presidency he remarked that there were a million men better able to discharge the duties of the office. He was undoubtedly aware of the opportunities presented by our rich group life for the preparation of rulers.

The significance of group life is not confined, however, to its contributions to an understanding of "politics" as that term is commonly used. Much of the actual government of the United States is to all intents and purposes by private associations. Examples of this are not far to seek. Local school boards and colleges and university governing bodies find themselves influenced and limited at every turn by the regional and national accrediting agencies—such as the North Central Association of Colleges and Secondary Schools. The standards for admission to graduate study everywhere are set in reality by the thirty-odd universities that are members of the Association of American Universities. Medical schools, public as well as private, are rated by the American Medical Association,

---

[1] *On Liberty* (Everyman edition), p. 167.

the judgment of which determines the standards of admission to the profession and thus the content of the premedical curriculum. Competence in the various medical specialties is certified by national boards the standards of which are frequently accepted by state legislatures and licensing authorities. To a greater or less degree this sort of thing is found in all the professions. The voluntary association takes the lead, governments follow. With respect to such commonplace but important matters as the strength of materials, the viscosity of lubricating oil, and the manufacture and use of electrical equipment, insulating and roofing materials, our effective rulers are engineering societies, fire insurance underwriters, and trade associations. What they regard as adequate or safe or of minimum efficiency is for the most part adopted without serious question by our formal rulers.

The importance of these facts in terms of distributing power and hence in erecting bulwarks against officialism and bureaucracy is very great. In a formal sense law is found in the statute books, in recorded judicial decisions, and in the decrees of administrators; in fact it is both made and to a degree enforced by the people themselves organized in groups formed primarily to advance those interests which affect them most closely.

There is, of course, another side to this. Everyone has observed that in all human organizations there is a tendency for affairs to get into the hands of an oligarchy of officials who, once in power, attempt to perpetuate their influence. In so far as they are successful, the rank and file are scarcely less free with respect to the affairs of the organization than they would be under oligarchical leadership in the State itself. The kind of oppression then possible may have to be corrected by law, as, for example, in the requirement that workers shall by ballot choose their own bargaining agency in labor controversies. Appeals to the law are infrequent, however, for members know that governmental assistance may be forthcoming only at the price of submission. It is well known that the "Nazification" of all significant private and professional associations in Hitler's Germany meant the end of freedom. So long as the right of free association is preserved men and women will be able to join other organizations which better reflect their real views. A society in which policies are debated, formulated, and struggled for in a never-ending series of battles within and between private associations may be shocking to the hyperesthetic, but it is well to remember that liberty is secreted in these unlovely contests: "Out of this nettle, danger, We pluck this flower, safety."

The more formal devices by which individual and group liberty has been preserved are discussed elsewhere in this book. Although our history has at times been disfigured by attempts to oppress the unconventional, we have in general favored the inquiring mind and sought improvement through the preservation of the experimental attitude. Even those extreme individualists, the criminals, have enjoyed, if anything, an excessive degree of protection before courts and juries, while those who are less drastically "different" have found us ordinarily hospitable to new ideas.

Government and the "Melting Pot"

The comparative absence of a demand for rigid conformity in thought and conduct is perhaps to be explained by the remarkable heterogeneity of our population—a heterogeneity greater than anywhere in the world except in the Soviet Union and in the Balkans. One of our most memorable achievements, in fact, has been the successful assimilation of millions of people alien to our social customs and political traditions. During the first century of our national existence immigration was actively encouraged not only because of the need for labor in developing a new country but also because of a genuine desire to extend the blessings of our free system to the oppressed of less-fortunate lands. Prior to 1930 nearly 40 million persons from every country in the world had come to the United States, most of them to remain.

It would be untrue to say, of course, that the "promise of American life" has been realized by all of these people. There have been and still are instances of the exploitation of groups and individuals and occasional outbreaks of violence against foreigners and other minorities. These things are an exemplification of a kind of suspicious tribalism which will be long in disappearing from a world organized in national states. On the whole, however, the rights and privileges guaranteed by the Constitution to all persons living under it have been extended even to foreigners. The acquisition of citizenship and thus of political rights has been made reasonably easy, and the traditional safeguards of property and criminal law are available for the most part even to noncitizens. More significant has been the absorption of these strangers into the political life of the community. Irish, Poles, Jews, Italians, Germans, and Scandinavians have—for selfish reasons perhaps—been welcomed by native party organizations and have in due time risen to places of influence or even dominance in our public life, as the ballot in many a state and local election will testify. Finally, those without political ambitions have, with less difficulty than might have been expected, adjusted themselves to new laws and customs and have become good Americans, Old World suspicions and enmities disappearing in the new climate of freedom. Negroes, Orientals, and Mexicans still await social acceptance as full citizens, but their exclusion is by now so greatly a matter of regret to thoughtful Americans that it may be regarded as likely to be ended before many years have passed.

Some Unfinished Business

It would be mere smugness to assert that these accomplishments are to be attributed to some high wisdom or virtue possessed exclusively by

Americans. Conditions for which we can claim no special credit have been largely responsible for them and for the development of a temper of mind which so far has preserved them intact. American political institutions were set up during the death throes of an old social and political order. Social classes were beginning to enjoy a fluidity which was new in the world. In Europe feudalism was dying and had no chance to lay its hand upon our future. Our Revolution was only one aspect of a world-wide revolt against overgovernment and was conducted by men who believed firmly in the potentialities of the individual and who rejected decisively the view that some were born to rule and others to serve. An unexploited continent challenged the energies and ingenuity of a vigorous people and tended to emphasize—perhaps beyond what was reasonable—the virtues of self-help and individual enterprise. All these factors, rather than any unique personal or national endowment, have been responsible for our distinctive achievements. But if disappearance of the physical frontiers makes necessary a new discipline of the individual for the good of the group, it may be hoped that our heritage of spiritual freedom will ensure that it shall be *self*-discipline.

The adventure of government is in its nature an endless one. Just as there is truth in the ancient philosopher's remark that "you cannot step twice in the same river, for fresh waters are ever flowing in upon you," so we find that political institutions are in a state of constant change. Unless the flow of the river is stopped—in which case it ceases *to be* a river—each successive step will be into something different, however little the difference may be.

Now in every society there are those who would dam the river and those who would find a new one, and, between them, those who are content to accept the fact of gradual change. The first class we may call reactionaries, men and women who cling to an order which has ceased to be, or better, to one which never existed, since such people are likely to believe that there were giants and sorcerers and fairy godmothers and perpetual Sunday-school picnics in some Golden Age of the past—probably around the year 1890! The second group we call radicals. These see the Golden Age in the future and to be reached by taking a completely new route. All that is past is a prologue filled with ogres and evil witches and the prolonged pestilence of tyranny and exploitation. These two groups are akin in having lively imaginations—which kinship accounts for their frequent alliances against the third group. These last, though apparently dull and uninventive, accept the values of both tradition and hope and, refusing to be wholly captivated by either, set to work to meet problems as they arise. The tendency of our history has for the most part been to follow this group. In practice our people and politicians have agreed with the great conservative, Edmund Burke, in regarding "a disposition to preserve and an ability to improve" as the standard of a statesman, and in looking upon extreme measures of either the Right or the Left as "vulgar in the conception, perilous in the execution." [2] It is because we believe in the strength of this tradition of moderation that we assume the continuance of our constitutional system and the avoidance of extreme measures.

We cannot get away from the fact, however, that our governmental machinery reflects views as to the nature of man and the sphere of government which are no longer widely held. The whole complicated machinery —consisting of checks and balances, the separation of powers, the federal system, and judicial review—is the typical product of an age in which the central figure was the *individual*. The period of the founding fathers was in process of throwing off age-old controls exercised by kings, feudal magnates, and economic monopolies enjoying governmental support. For more than a thousand years after the breakup of the Roman Empire men and women had significance principally or wholly as members of *classes*— as peasants, craftsmen, priests, lords—and it was the rare individual who escaped from the prison of his class to strike out on a new line for himself.

By the middle of the eighteenth century this system of social organization was rapidly breaking up, and for two hundred years the emphasis has been on the individual, not on the group or the class. The son of a tailor need not as of yore follow his father's craft but might *on his own* aspire to any calling to which his skill was adequate—even to that of ruling his fellows. It was commonly believed that the individual was free to get and to be what he could. Government was to exist for *him* and was to do nothing which he could do for himself. If he failed in the battle of life he had no one but himself to blame; if he succeeded it was because he had the brains, the skill, the strength, or the craftiness required for success, and failures had no right to envy or reproach him. In this sort of struggle he asked nothing of government except that it keep the battle a fair one. If it did more it was likely not only to favor some contestants over others but to do it badly and, what was more, charge him for it in the form of taxes. The less it did in any case the better and, so that it might not do too much, arrangements were devised to make it difficult to do anything at all beyond the obvious minimum of national defense and the preservation of internal order narrowly defined.

It requires no special wisdom to see that this view is no longer firmly held by the bulk of our population. Individualism was a doctrine involving grave risks to personal security and happiness. It required its followers to take literally the words of the poet James Graham, Earl of Montrose:

> He either fears his fate too much,
> Or his deserts are small,
> That dares not put it to the touch,
> To gain or lose it all.

[2] *Reflections on the Revolution in France* (Everyman edition), p. 153.

An incorrect estimate, an incautious movement might well end in disaster. "To gain or lose it all" poses hard alternatives—alternatives only the sturdy are willing to face. And so it has grown increasingly hard for the average man to find justice in a system which seems to him quite by accident to produce alternately millionaires and paupers. For two generations the tendency throughout the Western world has been toward using the power of government to minimize these accidents and replace the risks of individualism by guarantees of security. Hence we have nearly everywhere programs of old-age assistance, unemployment insurance, workmen's compensation, aid to widows, minimum wages and maximum hours, health insurance, and suggested programs to guarantee full employment. Corollaries to these are found in the growing influence of government in the conduct of private business both at home and abroad. Farming, traditionally the most individualistic of all callings, now receives price supports and a large measure of less obvious public aids, accompanied, to be sure, by public controls.

Individualism was the cult of the uncommon man; we seem now to be entering the age of the "common man," the mass man, the man willing to give up the zestful danger of competition in exchange for a minimum of economic security. If this is the popular philosophy of the future, then government must be adjusted to it. This means in our case that a government constructed with eighteenth-century conditions and beliefs in mind must somehow be made to fit the quite different beliefs and conditions of the twentieth century. In spite of our traditional optimism it will not be easy to make this adjustment within the framework of constitutionalism. Wisdom and insight and self-discipline of a high order will be required to do it with sufficient promptness. If it is not done it is hard to see how anything that is significant in our tradition can long survive.

Legislative-Executive Relationships. Perhaps the most important structural problem in American government has to do with the improvement of the relationships between Congress and the executive department. The existence of mutual suspicion and the working at cross-purposes resulting from it, while perhaps inevitable in a system based upon the separation of powers, are luxuries which we can no longer afford. Congress must be so organized as to enable it to perform its historic functions; and the executive branch must be equipped with the tools of administration needed to discharge its clear responsibilities. Both these problems are involved in the larger one of creating somehow a more responsible party system.

Congress, as is true of all representative bodies in free countries, has three principal functions. It makes laws, it appropriates money for the support of the functions assumed by government, and it watches over the performance of these functions by the various administrative agencies. Although the Reorganization Act of 1946 did much to rationalize the machinery of Congress, it did not complete the job. Largely because of its sectional character Congress has never developed within itself adequate and dependable leadership. It has therefore seldom been able to formulate clear-cut policies or to give clear instructions to the executive department. The absence of an organic union between the two branches means that neither accepts the other as national spokesman except on the basis of informal agreements likely to be upset at the very moment when unified and decisive action is essential. In an epoch when domestic and international crises succeed one another with great rapidity this is a perilous situation.

Admirers of the cabinet system have often urged its adoption in the United States. This would mean, of course, conferring upon the President a monopoly in the initiation of legislation as well as control over administration. Entirely apart from the difficulty of adopting the necessary amendments to the Constitution, our traditional suspicion of a strong executive is certain to prevent such a change. Nor, it must be urged, is there any reason to believe that our situation is sufficiently like that of Great Britain for us to profit by imitation. One of the witnesses before the Joint Committee on the Reorganization of Congress in 1946 spoke words of great wisdom [3] with respect to those conditions which make the cabinet system workable, conditions which emphatically do not exist in the United States.

A small and compact nation, a clear-cut social structure, a high regard for the proprieties, a general agreement on articles of faith, a zone of action narrow enough to blunt the edge of difference—such are the conditions of its success. But the conditions which make for success there do not exist here. Our population is made up of many elements; we have no class structure, no nucleus of first families, no common body of opinion which confines differences to nonessentials, no tendency for all members of Congress to think as one in the face of a crisis. There is no neat, well-ordered society here, such as England possesses, to which the system of cabinet government can be fitted.

The new philosophy of government now generally accepted imposes upon Congress a new role, a new organization, and a new relationship to the executive branch. Modern government is much less concerned with "enforcing the law" in the older sense of that phrase than with the day-by-day administration of complex social and economic programs and the conduct of what are essentially business enterprises. This sort of activity does not involve the relatively simple questions of what is right and wrong, legal or illegal, but rather a never-ending adjustment of interests amongst various segments of society. For this sort of task what is needed is a flexible

[3] Testimony of Walton Hamilton, printed in "Organization of Congress," *Hearings before the Joint Committee on the Organization of Congress*, 79th Cong., 1st sess., p. 703.

and expert administration subject to rational supervision but not exposed to the spasmodic and irresponsible intervention of amateurs.

It is not suggested that Congress is made up of incompetent and ill-disposed men and women. On the contrary, it contains the best talent that our public life produces and in industry, honesty, and public spirit it ranks high among national legislatures. The difficulty is that Congress is different from the sum of its members. It has taken a few steps toward setting its house in order, but on the whole it is still shackled by habits and devices of an earlier age. It is trying to do what no body so constituted can do and it is thereby losing the chance to do what it might do.

It is the principal business of a body like Congress to act as the great forum of the nation in the discussion of public problems. From the point of view of brains and experience it is well suited to serve in such a way—but only if it abandons some of its habits and revises some of its procedures. First of all, it must go further than it has in getting rid of the mass of petty business with which it now occupies itself. Some steps have been taken to reduce the number of private and local bills, but they have not gone far enough. A glance at the *Congressional Record* makes it obvious that the House of Representatives especially has relatively little time to devote to matters of national interest, the discussion of which is constantly interrupted by the insertion of the "small change" of personal or local politics. It may well be that debate changes few votes; yet it would be a tremendous gain if the people had some assurance that their representatives were talking about first-rate questions. If the credit of Congress with the voters is lower than it should be it is in part because of its habitual preoccupation with what we call "peanut politics." Closely connected with this is the time spent by members in the running of errands for their constituents and in the consideration of "pork barrel" legislation. In recent years the irresponsible use of the investigating function has not only reduced the effectiveness of Congress as a whole, but has had a good deal to do with the decline in its prestige among those who would like to see its vigor expended on genuinely public questions.

It may as well be admitted, of course, that only a public demand can bring changes with respect to these matters. So long as special interests in the states can create the impression that serving them is the way to re-election, individual Congressmen may be expected to respond as many of them now do. So long as the national treasury is pictured as something to be raided in order to favor local enterprises, some members will feel called upon to justify raids. Constituents themselves will have to show self-control if their representatives are to confine themselves to the discussion and supervision of truly national business.

Until the people show this sort of restraint the student must content himself with diagnosis. For it will do no good to upbraid Congress for not being like some picture in our minds. Precisely because it does reflect so adequately the breadth and variety of our interests, it is largely prevented from being the tightly organized, smoothly functioning body which ideally it could be if every problem before it had the same bearing upon every state and every district. The more responsible leadership which is universally regarded as important could only be *party* leadership, and yet it is hard to see how such a leadership can arise until Democrats or Republicans in Vermont and Montana and Florida see eye to eye on public questions—something which obviously seldom occurs.

What is "wrong" with Congress is what is "wrong" with the country. We are a loose congeries of sections and states, the conflicting interests of which are roughly compromised in an annual meeting of ambassadors called Congress. On very few issues is a truly national policy possible, and our statutes reflect the demands of local and sectional "politics" rather than the settled purposes of a homogeneous society. Congress *ought* to strengthen its agencies of leadership and give them disciplinary authority; it *ought* to prevent the proliferation of committees and subcommittees and their seizure of independent authority; it *ought* to abandon the seniority rule in the choice of committee chairmen. These things are easy to suggest and the gods on Olympus undoubtedly agree; but, as a matter of fact, every one of these proposals is highly artificial. They will come when we become a nation and scarcely before. Only when issues have much the same impact everywhere can Congress become a disciplined body willing and able to support a unified leadership within its own ranks or in the executive office.

Administrative Reorganization. That the executive branch should be given adequate tools with which to discharge its responsibilities is a commonplace generality until one analyzes it in the light of those responsibilities. The modern President is in charge, either directly or through subordinates of his own choosing, of vast expenditures of money. He must make decisions of frightening gravity in matters of both domestic and foreign policy. He cannot, as was possible for our earlier Chief Executives, know in detail what is going on in the farthest reaches of an administrative machine necessarily complicated and involving the services of literally millions of public servants, many of them performing extremely complex technical tasks. Yet for all of these things he is finally responsible both in law and before public opinion. How to make this responsibility real and the accompanying power effective involves, among other things, the problem which is now described as administrative reorganization—how to convert the administrative machine into a supple instrument of the Presidential will within the limits set by Congress.

Enough has been said in the proper place to indicate something of the *complexity* of the national administration below the level of the Presidential office itself. But it is essential to point out the new importance which our national administration has in the modern world and is likely to have in the future. For as far ahead as we can see the United States is likely to face appallingly intricate and critical problems of global diplomacy and perhaps military action, problems requiring an alert and powerful executive competent to act decisively and with complete knowledge of the pertinent facts. However great our homesickness may be for the secure and predictable world of the nineteenth century, all signs point to the need of our getting used to living in a much more dangerous one. The problems of such a world cannot be met by the ramshackle devices of another era. Equally staggering problems face us at home in such areas as the husbanding of our exhaustible natural resources, the threat of recurring depressions, and the elaboration and administration of schemes of social security. Simply because of the complicated technical nature of these problems, the administration occupies a key position. We may regret these complexities and we may deplore the expanding role of government, but there is little reason to believe that the complexities will disappear or that government will abandon these newer functions. Unless American democracy shows inventiveness and imagination in dealing with these problems, it will suffer a fatal loss of prestige before a world asked to choose between it and the apparently greater efficiency of dictatorship.

There has been at nearly every period of our history an awareness of the need for able and flexible national administration. Even when not formally investigating the administrative system, Congress has tinkered with its organization, changing it piecemeal, and, it must be confessed, in response to varying and often inconsistent pressures. During the past generation, however, the process of reform has been self-conscious and has been assisted by the application of the skills of management developed in private industry. Since the Efficiency and Economy Commission of 1909 the problem has seldom been out of the minds of Congress, the President, and private groups interested in governmental efficiency. Two able commissions—in 1937 and in 1948 to 1950—have produced thorough reports which have enjoyed favorable publicity and aroused wide interest. A body like Congress whose approval is needed to put into effect reforms proposed by such commissions moves slowly because various sections of its membership have, or feel that they have, a political stake in such changes, and hesitate, in any case, to take action that may add to the prestige of the executive branch. An able student of the subject, however, reaches this encouraging conclusion with respect to the fate of the recommendations of the Hoover Commission: [4]

[4] Herbert Emmerich, *Essays on Federal Reorganization*, p. 122, 1950. Since the Eisenhower administration came into power, further progress has been made.

Stimulated by the remarkable entente between ex-President Hoover and President Truman, an astonishing number of the recommendations of the Commission have already been put into effect. It is estimated that over 100 of the 277 specific suggestions have been effected by congressional or executive action. This has been the greatest show on earth in the field of government research. And appropriately so, for the Commission was looking into the biggest tent on earth and the one on which the safety, health, and welfare of this planet probably depend.

Administrative reorganization is hard to publicize in ways that reveal its true significance. The press has felt compelled to emphasize such things as the reshuffling of bureaus among the Cabinet departments or to capitalize on the shortcomings of "bureaucracy." Thus, when President Hoover many years ago complained that black bears were under the jurisdiction of one department, brown bears under another, and grizzly bears under a third, this was something from which the newspaper reader could infer that there was need of a more rational allocation of functions. When a reporter or a Congressman unearths some specially incomprehensible commission ruling or directive, it is easy to conclude that someone should take things in hand and bring some common sense into the conduct of affairs.

Perhaps there is no other way to dramatize, for a busy and largely indifferent public, questions and procedures which are really undramatic. Administrative reorganization, however, goes much farther than such matters. The power now possessed by the President—subject to Congressional disallowance—to shift and regroup agencies is significant simply as a step in the process of creating the capable and flexible administrative machine which the nature of the modern public service demands. The President as the responsible executive must have the authority to administer these services and enforce the laws in the light of his knowledge of concrete needs. This knowledge would normally exceed that of the other branches of the government if the President were actually at the head of the administration. A strong executive really in command of his subordinates would be in a position to enforce efficiency and economy against the efforts to defeat both which are invited by an administrative structure in which the lines of responsibility and control are tenuous and uncertain. Further than this, sound organization would make it possible for executive programs to be better planned and more consistent so that Congress itself would be in a better position to pass judgment upon them. This is true because, as everyone knows, Presidential proposals come not from the President himself but from his staff. This staff must in fact and not merely in theory be subject to executive control.

In short what we now at last face is the need of creating a strong administration. It may be argued in some quarters that government should not be doing some of the things for which it has assumed responsibility, but it *is* doing them and it ought to do them efficiently. Creating a strong administration will mean further departures from our heritage of a political and untrained administration, and these departures are certain to be resisted in some quarters. It is always easy to raise the cry of "bureaucracy" when it is proposed to introduce permanence of tenure and proved competence into the public service. The word has come to have sinister overtones which are emphasized by the unscrupulous in their efforts to preserve spoils or to frighten civil servants into compliance with the demands of special interests. The chief safeguard against such demagoguery will be found in a President capable of defending his own subordinates.

Responsible Party Government. The transactions of government in both the legislative and executive branches take place in an atmosphere of partisanship. No ways have been suggested by which in a free society public questions may be formulated and answers found except through the action of political parties. Ideally a party system should present to the voters alternate solutions to public problems; and each party should have enough internal cohesion and discipline to enable it to carry out, once it is in power, the program it has set forth in seeking office. In other words each party should have a meaningful program and, if it wins, the voters should be able to count on seeing that program carried into law.

Only a little observation is needed to show that we do not have such a party system. Probably no country has one that meets completely such ideal requirements. Except for brief periods the government of the American Union has been under a two-party system, as contrasted with the multiparty system found on the continent of Europe. Before we condemn out of hand our own system we do well to reflect that our politicians have after all shown great skill in intraparty negotiation over men and issues, and that this skill has prevented the kind of disorder in our politics which is the rule where small groups are able to set up housekeeping for themselves and ride their own hobbies. The differences between Democrats and Republicans may be no greater than cynics say they are, and yet we are perhaps better off than would be the case if the voters divided half a dozen ways on public questions. In any case we have been secure and prosperous enough to afford the luxury of a hit-or-miss party system, the inner logic of which is the despair of foreigners and a good deal of a puzzle even to Americans.

Most of the incoherence of our system springs from the immense variety of American life and society—a variety of national groups, of creeds, of social and political traditions, of economic interests, and of concrete problems. In a rough way this variety is taken into account by our federal organization which has added to the complexity of party life by encouraging the vested interest in patronage enjoyed now by our state political machines. The results of all this are evident even to the casual observer. If party platforms are so vague as to have little meaning, it is because they are the results of compromises which have to be made among the local and sectional interests within the party. If national statutes are often full of exceptions and generally lacking in definiteness, it is to be attributed to the same sort of compromises that have to be made among representatives in Congress. And Congress itself lacks effective organization and leadership because it faithfully reflects the varying and often mutually exclusive demands and loyalties of the states and the districts. The wonder is not that American politics is confused but rather that we get on as well as we do.

It is questionable whether we can much longer tolerate in safety the irresponsibility and incoherence of a system which has undergone few changes since the War between the States and which was geared to a social and economic order no longer in existence. The functions of modern government are so extensive and touch so deeply the economic and social life of the country that "the need for coordinated and coherent programs, legislative and administrative, has become paramount." [5] In view of the urgency of problems which impinge upon every section of the population, the time has passed when each state, section, or district can insist on its own views of policy and hold its representatives to no higher loyalty than that to local interests. In the face of national problems the parties as endorsers of policies and guarantors of officials should speak with a national voice. The national organs of the party should be relieved of the humiliating necessity of yielding to the demands of state and local machines little interested in anything beyond the spoils of victory in local elections. Finally, an effective national party leadership would make difficult the bypassing by pressure groups of the present party organizations, something which is encouraged by the fact that the titular leaders of the parties in Congress cannot actually command the support of their followers.

Some of these anomalies and abuses may presumably be remedied by law or by party action. State laws might well impose more rigorous tests of party membership and thus make more difficult the switching from one party to another which compounds the confusion of an already irresponsible system of loyalties. The national party conventions might be made more genuinely representative bodies than is now the case and also be given more authoritative control over the permanent executive organ of the party. The national party might well exercise a more rigorous supervision and a more stimulating leadership over state and local party organizations. In Congress itself much might be gained by formalizing the present devices of legislative leadership. This could be accomplished by creating

[5] *Toward a More Responsible Two-Party system,* report of the Committee on Political Parties of the American Political Science Association, p. 4, Rinehart and Co., Inc., 1950.

policy committees, by giving greater attention to the choice of committee chairmen and members so that the seniority rule will not work against the policy of the party as a whole, and by the more efficient staffing of the leadership group in each party. At a higher level, constitutional provisions with respect to the electoral-college system should be amended so as to give all sections of the country a proportional voice in the choice of the President and Vice-President, and thus encourage the development of a true two-party system in areas where one of the parties is now a permanent and hopeless minority.

While it is true that thoughtful party leaders are already aware of the weakness of the present system and disposed to attempt remedies, the system itself is the product of forces largely beyond the reach of formal legal treatment. Local and sectional factors have been important in American politics and have worked against unified leadership on the national level precisely because national policies have in the past affected differently the individual states and sections. Under the circumstances it is not surprising that local party organizations have insisted on local autonomy and have striven in every way open to them to see that particular interests are not threatened by a proposed national policy. Only rarely have national leaders felt it safe to oppose such forces either before the general public, within the party councils, or on the floor of Congress. The strength of these forces was shown in the failure of so popular a party leader as Franklin Roosevelt in 1938 to "purge" primary election candidates whom he regarded as hostile to the national party program.

The coming of a responsible party system may be aided by formal action of the party organizations themselves or by statute law, but the most effective influence in that direction will be found to be *the decline of localism and sectionalism,* and this decline seems to be under way.

Statistical evidence such as is available for the last generation shows that the most significant political trends in the country have been national, not sectional or local . . . Elections are increasingly won and lost by influences felt throughout the land. The measurable shift from sectional to national politics cannot fail to have a corresponding effect on party organization and the locus of power within the parties. *Party organization designed to deal with the increasing volume of national issues must give wider range to the national party leadership.*[6]

What this means is that the character of our traditional party system was determined by the fact that we were long a Union of *sections and states;* now that we are slowly and reluctantly becoming a *nation,* national party organs are being created. Laws and rules have had and probably will have little to do with it, except as they register decisions reached elsewhere.

[6] *Ibid.,* p. 33.

The People and Their Government

Democracy has usually been defined as government by the people. It is not accurate to call it self-government, for "self-government" is in reality a contradiction in terms. Obviously in no society does everyone do as he wishes; what happens always is that some persons exercise authority over others. A democracy is simply a form of government in which those who are ruled finally decide who their rulers shall be, or at any rate peaceably agree to their exercise of power. All governments, of course, are governments "of the people" in the sense that a few give orders and many obey. Governments commonly described as "aristocracies," "oligarchies," and "dictatorships" are "for the people" in the sense that their rulers are presumed to know what is best for the ruled. Government "by the people" may be said to exist only where the bulk of the people decide finally who shall rule, for what general purposes, and for how long. All the familiar devices of voting and debating in legislative bodies or before the people during campaigns are merely ways of finding the wishes of the majority.

Democratic government demands a great deal of the people who live under it. In the first place, it requires considerable active participation in the processes of government—voting, party work, service on juries and on legislative and administrative bodies, and attention to the work of those private organizations interested in public questions. In the second place, it requires our watching those chosen to rule us, acquainting ourselves with their official doings, passing judgment on their proposals, and withdrawing our support when they fail us. Most fundamental of all, it requires that our political activity shall be based upon some unselfish view of the *general* good, as distinct from purely personal wishes and ambitions. No doubt men and women generally vote as their interests seem to dictate; yet no government could survive if there were no willingness *at all* to sacrifice these interests to those of the community at large. Keeping these things in mind what do we find at the close of our survey?

On the credit side we are justified in saying that in no other country is there so wide a participation by the citizen in the processes of government. Americans, in contrast with the people of many other countries, are not accustomed to waiting for officials to take the lead—*they themselves make proposals and officials follow*. Many public functions have their origin in an individual's perception of a community need which is later widely publicized by some influential organization. There will readily come to mind such enterprises as public libraries, playground and recreational facilities, historical societies, symphony orchestras, community theatres, auditoriums and stadiums, community chests, and the vast network of welfare organizations. These things are the creations of the people, not of officeholders. The aggregate number of citizens directly concerned in such functions runs into the hundreds of thousands, and in every sizeable community there are dozens of persons interested in their efficient and impartial administration. On any showing the amount of public spirit which this indicates is amazing.

There is, to be sure, another side to this. Public functions, though popularly initiated, often get into the hands of narrow-minded and dogmatic persons who come to regard them as their private property or, in some cases, of persons who insist on starving them in the interests of "efficiency and economy." When this occurs the level of performance falls and general public interest lags. A library board that considers it its duty to censor the reading of the public is certainly no improvement over control by old-line politicians or bureaucrats. In many communities one of the unfortunate results of the movement to put "more business in government" has been to bring into the local service men whose primary interest is to keep city taxes low and city services at a minimum. If enlightened popular government is to survive one of our principal problems is how to attract to the public service persons who have no private or group axes to grind.

The widespread popular participation in government is a direct result of our tradition of self-help and our belief in individual responsibility for community well-being. American democracy will remain vigorous so long as conditions put a premium on what actual individuals think and do. And here we must take note of certain developments which may operate against individualism. A century ago John Stuart Mill [7] complained that "the greatness of England is now all collective; individually small, we only appear capable of anything great by our habit of combining . . . it was men of another stamp than this that made England what it has been; and men of another stamp will be needed to prevent its decline." It was Mill's belief that every improvement has its origin in the mind of an individual, and he is protesting against the influences in his day that erased the differences between individuals and compelled all to profess the same beliefs from fear to follow their own inclinations. He could see only intellectual stagnation and the despotic rule of commonplace public opinion as the results of such influences.

In the years since Mill wrote, standardizing influences have multiplied a hundredfold. The principal agencies for the spread of information in his day were the railways, the telegraph, cheap postal service, and the newspapers—the last not yet organized in "chains" but largely the properties of individual editors and publishers. "Applied psychology" was hardly known, with the result that advertising bore no resemblance in its modest chastity to the strident and yet insidious "art" which it has since become. The modern citizen, even if he wishes to "be himself," finds the going rough indeed. He is strongly tempted to take his political and economic views from his favorite radio commentator or syndicated columnist whose fol-

[7] *On Liberty*, p. 127.

lowers are numbered literally in the millions. Half a dozen newspapers and twó or three "newsmagazines" supply him with news, by no means always objectively. If he is too tired to read, "information" of a sort is given him by a dozen picture magazines. Even his books may be chosen for him by one of several book clubs. Finally there is national advertising—which apparently has as its object the turning out of a limited number of specimens of *homo sapiens* more or less alike in their preferences for hair oil, automobiles, toothpaste and shaving soap, cigarettes, and recipes for slimness, "charm," and "success," or for avoiding halitosis, falling hair, or the horrendous evils of the welfare state. And, quite forgetful of the value of dissenters in any free society, the citizen's political representatives are zealous in making it hazardous to hold or express unusual political or economic views at the very time when inventiveness is our chief need. In a society so regimented the only individualists likely to remain are those who do the regimenting.

Another development which is anti-individualistic and potentially dangerous to democracy is the growth of "pressure politics." Undoubtedly minority groups have at all times sought special favors from legislative bodies; what makes their tactics dangerous now is the greater facility with which opinion can be organized and brought to a focus on legislators. Pressure and lobbying groups may or may not represent the individuals whom they claim as members; the point is that the individual is manipulated by his leaders in ways which he may actually not approve. In any case this is another type of regimentation with real dangers to popular institutions.

There is really no way, consistent with the preservation of democratic processes, by which lobbying can be prevented. The demands of a "pressure group" arise from the real sources of power in society and are therefore in a sense democratic in their origin. The beneficiaries of the favors which they seek are not necessarily a minority of the population; what is requested may be quite consistent with the general good. There is always the possibility, however, that what is sought can be granted only at the expense of the majority whose representatives will be overawed by a well-financed and cleverly-directed campaign. Surely a Congress that simply recorded the desires of Big Business, Big Labor, Big Agriculture, or the veterans, would have abdicated its essential, though difficult, task of representing all of us.

There are, to be sure, mitigating factors. Congress cannot represent all of us without giving attention to those groups which represent at least *some of us.* The job of a congressman is, first, to judge the extent to which the lobby actually represents its membership and the degree to which its demands are consistent with those of competing lobbies, and, second, to weigh this appraisal against what he can sense to be the general interest. He is in reality a sort of judge or umpire. To make his task easier a number of things are needed. One of these is publicity. There should never be any doubt as to the identity of lobbyists, the precise character of the legislation they desire, the amount and sources of their financial support, and the origin and authorship of their printed and oral propaganda. It goes without saying that all this information should be available to the membership of lobbying organizations as well as to the general public, in order that minority groups may know whether or not their official leadership really expresses their views. Furthermore, every effort should be made to strengthen the organs of party leadership and the machinery for formulating official party policy so that the parties are not bypassed by the lobbies. Finally, it would be well if the growing healthy cynicism of consumers about commercial advertising could be transferred to the processes by which voters are persuaded to "buy" what they do not need or perhaps even want.

Another unsolved problem of popular government is posed by the rising cost of conducting elections. The very devices which tend toward standardization and away from individualism work also to minimize the electoral importance of the average voter. It is quite as expensive to advertise the alleged merits of a candidate or a platform as it is to call attention to commercial products. During the presidential campaign of 1952 it was reported that a one-hour television program cost the Republican party $750,000, while the coverage of the national convention was said to have been almost prohibitively expensive even to the prosperous concerns that sponsored it. Even if no corrupt methods are used the cost of campaigning is so great as to be beyond the reach of all but very rich organizations. And except at the local level individual candidacy for office is out of the question except for the well-to-do or for those who can gain the support of special interests. Such support may, of course, be quite disinterested, but there is always at least the suspicion that it is offered largely in expectation of legislative and other favors to those who supply it.

As this is written the principal threat to democracy as we have known it comes paradoxically from the activities of those who regard themselves as defending it. If anything is clear from our history, it is that we have gained in strength as well as in liberty by maintaining a free market in ideas. While a great part of the world has repudiated individualism, there are still areas ready to follow a clear lead if the free world will give it. It is folly to believe smugly that we can impose our system readymade upon peoples now faced with a choice between freedom and tyranny. It is equally foolish to believe that we can buy adherence to our way of life. Finally, the cost of imposing our system by force—even if we were sure we could do it—is frightful to contemplate. It is a time then for inventiveness, for a canvassing of ideas and devices of all sorts. If those who would defend us from strange beliefs by throttling discussion succeed in pouring us all into the same mold, it is hard to see why any wavering people elsewhere should follow us. There are critical and sensitive areas in our public service which must be protected from invasion by the criminal and the treasonous. The state has the right both in law and in morals to assure the loyalty of its servants. But if we can meet the threat of our enemies only by using their tactics we shall have adopted a craven attitude which is not only false to our heritage but actually self-defeating.

REFERENCES

Carl Becker, *Freedom and Responsibility in the American Way of Life* (1945).
Thomas K. Finletter, *Can Representative Government Do the Job?* (1945).
Ernest S. Griffith, *The Impasse of Democracy* (1939).
Arthur N. Holcombe, *Our More Perfect Union* (1950).
Walter Lippmann, *An Inquiry into the Principles of the Good Society* (1937).
Robert McIver, *The Web of Government* (1947).
William A. Orton, *The Liberal Tradition* (1945).
Henry B. Parkes, *The American Experience* (1947).
J. Roland Pennock, *Liberal Democracy: Its Merits and Prospects* (1950).
Arthur M. Schlesinger, *Paths to the Present* (1949).
Frederick Watkins, *The Political Tradition of the West* (1948).

Constitution of the United States of America

We, the people of the United States, in order to form a more perfect union, establish justice, insure domestic tranquility, provide for the common defence, promote the general welfare, and secure the blessings of liberty to ourselves and our posterity, do ordain and establish this Constitution for the United States of America.

ARTICLE I

Section 1. All legislative powers herein granted shall be vested in a Congress of the United States, which shall consist of a Senate and House of Representatives.

Section 2. (1) The House of Representatives shall be composed of members chosen every second year by the people of the several States, and the electors in each State shall have the qualifications requisite for electors of the most numerous branch of the State legislature.

(2) No person shall be a Representative who shall not have attained to the age of twenty-five years, and been seven years a citizen of the United States, and who shall not, when elected, be an inhabitant of that State in which he shall be chosen.

(3) Representatives and direct taxes shall be apportioned among the several States which may be included within this Union, according to their respective numbers, [which shall be determined by adding to the whole number of free persons,] [1] including those bound to service for a term of years, and excluding Indians not taxed, [three fifths for all other persons].[2] The actual enumeration shall be made within three years after the first meeting of the Congress of the United States, and within every subsequent term of ten years, in such manner as they shall by law direct. The number of Representatives shall not exceed one for every thirty thousand, but each State shall have at least one Representative; [and until such enumeration shall be made, the State of New Hampshire shall be entitled to choose three, Massachusetts eight, Rhode Island and Providence Plantations one, Connecticut five, New York six, New Jersey four, Pennsylvania eight, Delaware one, Maryland six, Virginia ten, North Carolina five, South Carolina five, and Georgia three.] [3]

(4) When vacancies happen in the representation from any State, the executive authority thereof shall issue writs of election to fill such vacancies.

(5) The House of Representatives shall choose their Speaker and other officers; and shall have the sole power of impeachment.

Section 3. [(1) The Senate of the United States shall be composed of two Senators from each State, chosen by the legislature thereof, for six years; and each Senator shall have one vote.] [4]

(2) Immediately after they shall be assembled in consequence of the first election, they shall be divided as equally as may be into three classes. The seats of the Senators of the first class shall be vacated at the expiration of the second year, of the second class at the expiration of the fourth year, and of the third class at the expiration of the sixth year, so that one third may be chosen every second year; [and if vacancies happen by resignation, or otherwise, during the recess of the legislature of any State,

[1] Modified by Fourteenth Amendment.
[2] Superseded by Fourteenth Amendment.
[3] Temporary provision.
[4] Superseded by Seventeenth Amendment.

the executive thereof may make temporary appointments until the next meeting of the legislature, which shall then fill such vacancies.] [1]

(3) No person shall be a Senator who shall not have attained to the age of thirty years, and been nine years a citizen of the United States, and who shall not, when elected, be an inhabitant of that State for which he shall be chosen.

(4) The Vice President of the United States shall be president of the Senate, but shall have no vote, unless they be equally divided.

(5) The Senate shall choose their other officers, and also a president pro tempore, in the absence of the Vice President, or when he shall exercise the office of President of the United States.

(6) The Senate shall have the sole power to try all impeachments. When sitting for that purpose, they shall be on oath or affirmation. When the President of the United States is tried, the Chief Justice shall preside: and no person shall be convicted without the concurrence of two thirds of the members present.

(7) Judgment in cases of impeachment shall not extend further than to removal from office, and disqualification to hold and enjoy any office of honor, trust, or profit under the United States: but the party convicted shall nevertheless be liable and subject to indictment, trial, judgment, and punishment, according to law.

Section 4. (1) The times, places, and manner of holding elections for Senators and Representatives shall be prescribed in each State by the legislature thereof; but the Congress may at any time by law make or alter such regulations, except as to the places of choosing Senators.

[(2) The Congress shall assemble at least once in every year, and such meeting shall be on the first Monday in December, unless they shall by law appoint a different day.] [2]

Section 5. (1) Each House shall be the judge of the elections, returns, and qualifications of its own members, and a majority of each shall constitute a quorum to do business; but a smaller number may adjourn from day to day, and may be authorized to compel the attendance of absent members, in such manner, and under such penalties, as each House may provide.

(2) Each House may determine the rules of its proceedings, punish its members for disorderly behavior, and, with the concurrence of two thirds, expel a member.

(3) Each House shall keep a journal of its proceedings, and from time to time publish the same, excepting such parts as may in their judgment require secrecy; and the yeas and nays of the members of either House on any question shall, at the desire of one fifth of those present, be entered on the journal.

(4) Neither House, during the session of Congress, shall, without the consent of the other, adjourn for more than three days, nor to any other place than that in which the two Houses shall be sitting.

Section 6. (1) The Senators and Representatives shall receive a compensation for their services, to be ascertained by law, and paid out of the Treasury of the United States. They shall in all cases, except treason, felony, and breach of the peace, be privileged from arrest during their attendance at the session of their respective Houses, and in going to and returning from the same; and for any speech or debate in either House, they shall not be questioned in any other place.

(2) No Senator or Representative shall, during the time for which he was elected, be appointed to any civil office under the authority of the United States, which shall have been created, or the emoluments whereof shall have been increased, during such time; and no person holding any office under the United States shall be a member of either House during his continuance in office.

Section 7. (1) All bills for raising revenue shall originate in the House of Representatives; but the Senate may propose or concur with amendments as on other bills.

(2) Every bill which shall have passed the House of Representatives and the Senate, shall, before it become a law, be presented to the President of the United States;

---

[1] Modified by Seventeenth Amendment.

[2] Superseded by Twentieth Amendment.

if he approve he shall sign it, but if not he shall return it, with his objections, to that House in which it shall have originated, who shall enter the objections at large on their journal, and proceed to reconsider it. If after such reconsideration two thirds of that House shall agree to pass the bill, it shall be sent, together with the objections, to the other House, by which it shall likewise be reconsidered, and if approved by two thirds of that House, it shall become a law. But in all such cases the votes of both Houses shall be determined by yeas and nays, and the names of the persons voting for and against the bill shall be entered on the journal of each House respectively. If any bill shall not be returned by the President within ten days (Sundays excepted) after it shall have been presented to him, the same shall be a law, in like manner as if he had signed it, unless the Congress by their adjournment prevent its return, in which case it shall not be a law.

(3) Every order, resolution, or vote to which the concurrence of the Senate and House of Representatives may be necessary (except on a question of adjournment) shall be presented to the President of the United States; and before the same shall take effect, shall be approved by him, or being disapproved by him, shall be repassed by two thirds of the Senate and House of Representatives, according to the rules and limitations prescribed in the case of a bill.

Section 8. (1) The Congress shall have power to lay and collect taxes, duties, imposts, and excises, to pay the debts and provide for the common defense and general welfare of the United States; but all duties, imposts, and excises shall be uniform throughout the United States;

(2) To borrow money on the credit of the United States;

(3) To regulate commerce with foreign nations, and among the several States, and with the Indian tribes;

(4) To establish a uniform rule of naturalization, and uniform laws on the subject of bankruptcies throughout the United States;

(5) To coin money, regulate the value thereof, and of foreign coin, and fix the standard of weights and measures;

(6) To provide for the punishment of counterfeiting the securities and current coin of the United States;

(7) To establish post offices and post roads;

(8) To promote the progress of science and useful arts, by securing for limited times to authors and inventors the exclusive right to their respective writings and discoveries;

(9) To constitute tribunals inferior to the Supreme Court;

(10) To define and punish piracies and felonies committed on the high seas, and offenses against the law of nations;

(11) To declare war, grant letters of marque and reprisal, and make rules concerning captures on land and water;

(12) To raise and support armies, but no appropriation of money to that use shall be for a longer term than two years;

(13) To provide and maintain a navy;

(14) To make rules for the government and regulation of the land and naval forces;

(15) To provide for calling forth the militia to execute the laws of the Union, suppress insurrections, and repel invasions;

(16) To provide for organizing, arming, and disciplining the militia, and for governing such part of them as may be employed in the service of the United States, reserving to the States respectively the appointment of the officers, and the authority of training the militia according to the discipline prescribed by Congress;

(17) To exercise exclusive legislation in all cases whatsoever, over such district (not exceeding ten miles square) as may, by cession of particular States, and the acceptance of Congress, become the seat of the government of the United States, and to exercise like authority over all places purchased by the consent of the legislature of the State in which the same shall be, for the erection of forts, magazines, arsenals, dock-yards, and other needful buildings; and

(18) To make all laws which shall be necessary and proper for carrying into execution the foregoing powers, and all other powers vested by this Constitution in the government of the United States, or in any department or officer thereof.

Section 9. [(1) The migration or importation of such persons as any of the States now existing shall think proper to admit, shall not be prohibited by the Congress prior to the year one thousand eight hundred and eight, but a tax or duty may be imposed on such importation, not exceeding ten dollars for each person.] [1]

(2) The privilege of the writ of habeas corpus shall not be suspended, unless when in cases of rebellion or invasion the public safety may require it.

(3) No bill of attainder or ex post facto law shall be passed.

[(4) No capitation, or other direct, tax shall be laid, unless in proportion to the census or enumeration hereinbefore directed to be taken.] [2]

(5) No tax or duty shall be laid on articles exported from any State.

(6) No preference shall be given by any regulation of commerce or revenue to the ports of one State over those of another: nor shall vessels bound to, or from, one State, be obliged to enter, clear, or pay duties in another.

(7) No money shall be drawn from the Treasury, but in consequence of appropriations made by law; and a regular statement and account of the receipts and expenditures of all public money shall be published from time to time.

(8) No title of nobility shall be granted by the United States: and no person holding any office of profit or trust under them, shall, without the consent of the Congress, accept of any present, emolument, office, or title, of any kind whatever, from any king, prince, or foreign State.

Section 10. (1) No State shall enter into any treaty, alliance, or confederation; grant letters of marque and reprisal; coin money; emit bills of credit; make anything but gold and silver coin a tender in payment of debts; pass any bill of attainder, ex post facto law, or law impairing the obligation of contracts, or grant any title of nobility.

(2) No State shall, without the consent of the Congress, lay any imposts or duties on imports or exports, except what may be absolutely necessary for executing its inspection laws: and the net produce of all duties and imposts, laid by any State on imports or exports, shall be for the use of the treasury of the United States; and all such laws shall be subject to the revision and control of the Congress.

(3) No State shall, without the consent of Congress, lay any duty of tonnage, keep troops, or ships of war in time of peace, enter into any agreement or compact with another State, or with a foreign power, or engage in war, unless actually invaded, or in such imminent danger as will not admit of delay.

ARTICLE II

Section 1. (1) The executive power shall be vested in a President of the United States of America. He shall hold his office during the term of four years, and, together with the Vice President, chosen for the same term, be elected, as follows:

(2) Each State shall appoint, in such manner as the legislature thereof may direct, a number of electors, equal to the whole number of Senators and Representatives to which the State may be entitled in the Congress: but no Senator or Representative, or person holding an office of trust or profit under the United States, shall be appointed an elector.

[The electors shall meet in their respective States, and vote by ballot for two persons, of whom one at least shall not be an inhabitant of the same State with themselves. And they shall make a list of all the persons voted for, and of the number of votes for each; which list they shall sign and certify, and transmit sealed to the seat of the government of the United States, directed to the president of the Senate. The president of the Senate shall, in the presence of the Senate and House of Repre-

[1] Temporary provision.

[2] Modified by Sixteenth Amendment.

sentatives, open all the certificates, and the votes shall then be counted. The person having the greatest number of votes shall be the President, if such number be a majority of the whole number of electors appointed; and if there be more than one who have such majority, and have an equal number of votes, then the House of Representatives shall immediately choose by ballot one of them for President; and if no person have a majority, then from the five highest on the list the said House shall in like manner choose the President. But in choosing the President, the votes shall be taken by States, the representation from each State having one vote; a quorum for this purpose shall consist of a member or members from two thirds of the States, and a majority of all the States shall be necessary to a choice. In every case, after the choice of the President, the person having the greatest number of votes of the electors shall be the Vice President. But if there should remain two or more who have equal votes, the Senate shall choose from them by ballot the Vice President.] [1]

(3) The Congress may determine the time of choosing the electors, and the day on which they shall give their votes; which day shall be the same throughout the United States.

(4) No person except a natural-born citizen, or a citizen of the United States, at the time of the adoption of this Constitution, shall be eligible to the office of President; neither shall any person be eligible to that office who shall not have attained to the age of thirty-five years, and been fourteen years a resident within the United States.

(5) In case of the removal of the President from office, or of his death, resignation, or inability to discharge the powers and duties of the said office, the same shall devolve on the Vice President, and the Congress may by law provide for the case of removal, death, resignation, or inability, both of the President and Vice President, declaring what officer shall then act as President, and such officer shall act accordingly, until the disability be removed, or a President shall be elected.

(6) The President shall, at stated times, receive for his services a compensation, which shall neither be increased nor diminished during the period for which he shall have been elected, and he shall not receive within that period any other emolument from the United States, or any of them.

(7) Before he enter on the execution of his office, he shall take the following oath or affirmation: "I do solemnly swear (or affirm) that I will faithfully execute the office of President of the United States, and will, to the best of my ability, preserve, protect, and defend the Constitution of the United States."

Section 2. (1) The President shall be commander in chief of the army and navy of the United States, and of the militia of the several States, when called into the actual service of the United States; he may require the opinion, in writing, of the principal officer in each of the executive departments, upon any subject relating to the duties of their respective offices, and he shall have power to grant reprieves and pardons for offenses against the United States, except in cases of impeachment.

(2) He shall have power, by and with the advice and consent of the Senate, to make treaties, provided two thirds of the Senators present concur; and he shall nominate, and by and with the advice and consent of the Senate, shall appoint ambassadors, other public ministers and consuls, judges of the Supreme Court, and all other officers of the United States, whose appointments are not herein otherwise provided for, and which shall be established by law: but the Congress may by law vest the appointment of such inferior officers, as they think proper, in the President alone, in the courts of law, or in the heads of departments.

(3) The President shall have power to fill up all vacancies that may happen during the recess of the Senate, by granting commissions which shall expire at the end of their next session.

Section 3. He shall from time to time give to the Congress information of the state of the Union, and recommend to their consideration such measures as he shall judge

[1] This paragraph superseded by Twelfth Amendment, which, i₂ turn, is modified by the Twentieth Amendment.

necessary and expedient; he may, on extraordinary occasions, convene both Houses, or either of them, and in case of disagreement between them, with respect to the time of adjournment, he may adjourn them to such time as he shall think proper; he shall receive ambassadors and other public ministers; he shall take care that the laws be faithfully executed, and shall commission all the officers of the United States.

Section 4. The President, Vice President, and all civil officers of the United States, shall be removed from office on impeachment for, and conviction of, treason, bribery, or other high crimes and misdemeanors.

ARTICLE III

Section 1. The judicial power of the United States shall be vested in one Supreme Court, and in such inferior courts as the Congress may from time to time ordain and establish. The judges, both of the Supreme and inferior courts, shall hold their offices during good behavior, and shall, at stated times, receive for their services a compensation, which shall not be diminished during their continuance in office.

Section 2. (1) The judicial power shall extend to all cases, in law and equity, arising under this Constitution, the laws of the United States, and treaties made, or which shall be made, under their authority;—to all cases affecting ambassadors, other public ministers, and consuls;—to all cases of admiralty and maritime jurisdiction;—to controversies to which the United States shall be a party;—to controversies between two or more States; [—between a State and citizens of another State;] [1]—between citizens of different States;—between citizens of the same State claiming lands under grants of different States, and between a State, or the citizens thereof, and foreign States, citizens, or subjects.

(2) In all cases affecting ambassadors, other public ministers, and consuls, and those in which a State shall be party, the Supreme Court shall have original jurisdiction. In all the other cases before mentioned, the Supreme Court shall have appellate jurisdiction, both as to law and fact, with such exceptions, and under such regulations, as the Congress shall make.

(3) The trial of all crimes, except in cases of impeachment, shall be by jury; and such trial shall be held in the State where the said crimes shall have been committed; but when not committed within any State, the trial shall be at such place or places as the Congress may by law have directed.

Section 3. (1) Treason against the United States shall consist only in levying war against them, or in adhering to their enemies, giving them aid and comfort. No person shall be convicted of treason unless on the testimony of two witnesses to the same overt act, or on confession in open court.

(2) The Congress shall have power to declare the punishment of treason, but no attainder of treason shall work corruption of blood, or forfeiture except during the life of the person attainted.

ARTICLE IV

Section 1. Full faith and credit shall be given in each State to the public acts, records, and judicial proceedings of every other State. And the Congress may by general laws prescribe the manner in which such acts, records, and proceedings shall be proved, and the effect thereof.

Section 2. (1) The citizens of each State shall be entitled to all privileges and immunities of citizens in the several States.

(2) A person charged in any State with treason, felony, or other crime, who shall flee from justice, and be found in another State, shall, on demand of the executive authority of the State from which he fled, be delivered up, to be removed to the State having jurisdiction of the crime.

[(3) No person held to service or labor in one State, under the laws thereof, escaping into another, shall, in consequence of any law or regulation therein, be discharged

---

[1] Limited by Eleventh Amendment.

from such service or labor, but shall be delivered up on claim of the party to whom such service or labor may be due.] [1]

Section 3. (1) New States may be admitted by the Congress into this Union; but no new State shall be formed or erected within the jurisdiction of any other State; nor any State be formed by the junction of two or more States, or parts of States, without the consent of the legislatures of the States concerned as well as of the Congress.

(2) The Congress shall have power to dispose of and make all needful rules and regulations respecting the territory or other property belonging to the United States; and nothing in this Constitution shall be so construed as to prejudice any claims of the United States, or of any particular State.

Section 4. The United States shall guarantee to every State in this Union a republican form of government, and shall protect each of them against invasion; and, on application of the legislature, or of the executive (when the legislature cannot be convened), against domestic violence.

ARTICLE V

The Congress, whenever two thirds of both Houses shall deem it necessary, shall propose amendments to this Constitution, or, on the application of the legislatures of two thirds of the several States, shall call a convention for proposing amendments which, in either case, shall be valid to all intents and purposes, as part of this Constitution, when ratified by the legislatures of three fourths of the several States, or by conventions in three fourths thereof, as the one or the other mode of ratification may be proposed by the Congress; provided [that no amendment which may be made prior to the year one thousand eight hundred and eight shall in any manner affect the first and fourth clauses in the ninth section of the first article; and] [2] that no State, without its consent, shall be deprived of its equal suffrage in the Senate.

ARTICLE VI

(1) All debts contracted and engagements entered into, before the adoption of this Constitution, shall be as valid against the United States under this Constitution, as under the Confederation.

(2) This Constitution, and the laws of the United States which shall be made in pursuance thereof; and all treaties made, or which shall be made, under the authority of the United States, shall be the supreme law of the land; and the judges in every State shall be bound thereby, anything in the constitution or laws of any State to the contrary notwithstanding.

(3) The Senators and Representatives before mentioned, and the members of the several State legislatures, and all executive and judicial officers, both of the United States and of the several States, shall be bound by oath or affirmation to support this Constitution; but no religious test shall ever be required as a qualification to any office or public trust under the United States.

ARTICLE VII

The ratification of the conventions of nine States shall be sufficient for the establishment of this Constitution between the States so ratifying the same.

Done in convention by the unanimous consent of the States present the seventeenth day of September in the year of our Lord one thousand seven hundred and eighty-seven, and of the independence of the United States of America the twelfth. In witness whereof, we have hereunto subscribed our names.

[1] Superseded by Thirteenth Amendment so far as it relates to slaves.
[2] Temporary provision.

AMENDMENTS

ARTICLE I

Congress shall make no law respecting an establishment of religion, or prohibiting the free exercise thereof; or abridging the freedom of speech, or of the press; or the right of the people peaceably to assemble, and to petition the government for a redress of grievances.

ARTICLE II

A well regulated militia, being necessary to the security of a free State, the right of the people to keep and bear arms shall not be infringed.

ARTICLE III

No soldier shall, in time of peace, be quartered in any house, without the consent of the owner, nor in time of war, but in a manner to be prescribed by law.

ARTICLE IV

The right of the people to be secure in their persons, houses, papers, and effects, against unreasonable searches and seizures, shall not be violated, and no warrants shall issue, but upon probable cause, supported by oath or affirmation, and particularly describing the place to be searched, and the persons or things to be seized.

ARTICLE V

No person shall be held to answer for a capital or otherwise infamous crime, unless on a presentment or indictment of a grand jury, except in cases arising in the land or naval forces, or in the militia, when in actual service in time of war or public danger; nor shall any person be subject for the same offence to be twice put in jeopardy of life or limb; nor shall be compelled in any criminal case to be a witness against himself, nor be deprived of life, liberty, or property, without due process of law; nor shall private property be taken for public use, without just compensation.

ARTICLE VI

In all criminal prosecutions the accused shall enjoy the right to a speedy and public trial, by an impartial jury of the State and district wherein the crime shall have been committed, which district shall have been previously ascertained by law, and to be informed of the nature and cause of the accusation; to be confronted with the witnesses against him; to have compulsory process for obtaining witnesses in his favor, and to have the assistance of counsel for his defense.

ARTICLE VII

In suits at common law, where the value in controversy shall exceed twenty dollars, the right of trial by jury shall be preserved, and no fact tried by a jury shall be otherwise re-examined in any court of the United States than according to the rules of the common law.

ARTICLE VIII

Excessive bail shall not be required, nor excessive fines imposed, nor cruel and unusual punishments inflicted.

ARTICLE IX

The enumeration in the Constitution of certain rights shall not be construed to deny or disparage others retained by the people.

ARTICLE X

The powers not delegated to the United States by the Constitution, nor prohibited by it to the States, are reserved to the States respectively, or to the people.[1]

ARTICLE XI [2]

The judicial power of the United States shall not be construed to extend to any suit in law or equity, commenced or prosecuted against one of the United States by citizens of another State, or by citizens or subjects of any foreign State.

ARTICLE XII [3]

The electors shall meet in their respective States, and vote by ballot for President and Vice President, one of whom, at least, shall not be an inhabitant of the same State with themselves; they shall name in their ballots the persons voted for as President, and in distinct ballots the persons voted for as Vice President, and they shall make distinct lists of all persons voted for as President, and of all persons voted for as Vice President, and of the number of votes for each, which lists they shall sign and certify, and transmit sealed to the seat of the government of the United States, directed to the president of the Senate;—the president of the Senate shall, in the presence of the Senate and House of Representatives, open all the certificates, and the votes shall then be counted;—the person having the greatest number of votes for President, shall be the President, if such number be a majority of the whole number of electors appointed; and if no person have such majority, then from the persons having the highest numbers not exceeding three on the list of those voted for as President, the House of Representatives shall choose immediately, by ballot, the President. But in choosing the President, the votes shall be taken by States, the representation from each State having one vote; a quorum for this purpose shall consist of a member or members from two thirds of the States, and a majority of all the States shall be necessary to a choice. And if the House of Representatives shall not choose a President whenever the right of choice shall devolve upon them, before the fourth day of March next following, then the Vice President shall act as President, as in the case of the death or other constitutional disability of the President.—The person having the greatest number of votes as Vice President, shall be the Vice President, if such number be a majority of the whole number of electors appointed, and if no person have a majority, then from the two highest numbers on the list, the Senate shall choose the Vice President; a quorum for the purpose shall consist of two thirds of the whole number of Senators, and a majority of the whole number shall be necessary to a choice. But no person constitutionally ineligible to the office of President shall be eligible to that of Vice President of the United States.[4]

ARTICLE XIII [5]

Section 1. Neither slavery nor involuntary servitude, except as a punishment for crime whereof the party shall have been duly convicted, shall exist within the United States, or any place subject to their jurisdiction.

Section 2. Congress shall have power to enforce this article by appropriate legislation.

ARTICLE XIV [6]

Section 1. All persons born or naturalized in the United States, and subject to the jurisdiction thereof, are citizens of the United States and of the State wherein they

[1] The first ten amendments appear to have been in force from November 3, 1791.
[2] Proclaimed January 8, 1798.
[3] Proclaimed September 25, 1804.
[4] This amendment modified by the Twentieth.
[5] Proclaimed December 18, 1865.
[6] Proclaimed July 28, 1868.

reside. No State shall make or enforce any law which shall abridge the privileges or immunities of citizens of the United States; nor shall any State deprive any person of life, liberty, or property, without due process of law; nor deny to any person within its jurisdiction the equal protection of the laws.

Section 2. Representatives shall be apportioned among the several States according to their respective numbers, counting the whole number of persons in each State, excluding Indians not taxed. But when the right to vote at any election for the choice of electors for President and Vice President of the United States, Representatives in Congress, the executive and judicial officers of a State, or the members of the legislature thereof, is denied to any of the male inhabitants of such State, being twenty-one years of age, and citizens of the United States, or in any way abridged, except for participation in rebellion, or other crime, the basis of representation therein shall be reduced in the proportion which the number of such male citizens shall bear to the whole number of male citizens twenty-one years of age in such State.

Section 3. No person shall be a Senator or Representative in Congress, or elector of President and Vice President, or hold any office, civil or military, under the United States, or under any State, who, having previously taken an oath, as a member of Congress, or as an officer of the United States, or as a member of any State legislature, or as an executive or judicial officer of any State, to support the Constitution of the United States, shall have engaged in insurrection or rebellion against the same, or given aid or comfort to the enemies thereof. But Congress may by a vote of two thirds of each House, remove such disability.

Section 4. The validity of the public debt of the United States, authorized by law, including debts incurred for payment of pensions and bounties for services in suppressing insurrection or rebellion, shall not be questioned. But neither the United States nor any State shall assume or pay any debt or obligation incurred in aid of insurrection or rebellion against the United States, or any claim for the loss or emancipation of any slave; but all such debts, obligations, and claims shall be held illegal and void.

Section 5. The Congress shall have power to enforce, by appropriate legislation, the provisions of this article.

Article XV [1]

Section 1. The right of citizens of the United States to vote shall not be denied or abridged by the United States or by any State on account of race, color, or previous condition of servitude.

Section 2. The Congress shall have power to enforce this article by appropriate legislation.

Article XVI [2]

The Congress shall have power to lay and collect taxes on incomes, from whatever source derived, without apportionment among the several States, and without regard to any census or enumeration.

Article XVII [3]

The Senate of the United States shall be composed of two Senators from each State, elected by the people thereof, for six years; and each Senator shall have one vote. The electors in each State shall have the qualifications requisite for electors of the most numerous branch of the State legislature.

[1] Proclaimed March 30, 1870.

[2] Passed July, 1909, proclaimed February 25, 1913.

[3] Passed May, 1912, in lieu of Article I, Section 3, Clause I, of the Constitution and so much of clause 2 of the same Section as relates to the filling of vacancies; proclaimed May 31, 1913.

When vacancies happen in the representation of any State in the Senate, the executive authority of such State shall issue writs of election to fill such vacancies:

Provided, That the legislature of any State may empower the executive thereof to make temporary appointments until the people fill the vacancies by election as the legislature may direct.

This amendment shall not be so construed as to affect the election or term of any Senator chosen before it becomes valid as part of the Constitution.

ARTICLE XVIII [1]

Section 1. After one year from the ratificaton of this article the manufacture, sale, or transportation of intoxicating liquors within, the importation thereof into, or the exportation thereof from the United States and all territory subject to the jurisdiction thereof for beverage purposes is hereby prohibited.

Section 2. The Congress and the several States shall have concurrent power to enforce this article by appropriate legislation.

Section 3. This article shall be inoperative unless it shall have been ratified as an amendment to the Constitution by the legislatures of the several States, as provided in the Constitution, within seven years from the date of the submission hereof to the States by the Congress.

ARTICLE XIX [2]

(1) The right of citizens of the United States to vote shall not be denied or abridged by the United States or by any State on account of sex.

(2) Congress shall have power, by appropriate legislation, to enforce the provisions of this article.

ARTICLE XX [3]

Section 1. The terms of the President and Vice President shall end at noon on the 20th day of January, and the terms of Senators and Representatives at noon on the 3rd day of January, of the years in which such terms would have ended if this article had not been ratified; and the terms of their successors shall then begin.

Section 2. The Congress shall assemble at least once in every year, and such meeting shall begin at noon on the 3rd day of January, unless they shall by law appoint a different day.

Section 3. If, at the time fixed for the beginning of the term of the President, the President elect shall have died, the Vice President elect shall become President. If a President shall not have been chosen before the time fixed for the beginning of his term, or if the President elect shall have failed to qualify, then the Vice President elect shall act as President until a President shall have qualified; and the Congress may by law provide for the case wherein neither a President elect nor a Vice President elect shall have qualified, declaring who shall then act as President, or the manner in which one who is to act shall be selected, and such person shall act accordingly until a President or Vice President shall have qualified.

Section 4. The Congress may by law provide for the case of the death of any of the persons from whom the House of Representatives may choose a President whenever the right of choice shall have devolved upon them, and for the case of the death of any of the persons from whom the Senate may choose a Vice President whenever the right of choice shall have devolved upon them.

Section 5. Sections 1 and 2 shall take effect on the 15th day of October following the ratification of this article.

[1] Passed December 3, 1917; proclaimed January 29, 1919. Repealed by the Twenty-first Amendment.

[2] Proclaimed August 26, 1920.

[3] Proclaimed February 6, 1933.

Section 6. This article shall be inoperative unless it shall have been ratified as an amendment to the Constitution by the legislatures of three fourths of the several States within seven years from the date of its submission.

<h2 style="text-align:center">ARTICLE XXI [1]</h2>

Section 1. The eighteenth article of amendment to the Constitution of the United States is hereby repealed.

Section 2. The transportation or importation into any State, Territory, or possession of the United States for delivery or use therein of intoxicating liquors, in violation of the laws thereof, is hereby prohibited.

Section 3. This article shall be inoperative unless it shall have been ratified as an amendment to the Constitution by conventions in the several States, as provided in the Constitution, within seven years from the date of submission hereof to the States by the Congress.

<h2 style="text-align:center">ARTICLE XXII [2]</h2>

Section 1. No person shall be elected to the office of the President more than twice, and no person who has held the office of President, or acted as President, for more than two years of a term to which some other person was elected President shall be elected to the office of the President more than once. But this Article shall not apply to any person holding the office of President when this Article was proposed by the Congress, and shall not prevent any person who may be holding the office of President, or acting as President, during the term within which this Article becomes operative from holding the office of President, or acting as President during the remainder of such term.

Section 2. This Article shall be inoperative unless it shall have been ratified as an amendment to the Constitution by the legislatures of three-fourths of the several States within seven years from the date of its submission to the States by the Congress.[3]

[1] Proclaimed December 5, 1933. This amendment was ratified by state conventions.
[2] Adopted February 27, 1951.
[3] Five amendments have been proposed but not ratified. The first and second were proposed on Sept. 25, 1789, along with ten others which became the Bill of Rights. The first of these dealt with the apportionment of members of the House of Representatives. It was ratified by ten states, eleven being the necessary three-fourths. The second provided that "No law, varying the compensation for the services of the Senators and Representatives, shall take effect, until an election of Representatives shall have intervened." It was ratified by six states, eleven being necessary. A third was proposed on May 1, 1810, which would have abrogated the citizenship of any persons accepting foreign titles or honors. It was ratified by twelve states, fourteen being necessary. A fourth was proposed on Mar. 4, 1861, which prohibited the adoption of any amendment "to abolish or interfere, within any state, with the domestic institutions thereof, including that of persons held to labor or service by the laws of that state." This was approved by three states. The fifth, the proposed child-labor amendment, was proposed on June 2, 1924. It provides:

> *Section 1*—The Congress shall have power to limit, regulate, and prohibit the labor of persons under eighteen years of age.
> *Section 2*—The power of the several States is unimpaired by this article except that the operation of State laws shall be suspended to the extent necessary to give effect to legislation enacted by Congress.

This has been ratified by twenty-eight states and rejected in eleven. The approval of thirty-six states is necessary to complete ratification.

List of Visual Aids

The visual aids listed below and on the following pages can be used to supplement much of the material in this book. For the convenience of users the films have been grouped by chapters, but it is recommended that each film be reviewed, before use, in order to determine its suitability for a particular group or unit of study.

Motion pictures and filmstrips are included in the following list, the character of each being indicated by the self-explanatory abbreviations "MP" and "FS." Immediately following this identification is the name of the producer and, if different, the distributor also. Abbreviations are used for these names and are identified in the list of sources at the end of the bibliography. Unless otherwise indicated, the motion pictures are 16-mm sound black-and-white films and the filmstrips are 35-mm black-and-white and silent. The length of motion pictures is given in minutes (min), of filmstrips in frames (fr).

Most of the films can be borrowed or rented from state and local film libraries, and users should consult *A Directory of 2660 16mm Film Libraries,* available for 50 cents from the Government Printing Office, Washington 25, D.C.

This bibliography is a selective one, and film users should examine the latest annual editions and supplements of *Educational Film Guide* and *Filmstrip Guide,* published by the H. W. Wilson Co., New York. The *Guides,* standard reference books, are available in most school, college, and public libraries.

CHAPTERS 1 AND 2

Democracy (MP, EBF, 11 min) Presents nature and meaning of democracy with emphasis upon the economic and social conditions required to make it succeed.

Despotism (MP, EBF, 11 min) Portrays characteristics of despotic governments with emphasis upon underlying economic and social phenomena.

Social Change in a Democracy (MP, USA/UWF, 29 min) Portrays students in a high-school social-studies class discussing the difference be-

tween conditions in a democracy and in a totalitarian state, then learning
first-hand how a problem in their own community, arising from a social
change, is solved by law and assembly of the people.

CHAPTER 3

Meet Your Federal Government (MP, YAF, 15 min) Explains power and
function of Federal government and its three main branches.

Our National Government (MP, KB, 11 min) Gives a graphic analysis
of the national government in all its branches.

CHAPTER 4

English Criminal Justice (MP, BIS, 22 min) Portrays court procedures
in England and the precedents upon which English law is founded.

Due Process of Law Denied (MP, TFC, 20 min) Dramatization of the
dangers of denying due process of law and of the necessity to recognize
the Constitutional rights of individuals. Adapted from the theatrical feature film, *The Ox-Bow Incident.*

CHAPTERS 7 AND 8

Benjamin Franklin (MP, EBF, 17 min) Events in the life of the great
American statesman, concluding with the Constitutional Convention.

Our Constitution (MP, Academic, 20 min) Dramatization of events
relating to the Constitutional Convention in Philadelphia and portrayal
of Franklin, Washington, Madison, and others in their historic roles.

Our Living Constitution (MP, Coronet, 10 min color) Shows how basis
of our government changes and how it grows to meet needs of the times
while holding to the original principles of thought.

Seed of the Constitution (MP, Nu Art, 10 min) Dramatizes Benjamin
Franklin's plan for a union of the colonies under the British Crown.

Servant of the People (MP, MGM/TFC, 20 min) Shows the background
and making of the Constitution.

CHAPTER 9

Bill of Rights (MP, Warner/TFC, 20 min color) Shows struggle to in-
corporate Bill of Rights in the Federal Constitution.

Does It Matter What You Think? (MP, BIS, 15 min) Depicts formation
of opinions and their importance.

Greenie (MP, MGM/TFC, 10 min) A story of a Polish immigrant child
learning about America.

Immigration (MP, EBF, 11 min) Describes immigration to United States and naturalization and induction to citizenship.

Our Bill of Rights (MP, Academic, 20 min) Dramatization of the arguments pro and con and the acceptance by Washington, Jefferson, Franklin, and others of the first 10 amendments to the U.S. Constitution.

Tuesday in November (MP, OWI/UWF, 20 min) Explains election process and significance of secret ballot.

The Universal Declaration of Human Rights (FS, UN/McGraw, 73 fr) Describes with pictures and accompanying script the contents of the Declaration.

CHAPTER 10

Political Parties (MP, Coronet, 10 min) Depicts organization and functioning of political parties.

You the People (MP, MGM/TFC, 21 min) Shows the operations of a corrupt political machine.

CHAPTER 11

Pressure Groups (MP, EBF, 20 min) Explains the nature and function of pressure groups, their importance in the democratic process, and the dangers inherent in such groups unduly influencing legislation.

Public Opinion (MP, EBF, 11 min) A realistic analysis of public opinion, what it is, and how it is formed.

CHAPTERS 12 TO 14

The Congress (MP, MOT/McGraw, 13 min) Shows the functions of the two houses of Congress.

Inside the Capitol (MP, Columbia/TFC, 10 min) Shows various parts of the capitol with commentary pertaining to its historical background.

CHAPTERS 15 AND 16

Executive Departments (FS, EBF, 54 fr color) Explains the organization and work of the executive departments of the Federal government.

Great American Presidents (FS series, SVE, 28 fr each, color) Five filmstrips on Presidents Jefferson, Jackson, Lincoln, T. Roosevelt, and Washington.

The Presidency (MP, MOT/McGraw, 10 min) Traces present position of presidency from Constitutional beginning of office through development of implied powers to status of presidency today.

The President (FS, EBF, 52 fr color) Drawings illustrating the duties of the President of the United States.

The Roosevelt Story (MP, Brandon, 80 min) A "film biography" of the life and times of Franklin D. Roosevelt. Covers over 40 years of American history.

The White House (MP, MOT/McGraw, 14 min) The house and its traditions.

CHAPTER 17

Administration of Military Justice and Courts-Martial (MP, USA/UWF, 45 min) Military court procedures illustrated through a case study of desertion, capture, imprisonment, and trial.

Federal Courts (FS, EBF, 55 fr color) Explains the organization and functions of the Federal courts.

John Marshall (MP, EBF, 20 min) Portrait of the founder of American constitutional law.

The Supreme Court (MP, MOT/McGraw, 10 min) How the court works, progress of a case to and through the court.

CHAPTER 18

Men around Eisenhower (MP, MOT/McGraw, 27 min) Presents the President and his new cabinet (1953).

President's Cabinet (MP, Coronet, 10 min color or b&w) Reviews the duties and functions of the President's cabinet.

CHAPTER 20

Department of the Treasury (FS, CAS, 51 fr) Work of the U.S. Treasury Department including customs, currency, banking, and purchasing.

Property Taxation (MP, EBF, 11 min) Portrays usefulness of property taxation, types of government expenditures supported by property levies, and procedure of levying taxes on property.

Federal Taxation (MP, Coronet, 10 min) Documents entire United States Federal system of taxation.

CHAPTER 21

Bob Marshall Comes Home (MP, USDA, 22 min) Story of Rural Electrification Administration activities.

Hoover Dam (MP, US State/UWF, 33 min) Reviews the building of

Hoover Dam and explains its values in furnishing irrigation power and electric power to the people in the southwestern United States.

No Place Like Home (MP, RKO/McGraw, 16 min) Depicts the current housing problem and the many factors involved in it.

Two Way Street (MP, US Rubber, 13 min) Government experts discuss many aspects of world trade.

Who Should Control Our Natural Resources? (MP, AFF, 15 min) Discussion film, moderated by Marquis Childs, on what types of projects should be developed by private interests and by the Government.

Your Postal Service (MP, MOT/McGraw, 18 min) Shows inner workings of United States Post Office.

CHAPTER 22

Conservation of Natural Resources (MP, EBF, 12 min) Shows steps being taken to conserve water power, forests, and farm lands, effects of wind and water erosion and unwise farming, and efforts to check these abuses.

Decision for Bill (MP, USDA, 25 min color) Depicts activities of United States Department of Agriculture.

Department of Agriculture (FS, CAS, 51 fr) Activities of the Agriculture Department including soil conservation, forestry, crop insurance, home loans, and commodity credit. (Made in 1947)

Forest Conservation (MP, EBF, 11 min color) Points out how the forests have been depleted and what must be done to save them.

The River (MP, USDA, 30 min) A dramatization of the Mississippi River down to recent floods and erosion disasters.

Soil Conservation (FS, ACE, 51 fr) Major factors in conservation program; flood and erosion control, tree planting, crop rotation, contour plowing, etc.

A Strand Breaks (MP, EBF, 15 min color) Consequences of a state of imbalance in nature and the need for conservation measures.

CHAPTER 23

They Need to Know (MP, SSA, 14 min) Through a dramatized story, emphasizes the importance to wives and children of knowing of the survivors' insurance benefits available to them, upon the death of the family head, under the 1954 social security law.

Union Local (MP, US State/UWF, 26 min) Operations of a machinist's union and its relationships to management.

Valley of the Tennessee (MP, OWI/UWF, 30 min) Flood control in the Tennessee Valley, work of TVA, and results to people in the Valley.

CHAPTER 24

Expanding World Relationships (MP, US State/UWF, 11 min color)
Shows development of economic and social interdependence from Jefferson's time to present, emphasizing need for nations to work out ways of settling their differences peacefully.

Foreign Trade (FS, Film Pub, 57 fr) Shows nature, extent, and importance of foreign trade in modern society.

Monroe Doctrine (MP, Warner/TFC, 16 min color) Shows the circumstances that surrounded announcement of the policy.

Round Trip: The U.S.A. in World Trade (MP, World Today/IFB, 20 min) Relationship of world trade to American life.

The United Nations in World Disputes (MP, USA/UWF, 21 min) Presents the part of the United Nations in attempting to resolve disputes in four countries (Indonesia, Palestine, India, and Korea) which have threatened world peace since 1945.

CHAPTERS 25 TO 30

A Bill Becomes a Law (MP, Mass Bd Ed, 14 min) How a bill becomes a law in the Commonwealth of Massachusetts.

California State Legislature (FS, Long, 26 fr) Drawings of composition and functions of the California state legislature.

Community Responsibilities (MP, McGraw, 11 min) Raises questions concerning an individual's responsibilities to the community in which he lives.

County Government (MP, USIA/UWF, 28 min) Explains the system of county government in the United States as illustrated by Westchester County, N.Y.; its legislative, executive, and judicial functions; and its relationships to the state and Federal governments.

County Magistrate (MP, CNFB, 20 min) Administration of justice on the local level in Canada, as seen in the activities of a magistrate in rural British Columbia.

Functions of a State: Institutions (MP, Prog Pic, 20 min) Describes the operations and services of state institutions including a prison, correction schools for juveniles, and a mental hospital.

Iowa General Assembly (MP, Iowa U, 27 min) Procedures of the house and senate; duties of the governor, lt. governor, speaker of the house, chief clerk of the house, and secretary of the senate.

Legislative Process (MP, Ind U, 29 min color) Describes the steps in the passage of a bill through the general assembly of Indiana.

Legislative Process in Michigan (FS, Mich U, 60 fr) Processes of enacting a law in Michigan.

Local Government (FS, EBF, 52 fr color) Drawings explaining the functions and organization of a typical local government in the United States.

Mr. Mayor (MP, CNFB, 11 min) Portrait of the activities and responsibilities of the mayor of Granby, Quebec, a mushrooming industrial community.

The Milwaukee Way (MP, Wis U, 22 min color) Describes the Milwaukee city government and its services.

Pennsylvania Local Government in Action (MP, PSU, 22 min) Shows local government activities, including recreation, welfare, housing, council and other meetings, etc.

Portrait of a County (MP, PSU, 20 min color) Depicts a county as a unit of government, using Montgomery County, Pa., as an example.

State Government (FS, EBF, 55 fr color) Drawings explaining the functions and organization of a typical state government in the United States.

Understanding the Law: Equal Justice for All (MP, EBF, 12 min) Rights of individuals to be protected from and by the law. Defines the roles of state and Federal courts.

U.S. Citizen and His Governments (FS series, ACE) Four filmstrips, color, showing the kinds of services rendered by local, state, and Federal governments of the United States, and their relationships to one another and to individual citizens. Titles are:

Meeting the Basic Needs of Citizens (59 fr)
Promoting Material Welfare (49 fr)
Promoting Personal Welfare (64 fr)
Securing the Blessing of Liberty (48 fr)

Voting Procedures (MP, Ind U, 14 min) Importance of and procedures in registering for and voting in national, state, and local elections.

Wisconsin Makes Its Laws (MP, Wis U, 30 min color) Social processes by which needs for laws arise, and how a proposed law goes through the legislative, executive, and judicial processes in Wisconsin. Short version, 22 min, entitled *State Legislature*, available from Academy Films.

Your Community (MP, MTP, 27 min) Case histories of community problems and the actions taken by community groups in helping solve them. Sponsored by the General Federation of Women's Clubs and the Sears-Roebuck Foundation.

Your State Trooper (MP, Ind U, 22 min) Typical daily incidents showing the duties of state troopers who patrol the highways.

FILM SOURCES

Academic—Academic Film Co., 516 Fifth Ave., New York 36, N.Y.
Academy—Academy Films, Box 3088, Hollywood, Calif.
AFF—American Film Forum, Inc., 516 Fifth Ave., New York 36, N.Y.

ACE—American Council on Education, 1785 Massachusetts Ave., N.W., Washington, D.C.

BIS—British Information Services, 30 Rockefeller Plaza, New York 20, N.Y.

Brandon—Brandon Films, Inc., 200 West 57th St., New York 19, N.Y.

CAS—Creative Arts Studio, Inc., 1223 Connecticut Ave., Washington 6, D.C.

CNFB—National Film Board of Canada, 630 Fifth Ave., New York 20, N.Y.

Coronet—Coronet Instructional Films, 65 E. South Water St., Chicago 1, Ill.

EBF—Encyclopaedia Britannica Films, Inc., 1150 Wilmette Ave., Wilmette, Ill.

Film Pub—Film Publishers, Inc., 25 Broad St., New York 4, N.Y.

Hoover—Citizens Commission for the Hoover Report, 15 West 46th St., New York 19, N.Y.

IFB—International Film Bureau, 57 E. Jackson Blvd., Chicago 4, Ill.

Ind U—Indiana University, Bloomington, Ind.

Iowa U—State University of Iowa, Iowa City, Iowa.

KB—Knowledge Builders, 625 Madison Ave., New York 22, N.Y.

Long—Long Filmslide Service, 7505 Fairmont Ave., El Cerrito 8, Calif.

McGraw—McGraw-Hill Book Co., Text-Film Dept., 330 West 42d St., New York 36, N.Y.

Mass Bd Ed—Massachusetts Board of Educational Television, Boston 8, Mass.

Mich U—University of Michigan, Ann Arbor, Mich.

MTP—Modern Talking Picture Service, 5 East 54th St., New York 22, N.Y.

NuArt—Nu Art Films, Inc., 112 West 48th St., New York 19, N.Y.

Prog Pic—Progressive Pictures, 6351 Thornhill Dr., Oakland 11, Calif.

PSU—Pennsylvania State University, University Park, Pa.

SSA—Social Security Administration, Bureau of Old Age and Survivors' Insurance, Baltimore, Md.

SVE—Society for Visual Education, 1345 W. Diversey Parkway, Chicago, Ill.

TFC—Teaching Film Custodians, Inc., 25 West 43d St., New York 18, N.Y.

USA—U.S. Department of the Army, Washington 25, D.C.

USDA—U.S. Department of Agriculture, Washington 25, D.C.

USIA—U.S. Information Agency, Washington 25, D.C. (Films distributed in the United States by United World Films, Inc.)

US Rubber—United States Rubber Co., 1230 Sixth Ave., New York 20, N.Y.

UWF—United World Films, Inc., 1445 Park Ave., New York 29, N.Y.

Wis U—University of Wisconsin, Madison, Wis.

YAF—Young America Films, Inc., 18 East 41st St., New York 17, N.Y.

Index to Judicial Decisions

Index